MEDICAL
SOCIOLOGY

Sixth Edition

MEDICAL
SOCIOLOGY

William C. Cockerham
University of Alabama at Birmingham

Prentice Hall, Englewood Cliffs, New Jersey 07632

Library of Congress Cataloging-in-Publication Data

COCKERHAM, WILLIAM C.
   Medical sociology / William C. Cockerham. — 6th ed.
      p.   cm.
   Includes bibliographical references and index.
   ISBN 0-13-063322-4
   1. Social medicine.   I. Title.
RA418.C657   1995
362.1—dc20   94-21970

Acquisitions editor: *Nancy Roberts*
Editorial assistant: *Pat Naturale*
Project manager and interior design: *Edie Riker*
Photo editor: *Lorinda Morris-Nantz*
Photo researcher: *Chris Pullo*
Cover design: *Deluca Design*
Buyer: *Mary Ann Gloriande*

Photo Credits: Hazel Hankin/Stock Boston, p. 1; Tim Barnwell/Stock Boston, p. 13; Mike
   Okoniewski, p. 35; Peter Southwick/Stock Boston, p. 67; Spencer Grant/Monkmeyer
   Press, p. 89; Michael Tamborrino/FPG International, p. 107; Glen Korengold/Stock
   Boston, p. 133; Michael Weisbrot and family/Stock Boston, p. 149; Photo 20-20, p. 173;
   Joseph Nettis/Photo Researchers, p. 187; Harriet Gans/The Image Works, p. 207; Ulrike
   Welsch/Photo Researchers, p. 225; Jeffry W. Myers/FPG International, p. 249; AP/Wide
   World Photos, p. 261; Hugh Rogers/Monkmeyer Press, p. 285; Francene Kerry/Stock
   Boston, p. 319.

Printed in the United States of America

10   9   8   7   6   5   4   3   2   1

ISBN 0-13-063322-4

Prentice-Hall International (UK) Limited, *London*
Prentice-Hall of Australia Pty. Limited, *Sydney*
Prentice-Hall Canada Inc., *Toronto*
Prentice-Hall Hispanoamericana, S.A., *Mexico*
Prentice-Hall of India Private Limited, *New Delhi*
Prentice-Hall of Japan, Inc., *Tokyo*
Simon & Schuster Asia Pte. Ltd., *Singapore*
Editora Prentice-Hall do Brasil, Ltda., *Rio de Janeiro*

To Cynthia,
and to Geoffrey, Sean, Scott,
Laura, and Laurinda Cockerham

Contents

Preface

The field of medical sociology has undergone considerable change since the first edition of this textbook appeared in 1978. At that time, much of the research in medical sociology was dependent upon the sponsorship of physicians and a clear division of labor existed between sociologists working in academic departments in universities and in health institutions. Today, that situation has changed drastically. Medical sociology is no longer highly dependent on the medical profession for funding or focus—although a strong alliance continues to exist in many cases. Medical sociologists exercise their craft in an increasingly independent manner, either working with a greater degree of partnership with health care professionals or functioning as medicine's critics should the situation warrant it. Furthermore, research and teaching in medical sociology in both universities and health institutions are increasingly similar in the application of theory and usefulness in addressing problems relevant to clinical practice. In sum, medical sociology has evolved into a mature, objective, and independent field of study and work.

Medical sociology has also experienced significant growth worldwide in numbers of practitioners. In many countries, including the United States, Canada, Great Britain, Germany, and the Netherlands, medical sociologists are either the largest or one of the largest specialty groups. The European Society for Medical Sociology is a large and active professional society, as are the medical sociology sections of the American, British, and German Sociological Associations. Elsewhere, in Japan, the Japanese Sociology of Health and Medical Sociology is working to further develop the field in that nation. Numerous books, journals, college and university courses, medical school programs, and lecture series in medical sociology now exist in different parts of the world. In the United States, four universities—the University of Alabama at Birmingham, the University of California at San Francisco, and the combined University of Akron-Kent University program—offer doctorates in medical sociology, while the University of Kentucky and the University of Miami (Florida) specialize in the field. Although development on a worldwide basis is uneven and problems remain, medical sociology has nevertheless become a major subdiscipline within sociology.

The major objective of this textbook since its inception has been to introduce students to medical sociology by reflecting the ideas, concepts, themes, and research findings in the field. This edition—the sixth—continues that approach. The last edition attempted to overcome Sharon Barnartt's (1990) charge that there was a lack of diversity among current textbooks by adding chapters on health behavior and doctor–patient interaction, along with increased material on illness as a social experience, medicine and religion, the decline in the professional power and status of physicians, and health care delivery systems in the Third World. This edition builds on those themes and provides a greater focus on health reform in the United States and international comparisons of health care delivery. The intent, as usual, has been to identify and discuss the most current issues, debates, and findings in medical sociology.

ACKNOWLEDGMENTS

The material contained in the pages of this book is my own responsibility in terms of perspective, scope, and style of presentation. Nevertheless, I am deeply grateful to several people for their assistance in preparing the six editions of this book. I would like to acknowledge the insightful comments of those colleagues who reviewed all or part of this work throughout the revision process. For sharing their views and helping to improve the quality of this book, my appreciation goes to Neil Smelser, University of California, Berkeley; Barry Edmonston, Cornell University; Daniel J. Klenow, North Dakota State University; Spencer Condie, Brigham Young University; Norman Denzin, University of Illinois; Morton Creditor, University of Kansas Medical Center; Jeffrey Salloway, University of New Hampshire; John Collette, University of Utah; Sharon Guten, Case Western Reserve University; Herbert Bynder, University of Colorado; Paul Berzina, County College of Morris; Alexander Rysman, Northeastern University; Eliot Freidson, New York University; Sol Levine, Boston University; Melvin Barber, Florida A&M University; Reed Geertsen, Utah State University; Robert Clark, Midwestern State University; Joseph Jones, Portland State University; and Robert Terry Russell, College of St. Francis.

William C. Cockerham
Birmingham, Alabama

Medical Sociology

1

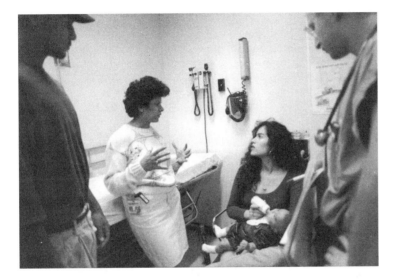

S ocial factors play a critically important role in health. Social conditions and situations not only promote the possibility of illness and disability, but they also enhance prospects for disease prevention and health maintenance. The greatest threats to an individual's health and physical well-being today stem largely from unhealthy lifestyles and high-risk behavior, and this is true for heart disease, cancer, AIDS, and a host of modern day health problems. Healthy lifestyles and the avoidance of high-risk behavior, on the other hand, advance the individual's potential for a longer and healthier life.

Social factors also are important in influencing the manner in which societies organize their resources to cope with health hazards and deliver medical care to the population at large. Individuals and societies tend to respond to health problems in a manner consistent with their culture, norms, and values. As Donald Light (Light and Schuller 1986:9) explains, "medical care and health services are acts of political philosophy"; thus, social and political values influence the choices made, institutions formed, and levels of funding provided for health. It is no accident that the United States has its form of health care delivery and other nations have their particular approach. Health is therefore not simply a matter of biology, but involves a number of factors that are social, cultural, political, and economic in nature.

The purpose of this book is to introduce the reader to the field of medical sociology. Recognition of the significance of the complex relationship between social factors and the level of health characteristic of various groups and societies has led to the development of medical sociology as an important substantive area within the general field of sociology. As an academic discipline, sociology is concerned with the study of the social causes and consequences of human behavior; thus, it follows that medical sociology is concerned with the social causes and consequences of health and illness. Medical sociologists study the social facets of health and disease, the social functions of health organizations and institutions, the relationship of systems of health care delivery to other social systems, the social behavior of health personnel and those people who are consumers of health care, and patterns of health services.

DEFINING HEALTH

The World Health Organization (WHO) defines health as a state of complete physical, mental, and social well-being, and not merely the absence of disease or injury. This definition calls attention to the fact that being healthy involves much more than simply determining if a person is ill or injured. To be healthy means also to experience a sense of well-being. As Canadian scholars Robert Evans and Gregory Stoddart (1990) point out, health not only means an absence of disease or injury, but also an absence of distress or an impaired capacity to carry out one's daily activities. Several European studies conducted in France (d'Houtaud and Field 1984; Herzlich 1973), Great Britain (Calnan 1987; Williams 1983), and the Netherlands (Joosten 1989) report, for example, that many individuals view health primarily as a state of functional fitness and apply this definition to their everyday social circumstances.

Good health is a prerequisite for the adequate functioning of any individual or society. If our health is sound, we can engage in numerous types of activities. But if we are ill, distressed, or injured, we may face the curtailment of our usual round of daily life and we may also become so preoccupied with our state of health that other pursuits are of secondary importance or quite meaningless. Therefore, as René DuBos (1981) explains, *health can be defined as the ability to function*. This does not mean that healthy people are free from all health problems; it means that they can function to the point that they can do what they want to do.

As Thomas McKeown (1979) explains, we know from personal experience that the feeling of well-being is more than the perceived absence of disease and disability. Many influences—social, religious, economic, personal, and medical—contribute to such a state. The role of medicine in health promotion is the prevention of illness and premature death and care of the sick and disabled. Thus, McKeown concludes that medicine's task is not to create happiness, but to remove a major source of unhappiness—disease and disability—from people's lives.

Contrasting Ideas about Health and Social Behavior

Attempts to understand the relationship between social behavior and health have their origin in history. DuBos (1969) suggested that primitive humans were closer to the animals in that they, too, relied upon their instincts to stay healthy. Yet some primitive humans recognized a cause and effect relationship between doing certain things and alleviating symptoms of a disease or improving the condition of a wound. Since there was so much that primitive humans did not understand about the functioning of the body, *magic* became an integral component of the beliefs about the causes and cures of health disorders. Actually, an uncritical acceptance of magic and the supernatural pervaded practically every aspect of primitive life. So it is not surprising that early humans thought that illness was caused by evil spirits. Primitive medicines made from vegetables or animals were invariably used in combination with some form of ritual to expel the harmful spirit from a diseased body. During the Neolithic age, some 4,000 to 5,000 years ago, people living in what is today the Eastern Mediterranean and North Africa are known to have even engaged in a surgical procedure called *trepanation* or trephining, which consists of a hole being bored in the skull in order to liberate the evil spirit supposedly contained in a person's head. The finding by anthropologists of more than one hole in some skulls and the lack of signs of osteomyelitis (erosion of bone tissue) suggest that the operation was not always fatal. Some estimates indicate that the mortality rate from trepanation was as low as 10 percent, an amazing accomplishment considering the difficulty of the procedure and the crude conditions under which it must have been performed (Mora 1985).

One of the earliest attempts in the Western world to formulate principles of health care based upon rational thought and the rejection of supernatural phenomena is found in the work of the Greek physician Hippocrates. Little is known of Hippocrates who lived around 400 B.C., not even whether he actually authored the collection of books that bears his name. Nevertheless, the writings attributed to him have provided a number of principles underlying modern medical practice. One of his most famous contributions, the Hippocratic Oath, is the foundation of contemporary medical ethics. Among other things, it requires the physician to swear that he or she will help the sick, refrain from intentional wrongdoing or harm, and keep confidential all matters pertaining to the doctor-patient relationship.

Hippocrates also argued that medical knowledge should be derived from an understanding of the natural sciences and the logic of cause and effect relationships. In his classic treatise, *On Airs, Waters, and Places,* Hippocrates pointed out that human well-being is influenced by the totality of environmental factors: living habits or lifestyle, climate, topography of the land, and the quality of air, water, and food. Interestingly enough, concerns about our health and the quality of air, water, and places are still very much with us in the twentieth century.

In their intellectual orientation toward disease, Hippocrates and the ancient Greeks held views that were more in line with contemporary thinking about health than found in the Middle Ages and the Renaissance. Much of the medical knowledge of the ancient world was lost during the Dark Ages that descended on Europe after the fall of the Roman Empire. What knowledge remained in the West was preserved by the Catholic Church. The Church took responsibility for dealing with mental suffering and adverse social conditions like poverty, while physicians focused more or less exclusively on treating physical ailments. The human body was regarded as a machine-like entity that operated according to principles of physics and chemistry. The result was that both Western religion and medical science sponsored the idea "of the body as a machine, of disease as a breakdown of the machine, and of the doctor's task as repair of the machine" (Engel 1977:131).

A few physicians, such as Paracelsus, a famous Swiss doctor who lived in the early sixteenth century, did show interest in understanding more than the physical functioning of the body. Paracelsus demonstrated that specific diseases common among miners were related to their work conditions. But Paracelsus was an exception and few systematic measures were employed to either research or to cope with the effects of adverse social situations on health until the late eighteenth and early nineteenth centuries.

Modern Medicine and Regulation of the Body

Modern medicine traces its birth to Western Europe in the late eighteenth century. In analyzing the development of French medicine at this time, social theorist Michel Foucault (1973) noted the emergence of two distinct trends in medical practice—what he called "medicine of the species" and "medicine of social spaces." Medicine of the species pertained to the strong emphasis in Western medicine upon classifying diseases, diagnosing and treating patients, and finding cures. The human body became an object of study and observation in order that physiological processes could be demystified and brought under medical control. Physicians perfected their so-called clinical gaze, allowing them to observe and perceive bodily functions and dysfunctions within a standardized frame of reference. Clinics were established both to treat patients and train doctors, with the clinical setting providing the optimal setting for physicians to exercise authority and control over their patients.

The medicine of social spaces was concerned not with curing diseases, but preventing them. This meant greater government involvement in regulating the conduct of daily life—especially public hygiene. Physicians served as advisors in the enactment of laws and regulations specifying standards for food, water, and the disposal of wastes. The health of the human body thus became a subject of regulation by medical doctors and civil authorities as social norms for healthy behavior became more widely established. In such a context, Foucault found that scientific concepts of disease had replaced notions that sickness had metaphysical (religious, magical, superstitious) origins. Disease was no longer considered an entity outside of the existing boundaries of knowledge, but an object to be studied, confronted scientifically, and controlled.

The Public's Health

Awareness that disease could be caused by unhealthy lifestyles and forms of social behavior spread through common sense and practical experience. A most significant development occurred when it was realized that uncontaminated food, water, and air, as well as sanitary living conditions could reduce the onset and spread of communicable diseases. Prior to the advent of modern medicine, high mortality rates from communicable diseases such as typhus, tuberculosis, scarlet fever, measles, and cholera were significantly lowered in both Europe and North America through improved hygiene and sanitation. Thus, the late eighteenth and early nineteenth centuries are conspicuous for the systematic implementation of public health measures.

Noting the link between lifestyle and health, some nineteenth-century European physicians argued that improvement was necessary in the living conditions of the poor. They advocated governmental recognition of the social as well as medical nature of measures undertaken to promote health. Rudolf Virchow, for instance, a prominent German physician known in clinical medicine for the development of cellular pathology, insisted that medicine was a social science. Virchow argued that the poor should have not only quality medical care, but also that they should have free choice of a physician. Improved medical care was also to go hand in hand with changed social conditions leading to a better life (Rosen 1979). However, these proposals had little effect outside Virchow's small circle of colleagues. Virchow's views were simply seen as too liberal by many European rulers and politicians of the period who feared that social reforms would erode their authority and lead to revolution. There was also a widespread bias in Europe among the educated classes in favor of a medical science that failed to acknowledge the possible benefits of health measures that were largely social.

This was rather ironic because several twentieth-century scholars have found that the decline in deaths from infectious diseases in the second half of the nineteenth century was mainly due to improvements in diet, housing, public sanitation, and personal hygiene instead of medical innovations (Levine, Feldman, and Elinson 1983; McKeown 1979; McKinlay and McKinlay 1981; McKinlay, McKinlay, and Beaglehole 1989; Sagan 1987). McKeown (1979), for example, notes that the decline in infant mortality was due more to improved nutrition for mothers and better care and feeding for infants than to improved obstetric services. Deaths from typhus also fell dramatically without a specific medical cause. A similar drop in mortality from typhoid and dysentery led McKeown (1979:53) to conclude that "the rapid decline in mortality from diseases spread by water and food since the late nineteenth century owed little to medical intervention."

The Germ Theory of Disease

Most physicians in the 1800s were primarily interested in treating their patients and improving the state of medical technology. They were not necessarily concerned with social reform. The success during this century of Louis Pasteur, Robert Koch, and others in bacteriological research that led to the conceptualization of the germ theory of disease, along with tremendous progress in the development of internal medicine, anesthesiology, pathology, immunology, and surgical techniques, convinced physicians to focus exclusively upon a clinical medicine grounded in exact scientific laboratory procedures. The practice of medicine in the twentieth century thus rested solidly upon the premise that every disease had a specific pathogenic cause whose treatment could best be accomplished by removing or controlling that cause within a biomedical framework. DuBos (1959) has pointed out that modern medicine's thinking has been dominated by the search for drugs as "magic bullets" that can be shot into the body to kill or control all health disorders. Because research in microbiology, biochemistry, and related fields has resulted in the discovery and production of a large variety of drugs and drug-based techniques for successfully treating many diseases, this approach became medicine's method for dealing with the problems it was called upon to treat.

Return to the "Whole Person"

As medicine moves toward the twenty-first century, it is increasingly called upon to return to the health problems of the whole person, which extend well beyond singular causes of disease. Contemporary physicians are often required to deal with health disorders more aptly described as "problems in living," dysfunctions that involve multiple factors of causation, not all of them biological in nature. The evidence is now quite striking that the manner in which people respond to social, psychological, and cultural influences has much to do not only with whether they become sick, but also with the form, duration, and intensity of their symptoms and disabilities (Albrecht and Levy 1984; Lubkin 1986). Thus, it has become clear that modern medicine must develop insight into the behaviors characteristic of the people it treats.

    To illustrate this point, consider that the major health disorders in urban-industrial countries are no longer a result of communicable diseases, but instead are the problems of chronic or long-term illnesses such as heart disease and cancer. Because chronic disorders can be influenced by many causes, health personnel should consider all aspects (social, psychological, and physiological) of a chronic condition.

    Also, it is not uncommon for an individual suffering from a chronic disease to feel perfectly normal, even when irreversible damage to organs and tissues has already occurred. Because of the irremediable damage done to the body by a chronic disease, patients may be required to permanently change their style of living and modify their social relationships. So, as Anselm Strauss (1975) has pointed out, health practitioners should know how patients with chronic disorders:

1. manage medical crises,
2. control their symptoms,
3. carry out their prescribed regimens,
4. adjust to changes in the course of the disorder,
5. attempt to normalize their interaction with others,
6. cope with the social isolation caused by reduced contact with others, and
7. seek the necessary money to pay for their treatment and possibly to support themselves and their dependents.

This is in addition to all else that physicians need to know about the behavior and lifestyles of individuals that influence whether they are likely to develop chronic disorders in the first place.

It is clear that social behavior plays a critically important role in causing disease through unhealthy lifestyles involving poor diets, lack of exercise, smoking, alcohol and drug abuse, stress, and exposure to sexually transmitted diseases like AIDS. Healthy lifestyles—the reverse of the above—help lessen the extent of chronic health problems, better control these problems when they appear, or allow the individual to avoid them until the onset of old age. However, adverse social conditions, namely, poverty, also promote health problems and reduced life expectancy. Howard Kaplan (1989:51) finds that the poor are more likely to engage in practices that induce ill health and less likely to engage in practices that forestall illness-inducing situations.

The poor are exposed to more violence in their daily lives and find themselves in situations where stress, inadequate diets and housing, and less opportunity for quality health care are common. They may also live in areas where chemical industries pollute the environment with cancer-causing agents or other chemicals causing skin and respiratory disorders, or have greater exposure to communicable diseases because of crowded living conditions, parasites, insects, and vermin. To be poor by definition means to have less of the good things in life; it also means the possibility of having more of the bad things and, with respect to health problems, this seems to be the case. The poor have the highest rates of disease and disability, including heart disease, of any socioeconomic group (Dutton 1986; Kaplan 1989; Susser, Hopper, and Richman 1983; Winkleby et al. 1992).

The need to understand the impact of lifestyles and social conditions on health has become increasingly important in preventing or coping with modern health disorders. This situation has promoted a closer association between medicine and the behavioral sciences of sociology, anthropology, and psychology. Medical sociologists are increasingly familiar figures not only in medical schools, but also in schools of nursing, dentistry, pharmacy, and public health, as well as in the wards and clinics of teaching hospitals. Medical sociologists now routinely hold joint teaching and research appointments between sociology departments and departments in various health-related educational institutions or are employed full time in those institutions.

THE RISE OF MEDICAL SOCIOLOGY

Medical sociology was established as a specialized field initially in the United States during the 1940s. The first use of the term *medical sociology* had appeared as early as 1894 in an article by Charles McIntire on the importance of social factors in health. Other early work included essays on the relationship between medicine and society in 1902 by Elizabeth Blackwell, the first woman to graduate from medical school in America, and James Warbasse in 1909. However, these early publications were produced by people more concerned with medicine than sociology and it remained for Bernard Stern to publish the first work from a sociological perspective in 1927, titled *Social Factors in Medical Progress*. A few publications followed in the 1930s, such as Lawrence Henderson's 1935 paper on the physician and patient as a social system which subsequently influenced Talcott Parsons' conceptualization of the sick role (Gerhardt 1989a); but it was not until after World War II that medical sociology began in earnest as significant amounts of federal funding for sociomedical research became available.

Under the auspices of the National Institute of Mental Health, medical sociology's initial alliance with medicine was in psychiatry. A basis for cooperation between sociologists and psychiatrists existed because of earlier research in 1939 on urban mental health conducted in Chicago by Robert Faris and H. Warren Dunham. A particularly significant cooperative effort that followed was the publication in 1958 of *Social Class and Mental Illness: A Community Study* by August Hollingshead and Frederick Redlich. This landmark research, conducted in New Haven, Connecticut, produced important evidence that social factors could be correlated with different types of mental disorders and the manner in which people received psychiatric care. Persons in the most socially and economically disadvantaged segments of society were found to have the highest rates of mental disorder in general and excessively high rates of schizophrenia—the most disabling mental illness—in particular. This study attracted international attention and is the best known single study in the world of the relationship between mental disorder and social class. This book played a key role in the debate during the 1960s leading to the establishment of community mental health centers in the United States, as did other significant joint projects involving sociologists and psychiatrists, such as the midtown Manhattan study of Leo Srole and his colleagues (1962).

Funding from federal and private organizations also helped stimulate cooperation between sociologists and physicians in regard to sociomedical research on problems of physical health. The Russell Sage Foundation funded a program in 1949 to improve the utilization of social science research in medical practice. One result of this program was the publication of *Social Science in Medicine* (Simmons and Wolff 1954). Other work sponsored by the Sage Foundation came later and included Edward Suchman's book *Sociology and the Field of Public Health* (1963). Thus, the direction of work in medical sociology in the United States when large-scale funding first became available was toward applied or practical problem solving rather than the development of theory.

This situation had important consequences for the development of medical sociology. Unlike law, religion, politics, economics, and other basic social processes, medicine was ignored by sociology's founders in the late nineteenth century because it was not an institution shaping the structure and nature of society (Ruderman 1981). Emile Durkheim, Karl Marx, Max Weber, and other major classical theorists did not concern themselves with the role of medicine in society. Medical sociology did not begin until after World War II, nor achieve any significant development until the 1960s (Turner 1987). The field therefore developed relatively late in the evolution of sociology as an academic subject and lacked statements on health and illness from the classical theorists. Consequently, medical sociology came of age in an intellectual climate far different from sociology's more traditional specialties with direct roots in nineteenth- and early twentieth-century social thought. As a result, it faces a set of circumstances in its development different from that of most other major sociological subdisciplines.

The circumstance that most affects medical sociology is the pressure to produce work that can be applied to medical practice and the formulation of health policy. This pressure originates from government agencies and medical sources, both of which either influence or control funding for sociomedical research and have little or no interest in purely theoretical sociology.

Yet the tremendous growth of medical sociology in both the United States and Europe in recent years most likely would not have been possible without the substantial financial support for applied studies provided by the respective governments. For example, in the United States, where medical sociology has reached its most extensive development, the emergence of the field was greatly stimulated by the expansion of the National Institutes of Health in the late 1940s. Particularly significant, according to Hollingshead (1973) who participated in some of the early research programs, was the establishment of the National Institute of Mental Health, which was instrumental in encouraging and funding joint social and medical projects. "It was through the impetus provided by this injection of money," notes Malcolm Johnson (1975:229), "that sociologists and medical men changed their affiliations and embraced the field of medical sociology." When Alvin Gouldner (1970) discussed the social sciences as a well-financed government effort to help cope with the problems of industrial society and the welfare state in the West during the post-World War II era, the prototype social science in this regard was medical sociology.

Parsons

However, a critical event occurred in 1951 that began the reorientation of American medical sociology in a theoretical direction. This was the appearance of Talcott Parsons' book *The Social System.* This book, written to explain a relatively complex structural-functionalist model of society in which social systems are linked to corresponding systems of personality and culture, contained Parsons' concept of the sick role. Unlike other major social theorists preceding him, Parsons formulated an analysis of the function of medicine in his view of society. Parsons presented an ideal representation of how people in Western society should act when sick. The merit of the concept is that it describes a patterned set of expectations defining the norms and values appropriate to being sick, both for the sick person and others who interact with that person. Parsons also pointed out that physicians are invested by society with the function of social control, similar to the role provided by priests, to serve as a means to control deviance. In the case of the sick role, illness is the deviance and its undesirable nature reinforces the motivation to be healthy.

In developing his concept of the sick role, Parsons linked his ideas to those of the two most important classical theorists in sociology—Emile Durkheim (1858–1917) of France and Max Weber (1864–1920) of Germany. Parsons was the first to demonstrate the controlling function of medicine in a large social system and he did so in the context of classical sociological theory. Some have argued that Parsons' concept of the sick role represents the most important single theoretical contribution to medical sociology to date (Fox 1989; Wolinsky 1988). Moreover, having a theorist of Parsons' stature rendering the first major theory in medical sociology called attention to the young subdiscipline—especially among academic sociologists. Not only was Parsons' concept of the sick role "a penetrating and apt analysis of sickness from a distinctly sociological point of view" (Freidson 1970b:62), but it was widely believed in the 1950s that Parsons and his students were charting a future course for all of sociology through the insight provided by his model of society.

This, of course, was not the case, as Parsons' ideas—including his concept of the sick role—were strongly criticized. Parsons nevertheless provided a theoretical approach for medical sociology that brought the subdiscipline the intellectual recognition it needed in its early development in the United States.

The institutional support for sociology in America was in the universities where the discipline was established more firmly than anywhere else in the world. Without academic legitimacy and the subsequent participation of such well-known, mainstream academic sociologists as Robert Merton, Howard Becker, and Erving Goffman, all of whom published research in the field, medical sociology would lack the credentials and professional position that it currently has in both academic and applied settings. Parsons' views on society may not be the optimal paradigm for explaining illness, but Parsons helped make medical sociology academically respectable.

Practical Application versus Theory

The direction taken by medical sociology early in its development is best summarized by Robert Straus (1957). Straus suggested that medical sociology had become divided into two separate but closely interrelated areas: sociology *in* medicine and sociology *of* medicine.

The sociologist in medicine is a sociologist who collaborates directly with the physician and other health personnel in studying the social factors that are relevant to a particular health disorder. The work of the sociologist in medicine is intended to be directly applicable to patient care or to the solving of a public health problem. Some of the tasks of the sociologist in medicine are to analyze the etiology or causes of health disorders, the differences in social attitudes as they relate to health, and the way in which the incidence and prevalence of a specific health disorder is related to such social variables as age, sex, socioeconomic status, racial/ethnic group identity, education, and occupation. Such an analysis is then intended to be made available to health practitioners to assist them in treating health problems. Thus, sociology in medicine can be characterized as *applied research and analysis primarily motivated by a medical problem* rather than a sociological problem. Sociologists in medicine usually work in medical schools, nursing schools, public health schools, teaching hospitals, public health agencies, and other health organizations. They may also work for a governmental agency like the U.S. Department of Health and Human Services in the capacity of biostatisticians, health planners, administrators, and advisors.

The sociology *of* medicine, on the other hand, has a different emphasis. It deals with such factors as the organization, role relationships, norms, values, and beliefs of medical practice as a form of human behavior. The emphasis is on the social processes that occur in the medical setting and how these contribute to our understanding of medical sociology in particular and to our understanding of social life in general. The sociology of medicine shares the same goals as all other areas of sociology and may consequently be characterized as *research and analysis of the medical environment from a sociological perspective.* Although some sociologists of medicine are employed in health institutions, the majority work as professors in the sociology departments of universities and colleges.

However, the division of work in medical sociology into a sociology of medicine and sociology in medicine eventually created problems. Medical sociologists affiliated with departments of sociology in universities were in a stronger position to produce work that satisfied sociologists as good sociology. But sociologists in medical institutions had the advantage of participation in medicine as well as research opportunities unavailable to those outside medical practice. A certain amount of tension began to develop between the two groups over whose work was the most important. What happened to change this situation was a general evolution in medical sociology, largely stimulated by funding from government agencies and private research foundations, toward work relevant to medicine and health policy. The division of the field as outlined by Straus lost its distinctiveness in the United States and never really developed in Western Europe (Bloom 1986, 1990; Claus 1983; Cockerham 1983, 1988; Fox 1985; Freeman and Levine 1989; Levine 1987; Olesen 1989; Wardwell 1982; Zola 1991). In Great Britain, Germany, and the Netherlands, where medical sociology has been developed more extensively than elsewhere in Europe, the subdiscipline is concentrated in medical schools. Most research in medical sociology today, regardless of whether it is in a sociology department in a university or in a medical institution, deals with practical problems. A major difference in comparison to the past is that the field has achieved a state of development that allows it to investigate medical problems from an independent sociological perspective. Contemporary medical sociologists are less concerned with whether work is in the sociology of medicine or sociology in medicine, but rather with how much it increases our understanding of the complex relationship between social factors and health.

At present, medical sociologists constitute the largest and one of the most active groups of people doing sociological work in the United States and Western Europe. Medical sociologists comprise the largest sections of the American, British, and German Sociological Associations. About one out of every ten American sociologists is a medical sociologist; in Germany, the German Society for Medical Sociology, an organization just for persons working in the field of medical sociology, has more members than the entire German Sociological Association. In Europe, medical sociologists have been identified in twenty-seven different countries (Claus 1983), and this population provided the basis for the European Society for Medical Sociology established in 1983. Not only have the numbers of medical sociologists increased in recent years, but as Renée Fox (1985) points out, the scope of matters pertinent to medical sociology has clearly broadened as issues of health, illness, and medicine have become a medium through which general issues and concerns about society have been expressed. One result is that numerous books and scientific journals dealing with medical sociology have been and continue to be published in the United States and Western Europe. The future of medical sociology itself is very positive.

SUMMARY

Throughout history human beings have been interested in and deeply concerned with the effects of the social environment on the health of individuals and the groups to which they belong. Today it is clear that social factors play a critically important role in health, as the greatest threats to the health and well-being of individuals stem largely from unhealthy lifestyles and high-risk behavior. Sociology's interest in medicine as a unique system of human social behavior and medicine's recognition that sociology can help health practitioners to better understand their patients and provide improved forms of health care have begun to bring about a convergence of mutual interest between the two disciplines. More and more, medical sociologists are being invited to join the staffs of medical institutions and to participate in medical research projects. Medical sociology courses and degrees are now more frequently offered by universities and colleges. The extensive growth of sociological literature in academic medicine is further evidence of the rising status of the medical sociologist. Although a considerable amount of work remains to be done, the medical sociologist at this time is in the enviable position of participating in and influencing the development of an exciting, significant, and relatively new field.

Epidemiology

2

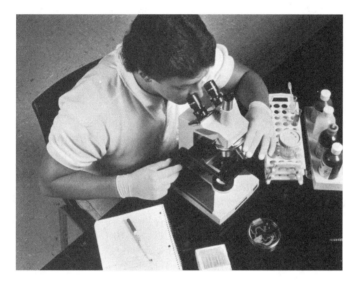

Many sociologists working in the field of medicine are epidemiologists. Epidemiology is a discipline which has evolved relatively specialized methods for investigating health problems. Depending upon the particular health hazard being investigated, epidemiology draws upon the knowledge and techniques of several scientific fields. Besides sociologists, one will find physicians, public health workers, biologists, biochemists, entomologists, ornithologists, mammalogists, veterinarians, demographers, anthropologists, and perhaps even meteorologists (in studies of air pollution) involved in epidemiological work. In its strictest sense, epidemiology is the science of epidemics; however, present-day epidemiologists have broadened their field to include not only epidemic diseases, but also all other forms of disease and bodily injury such as cancer, heart disease, alcoholism, drug addiction, suicide, and automobile accidents. The epidemiologist is concerned with exploring human ecology as it relates to the health of human beings and their environment.

The primary focus of the epidemiologist is not on the individual, but on the health problems of social aggregates or large groups of people. The epidemiologist studies both the origin and distribution of health problems in a population through the collection of data from many different sources. He or she then constructs a logical chain of inferences to explain the various factors in a society or segment of a society that cause a particular health problem to exist. Epidemiology is one of the most important investigative techniques in the study of health and disease.

The role of the epidemiologist can probably be best likened to that of a detective investigating the scene of a crime for clues. The epidemiologist usually begins by examining the sick person or persons and then extends the investigation to the setting where people first became ill and are likely to become ill again. What the epidemiologist is looking for is the common denominator that links all the victims of a health problem together so that the cause of the problem can be identified and eliminated or controlled.

EPIDEMIOLOGICAL MEASURES

Several important analytic concepts assist the epidemiologist in describing the health problems of human groups. One of these concepts pertains to the definition of a *case*. A *case*, in epidemiological terms, refers to an instance of a disorder, illness, or injury involving a person. Two other commonly employed concepts are those of *incidence* and *prevalence*. *Incidence* refers to the number of *new* cases of a specific health disorder occurring within a given population during a stated period of time. The incidence of AIDS during a particular month would be the proportion of persons within a population who are reported as having developed the illness during the month in question. *Prevalence*, in contrast, would be the *total* number of cases of a health disorder that exist at any given time. Prevalence would include new cases as well as all previously existing cases. Prevalence rates are sometimes expressed as *point prevalence* (the number of cases at a certain point in time, usually a particular day or week), *period prevalence* (the total number of cases during a specified period of time, usually a month or year), or *lifetime prevalence* (the number of people who have had the health problem at least once during their lifetime).

One way to distinguish between incidence and prevalence is to regard incidence as the rate at which cases appear, while prevalence is the rate at which all cases exist. To illustrate the difference between incidence and prevalence, consider that the incidence of influenza in a community might be low because no new cases had developed. Yet a measure of the disease's prevalence could be a larger figure because it would represent all persons who are currently sick from the illness. For chronic health disorders like cancer, cases initially reported in terms of incidence for a particular period may be reported later as prevalence because the duration of the disease has caused it to exist for a lengthy period of time. The cases are simply no longer new. The use of data on disease determines whether an analysis should be one of incidence or prevalence. An epidemiologist would use cases denoting incidence if he or she were analyzing the outbreak of a health problem. Cases specifying prevalence would be used to study the overall extent of a disorder.

Regardless of the size of the group under investigation, the epidemiologist is concerned with the computing of ratios. This is done to develop an accurate description of a particular health disorder in relation to a particular population. The epidemiologist accomplishes this task by collecting data from various sources such as face-to-face interviews or reports rendered by various health practitioners, institutions, and agencies. Once the relevant data are gathered, the epidemiologist computes a ratio which demonstrates the incidence and/or prevalence of the health problem. The ratio is always expressed as the total number of cases of a disease compared to the total number of people within a population:

$$\frac{cases}{population}$$

The simplest ratio computed by the epidemiologist is called the *crude rate,* which is the number of persons (cases) who have the characteristics being measured during a specific unit of time. Typical types of crude rates are birth rates and mortality rates. For example, the crude *mortality* (death) *rate* for a particular year is computed by using the number of deaths in that year as the numerator and the total number of residents in a specific population as the denominator. The results are then multiplied by either 1,000, 10,000, or 100,000 depending on whether the mortality rate being figured is for the number of deaths per 1,000, per 10,000, or per 100,000 people. The formula for computing the crude death rate in the United States for 1995 per 1,000 people would be as follows:

$$\frac{\text{Total deaths, all ages, 1995}}{\substack{\text{Estimated U.S. population} \\ \text{on June 30, 1995}}} \times 1,000 = 1995 \text{ death rate}$$

Crude death and birth rates, however, are usually too gross a measure to be meaningful for most sociological purposes. Sociologists are typically concerned with the effects of specific variables or social characteristics within a population such as age, sex, race, occupation, or any other measure of significant social differences. *Age-specific rates* are an example of rates used to show differences by age. Age-specific rates are computed in the same way as crude rates, except the numerator and the denominator are confined to a specific age group (a similar method can be used to determine sex-specific rates, race-specific rates, and so forth). In order to calculate an age-specific rate, the procedure is to subdivide a population by age and then compare the number of cases in this subpopulation with the total number of persons within the subpopulation. If you wanted to compute the age-specific mortality rate for all infants for a particular year in the United States, for example, you would need to know how many infants there were in that year and the number of deaths that occurred in this age-specific group. The *infant mortality rate,* a measure of the deaths of all infants in a geographical area under the age of one year, is a very common age-specific rate in epidemiology. You would compute the 1995 U.S. infant mortality rate in the following manner:

$$\frac{\text{Total number of deaths in 1995 among persons aged less than one year}}{\text{Number of live births during 1995}} \times 1,000 = 1995 \text{ infant mortality rate}$$

The infant mortality rate has special significance for a society because it is traditionally used as an approximate measure of a society's sanitary and medical standards. For instance, the infant mortality rate in the United States in 1900 per 1,000 infants was 162.4; by 1940 this rate had been reduced to 47.0 as a result of improvement in health care, diet, and living conditions. After World War II further advances reduced infant mortality rates per 1,000 infants to 29.2 in 1950, 27.0 in 1960, 20.0 in 1970, 12.6 in 1980, and 9.2 in 1990. Infant mortality rates during the twentieth century have traditionally been lowest in technologically advanced societies such as Japan, Sweden, the Netherlands, Great Britain, the United States, Canada, and Australia. The highest rates have usually been in the underdeveloped countries of Asia, Africa, and South America.

Another type of rate is the *standardized rate,* which is also known as the *standardized mortality ratio* (SMR). This rate is used to compare the mortality experience of different proportions of people grouped by age or sex with that of the total population. Rodney Coe (1978) provides us with an excellent example of a standardized rate in a comparison of mortality rates for the United States and Chile for 1972. The crude death rate for both countries that year was 9.4 per 1,000 persons. Can it therefore be assumed that the level of health in the two countries was about the same? The crude death rates may be the same, but the age distribution of the two populations were not. Utilization of a standardized rate shows us that the two countries differed significantly in deaths. By computing the age-specific rates for each sex and determining the number of deaths observed to the number expected, based on summing the number of deaths in each age group, a more precise measure was calculated. The principal difference between the two countries was that while the crude death rate was the same, the standardized rate showed that a significantly larger number of children under the age of five died in Chile than in the United States. In Chile, the death rate per 1,000 was 21.4 and 18.9, respectively, for young boys and young girls; in the United States, the figures were 4.6 for boys and 3.6 for girls. Hence, Chile had much higher mortality rates for the young and levels of health in the two countries could therefore not be considered equal in 1972. More children in Chile did not survive to reach old age.

THE DEVELOPMENT OF EPIDEMIOLOGY

As a method of measuring diseases in human aggregates, epidemiology has been a relatively recent development. So long as human beings lived as nomads or in widely scattered and isolated communities, the danger from epidemics and infectious disease was relatively slight. However, once people began to crowd into primitive cities with unsanitary living conditions and an abundance of rats and lice, the probabilities favoring the development of communicable diseases greatly increased. The crowded conditions of urban living also ensured that infectious diseases would spread more quickly and that disease-causing microorganisms would persist within the community for longer periods of time. In addition, the migration of peoples from one region of the world to another spread disease from geographic area to geographic area. Bubonic plague, for example, apparently reached Europe from China during the fourteenth century, cholera entered Great Britain by way of India in the seventeenth century, while Europeans brought smallpox to the Western Hemisphere during the exploration and settlement of the New World. History reveals numerous examples of explorers and travelers introducing the microorganisms of a dreaded disease to a community of unsuspecting people.

The bubonic plague that ravaged Europe between 1340 and 1750 marks one of the worst epidemic afflictions in all human history. It is estimated that one-quarter of the population of Europe died during its greatest prevalence (Paul 1966). During one single month (September 1665) in one city (London), approximately 30,000 people died from the plague. Describing conditions in the fourteenth century, historian Barbara Tuchman (1978:92) reports: "So lethal was the disease that cases were known of persons going to bed well and dying before they awoke, of doctors catching the illness at a bedside and dying before the patient." What made the disease especially frightening was that no one knew what caused it, how to prevent it, or how to cure it. Yet even though the pestilence affected the rich and poor alike, there was still a *social* difference in the death rates. The poor were much more likely to die from it than the rich. Tuchman says:

> Flight was the chief recourse of those who could afford it or arrange it. The rich fled to their country places like Boccaccio's young patricians of Florence, who settled in a pastoral palace "removed on every side from the roads" with "wells of cool water and vaults of rare wine." The urban poor died in their burrows, "and only the stench of their bodies informed their neighbors of their death." That the poor were more heavily afflicted than the rich was clearly remarked at the time, in the north as in the south. A Scottish chronicler, John of Fordum, stated flatly that the pest "attacked especially the meaner sort and common people—seldom the magnates." Simon de Covino of Montpellier made the same observation. He ascribed it to the misery and want and hard lives that made the poor more susceptible, which was half the truth. Close contact and lack of sanitation was the unrecognized other half of it.[1]

The cause of the plague was thought by many to be God's wrath upon sinners; however, the realization eventually came that diseases could be transmitted from person to person or between animals and people. The origin of the

---

[1] Barbara W. Tuchman, *A Distant Mirror: The Calamitous 14th Century* (New York: Random House, 1978), p. 98.

plague turned out to be the flea of the black rat, but the pneumonic plague, the most deadly form of the bubonic plague, was transmitted from person to person. What actually ended the plague about 1750 was the appearance in cities of the aggressive brown rat. The brown rat tended to avoid humans, had fleas that were less effective carriers, and drove most of Europe's black rats out of urban areas. Another very important factor was the development of improved housing and sanitation.

One of the earliest epidemiological studies was conducted by Sir Percival Pott in England in 1775 (Graham 1972). Pott observed that English chimney sweeps seemed to have a high incidence of cancer of the scrotum. He reasoned that the chimney sweep's occupation, which placed him in close and frequent contact with soot, might be the cause of cancer of the scrotum among those individuals who were susceptible to the disease. Pott suggested a relationship between a behavior (chimney sweeping) and a disease of a specific organ (cancer of the scrotum). He demonstrated that if behavior were changed by increased bathing, the incidence of the disease could be reduced. Pott's work showed that behavior can significantly affect susceptibility to a particular disease.

However, epidemiology as a form of systematic analysis did not develop until the nineteenth century. It was not until 1854 that the work of John Snow established the foundation of modern epidemiology. Snow was an English physician who plotted the geographic location of all reported cholera cases in London. He then went out into the neighborhoods of these victims and inquired into their day-to-day behavior. He wanted to know what they ate, what they drank, where they went, and the nature of all their activities. Eventually Snow began to suspect that cholera was transmitted by water, since the common factor in the daily lives of the victims was getting their water from the Broad Street pump. At that time, London obtained drinking water from several water companies, and a few of these companies apparently were providing water contaminated with cholera bacteria. By closing down the pump on Broad Street, Snow was able to stop the epidemic. He not only established a mode of investigation but also demonstrated that research could lead to positive action.

At the time of Snow's research, the development of scientific medicine was well underway. The work of Pasteur and his immediate followers during the latter part of the nineteenth century revolutionized medical thought with the germ theory of disease stipulating that bacteria were the source of infection in the human body. The findings of Snow, Pasteur, and others provided the epidemiologist with a framework of analysis. Recognition that germs were causal agents of disease served as a precursor to scientific determination that people come into contact with a variety of causal agents. These agents include (1) biological agents, such as bacteria, viruses, or insects; (2) nutritional agents, such as fats and carbohydrates as producers of cholesterol; (3) chemical agents, such as gases and toxic chemicals that pollute the air, water, and land; (4) physical agents, such as climate or vegetation; and (5) social agents, such as occupation, social class, location of residence, or lifestyle. What a person does, who a person is, and where a person lives can specify what health hazards are most likely to exist in that individual's life. The epidemiologist then identifies a particular host (person or group of persons or animals) most susceptible to these causal agents. Human hosts are examined in terms of characteristics that are both biological (age, sex, race, degree of immunity, and other physical attributes that promote resistance or susceptibility) and behavioral (habits, customs, and lifestyle). Next, the physical and social environment of the causal agent and the host is explored. The result is intended to be an identification of *what* is causing a group of people to become sick or suffer injury.

The term *social environment* in epidemiological research refers to actual living conditions, such as poverty or crowding, and also the norms, values, and attitudes that reflect a particular social and cultural context. Societies have socially prescribed patterns of behavior and living arrangements, as well as standards pertaining to the use of water, food and food handling, and household and personal hygiene. Therefore, the social environment provides information that can be used not only to identify causal agents and to trace the transmission process, but also to assist in ascertaining the most effective means of treatment and prevention within that particular environment.

THE COMPLEXITY OF MODERN ILLS: CORONARY HEART DISEASE

Many contemporary epidemiological problems are extremely complex, as the major health threat to contemporary society is from a variety of chronic and degenerative ills related to aging and the effects of man-made environments. The role of multicausality in disease causation is particularly apparent with respect to coronary heart disease.

Coronary heart disease is the leading cause of death in the United States, accounting for more than one-third of all deaths. As shown in the Framingham, Massachusetts research project (Dawber et al. 1963; Sytkowski, Kannel, and D'Agostino 1990), a number of factors are responsible for this disease. Begun during the 1950s, this study has shown that arteriosclerosis does not strike people at random as they age, but that highly susceptible individuals can be identified in advance. Some 5,000 persons initially participated in the study, and 5,000 of their children were added in a second-generation project beginning in 1970. They were all between the ages of thirty and sixty and were free from any form of heart disease at the time of their initial examination. They were given relatively complete physical examinations every two years. The data clearly suggest that male sex, advancing age, high blood pressure, cigarette smoking, diabetes, and obesity constitute significant risk factors in whether a person develops heart disease.

The proportion of risk that a person assumes with respect to each of these specific risk factors is unknown. For example, about twice as many males die from coronary heart disease than females. But even though men have the greater overall risk, they are more likely than women to have a favorable prognosis if they survive the first serious heart attack (Wenger 1982). Furthermore, women with diabetes do not show any special advantage over men when it comes to heart disease. In fact, as the Framingham study indicates, women who are diabetic, obese, and have a high level of harmful low density lipoprotein cholesterol are particularly prone to coronary heart disease. Therefore, when epidemiologists analyze heart disease, they must contend with a variety of relationships between the various risk factors.

However, not everyone with the attributes identified in the Framingham study gets the disease. It appears that there are social and psychological risk factors as well. One of the most thoroughly documented associations with heart disease is that of Type A behavior. Type A behavior is characterized as that of excessive drive, intense ambition and aggressiveness, and a strong sense of time urgency. Such persons tend to be intensely involved in competitive activities and a demanding schedule. Type A behavior is thought to be most common among middle- and upper-class males with a strong desire for overachievement, money, status, and personal recognition. However, Meyer Friedman and Ray Rosenman (1974) point out that Type A behavior is not limited to persons in high-status occupations; rather, janitors, truck drivers, shoe salesmen, and even florists can exhibit Type A personality traits.

Type B behavior, in contrast, is a more balanced and less intense approach to situational pressures. The Type B person may, in fact, be a highly successful person in his or her occupation but not be as harried, time sensitive, or compulsive as a Type A person. According to a series of longitudinal studies, men with Type A behavior, as compared with those who primarily show Type B behavior, have been found to have significantly higher risk of heart disease (Cohen et al. 1979; Drews 1986; Friedman and Rosenman 1974; Jenkins 1971). People with a tendency toward Type A behavior may be more likely to select stressful occupations or to perceive stress in the jobs they choose. The result is the same, however. Type A individuals suffer greater emotional strain in their daily lives and tend to enhance the probability of having a heart attack.

Yet recent findings indicate that if both Type A and Type B men have a heart attack, the Type A individual is more likely to survive it (Ragland and Brand 1988). Thus, it may be that Type A behavior promotes heart attacks but when this happens the Type A person is more likely to live through it than a Type B person. More research is needed to confirm this finding; however, such results underscore the complexity of understanding chronic illnesses like coronary heart disease.

Although coronary heart disease remains America's leading killer, since the mid-1960s there has been a rapid decline in deaths from the disease for both men and women. About 308 of every 100,000 persons in the general population died from heart disease in 1950 compared with a rate of 152 persons per 100,000 in 1990. Coronary heart disease comprises about 90 percent of all heart disease deaths. Improved medical services and surgical techniques, modified eating habits, increased exercise, decreased smoking, and improved control of blood pressure have been cited as responsible for this decline (Kannel 1982).

What is encouraging about this development and of particular interest is that the risk of coronary heart disease can be significantly reduced if people improve in just four areas: stop smoking, control high blood pressure, eat to lower cholesterol and avoid being overweight, and exercise. Moreover, in 1988, regular use of aspirin was identified as a possible means to reduce heart attacks through its action in preventing blood clots. It is apparent that coronary heart disease is a complex disorder and that changes in behavior can result in a substantially reduced risk. We see this, for example, in studies of diet and exercise.

Diet

A major study conducted in Oslo, Norway by I. Hjermann and his associates (1981) has shown exceptionally strong evidence that eating less fats and cholesterol can reduce the chances of a heart attack or sudden death from heart disease. The study also found that a small benefit could be derived from stopping smoking or reducing the number of cigarettes smoked. The research was begun in 1972 among 1,232 men forty to forty-nine years old who were selected because they faced a high risk of developing heart disease. Their blood pressure was normal but their cholesterol levels were high and 80 percent of them smoked cigarettes. An analysis of their normal diets showed that most consumed foods high in saturated fats and cholesterol. Foods like butter, sausage, high-fat cheese, eggs, and whole milk were prominent in their diets. The men were randomly assigned either to an experimental or control group. The experimental group was given advice to give up smoking and eat a cholesterol-lowering diet. The new diet included substituting skim milk for whole milk, eating no more than one egg a week, using polyunsaturated oil for cooking, having fruit for dessert, making sandwiches with high-fiber breads, fish, and low-fat cheese or meat, and using fish or low-fat meat with potatoes and vegetables for main dishes. No drugs were used and no recommendations were made to exercise or lose weight, which changed only minimally during the five-year experiment.

In 1977, cholesterol levels were 13 percent lower for the experimental group. Also, the ratio of protective high density lipoprotein cholesterol had risen in comparison to low density lipoprotein cholesterol. Hjermann and his colleagues found that the consumption of less saturated fat, usually animal fat, was the single most influential dietary change. They determined that this change accounted for 60 percent of the difference in the number of heart attacks and deaths from heart disease suffered by the two groups of men. Changes in smoking accounted for another 25 percent of the reduction in heart disease.

Altogether, the men in the experimental group had a 47 percent lower rate of heart attacks and sudden deaths than the men in the control group. In 1980, the Food and Nutrition Board of the National Academy of Sciences had concluded that no study had shown convincing evidence that reduced cholesterol levels in the blood through dietary change saved lives. The Oslo study, however, helped to reverse that conclusion because it produced strong evidence of the life-saving value of changing dietary habits.

Exercise

Another major study on coronary heart disease dealt with exercise and participation in sports. This study, conducted by Ralph Paffenbarger and his associates (Paffenbarger, Hyde, Wing, and Hsieh 1986) investigated the physical activity and lifestyle characteristics of 16,936 Harvard University alumni, aged thirty-four to seventy-four, for a period of twelve to sixteen years (1962–1978). It was found that exercise (such as walking, climbing stairs, and playing sports) improved life expectancy for all causes of mortality—but especially for heart disease. Death rates were one-fourth to one-third lower among Harvard alumni who expended 2,000 or more calories in exercise per week than among less active men. Risks of death were highest among those who did not exercise and who also had hypertension and smoked cigarettes. By the age of eighty, Paffenbarger estimates that regular exercise has provided an additional one to more than two years of longevity. In a subsequent study of Harvard alumni, Paffenbarger and his colleagues (1993) analyzed changes in lifestyle activities between 1977 and 1985 and determined that beginning moderately vigorous sports activity was associated with lower rates of deaths from all causes and particularly from coronary heart disease. Quitting cigarette smoking, avoiding obesity, amd maintaining normal blood pressure were also significant in reducing mortality rates.

However, Paffenbarger and his associates (1986, 1993) found that light sports did not influence the incidence of coronary heart disease; rather, moderately vigorous exercise was required. This same result was found in Great Britain and Germany as well. In Great Britain, an analysis of the physical activities and lifestyles of a group of 1,394 male factory workers disclosed that only relatively strenuous physical activity (especially cycling) in leisure time was related to fitness (Tuxworth, Nevill, White, and Jenkins 1986). Light exercise made no difference. Other researchers (Hollmann et al. 1985) in Germany likewise determined that endurance sports or training during leisure time can have a more positive effect on the cardiovascular system than heavy muscular work on the job.

Studies such as these have led to the conclusion that regular physical activity should be promoted in coronary heart disease prevention programs as vigorously as blood pressure control, diet, lowering of cholesterol levels, and smoking cessation (Blair et al. 1989; Powell, Thompson, Caspersen and Kenderick 1987). In a review of relevant studies published between 1980 and 1987, the Centers for Disease Control and Prevention (1987) determined that lack of physical activity is associated with coronary heart disease and recommended the promotion of a lifestyle for Americans that includes regularly scheduled physical activity. Figure 2-1, based upon Centers for Disease Control and Prevention estimates, shows that physical inactivity is a risk factor for coronary heart disease for 59 percent of all Americans, followed by cigarette smoking (18 percent), cholesterol (10 percent), and high blood pressure (10 percent). What is suggested by Figure 2-1 is that more Americans appear to be at risk for coronary heart disease because of physical inactivity than because of the other three major risk factors of blood pressure, cholesterol, and smoking.

FIGURE 2-1   Estimated percentage of population having selected
risk factors for coronary heart disease, by risk factor—
United States*

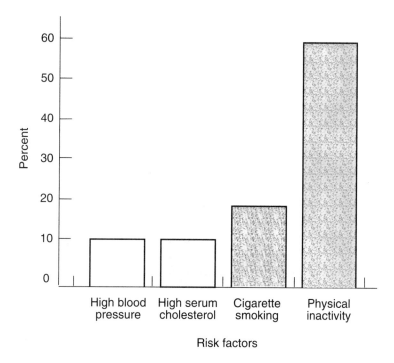

*Based on studies reported 1980–1987.

Source: Centers for Disease Control and Prevention, 1987, 1990, 1993.

In order to reduce the risk of heart disease, the Centers for Disease
Control and Prevention recommend approximately thirty minutes or more of
moderate physical activity—the equivalent of a brisk walk at three to four miles
an hour—at least five days a week. However, data collected by the Centers for
Disease Control and Prevention for 1991 show that some 57.7 percent of all men
and 58.5 percent of all women in the United States live a sedentary lifestyle. A
sedentary lifestyle is a way of living that involves no or irregular physical leisure-
time activity. Therefore, it appears that a majority of Americans do not exercise
despite lack of physical activity being such a significant risk factor for coronary
heart disease.

DISEASE AND MODERNIZATION

Although heart disease joins cancer, stroke, accidents, and mental disorders as the
leading causes of disability and death in advanced industrial societies, the underdeveloped nations of the world show somewhat different patterns of major health

problems. In these societies, the traditional diseases of human history influenced by poor sanitation and malnutrition often prevail. Underdeveloped nations usually are characterized by a high birth rate and a high death rate, with a relatively young population because various diseases do not allow large numbers of people to live a long life.

A major distinction, therefore, in how diseases are distributed among population groups becomes apparent when the health profiles of industrialized societies are compared to those of underdeveloped nations. Although malnutrition may occur in the United States and heart disease may occur in rural India, these cases do not follow general societal patterns. Many epidemiologists insist that there is a regular sequence of health problems corresponding to each stage of a nation's change in social organization from a rural to an urban society and from an agricultural to an industrial producer. For example, Table 2-1 shows the leading causes of death in the United States in 1900 were influenza and pneumonia, and tuberculosis. In 1992 these disorders had been replaced by heart disease, cancer, accidents, and cerebrovascular disease or stroke as the major causes of death in an increasingly urban and industrialized society. Improvements in living conditions and medical technology had all but eliminated disorders such as tuberculosis, gastroenteritis, and diphtheria as major threats to life in 1992, but smoking, excessive consumption of calories and animal fats, stress reactions, and inadequate physical activity had helped promote other health problems, such as heart disease and other cardiovascular disorders like cerebrovascular diseases. Homicide and AIDS, major health problems in the United States, had made their appearance as top ten killers by 1992.

The same type of pattern occurs in other countries as they experience modernization. For instance, Jamaica in 1920 had a level of health similar to that of the poorest country in Africa today (Cumper 1983). But once development was underway, Jamaica's traditional pattern of health problems changed. There was a remarkable fall, as statistics for the period 1945 to 1970 show, in mortality from infectious diseases (principally tuberculosis and syphilis) and parasitic disorders (mainly malaria). There were also declines in other diseases of the digestive and

TABLE 2-1   The Ten Leading Causes of Death in the United States, 1900 and 1992

1900	1992
Influenza and pneumonia	Heart disease
Tuberculosis	Cancer
Gastroenteritis	Accidents
Heart disease	Cerebrovascular diseases
Cerebral hemorrhage	Pulmonary diseases
Chronic nephritis	Influenza and pneumonia
Accidents	Diabetes
Cancer	Suicide
Diseases of early infancy	AIDS
Diphtheria	Homicide

respiratory systems with a communicable component. Life expectancy increased from fifty-three to sixty-eight years and infant mortality dropped from 90 to 32 per 1,000 live births. However, death rates increased for cancer and diseases of the heart and nervous system.

A similar situation occurred in Hong Kong. Up until the early 1950s, as Rance Lee (1983) points out, infectious diseases were the major causes of death. But in recent decades, the incidence of serious infectious diseases has been negligible. "Nowadays," states Lee (1983:1433), "people come to be concerned with noninfectious diseases such as cancer, heart diseases, strokes, mental disorders and occupational diseases." With infant mortality rates decreasing from 91.8 to 7.4 per 1,000 live births between 1951 and 1989 and life expectancy rising to seventy-two years for men and seventy-eight for women, the leading causes of death in Hong Kong are now those associated with aging rather than infection. The improvement in overall levels of health is due to socioeconomic progress and also reflects the development of better medical and health services.

Modernization, however, not only changes patterns of disease but introduces new health problems as well. In Nigeria, for instance, deaths from traffic accidents increased more than threefold since the start of an oil boom (Agbonifo 1983; Ungar 1989). By the mid-1980s, Nigeria had the world's highest mortality rates from automobile accidents (Ityavyar 1988). And, in several developing nations in Africa and Asia, there has been a growing concern with environmental pollution as chemicals and poisonous wastes begin to pollute the air and water as has happened in nations at a higher state of economic development. Health disorders associated with stress and psychological distress also become more prevalent as society becomes more modern (Lee 1983). Finally, it should be noted that the steady increase in cigarette smoking in developing countries has been accompanied by soaring rates of lung cancer and heart disease. Lung cancer is now the most common type of cancer among men in the Philippines and has jumped into first place among the cancers most often observed in Pakistan.

Moreover, modernization and improvement in health care delivery services take place at a different pace in different nations. Not every country has the wealth that a major oil-producing nation like Saudi Arabia can use to build hospitals and an extensive system of neighborhood clinics and hire large numbers of foreign doctors and nurses while their citizens are being trained. As Richard Kurtz and H. Paul Chalfant (1984) explain, a country like Tanzania may have the same basic philosophy as an oil-rich nation in improving the level of health of its people but may lack the resources to do more than make only limited progress. In Tanzania the emphasis has been on establishing rural health clinics and training local villagers to treat minor ailments, while sending out mobile health units to provide both medical treatment and education in preventive measures. Tanzania is one of the poorest countries in the world. Birth rates are high and life expectancy is low—about 50 years for males and 52.5 years for females. Yet the health situation in Tanzania appears to be getting better and its health system is considered one of the most promising among the poor nations of Africa (Elling 1980; Ungar 1989). Life expectancy has increased and infant mortality dropped from 197 deaths per 1,000 live births in 1967 to 106 in 1987.

Unfortunately, many of the people in Tanzania and elsewhere are trapped in a vicious circle. They are undernourished and sick because they are poor and they are poor because they are undernourished and sick. The link between poverty and poor health remains strong in most of the world. Even in highly developed countries like the United States and Great Britain, modern systems of health care delivery have not been entirely successful in mitigating or preventing health problems stemming from poverty. While modernization usually brings a higher overall standard of living and improved health, it also brings the diseases of advanced civilization, which the poor continue to share disproportionately.

The struggle against disease never ends. In some ways it becomes even more difficult as disease agents begin operating in more subtle and unanticipated ways—often in relation to certain forms of behavior and lifestyles. AIDS is a major example of this development.

AIDS

The Acquired Immune Deficiency Syndrome, known as AIDS, is a disease of society in the most profound sense (Nelkin, Willis, and Parris 1990). AIDS is a particularly deadly disease that destroys a person's immunity against infection, thereby leaving the individual defenseless against a variety of afflictions like cancer, pneumonia, and a host of viruses. AIDS is a virus itself—the human immunodeficiency virus (HIV)—transmitted through vaginal or anal intercourse, intravenous drug use, blood transfusions, or passed to newborn infants by infected mothers.

What makes AIDS a disease of society is that it is clearly grounded in the conduct of social life, and its potential for changing norms, values, sex habits, and lifestyles worldwide is enormous. Thus, AIDS is no "ordinary" epidemic; it is a lethal illness with far-reaching implications for individuals, families, health care providers and delivery systems, and societies across the globe (Bosk and Frader 1990; Brooks-Gunn and Furstenberg 1990; Conrad 1986a; Earickson 1990; Fox, Aiken, and Messikomer 1990; Kaplan et al. 1987; Le Blanc 1993; Levine 1990; Nelkin, Willis, and Parris 1990).

Signs of the disease appeared first in the autumn of 1979. Young homosexual men with a history of promiscuity began showing up at clinics in New York, Los Angeles, and San Francisco with an unusual array of ailments. Some had strange fungal infections and others had rare cancers, such as Kaposi's sarcoma that is found only among elderly men of Mediterranean extraction or young men from equatorial Africa. Some had a deadly pneumonia, *Pneumocystis carinii*, seldom seen except in cancer and organ transplant patients weakened from prolonged treatment with drugs. Information from physicians in Los Angeles and New York City alerted the Center for Disease Control in Atlanta to the problems in early 1981. Some fifty cases were initially identified around the country and each of these individuals was interviewed. But what caused the disease and how it could be treated remained unknown as the number of victims began to increase at an alarming rate.

By mid-1984, 4,918 persons in the United States had developed AIDS; many of them died. While homosexual organizations complained that the federal government had little interest in solving the outbreak since most of the victims were homosexuals, a task force was formed at the Center for Disease Control. At first, it was thought that the cause might be an inhalant, known as "Rush" or "poppers," containing either amyl nitrate or butyl nitrate, sometimes used by homosexuals to produce a "high" during sex. But this was ruled out after interviews with gay men who used the inhalants and did not come down with AIDS. This development directed the attention of the investigators toward a virus or some other infectious agent transmitted by sexual contact or dirty needles, since some of the victims used drugs. Support for this theory began to emerge after a few heterosexual drug abusers and a baby in San Francisco who received blood from a donor with AIDS contracted the disease. The strongest evidence on the means of transmission came from sexual histories obtained in Los Angeles. AIDS was consistently linked with the sexual encounters of the victims, with the agent possibly entering the blood stream through the anus. Three different men, for instance, none of whom were acquainted with each other, identified a man in New York City as a sexual partner; he was found to have AIDS.

The next clues were somewhat puzzling because AIDS turned up in immigrants from Haiti where homosexuality is considered exceptionally taboo. Many of these victims denied they were homosexual or drug users, but additional investigation showed they may have gotten the disease this way. One theory holds that AIDS may have originated in central Africa and was carried to Haiti where it reached the United States through homosexual contacts. But no scientific evidence has been produced that proves this theory.

AIDS research has confirmed that the disease is a virus, but attempts to find a cure have not been successful to date. It is now known that infection occurs when the virus enters the blood stream, with anal intercourse and intravenous drug use the most common means of transmission in Western societies. In the United States, Centers for Disease Control and Prevention data for 1991 show that 55 percent of all cases reported were homosexual and bisexual men, 24 percent were IV drug users, and 5 percent were homosexuals and IV drug users. Of the remaining AIDS cases, 7 percent resulted from heterosexual contacts, 1 percent were hemophilia cases, 2 percent were blood transfusion recipients, and the remaining 5 percent were from other causes or the origin of the infection could not be determined.

Routine, nonintimate contact in the home or workplace with persons with AIDS does not appear to spread the infection. Much of the fear about AIDS arises from the fact that many people who carry the virus are not aware of it. The virus can remain in the body without causing the disease, but among those who do develop AIDS, the average time between infection and diagnosis can be five years or longer. Thus, AIDS carriers can unknowingly infect other people for a number of years since the only method to determine if a person is HIV-infected in the absence of symptoms is through a blood test. As a study (Prohaska et al. 1990) in Chicago shows, some people consider themselves at risk for developing AIDS—especially if they have had multiple sex partners and know little about the partners' past sexual behavior.

Between 1984 and September 1993, the total number of AIDS cases in the United States rose from nearly 5,000 to 334,344. Some 201,775 persons have died. Figure 2-2 depicts the number of reported cases per 100,000 of the population for 1992. The District of Columbia had the highest rates in the nation in 1992 with 123.2 cases per 100,000 population. Puerto Rico was second with a rate of 48.4 cases per 100,000 population, followed by New York (45.0), Florida (41.8), and New Jersey (29.6). South Dakota had the lowest incidence of AIDS at 0.4 cases per 100,000.

For males, Centers for Disease Control and Prevention data for 1991 indicate that over 60 percent of all AIDS cases are non-Hispanic whites, about 25 percent are blacks, and nearly 16 percent are Hispanics. AIDS has continued to spread among young adult males to the point that, by 1992, it had become the leading killer of men twenty-five to forty-four years old in the United States.

FIGURE 2-2   Acquired immunodeficiency syndrome (AIDS)—Cases per 100,000 population, reported to CDCP by state, United States, 1991

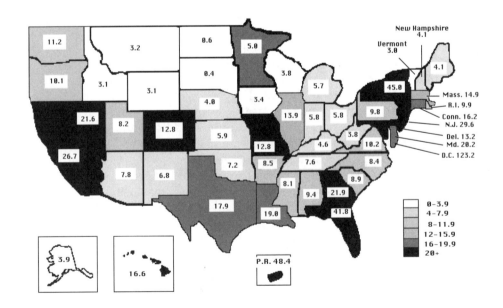

Source: Centers for Disease Control and Prevention, 1992.

From 1982 to 1992, the death rate for men aged twenty-five to forty-four has increased from 0.6 per 100,000 to 52.8 per 100,000. For females, over half of all AIDS victims are black, less than 30 percent are non-Hispanic whites, and nearly 20 percent are Hispanics. The Centers for Disease Control and Prevention has continued to report since 1990 that AIDS is increasing among women. AIDS rose from being the eighth leading cause of death for women between the ages of twenty-five to forty-four in 1987 to fourth place in 1992. From 1982 to 1992, deaths from AIDS rose from 0.1 per 100,000 to 7.8 per 100,000 for women in this age group. Most women become infected by AIDS from either IV drug use or sexual relations with men who are either bisexuals, IV drug users, or both.

The World Health Organization (WHO) estimated in 1992 that about one million Americans are carriers of the AIDS virus, but no one really knows for sure how many persons carry the virus but are not yet ill. Also, no one knows what proportion of those persons who are infected will ultimately develop the disease, nor how rapidly it will spread among American heterosexuals in the 1990s. The spread of AIDS among male homosexuals may be lessening through changes in sexual behavior, such as significantly reducing the number of sex partners and avoiding anal intercourse. New infections seem to be increasing the greatest among poor blacks and Hispanics in the inner city. They spread AIDS among themselves by sharing contaminated needles as they inject drugs and through sexual intercourse, either homosexual or heterosexual.

On a worldwide basis, WHO estimates that 10 million people were affected by the AIDS virus, with about 6.5 million of them in Africa. By the year 2000, WHO estimates that up to 40 million people may be infected. AIDS has been particularly prevalent in central Africa and is spreading rapidly throughout the African continent south of the Sahara Desert. About 5 to 20 percent of the adults in the major cities of central and east Africa are believed to be HIV-infected and the disease is moving into rural areas as well; African nations like Malawi, Burundi, Uganda, and Zambia have the highest rates per capita of AIDS in the world (Barnett and Blaike 1992; Earickson 1990; Ungar 1989; Obbo 1993; Walle 1990).

However, in striking contrast to Western society, AIDS is transmitted in Africa primarily by conventional sexual intercourse among heterosexuals. About 80 percent of all AIDS cases in Africa are believed to result from heterosexual relations. AIDS is especially prevalent among prostitutes, migrant workers, and long-distance truck drivers—but reaches up to include significant numbers of people in upper socioeconomic groups. The migrant labor system in sub-Saharan Africa plays a particularly important role in the transmission of AIDS (Hunt 1989; Obbo 1993). Whereas African women living in rural areas typically remain in their villages to work and care for their family, African men form a large migrant labor pool seeking greater economic opportunity in mining areas, large commercial farming areas, and some large cities. This system of labor, Charles Hunt (1989) explains, causes long absences, increased family breakdown, and increased numbers of sexual partners. This situation has created a large population that suffers from epidemics of sexually transmitted diseases—which has made it especially vulnerable to the AIDS virus. AIDS does affect women in Africa almost as often as men. Between 40 and 50 percent of all AIDS cases are women. Why the pattern of AIDS transmission seems to differ so drastically in Africa than elsewhere still remains a mystery. But it may be that sores and genital ulcers caused by other widespread sexually transmitted diseases like syphilis enhance the potential for AIDS transmission between men and women.

In Europe, the AIDS epidemic has followed the same pattern as in the United States, with the centers of infection found in major cities among homosexual and bisexual men and IV drug users. WHO estimated in 1992 that 500,000 people were HIV-infected in Europe. As for reported AIDS cases, Figure 2-3 shows the rates for thirteen Western European countries as of mid-March 1993. Switzerland had the highest rate with 43.6 AIDS cases per 100,000 of its population, followed by Spain (43.0) and France (40.6). Greece (7.2) and Norway (7.5) had the lowest rates. AIDS is principally transmitted by IV drug use in southern European countries like Italy and Spain but is passed in northern European countries like Denmark, Germany, and Great Britain largely through homosexual contact. Germany, however, had a major scandal in 1993 when a blood plasma company distributed blood contaminated with the AIDS virus to several German hospitals and clinics, as well as to foreign clients in Europe. Some employees were arrested for fraud and negligent manslaughter.

AIDS victims in Asia were few until the late 1980s when the disease began spreading rapidly. WHO estimates that over 1 million people in Asia were

FIGURE 2-3   AIDS cases in Western Europe per 100,000 people through mid-March, 1993

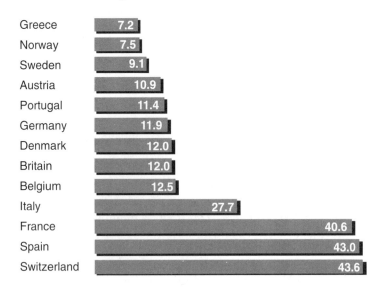

Source: World Health Organization data, 1993.

HIV-infected in 1992. Thailand and Myanmar (formerly Burma), which have many prostitutes and drug users, are centers of AIDS. The Thai government estimates that 200,000 to 400,000 people are infected out of a population of 58 million, but the number could reach 2 to 4 million or 6 percent of the population by 2000. Myanmar is believed to have about 100,000 people infected out of a population of 40 million. AIDS is also spreading in India where perhaps 1 million people—more than in Europe and about as many in the United states—are thought to be infected in a total population of 860 million. Prostitution in large cities like Bombay and Madras and drug use in northeast India are believed responsible for the spread of AIDS. The Indian Health Organization estimates that some 20 to 50 million Indians may be infected with HIV by 2000. Consequently, AIDS is emerging as a major health disaster in India.

Australia is estimated by WHO to have about 30,000 people HIV-infected. In Japan, only some 2,639 people had officially tested positive for HIV in mid-1992, but the government expects this figure to increase rapidly. Sexual intercourse with female prostitutes in Thailand, the Philippines, and other Asian countries by Japanese men is believed to be a major factor in spreading the disease in Japan. The Japanese public, however, does not view AIDS as a very serious problem, believing it to be associated with other countries and largely confined in Japan to small groups of homosexuals and hemophiliacs (Munakata 1992, 1994).

Another part of the world in which AIDS is on the increase is Central and South America and the Caribbean. AIDS first appeared among homosexuals and drug users in Haiti, Argentina, and Brazil. It is now spreading throughout the region. Bisexual activity by Latin American men is believed to be important in the infection of a large proportion of females. WHO estimates that about one million Latin Americans are HIV-infected. Some 60,000 of them have been diagnosed with AIDS. Brazil has the largest concentration of AIDS cases—nearly 35,000 in 1992—among Latin American countries. The number of recorded AIDS cases in Mexico has increased rapidly from 246 in 1986 to 11,034 in 1992. Latin America may be on the verge of a major AIDS epidemic.

AIDS thus stands as an example of how a certain type of behavior (especially homosexuality or drug use) provided a particular virus with the opportunity to cause a deadly disease. The sociological implications of the AIDS epidemic are enormous and involve not only the widespread modification of sexual behavior, but the deeply discrediting stigma attached to AIDS victims, the social rejection of AIDS patients, the subjective distress associated with becoming an AIDS patient, and the moral and religious debate centering on AIDS as a punishment for a deviant lifestyle (Bennett 1987; Fox, Aiken, and Messikomer 1990; Kaplan, Johnson, Bailey, and Simon 1987; Nisbet and McQueen 1993; Siegel and Krauss 1991; Turner, Hayes, and Coates 1993; Velmirovic 1987; Weitz 1989).

As Renée Fox and her associates (1990:239) observe: "The fact that a large proportion of people with AIDS are homosexual or bisexual men and intravenous (IV) drug users has evoked widespread stigmatizing, shunning, and discriminatory reactions to persons with AIDS." Thus, when one becomes infected with AIDS, that person in many ways becomes a social outcast—avoided by former friends and acquaintances. People often have a "master status," which is a general status that reflects an individual's most important position in society and typically comes from one's occupation. AIDS, however, can take on the attributes of a master status in that it becomes the single most important social characteristic of an infected person. Regardless of income, education, occupation, or other source of status, persons with AIDS will likely find that having the disease will negatively influence the attitudes and reactions of others. Rose Weitz (1989), for example, found in a group of homosexual and bisexual men with AIDS in Arizona that the disease had a highly negative impact on their social lives.

AIDS throws families into crisis as well. Carol Levine (1990) explains that not only do children with AIDS have families, but this is often the case with homosexuals and IV drug users. Family relationships can become strained as families cope with the stigma of AIDS, but families also involve themselves in the care and support of the infected member. For all concerned, dealing with AIDS is extremely stressful for families. AIDS is also stressful for the nurses, physicians, and other health care providers who work with AIDS patients (Bosk and Frader 1990; Fox, Aiken, and Messikomer 1990). Health personnel not only risk exposure to the virus, but they themselves may also be shunned by colleagues and friends, mourn the deaths of patients, and become frustrated at their inability to provide a cure. Charles Bosk and Joel Frader (1990) explain that the full impact of AIDS on modern health care delivery systems will not be clear for many years, yet they note that the impact is likely to be substantial.

Since AIDS results from a private act that has extreme social consequences, serious moral and legal questions also arise about the rights of individuals versus the welfare of society. The central public problem is how to alter behavior that occurs in the most private of settings and whether it can be done in such a way that does not violate civil liberties (Bayer 1986). The current public policy approach to dealing with AIDS is to limit its spread through educational programs stressing safe sex, yet the possibility of quarantines and universal testing remains in the background if the incurable and fatal disease races unchecked through society. There are no easy answers about public measures in coping with AIDS. Clearly, AIDS has become the major public health issue of our time.

SUMMARY

The epidemiologist is like a detective, investigating the scene of a crime in which the criminal is a disease or some other form of health menace. The epidemiologist is primarily concerned not with individuals but with the health profiles of social aggregates or large populations of people. Important tools of the epidemiologist are the ratios used to compute descriptions of mortality, incidence, and prevalence. These rates can be either crude rates or rates reflecting age-specific data, sex-specific data, and so on.

Many diseases in modern society such as coronary heart disease are very complex; the example of AIDS indicates how challenging health problems can be to the practice of epidemiology. Moreover, it has been noted that as underdeveloped societies modernize, the pattern of their diseases changes accordingly. Communicable diseases are replaced by chronic illnesses like heart disease and cancer. A demanding lifestyle, inadequate diet, smoking, drug and alcohol abuse, obesity, lack of exercise, and exposure to environmental pollution have become the principal risk factors for ill health in modern society. But people can change their behavior and reduce or eliminate their risk of becoming sick.

The Social Demography of Health

3

F our of the most important variables employed in epidemiological research are age, gender, race, and social class or socioeconomic status. It has been found that each of these four variables represents important differences between people that can be correlated with health and life expectancy. The purpose of this chapter will be to examine these variables and assess their relationship to health from a sociological standpoint.

AGE

A number of factors including improved medical care, nutrition, sanitation, and housing have combined in the twentieth century to help promote longer lives for most Americans. In 1990, for example, the average infant at birth in the United States could expect to live 75.4 years. This figure represents an increase in longevity of nearly 50 percent since 1900 when life expectancy was 47.3 years. The rise in life expectancy has brought a corresponding increase in the growth of the elderly population. Men and women are living to 65 years of age and older in greater numbers and proportions than ever before. In 1940, the elderly (those sixty-five and over) constituted 9 million people or about 7 percent of the total population. By 1991, their number had increased to 31.7 million or about 12.6 percent of the population.

The twentieth century can be described as a period of rapid growth of the aged population worldwide. In the United States, people are not only living longer, but since 1958 the fertility rate has been in a period of decline. The lower death rate coupled with the lower birth rate has produced a much higher proportion of older Americans in relation to the total population. Table 3-1 illustrates this trend by showing that in 1900 only 4 percent of the total U.S. population was age sixty-five or over. By 1980, however, older Americans constituted 11.2 percent of the total population and by 2050 it is projected that 21.8 percent of all Americans will be in this age bracket. This means that persons over age sixty-five will make up more than one-fifth of the population in 2050. The point is obvious: Americans are living longer and the percentage of the elderly in the population is significantly increasing.

This trend will undoubtedly bring about a marked change in American society in general and in health care delivery in particular. The aged population will be healthier, better educated, and more affluent than any groups of elderly persons in the past. They are likely to not only have a higher standard of living but also increased political power because of their larger numbers and experience with the political process. This means they will have the clout to bring about legislation for public services to meet their social and health needs. Even though elderly Americans will be healthier than ever before, more pressure is likely to be put on health care delivery systems and public health insurance, namely Medicare, to keep them fit. The need for health services, however, becomes greater as one ages because even minor ailments can more easily develop into serious problems or simply linger longer than usual. Demands for health and other services for the aged are therefore likely to increase in accordance with their proportion of the population.

Pressure also will be put upon the Social Security system to maintain or increase payments for old-age benefits. With relatively fewer children resulting from the baby boom generation in the United States that was born between 1946 and 1964 and is now passing into middle age, the financing of old-age benefits will require increasingly more money in the future from a smaller working population. In 1955, for example, there were 8.6 taxpayers per Social Security beneficiary; but by 2005 the ratio will be 2.7 taxpayers per retiree. By 2035, the ratio will drop to about 1.9 taxpayers for every retiree. Serious difficulties in the financing and provision of services for the elderly in the United States appear certain.

TABLE 3-1   Percent of Total U.S. Population Age Sixty-Five and Over for Selected Years

	1900	1930	1950	1970	1980	1991	2000 (projected)	2050 (projected)
Percent Age 65 and Over	4.0	5.4	8.1	9.7	11.2	12.6	13.1	21.8

Source: U.S. Bureau of the Census, 1989, 1993.

These trends are important because when people become very old they require a greater share of public services. In developed nations, the care of the elderly has generally shifted from being a family responsibility to being more of a societal responsibility. This change has come about for a number of reasons. One reason is the decline of the extended family, in which multiple generations of a single family continued to live with or near each other, and its replacement by the nuclear family, that is, a family consisting of one couple and their children. Other reasons include the high cost of health and nursing care, the type and degree of care required, and the increase in the number of persons needing such care. Although most old people will be relatively healthy in old age, there will come a time, particularly for the oldest of the old, when their health will fail, bringing about the requirement for extended care and greater public expenditures to meet this need.

Adequate health care for the aged is a particularly significant goal for public policy because the single most important determinant of the quality of an elderly person's life is health (Cockerham 1991). Older people who are unhealthy lead relatively shorter and less satisfactory lives than older people who are healthy, feel good, and have the physical capability to pursue their chosen activities. Especially among the elderly, health matters affect all other areas of life. Interestingly, older people often rate their health in a positive fashion. But how can this be since health deteriorates with age? Several studies have investigated this situation and found that many elderly in the United States nevertheless tend to rate their health status as very good (Cockerham, Sharp, and Wilcox 1983; Ferraro 1980; Fillenbaum 1979; Linn and Linn 1980; Mechanic and Angel 1987; Myles 1978; Stoller 1984). An exception is elderly blacks who tend to be more pessimistic about their health than elderly whites (Ferraro 1993; Krause 1987; Mutchler and Burr 1991).

The question thus arises as to whether such self-assessments are accurate measures of a person's health. Such ratings do indeed appear to be valid and reliable and match up as well or better than physician evaluations (Ferraro 1980; Fillenbaum 1979). Moreover, research in Canada (Mossey and Shapiro 1982) and Israel (Kaplan, Barell, and Lusky 1988) has found that elderly persons who rate their health high have tended to live longer than those who rate their health less positively. It may seem incongruent that many older people tend to rate their health positively, in spite of the fact that health declines with age. The reason for this is that judgments concerning one's health by aged individuals are relative. That is, in assessing their health, aged persons compare themselves with others of their own age and sex, and perhaps also in relation to the expectations others have of their health.

High self-ratings of health by the elderly most likely are rationalized in two ways. First, simply surviving to old age in a condition reasonably free of serious illness or disability would be evidence of relatively good health. Eleanor Stoller (1984) suggests, for example, that older persons may expect a decline in their health as they age, but when the deterioration does not take place at the rate or to the extent they had anticipated, they may begin to assess their health above the rating they would assign to their age peers. Second, subjective responses to a health problem tend to be determined by how much of a person's life is disrupted by the condition (Myles 1978) and elderly people usually are not required to maintain a highly active level of functioning. Thus, the aged are able to perceive their health as good enough to perform their daily activities. Therefore, as David Mechanic and Ronald Angel (1987) suggest, the elderly appear to adjust their perceptions of their health as they modify their expectations with age. As people become older, they tend to change their definition of what it is to be healthy in order to fit their circumstances.

Of course, the health of elderly people on the whole is not actually better than that of young adults in general. This is apparent when age differences in overall physical condition, stamina, hand and eye coordination, hearing and vision, and capacity for healing from disease and injury are considered. Although there are exceptions, older people generally cannot pursue a highly active physical lifestyle to the same extent as someone much younger. Rather, it is that the health of many older people is quite good for their age. The health of other older people, however, may be poor. The fact remains that health does deteriorate with age, and this occurs later in some people than in others. But eventually everyone's health declines if one lives long enough. The key to a positive quality of life in old age appears to be that of maintaining one's health as long as possible and as close as possible to the time of one's death.

There is also likely to be a different profile of illnesses in the United States. For example, the number of diabetics in America is expected to increase dramatically as the baby boom generation reaches middle age and beyond. The reason for this is that the prevalence of diabetes in the population increases with age. The number of diabetics in 1980 was 5.4 million and is expected to increase to 7.4 million by the year 2000. Another 5 million are estimated to have diabetes but are unaware of it. The fastest-growing segment of the population with diabetes will be persons between the ages of forty-five to sixty-four since the disease is most likely to develop at this time. Nearly a million new cases of diabetes will surface among persons in this age group in the 1990s. Diabetes, like cancer and heart disease, is incurable and persons undergoing medical treatment for these problems will be likely to do so for several years until they die. Thus, with an aging population, chronic and persistent health problems will become even more prevalent than they are today—requiring an increase in services and greater funding of those services.

However, although there will be an increased emphasis on meeting the health needs of the elderly in coming years, the aged population in the United States is likely to be more healthy overall than aged populations in the past. Factors like a more nutritious diet, exercise, and medical care that have helped raise life expectancy signify a probable trend toward better general health for the aged. So there will be something of a paradox in that the aged will be placing greater demands on the health care system (since there will be more of them), but they also are likely to be more healthy than previous generations.

Sociologists concerned with aging usually work in social gerontology, a subfield of gerontology that deals primarily with the nonphysical aspects of aging. These specialists study the ways in which the elderly adjust to their society and how society adapts to the elderly. As larger numbers of people live longer, this area will grow in importance.

GENDER

In preindustrial societies, including those in Europe, the life expectancy of men and women was approximately the same. This was the situation as late as 1850 in England and Wales where fifteen-year-old boys could expect to live another 43.2 years and girls an additional 43.9 years. By 1950, fifteen-year-old girls in England and Wales typically outlived boys of the same age by 6 years. Between 1850 and 1950, life expectancy for women had increased 41 percent as compared with 30 percent among men (Hart 1991). In the 1990s the gap in life expectancy between men and women in England and Wales persists. The same pattern exists in most of the world. Life expectancy has increased for both men and women in the twentieth century, but women live longer on average than men. As British sociologist Nicky Hart (1991) concludes, economic progress appears to have benefited the longevity of women the most.

The only exception worldwide is in South Asia in countries such as Bangladesh, India, Nepal, and Pakistan, where men outlive women (Cockerham 1991). In India, the difference is not great. Indian men, for example, lived about 55.6 years on the average compared to 55.2 years for women in 1985. However, in Pakistan, the difference was two years, with men averaging 51 years and women 49 years. Nutritional deprivation and lessened access to medical care are among the possible reasons for this reversal of the usual female superiority in life expectancy (Martin 1988).

Outside of South Asia, women have a definite advantage over men in longevity. Males typically exceed female death rates at all ages and for the leading causes of death such as heart disease, cancer, cerebrovascular diseases, accidents, and pneumonia. Women tend to suffer from more frequent illnesses and disability, but their usual health disorders are not as serious or as life threatening as those encountered by men. Yet women, especially in later life, also die from the same illnesses as men. So what should be kept in mind, as Lois Verbruge (1985:163) observed, is "that men and women essentially suffer the same *types* of problems; what distinguishes the sexes is the frequency of those problems and the *pace* of death." For example, coronary heart disease is the leading cause of death for women after age sixty-six, but becomes the number one killer of men after age thirty-nine.

The result is that as of 1990 the average life expectancy in the United States of white females was 79.4 years compared to 72.7 years for white males. The same advantage applies to black females who had an average life expectancy in 1990 of 73.6 years compared to 64.5 years for black males. Table 3-2 also demonstrates female superiority in life expectancy. For 1989, the U.S. National Center for Health Statistics projected that 99.2 percent of all white females and 99.0 percent of all white males would survive to age one from birth; by age sixty-five, however, only 75.9 percent of the white males would be alive compared to

86.3 percent of the white females. The lowest level of life expectancy belongs to the black male. Table 3-2 shows that 98.0 percent of the black males will survive from birth to age one compared to 98.4 percent of the black females; by age sixty-five the percentage of surviving black males is 57.4 and the percentage of surviving black females is 75.3. Whereas black females have a definite advantage in longevity over black males, white females have the longest life span in the United States.

Men have a substantial health inferiority in terms of life expectancy because of the combined result of two major effects: (1) biological and (2) social-psychological. The male of the human species is at a biological disadvantage to the female. The fact the male is weaker physiologically than the female is demonstrated by higher mortality rates from the prenatal and neonatal stages of life onward. Although the percentages may vary somewhat from year to year, the chances of dying during the prenatal stage are approximately 12 percent greater among males than females and 130 percent greater during the neonatal (newborn) stage. Examples of neonatal disorders common to male rather than female babies are such afflictions as hyaline membrane disease (a respiratory disease) and pyloric stenosis (a disorder of the pyloric muscle affecting the emptying of the stomach). Neonatal males are also more prone to certain circulatory disorders of the aorta and pulmonary artery and are subject to more severe bacterial infections. Females are less likely to get childhood leukemia and have a better chance for survival when they do. As an organism, the male appears to be more vulnerable than the female, even before being exposed to the differential social roles and stress situations of later life.

While the evidence is not conclusive, social and psychological influences are nonetheless presumed to play an important part in the determination of life expectancy. Accidents, for example, cause more deaths among males than females, which reflects a difference in sex roles. Men tend to be more aggressive than women in both work and play. High accident rates among males may be attributed to the male's increased exposure to dangerous activities, especially those arising from high-risk occupations. The most dangerous job in the United States (according to the Metropolitan Life Insurance Company) is sponge diving, followed by (in order) motorcycle racing, trapeze and high-wire artists, structural steel workers, lumberjacks, bank guards, munitions and explosive workers, anthracite coal miners, and state police officers. Being president of the United States is also hazardous. About one out of three U.S. presidents has lived to enjoy a normal life expectancy.

TABLE 3-2 Percent of Males and Females Surviving from Birth in the United States, 1989

Surviving from Birth	White Males	White Females	Black Males	Black Females
To age 1	99.0	99.2	98.0	98.4
To age 20	98.1	98.7	96.4	97.5
To age 65	75.9	86.3	57.8	75.3

Source: National Center for Health Statistics, 1992.

Another factor contributing to excess male mortality rates may be occupational competition and the pressure associated with a job. The lifestyle of the business executive or professional with an orientation toward "career" and drive toward "success," marks of the upwardly mobile middle-class male in American society, is thought to contribute strongly to the development of stress among such men. Middle-aged professional males in the United States today are noted by life insurance companies as a high-risk group, particularly if they smoke, are overweight, and tend to overwork. It would thus seem that both the male sex role and the psychodynamics of male competitiveness are significant factors affecting male longevity. Alcohol use, particularly heavy use, has also been identified as a risk factor for some diseases (such as cirrhosis of the liver) and deaths from automobile accidents. Men and boys continue to drink more frequently and drink more at one time than women and girls. Driving at high speeds and participating in violent sports is likewise more common for males. Males also tend to have higher levels of blood pressure. Thus, when occupational hazards are added, men are at greater risk in developing major degenerative diseases than women. This situation may change as women move into high-risk occupations and ambitious female executives and professionals experience career pressures.

While men have a higher rate of mortality, women appear to have a higher morbidity or sickness rate. According to the National Center for Health Statistics (1993), females have higher rates of acute illness—namely, infectious and parasitic diseases and digestive and respiratory conditions. The only category of acute health problems in which males had a higher incidence was injuries. Males, however, tended to not stay in bed for injuries as much as females. The rate for acute conditions not related to pregnancy is eleven times greater for females than males.

As for chronic (long-term) conditions, females show higher rates of hypertension, thyroid, anemia, and gallbladder conditions, chronic enteritis and colitis, migraine headaches, arthritis, diabetes and other diseases of the urinary system, and some skin conditions. Males, on the other hand, have more losses of limbs, gout, emphysema, and coronary heart disease. Males have higher rates of cancer at the youngest and oldest ages; women have the highest incidence rates between the ages of twenty and fifty-five. Overall, men are 1.5 times more likely to die from cancer. The pattern that emerges from these differences is that women are more likely to have a higher prevalence of chronic conditions that are not a leading cause of death (except for diabetes), while men have more of the chronic health problems that end one's life. Women also exhibit much greater use of health services than men (Andersen and Anderson 1979; Cleary, Mechanic, and Greenley 1982; Marcus and Seeman 1981; National Center for Health Statistics 1993; Wan and Soifer 1974). This pattern is consistent even when rates of utilization of maternity services are excluded from analysis. It is also consistent among special populations like the homeless, in that homeless women report more physical symptoms overall, but homeless men have more severe health problems (Ritchey, LaGory, and Mullis 1991).

It appears there is an inverse relationship between mortality and morbidity when sex differences are considered. Women may be sick more often, but live longer. Men may be sick less often, but die sooner. The possibility exists that women do not have more sickness but are just more sensitive to their bodily discomforts and more willing to report their symptoms to others. For chronic diseases like pain in the joints (Davis 1981) and cancer (Marshall, Gregorio, and Walsh 1982), researchers have not found a significant difference between men and women in the reporting of symptoms. The best evidence, however, indicates that overall differences in morbidity are real (Bird and Fremont 1991; Gove and Hughes 1979; Nathanson 1977a; National Center for Health Statistics 1990, 1993; Verbrugge 1985, 1986; Waldron 1981, 1983). And, as Verbrugge (1976:401) explains, "Whether the reasons for greater morbidity are mostly social and psychological, or mostly physical, the immediate social outcomes are the same." The outcome is that females report more illness and disability and, consequently, show a greater loss of productivity—whether their work is in the home or outside it. Employers cannot rely on females as readily as they can males to be at work or to feel like working while they are there. Females also spend more days at home in a sick role and thus tend to disrupt more family activities. And, since good health is generally considered to be a highly significant aspect of a good life, females are at a disadvantage compared to males. "Higher female morbidity, compared to males," states Verbrugge (1976:401), "means that females experience a less comfortable and satisfying life with regard to a cherished attribute. They simply do not feel as well as often as males."

While females are more fit biologically at birth, less often exposed to danger and highly stressful occupations, are more sensitive to their bodily states, and possibly enhance their life expectancy through increased use of medical services, the female advantage in longevity may be a mixed blessing. Women not only appear to feel physically ill more often than men, but many studies confirm that depression and anxiety are more prevalent among women, as is discussed in the next section. Female longevity has also resulted in an increasing number of widows faced with important decisions about remarriage, employment, family life, and dealing with loneliness.

There is, however, renewed interest in investigating the health differences of men and women because of changes in the way that people now live. The lives of men and women used to be more predictable in that men typically behaved in certain distinct ways and women in others. Thus, gender differences in activities, goals, and life expectancy were taken for granted and more or less anticipated. But Verbrugge (1985) indicates that important clues are emerging that show Americans may be moving toward greater equality in mortality between the sexes. This suggestion is based upon evidence that sex differences for some major causes of death like lung cancer have either decreased, stabilized, or only slowly widened. Considerable speculation exists with respect to the possible effects on female life expectancy posed by their increased participation in the labor force and changes in lifestyle. Women in recent years, as compared to the 1950s, are more likely to work in occupations that were once almost exclusively male, drink more alcohol, and smoke more cigarettes. It will be several years, until the present cohort of adult women dies, before these effects on women's health can be fully determined.

FIGURE 3-1   Age-adjusted death rates for lung, breast, colorectal, and stomach cancer among females: United States, 1950–1990.

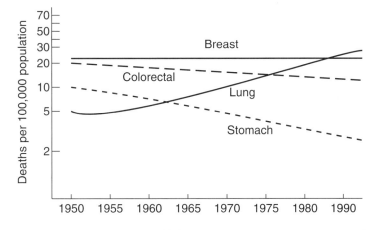

Source: National Center for Health Statistics, 1990, 1993.

Lung Cancer

Yet for lung cancer, there is already evidence of change. American women did not begin smoking in large numbers until after World War II and their rates of lung cancer are now matching those of males. Lung cancer ranked eighth among cancer deaths for women in 1961, but moved up to first by 1986. Figure 3-1 depicts this trend by showing the age-adjusted death rates for lung, breast, colorectal, and stomach cancer for American females for 1950 to 1990. Figure 3-1 shows that deaths from lung cancer were the lowest of the four major cancers in 1950 but rose to second place in the late 1970s and continued to rise to the point in 1986 that lung cancer had overtaken breast cancer as the leading cause of cancer deaths among women.

The death rate for lung cancer among women, as shown in Figure 3-1, rose very rapidly between 1960 and 1983 at an average rate of 6.2 percent annually. The National Center for Health Statistics (1985) attributed this rise to an aging of cohorts with a high prevalence of cigarette smoking. The trend in the United States, however, is toward a decrease in smoking for both sexes, but especially for men. As shown in Table 3-3, the proportion of men who smoke in the United States declined from 51.6 percent in 1965 to 27.5 percent in 1991. The percentage of smokers among both white and black males declined during the period, but black males still show the highest percentage (34.7 percent) of all smokers. For females, Table 3-3 shows that the proportion of women smoking dropped from 34 percent in 1965 to 23.6 percent in 1991. Whereas smoking by males began declining in the 1970s, the percentage of female smokers did not decrease significantly until the late 1980s. Smoking by both sexes and races is now decreasing. Today, the persons most likely to smoke are those with lower levels of education

TABLE 3-3   Percentage of Current Cigarette Smokers by Sex and Race, United States (Selected Years, 1965–1991)

	1965	1979	1983	1987	1991
Male	51.6	37.2	34.7	31.0	27.5
White	50.8	36.5	34.1	30.4	27.0
Black	59.2	44.1	41.3	39.0	34.7
Female	34.0	30.3	29.9	26.7	23.6
White	34.3	30.6	30.1	27.2	24.2
Black	32.1	30.8	31.8	27.2	23.1

*18 years of age and over, age-adjusted.
Source: Center for Health Statistics, 1990, 1993.

and income. Quitting smoking, even past the age of fifty, tends to increase longevity, but the death toll continues to rise each year as the habits of the past have their effects.

This trend is dramatically depicted in an international study of mortality from tobacco use in developed countries conducted by Richard Peto and his colleagues (1992). Peto and his colleagues projected death rates from smoking for the 1990s by analyzing trends in different countries over the course of several years. They predict that approximately twenty-one million people will die from smoking between 1990 and 1999 in developed countries alone: five to six million in the United States, five to six million in the European Union, five million in Russia, and two million elsewhere, including Australia, Canada, Japan, and New Zealand. These deaths will not just be from lung cancer but also from smoking-related cancers of the mouth, pharynx, and larynx, diseases of the cardiovascular system, and other diseases.

As shown in Table 3-4, it is projected that the percentage of deaths attributed to smoking in 1995 for thirty-five- to sixty-nine-year-old males will be as high as 45 percent in Russia, 37 percent in the United States, and 36 percent in the European Union. For thirty-five- to sixty-nine-year-old females, the United States

TABLE 3-4   Estimated Percentage of Deaths Attributed to Smoking in Developed Countries by Age Group, 1995

	MALE AGE GROUPS		FEMALE AGE GROUPS	
	35–69	70+	35–69	70+
United States	38%	25%	37%	18%
European Union	36	25	12	5
Russia	45	22	7	3
All Developed Countries	39	23	15	8

Source: Adapted from Richard Peto, Alan D. Lopez, Jillian Boreham, Michael Thun, and Clark Heath, Jr., "Mortality from Tobacco in Developed Countries: Indirect Estimation from National Vital Statistics," *Lancet* 339 (1992), 1268–1278.

leads the way with 37 percent of all deaths attributable to smoking compared to only 7 percent in Russia and 12 percent in the European Union. So while it is anticipated that the percentage of smoking-induced deaths in the United States will be the same for males and females, American females will have a dramatically higher mortality rate in comparison to Russian women and women in the European Union. Table 3-4 shows that American females also have strikingly higher death rates from smoking in the seventy-plus years age group. In sum, smoking is a serious health problem for women—especially in the United States.

Mental Health

As for mental health, there are no consistent differences between men and women in clinically diagnosed cases of mental illness, with two exceptions. Women have higher rates of mood (prolonged depression or elation) and anxiety disorders, while men have more personality disorders, which consist largely of impaired personality traits (Cockerham 1992; Kessler et al. 1994). Tendencies toward depression and anxiety that fall short of mental disorders in the full-blown clinical sense, but nonetheless cause people to feel psychologically distressed, are also more common among women than men (Mirowsky and Ross 1989). This is the situation both in the United States and in other countries around the globe (Cockerham 1992; Fuller et al. 1993).

These differences appear to be related to both biological and sociocultural factors. Much of the current research in medical sociology focuses on the everyday social roles of women. Women employed outside the home tend to show less psychological distress than housewives but more distress than employed men (Gove and Tudor 1973; Mirowsky and Ross 1989). Often working wives have to maintain the house as well as perform satisfactorily on the job, which, in essence is tantamount to having two full-time jobs. It may be that working wives are under greater strain than their husbands, although both employed men and women generally have fewer health problems than the unemployed (Nathanson 1980; Northcott 1980; Verbrugge 1983). Nevertheless, Catherine Ross, John Mirowsky, and Patricia Ulbrich (1983:681) conclude that "if a married woman gets a job to bolster the family income or find self-expression through occupational achievement, or both, she finds that the wife is now more like a husband but the husband is not more like a wife." There is research that shows the strain of working and doing the majority of work associated with raising children increases psychological distress among married women—particularly those from low-income families (Cleary and Mechanic 1983; Gore and Mangione 1983; Parry 1986; Ross and Huber 1985; Shehan, Burg, and Rexroat 1986; Simon 1992; Thoits 1987; Turner and Noh 1983). Women's employment can also be negative for their husbands' mental health if the men make less money from their job or have to do more housework because of it (Rosenfield 1992).

However, other studies have found that employment outside the home has tended to enhance the overall psychological well-being of women (Kessler and McRae 1981, 1982; McLanahan and Glass 1985; Rosenfield 1992), especially if they are able to exercise some control over what they do on the job (Lennon and

Rosenfield 1992). Other research suggests that women occupying nontraditional (typically male) roles may be better off psychologically than women in traditional female roles (Rosenfield 1980). But findings in this regard are controversial since some research shows that women have more depression than men in both nontraditional and traditional roles (Roberts and O'Keefe 1981). According to Ronald Kessler and James McRae (1982), women who like to combine a job with that of homemaker show the most positive levels of mental health among women working outside the home. Job satisfaction combined with a positive family life is cited as best for working wives. Unfortunately, many jobs that women perform have low levels of complexity, which reduce the possibilities for satisfaction (Lennon 1987). Consequently, the degree to which employment outside the home has resulted in improved mental health for women generally is not clear. What is clear is that increased employment for women has not had a widespread negative impact on the psychological well-being of women working outside the home.

As for marriage, some research suggests that women are more likely to show psychological distress than men regardless of whether they are married (Fox 1980), but among those who are married (women as well as men) the quality of the relationship with the spouse appears especially important in maintaining a positive level of mental health (Gove, Hughes, and Style 1983; Vanfossen 1981). Ross, Mirowsky, and Huber (1983) have found that both spouses are less depressed when the wife's employment outside the home is consistent with their preference. Wives are less depressed if their husbands help with the housework and helping does not appear to increase depression for men. Yet, whether in the home or on the job, the lives of women are often dependent on what others (usually men) do; hence they cannot control the possibilities for satisfaction as much as men can.

Some women are no doubt content to be wives and mothers; other women may find more satisfaction in establishing a career outside the home or combining a job with being a housewife. But others may experience conflict between being a homemaker or a career person or being both. Married women do have less control over their lives because of the demands of marriage and family and dependence on the careers of their husbands. This lack of control has been found to make women particularly vulnerable to psychological distress (Kessler and McLeod 1984; Mirowsky 1985; Rosenfield 1989; Thoits 1987). Therefore, in comparison to men, women are more prone to psychological distress in general and to anxiety and depression in particular. The social role of the woman appears highly significant in this process. Sarah Rosenfield (1989:77) summarizes the mental health differences between men and women by concluding that these differences exist "across cultures, over time, in different age groups, in rural as well as urban areas, and in treated as well as untreated populations."

RACE

One reflection of social inequality in the United States is the differences among the health profiles of racial groups. Asian Americans have typically enjoyed high levels of health, with blacks being especially disadvantaged. Hispanics and Native Americans also have health disadvantages relative to whites. Comparisons of the health of racial minorities with whites in the United States will be reviewed in this section.

Black Americans

The most striking change in the health of the American population in the late twentieth century is the dramatic decline in the health of blacks. Table 3-5 shows, for example, that life expectancy for black males decreased between 1987 and 1990. For black males, Table 3-5 indicates that life expectancy was 65.2 years in 1987—but dropped to 64.5 years in 1990. The life expectancy of black females during this period stayed the same at 73.6 years, while the life expectancy of both white males and females increased. The black male clearly has the lowest life expectancy among black and white men and women. Table 3-5 shows that the black male with a life expectancy of 64.5 years in 1990 lives, on the average, 8.2 years less than the white male (72.7 years) and 14.9 years less than the white female (79.4 years). The white female had a life expectancy in 1990 5.8 years greater than the black female.

Underlying the lessened life expectancy of blacks is a higher prevalence of several life-threatening illnesses, such as AIDS, cancer, heart disease, and hypertension (Braithwaite and Taylor 1992; Polednak 1989). Hypertension or high blood pressure has been a particular health problem for blacks. Although blacks constitute 12 percent of the American population, they have more than 28 percent of the diagnosed hypertension (Hildreth and Saunders 1992). Between the ages of twenty-five and forty-four years, hypertension kills black males 15.5 times more frequently than it does white males. The ratio of black to white females dying from hypertension in the same age category is 17 to 1. Nearly 26 percent of all black females seventeen and older have hypertension. The end result is that pro-

TABLE 3-5   Average Number of Years of Life Expectancy in the United States by Race and Sex, Since 1990

Year	White Males	White Females	Black Males	Black Females
1900	46.6	48.7	32.5*	33.5*
1950	66.5	72.2	58.9	62.7
1960	67.4	74.1	60.7	65.9
1970	68.0	75.6	60.0	68.3
1980	70.7	78.1	63.8	72.5
1987	72.2	78.9	65.2	73.6
1990	72.7	79.4	64.5	73.6

*Includes all nonwhites.
Source: National Center for Health Statistics, 1991, 1993.

portionately more black people than white have hypertension. Various hypotheses have been suggested to explain this situation:

1. The genetic hypothesis argues that blacks are genetically different from whites in ways that predispose them to hypertension.
2. The physical exertion hypothesis postulates that blacks are more likely than whites to be engaged in manual labor, and that greater physical exertion leads to high mortality from hypertension.
3. The associated disorder hypothesis asserts that blacks are more prone to diseases such as pyelonephritis and syphilis that may result in secondary hypertension.
4. The psychological stress hypothesis theorizes that blacks are severely frustrated by racial discrimination and that this stress and the repressed aggression associated with it lead to a higher prevalence of hypertension.
5. The diet hypothesis emphasizes that blacks may have dietary patterns that increase their susceptibility to hypertension.
6. The medical care hypothesis argues that blacks receive poorer medical care than whites and that this results in greater morbidity and mortality from hypertensive disease and perhaps a higher prevalence of secondary hypertension.

The exact cause of the higher rates of hypertension among blacks is not known. Some research suggests that the genetic hypothesis and the psychological stress hypothesis contribute the most to providing an answer, since blacks in general—not just low-income blacks—have higher rates of hypertension than whites (Howard and Holman 1970). Other research, however, suggests that socioeconomic factors are particularly important because low-income blacks have three times more hypertension than affluent blacks (Polednak 1989). Rates of hypertension among blacks had declined somewhat since 1960 but remained the leading cause of death from kidney failure and a major contributor to deaths from end-stage renal disease, heart disease, and stroke.

Blacks and whites also differ in relation to health problems other than hypertension. Diabetes, for instance, is particularly prevalent among blacks. The National Center for Health Statistics (1987a) found in 1987 that the prevalence of known (diagnosed) diabetes was increasing substantially among blacks. In 1963, an estimated 228,000 black Americans had diabetes for a rate of 11.7 per 1,000 blacks. But in 1985, approximately one million blacks had diabetes for a rate of 35.9 per 1,000. Whites, in contrast, showed rates of 24.1 per 1,000. Homicide is also a major problem for blacks since it was the leading cause of death between 1974 to 1990 for fifteen- to twenty-four-year-old black males. In 1978, the homicide rate for this group was 7.1 per 1,000; in 1980, the homicide rate had risen to 8.4 per 1,000 and then declined to 6.1 per 1,000 in 1984—only to increase to 13.8 per 1,000 in 1990. Thus, the period between 1984 and 1990 witnessed a doubling of homicide rates among young black men. The homicide rate for young whites, conversely, was 1.5 per 1,000 in 1990.

The extent of the disparity in health between blacks and whites is depicted in Table 3-6. Table 3-6 shows the age-adjusted death rates for selected causes of

TABLE 3-6   Age-Adjusted Death Rates for Selected Causes of Death, According to Sex and Race, United States, 1990*

	White Males	White Females	Black Males	Black Females
All causes	644.3	369.9	1,061.3	581.6
Heart disease	202.0	103.1	275.9	168.1
Cerebrovascular diseases	27.7	23.8	56.1	42.7
Cancer	160.3	111.2	248.1	137.2
Pulmonary disease	27.4	15.2	26.5	10.7
Pneumonia and influenza	17.5	10.6	28.7	13.7
Liver disease and cirrhosis	11.5	4.8	20.0	8.7
Diabetes	11.3	9.5	23.6	25.4
Accidents	46.4	17.6	62.4	20.4
Suicide	20.1	4.8	12.4	2.4
Homicide	8.9	2.8	68.7	13.0
AIDS	15.0	1.1	44.2	9.9

*Deaths per 100,000 resident population.
Source: National Center for Health Statistics, 1993.

death for black and white males and females in all age groups in 1990. For all causes, Table 3-6 shows black males with the highest death rates of 1,061.3 per 100,000, followed by white males (644.3 per 100,000), black females (581.6 per 100,000), and white females (369.9 per 100,000). Black males show higher death rates for each specific cause of death than white males and black and white females, except for pulmonary (lung) disease and suicide, where white males have the highest rates, and diabetes, in which black females have the highest rates. Overall, blacks lead whites in all categories except pulmonary disease and suicide. Particularly striking are the exceptionally high mortality rates for black males for heart disease, cancer, homicide and AIDS. Among all age groups, blacks are significantly more likely to suffer a heart attack and die than whites (Becker et al. 1993).

When it comes to infant mortality, blacks are again disadvantaged. Black infants have traditionally had almost twice as high an infant mortality rate as white infants. In 1960, there were approximately 43 infant deaths per 1,000 black infants compared to an infant mortality rate of 22.9 among whites. Although rates of infant mortality have declined significantly for both races since 1960, the gap remains, as 1990 data show an infant mortality rate of 18.0 for blacks versus 7.6 for whites. A major factor causing this difference is poverty. Blacks are overrepresented among the poor and the poor have the highest rates of infant mortality regardless of race (Brooks 1980; Gortmaker 1979; Hummer 1993; Polednak 1989).

Recent research shows that black infants born to college-educated parents also have higher mortality rates than similar white infants (Schoendorf et al. 1992). Black college-educated parents had somewhat lower levels of income, thereby identifying an important socioeconomic difference. However, the key factor in the higher infant mortality rates for blacks was low birth weights. Black and white infants of normal birth weight had equivalent rates. The low birth-weight infants were usually premature. The researchers concluded that the persistently higher level of premature infants born to the black parents was possibly due to a number of factors, namely, poor maternal health before pregnancy, psychosocial stress, poor health habits during pregnancy, insufficient access to health care services, substandard health care, or standard medical care that did not adequately address the needs of pregnant black women (Schoendorf et al. 1992:1525).

Mortality rates for blacks are higher than for any other racial group in American society, despite the significant increases in life expectancy for the black population in the twentieth century. Several sources report that blacks have higher death rates than non-Hispanic whites, Hispanics, Asians, and Pacific Islanders, and native Americans for heart disease, all forms of cancer, and other major causes of mortality (Braithwaite and Taylor 1992; U.S. Department of Health and Human Services 1985; National Center for Health Statistics 1988, 1990, 1991, 1993; Polednak 1989). Prior to the 1980s, native Americans appeared to have the worst health profile in American society, but today that position has been taken by blacks. What caused this situation? The exact causes have not been conclusively identified, but strong evidence indicates that blacks are at greater risk because of smoking, high blood pressure, high cholesterol levels, alcohol intake, excess weight, and diabetes (Otten et al. 1990). Low income appears to be an important risk factor as well because of its association with stress and the manner in which stress promotes smoking, high blood pressure, and high caloric intake. A limited supply of cardiac surgeons in predominately black communities—especially in rural areas—has been cited as one reason elderly blacks receive fewer coronary artery bypass operations than elderly whites (Goldberg et al. 1992). The availability of medical practitioners and facilities, as well as a lack of financial resources and information about the need for the care are also important health barriers for low-income blacks.

In 1993, the National Center for Health Statistics released data for 1986 showing mortality rates by race (blacks and whites only), sex, education, and income. These data are depicted in Figure 3-2. Not surprising, Figure 3-2 shows that those persons with the lowest education and income have the highest death rates. Black males with zero to eleven years of education have the highest mortality rates of all educational groups with 13.4 deaths per 1,000. In contrast, black males with four or more years of college had a rate of 6.0 deaths. Among whites, males with the lowest levels of education show the highest rates at 7.6 deaths per 1,000. Figure 3-2 generally shows that the higher the education, the lower the death rates for both blacks and whites. The only exception is that black males with four or more years of college have slightly higher rates compared to black men with one to three years of college.

For income, Figure 3-2 shows black males in the lowest income group (less than $9,000 annually) with the highest mortality rate of all income groups at 19.5 deaths per 1,000. This compares to 3.6 deaths for black males in the highest income group ($25,000 annually). Therefore, among black men, the death rate for the lower income group was 5.4 times greater than the highest income group. The death rate for poor black women was 3.3 times greater (7.6 versus 2.3 deaths per 1,000) than that of the most affluent black women. White males in the lower income category had the highest rates for whites at 16.0 deaths per 1,000 compared to 2.4 deaths for every 1,000 men in the highest income group. Poor white men

FIGURE 3–2   Deaths per 1,000 People 25 to 64 Years Old, by Education and Income, United States, 1986.

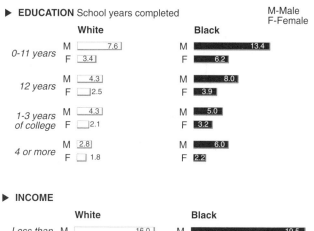

▶ **EDUCATION** School years completed

M-Male
F-Female

		White		Black
0-11 years	M	7.6	M	13.4
	F	3.4	F	6.2
12 years	M	4.3	M	8.0
	F	2.5	F	3.9
1-3 years of college	M	4.3	M	5.0
	F	2.1	F	3.2
4 or more	M	2.8	M	6.0
	F	1.8	F	2.2

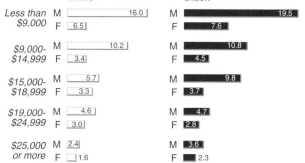

▶ **INCOME**

		White		Black
Less than $9,000	M	16.0	M	19.5
	F	6.5	F	7.6
$9,000-$14,999	M	10.2	M	10.8
	F	3.4	F	4.5
$15,000-$18,999	M	5.7	M	9.8
	F	3.3	F	3.7
$19,000-$24,999	M	4.6	M	4.7
	F	3.0	F	2.8
$25,000 or more	M	2.4	M	3.6
	F	1.6	F	2.3

Source: National Center for Health Statistics data, 1993.

had death rates 6.7 times greater than white men in the highest income group; poor white women had rates 4.1 times greater (6.5 versus 1.6 deaths per 1,000).

These data provide strong evidence that the life expectancy of blacks and whites can be explained almost entirely by differences in socioeconomic status. Jan Mutchler and Jeffrey Burr (1991:352) provide the best summary of this situation in their study of health differences between blacks and whites by noting that "most theoretical statements on the association between race and health highlight socioeconomic status as the critical intervening factor between race and health." Blacks have worse health than whites largely because they also have less education and income.

Hispanic Americans

Adverse levels of health relative to non-Hispanic whites are common among Hispanics. Because of immigration and high birth rates, Hispanics are the fastest growing minority group in American society and will replace blacks as the largest minority in the early twenty-first century. Health data on Hispanics in the United States are limited because, until 1976, federal, state, and local agencies included Hispanics with non-Hispanic whites in the white category. Hispanics were also not included as a separate category on death certificates nationally until 1988. The existing data on the health of Hispanics were summarized in a special report by the American Medical Association (AMA 1991), which determined that, in comparison with the general population, Hispanics have significantly higher mortality rates from stomach cancer. Compared to non-Hispanic whites, Hispanics have more diabetes, hypertension, tuberculosis, lung cancer, alcoholism and deaths from cirrhosis of the liver, and homicide.

Although Hispanics constitute 8 percent of the total U.S. population at present, they also account for nearly 20 percent of the reported AIDS cases among both males and females. "Hispanics are at greater risk for HIV infection," concluded the AMA (1991:251), "not because of their race and culture, but because of underlying factors such as living in high prevalence areas and exposure to intravenous drug use."

It should also be noted that Hispanics have lower mortality rates than either blacks or non-Hispanic whites for heart disease and most forms of cancer, but the mortality rates from diabetes are three times higher than that of non-Hispanic whites. Poverty, lack of education, and restricted access to health care play a major role in the disproportionate levels of illness suffered by Hispanics. Hispanics are more likely than non-Hispanics to not have a regular source of health care or to use hospital emergency rooms as their primary source of medical services. They are more likely than any other racial/ethnic group in American society to not have health insurance and many face cultural and language barriers in health care settings. Among Hispanics, Puerto Ricans report the worst health status and Cubans the best, with Mexican-Americans and other Hispanics in the middle.

Native Americans

Native Americans, consisting of American Indians and native Alaskans, have shown a dramatic improvement in their overall level of health in the last forty years. There is evidence, for example, that the health of elderly native Alaskans is not significantly different from elderly whites in Alaska (Seccombe 1989). Moreover, in 1950, the infant mortality rate for American Indians and native Alaskans was 82.1 per 1,000 live births; in 1987, the mortality rate had dropped to 13.0 per 1,000 births. Life expectancy for native Americans in 1950 was sixty years, but climbed to more than seventy in the 1990s. Furthermore, American Indians and native Alaskans have the lowest rates of cancer in the United States. Mortality rates from heart disease are lower than the general population as well, but heart disease is still the leading cause of death for native Americans.

However, American Indians have very high mortality rates from diabetes. The rate of deaths from diabetes are 2.3 times higher among Indians than non-Indians and one tribe, the Pimas, has the highest rates of diabetes in the world. Diabetes among Pima Indians is ten to fifteen times higher than the general American population. The complications of diabetes take a further toll on Indians by increasing the probability of kidney disease, blindness, and heart disease. Indians also suffer more dysentery, strep throat, venereal disease, and hepatitis than other Americans. Other significant health problems of American Indians are alcoholism, tuberculosis, dietary deficiency, cirrhosis of the liver, and gastrointestinal bleeding. In addition, chronic otitis media, a severe ear ailment that arises when simple ear infections are not treated, occurs among 10 percent of all Indian children.

So while American Indians have experienced a significant improvement in their overall level of health, important problems remain. The leading causes of death for Indians and Alaskan natives after heart disease are accidents, cancer, liver disease and cirrhosis, stroke, pneumonia, influenza, homicide, and diabetes. More American Indians die from accidents, primarily automobile accidents, than members of any other racial group in the United States.

Another major problem for Indians is suicide. The death rate from suicide among Indians is approximately 20 percent higher than suicide rates for the general population. American Indian suicide victims are typically younger than those in the general population with suicide peaking at ages fifteen to thirty-nine, compared with the non-Indian population in which suicides usually occur after the age of forty. For fifteen- to twenty-four-year-olds, the mortality rate from suicide during 1988 and 1990 was 7.5 per 100,000 compared to 4.1 nationally (Center for Health Statistics 1993). White fifteen- to twenty-four-year-olds were second in suicides with a death rate of 4.4 per 100,000, followed by Asians and Pacific Islanders (3.5), Hispanics (2.9), and blacks (2.6). In addition to particularly high rates of diabetes, accidents, and suicides, Indians have an exceptionally high prevalence of alcoholism, with most Indian families affected either directly or indirectly by the alcohol abuse of one or more of its members.

Asian Americans

Another example of the importance of socioeconomic factors in relation to health is found by examining data that include Asian Americans. Asian Americans have the highest levels of income, education, and employment of any racial/ethnic minority group in the United States, often exceeding levels achieved by the white population. Consequently, it is not surprising that the lowest age-adjusted mortality rates in the United States are those of Asian Americans. Asians and Pacific Islanders in the United States showed an age-adjusted mortality rate in 1988 to 1990 of 295.4 per 100,000, which was the lowest of any racial/ethnic group in the nation.

Heart disease is the leading cause of death for Asians, but mortality from this disease is less than that of whites and other minorities. Deaths from cancer, stroke, automobile accidents, AIDS, homicide, and suicide are lowest as well. Overall, Asians and Pacific Islanders are the healthiest racial group in American society.

When infant mortality rates for the United States are reviewed, the health advantage of Asian Americans becomes even more apparent. Table 3-7 shows

Japanese- and Chinese-Americans with the lowest rates. According to Table 3-7, infant mortality in the United States has drastically declined since 1950. The most striking decline, as previously noted, has been that of American Indians from 82.1 deaths per 1,000 live births in 1950 to 13.0 in 1987, the most recent year comparative data are available. The decline for Chinese- and Japanese-Americans has been almost as great in terms of relative proportion, but the rates were much smaller to begin with and therefore not as dramatic. In 1987, Table 3-7 shows that blacks had the highest infant mortality rates (17.8 per 1,000), followed by American Indians (13.0), whites (8.2), Japanese-Americans (6.6), and Chinese-Americans (6.2).

Besides illustrating the low infant mortality rates of Japanese and Chinese-Americans, with Japanese-Americans having the lowest rates of all, Table 3-7 also indicates some other patterns of interest. In 1950, American Indians had the highest infant mortality rates—almost twice as high as that of blacks. By 1970, Indian infant mortality rates had dropped so sharply that they were lower than the rates for blacks. While infant mortality rates for blacks had declined by more than one-half (43.9 versus 17.8) between 1950 and 1987, the black rate was twice as high as that of whites (17.8 versus 8.2) in 1987. Hence, the gap between black and white infant mortality rates has remained constant even though infant deaths from both racial groups have fallen.

Although infant mortality rates are only one indicator of health in a society, they are nevertheless an important measure of the quality of life available to a population. Such rates, along with the other data discussed in this section, point toward the fact that Asian-Americans enjoy the best health in the United States.

Race: Conclusion

Some afflictions such as hypertension, diabetes, and sickle cell anemia have a genetic basis, but living conditions associated with poverty influence the onset and course of most physical health problems (Hart 1991; Otten et al. 1990).

TABLE 3-7   Infant Mortality Rates by Race, United States, Selected Years 1950–1987*

			RACE			
Year	Black	American Indian	Chinese-American	Japanese-American	Hispanic	White
1950	43.9	82.1	19.3	19.1	—	26.8
1960	44.3	49.3	14.7	15.3	—	22.9
1970	32.6	22.0	8.4	10.6	—	17.8
1977	23.6	15.6	5.9	6.6	—	12.3
1984	18.7	14.3	8.3	6.0	9.3	8.9[†]
1987	17.8	13.0	6.2	6.6	8.2	8.2[†]

*Infant mortality rate is the number of deaths for infants under one year of age per 1,000 live births.
†Non-Hispanic whites.
Source: National Center for Health Statistics, 1986, 1993.

Tuberculosis, for example, was nearly extinct in the United States but resurfaced in the late 1980s and early 1990s with the greatest concentration among the poor. Alcoholism, drug abuse, suicide, homicide, lead poisoning, and influenza and pneumonia, along with heart disease and cancer are more prevalent among the lower class (Jenkins 1983; Susser, Hopper, and Richman 1983; Winkleby et al. 1992). Race becomes an especially significant variable for physical health in American society because many racial minority persons occupy a disadvantaged social and economic position. This is especially the case for blacks (Braithwaite and Taylor 1992; Mutchler and Burr 1991). As previously noted, the differences in life expectancy of blacks and whites can largely be explained by differences in socioeconomic status.

When it comes to mental health, a well-known study by George Warheit and his colleagues (1973) found, for example, that blacks, the aged, the poor, and those with the least formal education have the highest rates of depression. However, when race, sex, age, and socioeconomic status were correlated, only sex and socioeconomic status were statistically significant. The major difference in depression scores between whites and blacks was accounted for by socioeconomic differences, with most blacks occupying the lowest socioeconomic level. There is little or no support for the claim that there is a significant difference among races in overall rates of mental disorder, except the relatively low rates for Asian Americans (Cockerham 1992). A recent nationwide study by Ronald Kessler and his associates (1994) finds that there are no mental disorders where either lifetime or active prevalence is significantly higher among blacks than whites. Nor were there significant lifetime or active prevalence differences between Hispanics and non-Hispanic whites.

Social class, however, is an exceptionally strong predictor of mental distress (Cockerham 1990, 1992; Kessler 1979; Warheit, Holzer, and Arey 1975; Warheit, Holzer, and Schwab 1973). If race and socioeconomic status jointly influence depression, the effects appear limited to the lower class, with poor blacks possibly more psychologically distressed than poor whites (Kessler and Neighbors 1986; Ulbrich, Warheit, and Zimmerman 1989). Other research shows lower-class white males with higher rates of psychiatric illness than their black male counterparts (Williams, Takeuchi, and Adair 1992). Consequently, there is debate concerning the extent of differences in mental health between blacks and whites within the lower class alone. In general, socioeconomic status appears much more important than race in explaining mental disorder.

SOCIOECONOMIC STATUS

To be poor is by definition to have less of the things (including health care) produced by society. This situation is seen in the experience of the poor in obtaining health services in the United States. Before the 1930s, those who were unable to pay for health care were largely dependent on charity. In addition, many of the urban clinics providing treatment for the poor were established and maintained primarily as teaching facilities for medical and nursing students. In such cases, education was the primary goal of the institution. Since the 1930s, there has been a considerable increase in the number and types of facilities as well as an improvement in the quality of care available to the poor, yet many problems remain.

As Anselm Strauss (1970) pointed out, medical systems in the United States have not been designed to meet the needs of the poor. Large medical centers can be especially complex and confusing to people with low levels of education. The manner in which the poor live and conduct their daily lives is not always considered by health care providers. Strauss, for example, discussed communication problems between physicians and the poor by noting that many doctors assume that the poor (like themselves) have regular meals, lead regular lives, try to support families, keep healthy, and plan for the future. To prescribe the same type of treatment for all diseases for all people does not take into account the fact that people live their lives differently. Strauss (1970:16) illustrated this point by asking, "What does 'take with each meal' mean to a family that eats irregularly, seldom together, and usually less than three times a day?"

A review of relevant research discloses that a number of studies substantiate the relationship between poverty and lack of access to *quality* medical care in the United States (Dutton 1978, 1986; Kaplan 1989). Despite evidence of more frequent visits to physicians made possible by greater health insurance coverage through government-sponsored programs (Medicaid and Medicare), the poor are still treated within the framework of welfare medicine and still live on a day-to-day basis within an environment of poverty.

The health care reforms of the Clinton administration offered the promise of increased equity in access to health care by providing a basic level of medical benefits to all Americans. While the final form of this legislation is not known as this book goes to press, the clear direction of the preliminary proposals was for universal coverage regardless of one's socioeconomic status. Obtaining equal access to care is a major step in improving the health of the general population. However, improved access to health services is only part of the solution for advancing health. The fact remains that people at the bottom of society have the worst health of all, regardless of what country they live in and what type of health insurance they have.

In the United States and elsewhere in the world, socioeconomic status is one of the strongest and most consistent predictors of a person's health and life expectancy (Williams 1990; Winkleby et al. 1992). As Marilyn Winkleby and her colleagues (1992) determined, this finding persists across all diseases with few exceptions and throughout the life span. Socioeconomic status (SES) typically consists of measures of income, occupational status or prestige, and level of education. Although interrelated, each of these measures reflects different dimensions of a person's position in the class structure of a society. In studies of health and illness, income reflects spending power, housing, diet, and medical care; occupation measures status, responsibility, physical activity, and health risks associated with work; and education is indicative of a person's skills for acquiring positive social, psychological, and economic resources (Winkleby et al. 1992:816). While income and occupational status are important, the strongest single predictor of good health appears to be education. Well-educated people are generally the best informed about the merits of a healthy lifestyle and the advantages of seeking preventive care or medical treatment for health problems when they need it. In sum, education promotes healthy living and the ability to solve problems. For example, in a study of health in Finland, Denmark, Sweden, Norway, Hungary, and England and Wales, Finnish medical sociologists Eero Lahelma and Tapani Valkonen (1990) found that education allowed comparisons between countries more readily than income or occupation. In each country, persons with less education had the highest mortality rates.

A well-known study by Aaron Antonovsky (1972) on life expectancy and social class highlights the importance of the socioeconomic differential by suggesting that, on every measure, social class position influences one's opportunity for longevity. Antonovsky conducted a statistical investigation of approximately thirty studies of mortality rates in the United States and Europe. He found that the upper socioeconomic classes were favored in all dimensions of life expectancy. "The inescapable conclusion," stated Antonovsky (1972:28), "is that class influences one's chances of staying alive." The only major contradiction found by Antonovsky involved a Dutch study (DeWolff and Meerdink 1954); however, the population in this study demonstrated few social class differences and, as a whole, had one of the lowest death rates ever recorded. This research by the Dutch scientists suggests the important hypothesis that as differences between social classes decline, overall mortality rates of a population may similarly decline.

Three European studies, from Johannes Siegrist (1987a) in Germany, Sara Arber (1993) in Great Britain, and Tapani Valkonen (1987, 1989) in Finland illustrate the relationship between socioeconomic status and health. In a thorough review of the research literature in the United States and Western Europe, Siegrist concluded that education was an especially important determinant of health along with occupational status. Those persons with the highest education and occupational status invariably have the lowest mortality rates from chronic disease and this trend becomes apparent beginning in middle age. Higher education and occupational status translate into the level of knowledge and income that allows an individual to live in the most healthy circumstances. Siegrist suggested, accordingly, that the social dimensions of unequal health primarily result from two major factors: (1) greater stress among lower socioeconomic groups and (2) greater risk of exposure to unhealthy living and work environments.

Arber (1993) studied chronic illness over the life course and found that by the time lower-class British men and women reached old age, they were significantly less healthy than better educated and more affluent elderly persons. The highest levels of chronic illness were among unskilled workers and the lowest among higher professionals. Class differences in health were more modest below age twenty-five but increased thereafter. The lower class also had greater physical disability and the difference became especially pronounced among the elderly.

Valkonen focused on mortality rates in Great Britain, France, Hungary, Denmark, Norway, Sweden, and Finland. He found a particularly strong association between level of education and mortality, thereby suggesting that better educated persons have higher intelligence and greater motivation for disciplined behavior and a lifestyle that leads to enhanced health. In each of the countries studied, level of education was significant and, overall, the mortality rate for those persons with an elementary school education was double that of university graduates. Social class differences and mortality rates were lowest in Denmark, Norway, and Sweden, but class differences were greatest in France and Great Britain, and it was in these countries that differences in mortality by socioeconomic position were highest. Of particular interest is the situation in Hungary where the former communist system was oriented toward removing class distinctions as a fundamental principle of Marxist theory. Nevertheless, in Hungary, manual workers outside of agriculture and especially manual workers in agriculture had mortality rates well in excess of nonmanual workers.

Therefore, as several studies report, lower socioeconomic groups have the poorest health and the causes of this situation appear to be due primarily to social factors. These studies have been conducted in several European countries (Fox 1989; Illsley and Svensson 1986; Lahelma and Valkonen 1990; Leclerc 1989; Valkonen 1987, 1989), as well as in the United States (Dutton 1978, 1986; Kaplan 1989; Sagan 1987) and other countries like Great Britain (Hart 1986, 1991; Macintyre 1986; Morgan, Calnan, and Manning 1985; Smith 1987; Townsend, Davidson, and Whitehead 1990; Wilkinson 1986), Germany (Kirchgässler 1990; Siegrist 1987a, 1989), the Netherlands (Kunst, Looman, and Mackenbach 1990; Spruit 1990), Belgium (Lagasse et al. 1990), Italy (Piperno and DiOrio 1990), Spain (Rodríguez and Lemkow 1990), Israel (Shuval 1990), Poland (Wnuk-Lipinski 1990), and even Sweden (Diderichsen 1990; Lundberg 1986) where social equality in living conditions is among the best in the world. In Europe, as in the United States, women have a distinct advantage in life expectancy over men (Hart 1989), but lower-class European women live less long than women in higher socioeconomic groups (Arber 1989). Regardless of gender, persons living in poverty and reduced socioeconomic circumstances have greater exposure to physical (crowding, poor sanitation, extreme temperatures), chemical and biochemical (diet, pollution, smoking, alcohol and drug abuse), biological (bacteria, viruses), and psychological (stress) risk factors that produce ill health than more affluent individuals.

Equality of Care: The British Experience

Since many health disorders appear related to poverty, it is a logical assumption that if poverty were not a factor retarding the availability of quality medical care, the incidence and prevalence of illness in the lower social classes would be reduced. Following World War II, socialized medicine was introduced in Great Britain to provide the lower classes with the same medical care available to the upper classes. It should be noted, however, that poverty and social class differences remained—only health care was supposedly equalized. Results have shown that the equalization of health care alone has not reduced the disparity in health between social classes. Mortality rates remained higher for lower classes. According to Mervyn Susser and William Watson (1971), Britain's experiment failed to reduce health disparities precisely because living conditions and lifestyles could not be equalized; the physical environment of poverty and poor nutrition continued to adversely affect lower-class health.

Ivan Reid, in his book *Social Class Differences in Britain* (1989), examines the extent to which the British social classes differ with respect to health in a review of data taken largely from the British government's *General Household Survey*. Health in Britain has improved significantly for all social classes during this century, but mostly for the upper classes. The lower classes continue to show several health disadvantages, such as higher infant mortality, lower birth weight, more chronic disability, more absence from work due to illness, lower life expectancy, and higher ratios of risk factors like obesity and smoking. Reid attributes the health differences between the classes to a combination of factors, namely, wealth, personal habits, diet, home environment, exercise, mental stress, and differing occupational hazards. He also points out that the lower classes visit physicians more often than the other classes. This trend, which is similar to that in the United States, is consistent with the fact that the lower classes have more health problems.

Richard Wilkerson (1986) explains that prior to the 1980s, it was widely assumed in Britain that society was becoming more egalitarian. Social class differences were believed to becoming less important because of the growth of welfare services. This assumption was shattered, however, by the publication in 1980 of the Black Report which not only found very large differences between mortality rates among occupational groups but also that these differences were not declining. British workers in lower status occupations were clearly not living as long as those persons at the top of the occupational scale and this trend was not improving.

One of the better studies researching this situation is that of M. Marmot, M. Shipley, and Geoffrey Rose (1984) who investigated the mortality of 17,530 British male civil government employees who were ranked on the basis of their job position. The men were classified as either administrators, professionals/executives, clerical, or other (which consisted of jobs lowest in status such as messengers and other unskilled manual workers). These men, aged forty to sixty-four, were initially interviewed during 1967 to 1969 with respect to their health habits and then were reinvestigated ten years later in relation to mortality. Table 3-8 shows the results according to the percentage of each occupational group who died and the cause of death. Table 3-8 shows that for each cause of death, the percentage of men dying changed on the basis of occupational ranking. Those with the highest rank (senior administrators) had the lowest percentage of deaths and the percentages increased across job categories with the lowest ranked occupations (other) having the highest percentage of deaths. In other words, low status equaled high mortality. Most of the men died from coronary heart disease and Table 3-8 shows, for example, that 2.16 percent of the administrators died from this cause and the percentage of deaths increased across job ranks with other showing a percentage of 6.59. For deaths from all causes, Table 3-8 shows that 4.73 percent of the administrators died compared to 8.00 percent of the professionals/executives, 11.67 percent of the clerical workers, and 15.64 percent of other.

TABLE 3-8   Percentage of British Civil Government Employees Dying Over a Ten-Year Period (1969-1979) by Civil Service Grade and Cause of Death

Cause of Death	Senior Administrators	Professional/ Executive	Clerical	Other
Lung Cancer	0.35	0.73	1.47	2.33
Other Cancer	1.26	1.70	2.16	2.23
Heart Disease	2.16	3.58	4.90	6.59
Stroke	0.13	0.49	0.64	0.58
Other Cardiovascular	0.40	0.54	0.72	0.85
Chronic Bronchitis	0.00	0.08	0.43	0.65
Other Respiratory	0.21	0.22	0.52	0.87
Gastrointestinal	0.00	0.13	0.20	0.45
Genitourinary	0.09	0.09	0.07	0.24
Accidents/Violence	0.00	0.13	0.17	0.20
Suicide	0.11	0.14	0.15	0.25
Other Deaths	0.00	0.16	0.26	0.40
All Causes	4.73	8.00	11.67	15.64

Source: Adapted from M. G. Marmot, M. J. Shipley, and Geoffrey Rose, "Inequalities in Death—Specific Explanations of a General Pattern," *Lancet*, 83 (1984), 1004.

What is indicated by studies such as those of Marmot and his colleagues is that medical care alone cannot counter the adverse effects of low incomes on health. The evidence is clear that a significant gap in health and life expectancy continues to persist in Britain—despite improved access to medical care (Arber 1993; Blackburn 1991; Hart 1986, 1991; Macintyre 1986; Martin and McQueen 1989; Morgan, Calnan, and Manning 1985; Reid 1989; Smith 1987; Townsend, Davidson, and Whitehead 1990; Wilkinson 1986). As indicated by the 1980 Black Report, a government-sponsored assessment of trends in British health, the lower class had the highest rates of illness, disability, and infant mortality and the lowest life expectancy. The lower class also used prenatal and preventive health care services less frequently than members of more affluent classes. So while medical care was equalized and subsequently utilized more often by the poor, the use of services was directed significantly more toward treatment of existing health problems than prevention. The Black Report provided strong evidence that "the lower down on the social scale you are, the less healthy you are likely to be and the sooner you can expect to die" (Abercrombie et al. 1988:352).

The Black Report placed the blame for class differences in levels of health squarely on the socioeconomic environment—smoking, work accidents, overcrowding, poor living conditions, exposure to dampness and cold, and the like. An update of the Black Report for the decade of the 1980s was compiled by Margaret Whitehead (1990). She determined that, while the health of the British population in general and the lower class in particular continued to improve throughout the 1980s, serious social inequities in health remained. Whitehead concluded:

> Whether social position is measured by occupational class, or by assets such as house and car ownership, or by employment status, a similar pic-

ture emerges. Those at the bottom of the social scale have much higher death rates than those at the top. This applies at every stage of life from birth through to adulthood and well into old age.

Neither is it just a few specific conditions which account for these higher death rates. All the major killer diseases now affect the poor more than the rich (and so do most of the less common ones). The less favoured occupational classes also experience higher rates of chronic sickness and their children tend to have lower birthweights, shorter stature and other indicators suggesting poorer health status.

The unemployed and their families have considerably worse physical and mental health than those in work. Until recently, however, direct evidence that unemployment *caused* this poorer health was not available. Now there is substantial evidence of unemployment causing a deterioration in mental health, with improvements observed on re-employment.[1]

Equally poor housing, and even worse living situations, exist not only in Great Britain but in other industrialized nations like the United States—not to mention the miserable conditions of the poor who live in underdeveloped countries. The point is that equality in medical care alone cannot change differences in levels of health between social classes.

J. Rogers Hollingsworth (1981) investigated this situation in England and Wales for the period 1891 to 1971 and suggests that societies wishing to equalize levels of health across social classes should consider equalizing income and educational attainment. In a particularly well-designed study, Hollingsworth analyzed changes in technology and structure of the health care delivery systems in England and Wales in relation to changes in health (as measured by mortality) across social classes and geographic regions during the same time span. He hypothesized that as medical technology becomes more effective and the costs increase, there will be a rising public demand that the state increase its responsibility for providing health services. This will result in greater centralization of decision making. As medical care systems become more centralized, medical services will become more accessible to all social classes and regions, thereby suggesting that there should be a convergence in levels of health.

Public demand for greater government involvement in providing medical services (influenced by rising costs) resulted in the centralization of care under a National Health Service (NHS). The NHS made those services more accessible to all social classes. However, there was not a convergence in levels of health across classes though there was some convergence across regions. Mortality rates for all classes declined, but, as noted, the gap between the classes was not significantly reduced. In other words, everyone in Britain tended to live longer, but the upper classes continued to live longer than anyone else. This took place even though the lower classes over time began using medical services more than the middle and upper classes.

[1]Margaret Whitehead, *The Health Divide*, as reported in *Inequalities in Health*, P. Townsend and N. Davidson, eds., and M. Whitehead (London: Penguin Books, 1990), pp. 351–352.

Hollingsworth notes that income is inequitably distributed in Britain and this is reflected in a wide variation in lifestyles. Education also remains unevenly distributed, and educational levels may be more important than income in explaining differences in health. Hollingsworth (1981:281) concludes: ". . . that even though the British National Health Service is the most egalitarian one in the Western world, gross inequalities in levels of health are likely to persist across social classes as long as gross inequities in the distribution of income and education persist."

Modern Diseases and the Poor

The lower class, even in modern nations, suffers more from the typical diseases of past human existence, like influenza and tuberculosis, in comparison to the upper and middle classes. Coronary heart disease, on the other hand, has traditionally been associated with an affluent way of life. The incidence was usually high in rich countries and low in poor countries. Yet as Mervyn Susser, Kim Hopper, and Judith Richman (1983) observe in a review of relevant literature, there have been variations with respect to heart disease between different nations and within countries among people of the same ethnic background with different life experiences. Japan, for example, has shown a relatively lower rate of heart disease despite being one of the most technologically advanced nations of the world. Diet and stress-reducing activities like periodic group vacations and after-work socializing for Japanese males have been thought to contribute to the low mortality rates from heart disease. In recent years, however, heart disease has been increasing in Japan, especially with the spread of Western eating habits. Westernization of the Japanese diet is considered responsible for the replacement of stroke by heart disease as Japan's second leading cause of death (Powell and Anesaki 1990). This pattern underscores the significance of lifestyle in influencing the distribution of disease. Susser and his associates explain that as societies change and environments are modified, the style of living and types of activities available to members of the various social classes also change.

Consequently, in the United States there has been a change in the incidence of heart disease. Rates of coronary heart disease have declined dramatically in the past twenty-five years for all Americans, but the decline has been greatest among the upper and middle classes (Gatchel, Baum, and Krantz 1989; Polednak 1989; Susser, Hopper and Richman 1983). The result is that coronary heart disease is now concentrated more among the poor. The difference, as Susser and his associates show, is that more obesity, smoking, and stress occur in the lower class, in addition to higher levels of blood pressure, less leisure-time exercise, and poorer diets. Data from the National Center for Health Statistics (1989) confirm this situation by showing that persons earning $25,000 or less annually in the United States in 1986 were more likely to die from heart disease than persons earning over $25,000. Differences in mortality from heart disease were particularly dramatic in relation to education. Table 3-9 shows the percent distribution of deaths from all forms of heart disease in 1986 and—for all ages and both sexes—the

TABLE 3-9   Percent Distribution of Deaths from Heart Disease by Level of Education, According to Age and Sex, United States, 1986

Sex, and Level of Education	All Ages	25–64 Years	65 Years and Over
Both sexes (N = 699,778)			
All levels of education	100.0	100.0	100.0
Less than high school	55.2	44.1	57.9
High school	27.2	35.1	25.3
1–3 years of college	9.8	10.7	9.6
4 years of college or more	7.8	10.1	7.2
Male (N = 366,900)			
All levels of education	100.0	100.0	100.0
Less than high school	54.0	45.5	57.3
High school	26.0	31.9	23.8
1–3 years of college	9.8	10.8	9.3
4 years of college or more	10.2	11.8	9.6
Female (N = 322,878)			
All levels of education	100.0	100.0	100.0
Less than high school	56.4	40.4	58.4
High school	28.6	43.8	26.8
1–3 years of college	9.9	10.4	9.8
4 years of college or more	5.1	5.4	5.0

N = number of cases.
Source: National Center for Health Statistics, 1989.

largest percentage dying from heart disease were those persons with less than a high school education (55.2 percent), followed by high school (27.2 percent), one to three years of college (9.8 percent), and four years of college or more (7.8 percent). The same pattern holds true for persons between twenty-five and sixty-four years of age and sixty-five years and over, as well as for both males and females. The finding that persons with less education are significantly more likely to die from heart disease than more educated persons underscores the importance of socioeconomic status in health matters.

Other research shows that the risk of dying from cancer is higher than average for men who live in poor, overcrowded urban neighborhoods where there are few married families. According to C. David Jenkins (1983), there is a strong association between living in poverty and dying of cancer, especially for adult males who are unemployed or underemployed. Jenkins suggests that perhaps the lack of close relationships with other people is the critical factor, in that sharing one's life with someone else increases the likelihood of maintaining regular patterns of eating and sleeping and obtaining medical treatment in a timely fashion. Jenkins does not claim that being poor causes cancer but that being poor lessens the chances of early detection of cancer and promotes the health conditions that make death more likely once cancer occurs. Not only is the likelihood of getting cancer greater for lower-class males, but the poor in general also get more migraine headaches than the affluent (Stewart et al. 1992).

The lower class, therefore, appears to be especially disadvantaged in regard to health. This disadvantage extends not only to communicable diseases associated with unhealthy living situations but also to chronic health problems like heart disease that are more prevalent in modern, industrialized countries and strongly affected by how one lives. Clearly, there is more to health than the availability of medical care. Lifestyle and social/environmental conditions, along with preventive health measures, primarily determine health status. A healthy lifestyle includes the use of good personal habits like eating properly, getting enough rest, exercising, and avoiding practices like smoking, abusing alcohol, and taking drugs. However, the type of lifestyle that promotes a healthy existence is more typical of the upper and middle classes who have the resources to support it. The most important relationship between social class and health is the manner in which social class affects the opportunities a person has for a generally healthy life. Crowded living conditions, poor diet, inferior housing, low levels of income and education, and enhanced exposure to violence, alcoholism and problem drinking, and drug abuse—all combine to decrease the life chances of the poor.

The lower class is also disadvantaged with respect to mental health. The basic finding of most studies is that the highest overall rates of mental disorder are found in the lower class, including schizophrenia—the most severely disabling form of mental illness (Cockerham 1992; Dohrenwend 1975; Hollingshead and Redlich 1958; Kessler et al. 1994; Link, Dohrenwend, and Skodol 1986). Anxiety and mood disorders, on the other hand, tend to be more prevalent among the upper and middle classes, yet the lower class suffers from these problems as well. Why the relationship between mental disorder and social class position exists is not known, but it may be due to genetics or greater stress in coping with the conditions of poverty, or both. Consequently, for mental as well as physical difficulties, socioeconomic factors are major determinants of the types and extent of an individual's health problems.

SUMMARY

This chapter has discussed the social demography of health from the standpoint of age, sex, race, and social class. The section on age disclosed that as more and more persons live to older ages in American society, marked changes are likely to occur in society in general and health care delivery in particular. The new generation of the aged, however, is likely to be the most affluent, educated, and healthy in American history. As for sex differences, females generally have a very definite advantage over males with regard to life expectancy. This advantage involves both biological and social-psychological factors. White Americans also have a definite advantage in health over nonwhite Americans. However, the most significant sociodemographic variable affecting nonwhites is that they are likely to be poor, and poverty, as far as healthy living conditions and medical care is concerned, may be equated with second-rate circumstances. In Great Britain, socialized medicine failed to reduce health differentials between the social classes because social class differences themselves were not reduced. Equal access to medical care could not, by itself, overcome the adverse effects of poverty. The lower class suffers not only from more illness and disability, but also shows the highest rates of mental disorder.

Social Stress

4

S ocial influences upon the onset and the subsequent course of a particular disease are not limited to such variables as age, sex, race, social class, and the conditions of poverty as they relate to lifestyle, habits, and customs. It is also important to recognize that interaction between the human mind and body represents a critical factor in regard to health. As Barbara and Bruce Dohrenwend (1981:1) point out, "Life stressors can play a part in causing serious illness and even death." By way of illustration, the Dohrenwends cite a case (Engle 1971:774) involving "the death of the twenty-seven-year-old army captain who had commanded the ceremonial troops at the funeral of President Kennedy. He died ten days after the President of a 'cardiac irregularity and acute congestion' according to the newspaper report."

Stress can be defined as a heightened mind-body reaction to stimuli inducing fear or anxiety in the individual. Stress typically starts with a situation that people find threatening or burdensome (Pearlin 1989). Examples of stressful situations include divorce (Aseltine and Kessler 1993; Booth and Amato 1991), unpleasant work conditions (Pavalko, Elder, and Clipp 1993), and widowhood (Umberson, Wortman, and Kessler 1992). A review of selected sociological theories developed by Charles Cooley, William I. Thomas, Erving Goffman, and Emile Durkheim will serve to illustrate how social processes, from the standpoint of both the individual and the wider society, can lead to stress.

COOLEY, THOMAS, AND GOFFMAN:
SYMBOLIC INTERACTION

Cooley, Thomas, and Goffman reflect the symbolic interactionist approach to human behavior, which views human group life from the perspective of the individual. Based upon the work of George Herbert Mead (1865–1931), this approach sees the individual as a creative, thinking organism who is able to choose his or her behavior instead of reacting more or less mechanically to the influence of social processes. It assumes that all behavior is self-directed on the basis of symbolic meanings that are shared, communicated, and manipulated by interacting human beings in social situations. Of special relevance to a sociological understanding of stress is Charles H. Cooley's (1864–1929) theory of the "Looking-Glass Self." Cooley (1964) maintained that our self-concepts are the result of social interaction in which we see ourselves reflected in other people. Cooley compares the reflection of our self in others to our reflections in a looking glass:

> Each to each a looking glass
> Reflects the other that doth pass.

Cooley's looking-glass self-concept has three basic components: (1) We see ourselves in our imagination as we think we appear to the other person; (2) we see in our imagination the other person's judgment of our appearance; and (3) as a result of what we see in our imagination about how we are viewed by the other person, we experience some sort of self-feeling, such as pride or humiliation. The contribution of this theory to an understanding of stress is that an individual's perception of himself or herself as a social object is related to the reaction of other people. Quite obviously stress could result from the failure of the observer to reflect a self-image consistent with that of the subject. Thus, stress can be seen as having a very definite social and personal component based on perception of a social event.

The work of William I. Thomas (1863–1947) is also relevant for its understanding of crisis as residing in the individual's "definition of the situation" (Volkart 1951). Thomas stated that so long as definitions of a social situation remain relatively constant, behavior will generally be orderly. However, when rival definitions appear and habitual behavior becomes disrupted, a sense of disorganization and uncertainty may be anticipated. The ability of an individual to cope with a crisis situation will be strongly related to socialization experiences that have taught the person how to cope with new situations.

Consequently, Thomas makes two particularly important contributions concerning stress. First, he notes that the same crisis will not produce the *same effect uniformly in all people.* Second, he explains that adjustment to and control of a crisis situation result from an individual's ability to compare a present situation with similar ones in the past and to revise judgment and action upon the basis of past experience. The outcome of a particular situation depends, therefore, upon an individual's definition of a situation and upon how that individual comes to terms with that situation. As David Mechanic (1978:293) states, "Thomas's concept of crisis is important because it emphasizes that crises lie not in situations, but rather in the interaction between a situation and a person's capacities to meet it." Saxon Graham and Leo Reeder (1972:91) add that in Thomas's notion of adaptation ". . . the individual's repertoire of coping behavior is a crucial element in understanding the ways in which people come to terms with a given stressful situation."

Erving Goffman (1922–1982) is noted for the dramaturgical or "life as theatre" approach. Goffman (1959) believed that in order for social interaction to be possible, people need information about the other participants in a joint act. Such information is communicated through (1) a person's appearance; (2) a person's experience with other similar individuals; (3) the social setting; and (4) most important, the information a person communicates about himself or herself through words and actions. This fourth category of information is decisive because it is subject to control by the individual and represents the impression the person is trying to project—which others may come to accept. This information is significant because it helps to define a situation by enabling others to know in advance what a person expects of them and what they may expect of him or her. Goffman calls this process "impression management."

Goffman says people live in worlds of social encounters in which they act out a line of behavior, a pattern of verbal and nonverbal acts by which individuals express their view of a situation and their evaluation of the participants, particularly themselves. The positive social value individuals claim for themselves by the line that others assume they have taken during a particular encounter is termed a "face." This face is an image of self projected by the individual to other people. One's face is one's most personal possession and is the center of security and pleasure, but Goffman is quick to point out that a person's face is only on loan from society and can be withdrawn if the person conducts himself or herself in an inappropriate manner. A person may be in the "wrong face" when information about that person's social worth cannot be integrated into his or her line of behavior or a person may be "out of face" when he or she participates in an encounter without the line of behavior of the type that participants in the particular situation would be expected to take.

Goffman further explains that the maintenance of face is a condition of interaction, not its objective. This is so because one's face is a constant factor taken for granted in interaction. When people engage in "face-work," they are taking action to make their activities consistent with the face they are projecting. This is important because every member of a social group is expected to have some knowledge of face-work and some experience in its use, such as the exercise of social skills like tact. Goffman sees almost all acts involving other people as being influenced by considerations of face; for example, a person is given a chance to quit a job rather than be fired. A person must be aware of the interpretations that others have placed upon his or her behavior and the interpretations that he or she should place upon their behavior. Therefore, Goffman's view of the self is that it has two distinct roles in social interaction: first, the self as an image of a person formed from the flow of events in an encounter; and second, the self as a kind of player in a ritual game who copes judgmentally with a situation. This aspect of

Goffman's work identifies the calculative element in dealings between people and presents them as information managers and strategists maneuvering for gain in social situations (Manning 1992).

Goffman's principal contribution to our understanding of stress arises from his claim that the self is a sacred object. The self is more important than anything else to us because it is always with us and represents who we are. For someone to challenge the integrity of that self as a social object is an embarrassing situation. Each self is special, and in social relationships that very special self we have tried to nourish and protect for a lifetime is put on display. Goffman has said that role-specific behavior is based not upon the functional requirements of a particular role, but upon the *appearance* of having discharged a role's requirements. Thus, stress could be induced when people fail in their performance. Otherwise, people might not be so willing to take such great care that they act out lines of behavior considered appropriate to their situation.

The symbolic interaction perspective, as reflected in the work of Cooley, Thomas, and Goffman, contributes to our understanding of stress by identifying the key variable in the stress experience: the perception of the individual. People vary in their interpretation of situations, but ultimately it is the way in which they perceive the strains and conflicts in their roles, tasks, personal relationships, and other aspects of their life situation that causes them to feel stressed. How people feel about themselves (Cooley), define situations (Thomas), or manage impressions (Goffman) can lead to the creation of stressful conditions. People typically cope with stress by trying to change their situation, manage the meaning of the situation, or keep the symptoms of stress within manageable bounds (Pearlin 1989).

DURKHEIM: FUNCTIONALISM

While symbolic interaction theory emphasizes interpersonal forms of interaction, functionalist theory focuses on the influence of the larger society on individuals. Functionalist theory is derived from the initial work of the French sociologist Emile Durkheim (1858–1917). Durkheim was concerned with those social processes and constraints that integrate individuals into the larger social community. He believed that when a society was strongly integrated, it held individuals firmly under its control (Durkeim 1950, 1956). Individuals were integrated into a society as a result of their acceptance of community values reinforced through social interaction with others believing in the same value system. Especially important were participation in events celebrating a society's traditions and also involvement in work activities.

As members of society, individuals were constrained in their behavior by laws and customs. These constraints were "social facts," which Durkheim (1950:13) defined as "every way of acting, fixed or not, capable of exercising on the individual an external constraint." What Durkheim suggests is that society has an existence outside of and above the individual. Values, norms, and other social influences descend on the individual to shape his or her behavior. Social control is, therefore, real and external to the individual.

Among Durkheim's works, the most pertinent to an understanding of the social determinants of stress is his 1897 study, *Suicide* (1951). In explaining the differential rates of suicide among various religious and occupational groupings, Durkheim suggested that suicide was not entirely a matter of free choice by individuals. He believed that suicide was a social fact explainable in terms of social causes. Durkheim distinguished between three major types of suicide, each dependent upon the relationship of the individual to society. These three types were (1) egoistic suicide, in which people become detached from society and, suddenly on their own, are overwhelmed by the resulting stress; (2) anomic suicide, in which people suffer a sudden dislocation of normative systems where their norms and values are no longer relevant, so that controls of society no longer restrain them from taking their lives; and (3) altruistic suicide, in which people feel themselves so strongly integrated into a demanding society that their only escape seems to be suicide.

Durkheim's typology of suicide suggests how a society might induce enough stress among people to cause them to take their lives. Egoistic suicide is a result of stress brought about by the separation of a strongly integrated individual from his or her group. Durkheim uses the example of the military officer who is suddenly retired and left without the group ties which typically regulated his behavior. Egoistic suicide is based upon the overstimulation of a person's intelligence by the realization that he or she has been deprived of collective activity and meaning. Anomic suicide is characterized by an overstimulation of emotion and a corresponding freedom from society's restraints. It is a result of sudden change that includes the breakdown of values and norms by which a person has lived his or her life. Sudden wealth or sudden poverty, for example, could disrupt the usual normative patterns and induce a state of anomie or normlessness. In this situation a chronic lack of regulation results in a state of restlessness, unbounded ambition, or perhaps crisis, in which norms no longer bind one to society.

Whereas egoistic and anomic forms of suicide are both due to "society's insufficient presence in individuals" (Durkheim 1951:256), altruistic suicide represents the strong presence of a social system encouraging suicide among certain groups. Suicide in the altruistic form could be characterized as the avoidance of stress by people who prefer to conform to a society's normative system rather than risk the stress of opposing it. Examples of altruistic suicide are the practice of hara-kiri in Japan, where certain social failures on the part of an individual are expected to be properly redressed by his or her suicide, or the traditional Hindu custom of the widow's committing ritual suicide at her husband's funeral.

Although altruistic suicide is relatively rare in Western society, stories do appear in the mass media of people killing themselves for reasons that could be considered egoistic or anomic. Yet the significance of Durkheim's orientation toward social processes for the understanding of the stress phenomenon extends well beyond the issue of suicide, since this is only one of many possible ways a person might find to cope with social and psychological problems. What is particularly insightful is Durkheim's notion of the capability of the larger society to create stressful situations where people are forced to respond to conditions not of their own choosing.

For example, in a 1976 federal government report and subsequent research, M. Harvey Brenner (Brenner and Mooney 1983; Brenner 1987a, 1987b) linked increased incidence of heart disease, stroke, kidney failure, mental illness, and even infant mortality in the United States and several Western European countries to downturns in the economy. Brenner's thesis is that there are few areas of our lives not intimately affected by the state of the economy. He argues that economic recession increases the amount of stress on an individual by comparing economic cycles with health statistics. Brenner found that heart attacks increase during periods of recession. Usually the first wave of deaths follows the recession by three years, with a second wave occurring five to seven years after the recession. The lag was thought to be due to the length of time it takes heart disease to cause death. Waves of kidney failure deaths generally lagged two years behind a recession, while death from strokes took about two to four years to follow an economic downturn. Infant mortality rates were particularly striking during periods of recession, according to Brenner. Mothers suffering from the stresses of the recession tended to have higher blood pressure and be less healthy themselves, thereby giving birth to children whose chances for survival had likewise been weakened.

What causes stress during an economic recession was the intensified struggle for the basic necessities of life (food, clothing, shelter, health care, and education for children) and a possible loss of self-satisfaction and social status associated with unemployment while trying to survive on savings, welfare, and unemployment insurance. These stresses were often found to be enhanced by a rise in drinking and smoking at the same time. What is happening, suggests Brenner, is that social stress from economic conditions increases exposure to the major risk factors known to accompany many health disorders.

Earlier, Brenner (1973) focused on the relationship between the economy and mental health. He examined rates of employment and mental hospital admissions in New York over a period of 127 years from 1841 to 1968. He believed that regardless of the number and combination of factors that predispose certain individuals toward becoming mentally ill, a question that needed to be answered was why mental disorder appears *when* it does. Brenner found that rates of mental hospitalization increased during economic downturns and decreased during upturns, thereby suggesting that economic factors may precipitate mental disorder.

Brenner provided two explanations for his findings. He preferred a "provocation" hypothesis that stress resulting from being dislocated from one's usual lifestyle or prevented from improving it during a downward shift in the economy caused vulnerable people to reach the point at which they required hospitalization in a mental institution. Another explanation is also possible and is described by Brenner as an "uncovering" hypothesis. This alternate view suggests that economic downturns do not promote mental disorder but simply "uncover" those people already mentally ill by stripping them of their existing economic resources. These people who are mentally "borderline" may be able to support themselves during periods of economic affluence, only to become the first to lose their jobs when times are bad. In fact, in a declining economic cycle, mental hospitals may be an attractive source of food and shelter for these marginal individuals.

Although Brenner prefers the hypothesis that economic downturns "provoke" mental disorder, his data also support the finding that such downturns "uncover" mentally disordered people. Additional research is needed to determine whether "provocation" or "uncovering" is actually at work; to a significant degree both hypotheses may be relevant. The import of Brenner's work is that it shows that downward trends in economic activity may stress certain people to the point that they require mental hospitalization, particularly those with the fewest financial resources.

Another study of the effect of economic change on the psychological well-being of individuals is that by Ralph Catalano and C. David Dooley (1977) conducted in Kansas City, Missouri. This study examined the relationship between depressed moods and stressful life events as correlated with the rises in inflation and rates of unemployment. Catalano and Dooley found that unemployment was significantly related to depression and stress, but that inflation was related to neither. Thus, unemployment appeared to be an especially strong predictor of depressed mood and stressful life events. The study did not test Brenner's "uncovering" hypothesis and explored his "provocation" hypothesis only partially; yet the data tended to support the "provocation" explanation that economic change put enough stress on certain people to cause mental problems. In contrast to Brenner's study, economic upturns as well as downturns produced stress.

Even though the research of Brenner (1973), Catalano and Dooley (1977; Dooley and Catalano 1984), and others (Pearlin, Lieberman, Menaghan, and Mullan 1981) demonstrates how large-scale societal processes, specifically those of economic change, can be correlated with adverse physical and mental health, the relationship is not that simple. It is very difficult to substantiate a precise, cause-and-effect relationship between a major social event like an economic depression and health problems of a particular individual because of the wide range of variables that may intervene in the individual's situation and modify the effect. Possible intervening variables could be those of personality, social support, genetics, social class, or socialization. For instance, research on the effects of social support (feelings of being loved, accepted, cared for, and needed by others) on persons subjected to unemployment (Atkinson, Liem, and Liem 1986; Gore 1978), stressful life events (Ensel and Lin 1991; Haines and Hurlbert 1992; Lin and Ensel 1989; Lin, Simeone, Ensel, and Kuo 1979; Lin, Woelfel, and Light 1985; Matt and Dean 1993; Newman 1986; Norris and Murrell 1984; Turner 1981; Wethington and Kessler 1986), sexual assault (Ruch and Chandler 1983), and occupational stress (LaRocco, House, and French 1980; Loscocco and Spitze 1990) shows that social support can act as a buffer against stress. Those persons with the strongest level of social support had fewer health problems than did those with little or no support. Other research shows how the hardiness of a person's personality reduces the potential of stress-induced illness (Kobasa, Maddi, and Courington 1981; Kuo and Tsai 1986).

The advantage of macro-level forms of analysis like functionalism, however, is that this approach shows how social and economic conditions beyond the direct influence or control of the average person can create stressful circumstances that force people to respond to them. For vulnerable people, the stressful circumstances may promote ill health.

STRESS

The theories of Durkheim, Cooley, Thomas, and Goffman demonstrate a relationship between social interaction and stress, but they do not explain the effect of stress upon the human body. Embarrassment and psychological discomfort can be socially painful, yet the effects of stress can transcend the social situation and cause physiological damage as well. Hence, a physiological perspective of stress must be considered.

Walter Cannon (1932) believed that the real measure of health is not the absence of disease but the ability of the human organism to function effectively within a given environment. This belief was based upon the observation that the human body undergoes continuous adaptation to its environment in response to weather, microorganisms, chemical irritants and pollutants, and the psychological pressures of daily life. Cannon called this process of physiological adaptation *homeostasis,* which is derived from the Greek and means "staying the same." Homeostasis refers to the maintenance of a relatively constant condition; for example, when the body becomes cold, heat is produced; when the body is threatened by bacteria, antibodies are produced to fight the germs; and when the body is threatened by an attack from another human being, the body prepares itself either to fight or to run.

As an organism the human body is thus prepared to meet both internal and external threats to survival, whether these threats are real or symbolic. A person may react with fear to an actual object or to a symbol of that object—for example, a bear versus a bear's footprint. In the second case, the fear is not of the footprint but of the bear that the footprint represents. Threats in contemporary urban societies could include types of stimuli such as heavy traffic, loud noises, or competition at work, all of which can produce emotional stress related more to a situation than to a specific person or object.

Whether the stressful situation actually induces physiological change depends upon an individual's perception of the stress stimulus and the personal meaning that the stimulus holds. A person's reaction, for instance, may not correspond to the actual reality of the dangers that the stimulus represents; that is, a person may overreact or underreact. Thus, there is considerable agreement that an individual's subjective interpretation of a social situation is the trigger that produces physiological responses (Moss 1973). Situations themselves cannot always be assumed beforehand to produce physiological changes.

Physiological Responses to Stress

Cannon (1932) formulated the concept of the "fight or flight" pattern of physiological change to illustrate how the body copes with stress resulting from a social situation. When a person experiences fear or anxiety, the body undergoes physiological changes that prepare it for vigorous effort and the effect of possible injury. Physiological changes in the body as a result of stress situations primarily involve the autonomic and neuroendocrine systems. The autonomic nervous system controls heart rate, blood pressure, and gastrointestinal functions—processes that occur automatically and are not under the voluntary control of the central nervous system. The autonomic nervous system is delicately balanced between relaxation and stimulation and is activated primarily through the hypothalamus, which is located in the central ventral portion of the brain. It is composed of two major divisions, the parasympathetic and the sympathetic systems. The parasympathetic system is dominant when there is no emergency and regulates the vegetative processes of the body such as the storing of sugar in the liver, the constriction of the pupil of the eye in response to intense light, and the decreasing of heart rate. When there is an emergency, the sympathetic system governs the body's autonomic functions and increases heart rate so that blood flows swiftly to the organs and muscles that are needed in defense. It also inhibits bowel movements and dilates the pupil of the eye in order to improve sight.

Besides the autonomic nervous system, the endocrine glands perform an important role in the body's physiological reaction to stress. The neuroendocrine system consists of the adrenal and pituitary glands, the parathyroids, the islets of Langerhans, and the gonads. They secrete hormones directly into the blood stream because they lack ducts to carry their hormones to particular glands. The two glands that are the most responsive to stress situations are the adrenal and pituitary glands. The adrenal gland secretes two hormones, epinephrine and norepinephrine, under stimulation from the hypothalamus. Epinephrine accelerates the heart rate and helps to distribute blood to the heart, lungs, central nervous system, and limbs; it also makes the blood coagulate more readily so that as little blood as possible will be lost in case of injury. Norepinephrine raises blood pressure and joins with epinephrine to mobilize fatty acids in the blood stream for use as energy. The function of the pituitary gland is, upon stimulation by the hypothalamus, to secrete hormones that, in turn, stimulate other endocrine glands to secrete their hormones.

At first, most medical scientists believed that only the adrenal gland was involved in stress reaction; however, in 1936 Hans Selye demonstrated the existence of a pituitary-adrenal cortical axis as having a profound effect upon body metabolism. Selye (1956) developed a theory known as the *general adaptation syndrome*. He believed that after an initial alarm reaction, a second stage of resistance to prolonged stress was accomplished primarily through increased activity of the anterior pituitary and adrenal cortex. If stress continued and pituitary and adrenal defenses were consumed, Selye indicated that a person would enter a third stage of exhaustion. He described this third stage as a kind of premature aging due to wear and tear on the body. However, it now seems that the entire endocrine system, not just the pituitary and adrenal glands, is involved in some manner in stress reaction. Under acute stimulus, hormone secretions by the endocrine glands increase; under calming influences, secretions decrease.

Most threats in modern society are symbolic, not physical, and they do not usually require a physical response. Today the human organism faces emotional threats with the same physical system used to fight enemies, yet modern society disapproves of such physical responses as fighting. Socially the human organism is often left with no course of action, perhaps not even verbal insults. This inability to respond externally leaves the body physiologically mobilized for action which never comes, a readiness that can result in damage to the body.

A number of studies have shown that the human organism's inability to manage the social, psychological, and emotional aspects of life—to respond suitably to a social situation—can lead to the development of cardiovascular complications and hypertension, peptic ulcers, muscular pain, compulsive vomiting, asthma, migraine headaches, and other health problems (House 1974; House et al. 1979; House et al. 1986; Moss 1973; Sorensen et al. 1985). From Germany, a particularly impressive series of studies by medical sociologist Johannes Siegrist and his associates (Siegrist 1984, 1987a, 1987b; Siegrist et al. 1990; Siegrist, Dittman, Rittner, and Weber 1982; Siegrist, Siegrist, and Weber 1986) has documented the relationship between stress and cardiovascular disease among male blue-collar workers. These studies have demonstrated the effects of stress on the cardiovascular system through measures of quality of life, work load, job security, coping styles, emotional distress, and sleep disturbances. This research shows how the failure to cope with job-associated stressors promotes cardiovascular problems.

Social Factors and Stress

There is a considerable amount of empirical research in medical sociology dealing with stress and stress-related topics. Selected findings will be reviewed here, to include relevant research on social stressors, stress adaptations, group influences, death from overwork, and changes in life events. The intent of this section is to show how contemporary sociologists are helping to improve our understanding of stress.

Social Stressors

One way understanding is being improved is through the identification of social stressors. Leonard Pearlin (1989) suggests two major types: life events and chronic strains. First, there is the stress of life events like divorce, marriage, or losing one's job. Second, are chronic strains which are relatively enduring conflicts, problems, and threats that many people face on a daily basis. Chronic strain includes role overload, such as the strain associated with work and being a parent (Simon 1992) or trying to advance one's career over the life course (Pavalko, Elder, and Clipp 1993). It also involves conflicts within role sets, like those between husbands and wives (Aseltine and Kessler 1993; Booth and Amato 1991), interrole conflict where a person has too many roles, role captivity in which a person is an unwilling incumbent of a role like being trapped in an unpleasant job or marriage, or role restructuring in which a person changes relationships within roles. As Pearlin (1989:245) observes, role strains can have serious effects on individuals because the roles themselves are important, especially when they involve jobs, marriage, and parenthood.

Stress Adaptation

Mechanic (1962b, 1978) attempts to explain the stress experience from the standpoint of both society and the individual. He draws on the work of William I. Thomas (Volkart 1951), who pointed out that the meaning of crisis lies not in the situation, but rather in the interaction between the situation and the person's ability to rise above it. The outcome or effect of a crisis depends on how well a person comes to terms with the situation. Stress, therefore, refers to difficulties experienced by the individual as a result of perceived challenges.

Mechanic believes that in social situations people have different skills and abilities in coping with problems; not everyone has an equal degree of control in managing emotional defenses nor the same motivation and personal involvement in a situation. In analyzing any particular situation, an observer must consider not only whether an individual is prepared to meet a threat, but also whether he or she is motivated to meet it.

Extending his concept of stress from the individual to societal components, Mechanic states that a person's ability to cope with problems is influenced by a society's preparatory institutions, such as schools and the family, two organizations designed to develop skills and competencies in dealing with society's needs. A person's emotional control and ability to cope are also related to society's incentive systems—that is, society's rewards (or punishments) for those who did (or did not) control their behavior in accordance with societal norms. As for a person's involvement or motivation in a situation, Mechanic explains that society's evaluative institutions provide norms of approval or disapproval for following particular courses of action.

Hence, the extent of physiological damage or change within an individual depends on (1) the stimulus situation, which includes the importance of the situation to the individual and the extent of his or her motivation; (2) an individual's capacity to deal with the stimulus situation, such as the influence of genetic factors, personal skills, innate abilities, and past experiences; (3) the individual's preparation by society to meet problems; and (4) the influence of society's approved modes of behavior. Mechanic (1962b:8) emphasizes the contribution of society toward an individual's adaptation to stress by stating "... that whether or not a person experiences stress will depend on the means, largely learned, that [the person] has available to deal with his [or her] life situation."

Mechanic's model represents an important contribution toward our understanding of stress by showing the importance of adaptation and explaining how that adaptation is based on an individual's perception of life situations, combined with his or her degree of preparation by society to cope with stressful circumstances. Mechanic thus identifies adaptability as the key variable in whether a person will eventually suffer organic damage.

Stress and the Social Group

People's perceptions of an event may be influenced by their intelligence, past experience, socialization, and awareness of stimuli, but the influence of group membership is also important. Gordon Moss (1973) illustrates the significance of group membership in helping individuals cope with information they find stressful. He suggests that stress and physiological change are likely to occur when people experience information that goes against their beliefs or desires. Moss notes that information processing produces changes in the central nervous system, the autonomic nervous system, and the neuroendocrine system, all of which can alter the susceptibility to disease among certain people. The most vulnerable persons are those whose physiological responses are easily elicited and likely to be more pronounced and prolonged. Moss emphasizes the advantages of group membership in providing social support for the individual. Subjective feelings of belonging, being accepted, and being needed have consistently shown themselves to be crucial in the development of feelings of well-being and the relieving of symptoms of tension. Thus, Moss's work joins that of others (Atkinson, Liem, and Liem 1986; Ensel and Lin 1991; Dean, Kolody, and Wood 1990; Flaherty and Richman 1989; Gore 1978, 1981, 1989; Haines and Hurlbert 1992; Jacobson 1986; Lin and Ensel 1989; Lin et al. 1979; Lin, Woelfel, and Light 1985; Loscocco and Spitze 1990; Matt and Dean 1993; Stewart 1989; Turner 1981; and Wethington and Kessler 1986) to show how the social support rendered by families and groups helps reduce the potentially harmful effects of stress upon the body and mind.

Furthermore, there is often a tendency among members of small groups to develop a consensus about how social events should be perceived; this process minimizes individual differences, reduces uncertainty, and maintains group conformity. Conformity to group-approved attitudes and definitions has long been hypothesized in sociology and social psychology as reducing anxiety by ensuring acceptance from persons and groups important to the individual (Presthus 1978). Much of human behavior is seen as the result of an individual's search for relief from anxiety by conforming to authority and group norms.

Death from Overwork

Rising concern is developing in Japan over a phenomenon known as *karoshi* or death from overwork (Yamazaki and Sakano 1991). The true prevalence of the problem is unknown, but concern exists because over 1,800 cases of karoshi were reported in Japan between 1987 and 1989 (Kawahito 1990). *Karoshi* is defined as a "condition in which unpsychologically sound work processes are allowed to continue in a way that disrupts the worker's normal work and life rhythms, leading to a build-up of fatigue in the body and a chronic condition of overwork accompanied by a worsening of preexistent high blood pressure and hardening of the arteries and finally resulting in a fatal breakdown" (Uehata et al., cited in Kawahito 1990:8) It is an affliction that happens primarily to middle-age men in Japan who work exceedingly long hours and become so exhausted they literally die—usually from cardiovascular complications—from overwork.

What makes overwork different in Japan is that the average Japanese spends so much more time on the job than people in other advanced nations. For example, Japanese industrial workers averaged 2,139 actual work hours in 1991, compared to 1,847 hours for Americans and 1,499 hours for Germans. It is also typical for salaried middle-class white-collar workers, who are the most common victims of karoshi, to work overtime without extra pay. They do this to show dedication to their company. As Dutch journalist Karel van Wolferen (1989:162) explains, the "most common way [for Japanese male office workers] to demonstrate loyalty is by working late hours or by spending time after office hours with colleagues and business associates—which means limiting time spent with his family to the hours between eleven at night and seven in the morning." Table 4-1, based on the findings of Japanese medical sociologists Yoshihiko Yamazaki and Junko Sakano (1991; Sakano and Yamazaki 1990), illustrates the long work day of Japanese white-collar workers in the Tokyo area. Table 4-1 shows the average time spent at work in a sample of white-collar workers to be 12 hours and 7 minutes daily. Another hour and 40 minutes is spent commuting to and from work.

Time at work is only one major factor in karoshi; it is the combination of time with effort and the pressure of meeting deadlines and quotas that creates very stressful and unhealthy conditions. However, the amount of time spent working signifies a particularly demanding work situation and appears to be a decisive variable in death from overwork. Data from the Tokyo area for ninety-eight karoshi victims show that 22.4 percent had worked fifty to fifty-nine hours per week, 32.7 percent had worked seventy to ninety-nine hours weekly, and 21.4 percent worked over 100 hours a week (Uehata 1991). Moreover, Yamazaki and Sakano (1991) found that a third of the workers they interviewed in Tokyo continue to think about their job demands even when they are off work. Many felt guilty about taking holidays or any time off from work.

Yet, Yamazaki and Sakano point out that the custom of relaxing after work in bars, noodle houses, and elsewhere with their fellow workers is an important method of dealing with stress for some men. Wives also tend to assume the greatest responsibility for family affairs, leaving their husbands to devote

TABLE 4-1 Average Daily Time Schedule of 200 White-Collar Workers in Major Companies in the Tokyo Area, 1990

Activity	Time Schedule
Rise	7:02 A.M.
Depart home	7:54 A.M.
Commute to work (train)	(50 minutes)
Arrive at work	8:54 A.M.
Work hours	(12 hours and 7 minutes)
Leave office	9:01 P.M.
Commute to home (train)	(50 minutes)
Arrive home	10:26 P.M.
Go to bed	12:01 A.M.
Sleep	(7 hours and 1 minute)

Source: Adapted from Junko Sakano and Yoshihiko Yamazaki, *Survey of the Role of White-Collar Workers as Family Members in the Tokyo Area* (University of Tokyo: Department of Health Sociology, 1990).

time to their employer. Clearly, the majority of Japanese white-collar workers do not die from karoshi, but enough evidence exists to call attention to the problem of stress and overwork in their society.

Life Changes

Another important factor in the production of stress is the occurrence of significant changes in a person's life experiences. Research in this area has generally focused on the reactions of people both to extreme situations, like wars and natural disasters, and to ordinary life events. This research is reviewed in the next two sections.

Extreme situations.   Extreme situations like natural disasters would appear to be a likely source of stress because of the great anxiety people usually attach to being caught in such circumstances. But a common misconception about disasters is that people flee in panic from the site of a potential disaster area. In reality, it is usually difficult to get people to evacuate their homes, even when the possibility of damage or destruction is imminent (Tierney and Baisden 1979). Some people are even attracted to potential disasters and take risks to see a tidal wave, tornado, or hurricane. Trying to view a disaster and being a victim of one, however, are two entirely different matters. Past research has shown that such extreme situations as earthquakes and tornados can induce stress (Dohrenwend 1973). Mass media reports commonly show or describe people in large-scale disasters as experiencing intense feelings of grief, loss, anguish, and despair. When tornado victims in rural Arkansas were interviewed shortly after a severe twister had touched down in their community, the great majority (about 90 percent) reported some form of acute emotional reaction (Fritz and Marks 1954).

Thus, there is sound reason for understanding the social and psychological consequences of disasters, especially from the standpoint of developing and implementing programs to assist disaster victims. According to a review by Kathleen Tierney and Barbara Baisden (1979:35) for the National Institute of Mental Health, most researchers agree that "very few people become grossly psychotic in the face of major disasters and the incapacitating psychological reactions are unusual phenomena in catastrophes."

This is not to say that disaster victims generally escape all psychological trauma—quite the contrary. There is almost unanimous agreement that disasters do promote acute psychological stress, emotional difficulties, and anxiety related to coping with grief, property damage, financial loss, and adverse living conditions. Tierney and Baisden (1979:36) state that "while few researchers would claim that disasters create severe and chronic mental illness on a wide scale, victim populations *do* seem to undergo considerable stress and strain and *do* experience varying degrees of concern, worry, depression, and anxiety, together with numerous problems in living and adjustment in postdisaster." Groups of people with special needs in the aftermath of disasters are usually children and the elderly. Older people, in particular, find it difficult to adjust to life after a disaster. And, as research on elderly flood victims in Kentucky shows, they may also suffer from severe fatigue when great personal loss and high community destruction occurs (Phifer, Kaniasty, and Norris 1988). Low-income groups also present special problems in that often they are left without any material resources and become especially dependent on aid.

A pattern that emerges in studies of natural disasters and psychopathology is that the disaster experience, though severe, is usually short in duration, and the effects on mental health likewise tend to be short term and self-limiting. The question thus arises about the possible effects of stress in extreme situations lasting long periods of time, such as the experiences of people exposed to the brutalities of Nazi concentration camps and the horrors of war. There is evidence that many concentration camp survivors have suffered persistent emotional problems and are particularly prone to physical illness and early death (Eitinger 1964, 1973). However, as Aaron Antonovsky (1979) notes, other concentration camp survivors adjusted to the effects of having been subjected to a most terrible experience and are now living lives that are essentially normal. Antonovsky states:

> More than a few women among the concentration camp survivors were well adapted, no matter how adaptation was measured. Despite having lived through the most inconceivably inhuman experience, followed by Displaced Persons camps, illegal immigration to Palestine, internment in Cyprus by the British, the Israeli War of Independence, a lengthy period of economic austerity, the Sinai War of 1956, and the Six Day War of 1967 (to mention only the highlights), some women were reasonably healthy and happy, had raised families, worked, had friends, and were involved in community activities.[1]

When considering what differentiates people who are generally vulnerable to stress-related health problems (not just concentration camp survivors) from those who are not so vulnerable, Antonovsky argues that a strong sense of coherence is the key factor. Coherence, in his view, is a personal orientation that allows an individual to view the world with feelings of confidence, faith in the predictability of events, and a notion that things will most likely work out reasonably well. One achieves this sense of coherence as a result of life experiences in which one meets challenges, participates in shaping outcomes (usually satisfactory), and copes with varying degrees of stimuli. Hence, the person has the resources to cope with unexpected situations if they arise. On the other hand, people whose lives are so routine and completely predictable that their sense of coherence as previously defined is weakened will find it difficult to handle unpleasant surprises and events. They are likely to be more susceptible to stress-induced health dysfunctions as they are overwhelmed by events. What Antonovsky appears to be saying is that people who have the capability to come to terms with their situation rather than to be overcome by it are those who are most likely to emerge in a healthy condition.

---

[1] Aaron Antonovsky, *Health, Stress, and Coping* (San Francisco: Jossey-Bass, 1979), p. 7.

A similar conclusion can be made about soldiers fighting in combat. Environmental stresses faced by combat infantrymen are among the hardest faced by anyone. These stresses include the overt threat of death or injury, the sight and sounds of dying men, battle noise, fatigue, loss of sleep, deprivation of family relationships, and exposure to rain, mud, insects, heat, or cold—all occasioned by deliberate exposure to the most extreme forms of violence intentionally directed at the soldier by the opposing side. Charles Moskos (1970) has compared combat with the Hobbesian analogy of primitive life—both can be nasty, brutish, and short. Yet somehow men generally come to terms with the circumstances, since most combat soldiers do not become psychiatric casualties. Two factors may be largely responsible. First is the existence of external group demands for discipline and efficiency under fire. Observing helicopter ambulance crews and Green Berets in Vietnam, Peter Bourne (1970), a psychiatrist, found these soldiers were subject to strong group pressures to be technically proficient regardless of friendship ties. This finding was particularly true of the Green Berets, who urged their detachment leaders to prove themselves in combat in order to be worthy of their role. Although at times this social pressure added to the stress of the leaders, when the entire group faced an enemy threat there was unusual group cohesion and considerable conformity in the manner in which the threat was perceived and handled.

Second, Bourne suggests that there is a further psychological mobilization of an internal discipline in which the individual soldier employs a sense of personal invulnerability, the use of action to reduce tension, and a lack of personal introspection to perceive his environment in such a way that personal threat is reduced. Whether Bourne's findings are representative of other types of combat soldiers is subject to question, since helicopter ambulance crews and Green Berets are highly self-selected volunteers for hazardous duty. Nevertheless, Bourne's study supports the conclusion of others (Kellett 1982; Rado 1949) that one of the most efficient techniques that allows soldiers generally to adjust to battle is to interpret combat not as a continued threat of personal injury or death but as a sequence of demands to be responded to by precise military performances. In failing to find significant physiological change (excretion of adrenal cortical steroids) occurring among most soldiers during life-threatening situations, Bourne suggests that the men allowed their behavior under stress to be modified by social and psychological influences that significantly affected physiological responses to objective threats from the environment.

Some research has shown relatively long-lasting effects of stress on a few Vietnam combat veterans, such as posttraumatic stress disorders (intense feelings of demoralization, guilt, anger, active expression of hostility, perceived hostility of others) among soldiers exposed to particularly abusive violence usually involving civilians (Laufer, Gallops, and Frey-Wouters 1984) or, in the case of depression, among those who were predisposed to depression in the first place (Helzer 1981). For most people, however, the effects of stress resulting from exposure to extreme situations are that such situations are relatively rare, and whatever stresses are generated among those persons are usually temporary and disappear after a while. Many people are not emotionally affected at all, even though the circumstances are exceedingly stressful. Consequently, as Bruce Dohrenwend (1975:384) pointed out, if stressful situations play a major role in causing mental disturbance, the relevant events must be more ordinary and frequent experiences in the lives of most people, such as marriage, birth of a first child, death of a loved one, loss of a job, and so on. Though such events are not extraordinary in a large population, they are extraordinary in the lives of the individuals who experience them.

Life events. Life events research does not focus on one particular life event (for example, exposure to combat) and claim that it is more stressful than another life event (for example, unemployment). Rather, it is generally based on the assumption that the *accumulation* of several events in a person's life eventually builds up to a stressful impact. However, what types of events, in what combinations, over what periods of time, and under what circumstances promote stress-induced health problems is not at all clear at the present time.

An important area of contention in life events research, for example, is the issue of whether any type of change in one's life, either pleasant or unpleasant, produces significant stress, or whether stress is largely a result of unpleasant events only. Considerable evidence supports the idea that any type of environmental change requiring the individual to adapt can produce a specific stress response (Selye 1956). Barbara Dohrenwend (1973) concluded from her research on heads of families in the Washington Heights area of New York City that stressfulness is best conceived as emanating from life change itself rather than from just the undesirability of certain life events. Leonard Syme (1975) has reported on studies in North Dakota and California where it was found that rates of coronary heart disease were twice as high among men who had experienced several lifetime job changes and geographic moves as compared to men with no such changes. The findings were not attributable to differences in diet, smoking habits, obesity, blood pressure, physical activity, age or familial longevity, but to changes in the situations in which people lived.

Most research clearly comes down on the side of unpleasant events as being of prime importance. Lloyd Rogler and August Hollingshead (1965) compared a matched set of twenty "well" families with twenty "sick" families (defined as having either the husband or wife or both diagnosed as schizophrenic) of lower-class status in Puerto Rico. Based upon recall of life events by the subjects and others in the community, the study found no significant differences in the family lives of the normals and schizophrenics during childhood and adolescence. Members of both groups were exposed to the same conditions of poverty, family instability, and lower-class socialization. There was also a lack of difference in their respective adult lives, with the notable exception that for those persons who became schizophrenic, there was a recent and discernible period—*prior to the appearance of overt symptomatology*—during which they were engulfed by a series of insoluble and mutually reinforcing problems. Schizophrenia thus seemed to originate from being placed in an intolerable dilemma brought on by adverse life events largely stemming from intense family and sexual conflicts related to unemployment and restricted life opportunities.

Robert Lauer (1974) investigated whether the rate or speed of change and the type of change, either positive or negative, were the most important variables in stress produced by change. Though stress was directly related to the perceived rate of change, his findings indicated that the effect of rapid change can be moderated by whether the change was perceived to be desirable. Rapid change and undesirability were the most stressful conditions. Still other research by Catherine Ross and John Mirowsky (1979; Mirowsky and Ross 1989) found that the undesirability of events predicts distress better than change alone does. Ross and Mirowsky observed that the effects of desirable events, ambiguous events, change per se, and the number of events experienced are not especially significant. They conclude that undesirability is *the* characteristic of life events most associated with increased psychological distress. Moreover, research by George Brown and Tirril Harris (1978) on depression among women in London found that long-term depression results from negative circumstances, not positive ones. Losing one's job is an undesirable life event that can also have potentially harmful effects on a person's physical and mental well-being (Hamilton et al. 1990; Kessler, House, and Turner 1987; Kessler, Turner, and House 1989). Reemployment, however, produces positive emotional effects, leading to the conclusion that the worst psychological effects of job loss can be minimized if opportunities exist for reemployment (Kessler, Turner, and House 1989).

When it comes to health in general, research by Allan McFarlane and his colleagues (1983) in Canada found that undesirable life events cause the most stress which, in turn, causes poorer health. What determined the impact of life events on health was the perception of the nature of the change by the individual. Events considered to be undesirable and not controllable by the respondents were consistently followed by an increase in reports of distress, symptoms of illness, and physician visits. Many people are particularly prone to seek out the services of a physician after experiencing a stressful life event as observed by several researchers (Gore 1981; Gortmaker, Eckenrode, and Gore 1982; Tessler, Mechanic and Dimond 1976).

Besides the type of change and the speed with which it occurs, the extent to which change affects a person's life may also be important. Libby Ruch (1977) investigated this and suggests that life change actually has three dimensions: (1) the degree of change evoked, (2) the undesirability of change, and (3) the aspect of one's life that is affected (for example, personal, occupational). But Ruch found that the degree of change is more significant than either desirability or the area of life affected. That is, the greater the change, the more likely stress will result. In subsequent research, Ruch (Ruch, Chandler, and Harter 1980) found that women with changes in their lives prior to being raped had significantly more problems adjusting in the aftermath of the assault than rape victims with little or no changes in their lives before the attack. Although too much change may indeed be stressful, too little change in a person's life also may induce stress (Wildman and Johnson 1977). It is not at all clear, however, that too much or too little change is a determining factor in stress-related health problems. Thomas Rundall (1978), for instance, has found that patients with higher levels of life change prior to surgery did not have appreciably more difficulty or sickness when recovering than patients lacking changes in their lives. In sum, the research pertaining to life events is contradictory and in need of clarification.

Life events research also entails serious problems of accurately measuring the presumed relationship between stress and particular life experiences. The most influential instrument at present is the Social Readjustment Rating Scale developed by Thomas Holmes and Robert Rahe (1967). This scale is based on the assumption that change, no matter how good or bad, demands a certain degree of adjustment on the part of an individual: the greater the adjustment, the greater the stress. Holmes and Rahe have carried their analysis one step further and have suggested that changes in life events occur in a cumulative pattern that can eventually build to a stressful impact. Thus, the type of change does not matter so much; the extent to which change disrupts normal patterns of life is important.

The Holmes and Rahe Social Readjustment Rating Scale, an adaptation of which is shown in Table 4-2 lists certain life events that are associated with varying amounts of disruption in the life of an average person. It was constructed by having hundreds of people of different social backgrounds rank the relative amount of adjustment accompanying a particular life experience. Death of a spouse is ranked highest, with a relative stress value of 100; marriage ranks

TABLE 4-2 Life Events and Weighted Values

Life Event	Value	Life Event	Value
Death of spouse	100	Son or daughter leaving home	29
Divorce	73	Trouble with in-laws	29
Marital separation	65	Outstanding personal	
Jail term	63	achievement	28
Death of close family member	63	Wife beginning or stopping	
Personal injury or illness	53	work	26
Marriage	50	Beginning or ending school	26
Fired at work	47	Revision of habits	24
Marital reconciliation	45	Trouble with boss	23
Retirement	45	Change in work hours	20
Change in health of family	44	Change in residence	20
Pregnancy	40	Change in schools	20
Sex difficulties	39	Change in recreation	19
Gain of new family member	39	Change in social activity	18
Change in financial state	38	Loan for minor purchase	17
Death of close friend	37	Change in sleeping habits	16
Change of work	36	Change in number of family	
Change in number of		get-togethers	15
arguments with spouse	35	Change in eating habits	15
Mortgage or loan for		Vacation	13
major purchase	31	Christmas	12
Foreclosure of mortgage	30	Minor violations of law	11
Change of responsibility			
at work	29		

Source: Adapted from T. H. Holmes and R. H. Rahe, "The Social Readjustment Rating Scale," *Journal of Psychosomatic Research*, 11 (August 1967), Table 3-1, 213. Reprinted with permission from the authors and Pergamon Press Ltd.

seventh with a value of 50, retirement tenth with a value of 45, taking a vacation is ranked forty-first with a value of 13, and so forth. Holmes and Rahe call each stress value a "life change" unit. They suggest that as the total value of life change units mounts, the probability of having a serious illness also increases, particularly if a person accumulates too many life change units in too short a time. If an individual accumulates 200 or more life change units within the period of a year, Holmes and Rahe believe such a person will risk a serious disorder.

Although used extensively and found to measure stress and life events about as well or better than other scales (Dohrenwend et al. 1978; Ross and Mirowsky 1979), the Holmes and Rahe Social Readjustment Rating Scale nevertheless contains some serious flaws that need to be overcome in future research if the scale is going to be continued as a major research tool. Some studies have found that the scale does not adequately account for differences in the relative importance of various life events among ethnic and cultural subgroups (Askenasy, Dohrenwend, and Dohrenwend 1977; Fairbanks and Hough 1981; Hough, Fairbanks, and Garcia 1976; Rosenberg and Dohrenwend 1975). In other words, the Holmes and Rahe scale measures the quantity of change rather than the qualitative meaning of the event (Ruch 1977). Other research suggests that some life events, such as divorce, can be regarded as a *consequence* of stress instead of a *cause.* For example, events such as "change in sleeping habits," "change in number of arguments with spouse," "sex difficulties," and "fired at work" may result from stress rather than cause it (Holmes and Masuda 1974). This situation confounds the relationships being measured. Some respondents also have difficulty recalling past life events (Funch and Marshall 1984).

Another problem is that the scale does not account for intervening variables, such as social support, that might modify the effects of stress for many individuals. While interpersonal influence can be stressful in itself because of discrepancies, conflicting expectations, excessive demands to achieve or maintain a certain level of performance (Mettlin and Woelfel 1974), there is little doubt that supportive interpersonal influences help reduce stressful feelings (Dean, Kolodny, and Wood 1990; Ensel and Lin 1991; Gore 1978, 1981, 1989; Haines and Hurlbert 1992; Jacobson 1986; Lin and Ensel 1989; Lin et al. 1979; Lin, Woelfel, and Light 1985; Loscocco and Spitze 1990; Matt and Dean 1993; Turner 1981; Wethington and Kessler 1986).

Furthermore, as Canadian medical sociologists R. Jay Turner and William Avison (1992) discovered, life events that are successfully resolved may not be stressful. That is, it may be the case that mastery of an event provides a buffer to stress because successful resolution constitutes a personally meaningful positive experience. This situation, as Turner and Avision explain, can substantially counterbalance the stress associated with the event.

Obviously, life events research is in need of more extensive development. The relationship between stress and life events as a precipitating factor in causing or contributing to the onset of physical and mental disorders is a highly complex phenomenon and not easily amenable to a simple cause-and-effect explanation. Nevertheless, considerable progress has been made in improving measures of stressful life events, and work in this regard continues today (Avision and Turner

1988). Current findings indicate that persons at the lower end of the socioeconomic scale are particularly vulnerable to the emotional effects of undesirable life events (Gore, Aseltine, and Colten 1992; McLeod and Kessler 1990). There may also be important differences between men and women, with men more likely to be distressed by work and finances and women by negative events in the family (Conger et al. 1993). Consequently, there is general recognition in the behavioral sciences that psychological distress is a negative influence on health (Lin and Ensel 1989; Mirowsky and Ross 1989). Strong support comes from research in genetics where evidence has been accumulated that stressful situations trigger genetic predispositions toward mental disorder and other psychological problems (Weiner 1985). Debate is no longer centered on whether life events are important in influencing health; rather, the focus now is upon determining in which specific ways they are important.

SUMMARY

The study of the relationship between social factors and stress-related diseases has advanced significantly in the past fifteen years, but the precise nature of this relationship is not yet fully understood. It is clear from existing studies, however, that the experience of stress is a subjective response on the part of an individual as a result of exposure to certain social experiences. Before an assessment can be made of the effect of stress upon an individual, it will be necessary to know (1) the nature of the threat itself; (2) the objective social environment within which the threat appears; (3) the psychological style and personality of the individual involved; (4) the subjective definition of the threat by the individual; (5) the social influences acting upon the individual, particularly the psychological supports offered by group membership; and (6) the duration of the threat. Obviously, stress research represents a very complex investigative effort. But the potential contribution of such research to both the social and medical sciences is great. As House (1974) pointed out, stress research offers opportunities to learn more about a phenomenon that has implications not only for understanding disease processes but also for understanding a wide range of human behavior, such as suicide, delinquency, social movements, family violence, child abuse, mental health, and many other important social problems.

Health Behavior

5

Before discussing the behavior of people who feel sick and in need of medical treatment, we will examine the behavior of healthy people who try to remain that way. This is an important area of investigation in medical sociology because health-oriented behavior does not pertain just to those activities concerned with recovering from disease or injury, but also involves the kinds of things that healthy people do to stay healthy. Living a healthy lifestyle and promoting one's own health in the process has become an increasingly important component of life in modern societies. Consequently, medical sociologists divide health-oriented behavior into two general categories: health behavior and illness behavior. Health behavior is defined as the activity undertaken by a person who believes himself or herself to be healthy for the purpose of preventing health problems, while illness behavior is the activity undertaken by a person who feels ill for the purpose of defining that illness and seeking relief from it (Kasl and Cobb 1966).

In this chapter we will review the research pertaining to health behavior. The first part of the discussion will focus on the health lifestyles that people pursue on their own more or less independently of the medical profession. The second part will review the health behavior of individuals that places them in direct contact with medical doctors and other health professionals for preventive care intended to maintain their health and reduce the risk of illness.

HEALTH LIFESTYLES

Health lifestyles are patterns of voluntary health behavior based on choices from options that are available to people according to their life situations (Cockerham, Abel, and Lüschen 1993). Health lifestyles include contact with the medical profession for checkups and preventive care, but the majority of activities take place outside the health care delivery system. These activities typically consist of choices and practices, influenced by the individual's probabilities for realizing them, that range from brushing one's teeth and using automobile seat belts to relaxing at health spas. For most people, health lifestyles involve decisions about food, exercise, relaxation, personal hygiene, risk of accidents, coping with stress, smoking, alcohol and drug use, and having physical checkups.

According to the World Health Organization (1986), significant improvements in health in the nineteenth century were brought about by what might be called "engineering methods"—the building of safe water supplies and sewers and the production of cheap food for urban areas through the use of mechanized agriculture. These methods continue to improve the health of people in underdeveloped areas of the world. The first sixty years of the twentieth century was the "medical era" in which the dominant approach to health was mass vaccination and the extensive use of antibiotics to combat infection. At present, however, WHO suggests that advanced societies are entering into a "postmedical era" in which physical well-being is largely undermined by social and environmental factors. These factors include certain types of individual behavior (such as smoking, overeating), failures of social organization (loneliness), economic factors (poverty), and the physical environment (pollution) that are not amenable to direct improvement by medicine. WHO (1986:117) concludes: "Whereas in the 'medical era' health policy has been concerned mainly with how medical care is to be provided and paid for, in the new 'post-medical' era it will focus on the attainment of good health and well-being."

While the provision and financing of medical care remains a critically important health policy issue today, the role of health lifestyles as a means to improve the health of people in a postmedical situation is gaining in significance as the twenty-first century approaches. Robert Crawford (1984) helps us to understand why this is the case. First, as Crawford points out, there has been a growing recognition among the general public that the major disease patterns have changed from acute or infectious illnesses to chronic diseases—like heart disease, cancer, and diabetes—that medicine cannot cure. Second, numerous health disasters, such as AIDS and cigarette-induced lung cancer, are caused by particular styles of living. Third, there has been a virtual campaign by the mass media and health care providers emphasizing lifestyle change and individual responsibility for health. The result has been a growing awareness that medicine is no longer the automatic answer to dealing with all threats to one's health. Therefore, strategies on the part of individuals to adopt a healthier lifestyle have gained in popularity. As Crawford explains, when threats to health persist in the environment and medicine cannot provide a cure, self-control over the range of personal behaviors that affect health is the only remaining option. This means the person will be confronted with the decision to acquire or maintain a healthy lifestyle, or disregard the situation and perhaps be at greater risk for poor health.

Weber: Lifestyles

Before proceeding to a discussion of health lifestyles, it is useful to review the work of German sociologist Max Weber (1864-1920). Weber is one of the most influential sociological theorists of all time and his views on lifestyles in general help place the concept of a "health lifestyle" in perspective. Weber's notion of lifestyles appears in his discussion of status groups in his classic work *Economy and Society* (1978), originally published in 1922. Karl Marx had earlier suggested that a person's social class position is determined exclusively by his or her degree of access to a society's means of production. In other words, Marx claimed that one's location in a class structure results strictly from how much of society's goods and services that person is able to command. However, in Weber's view, Marx's concept of class is not the whole story in determining someone's social rank; rather, status (prestige) and power (political influence) are also important. Weber focused primarily on the difference between class and status in his analysis. He pointed out that, while class was an objective dimension of social life signified by how much money and property a person has, status was subjective in that it consists of the amount of esteem a person is accorded by other people. Typically, a person's occupation and level of education are the basis of such esteem.

A status group refers to people who share similar material circumstances, prestige, education, and political influence; moreover, members of the same status group share a similar lifestyle. In fact, a particular lifestyle is what distinguishes one status group from another. People with high socioeconomic status clearly lead a different style of life than those at the bottom of society and those somewhere in the middle. Weber also made the pertinent observation that lifestyles are not based upon what one produces, but on what one consumes. That is, one's lifestyle is a reflection of the types and amounts of goods and services one uses or consumes. Thus, for Weber, the difference between status groups does not lie in their relationship to the means of production as suggested by Marx, but in their relationship to the means of consumption.

This view applies to health lifestyles because, when someone pursues a healthy style of life, that person is attempting to produce good health according to his or her degree of motivation, effort, and capabilities. Yet the aim of this activity, as Weber's insight suggests, is ultimately one of consumption. People attempt to maintain or enhance their health in order to use it for some purpose, such as a longer life, work, sexual attractiveness, or enhanced enjoyment of their physical being. A. d'Houtaud and Mark Field (1984), for example, found in a study in France that health was conceptualized as something to be cultivated for increased vitality and enjoyment of life among the upper and middle class, and for the ability to continue to work among lower-class persons. The lower class viewed health largely as a means to an end (work), while persons with higher socioeconomic status regarded health as an end in itself (vitality and enjoyment). In both situations, however, health was something that was to be consumed, not simply produced.

Weber did not ignore the socioeconomic conditions necessary for a specific lifestyle. Weber deliberately used three distinct terms to express his view of lifestyles: "*Stilisierung des Lebens*" (stylization of *life*), "*Lebensführung*" (life conduct), and "*Lebenschancen*" (life chances). As shown in Figure 5-1, *Lebensführung* and *Lebenschancen* are the two components of *Stilisierung des Lebens* (Abel 1991; Abel and Cockerham 1993; Cockerham, Abel, and Lüschen 1993). *Lebensführung,* or life conduct, refers to the choices that people have in the lifestyles they wish to adopt, but the potential for realizing these choices is influenced by their *Lebenschancen,* or life chances. Ralf Dahrendorf (1979:73) notes that Weber is ambiguous about what he really means by life chances, but the best interpretation he found of what Weber meant is that life chances are the "probability of finding satisfaction for interests, wants, and needs." For Weber, the notion of life chances therefore refers to the probability of acquiring a particular lifestyle, which means the person must have the financial resources, status, rights, and social relationships that support the chosen lifestyle. One's life chances are shaped by one's social circumstances.

Of course, the life chances that enhance participation in a healthy lifestyle are greatest among upper and middle socioeconomic groups who have the best resources to support their lifestyle choices. Yet it was Weber's contention that lifestyles frequently spread beyond the groups in which they originate (Bendix 1960). A good example is the spread of the Protestant ethic (a lifestyle emphasizing thrift, effort, and the value of work as a good in itself) into the general culture of Western society. One result is that, in the modern world, the Protestant ethic is no longer distinctive to Protestants, nor the West (Jaspers 1988). While lifestyles set people apart, Weber suggests that lifestyles can also spread across society. And there is evidence that health lifestyles, emphasizing exercise, sports, a healthy diet, avoidance of unhealthy practices such as smoking and the like, which had their origin in the upper middle class—are beginning to spread across

FIGURE 5–1   Weber's lifestyle components

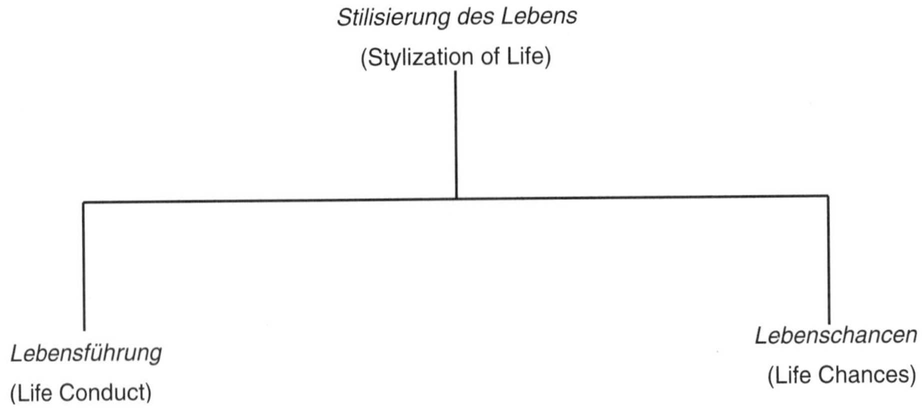

class boundaries in Western society (Featherstone 1987). It has become increasingly clear that most people try to do at least something (even if it is just eating sensibly, getting enough sleep, or relaxing) to protect their health (Harris and Guten 1979; Kickbusch 1989).

Weber's ideas about lifestyles are important for several reasons. First, his work led to the development of the concept "socioeconomic status," or SES in sociology, as the most accurate reflection of a person's social class position. Where a person is located in the social hierarchy of society is determined not by income alone, but typically by a combination of three indicators: income, education, and occupational status. Second, lifestyle is a reflection of a person's status in society, and lifestyles are based on what people consume, rather than what they produce. Third, lifestyles are based upon choices, but these choices are dependent upon the individual's potential for realizing them. And this potential is usually determined by one's socioeconomic circumstances. Fourth, although particular lifestyles characterize particular socioeconomic groups, some lifestyles spread across class boundaries and gain influence in the wider society.

Therefore, when it comes to health lifestyles, Weber's work suggests that, while such lifestyles are oriented toward producing health, the aim of the activity is ultimately toward its consumption as people try to be healthy so they can use their health to live longer, enjoy life, be able to keep on working, and so forth. Furthermore, while health lifestyles seem to be most characteristic of the upper and middle classes, the potential exists for them to spread across social boundaries. The quality of participation may differ significantly, but the level of participation in advanced societies may be spreading nonetheless. Regardless of one's particular socioeconomic position, an important feature of modern society appears to be the tendency for many people to adopt a healthy lifestyle within the limits of their circumstances and opportunities.

Health Lifestyle Motivation

An emphasis upon a healthy lifestyle is not a new development in the United States. What is new is the reawakened interest in health lifestyles that occurred in the mid-twentieth century because of the profound decline in infectious diseases and increase in chronic diseases associated with certain behavioral practices like smoking, overeating, and lack of exercise (Becker and Rosenstock 1989; Goldstein 1992). Prior to this time, as Harvey Green (1986) shows in an extensively documented history of health and fitness activities in the United States between 1830 and 1940, a long-term interest had existed on the part of Americans to be healthy. Green found that in the early nineteenth century, a strong religious sentiment was associated with health. Various Protestant reformers argued that the Second Coming of Christ might be advanced if humankind could achieve a state of grace and perfection, which included a healthy body. "Good health—the avoidance of disease, debility, and 'premature' death—thus took on extraordinary importance," states Green (1986:10). Sickness was therefore regarded by some people as a spiritual as well as a medical or physiological problem.

Other developments identified by Green during the nineteenth and early twentieth centuries included linking good health with the vitality of the nation; associating health with beauty; depicting athletics as a foundation for a "muscular Christianity" and a means to instill "team spirit" and an outlook necessary for success in business and war; and projecting health as vital to upward social mobility for new immigrants because of its close association with Americanism. Some groups and individuals also advocated good health as a means to avoid illness, reduce the chances of dying early, and gain an "edge" on competition in the workplace; but practical health goals were often not emphasized as much as idealistic values. The dominant view was that good health was an idealized end state that people should achieve for moral, religious, and patriotic reasons or as part of an overall effort to be a success in life (Gillick 1984; Green 1986).

Religion remains an important aspect of health lifestyles today for many people. Several studies suggest that religious attitudes and behaviors can have a positive effect on numerous health-related activities (Dwyer, Clarke, and Miller 1990; Idler 1987; Jarvis and Northcott 1987). This includes prohibitions on smoking, drinking, and multiple sexual relationships and the promotion of nutrition, hygiene, and exercise. In one study, Jeffrey Dwyer, Leslie Clarke, and Michael Miller (1990) observed lower mortality rates from cancer among religious groups emphasizing doctrinal orthodoxy and behavioral conformity. They suggest this development is due to the disapproval in such groups of behavior related to cancer mortality, like smoking.

In an extensive review of literature, Dwyer and his associates found other research supporting the positive effects of religion on health, such as the high life expectancy of Mormons in Utah, which, in the case of lung cancer, appears to extend to the non-Mormon population as well because of the prevalence of social situations in which smoking is strongly disapproved and fewer smokers causing secondary smoke for nonsmokers to breathe. Victor Fuchs (1974), in an earlier study, compared the death rates in Utah and Nevada, and observed that better health existed in Utah because of the lifestyles of a majority of its residents. People in Nevada had significantly higher rates of cigarette and alcohol consumption and family instability, along with less religiosity than found in Utah.

While religious values remain influential in regard to health lifestyles, most research on contemporary participation in a wide range of fitness activities shows that individual self-control over one's health is emerging as the principal rationale behind such participation (Crawford 1984; Harris and Guten 1979; Hayes and Ross 1987; Ransford 1986). This theme is also found in literature reviews and essays on fitness and the postmodern self (Glassner 1988, 1989). "By becoming fit," states Barry Glassner (1989:187), "persons are said to achieve a degree of independence from medical professionals and medical technology." Thus, the majority position in American literature today is that health lifestyles are pursued in modern society because they allow a person to assume some personal control over his or her health. A similar pattern appears to exist in Germany as well, where two concepts of health as a social value have developed. The predominant concept views health as a form of efficiency; the second concept, becoming more prevalent in recent years, depicts health as a form of individual emancipation (Rodenstein 1987).

Studies of wellness programs sponsored by American business corporations uncover a related theme. Relevant research shows most people participate in fitness activities provided by their employers because they want to stay in shape or lose weight largely just to look better (Conrad 1988a; Kotarba and Bentley 1988). That is, their health goals were limited to participating in workouts that would result in a positive body image and level of physical conditioning that would allow them to get more out of life (Conrad 1988a). A desire on the part of the individual to look and feel good through exercise and dieting was given priority over physical health.

Crawford (1984) suggests that health has indeed become a metaphor for consumption; that is, good health is a form of release in that it provides a person with the freedom to consume in order to satisfy individual needs. Furthermore, Crawford claims that the abundance of news and commentary in the media on lifestyles and health has reduced complacency about staying healthy; in fact, he notes that the media has declared health and fitness activity to be a lifestyle in itself. An important response to this situation is the virtual flood of commercial products in American society to help the individual "manufacture" health. Thus, states Crawford (1984:76), "the complex ideologies of health are picked up, magnified, and given commodity form by the image-makers." Commercial products associated with fitness not only produce profits, but also reinforce the general idea that health and fitness is a practical goal to be achieved through the use of these products.

Consequently, it appears that modern Americans wish to pursue health lifestyles largely for practical, not abstract, reasons. They want to be healthy in order to avoid disease, live longer, feel good, and look good. In other words, as suggested by Max Weber's (1978) work, health is something to be achieved (produced) so that it can be used (consumed) for some practical goal. As Joseph Kotarba and Pamela Bentley (1988:558) explain, workplace wellness programs "illustrate a more general trend in our culture that is transforming health from a status—something an individual has—to an accomplishment—something an individual does." Kotarba and Bentley point out that health becomes an accomplishment to the degree that an individual can rationally and systematically attempt to seek, nurture, and prolong it. Bryan Turner (1984, 1987) notes that religion dominated ideas about the physical use of the body in past Western history, but rationalization and secularization have produced a modern emphasis on the use of the outer surface of the body for desirable feelings and personal significance.

Therefore, as Glassner (1988) explains, greater self-control over one's quality of life through the medium of the body has emerged as a major component of modernism. The rationality underlying this development is what Weber (1978) refers to as "formal rationality." Formal rationality is the purposeful calculation of the most efficient means to achieve a goal. Weber made a major contribution to the development of social thought by explaining how formal rationality became the dominant mode of thinking in Western society and joined with the Protestant ethic to stimulate the rise of capitalism in the West. In the context of formal rationality, health is valued not so much as a substantive, idealized state; rather, health is valued because it has a practical function to perform. As Eugene Gallagher (1988a) points out, a distinctive feature of modernity in the health sphere is a more widespread and penetrating awareness of the value of health and individual efforts to achieve it—which stands in sharp contrast to the more fatalist and passive attitudes about health prevailing in many non-Western cultures.

Health Lifestyles in Western Society

Health professionals and the mass media have spread the message that healthy people need to avoid certain behaviors and adopt others as part of their daily routine if they want to maximize their life expectancy and remain healthy as long as possible. These statements are supported by ample evidence that a lack of exercise, diets high in fat and cholesterol, stress, smoking, obesity, alcohol and drug abuse, and exposure to chemical pollutants cause serious health problems and early deaths (Blair et al. 1989; Otten et al. 1990; Paffenbarger et al. 1986; Polednak 1989). It is also well known that lifestyles involving homosexuality and intravenous drug use increase the risk of AIDS, while smoking is linked to lung cancer, alcoholism to cirrhosis of the liver, and high fat diets to atherosclerosis and heart disease.

On the positive side, there is evidence that pursuing a healthy lifestyle can enhance one's health and life expectancy. Exercise has been found to reduce the risk of dying from heart disease (Blair et al. 1989; Paffenbarger et al. 1986), as have reductions in cholesterol levels, blood pressure, and cigarette smoking (Sytkowski, Kannel, and D'Agostino 1990). In other research, a ten-year survey of the health lifestyles of nearly 7,000 adults in Alameda County, California, identified seven good health practices: (1) seven to eight hours a night of sleep; (2) eating breakfast every day; (3) seldom if ever eating snacks; (4) controlling one's weight; (5) exercising; (6) limiting alcohol consumption; and (7) never having smoked cigarettes (Berkman and Breslow 1983). People reporting six or seven of these health practices were found to have better health and longer lives than people reporting fewer than four of them.

Such developments suggest that health lifestyles should be important for many people. Health lifestyles also should be more common in advanced societies where people have greater choices in their selection of lifestyles and a better opportunity to be healthy than in underdeveloped nations with relatively low standards of living and fewer health options. The author and his colleagues (Cockerham et al. 1986a) sought to determine whether lifestyles pertaining to the self-management of health had spread across class lines in American society. Using data collected from a statewide sample of adults in Illinois, it was found that considerable similarity existed between socioeconomic groups in certain lifestyles involving appearance, food habits, physical exercise, smoking, and alcohol use. Exercise, for instance, emerged as a behavioral pattern that people from all social classes accepted as something a person should do and that most people say they attempt in some form, ranging from short walks to participation in sports. When it came to food habits, most people, regardless of their socioeconomic situation, attempted to obtain the best nutritional value in the food available to them, avoid chemical additives, and the like. This latter finding is supported by Clare Blackburn's (1991) research in Great Britain where she found that low-income families spend a higher proportion of their total income on food and shop more efficiently for value and nutrients than higher-income families.

The United States and Germany. Subsequent research (Abel et al. 1989; Cockerham, Kunz, and Lueschen 1988a, 1988b; Cockerham et al. 1986b; Lueschen, Cockerham, and Kunz 1987) compared the health lifestyles of Americans living in Illinois to Germans in Northrhine-Westphalia and found a distinct lack of difference between social classes, races, and occupational groups in health behavior. Although the quality of participation may vary, health lifestyles in these studies appeared widely accepted and practiced.

One study (Cockerham, Kunz, and Lueschen 1988a) examined whether there were significant differences between people with comprehensive health care benefits provided by their government (Germans) and those generally lacking such coverage (Americans) in regard to participating in health lifestyles. Germany has an extensive system of national health insurance that covers 93 percent of the total population (the most wealthy are excluded and required to obtain private health insurance), while in the United States only some 20 percent of the population—the aged and the poor—have government-sponsored health insurance through Medicare and Medicaid. The study sought to determine whether Americans, who do not have the security of a national health insurance program, worked harder to stay healthy than Germans, who have their health care costs covered by a national health plan. The data showed a general lack of difference between Americans and Germans, as well as between social strata in the two countries, with respect to participation in health lifestyles. The more paternalistic German system of health insurance coverage did not appear to undermine personal incentives to stay physically fit in comparison to the American system, where people are more on their own in obtaining health insurance and covering their costs for health care.

These studies would suggest that—at least in the United States and Germany—health lifestyles are spreading across class boundaries in a manner similar to that suggested by Weber for the Protestant ethic. This does not mean that everyone is trying to live in a healthy manner, but many people are and they include persons in all social strata. Several other studies in the two countries support this conclusion. For example, in the United States, H. Edward Ransford (1986) found in a national sample that lower-class black adults were especially likely to adopt health-protective measures because of particular concern about heart disease. Well-educated whites were found to participate in health lifestyles because of a concern about their health in general. But the result was the same: Health behavior cut across class and racial lines. In Ohio, Daniel Harris and Sharon Guten (1979) found that practically everyone in their survey did something to protect their health. Other research in South Carolina found a lack of socioeconomic differences in health practices in a sample of state government employees in a health promotion program (the Carolina Health Lifestyle Project); most participants, regardless of class background, made positive changes in their health habits (Kronenfeld et al. 1988).

In Germany, the pattern of participation in health lifestyles is becoming increasingly similar to patterns in the United States. The number of Germans involved in sport and exercise has risen substantially in recent years, while diets have become more healthy and healthy work conditions have received more emphasis (Scheuch 1989). Jogging has clearly gained in popularity (Kimmerle 1987), and people are increasingly aware of the dangers of hard liquor and smoking (Noelle-Newman 1983; Wetterer and Troschke 1986). Moreover, the number of male smokers has significantly declined. With the exception of sports, where participation remains greater among members of the upper and middle class, there do not appear to be significant class differences in health lifestyles among Germans (Cockerham, Kunz, and Lueschen 1988a).

Other Western Countries. The situation in other Western countries has not been established because little research on health lifestyles has taken place to date and some of the existing studies contradict each other. In Great Britain, a major survey of health behavior indicates that important differences persist between the classes in the things they do to stay healthy, with the upper and middle classes tending to take better care of themselves than the working class and lower class (Blaxter 1990). However, Mike Featherstone (1987) suggests physical fitness activities are spreading increasingly throughout status groups in British society, and Michael Calnan (1989) found a lack of difference among socioeconomic groups in a large survey of health behavior in southern England. In addition, there is evidence of a significant decline in smoking among British males (Reid 1989), while participation in jogging (Crump 1989) and other forms of sport and exercise reached unprecedented levels in the 1980s (Mason 1989).

In other research involving a group of middle- and working-class women living on the outskirts of London, Calnan (1987) found that both groups agreed that the best way of keeping healthy was a good diet and physical exercise. However, there were different interpretations concerning diets and exercise that apparently resulted from differences in education and class-based life experiences. The middle-class women emphasized that diets should be high in fiber and low in fats and carbohydrates, while the working-class group placed greater emphasis upon having regular substantial meals that included meat and two vegetables. Both groups valued regular exercise, but the working-class women were most likely to regard household duties as meeting this requirement.

On balance, it appears that health lifestyles are spreading in British society, but distinct social class differences remain. This is not too surprising because class divisions in Britain remain more rigid than in the United States and Germany (Reid 1989). In France, little current data are available on health lifestyle participation, but health education programs have been strong advocates of changes in lifestyles for the general public (Letourmy 1986). There have been reports of increased spending on personal health care items and a significant increase in participation in sport and exercise generally in French society (Ardagh 1987). In fact, John Ardagh (1987:425) observes that "the French have become far more fussy about their health."

Claudine Herzlich and Janine Pierret (1987) identify a shift in French thinking toward a norm of a "duty to be healthy." Herzlich and Pierret find that this norm is strongest in the middle class, but they provide accounts of less socially advantaged persons espousing the same orientation and imply that this norm is spreading in French society. They describe health as a necessity for both society and the individual, and the means by which people achieve self-realization. "Today," state Herzlich and Pierret (1987:231), "the 'right to health' implies that every individual must be made responsible for his or her health and must adopt rational behavior in dealing with the pathogenic effects of modern life."

In Denmark, it was found that income failed to predict significant differences in some health-protective behaviors, except for greater routine physical exercise among higher-income persons (Dean 1989). The Danish study found few differences between socioeconomic groups overall, but many persons in the study indicated they took no particular action with respect to their health. Other research in Italy found that less-educated persons smoked more and drank more wine, while higher-educated persons were more likely to have quit smoking and be involved in physical exercise (Piperno and Di Orio 1990). However, it was also observed that, on the whole, relatively few Italians exercise for reasons of health and persons in the lower classes are even less likely to do so.

The case cannot be made that health lifestyles have spread completely throughout Western society on the basis of the existing studies. The most extensive participation appears to be in the United States and Germany; in Britain and France, health lifestyles show signs of spreading, but elsewhere in Western society little or nothing is known about the extent of health practices in the general population. Clearly, more research is needed to determine national, regional, and global patterns of health lifestyles. However, an emphasis on healthy living is an important part of modernity; and while it seems that persons in the upper and middle socioeconomic groups pursue this lifestyle more extensively in Western countries, data from America and Germany in particular show that participation also includes members of the lower social strata.

A Marxist Critique of Health Lifestyles. Marxist scholars like Howard Waitzkin and Vicente Navarro claim that an emphasis on individual responsibility for leading a healthy life excuses the larger society from direct accountability in health matters. Waitzkin (1983) maintains that capitalism puts the burden of being healthy squarely on the individual, rather than seeking collective solutions to health problems. The emphasis in capitalist societies on healthy lifestyles is seen as an effort to displace the responsibility for health from the social system and its health sector down to individuals. That is, capitalism promotes the philosophy that it is up to the individual to keep healthy by exercising, eating right, avoiding smoking and alcohol abuse, and obtaining medical care when needed. While not denying that individual lifestyles are important determinants of health, Waitzkin explains that individuals often lead unhealthy lives as a result of social inequality.

But when the responsibility for staying healthy is shifted to the individual, the social and medical system is not at fault if people become sick or die early deaths because of adverse social conditions.

Navarro (1986) also claims that the strategy of individual responsibility for health assumes that the fundamental cause of an individual's health problem is the individual, not the social system. Navarro argues that an emphasis on individual lifestyles assumes a degree of independence and freedom for the individual that is an illusion. He bases this view on his contention that a person's lifestyle is determined by their work position. Navarro (1986:34) states, "Here I am not only stressing what is obvious, that in our consumer society what *you have* depends on what *you do*, but even more important, that one's psychological framework—which determines one's level of expectation and behavior and pattern of interpersonal relations—is very much determined by one's work." Yet in capitalist society, the argument continues, workers do not have control over their work or their lives, including their health. Consequently, lifestyles are not left to the individual's discretion but are determined by one's work situation, which is controlled by the upper class and organized to protect their socioeconomic advantage.

The merit of the Marxist perspective on health responsibility, as advanced by Waitzkin and Navarro, is that it calls our attention to the fact that many health problems (the most obvious being those that stem from poverty) can have roots in the structure of society that cannot always be addressed by individual lifestyles alone. Therefore, societal-level responsibility for the health of individuals is an important component in the formulation of health policy. However, a problem with the Marxist view is that it assumes health behavior in particular and social behavior in general are not determined by the individual's choice and decision; rather, a person's behavior is essentially predetermined by the socioeconomic structure of society and the ideology that underlies it. Nonetheless, people do have choices, no matter how limited, in whether they want as healthy a life as possible given their circumstances. Decisions about smoking, alcohol use, diet, and exercise ultimately are made by the individual. To blame either society or the individual separately for poor health fails to recognize the interdependence of the two.

Downturn in Participation? Whereas the 1980s were a period of renewed public interest in living a healthy lifestyle, signs emerged in the early 1990s of a possible downturn in participation. A 1992 nationwide Harris Poll showed, for instance, that only 33 percent of Americans said they exercised strenuously compared to 37 percent a few years earlier. The respondents also indicated they were eating more of the wrong foods, driving too fast, and generally taking poorer care of themselves. Some 8 percent more stated they were fat compared to results a decade earlier. On the positive side, 70 percent said they used seat belts regularly, 75 percent did not smoke, and 88 percent either drank alcohol moderately or not at all.

Data such as these call attention to the relationship between economic conditions and health lifestyles. During the economic downturn of the late 1980s and early 1990s, some people may have adopted less healthy lifestyles because of longer work hours, less money, less time to prepare and eat healthy foods, and the influence of advertising for foods high in calories, fat, and other less healthy ingredients. Simply having a lower income would undermine a person's efforts to eat right. The people most affected by this situation would be the poor. Figure 5-2 supports this conclusion by showing weekly food spending by economic group in the United States between 1980 and 1988. The poorest one-fifth spent 13.1 percent less on food in 1988 than in 1980; the second poorest one-fifth spent 6.5 percent less. The wealthiest one-fifth, in contrast, spent 2.7 percent more. Given that the low-income families spend a greater proportion of their money on food than higher income families (Blackburn 1991), the economic downturn of the 1980s appears to have been particularly severe for the lower class. The results depicted in Figure 5-2 show that the eating habits of the wealthy are least affected when the economy enters a downturn. This finding suggests that when the economy is generally negative, participation in health lifestyles is likely to be diminished—especially for the poor.

However, even though some regression in participation in health lifestyles may have occurred in the United States during the late 1980s, Michael Goldstein (1992) claims the health movement is still strong. He summarizes the situation by pointing out that the proportion of the American population with some degree of awareness about the importance of health lifestyles is immense. Goldstein finds that considerable change has occurred in efforts to be healthy. Smoking, for example, has become a truly deviant behavior in the United States.

FIGURE 5–2 Change in Weekly Food Spending by Economic Group between 1980 and 1988, United States

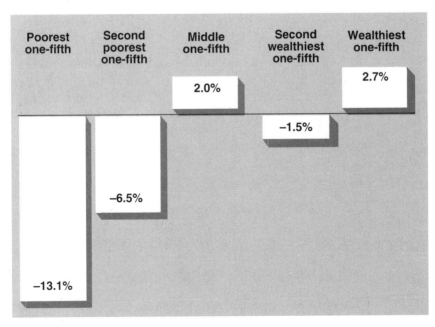

Source: U.S. Agriculture Department, 1992.

Moderation of alcoholic intake, seatbelt use, exercise and sports participation, and consumption of reduced-fat diets have all increased in recent years. Still, only a minority of Americans exercise, while the greatest failure of efforts to promote healthy lifestyles has been in the area of eating behavior. Many Americans still have poor health habits.

PREVENTIVE CARE

As noted earlier in this chapter, health lifestyles generally take place outside of the formal health care delivery system as people pursue their everyday lives in their usual social environment. However, an important facet of health behavior includes contact by healthy people with physicians and other health personnel for preventive care. Preventive care refers to routine physical examinations, immunizations, prenatal care, dental checkups, screening for heart disease and cancer, and other services intended to ensure good health and prevent disease—or minimize the effects of illness if it occurs.

Preventive Care and the Poor

While there is evidence that participation in health lifestyles that do not involve contact with physicians and other health personnel is spreading across social class boundaries in American and German society (Cockerham, Kunz, and Lueschen 1988a), there is other evidence from both countries showing that the poor are least likely to use preventive care (Dutton 1978, 1979; 1986; Siegrist 1988, 1989). As Johannes Siegrist (1989:359) points out for Germany, the most striking class differences in the use of health services are present in the field of prevention and screening programs. In the United States, Diana Dutton (1986) observes that, while the lower class visits physicians more frequently than members of other socioeconomic groups, their need for care is greater because of relatively poorer health and underutilization of preventive care. Regardless of the benefits from public health insurance programs, Dutton finds that the poor receive less preventive care whose utilization is at the discretion of the user.

Dutton's (1986) review of the literature shows that low-income women in the United States receive one-third less prenatal care, low-income children are four times more likely to have never had a routine physical examination, and other measures like dental care, breast exams, and childhood immunizations are considerably less common among the poor. The reason for this situation is that many low-income persons do not have a regular source of medical care, health facilities may not be near at hand, and the costs not covered by health insurance—which the individual must pay out of his or her own pocket—and this can be a significant barrier in visiting the doctor when one feels well. Moreover, for those 38.5 million people or approximately 15 percent of the American population without any health insurance, going to the doctor for preventive care may be an unaffordable luxury.

The underutilization of preventive care among the poor is common not just in the United States and Germany but also in several countries of Western Europe where the lower class has been found to use preventive medical and dental services significantly less frequently (Macintyre 1989). In Great Britain, for example, it is well established that those persons at the lowest end of the social scale make considerably less use of preventive services than do those higher up the social ladder (Calnan 1987; Martin and Mc Queen 1989; Townsend, Davidson, and Whitehead 1990).

Elsewhere, in underdeveloped countries in the Third World, preventive care for the poor is likely to be little or nonexistent, especially in rural areas. In the African nation of Guinea, for example, young mothers in rural villages are significantly less likely to obtain drugs to prevent or treat malaria because of a lack of access to clinics and pharmacies and a lack of awareness and knowledge about how to use such drugs (Glik et al. 1989). In Nigeria, as in Guinea and other African countries, physicians are rarely found in rural areas, regardless of the type of care needed by the local population (Ityavyar 1988). In such circumstances, preventive care is virtually unknown.

Consequently, it can be argued that preventive care is a behavior pattern most characteristic of the upper and middle classes in advanced societies. When explanations are sought for the significant disparity in health and life expectancy between the affluent and the poor in the world today, the conditions of living associated with poverty and the lack of preventive care among the lower classes are major factors.

The Health Belief Model

One of the most influential social-psychological approaches designed to account for the ways in which healthy people seek to avoid illness is the Health Belief Model of Irwin Rosenstock (1966) and his colleagues (Becker 1974). The Health Belief Model is derived to a great extent from the theories of psychologist Kurt Lewin, who suggested that people exist in a life space composed of regions with both positive and negative valences (values). An illness would be a negative valence and would have the effect of pushing a person away from that region, unless doing so would cause the person to enter a region of even greater negative valence (for example, risking disease might be less negative than failing at an important task). While people are pushed away from regions with negative valences, they are attracted toward regions of positive valences. Thus, a person's behavior might be viewed as the result of seeking regions which offer the most attractive values.

Within this framework, human behavior is seen as being dependent upon two primary variables: (1) the value placed by a person upon a particular outcome and (2) the person's belief that a given action will result in that outcome. Accordingly, the Health Belief Model, shown in Figure 5-3, suggests that preventive action taken by an individual to avoid disease "X" is due to that particular individual's perception that he or she is personally susceptible and that the occurrence of the disease would have at least some severe personal implications.

FIGURE 5–3   The Health Belief Model

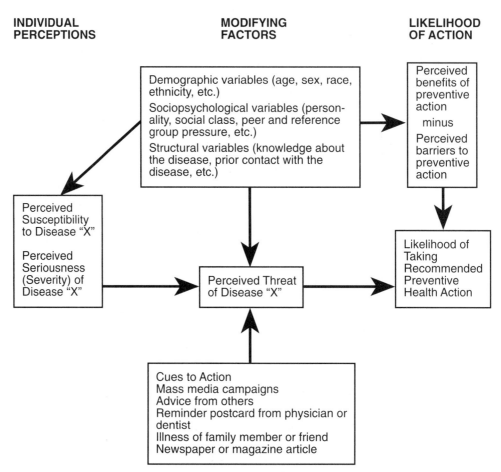

Source: Marshall H. Becker, ed., *The Health Belief Model and Personal Health Behavior* (San Francisco: Society for Public Health Education, Inc., 1974), p. 334. Reprinted with permission of Marshall H. Becker.

Although not directly indicated in Figure 5-3, the assumption in this model is that by taking a particular action, susceptibility would be reduced, or if the disease occurred, severity would be reduced. The perception of the threat posed by disease "X," however, is affected by modifying factors. As shown in Figure 5-3, these factors are demographic, sociopsychological, and structural variables that can influence both perception and the corresponding cues necessary to instigate action. Action cues are required, says Rosenstock, because while an individual may perceive that a given action will be effective in reducing the threat of disease, that action may not be taken if it is further defined as too expensive, too unpleasant or painful, too inconvenient, or perhaps too traumatic.

So despite recognition that action is necessary and the presence of energy to take that action, a person may still not be sufficiently motivated to do something. The likelihood of action also involves a weighing of the perceived benefits to action contrasted to the perceived barriers. Therefore, Rosenstock believed that a stimulus in the form of an action cue was required to "trigger" the appropriate behavior. Such a stimulus could be either internal (perception of bodily states) or external (interpersonal interaction, mass media communication, or personal knowledge of someone affected by the health problem).

The Health Belief Model has been employed successfully in several studies of (preventive) health behavior, such as the taking of penicillin prophylaxis for heart disease (Heinzelman 1962), vaccination against Asian influenza (Leventhal, Hochman, and Rosenstock 1960), the seeking of dental care (Gochman 1971; Kegeles 1963), dietary compliance among obese children (Becker et al. 1977), quitting cigarette smoking in Australia (Knight and Hay 1989), and engaging in self-care in the United States and Japan (Haug et al. 1989). Help-seeking behavior was observed in each of these studies to be based upon the value of the perceived outcome (avoidance of personal vulnerability) and the expectation that preventive action would result in that outcome. For example, the Gochman (1971) study found that if children are motivated to have good health in general, their perception of vulnerability to tooth disease and the benefits of visiting the dentist will result in their intentions to seek future dental care. Conversely, those children with low health motivation are not as likely to have the future intention of seeing a dentist. In the Becker et al. (1977) study, 182 pairs of mothers and their obese children were divided into three groups while the children participated in a weight reduction program. The groups consisted of (1) a high fear group (shown alarming material about the potentially unfavorable consequences of being fat in later life), (2) a low fear group (shown similar but less threatening information), and (3) a control group (shown no additional information). Children in the control group did not lose weight. Children in the low fear group lost some weight initially but also tended to put some of it back on. The high fear group lost the most weight and did not put any of it back on. The intervention of a fear-arousal cue in the high fear group had a marked effect on the mothers' notions of the perceived susceptibility, seriousness, and benefits of compliance for their children.

Unfortunately, the usefulness of the Health Belief Model is limited in that it has been applied mostly to preventive situations in which the behavior studied is voluntary. Obviously, however, many people who seek health services are motivated to take action only by the appearance of clear and definite symptoms.

Nevertheless, the Health Belief Model has demonstrated considerable utility in the study of health behavior (Becker 1979; Janz and Becker 1984; Kirscht 1974; Mullen, Hersey, and Iverson 1987). The merit of the model is that even when an individual recognizes personal susceptibility, he or she may not take action *unless* the individual also perceives that being ill will result in serious difficulty. Thus, the individual's subjective assessment of the health situation becomes the critical variable in the utilization of health services. In fact, a person's subjective assessment may be more important than an objective medical diagnosis. Several studies show no (sometimes even a negative) correlation between medical estimates of health and patient compliance (Becker and Maiman 1975). David Mechanic (1972) has noted that the difficulty in preventive medicine is that common sense approaches do not necessarily match clinical approaches, and common sense often determines whether health services are sought. Furthermore, once a patient subjectively feels well, physicians may be faced with the additional problem of encouraging the patient to continue to follow medical advice.

SUMMARY

Health behavior is the activity undertaken by a person who believes himself or herself to be healthy for the purpose of preventing health problems (Kasl and Cobb 1966). Health lifestyles, in turn, are ways of living that promote good health and longer life expectancy. Health lifestyles include contact with physicians and other health personnel, but the majority of activities take place outside of formal health care delivery systems. These activities include a proper diet, weight control, exercise, rest and relaxation, and the avoidance of stress and alcohol and drug abuse.

Max Weber, one of the most important theorists in the history of sociological thought, analyzed the general role of lifestyles in society and found that, while particular socioeconomic status groups are characterized by their own lifestyle, some lifestyles spread across social boundaries. He also observed that lifestyles are based on what people consume, rather than what they produce. There is evidence from the United States and Germany, and to a lesser extent from Great Britain and France, that health lifestyles are spreading throughout the class structure of these societies—although the quality of participation in the lower classes is undoubtedly less than that of the classes above them. And, while health lifestyles help produce good health, the aim of such lifestyles is ultimately one of consumption as health is used to avoid disease, live longer, feel better, work, or have a pleasing physical appearance.

Another important facet of health behavior is preventive care that involves contact by healthy people with health care providers. Preventive care consists of routine physical examinations, dental care, cancer and heart disease screening, immunizations, and the like intended to prevent or reduce the chance of illness or minimize its effects. Throughout the world, it appears that lower-class persons are significantly less likely to receive preventive care. The chapter concludes with a discussion of the Health Belief Model, which is one of the most influential approaches to the study of health behavior.

Illness Behavior

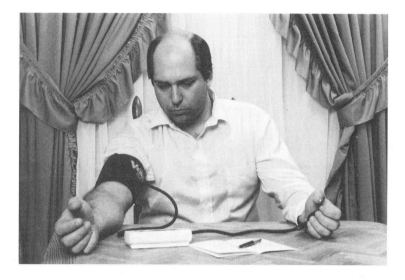

I llness behavior, in contrast to health behavior, is the activity undertaken by a person who feels ill for the purpose of defining that illness and seeking relief from it (Kasl and Cobb 1966). Some people recognize particular physical symptoms such as pain, a high fever, or nausea, and seek out a physician for treatment; others with similar symptoms may attempt self-medication or dismiss the symptoms as not needing attention. These differences in deciding whether to seek medical care have been and are continuing to be the subject of extensive investigation in medical sociology. Although the exact processes involved in making the decision to obtain medical care are not fully identified or understood at present, enough data have been collected in recent years to support a relationship between individual interpretation of deviation in physical functioning and social and psychological factors. As Susan Gore (1989) explains, we assume that the bodily changes—symptoms of illness that are disruptive, painful, and visible—are the basic determinants of medical help-seeking, and this is especially the case if the illness is severe. But sometimes physical changes are not obvious, particularly the early stages of chronic diseases. Gore (1989:311) explains, for example, that "the timing of the detection of diseases such as diabetes, heart disease, and cancer is determined by factors outside the disease process itself—social and psychological factors that shape the individual's response to the often subtle bodily changes that are experienced in daily living." Subjective interpretations of feeling states thus become highly medically significant.

For those individuals and groups concerned with the planning, organization, and implementation of health care delivery systems, the question of what social influences encourage or discourage a person from seeking medical treatment is of great significance. An understanding of the help-seeking process in medicine can have a tremendous impact upon the structuring of health services for the maximum utilization by people living in a community, both in terms of providing better medical care and making that care more accessible to the people who need it.

Medical sociologists and other behavioral scientists also want to find out how help-seeking behavior for medical care relates to the wider range of behaviors in which people attempt to obtain services generally. The focus of this chapter, however, will be upon reviewing the social pressures influencing the decisions of the ill to use professional medical services. First, self-care will be examined. Next, selected sociodemographic variables are discussed. These, however, explain only that variations in health services utilization exist, rather than *why* they exist. Thus, our third topic will be selected social-psychological models of medical help-seeking. Only when certain conditions are satisfied in a person's mind can we expect him or her to go to the doctor.

SELF-CARE

Self-care is the most common response to symptoms of illness by people throughout the world (Haug et al. 1991; Segall and Goldstein 1989). Self-care includes taking preventive measures (like consuming vitamin supplements), self-treatment of symptoms (such as taking home remedies or over-the-counter drugs), and managing chronic conditions (for instance, use of insulin by a diabetic). Self-care may involve consultation with health care providers and use of their services. As a way of acting in relation to one's health, self-care consists of both health and illness behavior. It essentially consists of a layperson's preventing, detecting, and treating his or her own health problems. What makes self-care distinctive is that it is a form of care which is self-initiated and self-managed (Segall and Goldstein 1989).

In modern societies, a number of factors have promoted renewed interest in self-care on the part of laypersons. According to Alexander Segall and Jay Goldstein (1989:154), these factors include (1) the shift in disease patterns from acute to chronic illnesses and the accompanying need to displace medical intervention from an emphasis on cure to care; (2) growing public dissatisfaction with medical care that is depersonalized; (3) recognition of the limits of modern medicine; (4) the increasing visibility of alternative healing practices; (5) heightened consciousness of the effects of lifestyle on health; and (6) a desire to exercise personal responsibility in health-related matters. Thus, it would appear that self-care is becoming increasingly important and commonplace.

Several sociological studies conducted in different countries have explored self-care practices. In Canada, Segall and Goldstein (1989) found that women, younger persons, and the well educated were more likely to treat their own symptoms than men, the elderly, and those with less education. In Denmark,

Kathryn Dean (1989) likewise found women more likely than men to take care of their health; when illness struck, social networks of family and friends become influential sources of information about self-care. In the United States and Japan, Marie Haug and her associates (Haug et al. 1991) found that self-care was common among both Americans and Japanese. However, the Japanese were especially likely to use self-care when they were sick, even for serious symptoms. Haug and her colleagues surmised that self-care gave the Japanese greater autonomy in matters of health. Japanese doctors tend to be authoritative and do not necessarily provide their patients with full information—even to the extent of not informing them they have cancer (Hattori et al. 1991). Japanese doctors believe disclosure of terminal cancer will cause unnecessary grief, so they typically inform the family but not the patient. Self-care therefore was a method by which the Japanese controlled their own health. Once they visit a doctor, the doctor assumes control and the patient is expected to follow orders.

Yet self-care is not an action that is completely independent of the medical profession. People engage in self-care in a manner consistent with medical norms, values, and insights. Often medical advice guides the actions taken. When laypersons lack knowledge, competence, or experience to proceed, or are simply more comfortable in allowing professionals to handle matters, they turn to doctors. The remainder of this chapter will discuss the social processes involved in seeking help from a physician.

SOCIODEMOGRAPHIC VARIABLES

A significant portion of past research in medical sociology has concerned itself with the effect of sociodemographic variables on the utilization of health care services. The reader should keep in mind that help-seeking behavior often involves interaction between several variables acting in combination to influence specific outcomes in specific social situations. Nonetheless, attempts to isolate some sociodemographic variables have resulted in studies of such factors as age, sex, ethnicity, and socioeconomic status, explaining how they relate to the behavior of people seeking medical care.

Age and Sex

The findings for age and sex have been consistent: Use of health services is greater for females than for males and is greatest for the elderly. As indicated in Chapter 3 on the social demography of health, it is clear from existing data that females report a higher morbidity and, even after correcting for maternity, have a higher rate of hospital admissions (Andersen and Anderson 1979; Cleary, Mechanic, and Greenley 1982; Gove and Hughes 1979; Marcus and Seeman 1981; Marcus and Siegel 1982; Nathanson 1977a; National Center for Health Statistics 1993; Verbrugge 1985, 1986, 1989; Waldron 1981, 1983; Wan and Soifer 1974; Weiss and Lonnquist 1994). If extent of knowledge about the symptoms of an illness is considered, it also appears that women generally know more about health matters than men and take better care of themselves (Dean 1989; Nathanson 1977b). In addition, the proportion of females in a household appears to be strongly related to the number of physician visits for that household. It has been shown, for instance, that the larger the proportion of females in a particular household, the greater the demand or requirement for physicians (Wan and Soifer 1974).

Perhaps it is obvious that people more than sixty-five years of age are in poorer health and are hospitalized more often than other age groups. Past studies on health care utilization, including research in Rhode Island (Kronenfeld 1978; Monteiro 1973), Los Angeles County (Galvin and Fan 1975), in five New York and Pennsylvania counties (Wan and Soifer 1974), Cleveland (Coulton and Frost 1982), St. Louis (Wolinsky et al. 1983), and a national survey (Wolinsky, Mosely, and Coe 1986), substantiates the supposition that elderly people are more likely to visit physicians than younger people. In Los Angeles County, Michael Galvin and Margaret Fan (1975) found public insurance and disability were directly related to the frequency of physician visits. Thus, since older people were more likely both to be physically disabled and to have public insurance (Medicare) coverage, they tended to visit a doctor fairly often. Studies of the utilization of medical services by the aged indicate that such use is determined more by actual need than any other single factor (Cockerham 1991; Coulton and Frost 1982; Wan 1982; Wolinsky et al. 1983). It is therefore not surprising that persons age sixty-five or older in the United States visited physicians an average of 10.3 times in 1991, much more than any other age group (National Center for Health Statistics 1993).

As for gender, males averaged 4.9 physician visits, compared to 6.3 visits for females in 1991. Females exhibit a lifelong pattern of visiting doctors more often than do males. There are three peaks in the visitation pattern for females. Initially, there are high rates during childhood, followed by a decline until a second rise during the childbearing years. After thirty-five, there is once again a decline, but physician visits by females steadily increase after age forty-five. For males, there are high rates of visits during childhood, followed by comparatively low rates of physician visits until a gradual increase begins at age forty-five.

Pregnancy and associated conditions do result in especially high rates of visits to physicians for women between the ages of fifteen and forty-four, but the woman's reproductive role accounts for less than 20 percent of all doctor visits. The higher visit rates by women are primarily the result of their greater number of ailments (Verbrugge 1985, 1986, 1989). More frequent utilization of physicians may have a substantial benefit for women in that they receive, on the average, earlier diagnosis and treatment for illness than men.

Ethnicity

Several early studies in medical sociology attempted to relate a person's utilization of health care services to his or her cultural background. One of the most systematic studies has been Edward A. Suchman's (1965a) investigation of the extent of the belief in and acceptance of modern medicine among several ethnic groups in New York City. Suchman sought to relate individual medical orientations and behaviors to specific types of social relationships and their corresponding group structures. He believed the interplay of group relationships with an individual's personal orientation toward medicine affected his or her health-seeking behavior.

Suchman categorized people as belonging to either cosmopolitan or parochial groups. Persons in a parochial group were found to have close and exclusive relationships with family, friends, and members of their ethnic group and to display limited knowledge of disease, skepticism of medical care, and high dependency in illness. They were more likely than the cosmopolitan group to delay in seeking medical care and more likely to rely upon a "lay-referral system" in coping with their symptoms of illness. A lay-referral system consists of nonprofessionals—family members, friends, or neighbors—who assist individuals in interpreting their symptoms and in recommending a course of action. The concept of the lay-referral system originated with Eliot Freidson (1960), who described the process of seeking medical help as involving a group of potential consultants, beginning in the nuclear family and extending outward to more select, authoritative laypersons, until the "professional" practitioner is reached. Freidson suggests that when cultural definitions of illness contradict professional definitions, the referral process will often not lead to the professional practitioner. The highest degree of resistance to using medical services in a lay-referral structure is found in lower-class neighborhoods characterized by a strong ethnic identification and extended family relationships. The decision to seek out a physician is based not just on professional standards of appropriate illness behavior but also on lay norms, and the two may be in conflict (Sawyer 1980).

By contrast, the cosmopolitan group in Suchman's study demonstrated low ethnic exclusivity, less limited friendship systems, and fewer authoritarian family relationships. Additionally, they were more likely than the parochial group to know something about disease, to trust health professionals, and to be less dependent on others while sick.

Social networks.   What is suggested by Suchman's (1965a) study is that, under certain conditions, close and ethnically exclusive social relationships tend to channel help-seeking behavior, at least initially, toward the group rather than professional health care delivery systems. Yet Reed Geertsen and associates (1975) replicated Suchman's study in Salt Lake City and found an opposite trend. They observed that the Mormon community, with its strong value on good health and education and its emphasis upon family authority and tradition, demonstrated that group closeness and exclusivity can increase, rather than decrease, the likelihood of an individual responding to professional health resources. They concluded that people who belong to close and exclusive groups, especially tradition- and authority-oriented families, are (1) more likely to respond to a health problem by seeking medical care if it is consistent with their cultural beliefs and practices or are (2) less likely to seek medical care if their cultural beliefs support skepticism and distrust of professional medicine.

Geertsen and colleagues focused on the family rather than the ethnic group as the critical social unit in determining help-seeking behavior; the family is the person's first significant social group and usually the primary source of societal values. Thus, knowledge of disease and family authority appear as the key intervening variables in a person's medical orientation, as knowledge assists in recognition of symptoms, while family authority impels the sick person into the professional health care system. Alternatively, low knowledge about disease and/or weak family authority could act as inhibiting factors in obtaining professional treatment.

In Boston, Jeffrey Salloway (1973) observed similar processes in the help-seeking behavior of the gypsy community. Gypsies, according to Salloway, are among the poor, uneducated, and ethnically distinct of American society whom most studies have found to exhibit the lowest rates of health care utilization. Salloway's study demonstrated, to the contrary, that gypsies were rather sophisticated when it came to obtaining treatment in Boston's complex, urban medical system. Although nonliterate or semiliterate, gypsies operated an extensive communication network in their community through which they informed each other on a regular basis who was sick, where they were being treated, who was treating them, and how pleased or displeased the patient, family, and other interested parties were with the treatment. Visits of gypsies to health practitioners or a visit by a practitioner to the gypsies were invariably a public affair. Information about the illness and its treatment was shared and became part of the group's general fund of knowledge.

Salloway points out the existence of an extensive accumulation of data among family and friends concerning past diagnoses, the treating agency, the prescription, and the prognosis for specific disorders. Gypsies were also very much aware of the differences in the quality of care available at local hospitals and out-patient clinics, including the specialties they offered, and the identity of care providers receptive to their needs. They were thus able to utilize available health care services more extensively than many disadvantaged minority groups because of an unusual intragroup network of communication.

What is suggested here is not that ethnicity per se is important, but that ethnicity represents a social experience that influences how a particular person perceives his or her health situation. Individuals are born into a family of significant others—significant because they provide the child with a specific social identity. This identity includes not only an appraisal of physical and intellectual characteristics but knowledge concerning the social history of a particular family and group with all that means in terms of social status, perspective, and cultural background. As the child becomes older and takes as his or her own the values and opinions of the immediate family or group, or those of the wider society as presented through the mediating perspective of the family, the child is considered to be properly socialized in that he or she behaves in accordance with group-approved views.

Admittedly, children can either accept or reject the social perspective put forth by their family as representative of their own social reality; yet the choices offered to them in the process of their socialization are set by adults who determine what information is provided and in what form it is presented. Thus, although children may not be entirely passive in the socialization experience, what is important, as Peter Berger and Thomas Luckmann (1967) explain, is that they have no choice in the selection of their significant others so that identification with them is quasi-automatic. This further means that children's internalization of their family's interpretation of social reality is quasi-inevitable. While this initial social world presented to children by their significant others may be weakened by later social relationships, it can nevertheless be a lasting influence on them. Parental influence, for example, has been found to be the most important and lasting influence on the preventive health beliefs of their children (Lau, Quadrel, and Hartman 1990).

Therefore, it is not surprising that a person's family or social group often guides the perceptual process or signals the perspective from which the total society is viewed. For this reason some studies in medical sociology have emphasized the social network as a major factor in help-seeking behavior (Geertsen et al. 1975; Gore 1989; McKinlay 1972, 1973; Pescosolido 1992; Radelet 1981; Salloway 1973). A social network refers to the social relationships a person has during day-to-day interaction which serve as the normal avenue for the exchange of opinion, information, and affection. Typically, the social network is composed of family, relatives, and friends that comprise the individual's immediate social world, although the concept of a social network can be expanded to include increasingly larger units of society.

The role of the social network and its specific values, opinions, attitudes, and cultural background act to suggest, advise, or coerce an individual into taking or not taking particular courses of action. While developing a theory of help-seeking behavior, Bernice Pescosolido (1992) stressed the importance of social networks in obtaining medical care. Table 6-1 depicts a list developed by Pescosolido of the various options and choices that people in virtually all societies can potentially turn to for consultation when ill. The most obvious choice are the modern medical practitioners, especially M.D.'s. But the realities of the marketplace, such as insufficient income or health insurance, may push the individual elsewhere. Therefore, alternative medical practitioners, like faith healers or chiropractors, may be a possibility. Nonmedical professionals like social workers, clergy, and teachers represent another option, along with lay advisors like family members, or self-care, or perhaps no choices are available.

Pescosolido points out that people often seek advice and help from a variety of sources until the situation is resolved. She finds that it is through contact with other people that individuals deal with their illnesses and obtain support for medical and emotional problems. "Individuals in social networks," adds Pescosolido (1992:1113), "are more than an influence on help seeking, they *are* caregivers and advisors, part of a 'therapy managing group.' " Consequently, the strategies that people employ for seeking health care are socially organized around the opportunities they have for interacting with people in a position to help.

As for ethnicity, its influence on physician utilization appears largely limited to its role in providing a cultural context for decision making within social networks. A variable that particularly confounds the effects of ethnicity on help-seeking is socioeconomic status. The higher an individual's socioeconomic position, the less ethnic the person often becomes (Hollingshead and Redlich 1958). In other words, middle-class Americans of European, African, Hispanic, Asian, and

TABLE 6–1   The Range of Choices for Medical Care and Advice

Option	Advisor	Examples
Modern medical practitioners	M.D.'s, osteopaths, allied health workers	Physicians, podiatrists, optometrists, nurses, opticians, psychologists, druggists, technicians, orderlies
Alternative medical practitioners	"Traditional" healers	Faith healers, folk healers spiritualists, herbalists, acupuncturists
	"Modern" healers	Chiropractors, naturopaths, nutritional consultants
Nonmedical professionals	Social workers Clergy Supervisors	Bosses, teachers
Lay advisors	Family Neighbors Friends Co-workers, classmates	Spouse, parents
Other	Self-care	Nonprescription medicines, self-examination procedures, home remedies, health foods
None		

Source: Adapted from Bernice A. Pescosolido. 1992. "Beyond Rational Choice: The Social Dynamics of How People Seek Help," *American Journal of Sociology*, 97:1113.

native origin descent tend to reflect the same middle-class norms and values as part of their mutual participation in middle-class society. Included in this pattern are similar perspectives toward the utilization of health services (Welch, Comer, and Steinman 1973). This situation suggests that the direct effects of ethnicity on decision making concerning health care are largely confined to the lower class as Suchman's (1965a) work indicated. Studies of racial/ethnic minorities in the United States, such as blacks and Hispanics, seem to support this conclusion. The next three sections will discuss some of this research.

Health insurance coverage.   To place this discussion of medical care for blacks and Hispanics into perspective, we should first note the extent of health insurance coverage in the United States by race. Persons age sixty-five and over are covered by Medicare. The major type of health insurance for the remainder of the American population (under the age of sixty-five) prior to current efforts at health reform was private insurance paid for by the individual, the individual's employer, or some combination thereof. Low-income families may qualify for Medicaid, the public health insurance program for the poor. Table 6-2 lists the proportion of health insurance coverage according to race for 1989. Some 53.3 percent of all Americans have private health insurance; 10.8 percent have Medicare; 8.3 percent have Medicaid; 4.2 percent have some other type of public health insurance, such

TABLE 6–2 Health Insurance Coverage, Hispanic Origin, and Race, United States, 1989

Insurance Type	Total U.S.	White Non-Hispanic	Black Non-Hispanic	Mexican-American	Puerto Rican	Cuban-American
Private	53.3%	68.2%	45.4%	43.7%	43.6%	55.6%
Medicare	10.8	12.5	7.0	2.9	3.9	10.0
Medicaid	8.3	5.0	23.3	13.7	32.5	11.9
Other public	4.2	4.1	4.6	2.8	4.5	2.2
Uninsured	13.4	10.2	19.7	36.9	15.5	20.3

Source: U.S. Bureau of the Census, 1990, 1992.

as military or Veterans Administration health benefits; and 13.4 percent have no health insurance. Table 6-2 also shows that 68.2 percent of all non-Hispanic whites have private health insurance compared to 45.4 percent of non-Hispanic blacks. Among Hispanics, Cuban-Americans have the highest percentage of private health insurance (55.6 percent), followed by Mexican-Americans (43.7 percent) and Puerto Ricans (43.6 percent).

For Medicaid, the public health insurance provided the poor, some 32.5 percent of all Puerto Ricans are covered along with 23.3 percent of all non-Hispanic blacks. Only some 5 percent of all non-Hispanic whites receive Medicaid. For those persons without any type of health insurance coverage, Table 6-2 shows that, among non-Hispanics, some 10.2 percent of whites and 19.7 percent of blacks fall into this category. However, the most striking disclosure is that the proportion of Mexican-Americans without health insurance is 36.9 percent, the largest percentage by far of any ethnic group in American society.

The figure of 13.4 percent without health insurance for the nation as a whole in 1989 compares to the figure of 11.6 percent for 1980; thus, it can be surmised that the proportion of persons in the total U.S. population lacking insurance coverage for health care increased during the 1980s. More recent data, which do not include a breakdown by race, show that 38.5 million Americans or 15 percent of the total population did not have health insurance in 1992. The uninsured are typically persons working in low-income jobs whose employers do not provide health insurance benefits for their employees. This would include many Mexican-Americans, as well as people from all other ethnic groups. These are near-poor who have a job and make enough money to be disqualified from welfare programs like Medicaid but who nevertheless are unable to purchase private health insurance because it remains too expensive for their low level of wages.

Black Americans. Ralph Hines (1972) suggested several years ago that preventive medicine is largely a white middle-class concept that provides a patient with an elaborate structure of routine prenatal and postnatal care, pediatric services, dental care, immunizations, and screening for the presence of disease. Hines blames the failure to use preventive health facilities on a lack of value orientation regarding such services. It can probably be attributed to a lack of financial resources as well. For those blacks living at a subsistence level, the only options seem to be welfare medicine, which by its very nature is often bureaucratic and impersonal, or no professional care at all.

However, while some blacks, namely those without any type of health insurance coverage, remain underserved with respect to professional medical care, the pattern of physician utilization by blacks in general has changed dramatically in the last few years. Prior to the mid-1970s, blacks tended to visit doctors significantly less often than whites and showed more negative attitudes toward seeking help from physicians (Dutton 1978). Since then it has been found that blacks have relatively positive attitudes toward doctors and are visiting physicians more often (Sharp, Ross, and Cockerham 1983; Stahl and Gardner 1976). Whites still generally visit physicians more than blacks, but the difference is not great. In 1991, for example, whites showed an average of 5.8 physician visits compared to 5.2 visits for blacks.

Even though blacks are utilizing physician services more than ever before (practically on a par with whites), they are more likely to receive that care in surroundings such as hospital outpatient clinics or emergency rooms that are relatively more public than private. As shown in Table 6-3, a higher percentage of whites (60.1 percent) than blacks (52.0 percent) received their care in 1991 in doctors' offices or consulted with doctors over the telephone (12.8 percent of whites versus 7.3 percent of blacks). But a higher percentage of blacks (21.2 percent) than whites (13.0 percent) visited physicians in hospital clinics or emergency rooms.

TABLE 6–3 Percent of Physician Visits, by Place of Visit and Selected Characteristics: United States, 1991

	PLACE OF VISIT				
Characteristic	Office (Including Prepaid Group)	Home	Hospital Clinic or Emergency Room	Telephone Consultation[1]	Other and Unknown	Total
All persons	58.9	2.7	14.2	12.2	12.0	100.0
Sex						
Male	57.8	2.4	16.0	11.1	12.7	100.0
Female	59.5	2.9	12.9	12.9	11.8	100.0
Race						
White	60.1	2.6	13.0	12.8	11.5	100.0
Black	52.0	3.6	21.2	7.3	15.9	100.0
Family Income						
Less than $14,000	48.7	3.8	20.2	10.1	17.2	100.0
$14,000–24,999	55.9	1.7	16.6	12.4	13.4	100.0
$25,000–34,999	60.7	1.7	13.6	12.8	11.2	100.0
$35,000–49,999	61.4	1.7	12.4	13.5	11.0	100.0
$50,000 or more	64.2	1.5	10.6	14.4	9.3	100.0

[1]Does not include calls for appointments and other nonmedical purposes.
Source: National Center for Health Statistics, 1993.

Major sites of care in relation to income, also shown in Table 6-3, fall into a pattern similar to that shown by race. A greater percentage of those persons reporting the highest incomes use the private doctor's office or group practice, or telephone. Whites had likewise preferred these same sources of health care. People with low incomes made more use of hospital outpatient clinics and hospital emergency rooms. Since many racial-ethnic minority groups tend to have low incomes, it is not a coincidence that utilization patterns by race and income are similar.

Patterns of help-seeking behavior for medical care by blacks in American society are not influenced as much by race or ethnicity as they are by conditions of poverty and the limitations of low incomes. For most purposes, visits to private doctors' offices and clinics are not covered by health insurance in the United States and the cost must usually be borne by the patient. Efforts by blacks to use public medical facilities and, in some cases, folk healers, can be seen as attempts to cope with health problems within the context of one's resources and social environment. Even though black Americans have made significant progress in obtaining equal opportunity in employment and education, largely as a result of the civil rights movement of the 1960s, the disparity between blacks and whites in regard to social and economic benefits still exists for many black people. This continued socioeconomic disadvantage translates into continued health disadvantages.

Hispanics. Some Hispanics are prone to use the services of nonprofessionals in health care matters. Instead they tend to favor the use of "folk" medicine, which involves treatment by friends, relatives, or neighbors who employ patent medicine and home cures for ailments. According to research reviewed by Ronald Andersen and his associates (1981), many Mexican-Americans are likely to initially try patent medicines, herbs, and teas when ill. If these fail to bring relief, they turn to members of the family for advice and assistance. Next they may visit a *curandero* or folk healer before dealing with a physician about their health problems; they may visit both a *curandero* and a physician.

William Madsen (1973) found in south Texas that even when Mexican-American patients consulted a physician, they would terminate the relationship unless the response to treatment was rapid. Yet when modern medicine produced a cure, Madsen observed that credit for that cure was often attributed to folk treatments which preceded, accompanied, or followed scientific treatment. Hospitalization, except in time of crisis, was also avoided like a plague. "To be separated from the family," Madsen (1973:95) states, "and isolated in an Anglo world is well-nigh intolerable for the conservative Mexican-American. Next to prison, the hospital is most dreaded as a place of isolation in an impersonal and enigmatic world."

However, research in Nebraska found that many Mexican-Americans are not exceptionally different from non-Hispanic whites in their attitudes toward health care (Welch, Comer, and Steinman 1973). This study found that Mexican-Americans have family doctors, go regularly to the dentist, and freely utilize other official health services. Madsen, too, mentions a greater frequency of physician visits among Mexican-Americans, particularly for the treatment of children. In south Texas, reliance upon modern medicine was most likely among more affluent Mexican-Americans and those with the highest level of education. The assimilation of mainstream American norms and values by Mexican-Americans apparently includes a tendency toward increased physician contact. Yet folk medicine is still a viable form of help-seeking behavior for those with lower-incomes. Large-scale social surveys of the help-seeking behavior of Mexican-Americans in regard to professional medical services still point toward the lowest rates of any racial/ethnic minority group in the United States. At least this is the trend suggested by studies conducted in the counties of Los Angeles (Berkanovic and Reeder 1973; Galvin and Fan 1975) and Alameda (Roberts and Lee 1980) in California, the southwestern United States (Andersen et al. 1981), and nationwide (National Center for Health Statistics 1984). Mexican-Americans appear to have somewhat lower rates than non-Hispanic whites and blacks for visits to physicians and substantially lower rates for physical examinations and eye examinations. Mexican-Americans have higher rates for visits to dentists than blacks, but these rates are markedly lower than those for non-Hispanic whites. Lower utilization rates for Mexican-Americans seem to be largely a function of socioeconomic status (lower income and education) rather than ethnicity (Roberts and Lee 1980).

Mexican-Americans are among those most likely to report that they could not afford health insurance as the main reason they did not have coverage (National Center for Health Statistics 1983). Several studies observe that low rates of private health insurance among Mexican-Americans (who have the lowest level of health insurance of any ethnic group) result from low income, education, and employment in firms that generally do not provide such coverage (Aday, Andersen, and Fleming 1980; Andersen et al. 1981; National Center for Health Statistics 1983). Uninsured Hispanics are less likely to have a regular source of health care, to have visited a physician in the past year, had a routine physical examination, and rate their health as excellent or very good in comparison to Hispanics with private health insurance (Treviño et al. 1991). Another factor in the low rates of physician utilization by Mexican-Americans in particular is the paucity of Hispanic health professionals; only 5.4 percent of all American physicians are of Hispanic origin and the percentage of Hispanic dentists, nurses, pharmacists, and therapists is even lower—about 3 percent of the national total in 1989 (Ginzberg 1991).

Socioeconomic Status

Another major approach to the study of help-seeking behavior has been its correlation with socioeconomic status. Several years ago, it was generally believed that lower-class persons tended to underutilize health services because of the financial cost and/or culture of poverty. The culture of poverty, as summarized by Thomas Rundall and John Wheeler (1979), is a phenomenon in which poverty, over time, influences the development of certain social and psychological traits among those trapped within it. These traits include dependence, fatalism, inability to delay gratification, and a lower value placed on health (being sick is not especially unusual). This, in turn, tends to reinforce the poor person's disadvantaged social position. The seminal study showing how the poor had developed a different perspective concerning their interpretations of symptoms was Earl Koos's *The Health of Regionville* (1954). Koos conducted his study in a small community in New York where he found it possible to rank the local residents into three distinct socioeconomic classes. Class I consisted of the most successful people in town in terms of financial assets. Class II represented middle-class wage earners who were the majority of citizens, while Class III represented the least skilled workers and poorest members of the community.

Members of each socioeconomic class were asked to indicate whether certain easily recognized symptoms were considered to be significant enough to be brought to the attention of a doctor. Class I respondents demonstrated a much higher level of recognition of the importance of symptoms than either Class II or Class III. Only two of the symptoms, loss of appetite and backache, were reported by less than three-fourths of Class I as needing medical attention. Otherwise, almost all Class I respondents were prepared to go to a physician if a symptom appeared. For only one symptom, persistent coughing, did Class I respondents not have the highest percentage and this difference was negligible.

Class III respondents, on the other hand, showed a marked indifference to most symptoms. Seventy-five percent of the lower-class respondents considered ten of the seventeen symptoms not serious enough to warrant medical attention. Only three symptoms (excessive vaginal bleeding and blood in stool and urine) achieved a response of 50 percent or more, and all of these were associated with unexplained bleeding.

Thus, in Regionville at the time of Koos's study in the early 1950s, symptoms did not necessarily lead to seeking medical treatment among the lower class. In addition, Class III persons were inhibited from seeking treatment because of cost, fear, and relative need as related to age and the role of the sick person. The very young, the elderly, and breadwinners were most likely to receive medical attention among the poor. Another important factor in help-seeking behavior for Class III persons was group expectations about symptoms, further suggesting the importance of the social network. Backache, for example, was a symptom the poor commonly defined as not being a serious ailment. For the poor, having a backache was nothing unusual.

At the time, Koos's study helped establish the premise that lower-class persons are less likely than others to recognize various symptoms as requiring medical treatment and that these beliefs contribute to differences in the actual use of services. This premise was supported by the conclusions of surveys by the National Center for Health Statistics in 1960 and 1965, which found that higher-income persons were utilizing the physician to a much greater extent than lower-income persons.

In 1968, however, the National Center found a changing pattern of physician utilization. It was now the middle-income group, consisting of those persons earning between $3,000 to $9,999 a year, who had become the underutilizers. Highest rates of physician visits were either persons with the lowest (under $3,000) level of income or the highest level (over $10,000). The higher rate for the low-income group was largely due to Medicaid and Medicare health insurance programs. Medicaid, administered at the state level, provides coverage intended to help pay the cost of health care for the poor. Medicare, a federal program, provides coverage for the elderly, who are overrepresented in the low-income group.

Since 1968 several studies (Andersen and Anderson 1979; Bellin and Geiger 1972; Benham and Benham 1975; Bice, Eichhorn, and Fox 1972; Cockerham et al. 1986a; Dutton 1986; Galvin and Fan 1975; Kaplan 1989; Monteiro 1973; Sharp, Ross, and Cockerham 1983; Sparer and Okada 1974) have confirmed that it can no longer be assumed that low-income persons underutilize physician services. Between 1963 and 1970, as the effects of Medicaid and Medicare became evident, the use of physician services by low-income persons increased to the point that the significance of the relationship between income and utilization was greatly diminished. In fact, by 1970, it could be demonstrated that the poor had higher rates of physician use than any other income group. For example, according to data collected by Ronald Andersen and Odin Anderson (1979) for selected years between 1928 and 1974, the low-income group had the lowest rates of physician utilization from 1928 to 1931. The middle-income group ranked in the middle and the high-income group had the highest number of visits. This pattern remained until 1970, when the low-income group emerged with the highest rates, followed by the high-income group and the middle-income group. The present pattern indicates the lowest income group visits physicians most often, followed by middle-income groups. The highest income group visits doctors the least.

Even though the poor are visiting doctors in greater numbers, this does not mean that they use the same sources of medical treatment in proportions equal to those of higher income groups. Differences between income groups in regard to where they seek care are obvious and consistent. People with higher incomes, as shown in Table 6-2, were more likely than those with lower incomes to have received medical services in private doctors' offices and group practices or over the telephone. However, the reverse situation was true for other sources of care. Table 6-3 shows that people with lower incomes were more likely to contact hospital outpatient clinics or emergency rooms. Although people of all income groups are seen to use each source shown in Table 6-3, a pattern emerges of a dual health care system—a "private" system with a greater proportion of the higher-income groups and a "public" system with a preponderance of lower-income groups. In the public system, the patient is likely to receive less quality medical care, spend longer amounts of time in waiting rooms, not have a personal physician, cope with more bureaucratic agencies, and return after treatment to a living situation that is less conducive to good health.

Furthermore, when actual *need* for health services is taken into account, low-income persons appear to use fewer services relative to their needs (Aday and Andersen 1975; Dutton 1978, 1986; Kravits and Schneider 1975; Newacheck and Butler 1983; Sudman and Freeman 1989). Diana Dutton (1978) points out that statistics showing increased use of health services by the poor can be misleading.

She argues that the poor have higher rates of disability due to illness and that the poor also tend to be more likely to seek symptomatic care. The nonpoor, in turn, are more likely to seek preventive care, which is aimed at keeping healthy people well, instead of waiting to seek help when symptoms appear. Thus, the poor appear to have more sickness and, despite the significant increase in use of services, still do not obtain as much health care as they actually need. Using data collected in Washington, D.C., Dutton tested three different explanations concerning why the poor would show lower use rates in relation to actual need than the nonpoor: (1) financial coverage, (2) the culture of poverty, and (3) the systems barrier.

The financial coverage explanation consists of the claim that the poor cannot afford to purchase the services they need—the cost is high, income is low, and insurance programs are inadequate. Dutton found this explanation to be weak. Public health insurance, notably Medicaid, had stimulated use of services by the poor to a much greater extent than private health insurance had done for the nonpoor. Unlike many private insurance plans, Medicaid paid for most physician services and thereby promoted physician utilization. Conversely, private insurance, with the exception of prepaid plans, had less impact on seeking physician services.

The culture of poverty explanation is derived from the premise that attitudes and norms characteristic of poor people tend to retard use of services. For example, the poor may view society and professional medical practices as less than positive as a result of their life experiences. The poor also may be more willing to ignore illness or not define it as such because they must continue to function to meet the demands of survival. Dutton found the culture of poverty explanation to have some validity when combined with measures of income. As income decreased, belief in preventive checkups and professional health orientation also decreased, while degree of social alienation increased. "Of course," says Dutton (1978:359), "these differences may not reflect cultural variation so much as realistic adaptation to economic circumstances; preventive care may well be less important than paying the rent, and purchasing a thermometer may be viewed as an unaffordable luxury." Nevertheless, Dutton argues that attitudes related to the culture of poverty do play an important role in explaining differences in the use of health services between income groups, particularly the use of preventive care.

In Dutton's view, the strongest explanation for low use of services by the poor in relation to need was the systems barrier explanation. This explanation focused on organizational barriers inherent in the more "public" system of health care typically used by the poor, such as hospital outpatient clinics and emergency rooms. This type of barrier pertains not just to the difficulty in locating and traveling to a particular source of care, but also includes the general atmosphere of the treatment setting, which in itself may be impersonal and alienating. For example, as Anselm Strauss comments:

> The very massiveness of modern medical organization is itself a hindrance to health care for the poor. Large buildings and departments, specialization, division of labor, complexity, and bureaucracy lead to an impersonality and an overpowering and often grim atmosphere of

hugeness. The poor, with their meager experience in organizational life, their insecurity in the middle class world, and their dependence on personal contacts, are especially vulnerable to this impersonalization.

Hospitals and clinics are organized for "getting work done" from the staff point of view; only infrequently are they set up to minimize the patient's confusion. He fends for himself and sometimes may even get lost when sent "just down the corridor." Patients are often sent for diagnostic tests from one service to another with no explanations, with inadequate directions, with brusque tones. This may make them exceedingly anxious and affect their symptoms and diagnosis. After sitting for hours in waiting rooms, they become angry to find themselves passed over for latecomers—but nobody explains about emergencies or priorities. They complain they cannot find doctors they really like or trust.

... To the poor, professional procedures may seem senseless or even dangerous—especially when not explained—and professional manners impersonal or brutal, even when professionals are genuinely anxious to help.[1]

Dutton (1978, 1979, 1986) found from her research that low-income patients in public health care systems confronted a lack of preventive examination (physicians had little time for counseling patients or providing preventive care), high charges for services, long waiting times, and relatively poor patient-physician relationships. Dutton's (1978:361-362) position was that this situation posed a highly significant barrier that discouraged low-income patients "from seeking care, *above and beyond* the deterrent effects of inadequate financial coverage and negative attitudes toward professional health care." Low utilization was therefore seen as a normal response to an unpleasant experience.

The majority of people in the Dutton study were black. Subsequent research by Rundall and Wheeler (1979) on the effect of income on use of preventive care involved a sample of respondents living in Washtenaw County, Michigan, who were mostly white. Dutton's findings were confirmed. There was no support for the financial coverage explanation. There was some support for the culture of poverty explanation in that the poor perceived themselves as relatively less susceptible to illness (they could tolerate unhealthy conditions) and therefore were less likely to seek preventive services. However, there was strong support for the systems barrier explanation. People with relatively high incomes were more likely to have a regular source of care and those individuals with a regular source of care were more likely to use preventive services.

Having a regular source of care has been identified as an important variable in help-seeking behavior (see also Aday and Andersen 1975; Andersen and Aday 1978; Kronenfeld 1978). Andersen and Aday (1978), for instance, have suggested that a variable having great impact on physician use is the presence of a particular physician who is the person's regular source of care. This situation implies that the patient is relatively comfortable with the relationship and has some trust in the physician's skills at diagnosis and treatment. Low-income people receiving medical care in the public sector are less likely to have a personal

---

[1]Anselm L. Strauss, "Medical Ghettos," in *Where Medicine Fails*, A. Strauss, ed. (Chicago: Aldine, 1970), pp. 14, 15.

physician and must be treated by whichever physician happens to be on duty in a hospital or clinic. If they have to maneuver between several clinics and public assistance agencies to obtain either treatment or authorization for treatment, low-income people will be subject to even more fragmented and ill-coordinated patterns of health care.

What is necessary to improve this situation, according to Rundall and Wheeler (1979), is increased health education for low-income people and changes in the organization of health care that will provide regular sources of treatment that respect the dignity of the patient. Simply expanding public health insurance programs does not seem to be a sufficient measure for increasing health services utilization by the poor in relation to their need for services.

Future Patterns of Physician Utilization by Social Class

For most Americans, the financial barrier to medical care is no longer as formidable as it once was (Crandall and Duncan 1981; Tanner, Cockerham, and Spaeth 1983). Studies conducted in the 1950s and 1960s suggest that the culture of poverty produces beliefs and values inhibiting the use of physician services. According to this argument, disadvantaged groups hold beliefs that are not consistent with scientific medicine; the poor are skeptical about medical care and less sensitive to the meaning of symptoms (Koos 1954; Strauss 1970; Suchman 1965a; Zola 1966). The potential strength of these attitudes is evident in research reported by Mervyn Susser and William Watson (1971) on physician utilization in Great Britain during the first ten to fifteen years after the introduction of socialized medicine. Even though improved medical care was available at no cost, the poor continued to persist in using self-treatment and to delay seeking professional care. Susser and Watson suggested that despite the change in the availability of services, cultural change lagged behind. Thus, it appears that beliefs can have an impact on the use of physician services that is independent of financial constraints and the structural organization of services.

One would expect, however, that removing the financial barriers to health care might eventually alter the attitudes of people in the lower social classes accordingly. With increasing opportunities for the less privileged to receive health care, such as socialized medicine in Great Britain and the availability of Medicare and Medicaid in the United States, it seems likely that the attitudes of the less privileged would become more positive. Since the utilization rates of the poor have increased significantly over the past twenty-five years, their attitudes about going to the doctor should have changed also.

The author and his colleagues (Sharp, Ross, and Cockerham 1983) investigated this situation and found that blacks and people with less education have positive attitudes toward visiting physicians and are more likely than whites and people with more education to think that various symptoms are serious enough to warrant the attention of a doctor. These data suggest that as blacks and those with less education have gained more equitable access to the health care system with the advent of Medicare and Medicaid, their beliefs did change in a direction that encourages physician utilization. At the same time, the well educated may be taking more responsibility for their own health and feeling less inclined to visit the doctor. Better educated persons may be very (perhaps overly) discriminating in deciding which symptoms warrant seeing a physician because they wish to maintain control over their own health.

What is suggested by this finding is that there is more of a consumer orientation toward health among socially advantaged persons. In a free market situation, health consumers typically have more freedom to choose their source and mode of health care than is the case in a system of socialized medicine. Laypersons, as Freidson's (1960) discussion of the lay-referral system made clear, do judge technical performance and the quality of service provided by physicians regardless of whether they are trained to do so. And they make decisions about doctors based upon these evaluations, usually in consultation with their friends and relatives.

The trend toward consumerism in medicine is similar to consumerism in other aspects of American life in which people make informed choices about the services available to them. This orientation is more likely a feature characteristic of middle- and upper-class persons than the socially and economically disadvantaged. Dutton (1978) has suggested that the United States has a two-track system of health care delivery—one private and the other public. What we may be seeing is that those persons at the bottom of society, who are the major participants in the public track, may have a much greater willingness to turn the responsibility for their health over to the health care delivery system itself. This development is consistent with research investigating Talcott Parsons' (1951) concept of the sick role where it was found that persons on the lower level of income are most likely to agree that people have a right not to be held responsible for their illnesses (Arluke, Kennedy, and Kessler 1979; Cole and LeJeune 1972; Wolinsky and Wolinsky 1981).

Arnold Arluke and his associates (1979:34) suggest that acceptance of the notion that illness is not the responsibility of the sick person may be related to broader social class differences in imputation of responsibility. That is, lower-class persons may tend to have a more passive orientation toward life in general and less willingness to take responsibility for problems. Certainly this is what is shown by research using locus-of-control measures in which it is reported that members of the lowest socioeconomic group have more fatalistic attitudes and are more accepting of external forces controlling their lives (Wheaton 1980).

Among those studies that have used a locus-of-control measure in relation to physical health, the work of Melvin Seeman and his colleagues appears to be the most relevant. Seeman and J. W. Evans (1962) found that tuberculosis patients with an internal locus of control (belief that one can master, control, or effectively alter the environment) knew more about their illness and took a more active role in coping with it than those with an external locus of control (belief that one is more or less at the mercy of the environment). Seeman and Teresa Seeman (1983) found that a low sense of internal control could be significantly associated with less self-initiated preventive care, less optimism about the effectiveness of early treatment, poorer self-rated health, more illness and bed confinement, and greater dependence on physicians.

In other research, the author and his colleagues (Cockerham et al. 1986a) found important differences between socioeconomic groups with respect to symptom perception, physician utilization, and sense of control over one's health situation. Persons with higher socioeconomic status were more consumer minded and expressed greater personal responsibility for their own health. The poor were less discriminating in deciding which symptoms warranted a doctor's attention. When ill, the poor reported they visited doctors more or less routinely, even for minor ailments, while the more affluent appeared more likely to engage in self-treatment or to recognize minor ailments as self-limiting and likely to disappear in a day or two without a physician's services. The poor also expressed a decreased sense of personal control over their health. Thus, the poor seemed to be relatively passive recipients of professional health services with a significantly greater likelihood of investing responsibility for their own health in the health care system than in themselves.

Consequently, when it comes to the self-management of one's health, studies such as the one just mentioned point to an interesting contrast in the health practices of the poor. Persons in lower socioeconomic groups may be attempting to participate in middle-class health lifestyles in accordance with their level of capability, but adopting a distinctly more dependent posture in interacting with physicians and the health care system. If middle-class values have spread to the lower class in regard to health-advancing behavior, why have they not also spread in relation to coping with medical doctors and institutions?

The answer seems to lie within the cultural context of both poverty and medical practice. The culture of poverty tends to promote feelings of dependence and fatalism. Thus, the poor are especially disadvantaged when they interact with physicians as authority figures and are confronted with modern medical technology. The development of a large array of medical equipment and procedures has increasingly taken away the self-management of health from laypersons, but particularly from those at the bottom of society with their more limited levels of education and experience with technology. When direct collaboration with medical practitioners is required, the poor become even more dependent.

However, other better educated persons have reacted to the professional dominance of physicians with increased skepticism of physicians' service orientation and an emerging belief that physicians should not always be completely in charge of the physician–patient relationship (Haug and Lavin 1981, 1983). They have assumed more of a consumer position with regard to health care. That is, they are making decisions on their own about which steps are most appropriate for them in dealing with doctors and maintaining their health. In doing so, they are becoming less dependent on physicians and rejecting the traditional physician–patient relationship for one of provider–consumer.

This leads us to consider the influence of the culture of medicine. The culture of medicine does not encourage consumerism among laypersons when direct physician–patient interaction is required, nor provide a context within which such an orientation can grow within the medical environment. Instead, physicians are portrayed as all-powerful individuals with the training and intellect to make life or death judgments and patients as completely dependent on those judgments. Consumerism and equality are not promoted because of the physician's need to have leverage over the patient. In the medical view, leverage is needed since treatment may be painful and discomforting and the patient typically lacks the expertise to treat the disorder (Parsons 1951).

This situation suggests that the culture of medicine is particularly important in explaining the health and illness behavior of the poor. One consequence of the increased frequency of contact between the medical profession and the poor appears to be that medical values have spread to the lower class. Accepting responsibility and self-management for diet, exercise, smoking, and other health-advancing behavior is strongly encouraged by the mass media and the medical profession. Physicians actively promote and reinforce the practice of health-advancing behavior. But consumerism and enhanced self-management in dealing with doctors and the health care system are not similarly encouraged or reinforced. Therefore, we have a circumstance in which self-management and responsibility for health among the lower class appear to develop when encouraged by social institutions, but fail to flourish where they are not encouraged.

The trend for the immediate future in the use of physician services seems to be one in which the more affluent and better educated are likely to be more discriminating in their use of doctors. They likely will take a consumer approach, shopping for the appropriate services, making their own decisions about their symptoms and what they mean, and dealing with physicians on a more equal basis than before. Conversely, the poor appear likely to continue seeing doctors more frequently than members of the other social strata, both because they have more illness and disability and because they have more of a tendency to invest responsibility for their problems in the health care delivery system itself. In doing so, they appear less likely to question the authority or judgments of doctors, while assuming doctors will alleviate their symptoms or cure them. Whether the lower class evolves toward having more of a consumer orientation in interacting with physicians will have to be determined by future research. The environment to support such a development does not appear to exist at present, since the poor remain especially dependent upon the medical profession as experts, and in this sector equality between doctors and patients is not encouraged.

Predisposing, Enabling, and Need Components

A major model of help-seeking for medical care is that developed by Andersen and his associates (Aday and Anderson 1975; Andersen, Kravits, and Anderson 1975). This model consists of predisposing, enabling, and need components that describe a person's decision to use health services. The predisposing component consists of sociodemographic variables and attitudes and beliefs about health care. The enabling component refers to factors such as family income, health insurance coverage, availability of services, and access to a regular source of care. The predisposing and enabling components establish the conditions within which a person is or is not likely to seek health services when stimulated by need (health status, disability, or diagnosis).

This model has been used in several studies and shown some success in describing variance in health services utilization on the basis of such variables as age, sex, education of head of household, and having a regular source of care. Almost all of the explained variance, however, is due to the need variables. That is, the perceived seriousness of one's symptoms has been found to be the most significant factor in whether a doctor is consulted (Berkanovic, Telesky, and Reeder 1981; Jones et al. 1981; Tanner, Cockerham, and Spaeth 1983).

It should be noted that Andersen's model is a prediction model, a major purpose of which is to maximize the amount of variance explained, regardless of why certain variables predict as they do. Prediction models provide useful insight by predicting levels of utilization and assisting researchers in describing the patterns they observe, but such models in themselves often do not explain *why* the process is occurring. They explain only *what* is occurring. Process models, as opposed to prediction models, are oriented toward increasing our understanding of why certain behaviors occur. These models consist of social-psychological approaches that measure the perceptual process guiding the seeking of health care discussed in the next section.

SOCIAL-PSYCHOLOGICAL MODELS OF ILLNESS BEHAVIOR

Studies in the United States, Great Britain, France, and the Netherlands suggest that laypersons generally conceive of health as either the relative absence of the symptoms of illness (Calnan 1987; Williams 1983), a feeling of physical and mental equilibrium or well-being (Herzlich 1973; Herzlich and Pierret, 1986, 1987; d'Houtaud and Field 1984, 1986; Joosten 1989), being able to carry out one's daily tasks (Apple 1960), or some combination of the above (Baumann 1961; Twaddle 1969). Conversely, to be ill means the presence of symptoms, feeling bad and in a state of disequilibrium, and functional incapacitation (not being able to carry out one's usual activities).

Thus, what laypersons recognize as illness is in part deviance from a standard of normality established by common sense and everyday experience. David Mechanic and Edmund Volkart (1961) have suggested that a given illness manifests specific characteristics with regard to symptom recognition and the extent of danger. Illness recognition is determined by how common the occurrence of the illness is in a given population and how familiar people are with its symptoms. Illness danger refers to the relative predictability of the outcome of the illness and the amount of threat or loss that is likely to result. When a particular symptom is easily recognizable and relatively devoid of danger, it is likely to be defined as a routine illness. When a symptom occurs infrequently, making identification more difficult, and is combined with an increasing perception of danger, there is likely to be a greater sense of concern.

Yet, as Mechanic (1978) has noted, recognition of a symptom, while certainly a necessary condition to motivate help-seeking behavior, is not in itself sufficient for a definition of illness. Some illnesses, such as appendicitis, may have obvious symptoms, while other illnesses, such as the early stages of cancer, may not. Also there are cases of persons who, despite symptoms, delay seeking health care. Cancer patients have been known to avoid cancer screening procedures because of their anxiety about learning the truth and being forced to confront what it means to have cancer (Becker and Maiman 1975). Therefore, the characteristics of illness recognition and illness danger can be significant influences on the manner in which people perceive a disease.

We can see an example of this in the experience of British sociologist Ann Holohan (1977), who visited a physician to receive treatment for what she thought would be diagnosed as an infection in her breast resulting from an injury a few months previously. She recognized she had a health problem but saw no particular danger from it. The physician discovered a lump in her breast and asked her to report to a hospital for a biopsy. The effect of this request was "shattering" because she had not even considered the possibility that she might have cancer. The discovery of the lump had come as a complete surprise and knowledge of its existence left her reeling with dismay. She suddenly had difficulty hearing her physician as he quoted the odds for and against the possibility of the tumor being malignant. She reports:

> His voice seemed to be coming from a distance, and I could only pick up stray words. Physically he appeared to become smaller and smaller, his voice fainter and fainter, while a jumble of thoughts about my family and survival pressed in on me. Inwardly I protested "it cannot be me." Yet I found myself writing automatically in my diary "hospital admission" and the date. It was sandwiched between the social commitments of a normal weekend—meeting friends, attending a concert, and I knew I would not be there.
>
> I got up, struggled to preserve normality (this seemed enormously important) and was astonished to hear myself asking mundane questions about admission procedures for tomorrow. He opened the door and still in a state of utter turmoil, I walked into the street. It seemed incredible that nothing had changed—the sun was still shining, the road sweeper gathering the leaves. I sat in my car, and with the conventional constraints removed, immense waves of panic engulfed me. I drove blindly home and recall very little of the actual journey. I felt this alien, pathological change was inexorable, gone was the reassuring external cause of my symptoms. Yet clearly I was no "sicker" than before my consultation. All that had changed was the possibility of a medical label for my symptom.[2]

[2]Ann Holohan, "Diagnosis: The End of Transition," in *Medical Encounters: The Experience of Illness and Treatment*, A. Davis and G. Horobin, eds. (New York: St. Martin's Press, 1977), pp. 87–88.

Upon her return home, Holohan did some housework as a form of denial. She reasoned that if she could still perform household chores she could not be seriously ill. She considered not going to the hospital for the biopsy, but she was unsure about what might happen if she declined to go. The thought of even touching the lump in her breast was repulsive to her. Her course was set. Illness recognition and danger were too strong to ignore. She felt she had to have the biopsy because the situation could be very serious. She entered the hospital and the results of the biopsy indicated that she did not have a malignant tumor. While leaving the hospital, however, another woman who was being discharged for the same reason remarked to her, "I wonder what would have happened if it had been the other way. It's like asking what's on the other side" (Holohan 1977:96).

Mechanic (1978:268–269) has formulated a general theory of help-seeking since his initial work with Volkart in the early 1960s. He suggests that whether a person will seek medical care is based on ten determinants: (1) visibility and recognition of symptoms; (2) the extent to which the symptoms are perceived as dangerous; (3) the extent to which symptoms disrupt family, work, and other social activities; (4) the frequency and persistence of symptoms; (5) amount of tolerance for the symptoms; (6) available information, knowledge, and cultural assumptions; (7) basic needs that lead to denial; (8) other needs competing with illness responses; (9) competing interpretations that can be given to the symptoms once they are recognized; and (10) availability of treatment resources, physical proximity, and psychological and financial costs of taking action. In addition to describing these ten determinants of help-seeking behavior, Mechanic explains that they operate at two distinct levels: other-defined and self-defined. The other-defined level is, of course, the process by which other people attempt to define an individual's symptoms as illness and call those symptoms to the attention of that person. Self-defined is where the individual defines his or her own symptoms. The ten determinants and two levels of definition supposedly interact to influence a person to seek or not seek help for a health problem.

The central theme that forms a backdrop for Mechanic's general theory of help-seeking is that illness behavior is a culturally and socially learned response. A person responds to symptoms according to his or her definition of the situation. This definition may be influenced by the definitions of others but is largely shaped by learning, socialization, and past experience as mediated by a person's social and cultural background. Although Mechanic's theory explains the decision-making process leading up to contacting a physician, it does not explain what happens after the initial contact is made (Wolinsky 1988). Nor does the theory detail the manner in which the determinants and levels of definition interact with one another. As a general theory of help-seeking behavior, Mechanic's theory has some shortcomings. As a theory of perceptual considerations relevant to an initial decision by a person to visit a physician for health care, Mechanic's work provides a good account of the decision-making process.

One approach that provides insight into the entire sequence of events involved in seeing a physician beyond the initial visit is Suchman's (1965b) description of the stages of illness experience. According to Suchman, when individuals perceive themselves becoming sick they can pass through as many as five different response stages, depending upon their interpretation of their particular illness experience. These stages, shown in Figure 6-1, are (1) the symptom experience, (2) the assumption of the sick role, (3) medical care contact, (4) the dependent-patient role, and (5) recovery and rehabilitation.

The illness experience begins with the symptom stage, in which the individual is confronted with a decision about whether "something is wrong." The decision of the person involved may be to deny the symptoms as not needing attention, to delay making a decision until the symptoms are more obvious, or to accept the symptoms as evidence of a health disorder. The person may also attempt to treat himself or herself through the application of folk medicine or self-medication.

If the decision is made to accept the symptom experience as indicative of an illness, the person is likely to enter Suchman's second stage of the sick role. Here the person is allowed to relinquish normal social obligations provided permission is obtained from the person's lay-referral system. The lay-referral system can grant the individual provisional permission to assume the sick role. "Official" permission to adopt the sick role, however, can come only from the physician, who acts as society's agent as the authority on illness. Thus, while lay remedies may continue, the individual is again faced with a decision to deny the illness and abandon the illness experience or accept the provisional sick role and perhaps seek medical treatment.

If professional assistance is sought, the person enters the third stage of medical care contact. At this stage, the person attempts to obtain legitimation of his or her sick role status and to negotiate the treatment procedure. The illness experience may be confirmed or denied by the physician. If there is a disagreement between physician and patient, the patient may go "shopping" for another physician's diagnosis that might prove more acceptable.

If both patient and physician agree that treatment is necessary, the person passes into the dependent-patient stage. Here the person undergoes the prescribed treatment, but still has the option either to terminate or to continue the treatment. Sometimes patients settle for the "secondary gain" of enjoying the privileges accorded to a sick person, such as taking time off from work, and do not seriously try to get well. Or both patient and physician may cooperate to allow the patient to enter the fifth and final stage of recovery and rehabilitation. In this stage the patient is expected to relinquish the sick role and resume normal social roles. This may not happen, as in the case of a chronic illness or when the patient chooses to malinger in an illness experience even though technically well.

Although an illness experience may not involve all of the stages described by Suchman and can be terminated at any particular stage through denial, the significance of Suchman's model is that each stage requires the sick person to take different kinds of decisions and actions. In evaluating the experience of illness, the sick person must interpret not only his or her symptoms but also what is necessary in terms of available resources, alternative behaviors, and the probability of success. Suchman's model is similar in its approach to the positions advocated by Rosenstock (1966), Mechanic and Volkart (1961), and Mechanic (1978), who

FIGURE 6-1 Suchman's stages of illness experience

	I Symptom Experience	II Assumption of the Sick Role	III Medical Care Contact	IV Dependent-Patient Role	V Recovery and Rehabilitation
Decision	Something is wrong	Relinquish normal roles	Seek professional advice	Accept professional treatment	Relinquish sick role
Behaviors	Application of folk medicine, self-medication	Request provisional validation for sick role from members of lay referral system—continue lay remedies	Seek authoritative legitimation for sick role—negotiate treatment procedures	Undergo treatment procedures for illness—follow regimen	Resume normal roles
Outcomes	Denial (flight into health) Delay Acceptance →	Denial Acceptance →	Denial Shopping Confirmation →	Rejection Secondary gain Acceptance →	Refusal (chronic sick role) Malingerer Acceptance →

Source: Rodney M. Coe, *Sociology of Medicine* (New York: McGraw-Hill Inc., 1970, 1978), p. 108. Reprinted with permission of McGraw-Hill, Inc.

likewise agree that individual perception is the key variable in assessing modes of coping with problems of health and illness. Rosenstock's Health Belief Model stressed the perception of personal susceptibility and the benefits of taking preventive action; Mechanic and Volkart emphasized perception from the standpoint of illness recognition and illness danger; and Mechanic, some years later, focused on illness behavior as a learned response.

SUMMARY AND CONCLUSION

This chapter has reviewed the major theories and findings of medical sociology concerning the process of seeking medical care and the utilization of health care services. While there is no single theory or approach that has earned general consensus, the existing literature reveals the two most important variables in health care utilization to be the perceived severity of symptoms and the ability to pay for the rendering of services.

Social-psychological models of help-seeking behavior have emphasized the importance of self-perception as it relates to a person's understanding of a particular symptom. Especially important is whether the person perceives himself or herself as able to perform normal social roles. Studies concentrating on ethnicity as a factor have pointed to the role of the social network in influencing the perceptual process according to the network's own sociocultural orientation. Although some patients, notably cancer patients, may delay seeing a doctor because they are fearful about having their perceptions confirmed, the generalization can be made that the more symptoms are perceived as representing a serious illness, the more likely it is that a person will seek professional services.

The ability to pay for health services has traditionally accounted for significant socioeconomic differences in health care utilization. Today it appears that public health insurance and social welfare monies have enabled the poor to visit physicians more frequently than the upper-income groups. However, whether increased physician visitation has resulted in a corresponding rise in the quality of health care provided the poor remains to be determined. Then, too, the poor still reside in an environment of poverty that perpetuates their increased risk to health hazards. Among those persons without public health insurance—those covered by private health insurance plans that still leave considerable cost for the individual consumer, or those without any health insurance—the ability to pay remains an important obstacle to help-seeking behavior. This chapter also discussed the sociodemographic variables of age and sex, which were found to be consistent predictors of seeking medical care. Elderly persons and females generally report more illness than younger persons and males and tend to consult physicians more readily.

Healing Options in American Society

7

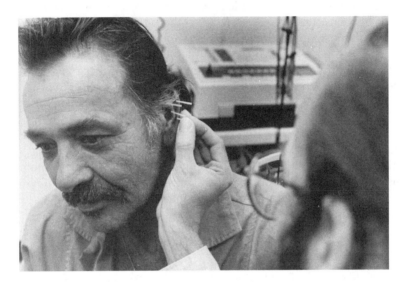

The majority of persons in American society turn to medical doctors for help when they are sick or injured. Other people, for reasons that may be religious, financial, or cultural, or simply because no doctors are available or because modern medicine may not meet their needs, seek treatment elsewhere. To complete our discussion of help-seeking, this chapter examines healing options in the United States. These healers exist because they provide a service to their clients. What these services are and why they are sought is our focus. First we will discuss the *osteopath,* who is a physician. Next, we will expand our discussion to include a consideration of *chiropractors, faith healers,* and *folk healers.*

OSTEOPATHS

Osteopathy began in the 1860s in Kirksville, Missouri, as little more than a pseudoscientific cult (Albrecht and Levy 1982; Eckberg 1987; New 1958; Wardwell 1979; Wolinsky 1988). Its founder, Andrew Taylor Still, a physician, had a "divine inspiration" that illness was caused by a dislocation of one or more bones in the spinal column. For many years, osteopathy was viewed by physicians and much of the general public as a form of quackery. But gradually osteopathy achieved respectability by moving away from its exclusive focus on spinal manipulation. By the mid-twentieth century, osteopaths were receiving scientific medical training in such areas as surgery and drug therapy. Training for osteopaths takes place at fifteen osteopathic colleges in the United States whose graduates are awarded the Doctor of Osteopathy Degree (D.O.). Further training as an intern and resident is required, and 34 percent of all osteopathic students are women. Osteopaths have also formed their own professional organization, the American Osteopathic Association, which serves to promote professionalism.

In 1953 the American Medical Association recognized osteopaths as another medical specialty and they now enjoy the rights and privileges of medical doctors. To date, osteopaths have been able to maintain their separate identity, yet the trend is toward absorption into medicine. Some sources, in fact, have identified osteopathy as a "backdoor" into medicine (Eckberg 1987); that is, osteopathy has been seen by some as an alternative way to become a physician. Osteopaths, for example, can specialize in surgery, anesthesiology, psychiatry, pediatrics, radiology, and other medical specialties. The most hotly debated question in osteopathy today, as noted by Fredric Wolinsky (1988) and others (Albrecht and Levy 1982; Eckberg 1987; Wardwell 1979) is whether "classical" osteopathy has given itself over totally to medicine as practiced by medical doctors. This argument remains unresolved at present as the osteopathic profession continues to resist complete assimilation into traditional medicine. Since osteopaths are trained to practice manipulation of the musculoskeletal system, they see themselves as able to provide this service as an added dimension of health care. In 1990, 28,100 osteopaths were professionally active in the United States.

Outside of the United States, osteopathy is less accepted. In Great Britain, for example, osteopathy is not available in the British National Health Service, nor qualifies for any public funding to cover the costs of care. Patients who visit osteopaths must pay the costs themselves, which is not the case when they visit medical doctors.

CHIROPRACTORS

The chiropractic approach to healing involves manipulation of bones in the spinal column. This type of treatment originated with Daniel Palmer in Davenport, Iowa, in 1895. It is based on the idea that manipulation of the spine can relieve pressure on the nerves and thereby alleviate illness and pain. While there is some dispute over whether the osteopathic and chiropractic approaches evolved independently of each other in terms of initial conceptualization, chiropractors today are restricted solely to nonmedical techniques. In 1991 there were seventeen chiropractic colleges in the United States. There are also chiropractic colleges in Canada, England, and Australia. Training is four years in duration, three in the classroom and one in practice at the college. There are no internships or residencies to serve.

While there is evidence that chiropractic techniques can help patients with back, shoulder, and neck pain (Wardwell 1980), the medical profession has traditionally opposed the extension of professional status to chiropractors. This opposition is based on the assertion that chiropractic methods are derived from inaccurate theories, chiropractic educational standards are low, and the techniques are of little or no therapeutic value to patients. Rather than attempt to absorb the chiropractor into medicine, some physicians have preferred to eliminate the field altogether. In 1987, a federal court ruled that the American Medical Association had conspired to destroy chiropractic medicine in violation of antitrust statutes. The AMA was ordered to cease undermining the public's confidence in chiropractic procedures.

Chiropractors are licensed to practice in all fifty states, are authorized to receive Medicare payments for treatments rendered to patients over the age of sixty-five and provide services covered by major private insurance carriers. In 1990 about 25,000 chiropractors provided services to their clients. Chiropractors are often favored because they charge less than physicians, are friendly, give more time to patients, and explain difficulties in words easily understood (Bauwens 1977; Wardwell 1980).

However, chiropractors have been hampered in their attempts at professionalization not only by physicians but also because of conflicts among themselves. Some chiropractors favor a more expanded role, using a variety of techniques, in which a wider range of health problems would be treated. Others prefer a more "pure" approach, in which chiropractors would limit themselves to spinal manipulation. Chiropractors must often strongly compete among one another for patients and have little control over who should be licensed to practice. Moreover, two organizations, the American Chiropractic Association and the International Chiropractor Association, have differing positions, although most chiropractors agree they should merge. Walter Wardwell summarized the overall chiropractic situation as follows:

> To the extent that they reject the basic conceptions of medical science as fundamentally wrong, and propound chiropractic as a completely different philosophy and science capable of treating nearly the entire range of human ailments, they inevitably find great difficulty in convincing the mass of informed citizens that medicine's evaluation of chiropractic is wrong. Such citizens, unless persuaded by personal experience, are unlikely to view chiropractic as scientific or chiropractors as qualified doctors. Lack of acceptance by the public and rejection by orthodox medical authorities explains why the word "marginal" has been used to describe the chiropractic profession ever since 1952. . . . However, from being "marginal," chiropractic could evolve, as has osteopathy, to being "parallel" to medicine if it becomes the equal of medicine in education, scientific research, public acceptance, and success in therapy.[1]

---

[1]Walter I. Wardwell, "The Present and Future Role of the Chiropractor," in *Modern Developments in the Principles and Practice of Chiropractic*, S. Haldeman, ed. (New York: Appleton-Century-Crofts, 1980), pp. 36–37.

Physicians rarely refer patients to chiropractors. Yet the National Center for Health Statistics (1983a) reported that 80 percent of the people who visit chiropractors also have seen a physician during the past year. Therefore, it appears that the majority of people who use chiropractic services do not depend entirely on this method of treatment. Instead, they use chiropractors and physicians in a complementary manner. Because physicians do not typically refer their patients to chiropractors, it must be assumed that most people visit chiropractors on their own initiative. Many people go to chiropractors for treatment in addition to that received from physicians, but some seek help from both chiropractors and physicians for the same conditions. Chiropractors are the second largest category of primary health care practitioners in the United States, following medical doctors, when the number of practitioners and patients is taken into account. Nevertheless, chiropractors remain outside the mainstream of medicine.

Elsewhere, in Great Britain, there are only 350 chiropractors in the entire country and chiropractic care is not available in the British National Health Service. Some private health insurance programs, however, do cover chiropractic care if treatment is recommended by a medical doctor.

FAITH HEALERS

Faith healers are people who use the power of suggestion, prayer, and faith in God to promote healing. According to John Denton (1978), two basic beliefs are prevalent in religious healing. One form of belief supports the idea that healing occurs primarily through psychological processes and is effective only with psychophysiological disorders. The other belief is that healing is accomplished through the intervention of God and constitutes a present-day miracle. Denton offers five general categories of faith healing: (1) self-treatment through prayer; (2) treatment by a layperson thought to be able to communicate with God; (3) treatment by an official church leader, for whom healing is only one of many tasks; (4) healing obtained from a person or group of persons who practice healing full time without an affiliation with a major religious organization; and (5) healing obtained from religious healers who practice full time and are affiliated with a major religious group, such as Christian Science healers. A common theme running through each of these categories is an appeal to God to change a person's physical or mental condition for the better.

An example of faith healing is found in the study conducted by Gillian Allen and Roy Wallis (1976) of members of a small congregation of a Pentecostal church, the Assemblies of God, in a city in Scotland. Members of the church subscribed to a belief that the devil caused illness and that even for such afflictions as mental illness, blindness, dumbness, and epilepsy a person could be possessed by evil spirits. Accepting the Bible as the literal truth, the Assemblies of God officially support the idea of *divine healing* based upon Biblical passages indicating that (1) some people have the power to transmit the healing forces of the Holy Spirit or to exorcise demons, and (2) healing can be obtained through faith the same way as salvation from sin. The healing procedure was described in this manner:

> Prayer for healing in the Assembly of God occurs at the end of normal services when those who need healing or help and advice, are asked "to come out to the front." There the pastor and the elders perform the laying on of hands and sprinkling with holy oil and pray simultaneously: "Oh Lord, heal this woman! Yes, Lord. We know you can heal her." The occasional case of demon possession is dealt with in a similar way when the pastor or evangelist addresses the demon along these lines: "Get out, foul demon! In the name of Jesus, leave her!"[2]

Although the Pentecostal church used divine healing as a central aspect of church dogma, it did not prohibit members from seeking professional medical care. Use of divine healing, however, was preferred because it offered the advantage of providing both spiritual and physical healing. It was also believed to work in many cases where orthodox medical practices failed. The members had a fund of knowledge attesting to spectacular cures, either through the specific effect of the emotional healing services or through the power of prayer in general. Yet since church members also believed that "God's methods are sometimes through men" and that "God put doctors in the world and gave them their skills," it was permissible to seek physician assistance. For serious illnesses in particular, divine healing was used in conjunction with professional medicine. Hence, church members held both religious and scientific beliefs about the causation and treatment of illness simultaneously, without any apparent conflict. "In serious illnesses," state Allen and Wallis (1976:134–135), "members were not faced with the choice between breaking their religious principles by fetching the doctor and refusing medical treatment altogether." Consequently, Pentecostalists were usually able to avoid the dilemma of whether to use *either* a religious *or* a medical curing process.

Deborah Glik (1990) interviewed several people who participated in spiritual healing groups in Baltimore, Maryland. The majority of respondents claimed they had experienced some type of healing and attributed it to their participation and belief in spiritual healing. Rather than cures, however, the most common form of healing was alleviation of symptoms, followed by relief from psychological distress, acceptance of one's health or life situation, or adoption of another perspective about one's situation. In some cases, people redefined what was wrong with them to better fit the outcome of their healing experience; that is, they redefined their ailments as less serious and less medical after religious healing. "While few persons claimed their healing had been complete," states Glik (1990:161), "most cited improvements in some health or life situation." Glik's data suggest that the benefits of religious healing primarily lay in relief from stress, enhanced feelings of support from God, and the adoption of a different viewpoint

---

[2]Gillian Allen and Roy Wallis, "Pentecostalists as a Medical Minority," in *Marginal Medicine*, R. Wallis and P. Morley, eds. (New York: The Free Press, 1976), p. 121.

about the meaning of their health problem in their lives. For example, as two of the respondents in the Glik study reported:

> A 61 year old female teacher going through a divorce and dealing with depression and arthritis said: "Faith and belief has made me accepting of problems. I have been able to fill up with God, and He will not let my problems get to me."
>
> A 34 year old male real estate broker suffering from stress and lower back pain noted, "I am now relaxed. I have learned to let go and let God be alive in my body, mind and all my affairs. Life has changed dramatically for the good."[3]

In the United States, some faith healers hold services in a church or in their homes; others travel from city to city holding meetings, perhaps in tents, and some appear on television or radio. The number of people who frequent such healing services and who are actually helped by this method is not known. But faith healers tend to be readily available and most cities and towns are visited by such healers at least once a year.

Most religious groups in the United States favor a combination of religious practices and professional medical care in treating health problems. The doctrines of a few religious groups, however, prohibit their members from seeking modern medical treatment. These groups utilize faith healing, laying on of the hands, and individual and communal prayers in treating illnesses. Sometimes there are accounts of "miracle" cures in which a deadly affliction like cancer is overcome. Other times there are tragic stories such as the 1982 court cases in Oklahoma against the parents of a young boy who died from a ruptured appendix, and against church midwives and parents of a newborn baby dying from injuries suffered at birth—who were all members of the same church. All parties were eventually acquitted. But even though the church elders had maintained that receiving medical attention from a doctor was a "forgivable sin," the parents in each case had refused medical treatment because it was against their religious beliefs. A similar case in Indiana in 1984, however, resulted in a prison sentence for the parents of a boy allowed to die of bacterial meningitis. The parents had refused to seek medical care because of their religion. In 1991, the city of Philadelphia threatened court action against two churches when five children died in a measles outbreak in their schools. Both churches maintained that prayer, not medicine, cured illnesses and none of the children in their schools had been inoculated against measles or other diseases.

The most prominent group in American society advocating religious healing in place of medical treatment is the Christian Science Church. Founded in 1866 in Boston by Mary Baker Eddy, the Christian Science Church maintains that sickness and pain are an illusion. Disease is not God given but is believed to be produced by a distorted view people have of their spiritual nature. All forms of

---

[3]Deborah C. Glik, "The Redefinition of the Situation: The Social Construction of Spiritual Healing Experiences," *Sociology of Health and Illness* 12 (1990), 157.

disease are considered symptomatic of an underlying spiritual condition that can be healed only through prayer. The key to life and health is thus obtained through spiritual discovery. Christian Scientists are believed to possess the capacity to heal themselves, although the assistance of a Christian Science practitioner, licensed by the church, is also available. Practitioners are not considered to be the equal of medical doctors but are intended to help the sick person find a cure through prayer. Healing consists of prayers meant to convey to individuals a deeper understanding of their spiritual being. This understanding is held to be the crucial factor in eliminating the mental attitudes from which all diseases are thought to originate. There are certain medical problems that are considered more mechanical than spiritual, such as broken bones or a need for surgery, that can be legitimately treated by a doctor. But generally speaking, Christian Science healing is thought to be incompatible with medical treatment.

In 1988 and 1989, however, four court cases resulted in convictions of manslaughter or neglect for Christian Science parents in the deaths of their children because of a failure to seek conventional medical care. One 1989 case involved the death of a two-year-old boy from a bowel obstruction in Boston when the parents relied exclusively on prayer to help the child find relief. In another case in Florida in 1989, a judge rejected a charge of manslaughter against a Christian Science couple after a jury found them guilty of allowing their seven-year-old daughter to die from diabetes. Instead, the judge accepted the more stringent conviction of third-degree murder, along with child abuse, and sentenced the parents to suspended four-year prison terms, fifteen years of probation, and ordered them to provide medical treatment for their surviving children. A Florida appeals court upheld the sentence in 1990 and stated that the right to practice religion freely does not include the liberty to expose a child to ill health or death and added that, while parents may be free to become martyrs themselves, they are not free to make martyrs of their children.

The legal issues in cases such as these are clear: On one side is the issue of religious freedom and parental autonomy and on the other is the state's right to protect children. The current trend in court decisions in this matter appears in a 1991 finding by the State Supreme Court in Massachusetts involving Jehovah's Witnesses who refused blood transfusions for their children in two separate cases, one where the child had leukemia and the other hemorrhage of an ulcer. The court held that, while adults have the right to refuse medical care, parents may be forced to have their children treated for life-threatening illnesses.

When it comes to faith healing, however, there is also considerable controversy about whether it actually works. Moreover, questionable ethics on the part of some television evangelists in recent years, including sex scandals, cannot have helped the overall image of faith healing among the general public. As Wolinsky (1988) points out, the medical profession in the United States does not hold faith healing in high esteem and the future of this mode of health care delivery in the United States is uncertain—at least with respect to its electronic version.

Nevertheless, the relationship between health and religion is an important area that needs to be studied in greater detail. Such studies should not be limited to faith healing, but should include the manner in which religious beliefs have an impact generally on health and medical care. It is clear that an appeal to a spiritual or divine being promotes a sense of psychological well-being in the individual (Ellison 1991; Idler and Kasl 1992; Pollner 1989). Among the few existing studies is that of Ellen Idler (1987) who investigated the health and degree of religious involvement among a sample of elderly persons living in New Haven, Connecticut. Idler found that those persons with the highest levels of religious involvement showed the least depression and physical disability. Another study is that by Jeffrey Dwyer and his colleagues (Dwyer, Clarke, and Miller 1990) who determined death rates from cancer were lower in those areas of the United States where there was a high concentration of religious persons. Dwyer and his colleagues suggest that the lifestyles associated with high religiosity emphasize activities that promote health, such as the avoidance of cigarettes, alcohol, and multiple sex partners and an emphasis on nutrition, hygiene, and—for most religions—preventive medical care. Studies such as these demonstrate that religion can be a major resource in coping with health problems.

FOLK HEALERS

Folk healers are not used to any significant extent in the United States except by some low-income persons belonging to racial and ethnic minority groups. Apparently few non-Hispanic whites go to folk healers, although some elderly persons living in poverty and rural areas may be prone to use "folk remedies" in treating ailments (Bauwens 1977). Common ingredients in folk remedies are such substances as whiskey, honey, sugar, lemon juice, baking soda, aspirin, kerosene, salt, butter, mustard, and sassafras (Denton 1978). Practicing folk healers are most likely to be found among blacks, Hispanics, and American Indians.

Black Folk Healers

The tendency of some low-income black people to seek the services of lay practitioners rather than physicians is illustrated in the work of Loudell Snow (1978), who studied black folk healers in Chicago. Black folk healers and their patients, according to Snow, subscribe to a belief system that—unlike modern medicine—does not differentiate between science and religion. All life events, including illness, are viewed in relation to the total environment as either natural or unnatural, good or evil. Being healthy is an instance of good fortune like having a good job or a faithful spouse. Being sick is an example of misfortune like unemployment and marital strife. Thus, life is *generally* good or bad and the cure for *one* problem, says Snow, might cure *all* problems.

Additionally, Snow notes that folk diagnosis of a health problem emphasizes the *cause* of the problem, not the symptoms. Having a body rash might initially be seen as stemming from a lack of cleanliness but come to be defined as the result of black magic. In this belief system, what is important is not the rash, but what or who brought on the rash. Snow gives the following example:

Even when a direct cause-and-effect relationship is known which is equivalent to the professional view this may be supported by religious or magical overtones. The sister of one of my informants died of bacterial meningitis, an etiology clearly understood by the family. But why did the organism invade her system at all? In their view to punish the father for "drinking and running around with women."[4]

Another prominent belief is that all illnesses can be cured, if not by medicine, then by magic. This belief is supported by the idea that illnesses are either natural or unnatural. Natural illnesses are those maladies caused by abusing the natural environment (staying out too late, eating too much, failing to wear warm clothing) or brought on as a punishment by God for sin or for not living up to the Lord's expectations. Thus, in the case of divine punishment, the afflicted person must make contact with God either directly or indirectly through an intermediary such as a faith healer. "Prayer and repentance," reports Snow (1978:73), "not penicillin, cure sin."

Unnatural illnesses are outside of "God's plan" and beyond self-treatment or treatment prescribed by friends and relatives. And if the mind is affected, unnatural illnesses are thought to be beyond the capabilities of physicians, who are usually associated just with the treatment of natural illnesses that have obvious physical symptoms. The cause of an unnatural illness can be worry or stress, but often the etiology is ascribed to evil influences or acts of sorcery. When black magic is suspected, it is necessary to find a healer with unusual magic or religious powers who can successfully intervene for the victim.

Snow observed that the term *healer* in Chicago's black community included a bewildering array of persons performing different healing roles. The variety of healers is reflected in the number of names used to describe them, such as healer, root doctor or root worker, reader, advisor, spiritualist, or conjure man or woman. If voodoo is practiced, a male healer may be called *houngan* or *papaloi,* a female healer would be a *mambo* or *maraloi.* Few of them refer to themselves as "doctor," since healing is only part of their services. Instead, their given name is likely to be prefaced by a kinship, religious, or political title, such as Sister, Brother, Mother, Reverend, Bishop, Prophet, Evangelist, or Madam. These healers depend on word of mouth for patient referrals or they may advertise by newspaper or leaflet. They claim to have received their ability to heal (1) as a result of learning (which confers little status since almost anyone can be expected to learn); (2) during an altered state of consciousness, such as a profound religious experience or a divine "call" to healing; or (3) at birth. Snow states (1978:79), "they will probably have in common only the assertion that the abilities are a gift from God."

Many healers do not require direct personal contact with the recipient of services but will conduct business over the telephone or by mail. If the individual's complaint involves sorcery, the use of some substance (such as oils, potions, or perfumes) will be required and may need to be purchased; if witchcraft is at

[4]Loudell F. Snow, "Sorcerers, Saints and Charlatans: Black Folk Healers in Urban America," *Culture, Medicine, and Psychiatry,* 2 (1978), 71.

work, a thought, prayer, or verbal spell is necessary. In the case of witchcraft, it might be necessary to purchase candles to assist the healer in effecting a solution. For example, when Snow complained in a letter to "Sister Marina" that she had problems sleeping and eating, was losing weight, and did not seem to enjoy life any more, Sister Marina replied in writing:

> I am so sorry I took so long to write but I had to take your letter into my church to see if what I suspected about your case was true. I had suspected an unnatural problem and I was right. But writing everything to you that I have learned would have to fill 10 pages of paper and maybe you still would not fully understand so I am asking you to phone me so that I can explain to you better the history of your case and let you know what will be needed to help you. I have lit a special candle for you and my spirits have told me since you have written to me you have felt slightly better. But if you want to be helped call me.[5]

Snow wrote back asking if Sister Marina could help her by mail and she received a warning by return mail that if she did not hurry it might be too late to save her. Sister Marina wrote:

> In order for me to take your case I must burn 9 candles for you to find out just what it is I must do to get rid of this UNNATURAL PROBLEM and remove this EVIL! And each candle costs $10.00 so it would come up to $90.00 to help and if you do not either bring it to Chicago or send it within a week and 1/2 which would be about 11 days I cannot except your case because you might get too bad off and then no one will be able to help if you decide to come to see me please call me a day ahead of time and let me know.[6]

How effective black folk healers like Marina are in treating their clients is not known. Some of these healers are likely to be frauds. Yet the advantage they offer to their clients is that they are readily available, results are usually quick and sometimes guaranteed, and they claim to be able to solve any problem. Their abilities are supposed to be derived from divine authority and, if they fail, they can attribute the failure to the will of God. In essence, what black folk healers appear to accomplish is to reduce the anxieties of their clients, and they are most effective in dealing with health problems that have some emotional basis. What is particularly significant in the reduction of anxiety, and what distinguishes their practice, is the recognition that health problems are an integral part of such other problems of daily life as lack of money, a strayed spouse, loss of a job, or envious relatives or neighbors. Consequently, black folk healers treat the whole person, not just a single symptom, which is often the case with a physician. Moreover, physicians tend to charge significantly higher prices for their services, are not as readily available in low-income areas, and may be unable to show quick results

[5]Snow, "Sorcerers, Saints, and Charlatans," p. 99.

[6]Snow, "Sorcerers, Saints, and Charlatans," p. 99.

because of the patient's delay in seeking treatment or the severity of the disorder or both.

While the Snow study dealt with low-income black Americans living in an urban area, other data on similar blacks living in a rural setting point toward the same kind of pattern. Julian Roebuck and Robert Quan (1976) compared the health practices of fifty black and fifty white lower-class households in a small town in Mississippi. Although the white households tended to have a somewhat higher average income, practically all of the households received supplemental income from public assistance and welfare programs. Overall educational levels for both black and white households were between the fifth and sixth grades, and those household members who were employed held jobs that were either semi-skilled or unskilled. There were important differences, however, when it came to seeking treatment for health problems. More white (68 percent) than black (48 percent) households sought health care only from physicians. More black (42 percent) than white (24 percent) households obtained care from a combination of practitioners—physicians, marginal healers, and illegal healers. Somewhat more whites (8 percent) than blacks (4 percent) went to marginal healers (defined as chiropractors, pharmacists, podiatrists, nurse-midwives). As for illegal healers (defined as folk practitioners, spiritualists, sorcerers), 6 percent of the black households used this source only compared to none of the white households.

In general, Roebuck and Quan found that lower-class blacks usually waited longer than lower-class whites before seeking the services of a healer when sick. Blacks were less oriented toward Western scientific medicine than whites and believed more in the effectiveness of illegal healers (who were sometimes used along with physicians). One black respondent, for example, stated: "The doctor thought I had a stroke because I couldn't move, but the hoodoo man said someone had placed stumbling blocks in front of me and he chased it away" (Roebuck and Quan 1976:157). Another black respondent said: "I saw Sister Cherokee [spiritualist] and she rubbed some olive oil on the back of my neck and told me I was suffering from high blood—exactly what the doctor told me!" (Roebuck and Quan 1976:157). Many of the blacks not only believed in the effectiveness of the illegal healers but had a corresponding lack of faith in physicians as well. None of the whites used the illegal healers in any capacity, nor expressed confidence in their methods.

Other research conducted by Snow (1977) among lower-class blacks in a community in the southwest United States showed health practices similar to those found by Snow in Chicago and Roebuck and Quan in Mississippi. Sick people were typically channeled through a lay-referral system of family and neighbors to a source of medical treatment, which in many cases was not a physician. Sometimes physicians were consulted only as a last resort.

There are two distinct types of black folk healing in the United States: traditional and Caribbean. The traditional form has been discussed in this section. The Caribbean form consists of several variations, such as *Voodoo* (Haiti), *Santeria* (Cuba), and *Obeah* (West Indies). What each of these Caribbean approaches to folk healing have in common is that they are based on native African beliefs and are part of the Caribbean's past slave culture. Each uses rituals, charms, herbs, concoctions, and prayer to prevent or cure illness by healing the mind and spirit, along with the body (Holloway 1990; Laguerre 1987; Robinson 1990). These healing practices are all part of a larger system of religious and spiritual beliefs that are limited in the United States to small numbers of black Americans with ties to the Caribbean. Miami, New Orleans, Chicago, Philadelphia, and New York show the largest concentrations of these practitioners.

Curanderismo

Male Mexican-American folk healers are known as *curanderos* and females as *curanderas*. Like black folk healers, curanderos and curanderas blend religion and folk medicine into a single therapeutic approach. They likewise classify illnesses primarily on the basis of *what* causes the disorder rather than the symptoms, and they do not separate the natural from the supernatural when it comes to diagnosis and treatment. Most of their patients are lower class. Unlike black folk healers, they do not charge for their services or they charge very little. They may ask for a small donation (perhaps a dollar or two) for expenses or they may accept a small gift such as vegetables or a chicken.

Curanderos and curanderas also appear to use religion to a much greater extent than black folk healers. Ari Kiev (1968) points out that religion, based upon a Spanish Catholic tradition, is central to the curandero, who believes life is ordained by the divinity, and good health and happiness can be achieved only by those who keep God's commandments. A patient who suffers, therefore, is seen as helping God's plan for the universe since it is believed that God allows men to suffer in order to learn. The example of Christ suffering on the cross is often used to illustrate that suffering and illness can be a worthwhile experience. Thus, the curandero views helping the patient accept suffering as a major task. In this context, suffering is explained as being part of the patient's burden for the world's sin and ignorance and a necessary role in God's plan for the universe. The more religious the curandero appears to be and the more convincing he or she is in influencing others to accept the will of God, the more highly regarded the curandero is as a healer. One effect the curandero uses to help accomplish this task is to establish a work setting that supports his or her image. Kiev describes it like this:

> Each curandero works in his own unique setting, depending usually upon his degree of affluence. The basic atmosphere created is invariably the same. In general, the curandero sees patients in part of his home set aside for treatment. These rooms, even in poor slums, are distinctive because of the great number of religious objects contained in them. The presence of numerous pictures and statues of the Virgin Mary and Jesus, of various sized crosses and religious candles, which are often arranged around an altar in a corner of the room, creates an atmosphere of religious solemnity which makes one forget the poverty of the slum or the humble shack of the curandero. Indeed, in such treatment rooms one feels as if in a church, and cannot help but view the curandero with awe and respect.

The therapeutic effect of this "temple in the home" cannot be minimized. The quiet calm can invoke a feeling of security and protectiveness in the frightened and anxious. . . . Perhaps most important is the authority the curandero derives through his relationship to the setting. It makes him the object of respect and awe and puts him in command of much of the power that derives from the patient's response to the setting and the symbolism. By relying upon religious symbols and objects that have great meaning for the patients, he can immediately establish himself as a man of wisdom and authority, which undoubtedly increases the patient's willingness to cooperate and his expectations of relief.[7]

Besides prayer and religious counseling, the curandero or curandera employs a variety of folk drugs and herbs to produce a cure (rattlesnake oil, mineral water, garlic, sweet basil, wild pitplant, licorice, camphor). To a very large extent this approach is based on sixteenth-century Spanish medicine, derived largely from Greek and Arabic sources, and influenced by beliefs of the Mayans and Aztecs. Prevalent in this view is the Hippocratic notion of bodily equilibrium. Hippocrates, the famous physician of ancient Greece, believed that good health resulted from the equilibrium within the body of four humors of blood, phlegm, black bile, and yellow bile. Important, too, was the harmony of the body with living habits and the environment. As long as the four humors were in balance, the body was healthy. If an imbalance occurred, however, and more of one type of humor than another was present, a person was sick. Because the body is perceived as being a mix of cold and hot conditions, curanderos and curanderas use "hot" foods and medicines to treat "cold" conditions (drowsiness, chills) and "cold" foods and medicines to treat "hot" conditions (fever, hypersexuality).

The most dreaded form of disorder, either physical or mental, is that caused by witchcraft. Witches, or *brujas,* are evil persons who supposedly have made pacts with the devil and use supernatural powers in the form of curses, magic, herbs, or ghosts to harm other people. According to William Madsen (1973), who studied Mexican-Americans living in south Texas, conservative lower-class Mexican-Americans showed an almost universal acceptance of the existence of witchcraft, even though belief in witchcraft is more strongly denounced than other folk theories of disease by the churches and in newspapers and schools. Hence, curanderos were needed to provide "good" power to offset "evil" influences.

Kiev (1968) points out that curanderismo persists in the American Southwest because it works in many cases. The advantage the curandero brings to the treatment setting is that he or she works in a subculture supportive of beliefs in the effectiveness of the curandero's methods. Especially important is the anxiety-reducing approach of the curandero, carried out within the context of family and friends, that defines the treatment as therapeutic and positive according to the norms and values of the Mexican-American community. While Anglos may view illness as impersonal and unemotional in origin caused by germs,

[7]Ari Kiev, *Curanderismo: Mexican-American Folk Psychiatry* (New York: The Free Press, 1968), pp. 129–130.

lower-class Mexican-Americans may see illness as related to one's interpersonal relationships, community life, and religion.

American Indian Healers: The Navajos and the Cree

There are few studies of American Indian healers. Exceptions, however, are Jerrold Levy's (1983) research on Navajo health beliefs and practices in Arizona and that of Janice Morse and her associates (1991) among the Cree in Canada. Levy notes that the rituals associated with traditional Navajo religion are predominantly health oriented and stem from an emphasis upon enhancing the well-being of the hunter. The principal figure in these rituals is the *singer*, whose knowledge of ceremonies is obtained through several years of apprenticeship with another practitioner. The singer, who is the most prestigious person among Navajo healers, is the ceremonial leader in rituals that may last several days and are intended to drive out of the body whatever is causing the illness. Diseases, according to traditional beliefs, are thought to be caused by soul loss, witchcraft, spirit possession, or improper behavior such as violating a tribal taboo. The singer is assisted by the *diviner* (or the singer may fill both functions), whose role is to diagnose illness and whose ability is believed to be a special gift. Upon making a diagnosis, the diviner may refer the patient to the singer, who performs the ceremony appropriate for the diagnosis. There are also *herbalists* and *bone setters* in Navajo communities who have knowledge of a practical nature about how to treat various common ailments and injuries.

Levy found that the number of singers has been declining over the years because fewer men (healers are males) are able to devote their time to learning the chants since they also must earn a living. The demands of a wage work economy and education about modern health practices may cause traditional healing to disappear, in Levy's view. Furthermore, the large traditional healing ceremonies last from five to nine nights and involve many guests, which makes the practice expensive for families with limited incomes. Some Navajos have substituted the peyote rituals of the Native American Church for traditional ceremonies, since these rituals serve the same purpose, last only one night, are more economical, and are consistent with basic Navajo beliefs about harmony with nature and the supernatural.

Like black folk healers and curanderos, Navajo healers are primarily concerned with the cause of an illness rather than its symptoms. In fact, Levy found it difficult to determine precisely what role symptoms play in diagnosis. Levy states:

> No Navajo disease is known by the symptoms it produces or by the part of the body it is thought to affect. Rather, there is bear sickness and porcupine sickness, named for the agents thought to cause them; or there is "that which is treated by the Shooting Chant," so named by the ceremonials used to cure it. Because the traditional health culture does not rely upon a knowledge of symptoms in the diagnostic process, Navajo patients often have difficulty understanding the purpose of history taking

and physical examination, a circumstance that often leads to misunder-standing in the clinical setting.[8]

Nevertheless, Navajos do recognize illness by personal discomfort and some symptoms have meaning for them. Also certain types of healing ceremonies are associated with certain symptoms and not others; some ceremonies are used to treat a broad range of symptoms. So knowledge and logic linking causes to solutions are an inherent feature of Navajo medicine and symptoms play a part in deciding upon which ritual is to be used.

Levy indicates that Navajos will often use both native healers and physicians because of the belief that modern medicine will remove symptoms and Navajo medicine will remove the cause of the illness. Among Christian Navajos, the tendency is to combine modern medicine with prayer and not go to native healers. Levy suggests that about half of the Navajo population uses physicians exclusively, about 40 percent use a combination of native healers and physicians, and 10 percent use native practitioners only. Fractures, cuts, and childbirth were treated most often by doctors, while fainting, vague symptoms, or culturally defined illnesses without symptoms were never treated by physicians alone. Since use of native healers conjointly with physicians was common, it was difficult to determine the effectiveness of traditional medicine, but Levy maintained that utilization of native healers was due more to a lack of access to medical facilities and poor communication with doctors than to adherence to native beliefs. The major factor affecting frequency of hospital use, for example, was distance from the hospital on a reservation the size of West Virginia. The declining number of singers, the growing tendency to shorten traditional ceremonies, the gradual replacement of herbalists by physicians among the population, and health education in the schools all point toward a demise in native healing for the Navajos.

In Canada, Janice Morse and her colleagues (Morse, Young, and Swartz 1991) identified five phases in the healing ceremony of the Cree tribe. First, was an initial ritual in which the healer, other people serving as the healer's spiritual helpers, and the patient participated. A ceremonial pipe was passed around three times to all who were present and smoke from a smoldering fungus, sage, or sweetgrass was carried around the room four times in a clockwise direction. This activity was a process of purification intended to open channels of communication to the spirit world and attract the attention of the Great Spirit. Purification is intended to foster a receptive attitude among the participants and place the healer in a position of control. All movements by the healer are clockwise, and like rituals in other native American tribes (Avery 1991) are oriented toward maintaining harmony with nature. Second, came a contract phase in which the patient formally requests healing and the healer agrees to mediate with the Great Spirit on behalf of the patient.

---

[8]Jerrold E. Levy, "Traditional Navajo Health Beliefs and Practices," *Disease Change and the Role of Medicine: The Navajo Experience*, Stephen J. Kunitz, ed. (Berkeley: University of California Press, 1983), p. 132.

Third, was the treatment component. This phase consisted of the patient drinking herbal tea and having a herbal solution applied to his or her skin. Throughout this stage, the healer provides vivid descriptions of what the medicine is doing to the cause of the disease, thereby providing visual imagery intended to facilitate the healing process in the patient's mind. Furthermore, the healer constantly offers reassurance to the patient that the treatment is effective and many people in worse condition have been healed in the past. The final treatment consists of a sweatlodge ceremony in which the patient sits in the dark around a pit of heated rocks and absorbs steam from herbally medicated water that is sprinkled on the stones. The healer sings and occasionally conveys messages to the patient from the spirit world. The fourth phase, which Morse and her colleagues call didactic, consists of the healer educating the patient about the healing process and the effectiveness of the treatment. And, finally, in the fifth phase, closure, the healer ends the healing but assures the patient of the continued healing and support of the Great Spirit.

Cree healing, like folk healing generally, treats the whole person, not just particular symptoms. It is probably very effective at reducing anxiety as the methods are consistent with Cree cultural beliefs. Moreover, the sweatlodge ceremony may be especially helpful for some respiratory ailments. Morse and her colleagues found, however, that the Cree have low rates of physician utilization and relatively poor health.

SUMMARY

This chapter has examined the role and function of alternative healers in American society. Other than osteopaths, such healers continue to maintain themselves because there is a demand for their services. Chiropractors, in fact, represent the second largest category (behind medical doctors) of primary health care practitioners in the United States, but they are not generally accepted by the medical profession. Folk healers work generally among persons from low-income backgrounds and racial minority group status. They provide a service consistent with the cultural beliefs of the people who go to them. Many people combine medicine with prayer, but faith healers actively work to achieve recovery from illness and injury through spiritual means. Some religious groups believe in working with doctors, while a few reject medical treatment as incompatible with their beliefs. Excluding osteopaths, the role and function of alternative healers are to meet the health needs of those persons not met by professional medicine. Generally, these are persons who are not affluent or well educated.

The Sick Role

8

E ach society's definition of illness becomes institutionalized within its cultural patterns, so that one measure of social development is a culture's conception of illness. In primitive societies illness was defined as an autonomous force or "being," such as an evil spirit, which attacked people and settled within their bodies in order to cause them pain or death. During the Middle Ages illness came to be defined as a punishment for sins, and care of the sick was regarded as religious charity. Today illness is defined as a state or condition of suffering as the result of a disease or sickness. This definition is based upon the modern scientific view that an illness is an abnormal biological affliction or mental disorder with a cause, a characteristic train of symptoms, and a method of treatment.

ILLNESS AS DEVIANCE

The medical view of illness is that of deviance from a biological norm of health and feelings of well-being. This view involves the presence of a pathogenic mechanism within the body that can be objectively documented. The diagnosis of a disease, for example, results from a correlation of observable symptoms with knowledge about the physiological functioning of the human being. Ideally, a person is defined as ill when his or her symptoms, complaints, or the results of a physical examination and/or laboratory tests indicate an abnormality. The traditional identifying criteria for disease are (1) the patient's experience of subjective feelings of sickness; (2) the finding by the physician that the patient has a disordered function of the body; and (3) the patient's symptoms conforming to a recognizable clinical pattern. The clinical pattern is a representation of a model or theory of disease held by the diagnostician. In diagnosis, logic is the basic tool.

The physician's function in the treatment of illness involves, first, arriving at a diagnosis and, second, applying remedial action to the health disorder in such a way as to return the patient to as normal a state as possible. The evaluation of illness by the physician contains the medical definition of what is good, desirable, and normal as opposed to what is bad, undesirable, and abnormal. This evaluation is interpreted within the context of existing medical knowledge and the physician's experience. On this basis the medical profession formulates medical rules defining biological deviance and seeks to enforce them by virtue of its authority to treat those persons defined as sick.

In medical sociology, *disease* is considered an adverse physical state, consisting of a physiological dysfunction within an individual; an *illness* is a subjective state, pertaining to an individual's psychological awareness of having a disease and usually causing that person to modify his or her behavior; while *sickness* is a social state, signifying an impaired social role for those who are ill. Although a major area of interest in medical sociology is illness behavior, the concept of sickness is of special interest because it involves analysis of factors that are distinctly sociological—namely, the expectations and normative behavior that the wider society has for people who are defined as sick.

Sickness has typically been viewed by sociologists as a form of deviant behavior. This view was initially formulated by Talcott Parsons (1951) in his concept of the sick role—characteristic behaviors a sick person adopts in accordance with the normative demands of the situation. Parsons saw being sick as a disturbance in the "normal" condition of the human being, both biologically *and* socially. Previously, the sociological study of health and illness had relied upon the medical perspective; efforts were in fact limited to correlating social factors with biological factors based on references provided solely by the health practitioner. This medically oriented approach emphasized the physiological reality of the human organism but neglected the sociological reality that a person is sick when he or she *acts* sick.

The basis for describing illness as a form of deviant behavior lies in the sociological definition of deviance as any act or behavior that violates the social norms within a given social system. Thus, deviant behavior is not simply a variation from a statistical average. Instead, a pronouncement of deviant behavior involves making a *social judgment* about what is right and proper behavior according to a social norm. Norms reflect expectations of appropriate behavior shared by people in specific social settings, or they may be more general expectations of behavior common to a wide variety of social situations. Conformity to prevailing norms is generally rewarded by group acceptance and approval of behavior; deviation from a norm, however, can lead to disapproval of behavior, punishment, or other forms of social sanctions being applied against the offender. Norms allow for variations of behavior within a permissible range, but deviant behavior typically violates the range of permissible behavior and elicits a response from other people intended to control that behavior. Most theories of deviant behavior in sociology are concerned with behavior common in crime, delinquency, mental disorders, alcoholism, and drug addiction. These forms of behavior typically *offend* someone.

It is important to note that not all forms of deviant behavior produce undesirable consequences for a society. Deviance from the usual norms in such fields as art, music, theatre, literature, and dance often provides very positive rewards both for the creative deviant and the society. However, sickness as deviance is typically regarded as an undesirable circumstance for both the sick person and for society. For the sick person, an illness obviously can mean discomfort and either permanent or temporary disruption of normal biological and social functioning, including death. Illness also entails the risk of economic hardship for the sick person's family. For society, illness can mean a reduction in the ability of a social group or organization to carry out its usual tasks and perform its normal social functions.

While sociologists have suggested that the explanation for sickness as a social event can be found outside of biology and medicine by including sickness within the general category of deviant behavior, this approach has been relatively recent. The early causal theories of deviance in sociology were essentially biological models that defined the source of deviance as something inherent in certain individuals. Undesirable behavior was thought to be caused by the genetic inheritance of criminal traits or perhaps a capricious genetic combination. The biological view of deviance has been generally rejected by contemporary sociologists as concentrating exclusively on the physiology of the individual and completely overlooking the implications of social norms and social judgments about an individual's behavior.

In turn, these social judgments are influenced by various aspects of social change. For example, in our past agrarian society, illness occurred largely in small-group contexts such as the family. It was a common occurrence and the roles of being sick or attending sick people were part of a role-set that included expectable variations in behavior as well as "normal" behavior. However, far-reaching changes have occurred in industrialized society: the decline of large families, changing theories in the treatment of disease, and the evolution of complex medical techniques that often require hospitalization. These developments have tended to draw disease out of the area of the expectable into a highly specialized, institutionalized context. Similarly, our methods of dealing with sick people have changed, transferring them to the care of specialists who operate outside the context of the familiar and over whom ordinary people have few powers of control. This transfer itself, coupled with our submission to hospital routines and medical procedures, creates a specialized set of circumstances that lead to a definition of sickness as deviance. The physically sick, like the insane and criminals, represent a social category of people removed from the mainstream of society if their illness is judged severe enough. Of course, the insane and criminals are much more stigmatized by society than the physically sick, but the point is that the pattern of treatment (removal from society and treatment by specialists) allows the person who is physically sick to be similar—though not identical—to an insane person who goes to an asylum or a criminal who goes to prison. Since the methods for dealing with the ill, the criminal, or the insane are in certain respects similar, we can see a basis for defining sickness as deviance.

THE FUNCTIONALIST APPROACH TO DEVIANCE

While sociologists reject biological models of deviance, present-day functionalism, stressing societal-level processes, systems, equilibrium, and interrelationships, represents a modern version of a homeostatic theory of deviance. This model is not organic or physiological. It does not find the causes of deviant behavior in individual needs, drives, instincts, genetic combinations, or any other purely individual patterns. It does find the source of deviant behavior in the relationships between individuals and social systems. This approach is based on the view that society is held together in a state of equilibrium by harmonious patterns of shared norms and values. What makes social life possible is the expectation that people will behave in accordance with the norms and values common to their particular social system. This process is "functional" because it results in social harmony and counterbalances "dysfunctional" processes, like crime and mental illness, that disrupt the social order. The tendency of a society toward self-maintenance through equilibrium is very similar to the biological concept of homeostasis in which the human body attempts to regulate physiological (internal) conditions within a relatively constant range in order to maintain bodily functioning. A person may suffer from warts, indigestion, a broken leg, or perhaps even from a nonmalignant cancer and still be generally healthy. Likewise, a social system is viewed in the functionalist perspective as maintaining social functioning by regulating its various parts within a relatively constant range. A social system may have problems with crime and delinquency but be "healthy" because of its overall capacity to function efficiently.

Because functionalist theorists perceive social systems as composed of various closely interconnected parts, they argue that changes, decisions, and definitions made in one part of the system inevitably affect to some degree all other parts of the system. Thus, a person's position within the social system subjects him or her to events and stresses originating in remote areas of the system. Behavior that is adaptive from one's own perspective and peculiar circumstances—like turning to crime—may be regarded as deviant by society at large. The individual then has the choice of continuing the adaptive behavior and being defined as deviant or trying to change that behavior even though the person sees it as necessary for his or her own survival. Many people, not surprisingly, continue the disapproved behavior and are therefore pressured by society into being deviant. Such people run the risk of confrontation with those authorities, such as psychiatrists, the police, and the courts, charged with controlling or eliminating dysfunctional social processes. Deviance in a social system is thus reduced through the application of social sanctions against the offender. These sanctions include the use of jails, prisons, and mental hospitals to remove the deviant from society to ensure social order and cohesion.

According to functionalist theory, sickness is dysfunctional because it also threatens to interfere with the stability of the social system. The medical profession functions to offset the dysfunctional aspects of sickness by both curing and preventing disease and by establishing technology by which handicapped persons can assist in self-maintenance and in maintenance of the social system. This analytical approach is the basis for Parsons' theory of the sick role, a central concept in medical sociology today.

THE SICK ROLE

Talcott Parsons (1902–1978) introduced his concept of the sick role in his book *The Social System* (1951) which was written to explain a complex functionalist model of society. In this model, social systems were linked to systems of personality and culture to form a basis for social order. Unlike other major social theorists preceding him, Parsons included an analysis of the function of medicine in his theory of society and, in doing so, was led to consider the role of the sick person in relation to the social system within which that person lived. The result is a concept that represents the most consistent approach to explaining the behavior characteristic of sick people in Western society.

Parsons' concept of the sick role is based on the assumption that being sick is not a deliberate and knowing choice of the sick person, though illness may occur as a result of motivated exposure to infection or injury. Thus, while the criminal is thought to violate social norms because he or she "wants to," the sick person is considered deviant only because he or she "cannot help it." Parsons warns, however, that some people may be attracted to the sick role in order to have their lapse of normal responsibilities approved. Generally, society accounts for the distinction between deviant roles by punishing the criminal and providing therapeutic care for the sick. Both processes function to reduce deviancy and change conditions that interfere with conformity to social norms. Both processes also require the intervention of social agencies, law enforcement or medicine, in order to control deviant behavior. Being sick, Parsons argues, is not just experiencing the physical condition of a sick state; rather, it constitutes a social role because it involves behavior based on institutional expectations and reinforced by the norms of society corresponding to these expectations.

A major expectation concerning the sick is that they are unable to take care of themselves. It thus becomes necessary for the sick to seek medical advice and cooperate with medical experts. This behavior is predicated upon the assumption made by Parsons that being sick is an undesirable state and the sick person wants to get well.

Parsons insists that sickness is dysfunctional because it represents a mode of response to social pressure that permits the evasion of social responsibilities. A person may desire to retain the sick role more or less permanently because of what Parsons calls a "secondary gain," which is the exemption from normal obligations and the gaining of other privileges commonly accorded to the sick. Hence, medical practice becomes a mechanism by which a social system seeks to control the illnesses of its deviant sick by returning them to as normal state of functioning as possible.

The specific aspects of Parsons' concept of the sick role can be described in four basic categories:

1. *The sick person is exempt from "normal" social roles.* An individual's illness is grounds for his or her exemption from normal role performance and social responsibilities. This exemption, however, is relative to the nature and severity of the illness. The more severe the illness, the greater the exemption. Exemption requires legitimation by the physician as the authority on what constitutes sickness. Legitimation serves the social function of protecting society against malingering.
2. *The sick person is not responsible for his or her condition.* An individual's illness is usually thought to be beyond his or her own control. A morbid condition of the body needs to be changed and some curative process apart from personal will power or motivation is needed to get well.
3. *The sick person should try to get well.* The first two aspects of the sick role are conditional on the third aspect, which is recognition by the sick person that being sick is undesirable. Exemption from normal responsibilities is temporary and conditional upon the desire to regain normal health. Thus, the sick person has an obligation to get well.
4. *The sick person should seek technically competent help and cooperate with the physician.* The obligation to get well involves a further obligation on the part of the sick person to seek technically competent help, usually from a physician. The sick person is also expected to cooperate with the physician in the process of trying to get well.

Parsons' concept of the sick role is based on the classical social theory of Emile Durkheim and Max Weber and the psychoanalytic theory of Sigmund Freud and especially Franz Alexander (Gerhardt 1989a, 1989b, 1989c). Psychoanalytic theories of the structure of the personality (id, ego, and superego) and the unconscious assisted Parsons in developing his thoughts on individual motivation. The sick person is presumably motivated to recover (as a result of socialization and the influence of the superego) and yet may perhaps also be motivated, either consciously or unconsciously, to desire the "secondary gain" of privileges and exemptions from daily tasks that accompany the sick role.

Durkheim's ideas on the function of moral authority and Weber's views on religious values are utilized by Parsons in describing the role of the physician. The physician, according to Parsons, is invested with the function of social control. This function, similar to that provided historically by priests and which originated in religion, is intended for the control of deviance. In this case, illness with its dysfunctional nature is the deviance. The designation of illness as an undesirable and illegitimate state is considered by Parsons to have the greatest implications for the healthy in that it reinforces their motivation to stay well. All of this is reflected in the position of health as an important social value in American society and the manner in which people are socialized to accept this value. By incorporating a consideration of health and illness into his analysis of social systems, Parsons was the first to demonstrate the function of medicine as a form of social control and did so within the parameters of classical sociological theory.

The Physician–Patient Role Relationship

A major contribution of Parsons' concept of the sick role is its description of a patterned set of expectations that define the norms and values appropriate to being sick in Western culture, both for the individual and for others who interact with the sick person. The sick role thus views the patient–physician relationship within a framework of social roles, attitudes, and activities that both parties bring to the situation. This allows us, with some exceptions, both to understand and predict the behavior of the ill in Western society. The patient–physician role, like all other roles, involves a basic mutuality; that is, each participant in the social situation is expected to be familiar with both his or her own and others' expectations of behavior and the probable sequence of social acts to be followed. *The sick role evokes a set of patterned expectations that define the norms and values appropriate to being sick, both for the individual and for others who interact with the person.* Neither party can define his or her role independently of the role partner. The full meaning of "acting like a physician" depends on the patient's conception of what a physician is in terms of the social role. The physician's role is, as Parsons tells us, to return the sick person to his or her normal state of functioning.

The role of the patient likewise depends on the conception the physician holds of the patient's role. According to Parsons, the patient is expected to recognize that being sick is unpleasant and that he or she has an obligation to get well by seeking the physician's help. The patient-physician role relationship is therefore not a spontaneous form of social interaction. It is a well-defined encounter consisting of two or more persons whose object is the health of a single individual. It is also a situation that is too important to be left to undefined forms of behavior; for this reason, patients and physicians tend to act in a stable and predictable manner.

The patient–physician relationship is intended by society to be therapeutic in nature. The patient has a need for technical services from the physician, and the physician is the technical expert who is qualified and defined by society as prepared to help the patient. The goal of the patient–physician encounter is thus to promote some significant change for the better in the patient's health.

Although the patient–physician relationship involves mutuality in the form of behavioral expectations, the status and power of the parties are not equal. The role of the physician is based upon an imbalance of power and technical expertise favorable exclusively to the physician. This imbalance is necessary because the physician needs leverage in his or her relationship with the patient in order to promote positive changes in the patient's health. Accomplishment of this goal sometimes requires procedures that can be painful or discomforting to the patient, yet the patient must accept and follow the treatment plan if the physician is to be effective. The physician exercises leverage through three basic techniques: (1) professional prestige, (2) situational authority, and (3) situational dependency of the patient. A physician's professional prestige rests upon technical qualifications and certification by society as a healer. The physician's situational power, on the other hand, refers to the physician's having what the patient wants and needs. By contrast, the patient is dependent because he or she lacks the expertise required to treat the health disorder.

The role of the physician is also enhanced by a certain mystique reflecting faith in the power to heal. This aspect of the physician role results from the dependence of the patient on the physician for life and death decisions. Since the physician has the responsibility to "do everything possible" and because the survival of the patient may be at issue, the patient may be likely to regard the physician with a strong emotional attachment in the hope or belief that the physician has a "gift" or natural skill in the healing arts. Since medical practice is sometimes characterized by uncertainty, a physician's presumed talent can be a very important dimension in the patient–physician relationship. Exact proof of the existence of many minor ailments and most chronic diseases is either not possible, or attempts to establish such proof may not be justifiable because of the hazards to the patient involved in the investigation. Despite the great advancement of the science of medicine during the twentieth century, the physician must still sometimes act on the basis of a hunch.

An interesting analog to the patient–physician relationship is the child–parent relationship. For some people an illness can foster a childlike state of dependency. However, while the role of the child is an immature role, the role of the patient represents a "disturbed" maturity (Wilson 1970). Both the child and the sick person lack the capacity to perform the usual functions of the adult in everyday life, and both are dependent on a stronger and more adequate person to take care of them. Also the physician can be like a parent figure in that he or she provides support and controls rewards significant to the dependent party. The primary reward for the child would be approval, while the primary reward for the sick person would be to get well. Yet the physician and the parent are unlike in the magnitude of their involvement with the dependent party and the depth of their emotional feelings. Obviously, the states of childhood and patienthood are not totally similar, yet the similarity is a striking one because the extremely sick person who is helpless, technically incompetent in treating his or her disorder, and perhaps emotionally disturbed over his or her condition of illness can be very dependent and fully capable of acting in childlike ways.

According to Eliot Freidson (1970a:206), physicians create the social possibilities for acting sick because they are society's authority on what "illness really is." They decide who is sick and what should be done about it. In essence, physicians are "gatekeepers" to most professional health resources since these resources (such as prescription drugs and hospitals) cannot be used without their permission. Thus, Friedson argues that the behavior of the physician and others in the health field constitutes the embodiment of certain dominant values in society. These dominant values were described by Parsons (1951, 1979) and include the idea that health is positive and should be sought after. Stipulated in his concept of the sick role is that the sick person is expected to cooperate with the physician and *work* to achieve his or her own recovery and return to normal functioning.

Medicine as an Institution of Social Control

Besides Parsons' analytical insight into the ramifications of the patient–physician relationship, implicit in his concept of the sick role is the idea that medicine is (and should be) an institution for the social control of deviant behavior. Some medical sociologists (Conrad 1975; Conrad and Schneider 1980; Freidson 1970a; Twaddle 1969; Zola 1972) have expressed concern that medicine is indeed an institution for the control of deviance and is taking responsibility for an ever greater proportion of behaviors defined as deviant. In other words, acts that might have been defined as sin or crime and controlled by the church or the law are increasingly regarded as illnesses to be controlled through medical care. Thomas Szasz explains this trend as follows:

> Starting with such things as syphilis, tuberculosis, typhoid fever, and carcinomas and fractures we have created the class, "illness." At first, this class was composed of only a few items all of which shared the common feature of reference to a state of disordered structure or function of the human body as a physical-chemical machine. As time went on additional items were added to this class. They were not added, however, because they were newly discovered bodily disorders. The physician's attention has been deflected from this criterion and has become focused instead on disability and suffering as new criteria for selection. Thus, at first slowly, such things as hysteria, hypochondriasis, obsessive-compulsive neurosis and depression were added to the category of illness. Then with increasing zeal, physicians and especially psychiatrists began to call "illness"... anything and everything in which they could detect any sign of malfunctioning, based on no matter what the norm. Hence agoraphobia is illness because one should not be afraid of open spaces. Homosexuality is an illness because heterosexuality is the social norm. Divorce is illness because it signals failure of marriage.[1]

If Szasz', view is correct, there appears to be a long-term trend toward making sickness and deviance not only synonymous but also toward treating deviance exclusively in a medical mode. Eliot Freidson (1970a) has argued that medicine has established a jurisdiction far wider than justified by its demonstrable capacity to "cure." Nonetheless, the medical profession has been highly successful in gaining authority to define deviant behavior as illness—behavior properly handled only by the physician. Andrew Twaddle (1973:756) points out that "today

---

[1]Thomas S. Szasz, *The Myth of Mental Illness*, rev. ed. (New York: Harper & Row, 1974), pp. 44–45.

there are few, if any, problems of human behavior that some group does not think of as medical problems."

According to Bryan Turner (1984, 1987, 1992), regulation of the human body is in the interest of society because of the need to protect public health, the economy, and the social order. Turner notes that disease can be contained through social hygiene and education in appropriate lifestyles. Yet people can also knowingly jeopardize their health through habits like drug addiction, overeating, smoking, lack of exercise, and alcoholism. These behaviors, he continues, are either already regarded as socially deviant or are well on the way to becoming regarded as such. When certain behavior threatens the health of people and the well-being of society, the state may be required to intervene, such as banning cigarette smoking from public places. Consequently, it is Turner's (1984:226) position that "medicine is essentially social medicine, because it is a practice which regulates social activities under the auspices of the state." Therefore, to the extent that the control of human behavior is the basis of social organization and to the extent that the control of deviant behavior is becoming the function of the medical profession, Parsons' concept of the sick role helps us understand contemporary mechanisms of social stability.

Research Applications of the Sick Role

Parsons' concept of the sick role, as Freidson (1970a:228) has explained, represents "a penetrating and apt analysis of sickness from a distinctly sociological point of view." This comment is particularly appropriate when it is recognized that the sick role has stimulated a considerable body of research in medical sociology. To mention only a few such studies, Paul Chalfant and Richard Kurtz (1971) utilized Parsons' sick role concept in explaining social workers' denial of the sick role to alcoholics. Social workers in this study felt that drinking was motivated behavior and that alcoholics could avoid their disorder if they desired to do so. Hence, the alcoholic was not entitled to exemption from normal responsibilities.

Another application of the sick role is found in Stephen Cole and Robert LeJeune's (1972) study of welfare mothers. Cole and LeJeune observed that among welfare mothers in New York City the general norm was to accept the dominant cultural view that being on welfare is a result of personal failure. Welfare mothers who had given up hope of getting off welfare were prone to adopt the sick role in order to legitimize their self-defined failure. This study concluded that the sick role may provide a "substitute" status by way of exemption from normal role responsibilities for persons who lack other socially approved statuses. What is implied here is that certain people may use the sick role because it is less stigmatizing than being regarded a failure.

A similar finding was noted in a study by Arnold Arluke, Louanne Kennedy, and Ronald Kessler (1979) of 1,000 patients discharged from two large New York City hospitals. Arluke and his colleagues found that low-income and elderly patients are most likely to agree that a person has the right not to be held responsible for his or her illness. For some elderly people, it was believed that the sick role provided a sense of legitimacy for an otherwise dependent state. Consequently, these elderly people were most unwilling to give up the role. Younger people were most likely to agree that a person has the duty to try to get well. In other research, Fredric and Sally Wolinsky (1981) found in a rural North Carolina county that those who expect sick-role legitimation are older, have relatively lower socioeconomic status, and perceive themselves in poor health. In Illinois, the author and his associates (Cockerham et al. 1980) studied the manner in which physicians treated their own minor ailments. The doctors tended to adopt aspects of the sick role by engaging in actions requiring a physician (or, in this case, being one), such as taking prescription drugs or ordering diagnostic tests on themselves. This finding suggests that both physicians and the public often act in a similar manner when dealing with their own physical discomforts. By treating their symptoms in a medical mode requiring some degree of physician skills, physicians are implying that patients should obtain similar services.

CRITICISM OF THE SICK ROLE

Although Parsons' concept of the sick role has demonstrated research utility as a framework for explaining illness-related behavior and has become a basic concept in medical sociology, the model has some serious defects which have led a few sociologists to suggest that it should be abandoned (Berkanovic 1972; Kosa and Robertson 1969). Gerald Gordon (1966) has pointed out that, while widely accepted, Parsons' sick role concept is not based upon systematic observation and has not been empirically validated. Gordon states that the sick role concept has been accepted primarily because of its prima facie reasonableness and logical construction.

Parsons' sick role theory can be criticized because of (1) behavioral variation, (2) types of diseases, (3) the patient–physician relationship, and (4) the sick role's middle-class orientation.

Behavioral Variation

Much of the criticism of the sick role theory has been directed toward its lack of uniformity among various persons and social groups. David Mechanic (1962a), for example, has suggested that age, sex, and the importance of social roles and learned responses to symptoms vary among individuals. In a 1964 study of illness behavior among children, he found important sex and age differences in attitudes toward illness. Boys appeared to have more stoical attitudes toward illness than girls, and older children appeared to have more stoical attitudes than younger children.

In a random sample of people living in New York City, Gordon (1966) found at least two distinct and unrelated statuses and complementary role expectations associated with being sick. When a prognosis was believed to be serious and uncertain, expectations of behavior generally conformed to Parsons' description of the sick role; however, when a prognosis was known and not serious, the notion of an "impaired role" emerged from Gordon's data, which required normal role responsibilities and rejected role exemptions despite sickness.

Twaddle (1969) reported at least seven configurations of the sick role, with Parsons' model being only one, in a study of Rhode Island married couples in late middle age. The exact configuration of the alternative sick roles discovered by Twaddle depended in part on cultural values and whether a person defined himself or herself as "sick." Not only were there differing personal definitions of "being sick," but also not all of the respondents stated they expected to get well and not all of them cooperated with the physician. Twaddle found that the sick role, as defined by Parsons, was much more applicable to Jews than to either Protestants or Italian Catholics. Jews were more likely to see themselves as being sick, as expecting to get well, and as cooperating with the physician. Protestants were the most resistant to seeing a physician, and Italian Catholics were generally the least cooperative with the physician. There were also other important ethno-cultural differences in the Twaddle study. Protestants, for example, were much more likely to regard functional incapacity (usually an inability to work) as the first sign of illness, while Italian Catholics were more likely to emphasize changes in feeling states such as pain. Jews, however, tended to emphasize fear of eventual outcomes rather than feeling states or functional incapacities.

A well-known study by Mark Zborowski (1952) demonstrated important group differences pertaining to pain. While pain is clearly a biological phenomenon, Zborowski observed that responses to pain are not always biological but vary among ethno-cultural groups. Zborowski's sample consisted of eighty-seven male patients and sixteen healthy males in New York City who were primarily of Jewish, Italian, and "Old American" ethnic backgrounds. The so-called Old Americans were defined as white, native-born, and usually Protestant patients whose families had lived at least two generations in the United States; they also did not identify with any particular foreign nationality. All of the patients suffered from neurological ailments, such as herniated discs or spinal lesions, which represented disorders where the pain involved would vary only within fairly narrow limits.

Although the level of pain was thought to be generally similar, Zborowski found significant variation in the responses to pain. Jews and Italians tended to be more sensitive to pain and more prone to exaggerate the experience of pain than Old Americans. While Jews and Italians were similar in responding to pain in the hospital, the two ethnic groups differed in the home setting. At home the Italian acted strong and authoritative, but in the hospital he was highly emotional. The Jewish patient was emotional in both settings. Zborowski observed that Jewish patients also used their suffering as a device for manipulating the behavior of others. But once satisfied that adequate care was being provided, the Jewish patient tended to become more restrained in his response.

In contrast, the Old American patients tried to conform to the medical image of the ideal patient. They cooperated with hospital personnel and avoided being a nuisance as much as possible. The Old American patients also avoided expressing pain in public, and when examined by the physician they tended to assume the role of a detached observer by becoming unemotional and attempting to provide an efficient description of their internal state to aid in a correct diagnosis. If their pain was too much for them to control, they would withdraw to their rooms and express their pain privately.

The attitudes toward pain also varied. Zborowski reported that Italians were more concerned with the discomfort of the pain itself and were relatively satisfied and happy when immediate relief was provided. The Italian patient also tended to display a confident attitude toward the physician. The Jewish patient, however, was not particularly confident about his physician, and he seemed to be more concerned about the significance of his pain for his general state of health rather than about any specific and immediate discomfort. While Italian patients sought pain killers, Jewish patients were reluctant to take drugs because they were apprehensive about the habit-forming characteristics of the drugs. The Old Americans, like the Jews, were also primarily concerned about what pain signified for their general state of health, but unlike the Jews, they were optimistic about the power of medicine and its ability to provide a cure. Hence, they displayed great confidence in the decisions made by the physicians.

In an effort to explain these ethno-cultural differences, Zborowski offered the opinion that Jewish and Italian mothers demonstrated overprotective and overemotional attitudes about their sons' health and that this socialization experience fostered the development of anxieties regarding pain among the Jewish and Italian patients. Zborowski believed that Jewish and Italian parents had tended to prevent physical injury to their sons by prohibiting them from playing rough games and sports, whereas Old American parents, on the other hand, had socialized their sons to expect to get hurt in sports and to fight back. Old American boys were taught "not to be sissies," "not to cry," and "to take pain like a man." If such a child were actually injured, he was expected not to get emotional but to seek proper treatment immediately.

Research by John Campbell (1978) involving a sample of 264 children and their mothers in Washington, D.C., supports Zborowski's findings in regard to the responses of the Old Americans. Although Campbell did not focus on the role of ethnicity, his data showed that those children who were older and whose parents were of higher socioeconomic background tended to take a "stiff-upper-lip" or "business-as-usual" approach to illness. "This Spartan orientation," says Campbell (1978:46), "bears more than a passing resemblance to the responses to pain that Zborowski described as typifying his 'Old American' subjects—responses that tended to be approved by members of the medical profession—who themselves, perhaps not coincidently, would be assigned to higher SES [socioeconomic status] levels." According to Campbell, parents *do* make a difference when it comes to socializing their children to handle their emotions and reject the sick role.

As for other studies of ethnic variation, Irving Zola's (1966) comparison of American patients of Irish, Italian, and Anglo-Saxon descent at two hospitals in Boston also supported Zborowski's findings. In general, the Italians tended to dramatize their symptoms, while Zola found that the Irish would often deny their symptoms and the Anglo-Saxons would speak of their health problems in a detached and neutral manner lacking in anxiety. Zola concluded that there were indeed distinct differences between cultural groups and the way in which they communicated complaints about their health.

Besides ethnic variation, there may be other ways in which people interpret the sick role. One study has shown that, among heart patients having surgery, women tend to adopt the sick role more frequently than men and to be less ready to resume their work roles after surgery (Brown and Rawlinson 1977). Thus, there may be differences by sex in regard to acceptance of the sick role as well. Emil Berkanovic (1972) studied sick role conceptions among Los Angeles city employees. Although his sample cannot claim to be representative of city employees generally, his findings do suggest that some people feel they are able to define appropriate illness behavior under certain circumstances. These people do not reject medical theories of illness, but simply feel competent to decide what is the correct behavior for the sick person, provided the symptoms are recognized and the outcome of the illness is known. Berkanovic points out that often the physician is consulted only as a last resort and only after all other sources of health information fail to provide an adequate explanation.

What is indicated by all of these studies is that Parsons' concept of the sick role does not account for all of the considerable variations in the way people view sickness and define appropriate sick role behavior for themselves and others.

Type of Disease

The second major category of criticism regarding Parsons' concept of the sick role is that it seems to apply only to acute diseases, which by their nature are temporary, usually recognizable by laypersons, and readily overcome with a physician's help. Yet chronic diseases, such as cancer and heart disease, are by definition not temporary, and often the patient cannot be expected to get well as Parsons' model suggests, no matter how willing the patient may be to cooperate with the physician. Therefore, temporary exemptions from normal role responsibilities for the chronic patient are both inappropriate and perhaps impossible.

Research on patients with chronic disorders (Kassebaum and Baumann 1965) has shown that they perceive the sick role differently from patients with acute illnesses. Chronic patients were faced with the impossibility of resuming normal roles and the necessity of adjusting their activities to a permanent health disorder. However, in a reconsideration of the sick role, Parsons (1975) argued that even if the goal of a complete recovery is impractical, many chronic diseases can be "managed" so that the patient is able to maintain a relatively normal pattern of physiological and social functioning. While diabetes, for example, cannot be cured in the sense that pneumonia can, Parsons insists that a chronic disease like diabetes should not be placed in a totally different category from that of "curable" diseases if the patient can be returned to a normal range of functioning. True, this explanation may allow the sick role concept to account for some chronic disorders; still it cannot be applied to a wide range of illness situations such as the bedridden patient or the terminally ill patient.

Problems also arise in applying the sick role to the mentally ill, in that while the sick role stipulates a person should seek professional care, people who go to psychiatrists for help may be stigmatized for doing just that (Segall 1976). People who admit to a history of mental illness often have problems finding jobs, and a considerable body of research literature describes the difficulties former mental patients have in coping with rejection from other people. In addition, many mental hospital patients refuse to accept the idea that they are mentally ill and most patients, rather than voluntarily seeking help, are admitted to mental institutions involuntarily (Cockerham 1992).

Patient–Physician Role Relationship

A third major area of criticism of Parsons' sick role model is that it is based upon a traditional one-to-one interaction between a patient and a physician. This form of interaction is common because the usual setting is the physician's office, where Parsons' version of the sick role is conceptualized. It is the setting where the physician has maximum control. Yet quite different patterns of interaction may emerge in the hospital, where perhaps a team of physicians and other members of the hospital staff are involved. In the hospital the physician is one of several physicians and is subject to organizational constraints and policies. If the patient is at home, the patient–physician relationship may also again vary because the patient and his or her family can much more clearly influence the interaction.

In addition, the pattern of relationships outlined in Parsons' sick role is modified if the client is a target of preventive techniques rather than strictly therapeutic measures. A considerable portion of contemporary medical practice is concerned not with restoring a single patient to normal social functioning but with maintaining and improving public health. The patient–physician relationship is different when the target is a group of individuals, particularly if the health problem is not a disabling illness but a behavioral problem such as smoking cigarettes or an environmental problem such as water or air pollution. In this situation the physician or health practitioner must usually be persuasive rather than authoritative, since he or she lacks the leverage to control the client group. The physician must convince the group that certain actions, such as physical examinations or X-ray examinations for tuberculosis, are good for them. In defense of Parsons' sick role, however, it should be noted that the behavior needing to be changed in such cases is often "normal" rather than "sick."

Middle-Class Orientation

Finally, it should be noted that Parsons' sick role model is a middle-class pattern of behavior. It emphasizes the merits of individual responsibility and the deliberate striving toward good health and a return to normality. It is oriented to the middle-class assumption that rational problem solving is the only viable behavior in the face of difficulty and that effort will result in positive gain. It fails to take into account what it is like to live in an environment of poverty where success is the exception to the rule.

Also, many people in the lower socioeconomic classes may tend to deny the sick role, not only because they may not have the opportunity to enjoy typically middle-class secondary gains but also because the functional incapacity of the poor person may render him or her less likely to be able to earn a living or survive in conditions of poverty (Kassebaum and Baumann 1965; Kosa, Antonovsky, and Zola 1969). Therefore, people living in a poverty environment might work, regardless of how sick they might be, as long as they feel able to perform some of their work activities.

Yet it should be noted that even though the notion of "striving toward good health" reflects a middle-class orientation, the lower class uses the sick role to justify their disadvantaged social position (Arluke, Kennedy, and Kessler 1979; Cole and LeJeune 1972). That is, some poor people claim they are poor because they are sick, and being sick (and poor) is not their fault. While being sick and working to get well may be typical of the middle class, being sick and using the sick role to excuse one's circumstances in life appear frequently among the lower class.

Parsons' Sick Role: Conclusion

Despite the considerable criticism of Parsons' sick role concept found in sociological literature, the reader should note that this model represents a significant contribution to medical sociology. Parsons insists that illness is a form of deviance and that as such it is necessary for a society to return the sick to their normal social functioning. Thus, Parsons views medicine as a mechanism by which a society attempts to control deviance and maintain social stability. In light of the trend toward classifying more and more social problems as medical problems, Parsons' explanation of the function of medicine has broad implications for the future treatment of deviants in our society.

While recognizing that some criticisms of Parsons' theory are valid, we should note that at least some of this criticism is based upon a misunderstanding of Parsons. Apparently some critics incorrectly assume that Parsons viewed the sick role as a fixed, mechanical kind of "cage" that would produce similarities of behavior among sick people regardless of variant cultural backgrounds and different personal learning experiences. Instead, what Parsons has given us is an "ideal type" of the sick role. By definition, ideal types do not exist in reality. They are abstractions, erected by emphasizing selected aspects of behavior typical in certain contexts, and they serve as bases for comparing and differentiating concrete behaviors occurring in similar situations in different sociocultural circumstances. Perhaps Eugene Gallagher (1976) said it best when he pointed out that whoever acquires a sociologically informed understanding of health and illness in contemporary society soon realizes how significantly sociological analysis has benefited from Parsons' formulation of the sick role and how, in comparison, many criticisms of it seem petty.

Therefore, it can be concluded that Parsons' model is a useful and viable framework of sociological analysis within certain contexts. Although the theory is an insufficient explanation of all illness behavior, it does describe many general similarities and should not be abandoned. In fact, writing in a later article, Parsons (1975) admitted that he did not believe it was ever his intention to make his concept cover the whole range of phenomena associated with the sick role. Two possibilities exist: (1) Using the model as an "ideal type" with which various forms of illness behavior can be contrasted or (2) expanding the concept to account for conditions generally common to most illness situations.

LABELING THEORY

By failing to account for the behavioral variations within the sick role, the functionalist approach to illness has neglected the various aspects of acting sick. Chapter 6, on illness behavior, pointed out that two people having much the same symptoms may behave quite differently. One person may become concerned and seek medical treatment, while another person may ignore the symptoms completely. Z. Lipowski (1970) has noted that individual strategies in coping with illness vary from passive cooperation to positive action to get well and from fear at being diagnosed as ill to actual pleasure in anticipation of secondary gains. Several writers, Freidson (1970a) in particular, have taken the position that illness as deviant behavior is relative and must be seen as such; this is the perspective of labeling theory.

Labeling theory is based on the concept that what is regarded as deviant behavior by one person or social group may not be so regarded by other persons or social groups. Howard Becker (1973), one of the leading proponents of labeling theory, illustrates the concept in his study of marijuana users. His analysis reveals a discrepancy in American society between those people who insist that smoking marijuana is harmful and that use of the drug should be illegal, and those who support a norm favoring marijuana smoking and who believe that use of the drug should be legalized. While the wider society views marijuana smoking as deviant, groups of marijuana smokers view their behavior as socially acceptable within their own particular group.

Becker's position is that deviance is created by social groups who make rules or norms. Infractions of these rules or norms constitute deviant behavior. Accordingly, deviance is not a quality of the act a person commits, but instead is a consequence of the definition applied to that act by other people. The critical variable in understanding deviance is the social audience, because the audience determines what is and what is not deviant behavior.

The applicability of labeling theory as a vehicle for explaining illness behavior is that, while disease may be a biological state existing independently of human knowledge, sickness is a social state created and formed by human perception. Thus, as Freidson (1970a) has pointed out, when a veterinarian diagnoses a cow's condition as an illness, the diagnosis itself does not change the cow's behavior. But when a physician diagnoses a human's condition as illness, the diagnosis can and often does change the sick person's behavior. Thus, illness is seen by labeling theorists as a condition created by human beings in accordance with their understanding of the situation.

For example, among the Kuba people of Sumatra, skin diseases and injuries to the skin are quite common because of a difficult jungle environment (Sigerist 1960). A person suffering from a skin disease would not be considered to be sick among the Kuba because the condition, while unhealthy, is not considered abnormal. In parts of Africa, such afflictions as hookworms may not be considered abnormal because of their prevalence. Margaret Clark (1959) points out that among the Mexican-Americans in her study conducted in the southwestern United States, such disorders as diarrhea and coughing were so common they were considered "normal," though not necessarily good. Examples such as these have led to the realization that an essentially unhealthy state may not always be equated with illness when the people involved are able to function effectively and the presence of the disorder does not affect the normal rhythm of daily life. Therefore, judgments concerning what is sickness and what is deviant behavior are relative and cannot be separated from the social situations in which people live.

Labeling Theory and Illness Behavior

Labeling theory has so far failed to develop a theory of illness behavior comparable to Parsons' model. The closest equivalent deriving from the symbolic interactionist view (labeling theory) is that of Eliot Freidson (1970a). Freidson indicates that the key to distinguishing among sick roles is the notion of legitimacy. He maintains that in illness states, there are three types of legitimacy, which involve either a minor or serious deviation. (1) *Conditional legitimacy*, where the deviants are temporarily exempted from normal obligations and gain some extra privileges on the proviso that they seek help in order to rid themselves of their deviance. A cold would be a minor deviation and pneumonia serious in this category. (2) *Unconditional legitimacy*, where the deviants are exempted permanently from normal obligations and are granted additional privileges in view of the hopeless nature of their deviance. Terminal cancer falls in this category. (3) *Illegitimacy*, where the deviants are exempted from some normal obligations by virtue of their deviance, for which they are technically not responsible, but gain few if any privileges and take on handicaps such as stigma. A stammer would be minor and epilepsy serious.

Freidson's classification system implies that there are different consequences for the individual and that his or her treatment by other people depends on the label of definition applied to the deviant's health disorder by others. Freidson's model accounts for the problematic aspects of illness relative to social situations. A person with a skin disease in the Kuba tribe or a person with hookworms in Africa could be classified as unconditionally legitimate, for example, because the afflicted person would gain no special privileges or changes in obligations since the disorder would be common to most people who functioned normally in their society. A person with cancer, on the other hand, would gain a permanent exemption from normal obligations because of his or her condition.

Freidson's concept, however, is strictly theoretical and has not been extensively tested. Whether it can account for variations in illness behavior is therefore still a matter of speculation. While Freidson's model is useful in categorizing illness behavior, it fails to explain differences in the way people define themselves as being sick and in need of professional medical care. The merit of Freidson's model, on the other hand, is that it does go beyond Parsons' concept of the sick role by describing different types of illness and by pointing out that illness is a socially created label.

Criticism of Labeling Theory

The labeling approach stresses that judgments of what is deviance are relative, depending upon the perceptions of others. Therefore, the critical variable in understanding deviant behavior is the social audience that has knowledge of the act in question because the audience determines what is and what is not deviance. But despite its merits in providing a framework to analyze the variety of perceptions people may hold about deviance, labeling theory contains some shortcomings.

First, labeling theory does not explain what causes deviance other than the reaction of other people to it. Few would deny that groups create deviance when they establish norms. Admittedly, the reaction of an "audience" to variant types of behavior influences the individual's self-concept and also influences society's response. But a label in itself does not cause deviance. Some situations— murder, burglary, drug addiction, and suicide—are generally defined by most people as deviant, yet people do these things regardless of how they are labeled, and their reasons for doing so may have nothing to do with the label that is attached to them. Second, if deviant acts and actors share common characteristics other than societal reaction, these common characteristics are not defined or explained. Yet people committing deviant acts may share many similarities such as stress, poverty, age, peer group relations, and family background. These characteristics may be as important as, if not more important than, the reaction of the social audience. Jack Gibbs (1971) thus raises the important question of *what* is being explained by labeling theory—deviant behavior or *reactions* to deviant behavior? Third, labeling theory does not explain why certain people commit deviant acts and others in the same circumstances do not. All this seems to pose the question of whether societal reaction alone is sufficient to explain deviant behavior; the answer seems to be that it is not. In a later reconsideration, Becker (1973: 179) agreed that labeling theory "cannot possibly be considered as the sole explanation of what alleged deviants actually do."

Labeling Theory: Conclusion

When compared to Parsons' concept of the sick role, labeling theory does address itself to the specific variations in illness behavior that seem to be present among differing socioeconomic and ethno-cultural groups in American society.

It also provides a framework of analysis for illness behavior according to the definition and perception of particular social groups and allows the social scientist to account for differences between social settings and types of illnesses as well. Over and against these advantages, labeling theory suffers from vagueness in its conceptualization, namely, what causes deviance other than societal reaction—which has little or nothing to do with disease. While Freidson's model has potential, it has not attracted the attention accorded to Parsons' sick role. But most important, there is serious doubt whether societal reactions in and of themselves are sufficient to explain the generalities of behavior occurring among the sick.

SICKNESS AS SOCIAL DEVIANCE?

This chapter discussed the various approaches to sickness as deviance. The question remains whether this perspective of sickness is useful or adequate for sociological studies. The conceptualization of sickness as deviant behavior does make sickness a sociologically relevant variable, but it also restricts the analysis of sickness to the framework of a social event. This is in accord with the major intention of the sickness-as-deviance perspective in sociology—to focus exclusively on the social properties of being ill and thus to exclude biological properties definable only by the physician. Yet by dwelling exclusively on the social properties of sickness, the deviance perspective severely limits its capacity to deal with the biological aspects of sickness as a condition of suffering.

It can also be argued that, while deviance is behavior contrary to the normative expectations of society, sickness itself does not counteract social norms (Pflanz and Rohde 1970). The members of any society are expected to become ill now and then during their lives. Accordingly, if sickness is deviance and since deviance is regarded as a violation of expectations of behavior, it would be necessary to assume that society expects people not to become ill, just as it expects them not to commit a crime or become a homosexual or drug addict. People who are sick are different from the norm of wellness, but this situation does not make them bad which the concept of deviance implies.

However, when people are sick they are not themselves. They are different (abnormal) in a negative sort of way that most people would prefer to avoid—just as they would like to avoid going to prison. Not only do sick people feel bad, but they may be physically disabled as well. They may also experience mental dysfunctions. According to Eric Cassell (1985), people with serious physical illnesses often lose their sense of perspective and are unable to think about situations from more than a single viewpoint. Their ability to reason and make decisions may change and they may become heavily dependent upon doctors and others to take care of them. They may also become so self-absorbed and childlike that they focus exclusively on themselves and ignore the outside world.

Kathy Charmaz (1983, 1991) has suggested that the chronically ill also experience a negative sense of self because their illness restricts their activities, isolates them from other people, discredits them by lessening their sense of worth, and causes them to be a burden to others. Some persons may, in fact, feel stigmatized as a result of their illness as seen in accounts of persons with physical handicaps (Zola 1982), Parkinson's disease (Lefton 1984), epilepsy (Scambler and Hopkins 1986), and other problems like diabetes, end-stage renal disease, and multiple sclerosis (Roth and Conrad 1987). Effects such as these would seem to place the ill in a position of deviance with respect to their sense of self, relations with other people, and role in society.

Therefore, when the sick role is considered along with society's method of dealing with the sick (that is, placing them under the control of doctors, putting them in hospitals), the concept of sickness as deviance may well apply. In the absence of other theoretical concepts in medical sociology that would provide a better approach to understanding the sociological aspects of illness, the illness-as-deviance perspective still remains the best sociological thinking on the subject.

BEING SICK AND DISABLED

Everyone becomes ill at some time. Susan Sontag, in her book, *Illness as Metaphor* (1978), puts it this way:

> Illness is the night-side of life, a more onerous citizenship. Everyone who is born holds dual citizenship, in the kingdom of the well and in the kingdom of the sick. Although we prefer to use only the good passport, sooner or later each of us is obligated, at least for a spell, to identify ourselves as citizens of that other place.[2]

As citizens of that other place—the realm of sickness—we typically feel bad or weak or both. We are unable to feel normal because we experience a sense of being less than our usual self. As Peter Freund and Meredith McGuire (1991:147) explain, "illness is upsetting because it is experienced as a threat to the order and meanings by which people make sense of their lives." What Freund and McGuire mean by this is that illness disrupts our daily routine, causes various degrees of suffering, and threatens our ability to plan for the future and control our activities. To be sick is to envy those who are well or envy our own past periods of wellness and hopefully be able to look forward to their return. The latter may not be possible if one has an incurable chronic condition. For example, in a study of HIV-positive homosexual men in New York City, Karolyn Siegel and Beatrice Krauss (1991) found that having AIDS meant having to confront the pos-

---

[2]Susan Sontag, *Illness as Metaphor* (New York: Farrar, Straus, and Giroux, 1978), p. 3.

sibility of a curtailed life span, dealing with reactions to having a highly discrediting and stigmatized illness, and developing strategies for maintaining physical and emotional health. Being sick is clearly an undesirable state despite the exemption from one's usual activities that are an inherent feature of the sick role.

As previously noted, there are two types of illness conditions. One is acute illness, which typically refers to the sudden onset or sharp increase in pain, discomfort, or inflammation; usually such problems last only a relatively short time and either disappear after a few days, or are moderated or cured by medical treatment (DeFriese and Earp 1989). An acute illness is often communicable and can be passed from one person to another, such as colds, flus, measles, and chicken pox. The other form of sickness is chronic illness, which is usually slow in developing, long in duration, and typically incurable (Lubkin 1986; Maddox and Glass 1989; Strauss 1975; Strauss and Corbin 1988). Chronic illnesses are not usually communicable, although there are exceptions, such as AIDS. Chronic disorders develop within the individual rather than being passed directly from someone else and are usually associated with genetic, environmental, and lifestyle influences. If the chronic disease is life-threatening, like cancer, diabetes, or heart disease, the afflicted person is likely to eventually die from it. Other chronic conditions, like arthritis, are uncomfortable but not life-threatening.

Regardless of whether one's affliction is acute or chronic, when people suffer, their sense of personal competency can be adversely affected. Freund and McGuire (1991) point out that an illness can be particularly damaging to a person's concept of self when it is experienced as overwhelming, unpredictable, and uncontrollable because it paralyzes the ability to act and manage one's life normally. Very sick people often sense a degree of alienation or psychological separation from their body because it no longer feels normal or functions adequately (Freund and McGuire 1991; Leventhal 1975). People who are sick often withdraw from others because they feel bad and are unable to pursue normal social relations.

Persons with chronic disorders, particularly those who are physically handicapped, are faced with additional problems of altered mobility, a negative body image, and social stigma (Bury 1991; Lubkin 1986; Radley 1989; Roth and Conrad 1987; Yoshida 1993). Consequently, Zola (1982, 1989) points out that the problems facing someone with a physical impairment are not just medical, but include social, attitudinal, economic, and other adjustments. Simply moving about can be a major challenge. Kathy Charmaz (1983, 1991) found in a study of chronically ill persons in northern California that such individuals frequently experience a deteriorating former self-image and are unable to assume an equally valued new one. As a result of their illness, they live restricted lives, are socially isolated, discredited as less than normal, and feel they are a burden to others. All of these factors combine to reduce the chronically ill person's sense of self-worth, unless some alternative means of satisfaction can be found.

Anselm Strauss (1975; Strauss and Corbin 1988) explains that the chief business of a chronically ill person is not just to stay alive or keep his or her symptoms under control but to live as normally as possible. A life-long illness, in Strauss's view, requires life-long work to control its course, manage its symptoms, and live with the disability. In this context, the sick role that the person assumes is a permanent condition.

SUMMARY

Two major theories have been advanced to date to explain the relationship between illness and society. Parsons' concept of the sick role has had the greatest impact on sociological perspectives thus far, but Freidson's labeling theory approach also represents an important contribution.

Parsons' concept of the sick role includes the following postulates: (1) An individual's illness is grounds for exemption from normal responsibilities and obligations; (2) an individual's illness is not his or her fault and he or she needs help in order to get well; (3) the sick person has an obligation to get well because being sick is undesirable; and (4) the obligation to get well subsumes the more specific obligation of the sick person to seek technically competent help. Parsons also demonstrates the utility of medicine as an institution of social control by virtue of its mission of treating the deviant sick.

Although Parsons' concept of the sick role has provided a useful framework for understanding illness behavior, it has not been generally sufficient because of its failure (1) to explain the variation within illness behavior; (2) to apply to chronic illness; (3) to account for the variety of settings and situations affecting the patient–physician relationship; and (4) to explain the behavior of lower-class patients. Nonetheless, if we realize the limitations of Parsons' sick role theory, we can continue to apply it to behavior as an ideal-type model.

The labeling approach to illness, as formulated by Freidson, provides a useful orientation for analyzing the problematic aspects of illness behavior and the social meaning of disease. However, a definitive sick role theory using labeling theory has yet to be developed. Both Parsons' sick role concept and Freidson's labeling theory are formulated within the framework of an illness-as-deviance perspective and currently this view contains the best work on the sociological aspects of being sick. For the chronically ill, the sick role can be a permanent state.

Doctor–Patient Interaction

9

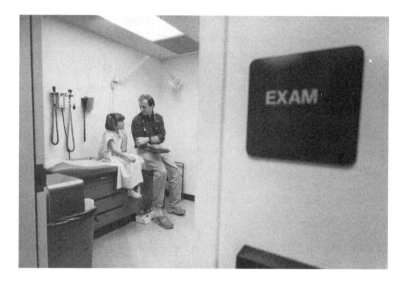

T alcott Parsons' (1951) concept of the sick role provided some basic guidelines for understanding doctor–patient interaction. Parsons explains that the reltionship between a physician and his or her patient is one that is oriented toward the doctor helping the patient to deal effectively with a health problem. The physician has the dominant role since he or she is the one invested with medical knowledge and expertise, while the patient holds a subordinate position oriented toward accepting, rejecting, or negotiating the recommendation for treatment being offered. In the case of a medical emergency, however, the options of rejection or negotiation on the part of the patient may be quickly discarded as the patient's medical needs require prompt and decisive action from the doctor.

Parsons' concept of the sick role details the obligations of patients and physicians toward each other. Patients cooperate with doctors and doctors attempt to return patients to as normal a level of functioning as possible. When people visit doctors for treatment and medical advice, doctors usually (but not always) take some type of action to satisfy the patient's expectations. Eliot Freidson (1970a) suggests that physicians tend to have a bias in favor of finding illness in their patients. He cites the *medical decision rule* as the guiding principle behind everyday medical practice. The medical decision rule, described by Thomas Scheff (1966), is the notion that since the work of the physician is for the good of the patient, physicians tend to impute illness to their patients rather than to deny it and risk overlooking or missing it. Although this approach may promote tendencies to prescribe drugs and order laboratory tests and X-rays, such consequences should not be surprising. Patients desire and demand services, and physicians are trained to meet these demands. As Freidson (1970a:258) points out: "While the physician's job is to make decisions, including the decision not to do anything, the fact seems to be that the everyday practitioner feels impelled to do something when [patients] are in distress."

Richard Tessler and his associates (Tessler, Mechanic, and Dimond 1976) remind us that the role of the physician in meeting the needs of patients is quite broad and that physicians should be attentive not only to a patient's complaints but also to whatever factors caused the patient to come to a doctor at a particular point in time. The distress may not be only physical; purely psychological needs can trigger a visit to a doctor as well (Cockerham, Kunz, and Lueschen 1988b; Tessler, Mechanic, and Dimond 1976). Therefore, to assume that interaction between physicians and patients always follows a preset course in which all parties work together under the same set of mutual understandings, overlooks the potential for misunderstanding, uncertainty, or disregard of the physician's method of treatment by the patient. The quality of physician–patient interaction is sometimes problematic, yet the process is important because of its potential for affecting the care being provided. This chapter will review models of interaction, misunderstandings in communication, cultural differences in presenting symptoms, and problems in patient compliance. These are topics of interest to sociologists since physician–patient interaction constitutes a structured relationship and mode of discourse that are inherently social.

MODELS OF INTERACTION

Since Parsons formulated his concept of the sick role, two additional perspectives on physician–patient interaction have added to our understanding of the experience. These are the views of Szasz and Hollender and Hayes-Bautista. Thomas Szasz and Marc Hollender (1956), both physicians, take the position that the seriousness of the patient's symptoms is the determining factor in doctor–patient interaction. Depending on the severity of symptoms, Szasz and Hollender argue that physician–patient interaction falls into one of three possible models: activity–passivity, guidance–cooperation, and mutual participation.

The *activity–passivity model* applies when the patient is seriously ill or being treated on an emergency basis in a state of relative helplessness due to a severe injury or lack of consciousness. Typically, the situation is desperate as the physician works in a state of high activity to stabilize the patient's condition. Decision making and power in the relationship are all on the side of the doctor, as the patient is passive and contributes little or nothing to the interaction. The *guidance–cooperation model* arises most often when the patient has an acute, often infectious illness, like the flu or measles. The patient knows what is going on and can cooperate with the physician by following his or her guidance in the matter, but the physician makes the decisions.

The *mutual participation model* applies to the management of chronic illness in which the patient works with the doctor as a full participant in controlling the disease. Often the patient modifies his or her lifestyle by making adjustments in diet or giving up cigarettes and is responsible for taking medication according to a prescribed schedule and seeking periodic checkups. The patient with diabetes or heart disease would be in this category. What Szasz and Hollender accomplish is to show how the physician–patient relationship is affected by the severity of the patient's symptoms.

David Hayes-Bautista (1976a, 1976b) focuses on the manner in which patients try to modify treatment prescribed by a physician. Hayes-Bautista finds that they either try to convince the physician that the treatment is not working or they counter the treatment with action of their own, such as deliberately reducing the amount of medication they are supposed to take or increasing it. Physicians respond by pointing out their expertise, that the patient's health can be threatened if the treatment is not followed, that the treatment is correct but progress may be slow, or simply appeal to the patient to comply. The relevance of the Hayes-Bautista model for understanding doctor–patient relations is that he views the interaction as a process of negotiation, rather than the physician simply giving orders and the patient following them in an automatic, unquestioning manner. The model is limited, however, to those situations in which the patient is not satisfied with treatment and wants to persuade the doctor to change it.

What is suggested by the Szasz and Hollender and Hayes-Bautista models is that in nonemergency situations, patients do not necessarily act passively when interacting with their doctors in health matters. Patients ask questions, seek explanations, and make judgments about the appropriateness of the information and treatment physicians provide. But the interaction that takes place appears to be strongly affected by social class differences. Lower-class persons tend to be more passive in dealing with doctors as authority figures and show a decreased sense of personal control over health matters; people with middle and upper socioeconomic status, on the other hand, tend to be more consumer oriented and active participants in the physician–patient encounter (Cockerham et al. 1986a). This circumstance suggests that it is middle- and upper-class patients who are most likely to try to negotiate with doctors and involve themselves as partners in decision making about their medical problem, while lower-class persons stand as more or less passive recipients of professional health services.

In their study of consumerism in the doctor–patient encounter, Marie Haug and Bebe Lavin (1981, 1983) found that better educated and younger adults tended to be more skeptical of physician motives in providing treatment. They were more likely to question whether the physician was ordering tests and providing services primarily to help the patient or to make money. These persons strongly believed that decision making in the doctor–patient relationship should not be left entirely to the doctor.

The results of the Haug and Lavin research, along with those of other studies (Cockerham et al. 1986a), indicate that in nonemergency situations, the tendency among middle- and upper-class patients is greater involvement and control in dealing with doctors about their health. Just as some people participate in healthy lifestyles in order to have greater individual control over their health, some people also seek greater parity with their physician in the decisions that are made about their medical care. Trends toward the expression of greater equality on the part of patients, as previously noted, are situated largely among more affluent and well-educated people.

As medicine moves into the twenty-first century, the most common mode of physician–patient relationship is likely to be that of Szasz and Hollender's (1956) mutual participation model in which patients and doctors share responsibility for decision making and treatment outcomes. This development is due both to growing demands on the part of patients for equity and the prevalence of chronic diseases as the most common health problems in modern society. Chronic diseases often require long-term treatment and modifications in living that push doctors and patients into greater partnership.

MISUNDERSTANDINGS IN COMMUNICATION

The interaction that takes place between doctor and patient is an exercise in communication. Medical treatment usually begins with a dialogue. As is the case in any face-to-face situation, the effectiveness of doctor–patient interaction depends upon the ability of the participants to understand each other. However, a major barrier to effective communication lies in the differences between physicians and their patients with respect to status, education, professional training, and authority. Several sources report that a failure to explain a patient's condition to the patient in terms easily understood is a serious problem in medical encounters (Allman, Yoels, and Clair 1993; Clair 1993; Coe 1978; Davis 1972; Fisher and Todd 1990; Mishler 1984). Physicians, in turn, state that an inability to understand or the potentially negative effect of threatening information are the two most common reasons for not communicating fully with their patients (Davis 1972; Howard and Strauss 1975). Consequently, as Fred Davis (1972) found in a study of the interaction between the parents of children who were victims of paralytic poliomyelitis and their doctors, the most common form of communication was evasion; the doctors tended to answer the questions of parents in terms that were either evasive or unintelligibly technical.

Yet some doctors are very effective communicators and, as Eric Cassell (1985) explains, information can be an important therapeutic tool in medical situations if it meets three tests: (1) reduces uncertainty, (2) provides a basis for action, and (3) strengthens the physician–patient relationship. Cassell provides an example of this situation in the following dialogue between a male physician and a female patient:

DOCTOR: Now, first I want you to start off by listening—listen to me, carefully. With your ears, not your fears. I'm very straight with people, as you know. What I tell you is everything, uh—right. Now, on your skull x-rays there is a place where the pituitary gland sits. I'll show it to you. That place right here—

PATIENT: Mm-hm.

DOCTOR: —is larger than it's supposed to be.

PATIENT: I see.

DOCTOR: The pituitary gland sits in there. Now the pituitary gland has a lot— does a lot of work in the body. It's very teeny and makes a lot of little hormones that tell the other glands of your body what to do.

PATIENT: Mm-hm.

DOCTOR: When it's large, like that, we think it has a tumor. The kind of tumor that it has is not a cancer tumor. That is not what makes that kind of tumor.

PATIENT: Mm-hm. . . .

DOCTOR: That would give you the headaches that you complain of. 'Cause tumors cause headaches, they grow very slowly. They're not cancer. They grow very, very slowly. . . . Where we sit right now is, there is a suggestion that you have a tumor of the pituitary gland.

PATIENT: Mm.

DOCTOR: The most common one—ah, name, is called chromophobe adenoma. You know, but the name is not important, except, as I say, it's not cancer.

PATIENT: Mm.

DOCTOR: Now. If that's what you have, you're going to be operated on for it.

PATIENT: Mm.

DOCTOR: Now, as scary as it may be when somebody points at your head and talks about tumors, this is NOT a scary tumor.

PATIENT: I see.

DOCTOR: I don't mean to say that on the way, you ain't going to get scared and worry and be frightened, and have things go on, doctors and all that, because you are. Until this is all settled, you're going to get frightened, and nothing I'm going to tell you is going to make you less frightened, except, I'm telling you the truth. You're going to come out all right, if that's what it is.

PATIENT: Mm-hm.

DOCTOR: All right? I don't mean come out all right, I mean alive, I mean all right.

PATIENT: Mm-hm.

DOCTOR: You know? Able to do your exercises, work, have sex, cook food, get mad at your children, and grow to be one hundred and ten years old like your mother. Nasty. With a nasty disposition.

PATIENT: (Laughs) OK.[1]

Other doctors do poorly when it comes to communicating with patients. Cassell provides further examples of physicians telling their patients they were not going to explain a disease because they would not understand what they were

---

[1] Eric J. Cassell, *Talking with Patients, Clinical Technique*, vol. 2 (Cambridge, Mass.: MIT Press, 1985), pp. 165–166.

told, or being vague and ultimately frightening the patient. In the following example from a British study, a woman with a neck problem resulting from a car accident sought reassurance that no serious difficulties existed. However, she was clearly not reassured as shown in this conversation with her doctor:

PATIENT: Could you tell me Doctor X, is it all right that my neck clicks now and then?
DOCTOR: Yes.
PATIENT: Is that all right?
DOCTOR: Yes, it may do. Yes.
PATIENT: Fine. Thanks.

> She continued to express her concern to the interviewer. "The doctor just asked if my neck was all right and dismissed it, although I would like to have discussed it—the pain I'm having. I mean, I don't know if it's all right."[2]

This, of course, is the type of situation that promotes misunderstandings between doctors and patients and leaves the patients dissatisfied with the relationship. Two groups in society, the lower class and women, have been identified as having the most communication problems with physicians. It has been found, for example, that poorly educated persons are the most likely to have their questions ignored and to be treated impersonally as simply someone with a disease instead of an individual to be respected (Ross and Duff 1982). Upper- and upper-middle-class persons tend to receive more personalized service from physicians (Link 1983). They are also more active in presenting their ideas to a doctor and seeking further explanation (Boulton et al. 1986).

Howard Waitzkin (1985, 1991), a physician and medical sociologist, studied information giving in medical care and found that social class differences were the most important factors in physician–patient communication. Noting that information often provides a basis for power by those who have it in relation to those who do not, Waitzkin determined that doctors did not usually withhold information to exercise control over their patients. Rather, doctors from upper-middle-class backgrounds tended to communicate more information to their patients generally than doctors with lower-middle- or working-class origins. Moreover, patients from a higher class position or educational level usually received more information. Socioeconomic status thus emerged as a determining factor in both providing and receiving medical information.

Mary Boulton and her colleagues (Boulton et al. 1986:328) explain that the influence of social class on the doctor–patient relationship is best understood in terms of social distance. Those patients who are similar to physicians in social class are more likely to share their communication style and communicate effectively with them; those with dissimilar class backgrounds are likely to find

---

[2]Freda Fitton and H.W.K. Acheson. *The Doctor/Patient Relationship: A Study in General Practice* (London: Department of Health and Social Security, 1979), p. 75.

communication more difficult because their communication style differs from that of the doctor and they lack the social skills to negotiate the medical encounter effectively.

As for women, Sue Fisher (1984) studied doctor–patient communication in a family practice clinic in a small southeastern American city staffed by white middle-class men. She found that many women patients were not satisfied with the explanations given them by their doctors. Fisher claimed that treatment decisions for women were not always in their best interest. She provided the following example:

> One quiet evening my phone rang. It was a fellow graduate student and she was in distress. For the past several years she used an intrauterine device (IUD) as her method of contraception. Recently she developed a pelvic inflammatory disease (PID) and was treated with antibiotics. The first regimen of antibiotics was unsuccessful and the doctor then recommended a hysterectomy. Faced with the doctor's recommendation my friend, Andrea, felt helpless. She didn't know how to determine whether or not the hysterectomy was necessary. She called to see if I could help. I suggested that she tell the doctor that she was engaged to marry a [physician] who wanted a family, and ask the doctor if there were any other ways to treat her problem.
>
> Several weeks later my phone again rang. Andrea had followed my advice. Once the doctor learned of her impending marriage his attitude changed. He assured her that there were alternative treatments available and they would work hard to avoid a hysterectomy. She was treated with another course of antibiotic, her infection cleared up, avoiding unnecessary surgery.
>
> Andrea's is a distressing, but not an isolated, tale. Repeatedly, while doing research in the Departments of Reproductive and Family Medicine, I saw physicians recommend treatments and patients, usually unquestioningly, accept them. My research gave me access to behind-the-scenes information typically reserved for physicians. Hardly a week passed without someone calling, as Andrea had, to tap into that stock of knowledge. The women who called were often well educated and articulate, yet they did not feel they had the information with which to make reasonable decisions or they felt they did not understand or could not trust the recommendation their physician made. Their feelings were exacerbated when their medical problems were related to reproduction. The women's questions were always of the same kind—How do I evaluate whether the treatment or procedure being recommended is really in my best interest?[3]

Fisher's basic message is to call for greater insight on the part of male doctors in dealing with female patients and their complaints. The lack of male sensitivity in providing health care to women patients was a major factor in the formation of the women's health movement to combat sexual discrimination in

[3]Sue Fisher, "Doctor-Patient Communication: A Social and Micro-political Performance," *Sociology of Health and Illness*, 6 (1984), 1–2.

medicine. As part of this movement, feminist health organizations have evolved which advocate natural childbirth, midwifery, home deliveries of babies, self-help, and recognition of the rights and intelligence of patients (Davidson and Gordon 1979). A particular focus has been on the manner in which some male physicians treat women patients and health workers as inferior because of their sex. Reviews of both past and present medical literature have found images of women patients that depict them as being naturally frail, sickly, incompetent, submissive, and in need of physician consultation fairly regularly. In examining the relationship between male physicians and female patients in the early twentieth century, Barbara Ehrenreich and Deirdre English noted:

> The doctors' view of women as innately sick did not, of course, *make* them sick, or delicate, or idle. But it did provide a powerful rationale against allowing women to act in any other way. Medical arguments were used to explain why women should be barred from medical school (they would faint in anatomy lectures), from higher education altogether, and from voting. . . . Medical arguments seemed to take the malice out of sexual oppression: when you prevented a woman from doing anything active or interesting, you were only doing this for her own good.[4]

Other research supports this theme. For example, in a review of gynecology textbooks over a 125-year period, Diana Scully and Pauline Bart (1979) found that very little had changed over the years in regard to stereotypes of women patients. There were consistent statements that attributed inferior sexuality and natural submissiveness to women, as well as relegating them to primary roles of reproduction and homemaking. One textbook, published in the early 1970s, cautioned gynecologists to inform their patients to be sure and follow the lead of their husbands in sexual relations but not to become completely passive since some overt advances are attractive and provocative. No one likes to "take a tone-deaf individual to a concert" was one reminder the gynecologists were told to give the women who came to see them for advice about their role in the sex act (Scully and Bart 1979:222).

Sometimes, for women doctors in a work situation, being a woman is a more meaningful status than being a physician. Candace West (1984) reports that some patients may perceive women physicians as less of an authority figure than male physicians. In one instance, West (1984:99) notes that a male patient was asked by his woman physician if he was having difficulty passing urine and the patient replied, "You know, the *doctor* asked me that." In this case, indicates West, it was difficult to tell who "the doctor" was because "the doctor" was evidently not the female physician who was treating him. And Judith Hammond (1980) suggests that women medical students deliberately develop personal biographies about themselves that show them as being no different than any other medical student. They do this in order to gain acceptance as colleagues from male stu-

[4]Barbara Ehrenreich and Deirdre English, "The 'Sick' Women of the Upper Classes," in *The Cultural Crisis of Modern Medicine*, J. Ehrenreich, ed. (New York: Monthly Review Press, 1979), pp. 127–128.

dents who question their motivation, skills, and potential for medicine. As one woman medical student described the attitude of a male counterpart:

> This guy had this theory. . . if you're a woman, obviously you're going to be the one to bring up the kids. . . . You know, maternal instinct and all that? Like you shouldn't spend all your time being a doctor. You can't do *both*. Well, that's what most of them think: you can't do both.[5]

There is evidence, however, that adverse attitudes and stereotypes about women are beginning to be modified among members of the medical profession. Visible changes are occurring in the approaches of some physicians and hospitals toward treating women (Davidson and Gordon 1979). A particularly significant source of change is found in the increasing numbers of women physicians. The first American woman to graduate from medical school was Elizabeth Blackwell in 1849, but her experience was atypical. While there is evidence that premedical students do not typically try to undercut each other in qualifying studies (Conrad 1986b) and that there has been an absence of sex discrimination by medical schools in accepting female students (Cole 1986), women have historically been underrepresented in medical school classes. Differences in socialization experiences (Cole 1986) and a greater degree of persistence among males whose academic records are marginal (Fiorentine 1987) seem to have produced this situation. It was not until the 1970s that women accounted for at least 10 percent of all first-year medical students. But in 1993, 40 percent of all students entering medical schools were women.

This is not to claim that sexism in medicine is no longer significant because several accounts of women medical students and physicians detail the problems women have in being recognized as equal colleagues by male physicians and as "real" doctors by male patients (Elston 1993; Hammond 1980; Lorber 1984, 1993; Riska and Wegar 1993; West 1984). But the trend is clear: Women physicians will be commonplace in the future and the impact should be significant. For example, Judith Lorber (1984) found that when male doctors assessed their accomplishments, they tended to speak only of their technical skills and choices of appropriate treatment. The personal side of the physician–patient relationship was rarely mentioned. Women doctors, on the other hand, stressed their value to patients and did so using words like "help" and "care." Steven Martin and his associates (Martin, Arnold, and Parker 1988) determined that men and women physicians have similar diagnostic and therapeutic skills, but there appear to be differences in their communication styles: Female physicians tend to be more empathic and egalitarian in their relationships with patients, more respectful of their concerns, and more responsive to patients' psychosocial difficulties.

Today, women physicians are not only entering specialties that have traditionally attracted them—namely, pediatrics, obstetrics-gynecology, and general practice—but also increasingly in male-dominated specialties like surgery,

---

[5]Judith M. Hammond, "Biography Building to Insure the Future: Women's Negotiation of Gender Relevancy in Medical School," *Symbolic Interaction*, 3 (1980), 39.

urology, and orthopedics. Thus, women physicians are adopting more specialties than before and are now entering areas of medicine where they deal with a
wider range of patients. Consequently, we have the beginnings of a new trend in
medicine that may not only affect the physician–patient relationship (in terms of
improved communication and willingness to relate to patients as people) but
may also have an impact on the general image of women held by the medical
profession.

CULTURAL DIFFERENCES IN COMMUNICATION

Physician–patient interaction can also be influenced by cultural differences in
communication. A major study in this area is Irving Zola's (1966) comparison of
Irish- and Italian-American patients in the presentation of symptoms at an eye,
ear, nose, and throat clinic. Zola found that Irish patients tended to understate
their symptoms, while Italian patients tended to overstate them. That is, the Irish
made short, concise statements ("I can't see across the street"), while Italians provided far greater detail ("my eyes seem very burny, especially the right eye. . . .
Two or three months ago I woke up with my eyes swollen. I bathed it and it did
go away but there was still the burny sensation")—for the exact same eye problem. The doctors were required to sort the differences in communication styles in
order to help them arrive at the appropriate diagnosis.

In contemporary American society, a particular problem in medical interviews is found among low-income and poorly educated Hispanics who speak little or no English, feel uncomfortable in impersonal social relationships, have no
regular source of care, and find it difficult to negotiate their way through an
Anglo health care delivery system (Andersen et al. 1981; Madsen 1973).

William Madsen provides an example of cultural misunderstandings in
the following exchange between a Mexican-American man who took his wife to
see a physician in south Texas. The man stated:

> We saw the doctor in his office after a long wait while many Anglos went
> in first. The doctor asked my wife, "What is wrong"? I told him. I said my
> wife had no energy and often no appetite. I told him how she had bad
> dreams and cried in her sleep. I explained she must have *susto* but had
> not responded to the treatment of a *curandero.* Therefore, she must have
> *susto pasado.* I said I had come to him because my brother thought he
> could probably cure this disease. The doctor sat there smiling as I talked.
> When I finished, he laughed at me. Then he sat up straight and said stern-
> ly, "Forget all that nonsense. You have come to me and I will treat your
> wife. It is my job to decide what is wrong with her. And forget about
> those stupid superstitions. I don't know how a grown man like you can
> believe such nonsense!" He treated me like a fool.[6]

---

[6]William Madsen, *The Mexican-Americans of South Texas,* 2nd ed. (New York: Holt, Rinehart,
& Winston, 1973), p. 94.

The doctor then asked the husband to go to the waiting room and the wife to disrobe for an examination. The husband refused to let his wife be examined in this manner and took her away—never to return. Madsen (1973) reported that increasing reliance on physicians had eased some social barriers as a few doctors explained illnesses in simple terms and treated their patients with respect. But others remained disrespectful of them and the culture surrounding folk medicine.

Other lower-class minorities, including blacks, can have communication problems with doctors as well. Beverly Robinson (1990:211) reports on one black woman who, when asked how she was feeling, told her doctor that "the pain gone." The physician thought the woman was recovering until someone else informed the doctor that the woman meant the pain had only left temporarily. The woman's use of English was influenced by an African dialect in which "gone" meant a temporary absence, "done gone" and "done been gone" meant something had indeed left but could return and "gone gone" meant a complete absence.

Modern-day medical practice is provided within the context of middle-class norms and values emphasizing scientific beliefs, the application of sophisticated technology, and cooperation with physicians. For patients with a different cultural perspective, interaction with doctors can be difficult and subject to misunderstanding on both sides.

PATIENT COMPLIANCE

Another important aspect of physician–patient interaction is patient compliance with medical regimens (Svarstad 1986; Thompson 1984). Physicians prescribe medications, diets, and the like and expect patients to follow them faithfully. Many, perhaps most, patients comply with a physician's instructions, but other patients do not; in fact, some patients may pay little attention to a doctor's guidance, and this is especially the case when they begin to feel better or when symptoms are not obvious.

For example, in a study in Scotland, Mildred Blaxter and Richard Cyster (1984) found that a majority of patients with liver problems caused by alcoholism in an outpatient clinic continued to drink—despite being advised by their physicians to reduce or give up alcohol intake. The physicians had either not adequately communicated the danger associated with continued drinking or the patients had misunderstood. One male patient had been told to drink no more than two glasses of sherry a day as an example of how much he could drink, but since he drank whiskey not sherry, he gladly gave up any thought of drinking sherry and proceeded to pursue his normal drinking pattern. Other patients refused to believe their doctors or simply did not want to change their drinking habits since it meant changing a preferred lifestyle.

Compliance requires comprehension by the patient, and communication is the key for avoiding noncompliance. The motivation to be healthy, a perceived vulnerability to an illness, the potential for negative consequences, effectiveness of the treatment, sense of personal control, and effective communication are the strongest influences on compliance (Thompson 1984).

THE FUTURE OF DOCTOR–PATIENT RELATIONS

The style of doctor–patient interaction has undergone a fundamental change in recent years. A 1989 nationwide Gallup Poll showed that 75 percent of the respondents believed doctors keep patients waiting too long, 67 percent concluded doctors are too interested in making money, and 57 percent stated doctors don't care about people as much as they used to. Some 56 percent indicated they respected doctors about the same as ten years ago, but 26 percent said they had less respect (because doctors are in it for the money, lack concern, don't take time for patients, or they had a bad personal experience with a doctor) and 14 percent said they respected doctors more (because doctors are more knowledgeable, are needed more because the respondent was getting older, do a good job, or have more pressures and challenges). On balance, there appeared to be greater dissatisfaction with physicians than in the past and a growing image of medicine as just a business.

Edward Shorter (1991) has traced the social history of the doctor–patient relationship. First, he explains how the medical profession evolved from being a relatively low-status occupation to a highly respected scientific field. The image of the ideal doctor–patient relationship—the caring physician and the trusting patient—was not lasting; it had ended, in Shorter's view, by the 1960s. Doctors had become increasingly distant in interacting with patients, while patients, in turn, had evolved from being willingly passive to active, informed clients who wanted to participate more equally in their care. The high cost of care, high salaries of many doctors and superior attitudes on the part of some, along with organized opposition to health reform, caused some patients to become disillusioned with the medical profession. Doctors, on their part, became resentful about patients and others who questioned their commitment. As result, Shorter concludes, doctor–patient relationships in the United States have seriously eroded in recent years.

Not all patients, however, are dissatisfied to the same degree and, as previously noted, social class differences appear to be the key variable in this situation. According to Freidson:

> Those of lower status than the doctor, who lack the resources of a higher education, who are not exposed to a broad range of media information, and who are not forced to make calculated choices are not likely to become troublesome for the doctor. On the other hand, those who consider themselves to be of equal or higher status than the doctor, who consider themselves to be well informed about the latest diagnoses, prognoses, and treatments for what ails them, and who are experienced in reading the language of contracts and dealing with bureaucratic procedures have the potential to become serious problems of management.[7]

[7]Eliot Freidson, *Medical Work in America: Essays on Health Care* (New Haven, Conn.: Yale University Press, 1989), p. 13.

Therefore, as Cassell (1986) explains, the belief among laypersons that the "doctor knows best" is no longer virtually accepted. Americans have become more knowledgeable about medicine and while they do not believe they are doctors, they do believe that they can understand and perhaps apply a piece of knowledge that is the same as the doctor's in their own health situation. Yet Cassell observes that simply having some knowledge about medicine is not enough to displace physicians from their previous preeminent status. Rather, he notes that during the 1960s, with the social turbulence associated with the civil rights movement and the Vietnam War, the relationship of individuals to authority began to change in the United States. Americans became more individualistic and questioning about the motives of those in authority, including physicians. Cassell states:

> During this era, the nature of the relationship between the doctor and patient has come under scrutiny, and it has become apparent that the relationship itself is a powerful force in medical care, that it can be endangered, and that it can change as a result of social as well as personal forces. From being seen as effectively passive in relation to the physician (except that patients have always been expected to be active in the sense of "fighting to get well"), patients now frequently believe themselves to be active partners in their care. They want to take part in decisions formerly reserved for the doctor; they want to exercise choice in therapy and they have high expectations about the outcome.[8]

Consequently, when it comes to health care, the evolving pattern among many Americans is one of consumerism in which the consumer wants to make informed choices about the services available and not be treated as inferior. The future direction of doctor–patient relations is one of greater mutual participation in decision making about the patient's health.

DOCTOR–PATIENT RELATIONS AND TECHNOLOGY

An important factor likely to have profound implications for the doctor–patient relationship in the future is new medical technology. The forthcoming development of computerized information highways connecting a patient's personal home computer to those of doctors, hospitals, drug companies, medical suppliers, health insurers, and medical databases will allow patients to obtain health information directly from their own computer rather than visiting a physician. Electronic monitoring devices will allow the patient to keep track of his or her physical and mental state and report these to physicians or databases by computer. Physicians may be consulted via home computers, electronic mail, or teleconferencing rather than in person. A computer can be used to diagnose the patient's

[8]Eric J. Cassell, "The Changing Concept of the Ideal Physician," *Daedalus*, 115 (Spring 1986), 196.

ills and determine treatment. Prescription drugs may be ordered electronically and delivered to the patient.

Other measures like the use of robotics and computer-guided imagery of a patient's body may increase efficiency and precision in surgery and reduce the need for extensive hospitalization. Doctors may have little direct involvement in certain surgeries as robots and teams of nurses handle most of the tasks. Also, gene therapy may anticipate an individual's susceptibility to various chronic diseases and eliminate many health problems in early stages. It may be the patient, however, who discovers the requirement for treatment through self-monitoring and computer-assisted analysis of his or her medical history. This situation significantly changes the traditional doctor–patient relationship because patients, not doctors, will cause health care to take place. Doctors will be responding to what patients themselves decide they need, rather than the other way around. Doctors and patients will still have contact, but much of that contact may be through computers. A new doctor–patient relationship is likely to emerge in which the patient initiates, determines, and controls much of the health services he or she consumes.

SUMMARY

This chapter has examined various social factors that affect doctor–patient interaction. The most likely model of interaction in future medical encounters is the mutual participation model suggested by Szasz and Hollender (1956). This model depicts the doctor and patient working together as more of a team than the patient simply following the doctor's orders in a more or less automatic fashion. However, it was found that a particularly significant barrier to effective interaction are differences in social class. Doctors from upper- and upper-middle-class backgrounds are likely to be better communicators than doctors from lower-middle- and working-class backgrounds, while patients from higher socioeconomic levels are more likely to demand and receive adequate information about their condition than patients with lower status.

Two groups in society are the most likely to have communication problems in medical encounters: One group is the lower class and the other is women who sometimes do not receive what they consider to be adequate information from male doctors. Cultural differences can also affect doctor–patient interaction and, in the United States, differences between Hispanic patients and non-Hispanic health care providers have been cited as a negative circumstance. Finally, patient compliance with a physician's directions is not always automatic and some patients fail to comply because of poor communication or other reasons. The doctor–patient relationship typically begins with dialogue and the quality of that dialogue is often affected by social factors.

Physicians

10

I n 1990 there were 589,500 doctors actively practicing medicine in the United States (National Center for Health Statistics 1993). This comes to 234 physicians for every 100,000 Americans. Medical doctors constitute less than 10 percent of the total workforce, yet the entire health care industry in the United States is subordinate to their professional authority, regardless of whether the task is patient care, research, or administration. Physicians not only control the conditions of their own work but also the work of most of the other members of the health profession as well. Consequently, the status and prestige accorded to the physician by the general public is recognition of the physician's monopoly of one of society's most essential functions: the definition and treatment of health disorders. As shown in comparisons of countries in North and South America, Europe, and Asia, as well as Australia, the medical profession is highly prestigious throughout the world (Quah 1989). Physicians are also relatively well paid; in 1991, for example, the average annual income of an American doctor was $170,600.

THE PROFESSIONALIZATION OF THE PHYSICIAN

The social importance of the medical function and the limited number of people with the training to perform as physicians are not the only criteria explaining their professional dominance. A particularly important factor is the organization of the medical profession itself. William Goode (1957, 1960) noted that two basic characteristics are sociologically relevant in explaining professionalism: prolonged training in a body of specialized, abstract knowledge and an orientation toward providing a service.

Moreover, once a professional group becomes established, Goode indicates that it begins to further consolidate its power by formalizing social relationships that govern the interaction of the professionals with their clients, their colleagues, and with official agencies outside the profession. Recognition on the part of clients, outside agencies, and the wider society of the profession's claim to competence, as well as the profession's ability to control its own membership, is necessary if professional decisions are not to be reviewed by outside authorities. Once this situation (public acceptance of claims to competence and the profession's control of its membership) occurs, Goode (1960:903) believes that additional features of the profession can be established:

1. The profession determines its own standards of education and training.
2. The student professional goes through a more stringent socialization experience than the learner in other occupations.
3. Professional practice is often legally recognized by some form of licensure.
4. Licensing and admission boards are manned by members of the profession.
5. Most legislation concerned with the profession is shaped by that profession.
6. As the occupation gains income, power, and prestige, it can demand high-caliber students.
7. The practitioner is relatively free of lay evaluation and control.
8. Members are strongly identified by their profession.

What Goode has accomplished, for our purposes, is the development of guidelines for analyzing the development of the medical profession in American society. While physicians in the United States have traditionally shared a basic service orientation, the second requirement, that of lengthy training in a specialized and abstract body of knowledge, was initially lacking. Most American medical practitioners in the period before the American Revolution were ship's surgeons, apothecaries, or clergy who had obtained a familiarity with medical knowledge in Europe. Few practitioners had been educated in either a university setting or a medical school. Anyone who wanted to practice medicine could do so and could claim the title of "doctor," which in Europe was reserved exclusively for persons educated at a university. The most distinguished early American physicians were those trained at the University of Edinburgh, Great Britain's foremost medical school in that era. From this small group of British-trained physicians came the impetus for establishment of the first American medical school in 1765 at the College of Philadelphia. This medical school, which later became part of the University of Pennsylvania, was subsequently joined in the years prior to

1800 by the organization of other medical schools at King's College (Columbia), Harvard, and Dartmouth.

After 1800, American medical schools virtually mushroomed, as school after school was established. But the quality of medical education in the United States remained low and physicians themselves had little prestige as late as 1850. Not only did the doctors of the day offer little hope in curing disease, but sometimes their methods were either unpleasant or fatal. Often patients were bled, which tended to weaken their condition, or they were administered purgatives, which caused them to vomit. By the middle of the nineteenth century, states E. Richard Brown (1979:62–63), "cholera victims were given an even chance of being done in by the disease or by the doctor."

The best medical training at this time was in Europe, especially in France and Germany where medical research was flourishing. In France, Louis Pasteur's germ theory of disease, advanced during the mid-1800s, revolutionized medicine and provided the foundation for the discovery, classification, and treatment of numerous diseases. By the last quarter of the century, however, Germany assumed the leading role in the scientific development of medicine. Medical scientists in Germany like Rudolf Virchow, who unveiled a general concept of disease based on cellular pathology (1858), and Robert Koch, whose work in bacteriology led to the discovery of the bacillus for anthrax (1876), tuberculosis (1882), and cholera (1883), became important figures in medicine. Their work, and the work of their colleagues, stimulated the growth of clinics and university-affiliated laboratories and promoted high standards of admission for medical training in Germany and Austria. Beginning in 1870, large numbers of American students flocked to the famous clinics and laboratories of German and Austrian universities. First Vienna and then Berlin became *the* centers of medical knowledge. It is estimated that between 1870 and 1914 approximately 15,000 American doctors received at least part of their training in German-speaking universities (Stevens 1971). Most of these doctors returned to the United States to set up lucrative private practices by introducing into their work the latest scientific techniques, which, as Brown (1979:73) explains, "at least *seemed* effective in reducing suffering and ameliorating the symptoms of disease." Brown describes the situation as follows:

> Physicians who had the money to take an extra year's study in Europe were able to build more prestigious practices than the ordinary American-trained doctor. Usually they would take themselves out of direct competition with the majority of physicians by specializing in gynecology, surgery, ophthalmology, or one of the other new branches of medicine. They quickly formed a new elite in the profession with reputations that brought the middle and wealthy classes to their doors.[1]

Other European-trained physicians returned to develop medical laboratories and pursue the scientific investigation of disease. Henry Bowditch, for exam-

---

[1]E. Richard Brown, *Rockefeller Medicine Men: Medicine and Capitalism in America* (Berkeley: University of California Press, 1979), p. 73.

ple, founded the first experimental physiology laboratory in the United States at Harvard University in 1871, while William Welch, who discovered staphylococcus in 1892, began the first pathology laboratory in America at Bellevue Hospital medical school in New York City in 1878. By 1900, the entire medical school faculties of Harvard, Johns Hopkins, Yale, and Michigan had been trained in Germany.

In the meantime, medical science continued to record impressive technical achievements. During the 1800s these achievements included René Laennec's (1816) invention of the stethoscope; the work of Crawford Long (1842), Robert Liston (1846), and William Morton (1846) on ether as an anesthetic; Claude Bernard's (1849) discovery of glycogen and the development of a theory of hormonal secretions providing the basis for endocrinology; Joseph Lister's (1866) use of antiseptic procedures in surgery; William Welch's discovery of staphylococcus (1892), Wilhelm Roentgen's (1895) development of the X-ray; and Ronald Ross' (1895) research on the cause of malaria. Thus, by the beginning of the twentieth century, American medical doctors were clearly able to claim the two core characteristics of a profession as outlined by Goode—a service orientation and a body of specialized knowledge.

Moreover, at the beginning of the twentieth century, medical research in the United States began to surpass that of Europe. American medicine had been influenced by the British until 1820, the French until the American Civil War, and then the Germans. By 1895, however, the Americans were ready to forge ahead thanks to the vast sums of money poured into medical research by private American philanthropic foundations, such as those funded by the Carnegie and Rockefeller families. According to Brown, physicians in America strongly supported the rise of scientific medicine because it gave them greater effectiveness in a rapidly industrialized society and provided them with higher status, prestige, and income. Wealthy industrialists supported scientific medicine because it appeared to be a good investment in maintaining the moral, social, and economic order of corporate capitalism. Nevertheless, the result was, to quote Rosemary Stevens (1971:135), that "under the impact of new knowledge, the rapid improvement of medical schools, and the proliferation of hospitals and clinics which in turn generated new information, medicine was becoming vastly more efficient."

The American Medical Association

Another important step was necessary before American physicians could take advantage of their evolving professional status—the organization of physicians into a professionally identifiable group. With the founding of the American Medical Association in Philadelphia in 1847 physicians could mark the beginning of a new era in medicine. Weak and ineffectual in the beginning, the American Medical Association gradually extended its authority to become the single greatest influence on the organization and practice of medicine in the United States.

Two internal organizational measures were highly significant in this process. First, in 1883 the *Journal of the American Medical Association* appeared. This journal not only disseminated the latest medical knowledge and contributed to the prestige of the association, but also developed an awareness among the members of the AMA of their primary allegiance to the medical profession. Second, in 1902 an important reorganization took place when the AMA was divided into component societies on the local level (district or county medical societies), constituent societies (state or territorial medical associations), a national House of Delegates, a Board of Trustees, and national officers.

As a result of this change, the basic unit of the AMA had become the local society. Most important, it had the authority to set its own qualifications for membership. In theory, all "reputable and ethical" licensed physicians were eligible to join the local society, but final approval of membership was dependent upon the local society's arbitrary discretion. The power of the local society was further enhanced because AMA organizational structure permits no formal right to a hearing or right to appeal the local society's decisions. Thus, threats of denial of membership or of expulsion from the local society represent powerful sanctions, since there is no alternative medical association and AMA membership can be important to a physician's career. Often such membership influences patient referrals, consultations, specialty ratings, and other professional and social contacts important to a highly successful medical practice.

In 1992 the AMA had a membership of 290,000 physicians. This figure represents 43 percent of all active doctors. Nonmembers include those who have retired, who have not satisfied local residence requirements, and who are employed by the government, the armed forces, research agencies, or universities and thus believe they do not need the benefits of membership. Other physicians may not belong because for some reason they are unacceptable to the local society, because they themselves disapprove of the AMA's policies, or because such membership is not important to them. Only about one-fourth of all women doctors belong to the AMA, suggesting a lack of appeal by the organization for female practitioners. Women doctors also have their own professional organization—the American Medical Women's Association—which addresses issues of interest to them.

Local societies have the power to enforce conformity at their level because they determine membership qualifications. However, despite the strength of local societies, there is little dispute within the AMA concerning its national objectives. As Eliot Freidson (1970a) and others have pointed out, the actual exercise of power in the American Medical Association is concentrated in the hands of a relatively limited number of physicians. Many members have either not been interested in the association's internal politics or have been too busy with their own medical practices to devote time to professional problems. The vast majority has usually been content to let the AMA represent the medical profession with Congress and other governmental agencies. The association in turn keeps its membership informed about significant medical and health legislation on both state and national levels.

Additionally, there is no forum for effective dissent within the AMA because public debates are disapproved in order to project an image of a united profession in the association's interaction with outside agencies. Dissenting issues within the AMA must first win major support at the local level or they are not considered further. And the Journal of the American Medical Association seldom publishes views other than official policy. Opposition groups within the AMA are further prevented from gaining power because of the indirect system of elections for national officers. Only the House of Delegates, which consists of representatives from each state, elects people to the top offices and to the Board of Trustees, which exercises day-to-day control over the association. Many influential appointments to AMA councils and committees are made directly by the Board of Trustees and are not voted upon by either the general membership or the House of Delegates.

In an examination of the American Medical Association by David Hyde and Payson Wolff in the *Yale Law Journal* (1954), the overall power base of the AMA was described as resulting from three primary sources: (1) power over the medical profession, (2) a strong economic position, and (3) the social status of the physician. The power of the AMA over the medical profession was described as the power of *consent, monopoly,* and *coercion.* Hyde and Wolff speculated that the AMA did have the consent of many physicians to represent organized medicine. This consent was derived from awareness that a formal organization was needed to enforce professional integrity, to advance professional interests, and to resist lay attempts to control medical matters. Monopoly resulted from the AMA's position as the only nationally recognized professional association available to the physician. The AMA's power of coercion was due to its authority to ostracize offending physicians and also to the incorporation of AMA guidelines into state medical practice laws and licensing procedures.

One of the most significant guiding principles of the AMA had been its view of the physician as an independent practitioner largely free of public control who engages in private medical practice on a fee-for-service basis. Since the 1920s a considerable portion of the AMA's energies has gone toward maintaining this situation. One major result is that the public image of the American Medical Association has become that of a protective trade association seeking to ensure that the position of the physician as an individual entrepreneur of health services is not undermined. Yet the AMA's claim that it speaks for the majority of medical doctors is somewhat misleading as less than half of all physicians are members. In 1963, 79 percent of all doctors belonged to the AMA; in 1992, the figure of 43 percent represents a substantial decrease.

Consequently, there may be considerably more variation in the medical and political attitudes of medical doctors in the United States than has previously been assumed. If this is the case, then the reputation of the AMA as a powerful lobby in Washington, D.C., may, to some extent, be spurious. David Mechanic (1972:28) seems to find for a weaker AMA when he explains that the idea of any particular political group's being able to dominate health policy is not consistent with the history of recent social legislation in health care. Although the AMA opposed both Medicare and other federal medical programs, these programs became law.

However, the evidence does not go so far as to conclude that the AMA no longer yields significant influence in health legislation. In fact, as Mechanic has also pointed out, even legislation that passed Congress over the objections of the AMA has taken those objections into account and attempted to protect the interests of the medical profession as much as possible. With its organization, influence, and financing, the AMA will likely remain a very important factor in future legislative battles in the health sector and will continue to be instrumental in shaping the overall direction of the medical profession. As Stevens (1971:532) has surmised in her analysis of the medical profession, the primary future role of the AMA seems likely to be that of a negotiating body with government and a governmental agent (by way of providing professional standards and discipline), rather than a protective trade association or the spokesman for medical education and health workforce development. The AMA still has a critical role in policy development and administration of any national programs dealing with health care.

The Control of Medical Education

The professionalization of medicine would not have been possible without control over the standards for medical education (Ludmerer 1985; Stevens 1971). At the beginning of the nineteenth century, the United States had seen the emergence of a vast number of proprietary medical schools. These schools, in the absence of any educational controls, were designed to offer medical degrees as part of a profit-making venture. It is estimated that about 400 proprietary medical schools existed during the 1800s; generally they had low standards of instruction, poor facilities, and admitted any student who could pay the required tuition. Since proprietary schools competed with other schools of this type and with schools affiliated with universities, they attempted to make their programs as attractive as possible. One school, for example, gave free trips to Europe upon graduation to any students who paid fees regularly and in cash for three years (Stevens 1971). Anyone who had the financial resources could obtain a medical degree and practice medicine, especially in the developing American West.

In 1904 the AMA established the Council on Medical Education to originate suggestions for the improvement of education and to become the association's agency for implementing educational change. The council eventually became an important regulating agency that operated both to establish high standards in medical schools and to strengthen the AMA's influence in medical education. The subsequent success of this effort was stimulated by one of the most important events in the history of medical education: the Flexner Report.

Sponsored by the Carnegie Foundation for the Advancement of Teaching, Abraham Flexner visited every medical school in the country and issued his famous report in 1910. Hoping to obtain funds from the prestigious Carnegie Foundation, most medical schools were anxious to discuss their problems and shortcomings while extending their full cooperation to Flexner in assessing their particular situation. The Flexner Report came out as a devastating indictment of the lack of quality medical education in the United States. Only three medical schools—Harvard, Western Reserve, and Johns Hopkins—were given full approval; many other schools were characterized by Flexner as "plague spots," "utterly wretched," "out-and-out commercial enterprises," "wholly inadequate," and so forth (Stevens 1971:67).

Flexner strongly recommended that medical schools consist of a full-time faculty and that both laboratory and hospital facilities be made available to medical students. He also urged that standards concerning the admission of students to medical schools be established and that the qualifications of medical school faculty be raised significantly. He likewise believed that medical education should be conducted by universities on a graduate level and that teaching and research functions be integrated within the institution offering the instruction. The example of a model medical school was Johns Hopkins University, with its medical education system containing a medical school, a nursing school, and a university hospital. Johns Hopkins required the bachelor's degree or its equivalent for admission as well as specific premedical college-level courses.

Although widespread protests arose from the affected schools, the Flexner Report induced considerable improvement in medical education. The better schools improved their programs and the lesser schools eventually closed because of the bad publicity, financial adversity, and failure to meet the requirements of state licensing boards. Many states refused to certify the graduates of inferior medical schools, and money from various foundations was usually channeled only into those schools with good reputations. Since the sole source of medical school ratings continued to be the AMA's Council on Medical Education, the medical profession was able to retain an effective monopoly over educational regulation.

In summary, by the mid-1920s, the medical profession had consolidated its professional position to the point that it clearly had become a model of professionalism. According to Goode's analysis of the characteristics of a profession, the medical profession had not only met the basic criteria of being a service occupation supported by prolonged training in a specialized knowledge, but furthermore, it had determined its own standards of education and training, had successfully demanded high-caliber students, had staffed its own licensing and admission boards, had shaped legislation in its own interests, had developed stringent professional sanctions, had become a terminal occupation, and was free of formal lay evaluation and control. Although threatened by social legislation regarding reforms in health care, physicians constitute, and will in all probability remain, the dominant professional group in the rendering of medical service in the United States.

THE SOCIALIZATION OF THE PHYSICIAN

To understand the perspectives of physicians as a professional group, it is important also to consider the manner in which physicians are selected and trained as medical professionals. In the 1990s, about 16,500 students will be selected annually out of more than 40,000 applicants to begin training at 126 medical schools in the United States. The number of applicants to medical schools declined from a high of 36,727 in 1981 to 26,721 in 1988; however, the most recent figures available disclose that applications to medical schools have shot up dramatically as 33,600 students applied in 1991 and over 40,000 in 1993. Some 60 percent of first-year students will be male; the remaining 40 percent represents a significant increase for females. In the 1970s only about 10 percent of all first-year medical students were female. There has also been an increase in the percentage of racial minority students. Since 1969, the percentage of racial minorities in first-year classes has risen from 3 to 27 percent. Because of these changes, about 40 percent of the medical students in the United States are white males.

Typically, first-year medical students will be between the ages of twenty-one and twenty-three and will have at least a bachelor's degree with a 3.4 (on a 4.0 scale) premedical grade point average. Most likely the undergraduate college major will be in biology, chemistry, zoology, premedical, or psychology. Because these students are motivated and committed to a well-defined, terminal career goal, they have a high probability of successfully completing medical school once accepted; about 95 percent of all entering medical students currently attain the M.D. degree.

Several studies on the social origins of American medical students clearly show that most are from upper- and upper-middle-class families. Although increasing numbers of lower-middle- and lower-class students are entering medical school, most medical students are homogeneous in terms of social class affiliation. For instance, Howard Becker and his associates (1961), in a major study of students at the University of Kansas Medical School in the late 1950s, found that lower-class medical students, by virtue of their undergraduate education and commitment to becoming successful physicians, had clearly assimilated middle-class norms and values.

Oswald Hall (1948) has pointed out that the decision to study medicine is largely social in character; that is, it originates in a social group that is able to generate and nurture the medical ambition. Family influence is an especially important variable in encouraging and reinforcing the ambitions of the future recruit to the medical profession, and having a parent, close relative, or family friend who is a physician also seems to be a distinct advantage promoting the desire to be a doctor (Bloom 1973; Rogoff 1957).

The reason given by many medical students for choosing a career in medicine has been generally that of wanting "to help people." Becker and his associates, for example, found that first-year medical students had idealistic long-range perspectives about why they selected medicine as a career. These perspectives were summarized as follows (Becker et al. 1961:72):

1. Medicine is the best of all professions.
2. When we begin to practice, we want to help people, have enjoyable, satisfying work while upholding medical ideas. We want to earn enough money to lead comfortable lives, but this is not our primary concern.

Some medical students no doubt enter medical school in order to make money or for the prestige of the M.D. degree or both. According to John Columbotos (1969), physicians from a lower-class social origin were more likely than upper-class doctors to emphasize success values as reasons for going into medicine. But once in medical practice, social class background became less significant. Those physicians who were initially success oriented became less so after commencing their practices, while the reverse occurred with those who were less success oriented. Columbotos suggested this trend was most likely due to socialization by colleagues. Success-oriented physicians were probably encouraged to be less obvious about their ambitions, and the less success oriented were most likely encouraged to strive for the level of status indicative of their professional group. Becker and his associates noted that most entering medical students *assumed* they would be well paid. Hence, making money was apparently secondary to helping patients. Many resented the notion that they were solely out to make money.

Once the medical student begins training, he or she is expected to acquire a foundation of knowledge in the basic medical sciences and the techniques employed in the actual practice of medicine. Included in this process is the internalization of ethical and moral principles that are essential if the physician is to be trusted by patients, colleagues, and the community and is to maintain professional autonomy. Most courses of study range from thirty-two to forty-five months, and the educational experience is usually divided into basic medical science studies and clinical studies. Basic medical science studies consist of courses in anatomy, biochemistry, physiology, pathology, pharmacology, microbiology, physical diagnosis, clinical laboratory procedures, and often behavioral science. The clinical programs consist of learning to use basic medical science to solve clinical problems by working with patients under the supervision of the faculty. The students also rotate through clerkships in various medical services, such as medicine, surgery, pediatrics, obstetrics-gynecology, psychiatry, and other specialties.

Much of the sociological research concerning medical education has focused on the consequences of that experience other than mastery of medical knowledge. Among the major studies, Renée Fox (1957) found that medical students at Cornell Medical School acquired basically two traits as a result of their medical training: ability to be emotionally detached from the patient and to tolerate uncertainty. Fox, whose work was part of an extensive study of student physicians (Merton, Reader, and Kendall 1957), noted that the medical student experienced three types of uncertainty. First, there was uncertainty resulting from an awareness of not being able to learn everything about medicine. Second, there was the realization that limitations existed in current medical knowledge and techniques. The first two uncertainties led to a third type of uncertainty in which medical students had problems distinguishing between personal ignorance and the limits of available knowledge. However, Fox observed that as the student acquired medical knowledge and gained experience, along with a sense of personal adequacy in medicine, he or she learned to cope with the uncertainty and to assess conflicting evidence objectively in arriving at a diagnosis. This process was assisted by the realization that other medical students were coping with the same problems and that the faculty also experienced uncertainty in their everyday work.

At the University of Kansas Medical School, Becker and his colleagues (1961) determined that the students developed a strong appreciation of clinical experience (actually working with patients rather than reading about disease and studying it in the laboratory) and that they acquired a sense of responsibility about patients. They also learned to view disease and death as medical problems rather than as emotional issues. The focal point of their passage through medical school was to graduate; since they could not learn everything they needed to know to practice medicine, they directed their efforts toward finding the most economical ways of learning. Generally, they tried to guess what the faculty wanted them to know, and then they studied this material for the examinations. Even so, they found that they put in an eight-hour day of classes and laboratories. They also studied four to five hours on week nights and continued studying on the weekends.

One aspect of medical training that appears in several more recent studies of medical students in the United States (Broadhead 1983; Conrad 1988b; Coombs 1978; Mizrahi 1986; Smith and Kleinman 1989), Canada (Haas and Shaffir 1977, 1982; Shapiro 1978), and Israel (Adler and Shuval 1978) is the finding that the experience tends to promote impersonal attitudes toward patients. Robert Coombs, for example, found that in a California medical school the faculty gave little real guidance in how to manage patients except to serve as role models for emotional control and a businesslike demeanor. In Canada, Jack Haas and William Shaffir found the students to be initially dismayed by how the teaching faculty and other hospital staff members treated patients. One student reported:

> What I do remember about Phase II that really got me when I did go to a cancer clinic at the Fensteran and I saw the way they were just herding in ladies that had hysterectomies and cancer, and just the way the doctors would walk right in and wouldn't even introduce us as students, and just open them up and just look and say a lot of heavy jargon. And the ladies would be saying, "How is it," "Am I better, or worse?" And they say in this phony reassuring tone, "Yes, you're fine," and take you into the hallway and say how bad the person was.
>
> They hardly talked to the patient at all. Like this was a big check up after waiting three months or six months and then the doctor whips in for two minutes to take a quick look and then they're gone. We would get in there and he'd hold the speculum and we'd all take a look and we would just herd right out again into another room and have a look and herd out again. I thought the dehumanization was awful.[2]

In trying to cope with the situation, the students began to rationalize that the large number of patients seen by the physicians precluded them from doing anything more than attending to the patient's medical condition. There were just too many patients and not enough time to deal with psychosocial problems. In fact, in their own work, the students found themselves depersonalizing patients so they could concentrate on learning what was medically important. A student described the situation this way:

[2]Jack Hass and William Shaffir, "The Professionalization of Medical Students: Developing Competence and a Cloak of Competence," *Symbolic Interaction*, 1 (1977), 82.

I think you realize that there is a structural problem, and there are a lot of demands made on you and you are forced to act in certain ways just to accomplish your work. But right now in the training phase, I find if the clinical preceptor takes me around to listen to six patients with heart murmurs and I only have five minutes with each patient, I don't get concerned that I'm not getting it on with the patient, because I'm trying to learn about heart murmurs.[3]

Previously, the Becker study had attempted to assess the general impact of such attitudes by exploring the charge that medical students become cynical as a result of their medical education. In reply, Becker and his colleagues noted that medical students did appear to enter medical school openly idealistic, but once in medical school, their idealism was replaced with a concern for getting through. Becker observed that medical students may in fact become cynical while in school, but he also pointed out that attitudes are often situational. Thus, when graduation approached, idealism seemed to return as the students could set aside the immediate problem of completing their program of study. What had happened was that medical students had been isolated in an institutional setting and forced to adjust to the demands of that setting. But once the medical student was ready to return to the mainstream of society, the student again became concerned about service to humanity. In an earlier article, Becker and Blanche Greer (1958) had argued that cynicism on the part of medical students represented growth toward a more realistic perspective. What appeared as a harmful change of attitude was actually part of a functional learning process fitted to the physician's role of maintaining an objective perspective of health and disease. The Coombs (1978) study likewise found that medical students' cynicism did not develop into a generalized personality trait. The students in this study learned to balance emotional attitudes with sensitivity toward patients.[4]

---

[3]Haas and Shaffir, "The Professionalization of Medical Students," p. 71.

[4]Some physicians do not need to spend a lot of time with patients. Consider, for example, the report of William Nolen (1970:191–192), who was undergoing training as a resident in surgery at a hospital on Long Island, New York:

> Steel was no slouch as a diagnostician. He was one of those surgeons who have a sixth sense about symptoms and could learn more about a patient in five minutes than most doctors do in an hour. I took him to see one of our rare service cases, an eight-year-old boy admitted for possible appendicitis. Steele spent two minutes with him and we stepped back into the corridor.
> "Did you notice the way he kept his right knee bent? Did you see that he wasn't moving his abdomen at all when he breathed? Did you get a look at how dry his tongue was? That kid's got peritonitis. Put him on [surgery] schedule."
> "But his white count is only nine thousand and his temperature is normal," I objected.
> "Nolen, let me tell you something," Steele said. "Try looking at the patient instead of the chart. The chart isn't sick."
> The boy had a ruptured appendix with peritonitis.

Yet Robert Broadhead (1983) observed in his study of medical students in California that while idealism returned at the end of their education, it was modified to allow for personal success. Though appearing idealistic, the students did not choose to provide basic medical care for the poor or select to practice medicine in geographic areas that most needed doctors. Elsewhere in two midwestern schools, Bebe Lavin and her colleagues (Lavin et al. 1987) found medical students developing more egalitarian attitudes toward patients in order to deal effectively with the new consumerist patients.

For some physicians the possibility still remains that medical training has focused their attention more on technical procedures than on dealing with patients as people. As Donald Light (1979) points out, in emphasizing clinical judgments and techniques physicians run the danger of becoming insensitive to complexities in diagnosis, treatment, and relations with patients. The result can be errors and malpractice suits. Light (1979:320) explains: "Their emphasis on techniques can make them oblivious to the needs of clients as *clients* define them; yet it is clients' trust that professionals will solve their complex problems which provides the foundation of professional power." Zeev Ben-Sira (1980), for instance, has found in Israel that, especially for lower-class patients, some emotional support by the physician will not only reduce the patient's uncertainty about the type and outcome of treatment but will also have a significant impact on the patient's evaluation of treatment. In the United States, Catherine Ross and Raymond Duff (1982) found that poorly educated persons were most likely to have their questions ignored by physicians and be treated as a disease entity instead of an individual to be respected. While there are signs of change among doctors, the narrow technical orientation of medical training and practice still shows some inherent tendencies to depersonalize patients (Anspach 1988; Bloom 1988; Conrad 1988b).

As medical education heads into the twenty-first century, significant changes are taking place. Since 1975, the number of male applicants has declined almost 50 percent and medical school classes are no longer composed almost entirely of white males. Females and racial minority students have taken their place, which indicates that the image of the medical profession as white and male is changing toward one of greater diversity. Admissions criteria also have been broadened to include a greater mix of students, not just women and racial minorities, but students whose background and undergraduate experiences suggest they will be likely to take a humanistic approach in dealing with patients (Gallagher and Searle 1989).

Furthermore, as Light (1988) and others (Gallagher and Searle 1989; Kendall and Reader 1988) indicate, medical education is having to adjust to new realities in medical practice. These realities, as Light points out, include the transition in American health care delivery from (1) a system run by doctors to one shaped by the purchasers of care and the competition for profits; (2) a decline in the public's trust in doctors to greater questioning and even distrust; (3) a change in emphasis on specialization and subspecialization to primary care and prevention; (4) less hospital care to more outpatient care in homes and doctors' offices;

and (5) less payment of costs incurred by doctors' decisions to fixed prepayments, with demands for detailed accounts of decisions and their effectiveness. Even though the medical profession and medical schools have a long tradition of conservatism, medical education is gradually adjusting to the realities of medical practice in order to better prepare medical students for the changing environment they will face in the next century (Bloom 1988; Gallagher and Searle 1989; Light 1988).

THE POWER STRUCTURE OF AMERICAN MEDICINE

Like any other profession, medicine has its own power structure. One of the early studies concerning the power structure of the medical profession was done by Oswald Hall (1946, 1948) in an eastern American city. Hall identified three factors important in establishing prestige within the medical profession: (1) hospital affiliation, (2) clientele, and (3) the inner fraternity.

The Hospital

A most significant factor in a successful urban medical career, according to Hall, was affiliation with a prestigious hospital because the more important hospital positions were usually associated with the more financially rewarding medical practices. Therefore, gaining an appointment at a prestigious hospital represented a crucial point in the career development of the urban physician.

Of particular significance was the initial appointment because, as Hall (1948:330) explains, "the internship that a doctor has served is a distinctive badge; it is one of the most enduring criteria in the evaluation of his status." In a study of the Harvard Medical Unit at Boston City Hospital, Stephen Miller (1970) found that the "best" internship was not necessarily determined by the quality of teaching, the type of patient, or the range of responsibility interns were allowed to assume, though these factors were important. The "best" referred to the reputation of the program and its location.

The reputation of an internship or residency in major medical and research institutions assists the candidate's entry into academic medical circles. For those physicians wishing to become general practitioners, the optional setting for an internship would be in communities where they hoped to build a medical practice. Even at the local level, the initial hospital appointment was important in that it facilitated the formation of friendships and professional relationships that could help to enhance a career. Usually the location of an internship or residency determines the system of medical institutions and group of physicians the new doctor will be associated with in the future.

For example, Miller observed that the Harvard program of graduate medical training was much more than a way to meet licensing requirements; it was a means by which an academic appointment at a "name" medical school could be secured. As one of the Harvard interns explained to Miller:

I'm going into academic medicine, and I wanted the internship which was the best or very good; I think of the word "prestige," a great deal of prestige in being part of this group. It just has a very good reputation, you know. It will look good on paper.[5]

All interns, however, do not receive their first choice for an internship since there are usually many more applicants than positions in the programs with the best reputations. Hall found that the likelihood of gaining an appointment depended much less on superior technical competence than on the future intern's acceptability to the institution of choice. It was not the individual traits that were important, but whether those traits could be assimilated by the institution itself. The department head of a large Catholic hospital told Hall that:

One of our most important problems here is picking interns. The main qualification as far as I can see is "personality." Now that is an intangible sort of thing. It means partly to mix well, to be humble to older doctors to the correct degree, and to be able to assume the proper degree of superiority toward the patient. Since all medical schools are now Grade A, there is no point in holding competitive examinations. So the main problem confronting the selection committee is that of getting interns who will fit well into the pattern of the hospital.[6]

A similar pattern of attitudes toward applicants was apparent in the Miller study in Boston. One of the senior resident physicians in the study informed Miller that:

. . . interviews here do not carry a great deal of weight, and people are accepted or rejected mostly in terms of where they stood in their medical school class and the kind of recommendations they get. But I suppose, in general, what we look for in the interview is some assurance that the [person] is reasonably mature and sensible. The people coming here obviously are all intelligent. We look for what their interests in the future might be. I think, by and large, people coming here are interested in academic careers, and somebody who is interested in general practice in Rudolph Junction, probably, this isn't the internship for him.[7]

Many of the interns in the Harvard program were graduates of "name" medical schools. About 50 percent had graduated from Harvard and another 30 percent were from schools like Cornell, Yale, and Johns Hopkins. The remaining 20 percent were from other medical schools. Thus, it was possible for the graduate of a "lesser" school to begin an internship with the Harvard group in order to ac-

[5]Stephen J. Miller, *Prescription for Leadership: Training for the Medical Elite* (Chicago: Aldine, 1970), p. 81.

[6]Oswald Hall, "The Stages of a Medical Career," *American Journal of Sociology*, 53 (March 1948), 330.

[7]Miller, *Prescription for Leadership*, pp. 59–60.

quire the background for an academic appointment at higher-level medical institutions. As Miller explained, there were not enough "name" medical school graduates for all the internships available; then, too, the Harvard Medical Unit limited the number of Harvard graduates it would accept in order to avoid the "inbreeding" of its faculty.

Yet the process of selection for the Harvard Medical Unit was not entirely democratic. Since many graduates of the program had gone on to the faculties of other medical schools, a large number of schools featured alumni of the unit, in effect a "colony" of physicians with the same medical background. Their letters of recommendation as former students, graduates, and people known to the Harvard Medical Unit greatly assisted the acceptability of applicants. Miller noted that all of the interns from lesser known schools in his study of the Harvard Medical Unit program were graduates of medical schools where Harvard alumni constituted a colony. Miller (1970:70) stated: "Most learned about the program from, discussed it with, and were advised to choose it by Harvard Medical Unit alumni." So not only were initial appointments important for the future careers of the interns, but also the gaining of these appointments was influenced to a certain degree by having recommendations from the "right" people. Hall found a similar trend in his study of the medical career.

Another consideration in understanding the importance of the hospital is that within the hospital, physicians are arranged in a hierarchy of status—intern, resident, staff member, and associate staff member. Each level represents progress in a medical career and indicates the status and privileges of the doctors involved. There are differences in status not only within hospitals, but also between hospitals. Hall noted in his study that the major hospitals were organized according to social class and ethnic differentials. The leading physicians in the community were characterized by Hall as upper-class Yankees who attended expensive universities as undergraduates and the better known medical schools, especially Harvard. Then they held internships at the dominant Yankee hospital. These Yankee physicians entered the practice of medicine in their community from the vantage point of being associated with the "best" hospital.

In contrast, Hall found that Italian M.D.'s found it difficult to gain a position at Yankee hospitals. Instead they sought an alternate route of career advancement in Catholic hospitals, which could both provide a good career and protect the Italian physician from Yankee competition. The point made by Hall was that the successful practice of medicine involved participation in a hospital system, which in turn provided the physician with integration into the other medical institutions in the community. The marginal people in medical practice, according to Hall, were those who had abandoned the shelter of a hospital affiliation and had gone out on their own in the wider competitive field of medicine. The same pattern appeared in the Miller study. One of the Harvard Medical Unit interns, who was a native of Boston and wanted to practice medicine there, made it quite clear that being without "connections at the Harvard hospitals" was like being in "exile" (Miller 1970:80).

Paul Starr (1982) adds that in the decades since World War II there has been a steady extension of the power of medical schools into the hospital systems of metropolitan areas. Noting that some critics depicted these schools as "empires," Starr found that the schools held a powerful position in medical affairs because of their control over academic appointments, hospital privileges, and hospital equipment and labor. Such medical centers, states Starr (1982:361): "typically would not only have a medical and dental school but also schools in pharmacy, public health, nursing, and other paramedical occupations; research institutes for heart disease, mental illness, cancer, rehabilitations, and other fields; several general teaching hospitals, perhaps a women's hospital, a children's hospital, a psychiatric hospital, various clinics, doctors' office buildings, and so on."

Consequently, universities became the hubs for the nation's regional medical centers even though their primary orientation was toward research and training rather than patient care. The most powerful figures in these medical centers were the professors who chaired the major medical school departments and were chiefs of medicine, surgery, psychiatry, obstetrics-gynecology, and pediatrics in the teaching hospitals. They were the ones who controlled policy-making boards and determined the careers of interns and residents. As one administrator put it: "It is inconceivable that the university would try to carry out a policy contrary to the wishes of the department chairmen of the Medical School and damned difficult for the hospital to carry out a policy contrary to the wishes of the chiefs" (Duff and Hollingshead 1968:46). Such a situation, as Starr observes, is practically a textbook definition of power.

The Clientele

The next stage described by Hall is that of acquiring a clientele and retaining and improving it. Hall likened this process to that of a commercial enterprise in that the physician needed to play the role of a promoter. In other words, the physician was required to interact with patients so as to secure their approval of the services provided. Freidson (1960) has pointed out that the lay-referral system not only channels the patient to certain doctors, but also helps the patient to make a decision about returning to a particular doctor. Freidson notes that the first visit to a doctor is often tentative, especially in a community large enough to support more than one doctor. Freidson (1960:378) states: "Whether the physician's prescription will be followed or not, and whether the patient will come back, seems to rest at least partly on his retrospective assessment of the professional consultation." Thus, the patient not only passes through the lay-referral system on the way to the physician, but also on the way back by discussing the doctor's behavior, diagnosis, and prescription with family and friends. In a given community, certain doctors are often chosen more frequently than others merely because they are fashionable or popular. Most physicians become aware of lay expectations and learn to deal with them if they expect patients to return.

Furthermore, Hall observed that success in medicine involves improving the practice by attracting the desired type of patient and discouraging those patients who do not fit into the physician's conception of his or her practice. It may also be true that more affluent patients desire to be treated with others of their kind, so a physician who treats both the rich and the poor in the same setting and under the same circumstances would run the risk of offending the rich. Michael Miller (1973) has observed that upper-class patients will change physicians sooner than lower-class patients.

Although the evidence is not conclusive, existing studies generally suggest that physicians tend to favor upper- and middle-class patients. Physicians who routinely treat more affluent patients tend to have greater status among their colleagues (Link 1983). Besides being perceived as more likely to pay their bills, upper- and middle-class patients also reflect values, norms, and attitudes similar to those of the physician. Duff and Hollingshead (1968), for example, found that physicians tended to be more attentive to upper-class patients by "overidentifying" with them.

The best medical practice in Hall's study was the specialized practice because Hall believed the specialist was accorded superior status by others in the medical profession. Other observers (Stevens 1971; Mechanic 1972) have also pointed toward the trend in specialization, which has resulted in the decline in number of general practitioners and the domination of the medical profession by speciality groups. A specialized practice, however, is dependent on having a group of colleagues who refer patients to the specialist. Generally, referring physicians are reciprocated by fee sharing or by the referral of patients back to the general practitioner. A specialized practice also requires access to hospital facilities, and hospital connections in themselves facilitate the development of referral relationships between physicians.

In a study of internists (specialists in internal medicine) in private practice in Chicago, Stephen Shortell (1973) found that they tended to refer their patients to other specialists on the hospital staff where they held a primary appointment. The influence of the hospital appointment was such that it provided both formal and informal channels of communication about who was available in the various specialties and what relative advantages they had to offer. Furthermore, the ability to follow up on a patient after care had been turned over to another specialist or specialists depended on the internist's being on the same hospital staff.

Shortell's study traced the informal organization of medical practice by extensively examining the referral process. He found that patterns of referrals were related to the professional status of the physicians and operated according to the relative rewards and costs perceived by physicians at different levels of the status hierarchy. High-status internists, for example, tended to refer their patients to other high-status colleagues, while lower-status internists also more often referred their patients to higher-status physicians than to their peers. Higher-status physicians thus tended to be the major recipients of referrals. High-status physicians primarily choose each other as referral partners because the exchange helps validate their own personal status and maintains the status structure of their own group as well. Lower-status physicians, however, tend to refer patients outside their group because of the prestige rewards of dealing with higher-status physicians and because of a potential loss of clientele to fellow low-status competitors. The reasoning was that low-status physicians were much more likely to be concerned about building their medical practice and thereby might tend to retain patients sent to them. High-status physicians, on the other hand, would already have a successful practice and would not be so desirous of acquiring more patients on a regular basis.

The "Inner Fraternity"

Hall's study pointed toward the existence of an "inner fraternity" in medicine that operated to recruit new members, to allocate these new members to positions in the various medical institutions, and to help them secure patients through referrals. Hall believed that the urban power structure of the medical profession consisted of four major groups of physicians. The first group was the "inner core," which Hall described as the specialists who have control of the major hospital positions. Immediately outside this inner core were the new recruits at various stages of their careers who were intended to inherit positions in the inner core at some time in the future. Next were the general practitioners who were linked to the inner core by the referral system. Women physicians tend to fall into this second group of "friendly outsiders"—that is, not members of the inner core (Lorber 1993). Besides these two groups were the marginal physicians, those who would remain on the fringes of the system because the inner core had its own methods of selecting recruits. According to Hall, the key to understanding the power structure of the medical profession was found in the system of control exercised by the inner core. The inner core displayed three major characteristics that enabled it to control the medical profession. First, it was a highly cohesive group of specialists with relatively identical educations and socioeconomic backgrounds, technical interdependence, and daily working relationships. Second, the social bonds between different specialists allowed these powerful physicians to integrate the various specialties into a cohesive body. And third, the inner core was able to organize the medical market by controlling the process in which patients were referred from one physician to another.

What Hall's analysis has provided in terms of understanding the power structure of the medical profession is the realization that a doctor's career takes place in a system of formal and informal relationships with colleagues. Formal relationships develop as a result of a physician's position within the prevailing medical institutions in a particular community. The control of the dominant posts within these institutions, especially hospital appointments, is the critical variable that distinguishes influential from noninfluential doctors. Informal relationships also develop over time as physicians interact with one another frequently and arrive at definitions of the quality of each other's work and personal characteristics. Thus, claims to position, status, and power become recognized and are perpetuated within the profession, and mechanisms for recruitment into the inner core become established in both formal and informal ways.

The most significant variable to emerge from this discussion of the power structure of the American medical profession is that of institutional position. The medical profession is based upon a variety of institutions—hospitals, clinics, medical schools, the AMA, and so forth. The policies and practices of these institutions are determined by those individuals who occupy decision-making positions within them. Power and influence among physicians (as in any other professional group) derive from being in a position to direct or at least share in a decision-making process that formulates significant professional policies.

SUMMARY

This chapter has examined the professional development of physicians by highlighting the manner in which an initial service orientation and development of a specialized body of knowledge resulted in power and status in American society. Instrumental in this evolution was the organization of the American Medical Association which expanded and protected the rights and privileges of doctors. In recent years, however, the AMA has sometimes been perceived as a protective trade association for physicians rather than having public welfare as its central interest. Although still influential, the AMA has lost power. There are increasing signs of changed attitudes toward their professional position on the part of many physicians, which suggests that greater attention to the needs of society may be ahead. The power structure of American medicine was also discussed from the standpoint of hospitals, clientele, and the "inner fraternity." The most powerful positions in medicine are those associated with prestigious academic appointments in the university medical centers of large urban areas.

Nurses, Physician Assistants, and Midwives

11

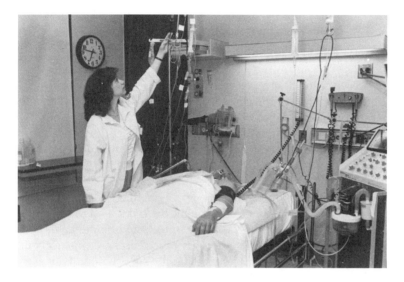

A lthough the dominant form of social interaction in the health care relationship
has traditionally been that of the one-to-one encounter between the physician
and the patient, the technical complexity and range of contemporary medical care
have evolved well beyond this exclusive two-person social system. Modern medical treatment has come to involve a great variety of health personnel who specialize in treatment, laboratory procedures, therapy, rehabilitation, and administration. More than four million people in the United States are currently employed in
nonphysician tasks related to health care.

Other than a few consulting professions such as clinical psychology, the
occupations performing tasks of patient care are organized around the work of
the physician and are usually under the physician's direct control. Eliot Freidson
(1970a:49) claims that these occupations—such as nurse, pharmacist, laboratory
technician, physical therapist—reflect four characteristic features that account for
their subordinate position in the practice of medicine. First of all, Freidson notes
that the technical knowledge employed in health occupations needs to be approved by physicians. Second, these workers usually assist physicians in their
work rather than replace the basic skills of diagnosis and treatment. Third, such
workers are subordinate to the physician because their work largely occurs at the
"request of" the physician; the "doctor's orders" provide them with their work re-

quirements. And fourth, among the various occupational roles in the health field, physicians have the greatest prestige.

However, just as the physician–patient relationship appears to be moving toward less dependency and increased equality for the patient, signs of a similar trend have begun to appear in the physician–registered nurse relationship. The time may come when patients will be treated by a medical team in which the physician is no longer an all-powerful figure and nurses will have greater autonomy in their role (Porter 1992).

NURSING: PAST AND PRESENT

Nursing represents the largest single group of health workers in the United States, with an estimated 1,715,600 people employed as licensed registered nurses in 1990; another 180,000 people were estimated to be employed as licensed practical nurses. About 75 percent of all licensed registered and practical nurses in the United States work in hospitals and nursing homes, while the remainder are employed in doctors' offices, public health agencies, schools, industrial plants, programs of nursing education, or as private duty nurses.

Registered nurses are responsible for the nature and quality of all nursing care patients receive, as well as for following the instructions of physicians regarding patients. In addition, they supervise practical nurses and other health personnel involved in providing patient care. The primary task of licensed practical nurses is the bedside care of patients; they may also assist in the supervision of auxiliary nursing workers such as nurse's aides, orderlies, and attendants. These auxiliary nursing personnel, who numbered 268,113 in the United States as of 1990, assist registered and practical nurses by performing less skilled medical care tasks and by providing many services designed for the overall personal comfort and welfare of patients.

Whereas the licensed registered and practical nurses and nurse's aides are generally women, orderlies and attendants are usually men employed to care for male patients and perform whatever heavy duties are required in nursing care. Nursing tasks obviously occur in a system of social relationships that are highly stratified by sex. The registered nurse, who has the most advanced training and professional qualifications of any of the nursing workers, is generally a female who is matched occupationally with a physician, whose role is dominant and who, in the past, was likely to be a male. The registered nurse, in turn, supervises lesser trained females (practical nurses and nurse's aides) and lesser trained males (orderlies and attendants). Thus emerges the traditional stereotype of the physician as father figure and the nurse as mother figure.

The Early Development of Nursing as an Occupation

While males perform nursing tasks, the social role of the nurse has been profoundly affected by its identification with traditionally feminine functions (Carpenter 1993; Davis 1966, 1972; Freidson 1970a, 1970b; Mauksch 1972; Olesen and Whittaker 1968;

Porter 1992; Strauss 1966). For instance, Hans Mauksch (1972:208) pointed out that in many European languages the very word *sister* not only refers to nuns but also generically identifies the nurse. In the English language, the word *nurse* carries with it a connotation of the mother's relationship to her child. Accordingly, the initial image of the nurse in Western society was that of a "mother-surrogate," in which nursing was equated with the mothering function (Schulman 1972).

Following the rise of Christianity in the Western world, the practice of nursing as a formal occupation was significantly influenced by the presence of large numbers of nuns who performed nursing services under auspices of the Roman Catholic Church. Prior to the late nineteenth century, hospitals were generally defined as places for the poor and lower social classes, often little more than "flophouses"; anyone who could afford it was usually cared for at home. Nursing activities in hospitals were thus viewed as acts of charity because they were usually carried out under difficult and unpleasant circumstances, as nurses served the personal needs of patients who were usually dirty and illiterate as well as diseased. Nursing under these conditions was regarded by the Church as a means by which those persons providing the services could attain spiritual salvation by helping those less fortunate. Hence, the original concept of nursing was not as a formal occupation with its own body of knowledge and specialized training procedures; rather, its primary focus as religious activity was in spiritual considerations. Nuns were not under the authority of doctors and they could refuse any orders they did not believe appropriate for themselves or their patients. Nuns were also reported to have refused to treat certain categories of patients such as unwed mothers or persons with venereal disease (Freidson 1970a).

Besides nuns, there were secular nurses working in public hospitals. But these women were characterized as "women off the streets" or "of bad character," who were considered as little or no better than the low class of patients for whom they provided their services. Well into the nineteenth century, nursing could be described as an activity for women who lacked specialized training in medical care, a supportive work role that was not officially incorporated into the formal structure of medical services. Moreover, nursing was not an occupation held in high regard by the general public.

Florence Nightingale

The role of nursing in Western society was changed in the middle of the nineteenth century through the insight and effort of Florence Nightingale. Nightingale, an English Protestant from a respectable middle-class family, believed that God had called her to the service of Christianity as a result of a vision she had experienced in 1837. There was some confusion, however, on Nightingale's part as to exactly what service she was expected to render. Being a Protestant, she could not choose to become a Catholic nun. She solved her dilemma by deciding to become a nurse. Over the strong objections of her family and after a delay of several years, she was finally able to secure training as a nurse from a Protestant minister in Germany.

Returning to England in 1853, Nightingale established a hospital for "Sick Gentlewomen in Distressed Circumstances" and staffed it with trained nurses from good families. She insisted that nursing was intended to become an honorable and respected occupation and she sought to achieve this through a formal training program with recruits from upper- and middle-class social backgrounds. Good intentions notwithstanding, Nightingale's hospital was not entirely successful because of the role conflict between the duties of the nurse and the prevailing standards of proper behavior for "ladies." Some of her nurses, for example, were reluctant to view nudity or to be present at physical examinations (Freidson 1970a).

However, in 1854 the Crimean War afforded Nightingale a much better opportunity to establish nursing as a formal occupation. She organized a contingent of nurses and, assisted by money raised by public subscription, she and her group sailed for the Crimea, where Great Britain, France, and Turkey were involved in war with Russia. Once there, Nightingale offered to the British military authorities the nursing services of her women for sick and wounded troops.

At first the military refused to employ her nurses and she retaliated by refusing to allow any of the nurses to provide patient care on their own initiative. Instead the nurses worked only when their assistance was specifically requested by physicians. Eventually such requests were forthcoming and Nightingale's nurses received considerable publicity in the British press as "angels of mercy." In fact, Nightingale's nurses had captured the imagination of the British public and when Nightingale returned to England after the war she found herself hailed as a heroine. Capitalizing upon her fame and popularity, she instigated a successful fund-raising effort that brought in enough money to organize a nursing school at St. Thomas Hospital in London. Other schools were also established and within a few years the "Nightingale system" became the model for nursing education.

Nightingale's approach to nursing training emphasized a code of behavior that idealized nurses as being responsible, clean, self-sacrificing, courageous, cool headed, hard working, obedient to the physician, and possessing the tender qualities of the mother; this idealized portrayal of nurses saw them as nothing less than "disciplined angels" (Strauss 1966). In reality, Nightingale had incorporated the best attributes of the mother and the housekeeper into her ideal nurse. This image did little to establish the view of nurses as having the qualities of leadership and independence necessary for true professional status. Although Nightingale had been able to establish nursing as a distinct and honorable occupation, her philosophy perpetuated the traditional social role of the nurse as a female supervised and controlled by a male physician. Perhaps in her time there was no other way to gain access to an official position within the male-dominated field of medicine, but the overall effect of subordination to the physician's orders weakened nursing's efforts in its struggle to achieve professionalization.

Nursing Education

Florence Nightingale's ideas formed the basis for establishing the first accredited schools of nursing in the United States. These schools, founded in 1873, were located at Bellevue Hospital in New York City, the Connecticut

Training School in New Haven, and the Boston Training School. Although they were intended to be separately administered, the new nursing schools were affiliated with hospitals that provided financial support and required, in turn, that the students furnish much of the nursing services on the hospital wards. During the late nineteenth and early twentieth centuries, the number of hospitals and hospital nursing schools grew rapidly. At the same time, increasing numbers of women entered the labor market due to immigration from abroad or migration from rural to urban areas. Nursing was an attractive occupation for many of these women because it afforded an opportunity for a woman to make a living and to also have a respectable position in the community.

But as Anselm Strauss (1966) and others have pointed out, many of the students in these early nursing schools did not receive the training that the Nightingale system required. Since only a few trained nurses were available and money was often in short supply, many hospital administrators and physicians, perhaps also unaware of Nightingale's techniques for training nurses, used nursing students as inexpensive and exploitable sources of hospital labor. As a result, much of the effort of nursing educators during the first decades of the twentieth century was directed at securing less hospital service and more education for nursing students in hospital schools. They also sought a university-based nursing school, with the first one being formed at the University of Minnesota in 1909.

While nursing educators were able to improve the standards of education for their students, they failed to obtain centralized control over educational programs. Unlike medical schools, which follow a prescribed and generally similar program of education leading to the M.D., nursing has been characterized by different types of educational experiences—all of which can qualify the student as a registered nurse. For example, there are currently three types of programs available for R.N.s: (1) two-year associate degree programs usually located in junior or community colleges; (2) hospital-based diploma schools requiring two and one-half to three years of study; (3) four-year and five-year university baccalaureate programs.

The most prestigious of the nursing education programs is the baccalaureate program, which is intended to provide training not only in nursing skills and theory, but also to provide the background for becoming a nursing educator or leader. But, as Mauksch (1972:211) makes clear, the graduates of any nursing program—despite the differences in time, money, effort and, supposedly, intellect demanded by their program—are virtually identical in terms of the basic skills required for their jobs.

The major source of nurses in the United States has traditionally been the hospital-based diploma school. College-based programs, with their combination of occupational training and liberal arts education, have become increasingly popular with nursing students in the last few years, although diploma schools provide more day-to-day experience with patients. As Table 11-1 shows, in 1961 diploma schools accounted for more than 80 percent of all nursing graduates, but by 1970 this percentage had declined to 52.3 percent and the period between 1970 and 1991 witnessed a further rapid decline to 8.5 percent. Although the percentage of graduates from baccalaureate programs increased over the period covered by Table 11-1, the primary beneficiary of declining numbers of diploma graduates had been the associate degree programs. With only 3 percent of the total number of nursing graduates in 1961, associate degree programs had grown to produce 64.9 percent of the total by 1990–1991.

The associate degree programs are relatively inexpensive, require only two years of training, and yet place their graduates on the same career track as graduates of diploma and baccalaureate degree schools. Originally conceived as a middle-range level of nursing education somewhere between the training required to perform simple or assisting nursing tasks and that required for complex tasks, the work role of the associate degree graduate has expanded into supervisory and management functions. Some controversy has arisen over this trend since it requires associate degree (AD) nurses to function beyond their intended level of training. Although problems regarding the work role persist, AD programs have become the largest single source of nurses in the United States.

Despite the remarkable growth of the associate degree programs and the growing acceptance of their graduates in nursing, their appearance has presented a special problem in terms of nursing's claims of professional status since the AD programs are essentially vocational rather than professional. A strategy to avoid this situation was to designate associate degree nurses as "technical" nurses and baccalaureate degree nurses as "professional" nurses, while advocating that all nurses be graduates of college programs at some time in the future. Although this became the official position of the American Nurses' Association in 1965, it was not accepted by the majority of its membership, who had graduated from diploma schools. These nurses replied that it would be a hardship for them to quit work and return to college and they pointed out that a liberal arts education did not help a nurse perform better nursing procedures (Olesen and Whittaker 1968). The end result was that among R.N.s the baccalaureate nurses are regarded as the *most* professional—leaders of organized nursing—yet associate degree and diploma nurses consider themselves to also be professionals.

In the late 1980s, however, nursing received a considerable boost in status and income with the development of a severe nursing shortage in American hospitals. The number of nursing school graduates declined significantly from more

TABLE 11-1   Schools of Nursing (R.N.) by Types of School and Percentage of Graduates (1961, 1970, 1983–1984, 1990–1991)

Type of School	1961 (N = 30,267)	1970 (N = 43,639)	1983–1984 (N = 80,312)	1990–1991 (N = 72,230)
Diploma	83.6	52.3	15.2	8.5
Associate Degree	3.0	26.8	55.3	64.9
Bachelor's Degree	13.4	20.9	29.5	26.6
TOTALS	100.0%	100.0%	100.0%	100.0%

Sources: National Center for Health Statistics, *Health Resources Statistics* (Washington, D.C.: U.S. Government Printing Office, 1978); *Nursing Data Review, 1992* (New York: National League of Nursing, 1993).

than 80,000 in 1983–1984 to less than 65,000 in 1987–1988. Long hours, stress, and low pay had reduced the attractiveness of nursing as a career field. In 1990–1991, as shown in Table 11-1, the number of graduates had increased to over 72,000. The enrollment in nursing schools had increased dramatically along with higher salaries. In 1980, starting salaries for nurses were $14,000; in 1992, the average beginning salary for a nurse was over $25,000 annually. In some large cities, experienced nurses earned over $50,000. As salaries and demand for nurses soared, nursing school enrollments reached 221,000 in 1990 compared with 187,000 in 1987. While the nursing shortage is likely to ease in the 1990s, an enhanced image of nursing as a career has taken place.

Nursing Students

In 1991, 1,484 schools of nursing offered programs leading to the R.N., with a total of 221,000 students enrolled in their courses. Nursing students have traditionally been characterized as having lower-middle-class and working-class social origins, often from small towns or rural areas, who are attracted to nursing as a means of upward social mobility (Hughes, MacGill, and Deutscher 1958). Although this pattern still persists today, there have been increasing numbers of students from upper- and upper-middle-class families and urban areas entering nursing schools (Davis 1972; Mauksch 1972), with the result that nursing, like teaching, has become a distinctly middle-class occupation.

There have been several studies of student nurses and their reasons for seeking training as a nurse. These studies, as summarized by Mauksch (1972), suggest that the objectives of a majority of nursing students are to be needed and to be engaged in personal helping relationships. However, some studies have suggested that a serious conflict often develops within new students concerning the lay image of the nurse as mother-surrogate (an image the students usually bring with them to the school) and the refusal of the nursing faculty to reinforce this image (Davis 1972; Olesen and Whittaker 1968; Psathas 1968; Warnecke 1973). Nursing faculties have tended to insist on students viewing their patients objectively, which has operated to deemphasize an intimate nurse–patient relationship. The prevailing reward system also places greater emphasis on removing the nurse from patient care and placing her in a supervisory position over auxiliary nursing workers.

In a major study of nursing students on the West Coast, Fred Davis (1972) observed six distinct stages of socialization. First was the stage of *initial innocence,* which consisted of the nursing students wanting to do things for patients within a secularized Christian-humanitarian ethic of care and kindness consistent with the lay (mother-surrogate) image of nursing. This stage was characterized, however, by feelings of inadequacy, worry, and frustration, as the nursing instructors failed to support the lay image of the nurse. Instead, the students were directed toward seemingly inconsequential tasks of patient care such as making beds and giving baths. These feelings of frustration, which usually came during the first semester of training, generated the second stage, which Davis called *labeled recognition of in-*

congruity. In this stage, the nursing students began collectively to articulate their disappointment and openly to question their choice of becoming a nurse. At this point a number of the students resigned from the school because they did not or could not adjust to the incongruity between lay expectations and actual training.

For those that remained, the third stage of *"psyching out"* began, in which the nursing students, like the medical students in the study by Becker and his associates (1961), attempted to anticipate what their instructors wanted them to know and to concentrate upon satisfying these requirements. Whereas some students may have attempted to "psych out" the instructors from the very beginning, it now became a group phenomenon with the entire class collectively participating in the process. The fourth stage, termed *role simulation,* was characterized by students performing so as to elicit favorable responses from the instructors. The approved mode of behavior was the exhibition of an objective and "professional" (detached) attitude toward patient care, which included an understanding of the principles behind nursing techniques as well as mastery of those techniques. Many of the students felt they were "playing at acting like a nurse" and they questioned their lack of conviction about the role. But Davis points out that the more successful they became at convincing others that their performance was authentic, the more they began to gain confidence in themselves as nurses. This stage usually came at the end of the first year. The last two years of their program were characterized as the fifth stage of *provisional internalization* and the sixth stage of *stable internalization.* During these final two stages, the nursing students took on a temporary self-identity as a "professional" nurse, as defined by the faculty, and finally settled into a stable and consistent identification of self by the time of their graduation.

The Davis (1972) study was conducted several years ago and ranks, with that of Virginia Olesen and Elvi Whittaker (1968) as perhaps the best known sociological studies of nursing education. Some of the findings, however, may not reflect conditions today. Davis found that unlike medical students, who desire a medical education as a terminal career, not all nursing students, perhaps even a majority, view a career in nursing as their primary life goal. Davis, along with Olesen (Davis, 1972; Davis and Olesen 1963), observed that several nursing students did not, either upon entry into nursing school or upon graduation, see themselves as being fully committed to a career in nursing. Their major life goal was that of marriage and family. This was so despite the influence of the women's movement and the encouragement of the nursing faculty to view nursing as a lifelong career. Davis (1972:46) found that the majority of students sought nursing training "as a kind of life insurance," should marriage and having a family not occur or should the marriage be less than ideal and result in "childlessness, divorce, premature widowhood, excessive financial burdens, or boredom with the home."

Therefore, the contingency of marriage became the decisive factor upon which all other decisions were based. Davis noted that a student's announcement of an engagement to be married was a great occasion for both the student and her classmates. Not only did it indicate that the major concern was resolved in a positive manner for the engaged student, but it also served to remind those not engaged of their less positive circumstances. Davis (1972:46) found that during the senior year there was "a veritable marital sweepstakes," in which the announcements of some engagements acquired the "theatrical overtones of a last minute rescue."

The overall image of nursing projected by such studies is that of an occupation dominated by a small group of older, career-oriented R.N.'s who serve as leaders, policy makers, and educators for a large and transient mass of younger nurses whose career aspirations are often affected by outside influences such as marriage (Freidson 1970b).

More recent research by Sam Porter (1992) in Northern Ireland presents a different view. Porter, who worked as a nurse, conducted a participant observation study of the nursing staff at a large urban hospital in Belfast. He finds that, contrary to the conclusions of previous studies, many nurses today regard their employment as a career. "A number of nurses," comments Porter (1992:523), "explicitly stated that, notwithstanding their desire to marry, they saw their job as a career which they expected to follow throughout their working lives." He concludes that with the increasing perception of nursing as a career in itself, the notion that nurses regard their first priority as finding a spouse to be out-of-date.

National Associations

Nurses have sought to improve the conditions of nursing practice and move toward enhanced professionalism through the organization of national associations representing nursing interests. The most prominent of these organizations have been the National League of Nursing and the American Nurses' Association.

The National League of Nursing is composed mainly of nursing educators and formal agencies interested in nursing education. Its primary aim is to promote quality standards for nurses' training. The American Nurses' Association (ANA) has become the major organization for registered nurses and is the official representative of nursing in relations with outside organizations. The ANA has not been a powerful organization, nor has membership played an important role in the ability of individual nurses to establish professional relationships with nursing colleagues. Only during the last few years has the ANA enjoyed the increasing support of a number of concerned nurses, who see in it the potential to enhance the professional status of nurses.

Gender and "The Doctor–Nurse Game"

As Porter (1992) observes, issues of gender have been of considerable importance in explaining the role of nurses. Nursing has traditionally been one of the world's major occupations for women. But unlike other jobs dominated numerically by women—elementary school teachers, librarians, and secretaries—nursing is paired with a powerful male-dominated profession. Sociologists have long recognized that nursing, as a historically subordinated occupation, has been constrained in its development by the medical profession (Carpenter 1993; Freidson 1970b). However, there are signs that gender inequality is losing some of its power in nurse–doctor relationships. The changes appear to be the result of three developments: (1) greater assertiveness by nurses, (2) increased numbers of male nurses, and (3) the growing numbers of female doctors.

The formal lines of authority that exist in the medical setting operate to place nurses at a disadvantage in acting upon their judgments regarding medical treatment. Yet there are times when nurses do go ahead and exercise their own judgment in opposition to the orders of physicians. An example of this situation is found in the experiment conducted by Steven Rank and Cardell Jacobson (1977) in two hospitals in a large midwestern city. The experiment consisted of having an assistant, using the name of a little known staff surgeon at the hospital who had given permission to use his name, telephone eighteen nurses who were on duty and order them to administer a nonlethal overdose of Valium to appropriate patients. The call was made in a self-confident manner, using medical terminology and familiarity with hospital routine. None of the nurses questioned the telephone request and all but one suspicious nurse entered the request on a medication chart. One of the experimenters, posing as a contractor working on a bid to install some new equipment on the ward, was present at the time of the call with the duty of terminating the experiment should the nurse actually proceed to administer the drug, refuse to comply, fail to take action after fifteen minutes, or try to call the "doctor" back. As a further safeguard, nursing supervisors were stationed in each of the patient's rooms to prevent the medication from being administered. Sixteen out of eighteen nurses refused to administer the Valium. One nurse (Rank and Jacobson 1977:191) said, "Whew! 30 mg—he [the doctor] doesn't want to sedate her [the patient]—he wants to knock her out." Twelve of these nurses tried to recontact the doctor; only two appeared ready to comply with the order. Rank and Jacobson suggest that the high rate of noncompliance was due to an increased willingness among hospital personnel to challenge a doctor's orders in contemporary medical practice (a 1966 study had found twenty-one out of twenty-two nurses willing to give an overdose), rising self-esteem among nurses, and a fear of lawsuits for malpractice.

However, rather than challenge physicians' orders directly, which can have unpleasant consequences for the nurse (being "chewed out," fired), most nurses have been able to develop an extremely effective informal interactional style with physicians. This interaction has been described by Leonard Stein (1967) as the "doctor–nurse game" because it has all the features of a game—an object, rules, and scores. The object of the game is for the nurse to be bold, show initiative, and make significant recommendations to the doctor in a manner, however, that appears passive and totally supportive of the "super-physician." The central rule of the game is to avoid open disagreement between the players. This requires the nurse to communicate a recommendation without appearing to do so, while the physician, in seeking a recommendation, must appear not to be asking for it. Stein notes that the greater the significance of the recommendation, the more subtly it must be conveyed. Both participants must therefore be aware of each other's nonverbal and verbal styles of communication.

Stein illustrates the doctor–nurse game with an example of a nurse telephoning and awakening a hospital staff physician who is on call with a report about a female patient unknown to the doctor. The nurse informs the doctor that the patient is unable to sleep and had just been informed that day about the death of her father. What the nurse is actually telling the doctor is that the patient is upset and needs a sedative in order to sleep. Since the doctor is not familiar with the patient, the doctor asks the nurse what sleeping medication has been helpful to the patient in the past. What the doctor is actually doing is asking the nurse for a recommendation; however, the sentence is phrased in such a way that it appears to be a question rather than a request for a recommendation. The nurse replies that phenobarbital 100 mg has been effective for this particular patient, which Stein interprets as a disguised recommendation statement. The doctor then orders the nurse to administer phenobarbital 100 mg as needed and the nurse concludes the interaction by thanking the doctor for the order. The nurse has been successful in making a recommendation without appearing to do so, and the doctor has been successful in asking for a recommendation without appearing to do so.

While all of this may seem silly to persons unfamiliar with the physician–nurse relationship, it nonetheless represents a significant social mechanism by which the physician is able to utilize the nurse as a consultant and the nurse is able to gain self-esteem and professional satisfaction from her work. A successful game creates a doctor–nurse alliance and allows the doctor to have a good "score" by gaining the respect and admiration of the nursing staff; the nurse, in turn, scores by being identified by the physician as "a damn good nurse." If the doctor fails to play the game well, pleasant working relationships with the nurses may become difficult and the doctor may have problems of a trivial yet annoying nature when it comes to getting his work done. Nurses who do not play the game well (are outspoken in making recommendations) are either terminated from employment if they also lack intelligence, or are tolerated but not liked if they are bright. Nurses who do not play the game at all, according to Stein, are defined as dull and are relegated to the background in the social life of the hospital. The essence of the doctor–nurse game is that physicians and nurses agree that the physician is superior and this hierarchical structure must be maintained; however, nurses may make recommendations to doctors as long as they *appear* to be initiated by the physician and disagreement is avoided.

Stein and his colleagues (Stein, Watts, and Howell 1990) reexamined the doctor–nurse game several years later and determined that a different situation now exists. Stein and his colleagues and others (Carpenter 1993; Porter 1992; Weiss and Lonnquist 1994) find that many nurses are no longer willing to be treated as mere subordinates by physicians. Several reasons are offered for this change. First, are declining public esteem for doctors due to widespread questioning of the profit motive in medical practice and greater recognition that physicians make mistakes. Second, is the increased number of women doctors. When female doctors and nurses interact, the stereotypical roles of male domination and female submission are missing. Third, the nursing shortage has emphasized to doctors the value of highly trained, competent nurses. Fourth, most nurses today are educated in academic settings. Nurses are recognizing that academic qualifications—as opposed to practical on-the-job training—means enhanced skills and status. Fifth, the women's movement may be encouraging nurses to define their own roles with greater autonomy. Instead of trying to professionalize the entire occupation of nursing, nurses are turning to "clinical nursing" as an exclusive specialty within general nursing that emphasizes specific nursing procedures, management of basic-skill nurses, and the central role of the nurse as the responsible worker for groups of patients.

Besides more assertiveness by female nurses, nursing has attracted larger numbers of males in recent years with increasing pay. For years, men have comprised 4 to 5 percent of all registered nurses or about 90,000 of the 1.7 million nurses. In 1988, men made up about 6 percent of all student nurses. However, in 1992, some 10 percent of nursing students were male, attracted to not only the higher pay but also to availability of jobs. Greater numbers of male nurses disrupt traditional gender role of submission for nurses since male nurses are not as likely to play the doctor–nurse game. Liliane Floge and Deborah Merrill (1986) found that while female nurses were supposed to appear passive in making recommendations to physicians, this did not seem to be the case for male nurses. Floge and Merrill state:

> We found that male nurses were more likely to voice their opinions than female nurses and to have their opinions accepted by male physicians. One typical example was a male nurse saying to a physician, "You'll find that _____." ... It was also common to hear a physician asking a male nurse for his opinion. In addition, one male nurse recalled a time when a female nurse was called a "bitch" after she pointed out a male physician's mistake to him, while the male nurse was thanked and told to change the medication when the same physician repeated the same mistake at a later time.[1]

While male physicians tended to regard male nurses as more competent than female nurses and to treat them accordingly, Floge and Merrill (1986) found that female physicians were not as likely to play the doctor–nurse game with either male or female nurses. But female physicians were also more likely than male physicians to have their actions questioned by nurses. Consequently, when it comes to physician–nurse relationships, gender still plays a significant role in shaping the nature of the interaction.

While it might be inferred that gender issues have promoted poor relationships between physicians and nurses, this does not appear to be the case. Extensive research shows considerable satisfaction among both groups and generally positive working relations (Prescott and Bowen 1985). Nurses valued trust and respect on the part of doctors and being regarded as intelligent participants in patient care; doctors, on their part, appreciated nurses who were competent, helpful, and had good communication skills.

[1]Liliane Floge and Deborah M. Merrill, "Tokenism Reconsidered: Male Nurses and Female Physicians in a Hospital Setting," *Social Forces*, 64 (1986), 939.

NURSING: FUTURE TRENDS

Nurses have achieved status through their high standards and professional orientation toward their work role and the extension of nursing tasks beyond bedside care. Typically, lower-echelon workers like nurse's aides provide the majority of bedside care under the supervision of a registered nurse, while R.N.'s, especially those with baccalaureate degrees, have expanded their range of services to include hospital administration, primary-care healing, nurse anesthetists, cardio-vascular nurse specialists, and other areas of specialization in nursing.

Hospital Administration

One significant change in the work role of nursing has been the evolution of the R.N. into an administrative role. Competent nurses cannot be rewarded by promotion to the higher rungs of the medical profession; in order to reach the top of the medical structure, the nurse is forced to leave nursing altogether and become a doctor. Since this is usually impractical, many nurses have sought a career in hospital administration. From the perspective of hospital administrators, registered nurses can be used more economically in managerial and supervisory positions because lower paid personnel are available for bedside tasks.

The paradox in this development, however, is that while it allows the nurse to gain a somewhat more secure claim of professional status, it greatly reduces or eliminates the contact with patients for which nursing was organized in the first place. Yet it has been suggested that patients usually cannot tell one type of nurse from another and generally do not overtly request emotional support (Elder 1963). Instead, patients typically request simple tasks—such as medications to ease pain or assistance in moving to a more comfortable body position—which can be accomplished by less qualified nursing aides. As Sam Schulman (1972:236) points out, in hospitals "mother-surrogateness is seldom encountered: in large measure, it is not asked for by patients nor is it given by nurses." Schulman concludes that, in an indirect sense, patients are supportive of the removal of most professional nurses from their bedsides because they want the most professional persons in charge of their care. Whether patients do approve of removing the best qualified nurses from their bedside is an arguable point; nevertheless, it is happening.

The Nurse Practitioner

The most recent change in nursing has been the emergence of another kind of nurse—the nurse practitioner or nurse clinician. This change is not intended to create a new type of health worker, but instead to use more fully the skills and capabilities of the well-trained nurse. The nurse practitioner is intended to occupy a work position similar to that of the new physician assistant role. The nurse practitioner is trained to assume many of the primary and routine tasks of patient care normally handled by the physician, such as giving physical examinations, taking medical histories, ordering laboratory tests and X-rays, providing health education to patients and their families, and making the decision as to whether the patient needs to consult with a physician. This role for the nurse allows the physician to assume the more realistic position of a highly trained specialist. It frees physicians from the routine tasks of medical practice and allows them to concentrate more fully on the complex medical problems for which their training has prepared them.

Although the role of nurse practitioner has not been fully conceptualized in terms of the training, qualifications, and responsibilities, existing studies (Light 1983; Merenstein, Wolfe, and Barker 1974; Taller and Feldman 1974) suggest that nurse practitioners have met with a high degree of acceptance among patients who have used their services, and that patient care can indeed be made more efficient by involving paramedical personnel.

Hence, a formal role for nurses who practice medicine as well as nursing is beginning to develop within the context of patient care. In the future, nurse practitioners may provide most or even all primary care for patients, leaving physicians to further consolidate their role as specialists. Although this would not effect a change in nursing's subordinate work role, it would allow the practitioners a greater degree of decision making. A major concern, however, with this projection of an expanded role is that the nurse practitioner may simply be "consumed" by the medical profession as a "lesser" doctor or given only a more complex form of tasks delegated by the physician. Research in Great Britain by Anne Bowling (1981) found nurses generally no more in favor of performing clinical tasks delegated to them than doctors were of doing the delegating. Bowling suggests that, in striving for personal autonomy, nurses tend to reject performing part of the doctor's duties in favor of emphasizing the uniquely "caring" functions of the nurse. The basis of this attitude was a narrow professionalism on the part of both nurses and doctors. The nurses clearly wanted to maintain their occupational identity by separating their work role from that of physicians. Bowling indicates that an appropriate use of nurses would be to increase their involvement in preventive medicine, health maintenance, and patient education rather than merely treating illness.

Current trends suggest, however, that the new generation of R.N.'s in the United States will play an expanded role in medicine through increased decision making and direct responsibility for decisions made as either administrator or practitioner. They will do so, however, within the overall structure of medical practice, and their position will remain subordinate to that of the physician. Direct bedside care of patients will increasingly come to be the domain of the practical nurse and the nurse's aide.

PHYSICIAN ASSISTANT

While the concept of the nurse practitioner derives from the expansion of a traditional occupation, that of physician assistant (PA) represents a new form of paramedical practitioner. This relatively new occupation results from the recognition by American physicians that specialization has reduced them to narrower and narrower competencies and that the pressure of increasing case loads has reduced the time available for attending to many minor and routine patient demands. It has been charged that some physicians have relied upon excessive use of laboratory and diagnostic tests (thus increasing the costs of medical treatment) as a partial substitution for physician–patient interaction. It has also been suggested that decreased physician–patient time per visit has contributed to patient dissatisfaction and thus to malpractice suits. Ideally physician assistants will handle many routine medical problems, thereby releasing the physician for increased physician–patient contact and more attention to difficult and complex problems. A general job description of the physician assistant would be to provide a level of primary patient care similar to or higher than that of nurse practitioners. Moreover, as James Cawley explains:

> A key corollary to the emergence of the PA was the notion that these providers could also bring new attributes to medical practice. Apart from the pressing reality of the shortage of physicians, there was also the problem that physicians were often too unconcerned with the routine illnesses of many patients. Patients tended to place little emphasis on important elements of primary care, such as counseling, patient education, and preventive service. A growing need was expressed for a new type of health provider, harking back to the days of the "old GP." These providers, working with physicians, could offer skills not only in medical diagnosis and management, but also in the caring and preventive aspects of practice.[2]

By 1992, there were over 25,000 physician assistants in the United States, of whom 42 percent were women. Their training was either in primary care or in specialties, especially ophthalmology and orthopedics. Typically, they worked directly for physicians, either in private medical practices or in hospitals providing in-patient services. They spend the largest part of their workday providing direct patient care, divided about equally between those tasks directly supervised and those indirectly supervised by physicians; considerably less time was spent in technical or laboratory work or in the supervision of other health workers. The physician assistant is becoming an established occupation within medicine (Cawley 1985; Hooker 1991). Most important for patient care, the physician's assistant, in conjunction with the nurse practitioner, may be able to resolve the significant issue of providing more primary care practitioners in the American system of health care delivery. It appears that the use of nurse practitioners and physicians' assistants will increase as long as they extend the medical functions of physicians without competing for or challenging their authority and autonomy (Ferraro and Southerland 1989:200).

---

[2]James F. Cawley, "The Physician Assistant Profession: Current Status and Future Trends," *Journal of Public Health Policy*, 6 (1985), 79.

MIDWIVES

Midwives are women who assist a mother during childbirth. There are two types of midwives, nurse-midwives who deliver babies under the supervision of a physician and lay midwives who assist births on their own. Midwifery is one of the earliest forms of care available to women. As Rose Weitz and Deborah Sullivan (1986) describe the history of midwifery, midwives attended practically all births in colonial America. In fact, as late as the eighteenth century it was considered undignified for male physicians to care for pregnant women and attend to the delivery of babies. That function was considered "women's work." What changed this situation was a growing belief in scientific progress among the general population and the development of obstetrics as a new medical specialty. Births attended by midwives began to drop rapidly as physicians took over responsibility for delivering babies. In the meantime, the medical profession developed strong opposition to midwifery, arguing that surgical skills and knowledge of drugs, as well as more sanitary conditions found in hospital delivery rooms, were far superior to any service midwives could provide. Weitz and Sullivan found that, by 1900, only about half of all births in the United States were attended by midwives; by 1950, midwifery ceased in all but remote areas.

However, midwifery has slowly made a comeback in American society despite the opposition of the medical profession. Midwives have become available to women in some locales who wish to have a natural childbirth, featuring breathing and relaxation techniques and emotional support in the place of pain-killing drugs. Many physicians, in turn, now practice many of the same techniques for women who opt for natural childbirth. Lay midwives have remained in existence because they deliver babies in the home which physicians typically refuse to do and they can prevent nurse-midwives from doing so because of the requirement for physician supervision. Midwives also serve women whose religious beliefs prevent them from using doctors (DeVries 1993). While opposition to midwifery by the medical profession continues, today some twelve states license or register lay midwives and lay midwifery is legal in three other states. Some twenty-four states allow nurse-midwives to deliver babies under a doctor's supervision and approximately 4,000 nurse-midwives are certified to practice in the United States as of 1990. In other states, midwifery is illegal or the law is unclear.

Weitz and Sullivan studied the development of midwifery in Arizona. They found that to become a midwife, a woman had to show evidence of formal training in midwifery, observations of live births, supervised experience, and pass oral, written, and clinical examinations developed by a nurse-midwife in consultation with physicians. These rules were developed in Arizona in the late 1970s after controversy emerged over the legal requirements for licensing. Earlier requirements had not been stringent, but when the number of midwives in the state increased and began serving middle-class clients, physicians objected. The new rules, as Weitz and Sullivan point out, gave the medical establishment substantial control of the licensure process, but midwives are able to practice. Weitz and Sullivan characterize the conflict with doctors as a struggle for women's rights and note continued problems with physician acceptance of midwives.

SUMMARY

Nursing as an occupation has evolved from being an informal exercise of charity ("sisterhood") into a formal occupational role subordinate to the authority and control of the physician. Many social factors have contributed to the maintenance of this situation, especially the stereotype of the mother-surrogate. It has also been noted that nurse's training is not always viewed by nursing students as a means to a career but also as a kind of "life insurance" should they be disappointed in their primary goals of marriage and family. Nevertheless, nurses have continually struggled to achieve formal colleagueship with the physician and they have achieved professional-like status, especially through their role in hospital administration and primary care delivery.

The role of nurse practitioner seems particularly promising because it would enable nurses to gain some autonomy over what they do and to share more fully in medicine's specialized body of knowledge. Both the nurse practitioner and the physician assistant roles result from a trend toward physician specialization that has made doctors less accessible to patients with minor and generalized ailments who nonetheless demand attention. These relatively new roles represent evidence that physicians have begun to modify their position in the medical work hierarchy by sharing once jealously guarded tasks of primary medical care. Perhaps the time may come when the physician will lead a balanced team of health personnel who are involved in decision making and limited independent action. Midwives, however, find their services constrained by doctors and their occupation relegated to a marginal role in medicine.

Hospitals

12

Since many health problems require a level of medical treatment and personal care that extends beyond the range of services normally available in the patient's home or in the physician's office, modern society has developed formal institutions for patient care intended to help meet the more complex health needs of its members. The hospital, the major social institution for the delivery of health care in the modern world, offers considerable advantages to both patient and society. From the standpoint of the individual, the sick or injured person has access to centralized medical knowledge and the greatest array of technology in hospitals. From the standpoint of society, as Talcott Parsons and Renée Fox (1952) suggest, hospitalization both protects the family from many of the disruptive effects of caring for the ill in the home and operates as a means of guiding the sick and injured into medically supervised institutions where their problems are less disruptive for society as a whole.

The purpose of this chapter is to consider the social role of the hospital. Besides serving the prescribed social function of providing medical treatment, hospitals can be viewed from the perspective of a functionally specific world. This chapter will examine the organizational aspects of that world in the following order: (1) development of the hospital as a social institution; (2) the hospital system in the United States; (3) social organization of hospital work, including its effect on the patient role; and (4) rising cost of hospital services.

THE DEVELOPMENT OF THE HOSPITAL
AS A SOCIAL INSTITUTION

The development of hospitals as institutions providing medical services for the general public proceeded in pace with the prevailing needs, beliefs, values, and attitudes of the societies they served (Coe 1978; Rosenberg 1987; Stevens 1989). Historically, hospitals have passed through four distinct phases of development: (1) as centers of religious practice, (2) as poorhouses, (3) as deathhouses, and (4) as centers of medical technology.

Hospitals as Centers of Religious Practice

Although the Romans were the first to establish separate medical facilities (for economic and military reasons) that have been described as hospitals, the origin of the institution we know today as the hospital has usually been associated with the rise of Christianity. Christian theology emphasized that human beings were duty bound to provide assistance to the sick and needy; this belief was reinforced by the notion that spiritual salvation could be obtained by whomever provided such a service. Consequently, the Roman Catholic Church encouraged its clergy to found hospitals and to locate these hospitals near churches as an integral feature of Christian religious endeavor. Furthermore, during the period of the Crusades between 1096 and 1291, many hospitals were established along the routes taken to the Holy Land by the Christian armies. Secular benefactors, such as kings, queens, and other members of the nobility, wealthy merchants, artisan and craftsmen's guilds, and municipalities also founded hospitals. By the end of the fifteenth century, an extensive network of hospitals existed throughout Western Europe.

The medieval hospital, however, was not a hospital by any modern standard. True, these hospitals were community centers for the care of the lower-class sick; yet the medical care, supervised and largely performed by clergy and nuns, consisted primarily of a rudimentary form of nursing. The primary functions of the medieval hospital were the exercise of religious practices and the extension of charity and welfare services to the poor, including both the able-bodied and the sick. These early hospitals, therefore, provided a wide spectrum of social tasks for the benefit of the lower classes, especially the provision of food, shelter, sanctuary, and prayer as well as nursing.

During the Renaissance and the Reformation, the religious character of the hospital began to disappear as increasing numbers of hospitals were placed under the jurisdiction of secular authorities. Nevertheless, as Rodney Coe (1978) has observed, three basic features of the modern hospital are derived from the influence of the Church. First, the concept of a service oriented toward helping others has become a guiding principle for the manner in which hospital personnel are required to approach their work. Second, hospitals are supposed to have a "universalistic" approach—that is, to accept for treatment all people who may be sick or injured. And third, the custodial nature of hospital care has been facilitated by housing patients within the confines of a single location.

Hospitals as Poorhouses

The secular control of hospitals marked a period of decline for the development of Europe's hospital system. Even though monks and nuns continued to work in hospitals, the removal of the centralized authority of the Church left hospitals under many separate administrations, usually those of municipal governments. Without general regulations pertaining to hospital administration, individual hospitals were free to pursue any course of action they desired. This situation encouraged abuse, particularly in regard to neglect of facilities, misappropriation of funds, and the lowering of prevailing standards of patient care. In England the suppression of the monastery system in the mid-1500s led to the collapse of the English hospital system as many hospitals, left without personnel or money, were forced to close. The few remaining hospitals limited their services to people who were actually sick and who could be cured. While this policy relegated the poor, both the incurably ill and the able-bodied, to poorhouses or to the streets for their support, it marked the beginning of a new definition of hospitals as institutions active in curing the sick and injured so that they could return to society.

However, by the end of the sixteenth century, the economic and social conditions of the poor worsened to a considerable degree. Unemployment, higher prices, and the loss of land created a serious problem of vagrancy throughout Europe. Many vagrants claimed to be sick or crippled, and they crowded whatever hospital facilities were available. In accordance with the new definition of social welfare as a community rather than a church responsibility, measures were eventually taken by city and national authorities to provide public assistance. Many hospitals were reopened, but they soon acquired the characteristics of boarding houses because they offered food and shelter to the poor, regardless of whether they were sick or healthy. Those persons living in hospitals who could work were required to pay for their lodging, while hospitals received further financial support through public taxation. Hospitals became little more than social "warehouses," where invalids, the aged, orphans, and the mentally defective could be sent and thus removed from the mainstream of society. Even today in the United States, people with chronic health problems requiring long-term hospitalization—the insane, the incurable, and individuals suffering from highly infectious diseases—tend to be sent to public institutions, while private hospitals tend to accept patients with acute disorders. And some hospitals, like Cook County in Chicago, Philadelphia General, Bellevue and Kings County in New York, and San Francisco General, were established and remain institutions for the very poor (Stevens 1989).

Hospitals as Deathhouses

Following the Renaissance and the Reformation, the outward character of hospitals appeared to change very little from that of a public institution whose purpose was to provide welfare services for the lower social classes on behalf of the communities in which they were located. Nonetheless, changes were taking place as physicians discovered that hospitals contained large numbers of sick and injured (and also generally powerless) people whose health problems could be studied and upon whom the various evolving techniques of medical treatment could be practiced.

Physicians had first begun to associate themselves with hospitals during the fourteenth century; initially they had little influence because they were not members of the hospital staff and provided their services on a purely voluntary basis. By the seventeenth century, however, physicians acquired a virtual monopoly over the existing body of medical knowledge that placed them in the position of first advising and eventually directing all patient care within the hospital. As physicians became increasingly influential, nonmedical hospital tasks gradually disappeared. By the early nineteenth century, hospitals had clearly assumed their present-day role as institutions for medical care, for medical research, and for the education of medical students.

Although medical treatment was recognized as the primary function of the hospital in the eighteenth century, the primitive level of that treatment produced few cures. Trained physicians were unable to achieve consistent results with their techniques and, accordingly, neither they nor hospitals were held in high esteem by the general population. Because so few patients survived treatment despite occasional heroic efforts, hospitals acquired an image as places where the poor went to die.

According to Coe (1978), the high death rate in hospitals was also related to the appalling living conditions provided patients. Typically, hospitals were dirty, poorly ventilated, and filled to capacity. Often more than one patient was placed in a single bed regardless of the patient's disorder, and treatment was usually carried out publicly on the ward itself. Surgery, which Coe points out was limited at that time mostly to amputations and childbirth, plus the purging of fevers with various potions, bloodletting to eliminate "excess" blood, and the removal of the dead all occurred in the same general area where patients ate and slept. Nor did the attending physicians and surgeons practice even the most rudimentary standards of sanitation, moving from bed to bed and treating a great variety of diseases, including those that were infectious, without washing their hands or changing their clothes. Thus, it is not surprising that hospitals were regarded by most people as places where only the lower social classes went to die.

Hospitals as Centers of Medical Technology

Since the end of the nineteenth century, a new image of hospitals evolved as institutions where patients of all social classes could generally expect to find the highest quality medical care and could reasonably expect to be cured of their disorders. Three major factors were responsible for this change. First was the fact that medicine had indeed become a science in terms of employing the scientific method to seek out accurate medical knowledge and to develop successful techniques that could be employed in a consistent manner. Of particular importance were increased knowledge about human physiology and the development of the science of bacteriology; also important was the perfection of ether as an anesthetic, which allowed surgery to be performed in a relatively painless fashion. Since the new medical technology required extensive and often expensive facilities, these facilities were centralized in hospitals so that they could be available to most physicians. Hospitals eventually became places where physicians also referred their upper- and middle-class patients, since the most advanced medical technology was located there. While the poor generally remained in a charity status as hospital patients, a new type of patient came into being—the private patient—who required private accommodations, usually had a private physician, and who paid for hospital services.

A second important factor, concomitant with the development of medical technology, was the discovery and use of antiseptic measures in the hospital to help curtail infection. Hospitals were not only properly cleaned and ventilated, but also patients with infectious diseases were isolated in special areas of the hospital, and hospital staffs were required to wash their hands and change their clothing after working with these patients. The use of such items as surgical masks, rubber gloves, and sterilized surgical instruments became commonplace. These procedures not only reduced the number of deaths among hospital patients but also reduced the amount of time required for patient recovery.

Third, there was a significant improvement in the quality of hospital personnel. Especially important was the entry on the scene of the trained nurse and the laboratory technician, whose specialized skills were able to support the physician in his or her primary role of diagnostician and practitioner. As Charles Rosenberg (1987) points out in his historical analysis of the development of American hospitals, no single change has transformed the day-to-day work in a hospital more than trained nurses. In the twentieth century, the hospital has become the major institutional resource available to society for coping with problems of health and illness.

HOSPITALS IN THE UNITED STATES

The first hospitals were founded in the United States more than two hundred years ago. Generally their development paralleled that of Western European institutions in the 1700s. The first such hospital was established by William Penn in Philadelphia in 1713, with the care of the sick being incidental to the main purpose of providing shelter for the poor. The well-known Charity Hospital in New Orleans was founded by the Catholic Church in 1737 for similar reasons. The first hospital to be established in the United States solely for the purpose of treating the sick was the Pennsylvania Hospital, founded by Benjamin Franklin and a group of interested citizens in 1751. These early hospitals were not governmental undertakings but were largely based on voluntary initiative by private citizens who wanted medical care available on a nonprofit basis. They were generally intended to provide treatment for those patients who had curable disorders.

Federal government participation in health care did not actually begin until 1798 with the U.S. Public Health Service hospital program for merchant sea-

TABLE 12-1   Types of Short-stay Hospitals, United States, 1960–1991

Type of Ownership	NUMBER			
	1960	1970	1980	1991
Total	5,768	6,193	6,229	5,675
Federal	361	334	325	308
Nonfederal	5,407	5,859	5,904	5,370
Nonprofit	3,291	3,386	3,339	3,184
Proprietary	856	769	730	738
State-local government	1,260	1,704	1,835	1,448

NOTE: Excludes psychiatric and tuberculosis and other respiratory disease hospitals.
Source: Adapted from American Hospital Association data.

men. State governments did not enter into health care delivery until the 1800s, and their efforts were largely confined to the establishment of state mental institutions. By 1873 there were only 178 hospitals of all types in the United States; in 1991, the number of hospitals was 5,675.

Hospital Ownership

The ownership of hospitals in the United States may be classified into three major types: (1) nonprofit; (2) proprietary (profit-making); or (3) government (federal, state, or local).[1] Table 12-1 shows the number of short-stay hospitals for the years 1960 to 1991. Short-stay hospitals are those in which patients are expected to stay for only a few days or weeks. This is the most common type of hospital. The figures in Table 12-1 show that the total number of short-stay hospitals in the United States rose from 5,768 in 1960 to 6,229 in 1980. For 1991, there were 5,675 short-stay hospitals. Some 308 or 5 percent of the short-stay hospitals in 1991 were owned by the federal government, while the remaining 5,370 hospitals were nonfederal. Nonprofit hospitals stood at 3,184, which represents 56 percent of all American short-stay hospitals.

Controlled by a board of trustees, nonprofit hospitals are exempt from federal income taxes and many other forms of state and local taxes. These hospitals have generally been characterized as emphasizing high-quality care for the upper and middle social classes, while also allowing access to their facilities by lower-class patients. Nonprofit hospitals are highly dependent on community physicians for membership on their staffs and for the referral of patients. Large nonprofit hospitals, however, are somewhat less dependent than smaller hospitals on local physicians because of their greater prestige, more extensive facilities, and higher ratio of staff positions for doctors.

[1] A hospital is defined as a facility with at least six beds that is licensed by the state as a hospital or that is operated as a hospital by a federal or state agency.

Table 12-1 shows that 738 short-stay hospitals (13 percent of the total) were classified in 1991 as proprietary or profit making. In the past, these hospitals have usually been small and highly dependent on local physicians for staff membership and patient referrals. However, Paul Starr's (1982) research demonstrated that the trend for proprietary hospitals is to merge into a multihospital chain owned by a large corporation. In this situation, physicians on the hospital staff are generally employees of the corporation, but doctors outside the hospital are encouraged to also place their patients in the profit-making hospitals through incentives like hospital staff privileges and higher-quality care for their patients by the hospital staff. The usual source of income for proprietary hospitals is internal and generated from patient care, especially payments from private insurance companies.

The number of state and local government-owned short-stay hospitals in Table 12-1 for 1991 is 1,448 which is 26 percent of the total. Government hospitals tend to lack prestige in comparison to other hospitals. They are the major source of health care for people with low incomes, particularly in urban areas. Noralou Roos and associates (1974) describe government hospitals as "hospitals of last resort" because they place their greatest emphasis on public access to their facilities rather than on the quality of their care. Yet the increased affiliation of government hospitals with medical schools portends a shift in emphasis toward quality care and modern facilities. Nevertheless, America's hospital system is a two-class system of medical care—one primarily for the relatively affluent and the other generally serving the poor (Albrecht 1984).

There are also long-term hospitals in the United States and Table 12-2 shows the number and ownership of these hospitals. There are 30 general hospi-

TABLE 12-2   Long-term Hospitals, United States, 1970–1991

Type of Hospital and Ownership	NUMBER		
	1970	**1980**	**1991**
General	75	17	30
Federal	38	9	9
Nonfederal	37	8	21
Psychiatric	459	381	354
Federal	33	23	15
Nonprofit	56	47	39
Proprietary	39	57	76
State-local government	331	254	224
Tuberculosis and other respiratory diseases	103	10	3
All other	200	150	109
Federal	1	1	4
Nonprofit	110	66	45
Proprietary	2	11	19
State-local government	87	72	41

Source: Adapted from American Hospital Association data.

tals; 9 are federal and 21 nonfederal. There are 354 psychiatric hospitals and the majority (224) are owned by state and local governments. Only three hospitals for tuberculosis and other respiratory diseases remained in 1991 out of a total of 103 in 1970, which is a testimonial to the decline of tuberculosis in the United States. Among the remaining long-term hospitals, 45 were owned in 1991 by nonprofit organizations and 41 by state and local governments. The largest number of proprietary long-term hospitals is the 76 psychiatric hospitals.

THE ORGANIZATION OF THE GENERAL HOSPITAL

Certainly not all hospitals are alike in their organization of services, but general hospitals, as the most common single type of hospital in the United States, exhibit organizational features similar to most other types of hospitals. Figure 12-1 shows the typical organization of large general hospitals. As a social organization, the general hospital has been described as being formal, highly stratified, quasi-bureaucratic, and quasi-authoritarian (Croog and Ver Steeg 1972; Georgopoulos and Mann 1972). General hospitals have also been described as "multipurpose institutions" in that they provide a variety of health-related functions for society such as (1) treating patients; (2) conducting medical research; (3) training health practitioners; (4) providing laboratories and other medical facilities to the community; and (5) sponsoring health education and preventive medicine programs for the general public (Coe 1978; Heydebrand 1973). Robert Wilson (1963), for example, describes the hospital as a hotel, a school, a laboratory, and a stage for treatment. The *primary* goal of the hospital, however, is that of providing medical treatment to its patients within the limits of contemporary medical knowledge and technology and the hospital's available resources.

To accomplish its tasks and coordinate its various activities, the hospital relies on a prescribed hierarchy of authority (as shown in Figure 12-1), which is operationalized through formal rules, regulations, and administrative procedures. The key to hospital efficiency and overall effectiveness is coordination of the various departments and individuals. They represent a complex and highly specialized division of labor that is both interlocking and interdependent.

Consider what happens when a staff doctor prescribes medication for a patient. The doctor's order for medication is written in the patient's medical records by a floor clerk, and the clerk, or a nurse's aide or orderly, takes the request to the pharmacy. When the medication is sent by the pharmacy, it is most likely administered by a nurse. A record is then forwarded to the accounting office so that the proper charges for the drug can be entered on the patient's bill; another written order might be sent from the pharmacy to purchasing (through the appropriate administrative channels) to reorder the medication and replace it for future use by another patient. So the rather routine activity of one particular member of the hospital staff (in this case a doctor) initiates a chain of events that affects the work of several other hospital employees.

FIGURE 12-1 Typical large general hospital organized into five divisions

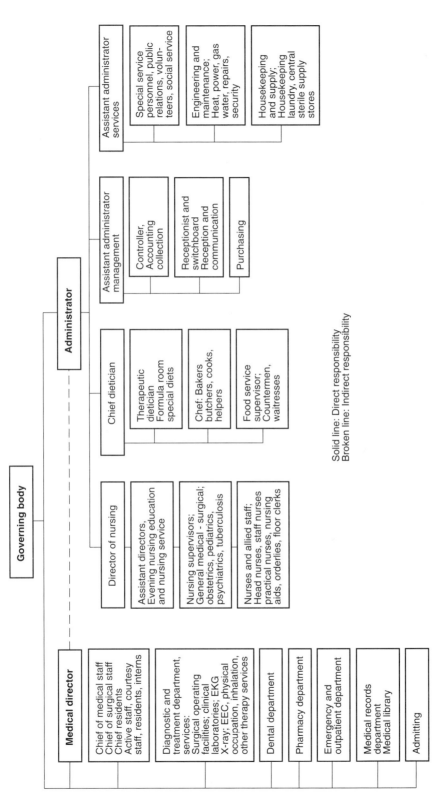

Solid line: Direct responsibility
Broken line: Indirect responsibility

Source: *Technology and Manpower in the Health Service Industry,* Manpower Research Bulletin, No. 14 (Washington, D.C.: U.S. Department of Labor, Manpower Administration, May 1967).

233

The Hospital: Dual Authority

According to Figure 12-1, the overall supervision of the general hospital comes under the auspices of its governing body. In most nonfederal hospitals, that governing body is a board of trustees. Figure 12-1 also shows that, whereas the medical director and the hospital administrator are linked to the governing body by a direct line of responsibility, they are only indirectly responsible to each other. What this type of arrangement indicates is that the authority system of the general hospital operates on a dual level (Alexander and Fennell 1986). This system is an outgrowth of the organizational conflict in the hospital between bureaucracy and professionalism.

Several sociologists (Goss 1963; Heydebrand 1973; Hillier 1987) have noted that Max Weber's (Gerth and Mills 1946) concept of bureaucracy is not totally compatible with the norms of hospital authority. Weber described bureaucracy as a rational and impersonal division of labor characterized by the principles of *office hierarchy* and levels of graded authority (lower offices are supervised by higher ones), and by *fixed and official areas of jurisdiction* governed by laws or administrative regulations. The essence of the conflict between bureaucracy and the professional consists of the professional's insistence on exercising an autonomous individual judgment within the limits prescribed by the profession itself. As Mary Goss (1963) points out, the work norms of the professional (in this case, the medical doctor) emphasize self-determination for each practitioner, that is, exclude control by those outside the profession. The bureaucrat (here, the hospital administrator), on the other hand, seeks to follow a rationalistic management approach that favors the efficient coordination of the hospital's activities through formal rules and impersonal regulations applicable to all persons in all situations.

Charles Perrow (1963) has traced the evolution of this conflict in his study of one voluntary general hospital he believes to be representative of most other hospitals of this type. Perrow noted that in the late 1800s and early 1900s the voluntary general hospital was dominated by its board of trustees, because this was an era when securing capital funds and gaining community recognition were critical hospital goals. Since community involvement was the pivotal factor, individual members of boards of trustees were usually laypersons selected at large from the community. Legally they were responsible for protecting the community's interests, but they also sought to incorporate hospital services into the general pattern of community life. Perrow believes this approach ultimately derives from seventeenth-century attitudes toward hospitals as state institutions operated on public funds, that is, as community welfare agencies and poorhouses.

In the 1930s trustee domination succumbed to medical domination. Perrow cites three major reasons for this change: First, the emphasis on free care declined significantly as hospital services became oriented toward patients who could pay; second, the facilities to support a complex system of medical technology were developed and the quality of care provided patients was improved; and third, the hospital sought prestige through medical research in terms defined by physicians. Hence, medical domination went hand in hand with increasing medical knowledge. During this period, however, Perrow also noted the appearance of several abuses that could be attributed to the great personal power of the medical director and department heads. Especially deficient was the out-patient care afforded to people with low incomes; also conspicuous was the favoritism shown toward certain physicians in the use of hospital facilities and staff promotions. Perrow observed:

> There was little to prevent such abuses. The doctor is an individual entrepreneur, selling his services for a profit. His income is affected by the facilities he commands in the hospital, his freedom from scrutiny, and by the price he must pay in the form of reciprocal duties such as teaching or committee work. Reliance upon professional ethics, even buttressed by the atmosphere created by teaching and research activities, is not sufficient in itself to guarantee a disinterested, ethical non-economic point of view. Nor will it prevent abuses stemming from the enormous concentration of power in the hands of the chief of staff and department heads who also control the hospital.[2]

What was needed, said Perrow, was a system to limit these powers, to establish objective criteria for promotion and to provide for more effective representation of patient and organizational interests. That system gradually emerged during the 1940s and 1950s as the role of hospital administrator gained in importance; through a constitutional system, the administration was able to define the medical staff's official power, standardize the hospital's administrative procedures, and establish a level of quality for the hospital's medical services. These early administrators were often physicians who could be expected to further the interests of the medical staff, but in doing so began to curtail their power. As authority became centralized in the administrator's office, there often developed a blockage of communication between the staff and the board of trustees. This period, according to Perrow, was characterized by a complex power struggle which eventually led, in the 1950s, to a system of multiple leadership common among general hospitals today.

Multiple leadership, at least in its hospital version, is actually a system of dual authority, one administrative and the other medical. Perrow notes the high probability of such a system developing in the hospital, because goals are generally multiple (trustees, administration, and medical staff often have diverse interests), the criteria for achieving them broad, and the power of each group to protect its interests is considerable. Since the physician's professional norms can set specific limits on the hospital administrator's authority and vice versa, the result has been to reconcile the physician-professional with the administrator-bureaucrat by establishing a system of dual authority.

The board of trustees still remains the nominal center of authority in the general hospital. It usually meets on a periodic basis, weekly or monthly, to review the hospital's operations and act upon those matters brought to its attention.

[2]Charles Perrow, "Goals and Power Structures: A Historical Case Study," in *The Hospital in Modern Society*, E. Freidson, ed. (New York: The Free Press, 1963), p. 123.

Generally the trustees themselves are people who are influential in the wider community. But despite their position as the hospital's ultimate source of authority, the trustees have only limited de facto authority over the medical staff, who usually make all health-related decisions. The board of trustees typically concerns itself with administrative matters and public relations while working closely with the hospital administrator, who acts as their agent in exercising authority and supervising the day-to-day routine of the hospital.

The medical staff maintains control over medical matters. As Basil Georgopoulos and Floyd Mann (1972) point out, physicians are subject to very few nonmedical restrictions because (1) private physicians are not employees of the hospital (they are "guests" with the privilege of practicing medicine there); (2) they have considerable social status and prestige; and (3) they have supreme authority in all matters of patient care and medical professionalism. Thus occurs a rather curious situation where the primary function (medical treatment) of an organization (a hospital) is carried out by people (nurses and other health professionals) employed by the organization, but who are supervised by self-employed individuals (private practitioners). The primary "customer" of the hospital is the physician, who does not pay for its services. Eliot Freidson describes this situation by making the following comparison:

> It is as if all professors were self-employed tutors, sending individual pupils to universities where they can themselves administer some special training, but most particularly where they can count on having their pupils trained specially by lesser personnel employed by the university rather than by the professor.[3]

The occupational group in the hospital most affected by its system of dual authority are the nurses and auxiliary nursing workers who perform health care tasks on the hospital's wards. Nurses are responsible to the physician for carrying out the physician's orders, but they also are responsible to the nursing supervisors and the upper echelons of the hospital's administration. Even though the communication and allegiance of ward personnel tend to be channeled along occupational lines within and toward the "administrative channel of command," medical authority can and does cut across these lines. While this system can at times cause interpersonal stress, inconsistency, overlapping of responsibility, and inadequate coordination, it also allows ward personnel to "play off" one authority against the other if one appears unreasonable (Wessen 1972) and acts to reduce organizational inflexibility and authoritarianism (Georgopoulos and Mann 1972). In fact, Georgopoulos and Mann further argue that the hospital's system of dual authority is virtually inevitable in light of its high degree of functional specialization and professionalism. Nonetheless, hospital personnel share a common goal of providing quality patient care through competency, devotion to duty, and hard work, qualities Georgopoulos

[3]Eliot Freidson, *Professional Dominance* (Chicago: Aldine, 1970), pp. 174–175.

and Mann suggest have had the effect of producing many common norms, values, and complementary expectations. The hospital's normative system, they argue, underlies its administrative structure and

> ... enables the hospital to attain a level of coordination and integration that could never be accomplished through administrative edict, through hierarchical directives, or through explicitly formulated and carefully specified organizational plans and impersonal rules, regulations, and procedures.[4]

In a separate study of a psychiatric hospital, Anselm Strauss and his associates (1963) noted a similar process wherein the hospital rules governing the actions of the professionals who worked within its setting were far from extensive, clearly stated, or clearly binding. These researchers contended that the social order of the hospital was not fixed or automatically maintained, but was the result of continual negotiation between the administration, the medical staff and other hospital employees, and patients. The individuals involved had varying degrees of prestige and power, were at different stages in their careers, and had their own particular goals, reference groups, and occupational ideologies. In addition, hospital rules governing physicians' conduct were not clearly stated, extensive, or binding. The hospital administration tended to take a tolerant position toward institutional rules in the belief that good patient care required a minimum of "hard and fast" regulations and a maximum of "innovation and improvisation." Thus, there was continual negotiation of the medical rules—what they were and whether they applied in a particular situation. What held the hospital staff together was the sharing of a common goal to return their patients to the outside world in a better condition than when they entered the hospital. Strauss and associates explained:

> This goal is the symbolic cement that, metaphorically speaking, holds the organization together: the symbol to which all personnel can comfortably, and frequently point—with the assurance that *at least* about this matter everyone can agree! Although this symbol ... masks a considerable measure of disagreement and discrepant purpose, it represents a generalized mandate under which the hospital can be run—the public flag under which all may work in concert.[5]

Although it might appear from the Strauss study that the hospital was in a state of chaos, held together by only a single, idealistic agreement, actually the process of negotiation was observed to have definite pattern. In following their

---

[4]Basil F. Georgopoulos and Floyd C. Mann, "The Hospital as an Organization," in *Patients, Physicians and Illness*, 2nd ed., E. Jaco, ed. (New York: Macmillan, 1972), p. 308.

[5]Anselm Strauss, Leonard Schatzman, Danuta Ehrlich, Rue Bucher, and Melvin Sabshin, "The Hospital and Its Negotiated Order," in *The Hospital in Modern Society*, E. Freidson, ed. (New York: The Free Press, 1963), p. 154.

own particular approach to their work, the physicians were able to originate relatively stable understandings with the nurses and other hospital employees; this resulted in efficient and standardized forms of behavior not dependent on special instructions for all contingencies. Consequently, the process of negotiation not only created new meanings, but also reinforced the significance of the more formalized rules through a process of periodic appraisal.

In summary, the hospital's organization consists of a varied group of professionals and allied health workers with different functions, training, and occupational values. To make this social organization function effectively, it has been necessary to construct a decentralized system of authority organized around a generally acceptable objective of service to the patient. While the administrator directs and supervises hospital policy, the medical staff retains control over medical decisions.

However, the dual system of authority that has existed in hospitals is in jeopardy as a result of the precedent-setting *Darling* case in Charleston, Illinois.[6] The *Darling* case involved a suit for damages sought by the plaintiff for alleged medical and hospital negligence. The patient, Dorrence Darling, broke his leg while playing football and was taken to the emergency room of Charleston Community Hospital. A general practitioner put the leg in the cast. The leg became discolored, pulseless, and a foul odor developed. The nursing staff complained to the administrator and the physician in charge. The cast was ventilated but the odor continued. Ultimately the leg was amputated. The physician settled out of court. The nurses were not held negligent because they followed the accepted guidelines and procedure. The hospital bylaws provided for the consultation of another physician upon the request of the administrator. The administrators maintained that the hospital had provided the "brick" and "mortar" (the facilities) in which health care took place and that they had acted as all other hospital administrators would have done. The court found the administrators negligent in their relationship to the patient by not requiring a consultation as provided in the hospital bylaws. It held that hospitals do much more than just furnish treatment facilities; they also assume certain responsibilities for the care of the patient.

Therefore, as Richard Durbin and W. Herbert Springall (1974) have pointed out, if the hospital is going to be held liable for professional medical decisions, the administrators will attempt to gain greater control over the practice of medicine within its facilities. Durbin and Springall predicted that liability for patient care will result in the hospital's imposing more of its rules and regulations on the physicians, raising the standards of qualification required for staff privileges, and generally reducing the amount of professional discretion and autonomy physicians have traditionally been allowed to exercise. Moreover, research by Ann Barry Flood and W. Richard Scott (1978) found that the greater the power of the

[6]See *Darling v. Charleston Community Hospital* 33 Ill. 2d 326, 211 N.E. 253 (1965), 50 Ill. App. 2d 253, cert. denied, 383 U.S. 946 (1966).

hospital administration, the greater the quality of surgical care rendered to patients. "The strongest and most consistent factor related to quality of care," state Flood and Scott (1978:251), "was the power of the hospital administrators to influence decisions within their own domain."

Thus, control by hospital administrators may not only affect professional discretion, but also professional effectiveness as the practitioners within the hospital are provided with better coordination of services and staff support. Enhanced coordination and control of services are already being provided hospital administrators through the information systems provided by modern computer technology. In all probability, the hospital administration in both nonprofit and profit-making hospitals is likely to have increased control over the staff in the future through computerization of information used as a basis for decision making. Current trends in hospital management indicate that increased sharing of authority and decision making among physicians and hospital administrators is taking place (Alexander, Morrisey, and Shortell 1986; Scott 1982).

THE HOSPITAL–PATIENT ROLE

While hospital services are oriented toward a supportive notion of patient welfare, hospital rules and regulations are generally designed for the benefit of hospital personnel so that the work of treating large numbers of patients can be more efficient and easier to perform (Coe 1978; Freidson 1970a; Lorber 1975). Consequently, the sick and the injured are organized into various patient categories (maternity-obstetrics, neurology, orthopedics, urology, pediatrics, psychiatry) that reflect the medical staff's definition of their disorder and are then usually subject to standardized, staff-approved medical treatment and administrative procedures.

While it can be argued that standardizing patient care results in increased organizational efficiency—and ultimately serves the best interest of the patient—a prominent theme of the hospitalization experience noted by medical sociologists has been that of depersonalization. Erving Goffman (1961), for example, describes the status of mental hospital patients as akin to being a "nonperson," while Coe (1978) believes that patients in general tend to be devalued by hospital personnel because they are sick and dependent. H. Jack Geiger, an M.D., illustrates the feelings of depersonalization in hospital care by commenting on his own experience as a patient:

> I had to be hospitalized, suddenly and urgently, *on my own ward*. In the space of only an hour or two, I went from apparent health and well-being to pain, disability, and fear, and from staff to inmate in a total institution. At one moment I was a physician: elite, technically skilled, vested with authority, wielding power over others, affectively neutral. The next moment I was a patient: dependent, anxious, sanctioned in illness only if I was cooperative. A protected dependency and the promise of effective

technical help were mine—if I accepted a considerable degree of psychological and social servitude.[7]

Geiger was subsequently placed in the ward's only private room, which he believed was more for the benefit of the staff than for himself. He felt that had he been placed among the other patients, lending objective credence to physician "mortality," the patients might have used the situation to reduce status and role barriers between themselves and the staff. Furthermore, Geiger learned what he now believes is the major reason why physicians make such "notoriously terrible patients." It was not because their technical knowledge caused them to be more fearful of the consequences of their disorder or more critical of the way it was treated. Instead it was the loss of their professional role and authority in the medical setting, which Geiger surmises is an integral part of their self-concept.

Personnel in hospitals do not necessarily have the express goal of making their patients feel depersonalized, but the organization of the hospital's work does favor rules and regulations that reduce patient autonomy and encourage patient receptivity of the hospital routine. Another important factor is the work situation itself. Jeanne Quint Benoliel (1975:180) has pointed out that nurses who had difficulty tolerating the work in intensive care hospital units felt oppressed by "repetitive exposure to death and dying, daily contact with mutilated and unsightly patients, formidable and demanding work loads, limited work space, intricate machinery, and communication problems involving physicians, staff, and families." The intensive care ward is thus an example of a work situation that generates pressures of a dehumanizing nature as a result of staff attempts to cope with inherently intense psychological stress.

Yet it should be noted that the process of depersonalization is not just a result of the manner in which large numbers of patients are managed or the work conditions; it is also related to the patient's subjective experience of feeling sick. Howard Leventhal (1975) has explained that most reports of depersonalization commonly cite the experience of one's self as a physical object or thing. A second common experience is the feeling that one's own psychological self is isolated from other psychological selves (other people). Furthermore, Leventhal suggests that bodily symptoms such as pain can create a sense of separation within the individual of the physical self from the conscious psychological self. This inner alienation, in addition to the feeling of isolation from others, compounded by the doubt, uncertainty, and confusion that often accompany feelings of illness, can create for patients a sense of inadequacy and inability to control their lives. Leventhal's argument is that this attitude of incompetency is further intensified by the patient's having to assume an institutional role like the sick role, in which he or she is officially dependent and excluded from decision mak-

[7]H. Jack Geiger, "The Causes of Dehumanization in Health Care and Prospects for Humanization," in *Humanizing Health Care*, J. Howard and A. Strauss, eds. (New York: Wiley-Interscience, 1975), p. 13.

ing. The process of depersonalization is undoubtedly enhanced by the need of the physician or nurse to have access to the patient's body. However legitimate this may be, Coe (1978) points out that the exposure and giving over of one's body to strangers can be a degrading and humiliating experience, even though it is intended to be therapeutic.

Stripping, Control of Resources, and Restriction of Mobility

Coe (1978) states that patients are alienated from their usual lives and reduced to a largely impersonal status in the hospital through three basic mechanisms of hospital processing: (1) stripping, (2) control of resources, and (3) restriction of mobility. Coe explains that when patients present themselves for treatment in a hospital, they bring with them a particular social identity, what Goffman refers to as a "face" (see Chapter 4); this represents their attitudes, beliefs, values, concept of self, and social status, all of which form the basis for their manner of presenting themselves to the world. *Stripping* occurs when the hospital systematically divests the person of these past representations of self. The patient's clothes are taken away and replaced with a set of pajamas; regardless of whether the pajamas are the property of the hospital or the patient, the simple fact of wearing pajamas serves as a uniform that identifies that person as sick and restricts movement to those areas of the hospital in which pajamas (patient dress) are authorized. Personal belongings of value are taken away and locked up for safekeeping by the staff. Visiting regulations control not only when patients are allowed to have visitors, but also who is allowed to visit (children under age fourteen are typically excluded). In addition, the staff supervises the patient's diet, decides when the patient should be asleep or awake, and in essence controls the general conduct of the patient's social life in the hospital. The hospital routine for one patient is very similar to the routine of others having the same or similar health problems.

Another important feature of hospitalization is the *control of resources* by the staff. Coe includes under the control of resources not only physical items, like bedclothes and toilet paper, but also the control of information about the patient's medical condition. Patients are normally not aware of their prognosis or the results of laboratory tests and X-rays unless the physician decides to inform them.

The third aspect of depersonalization outlined by Coe is the *restriction of mobility*. In most hospitals patients are not allowed to leave their wards without the permission of the head nurse, who is usually required to know the location of all patients at all times; when patients do leave the ward to travel to another area of the hospital, they are generally accompanied by a nurse, nurse's aide, or orderly. When patients are admitted to the hospital and also when discharged, they are taken in a wheelchair between the ward and the hospital entrance regardless of their ability to walk because the hospital is "responsible" for them whenever they are inside its walls. The result is that even the ability of patients to move about is supervised and controlled.

Conforming Attitudes

Some patients may be so seriously ill that feelings of depersonalization do not enter the picture. All they desire is to get well and they are happy to do or experience whatever is necessary to accomplish that goal. That is, they are quite willing to conform to the situation.

Yet this assumption may not be entirely correct. In a study of hospital patients in New York City, Judith Lorber (1975) found that conforming attitudes were common among cancer patients but not among patients hospitalized for very serious surgery. Lorber suggests that the cancer patients may have been scared by the ambiguities of the information they received. One woman, for example, refused to believe her doctor was telling her the truth after she had a tumor removed and it was found to be benign. Serious surgery patients, on the other hand, were much better informed about their illnesses, yet they behaved more "deviantly" (were troublesome, uncooperative, and complaining) than the cancer patients. Their somewhat lengthy stays in the hospital had not generally resulted in their complete acceptance of the staff's model of the "good" (obedient) patient. Thus, seriousness of a patient's illness was not a good predictor of whether a patient would conform to hospital routine.

The best attitude predictors, according to Lorber, were age and education: The younger and better educated the patient, the less likely was the patient to express highly conforming attitudes. Conversely, the older and more poorly educated patients were the least likely to express deviant attitudes. Yet among college-educated patients, Lorber found those patients over sixty years of age to be moderately conforming, while those under sixty tended to adopt "deviant" attitudes. This latter finding is consistent with other studies (Cartwright 1964; Coser 1956), which suggest that younger patients tend to be more aggressive about seeking information in the hospital and less conforming, while older patients tend to be more submissive to hospital rules.

Lorber (1975:220) also examined the attitudes of the doctors and nurses toward the patients, and her analysis of staff evaluations suggested the important finding that "ease of management was the basic criterion for a label of good patient, and that patients who took time and attention felt to be unwarranted by their illness tended to be labeled problem patients. In short," Lorber (1975:220) says, "the less of a doctor's time the patient took, the better he or she was viewed." Patients who had a tendency to complain or be uncooperative or overemotional were generally considered to be a problem only by the particular staff member who had cause to interact with them. The key variable, therefore, in how the doctors and nurses defined the patients was the amount of time from the staff that the patient demanded. Interestingly enough, Lorber reported that some staff members labeled certain patients as "good" if they couldn't remember them too well.

A question remains as to what actions physicians and nurses take to deal with troublesome hospital patients. Some studies (Glaser and Strauss 1965) suggest that staff members tend to avoid patients who are not liked or who are uncooperative; sometimes particularly bothersome patients will be reprimanded or scolded. Lorber found that the usual method of handling difficult patients in a New York City hospital was to prescribe tranquilizers or sedatives. If drugs did not accomplish the desired cooperation, then disruptive patients might on occasion be sent home or transferred to a convalescent center with trained psychiatric nurses. Lorber's general impression was that the hospital staff tended to treat the short-term, paying patients in a permissive fashion and put up with the problems they caused. It remains to be seen if the staff would have been as tolerant had the patients been hospitalized on a long-term, charity basis.

The Sick Role for Hospital Patients

To Parsons' (1951) concept of the sick role, which emphasizes patient cooperation and striving to get well, we may now add that of the hospitalized sick role, which apparently includes an obligation to accept hospital routine without protest. Lorber (1975:214) notes the similarities between Parsons' sick role and the role of the hospital patient. Both are universalistic, affectively neutral, functionally specific, and collectivity oriented. However, a major difference between them, Lorber observes, is that the idea of voluntary cooperation, one-to-one intimacy, and conditional permissiveness (being temporarily excused from normal social activities on the condition of seeking medical advice and care) applies primarily to the relationship between an out-patient and a private physician. In-patient care subjects the hospital patient to a role additionally characterized by submission to authority, enforced cooperation, and depersonalized status.

Coe (1978) has suggested that acquiescence is the most common form of patient adjustment to hospital routine and the most successful for short-stay patients in terms of the quality of their interaction with the hospital staff. Basically, all the attitudes of the hospitalized sick role are results of the necessity for a well-established work routine for hospital staff. As Rose Laub Coser (1956) has pointed out, in meeting the medical needs of patients, the hospital demands that its patients give up substantial rationality about the direction and nature of their personal activities in favor of the functional rationality of organizational life.

THE RISING COST OF HOSPITALIZATION

Any discussion of American hospitals would be incomplete without considering the financial cost of hospitalization, which has risen more sharply in recent years than any other aspect of medical care. For purposes of comparison, John Knowles (1973) indicates that in 1925 the cost of one day's stay as a patient at the Massachusetts General Hospital in Boston was $3.00, and the bill was paid entirely by the patient. By 1991, however, the average one-day cost of hospitalization had risen to $745, with most of the expense paid by a third party such as a private health insurance company—Blue Cross, Blue Shield, or some other hospital-medical plan—or Medicare, Medicaid, or a state welfare agency. Not only did costs increase significantly, but the manner of payment has also changed, as about 90 percent of all expenses for hospital services are now paid by third-party sources. In some cases, third-party coverage has led to increased hospital admission rates, since health needs that are met in the physician's office are often not covered by insurance. Hospitalization can therefore reduce the patient's direct cost of health care. But this does not mean that patients escape paying hospital bills. Government expenditures are paid out of tax revenues, while private health insurance costs must also be covered and private companies are set up to make a profit.

Overall health expenditures in the United States in 1991 amounted to $752 billion, of which $240.2 billion was spent on hospital care. Thus, about 38.4 percent of all the money spent on health in the United States is spent on hospital services. What does the hospital do with its income? Knowles explains that hospital expenses are categorized as either routine or ancillary costs. Routine costs are those expenses of providing room and board, including the provision of several different diets of three meals a day served in bed; the cost of nonmedical supplies and equipment; the salaries of all members of the hospital's nonmedical staff; and the salaries of medical technicians, nurses, auxiliary nursing workers, interns, and residents who are available to patients on a twenty-four-hour basis, seven days a week. Ancillary expenses include the cost of laboratories, the pharmacy, operating rooms, X-ray rooms, cast rooms, and other specialized hospital facilities, plus the cost of all medical supplies. Even though patients do not get to see or even use all of a hospital's facilities, the cost of maintaining and operating these facilities for those patients who do use them continues regardless.

The most expensive hospitals in the United States are located in New England and on the Pacific Coast, while the least expensive are found in the South and in some of the Rocky Mountain states. Supposedly, regional differences in the cost of hospitalization are related to regional differences in the overall cost of living. Other factors that have been found to be important in determining hospital costs are the ratio of personnel to total expenses (the cost of labor is higher in high-cost hospitals) and the patient occupancy rate (low-cost hospitals tend to have relatively high occupancy rates). Even the type of hospital administrator may be a significant factor, as administrators with medical qualifications (M.D.'s) may be able to negotiate to the administration's advantage in controlling the staff's demands for more and/or improved equipment and facilities.

It has also been found that one of the most significant factors affecting costs is the structure of the decision-making process. Edward Morse and his associates (1974) argue that decentralization of decision making tends to facilitate a hospital's adoption of modern medical technology. But while the application of new technology usually reduces the average length of stay and may increase the average occupancy rate, it has little direct impact upon the hospital's total expenses. Instead, Morse suggests that the more centralized the hospital's decision-making structure, the more efficient it will be in controlling expenses by selecting those organizational practices that facilitate goal achievement at the lowest cost.

Other factors contributing to higher hospital expenses have been inflation and increased costs. Between 1982–1984 and 1992, the cost of hospital care in the United States has more than doubled. The rise in hospital costs stems not only from inflation but also from increased costs for labor, medical equipment, supplies, and new construction. Labor constituted 53.8 percent of a hospital's total expenses in 1991 and represents the single greatest expense for a hospital.

However, the cost of paperwork is also significant. A study by Steffie Woolhandler and his associates (Woolhandler, Himmelstein, and Lewontin 1993) found that nearly 25 percent of all hospital costs nationwide were for administration. Minnesota had the lowest administrative costs (18.6 percent) as a percentage of total hospital spending and Hawaii the highest (30.6 percent), with the national average standing at 24.8 percent. This research also provided dramatic evidence of the growth in medical bureaucracy. In 1968, American hospitals employed 435,100 administrators and clerks while caring for an average of 1,378,000 patients daily; by 1990, 1,221,600 administrative personnel performed services for a daily average of 853,000 patients. Although the number of patients decreased, the number of hospital employees doing paperwork skyrocketed. Woolhandler and his colleagues suggest that hospitals in the United States could save $50 billion annually if they required less paperwork and utilized one form for all health insurance claims as is done in Canada.

For example, a hospital in the Canadian province of British Columbia employed one clerk in 1992 to process insurance claims; a few miles away in an American hospital of the same size in the state of Washington, forty-five clerks were employed full time to handle insurance claims. Canada, with its system of national health insurance, uses a single claim form. Yet the United States—with government-sponsored Medicare and Medicaid health insurance programs and numerous private health insurance companies requiring various deductions and copayments and providing different levels of coverage—has a complex and administratively burdensome approach to filing claims. As the Clinton administration's White House Domestic Policy Council describes the situation:

> American health care is choked by paperwork and strangled by bureaucracy. Administrative costs are higher in the American health care system than in any other country, and rising rapidly.
>
> Confusion, complexity and increasing costs stem from the peculiarities of our health insurance system. . . . Hospitals, clinics, doctors and other health providers must deal with hundreds of different insurance plans, each with its own benefit package, exclusions and limitations—and mountains of forms, rules, rates and payment procedures to follow. . . . Hospitals have been forced to establish whole departments, create new occupational categories and hire special clerks to handle the paperwork.
>
> . . . Every doctor's office and hospital must hire staff to document every service provided, enter record codes, send out bills, and process other paperwork. They must determine whether an individual qualifies for health coverage, which company carries the primary policy, whether the services are covered, whether another policy covers the same care, how

much each company is willing to pay, and how forms need to be filled out. Those staff spend hours on the telephone with insurers arguing about what's covered and what's not. In many cases, these steps are only the beginning; receiving payment can take weeks.[8]

Technological innovations have also been identified as an important cause of rising hospital costs. However, as William Rushing (1984) points out, innovations in technology are not automatically translated into higher hospital costs. Expenses from new technology increase because the public expects such innovations to be effective and therefore needed—even though costs are driven up because the innovations may be used by only a few patients and require the training and employment of increased numbers of specialists and superspecialists. Furthermore, physicians are often dependent upon the technology based in hospitals and the technology needs to be available for the hospital to support its relationships with doctors. Consequently, public expectations, the nature of hospital services, and physician–hospital relationships all combine to encourage a hospital to have the most recent innovations regardless of whether such innovations are cost effective.

What can be done about controlling hospital costs? The Clinton administration's proposed health reform program would provide several measures. One improvement would be a single uniform insurance claim form that would reduce the amount of paperwork and the need for armies of clerks to process claims. Another improvement would be basic health insurance coverage for everyone. If all patients carry a basic coverage, hospitals could rely on a steady stream of income and not suffer serious financial losses for treating the uninsured. Many of America's 38.5 million people without health insurance rely on hospital emergency rooms for primary care. Inappropriate use of costly emergency services contributes to the rising cost of health care—especially when the cost of care cannot be recovered. Federal law requires hospitals to accept patients in emergency rooms and prevents them from turning away emergency patients who cannot pay until their condition is stabilized. This forces hospitals to accept acutely ill or injured patients through their emergency rooms regardless of insurance status. It also encourages the uninsured to use emergency rooms for primary care since they know it is difficult or impossible to be treated at a private doctor's office without adequate funds or insurance coverage. With universal coverage, everyone could visit doctor's offices or use less expensive hospital facilities during normal working hours.

While support for the health reform is welcomed by many hospitals, the Clinton plan would require a difficult transition for some. The emphasis would be on care outside of hospitals, not in them, as a cost-saving measure. This would mean increased use of outpatient and ambulatory services, along with home health care which is increasing in the United States. Home care involves treatment on a full- or part-time basis by nurses in the home and visits to doctors' of-

[8]White House Domestic Policy Council, *Health Security: The President's Report to the American People* (New York: Touchstone, 1993), pp. 6–7.

fices or clinics if the patient is physically able. Otherwise, the doctor and other health care workers would make home visits. Hospitals would also need to trim their costs and offer quality care at the same time in order to be competitive and attract customers. Some hospitals might not survive reform.

One current measure, instituted in 1983, is federal legislation that establishes a fixed rate for each procedure (according to which DRG or Diagnostic Related Group the procedure falls under) that the government will pay hospitals for patients insured by Medicare. In the past, Medicare, which covers the elderly, paid hospitals for whatever it reasonably cost them to treat Medicare patients. The more hospitals spent, the more the government paid. If the spending had continued unchecked, the Medicare hospital insurance trust fund would have been depleted by 1988. Some states passed legislation aimed at regulating hospital rates, limiting construction of hospitals and nursing homes, and encouraging doctors to lower their fees. Private insurance companies also took steps to set fixed rates so hospital expenses for publicly insured patients would not be passed on to them.

Hospitals responded by expanding services and controlling costs in ways that ensured their survival (Gay et al. 1989; Stevens 1989). While some hospitals have been more successful than others in this regard, Rosemary Stevens (1989:324) points out that "hospitals naturally responded to DRGs, as they had to other government programs in the past, with an eye to maintaining their own income, expanding rather than contracting their overall services, and to solidifying their competitive position." Even not-for-profit hospitals have to buy new technology, replace worn equipment, and maintain or improve their physical plant— besides meeting rising labor and energy costs and dealing with inflation. Throughout the twentieth century, as Stevens observes, not-for-profit hospitals have been profit-maximizing enterprises, even though they viewed themselves as charities serving the community and still, to some extent, are charities in that they discount or write off some services for the poor. On balance, however, the record of American hospitals in meeting the health needs of the socially disadvantaged is not good and Stevens explains that disparities in services between social classes is a major challenge to the ideals of hospital services today.

As long as the prices of goods and services in general continue to increase, the cost of health care and hospitalization can be expected to rise accordingly. The principal social policy issues today with respect to American hospitals are to limit costs in such a way that hospital care is kept within a reasonable relationship to the rest of the economy and the needs of all Americans for hospitalization are met.

SUMMARY

This chapter has reviewed the hospital's evolving role as a community institution intended to serve the needs of sick and injured people as a form of social responsibility. Passing through stages of being a center for religious practice, a poorhouse, and a deathhouse, the hospital has finally come to be a center for medical technology designed to handle the health problems of all members of society, not just the lower classes.

Today in the United States hospitals can be classified in terms of their type of ownership (voluntary or nonprofit, proprietary or profit making, or government owned) and by their type of service (general medical-surgical or specialty). The largest single type of hospital in the United States is voluntary and general medical-surgical. These hospitals are nominally supervised by a governing body, such as a board of trustees, but actually exhibit a dual system of authority: administrative and medical. Although hospitals are supposedly oriented toward the welfare of the patient, a significant body of literature in medical sociology is concerned with the fact that treating large numbers of people has resulted in organizational procedures that tend to depersonalize the individual patient. The final section of the chapter dealt with the rising cost of hospitalization, which has become a major social issue.

The Physician in a Changing Society

13

Public dissatisfaction with the medical profession and its provision of health care in the United States is generally viewed as having largely economic and social origins. The specific issues usually cited are those of the rising financial costs of services and the failure to provide quality care for all Americans despite the medical profession's claims of excellence and technological achievement. Both of these issues are based on the organization of medical practice around the concept of financial profit in a free enterprise system. Advocates of this system, notably physicians, claim that the profit motive leads to enhanced efficiency in providing services, increased incentive for research and development, and greater responsiveness to patients. Opponents argue, in rebuttal, that the present system should be changed because the profit motive discriminates against the poor, fosters the unnecessary duplication of services (thereby increasing costs), and introduces a dehumanizing connotation to a service intended to relieve human suffering. Nevertheless, economic considerations, as Bradford Grey (1991) found, have become a primary motivation among physicians and hospitals. The profit motive, in turn, has bred increasing resentment among consumers and demands that the professional power of doctors be reduced.

       Part of the blame for this situation may lie in medicine's development as a profession. Howard Rasmussen (1975) has pointed out that professionalism in American medicine has resulted in at least three undesirable consequences. First, it has fostered the development of a view of disease largely confined to specific organs or physiological systems, but which fails to consider a more holistic view of patients as people. This conflicts directly with a major societal demand that contemporary practice come to terms with a wide spectrum of disorders related more to problems of living than to specific chemical and physical abnormalities of the body. Second, professionalism has led to the development of a highly rigid stratification system in medical practice which has promoted an increasingly large gap between physicians and nonphysician medical personnel. And for certain functions the nonphysician health worker may have a more important service to provide the patient than the physician. Third, professionalism has resulted in the separation of professional training so that a common educational base is lacking between physicians and paramedicals that might allow a health care team to work more effectively as a cohesive group. Overall, the physician has emerged in the role of a "super-physician" in a "super-hospital" with ultimate responsibility for the patient. But, as individuals, some physicians may not have the time, interest, training, or ability to cope with the entire range of modern patient care. Thus, while the health care needs of American society are those of the late twentieth century, organized medicine has continued to pursue a pattern of professional behavior based upon the image of medical practice at the turn of the century when the physician worked on a solo basis as an independent, fee-for-service, private practitioner.

SOCIAL CONTROL OF MEDICAL PRACTICE

The social control of medical practice has traditionally presented special problems for American society. It has been argued that since physicians themselves have established the medical standards enforced by governmental regulating agencies and since laypersons are generally unable to judge technical performance, the two most common forms of social control in an industrial society—bureaucratic supervision and judgment by the recipient of services—are lacking (Rueschmeyer 1972). However, the argument continues that the problem of controlling organized medicine is solved by the medical profession's emphasis on the strong self-control of the individual physician, an ethical stance reinforced by both the formal and informal sanctions of a community of colleagues. Society is thus justified in granting the physician professional autonomy because he or she is a member of a self-controlled collectivity providing a vital function for society's general good. This argument contains three serious defects.

　　First of all, it is important to note that laypersons do judge technical performance regardless of whether they are competent to do so. Eliot Freidson's (1960, 1989) discussion of the lay-referral system made it quite clear that lay avenues of influence and authority exist independently of the physician and operate to guide the patient either toward or away from the services of a particular physician. This activity may not only determine the physician's success in attracting patients but also affects the physician's mode of medical practice. As Freidson (1960:379) has stated, "in being *relatively* free, the medical profession should not be mistaken for being *absolutely* free from control by patients." The choices of clients act as a form of social control over professionals and can militate against the survival of a group as a profession or the career success of particular professionals (Goode 1957:198).

Several studies show that patients do terminate their relationships with physicians and actively shop around for other doctors who are more able to meet their expectations (Ben-Sira 1976, 1980; Hayes-Bautista 1976b; Kasteler et al. 1976). Besides lack of confidence in a physician's technical competence, other factors commonly identified as influencing patients to change doctors are the unwillingness of doctors to spend time talking to them, the high cost of services, the possible inconvenience of a particular doctor's office location and hours, and unfavorable assessments of the doctor's personality.

A second major defect in the argument legitimizing the medical profession's autonomy has to do with physician's efforts at peer regulation. In a study of a medical group practice, Freidson (1975, 1989) found indeed that rules and standards existed to define the limits of acceptable performance by physicians associated with the group. However, norms governing colleague relations, essentially *rules of etiquette,* restricted the evaluation of work and discouraged the expression of criticism. Etiquette was a more important norm than accountability, and it undermined attempts at critical evaluation and control by overlooking fault in order to maintain group harmony. Confrontation with a colleague was considered distasteful even in private and was unthinkable in public. In this medical practice setting, the norms of etiquette had not only seriously limited the exercise of professional control, but had also reduced the scope of procedures colleagues were willing to review.

Marcia Millman (1977a, 1977b) noted a similar situation in her study of three private, university-affiliated hospitals. Many doctors in this study were willing to criticize their colleagues for errors in small group discussions and behind the other's back. But they were strongly reluctant to criticize another doctor's mistakes at any official meeting because of what Millman termed "a fear of reprisal" and "a recognition of common interests."

Millman's examination of medical mortality and morbidity conferences, in which patient deaths were reviewed as a regular hospital procedure, was particularly illustrative of the collective rationalization of mistakes. The atmosphere of these conferences was likened to such social events as weddings or funerals, in which the participants were expected to show tact and restraint in order to remain on friendly terms. Restricted to members of the hospital's medical staff, the conferences were intended to be educational, not punitive. Only certain cases (conspicuous was the absence of cases involving patient deaths by gross medical mismanagement) were picked for review because as one hospital chief of medicine stated, "it's got to be a cordial affair." Millman described the meeting as follows:

> At Lakeside Hospital, the chief of medicine stands on the stage and presides as a master of ceremonies. As one member of the staff after another testifies about how he or she was led to the same mistaken diagnosis, the

responsibility for the mistake is implicitly spread around. As in a good detective story, the case is reconstructed to show that there was evidence for suspecting an outcome different from the one that turned out to be the true circumstance. Responsibility for the error is also neutralized by making much of the unusual or misleading features of the case, or by showing how the patient was to blame because of uncooperative or neurotic behavior. Furthermore, by reviewing the case in fine detail, the physicians restore their images as careful, methodical practitioners, and thereby neutralize the sloppiness and carelessness that are made obvious by mistakes.[1]

Millman contended that a "gentlemen's agreement" existed among the hospital physicians to overlook each other's mistakes. According to Charles Bosk (1979), in a study of physicians in a surgical training program at a major university medical center, there was a general recognition that honest errors exist and all physicians make them. Technical errors, if they were made in "good faith," were less serious than moral errors. A moral error was making the mistake of being unreliable, uncooperative, lacking in responsibility to patients, and failing to acknowledge subordination to superiors on the staff. Technical errors, on the other hand, could be forgiven and often had the result of motivating the offending physician to work harder, spend more time with patients, double check procedures, and learn from the mistake. By admitting mistakes and trying to make up for them, the physician remained a good colleague. Moral errors, conversely, resulted in unfavorable letters of recommendation for those seeking jobs and social isolation from other physicians in the hospital.

Other studies (Grey 1991) suggest that the lack of physician peer control described by Freidson and Millman and the rather weak control studied by Bosk are typical of most medical practice settings. Furthermore, if lawsuits for malpractice can be regarded as any kind of valid indicator, it would appear that incompetence in medicine, or at least a greater public awareness of medical malpractice, is common. Certainly physicians can be the victims of malpractice suits that have no merit in fact. Yet malpractice suits rose dramatically from a few hundred in the 1950s to more than 10,000 a year in the 1980s until 1988 when claims began to drop. There is evidence that doctors have adopted improved standards to reduce patient injuries, as well as develop better rapport with patients, share decision making, and persuade patients to take more responsibility for their health (Annandale 1989). Rates for malpractice insurance declined 5 to 35 percent in 1990 as states have set limits on the amount of money awarded in malpractice lawsuits and physicians have become more careful in dealing with patients.

This does not mean that there are not incompetent or dishonest doctors. A national data bank was established in 1989 to identify incompetent physicians, dentists, and other licensed health practitioners. The data stored consists of suspensions and other serious disciplinary actions and malpractice settlements or judgments. The action to establish the data bank represents one of the most im-

[1]Marcia Millman, "Masking Doctors' Errors," *Human Behavior*, 6 (1977), 17.

portant efforts by the federal government to discipline doctors. Hospitals can be fined or subjected to lawsuits for failing to report disciplinary actions, while other information comes from court decisions, insurance companies, and medical societies. In addition to malpractice, another sign of ineffective control over medical practice is the high cost to the government of Medicare and Medicaid due to physician corruption. Some physicians have been arrested and sentenced to prison for misrepresenting care they supposedly gave Medicare and Medicaid patients.

This discussion is not intended to convey the impression that physicians are generally untrustworthy. Instances of corruption and fraud appear to be rare. In fact, Freidson (1975) argues that it can be assumed that physicians are usually dedicated to their patients. State medical societies do cooperate with state licensing agencies to remove the medical licenses of demonstrably incompetent physicians, thus preventing them from legally practicing medicine. Furthermore, Professional Standards Review Organizations were established in 1970 in conjunction with Medicaid and Medicare to review and evaluate the medical care given to patients eligible to use these services. PSROs are composed of licensed physicians and osteopaths who determine if the services rendered are medically necessary, meet professional standards of quality, and are provided as efficiently and effectively as possible. Although some latitude in the interpretation of standards is likely in any diagnostic category, Freidson (1975:251) points out that a consensus of opinion will at least exclude "the blatant, gross, or obvious deviations from common knowledge and practice."

Nevertheless, medical standards and practices continue to be regulated by the practitioners themselves. Thus, it is generally difficult to find a physician who will be openly critical of another physician or who will publicly testify against a colleague. Mistakes and errors in medical practice, either through neglect or ignorance, can sometimes be defended as "a difference of opinion." Millman (1977a) suggests that possibly all doctors have at some time made a terrible mistake in their careers and realize that they may do so again. Therefore, in matters of peer regulation, they tend to follow the Golden Rule: "Do unto others as you would have them do unto you."

The third major defect in the professional autonomy argument arises from the fact that the autonomy granted the medical profession is granted *conditionally*, on the assumption that it will resolve significant issues in favor of the public interest. However, traditional AMA resistance to innovations in medical care that might threaten the fee-for-service pattern has been cited as an example of greater professional concern with matters of self-interest than with public welfare (Stevens 1971). This situation has reduced public confidence in medicine more than any other single issue since physicians in general are often viewed as placing the desire for financial profit ahead of the desire to help people.

For example, in 1984, the AMA endorsed a one-year freeze on physicians' fees to show it was serious about holding down health costs. Participation by individual physicians, however, was strictly voluntary. But six months later, the AMA unsuccessfully sued the federal government for formally freezing Medicare payments to doctors as a cost containment measure. The AMA claimed the government did not have the authority to impose limits on physicians' fees and such action interfered with the right to contract for services. Court action, such as this by the AMA, to overturn legislation intended to contain costs, seriously undermines the AMA's assertions that it supports the public interest. In fact, some critics argue that the AMA supported a voluntary freeze simply to forestall government control of Medicare fees.

At present, challenges to the autonomy of the medical profession come principally from three sources: (1) government regulation, (2) corporations in the health care business, and (3) changes in the traditional physician–patient relationship associated with consumerism.

GOVERNMENT REGULATION

Rising costs of health care do appear to result in increased public demands for government intervention (Hollingsworth 1981). The response of the federal government to these demands has been to support improvements in health care delivery for all segments of the population, exert limited controls over physicians, and initiate efforts to reform the health care delivery system. The passage of legislation establishing Medicare and Medicaid public health insurance in the 1960s to provide for the medical needs of the elderly and the poor was accomplished despite the opposition of the AMA.

Other legislation (also initially opposed by the AMA) followed in the 1970s. Professional Standards Review Organizations (PSROs), as previously discussed, were established to evaluate the care given to Medicare and Medicaid patients. Even though PSROs were controlled by doctors, their function was a signal that the government wanted to ensure a standard of quality care. Support through planning grants and loan guarantees was also provided to encourage the development of health maintenance organizations (HMOs)—a form of prepaid group practice emphasizing preventive care. One-half of the funds earmarked for HMOs were allocated for areas that were medically underserved. Although doctors and hospitals still controlled the efforts of PSROs, the sum total of regulatory efforts, as Paul Starr (1982:403–404) notes, went far beyond what physicians and hospitals wanted. Planning was aimed not at expansion but at containment and was formally linked for the first time with regulation.

Further regulation came in the early 1980s with the establishment of Diagnostic Related Groups by the federal government. DRGs are a schedule of fees placing a ceiling on how much the government will pay for specific services rendered to Medicare patients by hospitals and doctors. This action continued the government's attempts to meet public demands to control the cost of health care, even though it was bitterly contested by hospitals and the AMA.

The most extensive changes are yet to come, however. The Clinton health plan would reorganize health care delivery in the United States into systems of managed care. *Managed care* refers to health care organizations—like Health Maintenance Organizations or Preferred Provider Organizations—that "manage" or control the cost of health care by monitoring how doctors treat specific illnesses, limit referrals to expensive specialists, and require authorization prior to hospitalization, among other measures. The Clinton proposal would have patients choosing from managed care plans. If doctors wanted patients, they would have to join as well. They would have to work in accordance with the regulations and fee structure set by the managed care plan that employed them. Even when they treated patients who were not members of such plans, they would be required to charge them on the basis of a fee schedule approved by the government. Physicians will find, if this measure is enacted, that they will have even less autonomy to control their practice and income than anytime in the past.

The effect on some physicians has been discouragement. A 1989 nationwide Gallup Poll of doctors determined that nearly 40 percent would probably or definitely not go to medical school if they had been in college today, knowing what they now know about medicine. The most common reason was government or insurance regulations that interfered with their work and undercut their autonomy. Some 63 percent indicated that their control over patient treatment decisions had decreased in the last several years. This perception appears accurate, as greater government regulation of medical practice has led to an erosion of the authority of physicians over their work (Ritzer and Walczak 1988). This process is continuing and will be accelerated if the Clinton plan is put into effect.

THE COMING OF THE CORPORATION

The "Coming of the Corporation" is the title of a chapter in Paul Starr's influential book *The Social Transformation of American Medicine* (1982). In it, Starr describes how America may be on its way to a major change in its system of health care delivery through the intervention of large health care conglomerates. Starr states:

> This transformation—so extraordinary in view of medicine's past, yet so similar to changes in other industries—has been in the making, ironically enough, since the passage of Medicare and Medicaid. By making health care lucrative for providers, public financing made it exceedingly attractive to investors and set in motion the formation of large-scale corporate enterprises. Nursing homes and hospitals had a long history of proprietary ownership, but almost entirely as small, individually owned and operated enterprises. One of the first developments in the corporate transformation was the purchase of these facilities by new corporate chains. This, in a sense, was the first beachhead of for-profit corporations in the delivery of medical care.[2]

Next came a virtual wave of mergers, acquisitions, and diversifications by the health care corporations in which not only hospitals and nursing homes were acquired but also emergency-care centers, hospital supply companies, hospital restaurants, medical office buildings, alcohol and drug abuse centers, health

[2]Paul Starr, *The Social Transformation of American Medicine* (New York: Basic Books, 1982), p. 428.

maintenance organizations, health spas, psychiatric hospitals, home health care services, and hospital management systems. For the first time in the United States, health care became regarded as a major business arena. Profit-making corporations expanded into markets that were either underserved or into areas where their services could successfully compete with existing nonprofit-seeking institutions. The profit-seeking hospital chains, for example, would provide attractively furnished rooms, good food, a friendly staff, and more efficient services. With health insurance paying the majority of the cost for hospital care, some patients evidently prefer the surroundings and more expensive services of the for-profit hospital. In the context of corporate health care, the physician is an employee rather than an independent practitioner. The doctor is bound to the rules and regulations of the corporation which, in all probability, is managed by people trained in business, not medicine.

At present, about 13.3 percent of all U.S. hospitals are owned by profit-making organizations. What attracted corporations to health care delivery is that it is an area where sound business practices can realize profits. The federal government, through Medicare and Medicaid, has poured billions of dollars into health care since the mid-1960s. In 1991, $222.9 billion was spent by the federal government on health. Much of this money went to pay for doctor and hospital services. The corporations, however, have not been as interested in this public money as they have in the private health insurance companies. Private insurance companies reduce the risk of nonpaying patients through the coverage they provide. Medicare and Medicaid, in recent years, have become financially strained and in 1983 limits were set by the government on how much they would pay for specific health services. So the goal of the health care corporations is to attract patients with private health insurance which will cover the relatively higher charges of the profit-making hospitals.

Another new development has been the expansion of free-standing emergency centers that take business away from hospitals. Sometimes referred to as "Docs-in-a-Box" or "7-Eleven Medicine," these centers (called free-standing because they are not affiliated with a hospital) are typically open seven days a week, eighteen to twenty-four hours a day, and try to attend to their patients with a minimum of waiting time. They treat the cuts, broken bones, bruises, and minor ailments usually treated in doctors' offices or hospital emergency rooms. Sometimes these facilities are located in shopping centers or other convenient locations. They are generally open for business, accessible, reasonably priced, and provide fast service.

In an era of cost containment, cost-efficient innovations like the free-standing emergency centers and the multihospital corporate systems may have an advantage in attracting privately insured patients. They can offer quick and efficient service. In addition, the large multihospital systems can consolidate their resources and not duplicate services available elsewhere in the system, thereby saving them money. As not-for-profit hospitals find it increasingly difficult to contend with rising costs and limits on reimbursements from public health insurance, Starr suggests that there will be more pressure to sell out to the corporations with greater financial resources. There are, however, some limits to growth. Starr indicates that the large chains avoid owning hospitals in depressed areas with large numbers of Medicaid patients, nor do they seek to own teaching hospitals. The market for these chains is considered to be in the more attractive neighborhoods where the hospitals serve relatively affluent patients. What this means is that the poor will not generally benefit since the for-profit hospitals, with their higher prices, try to attract those who can afford their services. As Starr (1982:436) notes: "The for-profit chains have an undisguised preference for privately insured patients."

Physicians have not shown strong objections to being employed by the corporations or in sending their patients to the for-profit hospitals. There are two major reasons for this development. One is the availability of doctors for such jobs. Second, health care corporations provide jobs, offices, equipment, hospital privileges, and perhaps even a salary guarantee. Starr points out that because of their dependence on doctors, the corporations will be generous in granting them rewards, including more autonomy than they give to most corporate employees. More part-time and intermittent employment may also be available, especially for women doctors who wish to spend time with their children. Starr comments:

> . . . the profession is no longer steadfastly opposed to the growth of corporate medicine. Physicians' commitment to solo practice has been eroding; younger medical school graduates express a preference for practicing in groups. The longer period of residency training may cultivate more group-oriented attitudes. Young doctors may be more interested in freedom *from* the job than freedom *in* the job, and organizations that can provide more regular hours can screen out the invasions of private life that come with independent professional practice.[3]

Nevertheless, there will be a loss in autonomy for those physicians who do corporate work. Starr explains that doctors will no longer control such basic issues as time of retirement and there will likely be more regulation of the pace and routines of work. There will also be standards of performance in which doctors will be evaluated and paid on the basis of the amount of revenues they generate or number of patients treated per hour. Physicians who do not meet corporate standards are likely to lose their jobs. Moreover, there is likely to be a close scrutiny of mistakes in order to not only ensure quality medical care but also to avoid corporate liability for malpractice. Corporate management, utilizing data supplied by statisticians monitoring quality-of-care programs, will probably not be particularly concerned about professional norms of etiquette when it comes to dealing with doctors who are careless or incompetent. The locus of control will be outside the immediate health care facility and in the hands of a management system that is primarily business oriented. In corporations, doctors are not as likely to play the decisive role in decision making about policy, hospital budgets, capital investments, personnel appointments, salaries, and promotions.

---

[3]Starr, *The Social Transformation of American Medicine*, pp. 445–446.

To what extent the large health care corporations will be able to extend their control over the medical marketplace is not known. But it seems apparent that those doctors who practice corporate medicine will constitute a physician group with less control over the conditions of their practice than American physicians in the past. In successfully avoiding government regulation of their work, physicians may have established the circumstances for corporations to move in and dominate an unregulated area of the economy. This process is materially aided by a growing surplus of physicians desiring the benefits and work schedule a corporate practice can provide. As Starr (1982:445) explains: "The great irony is that the opposition of doctors and hospitals to public control of public programs set in motion entrepreneurial forces that may end up depriving both private doctors and voluntary hospitals of their traditional autonomy." Future studies of physicians may have to distinguish between owning, managing, employed, and independent physicians. Physicians who own hospitals and clinics or who are in independent private practice will have considerably more autonomy than physician managers of corporate facilities and doctors employed as practitioners by a corporation. The future direction that this situation will take, however, is not entirely clear. But the change appears to have a high probability of occurring nonetheless.

THE CHANGING PHYSICIAN–PATIENT RELATIONSHIP

Leo G. Reeder (1972) has formulated the clearest case to date that shows the changing relationship between physicians and their patients. He identifies three significant trends in contemporary society. One is the *shift in medicine away from the treatment of acute diseases toward preventive health services* intended to offset the effects of chronic disorders. Since the control of acute diseases has largely been accomplished, it is no longer the most important task for modern medical practice. Reeder explains:

> In a system dominated by curative or emergency care there is a "seller's market." The customer is suspect; client-professional relationships tend to be characterized by the traditional mode of interaction so well described in the literature. On the other hand, when prevention of illness is emphasized, the client has to be persuaded that he has a need for medical services such as periodic check-ups. The person has to be encouraged to come into the physician's office for medical care. Under these circumstances, there are elements of a "buyer's market"; in such situations there is more of a tendency for the "customer to be right."[4]

The other two features of societal change noted by Reeder are the *growing sophistication of the general public with bureaucracy* and the *development of consumerism.* Reeder claims that the increased development of large-scale bureau-

[4]Leo G. Reeder, "The Patient-Client as a Consumer: Some Observations on the Changing Professional-Client Relationship," *Journal of Health and Social Behavior*, 13 (December 1972), 407.

cratic industrial systems has ensured a similarity of experiences and attitudes in contemporary society and this has tended to "level" or make more familiar the bureaucratic aspects of modern medicine. Also highly significant is the development of consumerism. Reeder states that during the 1960s, the concept of the person as a "consumer" rather than a patient became established; doctors were regarded as "health providers," so a new relationship of provider–consumer emerged in direct opposition to the old relationship of physician–patient with its emphasis upon patient dependency. The new concept places the consumer on a more equal basis with the physician in the health care interaction. It also provides the philosophy behind the increased consumer involvement in health legislation and other matters as consumer interest groups.

In an age of consumerism, the social role of the physician and the overall physician–patient relationship can hardly escape modification. In general, this modification will take the form of physician and patient interacting on a more equal footing in terms of decision making and responsibility for outcome. There is already evidence that the physician–patient relationship is turning into more of a provider–consumer relationship, especially among patients who are relatively well educated and have middle- and upper-class social backgrounds (Cockerham, Kunz, and Lueschen 1988a; Cockerham et al. 1986a; Freidson 1989; Haug and Lavin 1981, 1983; Sharp, Ross, and Cockerham 1983; Sorenson 1974). More affluent persons appear to be increasingly oriented toward taking control over their lives, including their health.

THE DEPROFESSIONALIZATION OF PHYSICIANS

Increased consumerism on the part of patients and greater government and corporate control over medical practice suggest that the professional authority of physicians is in a state of decline. That is, doctors are moving from being the absolute authority in medical matters toward having somewhat lessened authority. With many patients insisting on greater equality in the doctor–patient relationship and health organizations that employ doctors seeking to control costs, maximize profits, and provide efficient services that are responsive to market demand, physicians are caught in the middle.

George Ritzer and David Walczak (1988) indicate that medical doctors are experiencing a process of deprofessionalization. Ritzer and Walczak (1988:6) define deprofessionalization as "a decline in power which results in a decline in the degree to which professions possess, or are perceived to possess, a constellation of characteristics denoting a profession." Deprofessionalization essentially means a decline in a profession's autonomy and control over clients. In the case of physicians, they still retain the greatest authority in medical affairs but that authority is no longer absolute and medical work is subject to greater scrutiny by patients, health care organizations, and government agencies. As Donald Light (1989:470) notes, buyers of health care "want to know what they are getting for their money" and it did "not take long for them to demand detailed accounts of what services are being rendered at what cost." This situation has led to greater control and monitoring systems by the government seeking to control costs, businesses attempting to constrain the expenses of employee health care, and insurance companies and profit-seeking health care corporations looking to increase maximize income.

Ritzer and Walczak argue that government policies emphasizing greater control over health care and the rise of the profit orientation in medicine identify a trend in medical practice away from substantive rationality (stressing ideals like serving the patient) toward greater formal rationality (stressing rules, regulations, and efficiency). Formal rationality, as discussed in Chapter 5, is defined by Max Weber (1978) as the purposeful calculation of the most efficient means to reach goals and substantive rationality, which, in turn, is an emphasis on ideal values and situations—rather than efficiency and practicality. Ritzer and Walczak join others (Ritchey 1981) in claiming that formal rationality has become dominant in medical practice. The result is that greater external control over physicians by the government and corporations now exists and lessens the professional power and authority of doctors.

Hence, pressure on physicians from below (consumers) and above (government and business corporations in the health field) forecasts a decline in their professional dominance. Doctors are still powerful in health matters but not to the extent they were earlier in the twentieth century. Government policies, market forces, and consumerism have required greater accountability and placed constraints on the exercise of professional power in an ever-increasing manner.

SUMMARY

There are increasing signs of influences outside the medical profession that the professional dominance of the physician may be modified in the future. This change originates from three directions. First, there are signs of increasing government regulation. Second, corporations are taking over more of the medical market and hiring physicians as employees to provide medical services. In this situation, decision making is vested in the hands of corporate management and not physician practitioners. Just what type of role doctors will play in a corporate system of health care delivery is not fully established, but it seems likely that physicians will lose some of their autonomy. Lastly, more affluent and educated persons appear to be increasingly consumer oriented toward health care. That is, they are making decisions on their own about which steps are most appropriate for them in dealing with their health. In doing so, they are becoming less dependent on physicians and changing the traditional physician–patient relationship to one of provider–consumer.

Health Care Delivery and Social Policy in the United States

14

T he central issues in the public debate about health care delivery in the United States are those of cost, equity, and the distribution of services. No other single issue in medicine has attracted more public attention in recent years than the rising cost of health care and the diminished ability of certain segments of American society to obtain health services adequate for their needs. The paradoxical nature of this situation, as Rodney Coe (1978) noted, is that the United States—one of the wealthiest countries in the world—has developed a technology to provide high-quality health care and has the resources to implement it on a large scale, yet a substantial portion of the population does without even minimally adequate health care. The Americans most affected by the sharply escalating costs of medical services include not only the poor but also the near poor who are unable to contend with rising costs. Furthermore, the proportion of the population without health insurance increased during the 1980s. About 13.4 percent of the population did not have health insurance in 1990; this figure rose to 15 percent by 1992.

RISING COSTS

In 1980, an average of $1,063 per person was spent on health care in the United States; by 1991 this figure had risen to $2,868—the highest in the world. Next highest was Canada which spent $1,915 per person on health care in 1991, nearly $1,000 less per capita than in the United States. Also, in 1980, Americans spent a total of $250.1 billion on health needs, as compared to 1991 health expenditures of $751.8 billion. Federal Government estimates, as depicted in Figure 14-1, show that health costs will be $942.5 billion in 1993 and reach $1,060.5 trillion in 1994. Hospital costs alone in 1994 are projected at $408.8 billion and physician costs at $194.9 billion. Figure 14-1 also shows 9.6 percent of the Gross Domestic Product (GDP) was spent on health in 1981 but is expected to reach 15.0 percent by 1994 in a continual upward escalation.

Beyond 1994, health costs are expected to soar. Without reform, health expenditures are projected to rise by an average annual rate of 13.5 percent between 1995 and 2000. This means that health spending will reach $1.7 trillion by the year 2000 which will be about 18 percent of the GDP. Some $5,551 per person would be spent on health in 2000.

Another illustration of the increase and the magnitude of the cost of health care in American society can be found in an examination of the U.S. Consumer Price Index. As in most other nations of the world, the cost of goods and services has been steadily rising. Table 14-1, however, shows that between 1950 and 1992 the cost of medical care increased more (90.1 percent) than any other major category of personal expense. The increase in the cost of medical care exceeded the rise in cost of all items combined between 1982–1984 and 1992.

FIGURE 14-1   Health Spending, United States, in Billion of Dollars

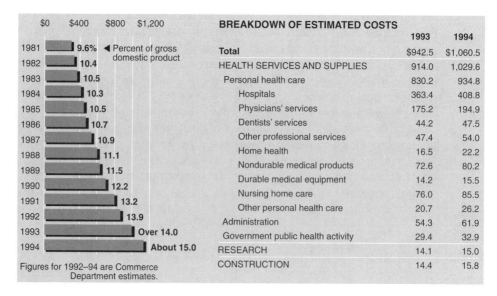

BREAKDOWN OF ESTIMATED COSTS	1993	1994
Total	$942.5	$1,060.5
HEALTH SERVICES AND SUPPLIES	914.0	1,029.6
Personal health care	830.2	934.8
Hospitals	363.4	408.8
Physicians' services	175.2	194.9
Dentists' services	44.2	47.5
Other professional services	47.4	54.0
Home health	16.5	22.2
Nondurable medical products	72.6	80.2
Durable medical equipment	14.2	15.5
Nursing home care	76.0	85.5
Other personal health care	20.7	26.2
Administration	54.3	61.9
Government public health activity	29.4	32.9
RESEARCH	14.1	15.0
CONSTRUCTION	14.4	15.8

Figures for 1992–94 are Commerce Department estimates.

Sources: U.S. Department of Health and Human Services and Department of Commerce, 1993.

TABLE 14-1 Consumer Price Index, United States, Selected Years, 1950–1992

Year	All Items	Medical Care	Food	Apparel and Upkeep	Housing	Energy	Personal Care
1950	24.1	15.1	25.4	40.3	—	—	26.2
1955	26.8	18.2	27.8	42.9	—	—	29.9
1960	29.6	22.3	30.0	45.7	—	22.4	34.6
1965	31.5	25.2	32.2	47.8	—	22.9	36.6
1970	38.8	34.0	39.2	59.2	36.4	25.5	43.5
1975	53.8	47.5	59.8	72.5	50.7	42.1	57.9
1980	82.4	74.9	86.8	90.9	81.1	86.0	81.9
1981	90.9	82.9	93.6	95.3	90.4	97.7	89.1
1982	96.5	92.5	97.4	97.8	96.9	99.2	95.4
1983	99.6	100.6	99.4	100.2	99.5	99.9	100.3
1984	103.9	106.8	103.2	102.1	103.6	100.9	104.3
1985	107.6	113.5	105.6	105.0	107.7	101.6	108.3
1986	109.6	122.0	109.0	105.9	110.9	88.2	111.9
1987	113.6	130.1	113.5	110.6	114.2	88.6	115.1
1988	118.3	138.6	118.2	115.4	118.5	89.3	119.4
1989	124.0	149.3	125.1	118.6	123.0	94.3	125.0
1990	130.7	162.8	132.4	124.1	128.5	102.1	130.4
1991	136.2	177.0	136.3	128.7	133.6	102.5	134.9
1992	140.3	190.1	137.9	131.9	137.5	103.0	138.3

NOTE: 1982–1984 = 100.

Source: U.S. Department of Labor, as quoted in National Center for Health Statistics, *Health, United States, 1992* (Washington, D.C.: U.S. Government Printing Office, 1993).

Within the general category of medical care, Table 14-2 shows the increase in the costs of various subcategories of items. The greatest single increase has been in the cost of prescription drugs (114.7 percent); this category is followed by increases in hospital and related services (114.0 percent). Physician services rose 81.2 percent.

The greatest innovation in the delivery of health services during the 1980s was in the area of cost containment and very little was accomplished with respect to problems of equity and distribution of services (Brown 1986; Grey 1991). In the public sector, the federal government instituted cost controls for services to Medicare patients by establishing set fees for Diagnostic Related Groups (DRGs). As Mary Ruggie (1992) points out, the use of DRGs demonstrates the government's increasing role in controlling costs. "Government" states Ruggie (1992:939), "is no longer inclined to accept charges set by health care providers but is instead prepared to lead the pattern of funding in its own direction." In the private sector, business corporations increasingly turned to lower-cost health maintenance organizations and preferred provider organizations (PPOs) to provide health care to their employees. Some corporations required second opinions from other doctors before surgery could be scheduled and some required data from insurance carriers to enable them to evaluate the performance of doctors and hospitals serving their employees. Many firms also increased the amount that their employees had to pay

TABLE 14-2 Consumer Price Index for All Items and Medical Care Components, United States, Selected Years, 1950–1992

Item and Medical Care Component	CONSUMER PRICE INDEX									
	1950	1960	1965	1970	1975	1980	1985	1990	1991	1992
CPI, all items	24.1	29.6	31.5	33.8	53.8	82.4	107.6	130.7	136.2	140.3
Less medical care	—	30.2	32.0	39.2	54.3	82.8	107.2	128.8	133.8	137.5
CPI, all services	16.9	24.1	26.6	35.0	48.0	77.9	109.9	139.2	146.3	152.0
All medical care	15.1	22.3	25.2	34.0	47.5	74.9	113.5	162.8	177.0	190.1
Medical care services	12.8	19.5	22.7	32.3	46.6	74.8	113.2	162.7	177.1	190.5
Professional medical services	—	—	—	37.0	50.8	77.9	113.5	156.1	165.7	175.8
Physicians' services	15.7	21.9	25.1	34.5	48.1	76.5	113.3	160.8	170.5	181.2
Dental services	21.0	27.0	30.3	39.2	53.2	78.9	114.2	155.8	167.4	178.7
Eye care[1]	—	—	—	—	—	—	—	117.3	121.9	127.0
Services by other medical professionals[1]	—	—	—	—	—	—	—	120.2	126.6	131.7
Hospital and related services	—	—	—	—	—	69.2	116.1	178.0	196.1	214.0
Hospital rooms	4.9	9.3	12.3	23.6	38.3	68.0	115.4	175.4	191.9	208.7
Other in-patient services[1]	—	—	—	—	—	—	—	142.7	158.0	172.3
Outpatient services[1]	—	—	—	—	—	—	—	138.7	153.4	168.7
Medical care commodities	39.7	46.9	45.0	46.5	53.3	75.4	115.2	163.4	176.8	188.1
Prescription drugs	43.4	54.0	47.8	47.4	51.2	72.5	120.1	181.7	199.7	214.7
Nonprescription drugs and medical supplies[1]	—	—	—	—	—	—	—	120.6	126.3	131.2
Internal and respiratory over-the-counter drugs	—	—	39.0	42.3	51.8	74.9	112.2	145.9	152.4	158.2
Nonprescription medical equipment and supplies	—	—	—	—	—	79.2	109.6	138.0	145.0	150.9

NOTE: 1982–1984 = 100, except where noted.

[1] Dec. 1986 = 100.

Source: U.S. Department of Labor, as quoted in National Center for Health Statistics, *Health, United States, 1992* (Washington, D.C.: U.S. Government Printing Office, 1993).

out of their own pocket for health care. All of these measures were intended to discourage the unnecessary use of health services and contain rising costs.

However, health spending continued to escalate into the 1990s and demands for reform increased. Of all the various factors promoting health reform, the single greatest force for change was the adverse reaction to high costs. A major source of the demand for reform was the corporate business community which paid over $130 billion annually in health insurance premiums for their employees in the late 1980s. General Motors alone paid $3 billion for employee health care in 1988, while Ford Motor Corporation paid $1.2 billion and Chrysler $702 million. Chrysler estimated that its health care costs add $700 to the price of each automobile the company sells, while General Motors placed its costs at about $689 and Ford $537 per car.

Overall, the United States spends more on health care than any other nation in the world. However, in comparison to all other industrialized countries, the United States has the highest proportion of people without any health insurance and the typical health insurance policy provides less coverage than found elsewhere. The need for reform is clear.

EQUITY IN HEALTH SERVICES

The problem of equity with respect to health services is and remains a serious problem in American society. In a free market system lacking national health insurance, those persons who are economically disadvantaged are also medically disadvantaged when it comes to obtaining quality services. As discussed in Chapter 6, the United States has a two-track system of health care delivery divided into a private track and a public track. The public track is a system of welfare medicine supported by public health insurance, especially Medicaid (for the poor) but also Medicare (for the elderly).

As Bruce Vladeck (1983) explains, although public health insurance has provided access to the American health care delivery system for the poor, the character of the services rendered—that of welfare medicine—has not changed dramatically. The urban poor have historically been dependent on public hospitals and clinics rather than private hospitals and practitioners for providing patient care. And that is still the case today for many of the poor and near poor as physicians, pharmacists, and hospitals have joined banks, supermarkets, and department stores in migrating out of inner-city areas where the poor are concentrated. Vladeck describes the situation as follows:

> Apart from whatever esthetic differences such a pattern might imply, the fact remains that the poor—and to an even greater extent, the near-poor, who lack even the limited access to private physicians Medicaid provides—have no continuing relationship with individual physicians. This means that access to other services resides in the hands of bureaucratic strangers. The poor and near-poor are more likely to be admitted to hospitals through emergency rooms than a scheduled admission, and more

likely to be sicker when they are admitted. They are more likely to be treated by a foreign medical graduate, or a house staff physician still in training (or both) than a fully trained American graduate. Their drug prescriptions are written by physicians with less personal knowledge and understanding of the patients' characteristics and problems, and they are likely to be seen on a follow-up visit by a physician other than the one who treated them originally.[1]

The rural poor likewise have problems of access to health care as medical facilities and health practitioners may not be available locally. And the rural poor (as other people living in rural areas) also may be more likely to be treated by foreign medical school graduates. This situation is brought on by the doctor shortage in these areas caused by a reluctance of many American-trained physicians to work in small communities.

Another segment of society particularly affected by problems of equity is the large number of Americans—over 15 percent of the population—who do not have health insurance. The largest proportion of persons without health insurance in 1989 were those whose family income was less than $14,000. Some 37.3 percent of all persons in this income category had no health insurance (National Center for Health Statistics 1993). Most individuals and families without health insurance make too much money to qualify for Medicaid but still live in or near poverty.

Without health insurance or available cash, people can be and are turned away from American hospitals, even in emergency situations. Ultimately, they may be denied treatment altogether or are sent to "hospitals of last resort," which are generally public hospitals under the jurisdiction of city, county, or state governments. These hospitals typically accept patients that private hospitals refuse to treat because of an inability to pay for services.

Cook County Hospital in Chicago is an example of such a hospital. Robert Schiff and his associates (1986) studied the transfer of patients to Cook County Hospital from other hospitals in the Chicago area. They note that hospital transfers are widespread in the United States and take place if there is a need for special care or the patient is unable to pay for treatment. In the case of Cook County Hospital, the researchers found that during the period of their study (six weeks in 1983) forty-two hospitals transferred 602 adult patients to the Cook County Hospital emergency room. Data were available on 467 patients who were admitted and it was found that 89 percent of these patients were either black or Hispanic and 81 percent were unemployed. Most (87 percent) were transferred because they did not have adequate health insurance. Only 6 percent of the patients had given written consent for the transfer and 22 percent were admitted to intensive care within 24 hours after their arrival. The mortality rate for these patients (9.4 percent) was significantly higher than for other medical-service pa-

---

[1]Bruce C. Vladeck, "Equity, Access, and the Costs of Health Services," in *Securing Access to Health Care*, vol. 3, President's Commission for the Study of Ethical Problems in Medicine and Biomedical and Behavioral Research (Washington, D.C.: U.S. Government Printing Office, 1983), p. 9.

tients (3.8 percent) who were not transferred. This study suggests that patients are transferred to public hospitals primarily for economic reasons, even though many of them are in an unstable condition at the time of transfer. Schiff and his associates state:

> We conclude that patients are transferred to Cook County Hospital from other hospital emergency departments predominantly for economic reasons. The fact that many patients are in a medically unstable condition at the time of transfer raises serious questions about the private sector's ability to consider the condition and well-being of patients objectively, given the strong economic incentives to transfer the uninsured. The delay in providing medical services as a result of the transfer process represents a serious limitation of the access to and quality of health care for the poor.[2]

It is clear from studies such as those by Schiff and his associates that equity in the access to health services in the United States is lacking.

DISTRIBUTION OF SERVICES

Besides problems with rising costs and equity, the American system of health care delivery is not evenly distributed geographically and primary care or family practitioners are underrepresented among physicians.

A major factor in obtaining adequate medical care for some people is the numerical shortage of physicians serving patients in rural areas and urban slums. Physicians generally prefer to practice medicine in urbanized settings where they are close to cultural, educational, and recreational facilities. Another advantage of an urban practice is its proximity to extensive technological resources in the form of well-equipped hospitals, clinics, and laboratories staffed by well-trained personnel. Also important are the relationships with colleagues, which tend to enhance professional life, and these relationships are more readily available in urban areas where there are greater opportunities for professional recognition. And finally, it should be recognized that the more financially rewarding medical practices are those in large cities.

The maldistribution of physicians in the United States can be illustrated by comparing differences between predominantly urban and rural states. Differences within states are even larger. One out of every twenty counties in the United States does not have a single doctor and more than half of all counties do not have a pediatrician. Even though small communities often advertise and try actively to recruit physicians, many doctors remain attracted to urban life.

The physician shortage is not limited to rural areas, however; it also extends into certain urban locales. Physicians in private practice are seldom found

[2]Robert L. Schiff, David A. Ansell, James E. Schlosser, Ahamed H. Idris, Ann Morrison, and Steven Whitman, "Transfers to a Public Hospital," *New England Journal of Medicine*, 314 (1986), 556.

in neighborhoods characterized by large numbers of poor and nonwhite residents. Areas whose residents have relatively low levels of education and income tend to have proportionately fewer medical doctors in private practice. Consequently, shortages of physicians may exist in parts of New York City as well as in rural Alaska and Texas.

But there are a few signs that the distribution of physicians is beginning to improve. Part of this development is due to market conditions. Some areas have an oversupply of doctors, which encourages others to look elsewhere for establishing their practice. Also, rural areas with only one physician for every 3,500 or more people and poverty areas with only one doctor per 3,000 or more are eligible to apply for doctors under the National Health Service Corps. The National Health Service Corps (NHSC) is a federally funded program designed to recruit and help organize the practices of health providers such as physicians, osteopaths, dentists, and physician's assistants for isolated and low-income areas. Physicians who volunteer for NHSC service are paid financial incentives for joining and medical students are given scholarships in return for participation in the program after graduation. For every year of support, the medical student is required to serve a year in the Corps. In addition, other programs exist, such as the rural Practice Project funded by the Robert Wood Johnson Foundation and administered by the School of Medicine at the University of North Carolina. This project, which has pilot programs in several states, matches a physician in a rural area with a health care administrator to provide improved services to medically deprived people.

Another factor that presents an intriguing situation for medical economists is the projection that the United States will have more physicians than it needs by 2000. The Graduate Medical Education National Advisory Committee predicted in 1980 that in 2000, the number of physicians was likely to increase to 634,000, or 145,000 more than are needed if the trend continued. The ratio of physicians to the general population, which was 197 per 100,000 in 1980, would grow to 247 per 100,000 in 2000. More recent predictions by the National Center for Health Statistics (1993) show there were already 234 physicians per 100,000 persons in 1990, with estimates of 271 per 100,000 in 2000. In either of these estimates, the number of physicians in relation to the general population is predicted to increase in coming years.

It may mean that the impact of larger numbers of physicians will be increased competition, possibly leading to reduced fees, more doctors in inner-city and rural areas, and more primary care practitioners as specialties become more crowded. Or it may be that more doctors will mean more medical spending—possibly without a noticeable improvement in the overall health of the population. William Rushing (1985), in a detailed study of physician oversupply, suggests that the increase in the number of physicians will indeed provide pressure to increase national expenditures for medical care in the years ahead. An attempt may be made to offset the projected doctor surplus by limiting medical school enrollments and restricting the number of foreign medical graduates who are allowed to practice medicine. Just how many physicians constitute too many doctors in view of current shortages of primary care physicians in particular and of doctors generally in rural and urban poverty areas may not have been fully determined. Yet the perception that an oversupply of doctors is coming in the near future has been widely accepted (Hafferty 1986).

Another factor in the maldistribution of physicians is that of overspecialization, which has reduced the number of doctors engaged as general practitioners in primary care and family practice. The number of general and family practitioners declined substantially from 112,000 in 1950 to 47,266 in 1980; but, by 1990, there was a slight increase to 55,571. In 1990, there were only forty-six general or family practitioners for every 100,000 persons in the United States.

A major reason for the trend in specialization has to do with the complexities of modern medicine. At Cornell Medical School, Patricia Kendall and Hanan Selvin (1957) noted some years ago that as medical students progressed through medical school, more and more of them began to express a preference for specialized training. Kendall and Selvin found that the reason for the tendency to specialize was the students' desire to restrict themselves to a particular area of knowledge with which they could be highly skillful, rather than trying to deal with an insurmountable body of knowledge. In addition, a specialized and more manageable area of medicine may be less demanding of personal time, has more prestige, and provides a greater income (Fuchs 1974; Ludmerer 1985; Macgraw 1975).

There are twenty-two specialty boards affiliated with the American Medical Association that certify physicians to practice in fifty-two medical specialties such as internal medicine, pediatrics, anesthesiology, family practice, obstetrics, gynecology, dermatology, psychiatry, general surgery, orthopedic surgery, urology, ophthalmology, and neurology. While medical specialization has produced positive benefits by allowing physicians to concentrate their efforts upon treating certain parts of the body, it has produced negative side effects in that it has become increasingly difficult to find a physician to take on continuing responsibility for the "whole" patient. Victor Fuchs describes the situation as follows:

> What the typical patient wants is easy, quick, reliable access to a source of care seven days a week, twenty-four hours a day. Moreover he wants this source of care to know him, have all his records, care about him, take continuing responsibility for him, and guide him through the labyrinth of whatever specialty care may be available. Such access is indeed rare. Instead, the medical care industry offers him a multitude of highly trained specialists, each of whom can provide better care than was previously available—but only within his specialty and only during office hours.[3]

It is clear that the relatively low number and availability of primary care practitioners inhibit the access of patients to the health care delivery system in the United States. Hospital emergency rooms are becoming centers of primary care

[3]Victor R. Fuchs, *Who Shall Live?* (New York: Basic Books, 1974), pp. 68–69.

because of the lack of general practitioners, the reluctance of physicians to make house calls, and the unavailability of private physicians in the urban inner city. Also significant is the fact that hospital emergency rooms are accessible, have a minimum of administrative barriers, and have the resources of an entire hospital behind them. The people who tend to utilize emergency rooms for primary care are the underprivileged who have minimal social ties and no other regular source of medical care (Vladeck 1983).

The medical specialty that has drawn the greatest amount of criticism in recent years is surgery. About 25 percent of all beginning physicians enter surgical training programs, which, in the face of the growing shortage of primary care physicians, is too large a percentage. Not only are there too many surgeons, but the question has also arisen whether all the surgical operations ordered are necessary. Lynn Payer (1988) confirms that more surgery is performed in the United States than in England, Germany, or France. While some argue that society should be more concerned with situations in which there is "too little" care, including surgery, instead of "too much" (Schwartz 1984), the fact remains that the United States appears to have too many surgeons in relation to other physician specialties such as family practitioners.

OVERVIEW OF HEALTH CARE DELIVERY

The existing health care delivery system in the United States is a conglomerate of health practitioners, agencies, and institutions, all of which operate more or less independently. The greatest portion of all patient services, approximately 80 percent, is provided in the offices of private physicians, who sell their services on a fee-for-service arrangement. About two-thirds of the 589,500 active physicians are involved in direct patient care work in an office- or clinic-based practice, while the remainder are mostly residents in training, or full-time staff members of hospitals. Direct payments by patients represent about 18 percent of all expenditures for physicians' services; private insurance pays 47 percent, and the government pays 35 percent. The total amount of expenditures for physician services in 1991 was $142 billion.

The next most prominent form of health care delivery consists of services provided by hospitals. With the exception of tax-supported government institutions, hospitals, like physicians, charge patients according to a fee-for-service system. Nonprofit hospitals charge patients for hospital services from the standpoint of recovering the full cost of services provided and meeting the hospital's general expenses. Proprietary hospitals calculate not only the cost of services rendered but also function to realize a profit from those services. Nonprofit and proprietary hospitals rely heavily on third-party sources, either private health insurance or government agencies, to pay most or all of a patient's bill. Americans spent $288.6 billion in 1991 for hospital care.

Besides office-based medical practices and hospitals, the other types of organizations involved in the delivery of health care to the American public are official agencies, voluntary agencies, health maintenance organizations, preferred provider organizations, neighborhood health centers, and allied health enterprises in the business community.

Official agencies are public organizations supported by tax funds, such as the U.S. Department of Health and Human Services, the U.S. Public Health Service, and the Food and Drug Administration, which are intended to support research, develop educational materials, and provide services designed to minimize public health problems. Official agencies also have the responsibility for the direct medical care and health services required by special populations like reservation Indians, the military, veterans, the mentally ill, lepers, tuberculosis patients, alcoholics, and drug addicts.

Voluntary agencies are charitable organizations, such as the Multiple Sclerosis Society, the American Cancer Society, and the March of Dimes, who solicit funds from the general public and use them to support medical research and provide services for disease victims.

Health maintenance organizations (HMOs) are prepaid group practices, like the Kaiser-Permanente program, in which a person pays a monthly premium for comprehensive health care services. HMOs are oriented toward preventive and ambulatory services intended to reduce hospitalization. Under this arrangement, HMOs derive greater income from keeping their patients healthy and not having to pay for their hospital expenses than they would if large numbers of their subscribers were hospitalized. There is evidence that HMOs do reduce hospital use and produce lower overall medical costs than the traditional open-market fee-for-service pattern (Gold, 1991). Most of the savings are due to lower rates of hospitalization, but surgical rates are also especially low for HMO populations. Physicians participating in HMOs may be paid according to a fee-for-service schedule, but many are paid a salary or on a capitation (set amount per patient) basis. In 1993 it cost an individual between $100 to $150 per month to belong to an HMO, while families paid between $150 and $250 monthly. Membership entitled them to receive physicians' services, hospitalization, laboratory tests, X-rays, and perhaps prescription drugs and other health needs at little or no additional cost.

There are some disadvantages to HMOs, namely that a patient (especially at night or on weekends) may be treated by whomever is on duty rather than their "own" doctor and patients may have a referral from their primary care practitioner to consult a specialist. HMOs have attracted considerable attention because of their cost control potential and emphasis on preventive care. The number of HMOs and their enrollment have been rapidly increasing in the last few years. In 1970 there were 37 HMOs serving 3 million people; in 1992 there were 544 HMOs enrolling 41.4 million people.

Preferred provider organizations (PPOs) are a relatively new form of health organization in which employers who purchase group health insurance agree to send their employees to particular hospitals or doctors in return for discounts. PPOs have the advantage of being imposed on existing networks of hospitals and physicians without having to build clinics or convert doctors into employees. Doctors and hospitals associated with a PPO are expected to provide their usual services to PPO members, but lower charges are assessed against the members' group health insurance. Thus, the health care providers obtain more patients and in return charge less to the buyer of group insurance. Some 38 million Americans belonged to PPOs in 1990.

Allied health enterprises are the manufacturers of pharmaceuticals and medical supplies and equipment which play a major role in research, development, and distribution of medical goods.

The majority of Americans have health insurance benefits provided through their place of employment and paid for by contributions from both the employee and employer. In 1984, some 96 percent of all insured workers were enrolled in traditional health plans that allowed them to choose their own doctors and have most of their costs for physician and hospital services covered in an unmanaged fee-for-service arrangement. By 1988, however, this situation had changed dramatically due to soaring costs of health care and limitations being placed on the insurance benefits provided. Only 28 percent of all insured workers had unmanaged fee-for-service health plans, while the remainder had managed fee-for-service plans in which utilization was monitored and prior approval for some benefits, like hospitalization was required. The day in which doctors and their patients decided just between themselves what care was needed without considering cost appears over, as financial concerns are increasingly influencing how patients are cared for.

Traditionally, doctors and hospitals have been paid on a fee-for-service basis. This approach is consistent with the principles of the open market, in which the consumers of health care, like the consumers of other products, are free to choose which health care providers offer the best services at prices they can afford. High-quality services and affordable prices are supposed to result from competition among providers. Theoretically, physicians who are incompetent or who charge excessive fees and hospitals with lower-quality services would be driven out of the market by more competent, reasonably priced, and more effective physicians and better hospitals. To eliminate or reduce free choice would supposedly undermine the incentive of physicians and hospitals to satisfy patients.

The fee-for-service system is a highly attractive situation for doctors, and it is no coincidence that it is the dominant form of payment for medical care. It allows physicians to decide how much money they should charge for their services, how many patients they should have, how many hours they should work per week, what branch of medicine they should specialize in, and where they should practice medicine. The market, professional ethics, and sense of duty to their patients are supposed to block any desire to make as much money as possible.

Fee-for-service health care delivery, however, is not a good example of a competitive marketplace. The fundamental law of the marketplace is supply and demand. When the supply of a product exceeds the demand for it, prices should drop. However, that law does not apply to medicine because physicians define what patients need and provide their services at prices they set. Therefore, doctors and hospitals create their own demand. Organized medicine has traditionally opposed changing the fee-for-service system because of the advantages it provides the profession. Yet fee-for-service discriminates against those people who are unable to pay the fees, making them dependent on welfare or charity. It also contributes to increased costs through high fees and the unnecessary duplication of technology and services by various providers and hospitals seeking to gain or maintain income. Rising costs and lack of universal access to quality care finally forced changes, beginning with Medicare and Medicaid in the 1960s.

SOCIAL LEGISLATION IN HEALTH CARE

The medical profession in the United States has had a consistent record of resistance to social legislation seeking to reduce the authority, privileges, and income of physicians (Saward 1973; Starr 1982; Stevens 1989). With the exception of some individuals, the profession as a group has opposed workmen's compensation laws, social security and voluntary health insurance in their initial stages, Medicare and Medicaid, and the creation of Professional Standards Review Organizations (PSROs) to review the work of those physicians involved in federally funded programs. The medical profession has also opposed the expansion of health maintenance organizations and strongly resisted proposals for national health insurance, even in the light of overwhelming evidence of their inevitability. "In short," Ernest Saward (1973:129) states, "the organized medical profession has repeatedly been on the negative side of social issues where the general public has been on the affirmative side."

Medicare and Medicaid: Passage and Programs

For more than forty years, the American Medical Association fought successfully to block the passage of any federal health care legislation that threatened the fee-for-service system or that advocated national health insurance. By the early 1960s, however, it was clear to most segments of society that private health insurance had not met the needs of the aged and the poor (Burdys 1987; Starr 1982). A considerable portion of the literature in medical sociology during the 1950s and 1960s, for instance, documented the disadvantaged position of the elderly and the poor in obtaining adequate health care in American society. Several sociological and political factors thus combined to influence the drafting of laws to provide hospital insurance for the aged—the commitments of Presidents John F. Kennedy and Lyndon B. Johnson; the changed composition of the U.S. Senate in 1962 and the U.S. House of Representatives in 1964; the lack of past effective health care legislation; the continuing increase in the cost of medical care; and perhaps the lessening credibility of the AMA, which claimed that "physicians cared for the elderly" and "knew their health needs better than anyone else" or that federal health insurance was incompatible with "good" medicine (Stevens 1971:438–439).

Despite the strong resistance of the medical profession, Congress passed the Medicare and Medicaid amendments of the Social Security Act in 1965. Although these amendments were compromises between what was ideal and what was politically feasible, their passage marked a watershed in the history of medical politics in the United States as the general public for the first time emerged as a dominant voice in health care delivery and demonstrated that the direction of medical practice might no longer be the sole prerogative of organized medicine (Burdys 1987; Starr 1982; Stevens 1971, 1989). In addition, the resistance of the medical profession to Medicare brought home the point to the general public that the medical profession could not always be relied upon to place the public's interest ahead of the profession's interest.

Medicare.   Medicare is a federally administered program providing hospital insurance (part A) and supplemental medical insurance (part B) for people sixty-five years or older, regardless of financial resources; disabled people under the age of sixty-five who receive cash benefits from Social Security or railroad retirement programs; and certain victims of chronic kidney disease. Hospital insurance benefits include (1) in-patient hospital services for up to 90 days a year for an episode of illness, plus a lifetime reserve of 60 additional days after the initial 90 days have been used; (2) care in a nursing home for up to 100 days after hospitalization; and (3) up to 100 home health visits after hospitalization.

Supplementary Medicare insurance benefits include (1) physicians' and surgeons' services, certain nonroutine services of podiatrists, limited services of chiropractors, and the services of independently practicing physical therapists; (2) certain medical and health services, such as diagnostic services, diagnostic X-ray tests, laboratory tests, and other services, including ambulance services, some medical supplies, appliances, and equipment; (3) outpatient hospital services; (4) home health services (with no requirement of prior hospitalization) for up to 100 visits in one calendar year; and (5) outpatient physical and speech therapy services provided by approved therapists.

There are specified deductible and coinsurance amounts for which the beneficiary is responsible. The deductible in 1993 on the hospital insurance (part A) was $696 and on the medical insurance (part B) was $100, with a 20 percent coinsurance amount also required for most part B services. After a beneficiary pays the first $100 for part B services, Medicare pays 80 percent of the charges it approves. The hospital insurance is financed primarily through social security payroll deductions, while the medical insurance plan, whose participation is voluntary, is financed by premiums paid by the enrollees and from federal funds. The medical insurance premium in 1995 was $46.10 a month.

The Medicare program is under the overall direction of the Secretary of Health and Human Services and is supervised by the Bureau of Health Insurance of the Social Security Administration. Most of the day-to-day operations of Medicare are performed by commercial insurance companies and Blue Cross/Blue Shield plans that review claims and make payments. Requests for payment are submitted by the provider of services and signed by the beneficiary; reimbursement is made on the basis of reasonable charges as determined by the private insurance companies who issue the payments. In 1992, a total of $129 billion in Medicare benefits were paid under coverage that extends to thirty-six million people.

Medicaid.   Medicaid, as Rosemary Stevens (1971) points out, is technically a welfare program. It provides for the federal government's sharing in the payments made by state welfare agencies to health care providers for services rendered to the poor. Medicaid provides, to the states, federal matching funds ranging from 50 to 78 percent, depending on the per capita income of the states involved. Each state is required to cover all needy persons receiving cash assistance. Eligible health care services include inpatient and outpatient hospital services, laboratory and X-ray services, skilled nursing home services, and physicians services, plus other forms of health care covered at the option of the individual states. For instance, it permits states to include not only the financially needy but also the medically needy, the aged, blind, and disabled poor, as well as their dependent children and families. In 1986, Congress passed legislation extending Medicaid coverage to children under five years of age and pregnant women with incomes below the poverty level, which in 1992 was $14,335 annually for a family of four or $7,143 for an unmarried person.

In 1992, 31.6 million people received Medicaid benefits and the cost to federal and state governments was $118 billion. Medicaid was originally intended to cover people on welfare, but the extension of benefits to children and pregnant women from low-income families, who may or may not be on welfare, indicates that the insurance is also being used to cover people with medical expenses who have no other source of health insurance. However, since Medicaid is administered by the states, not the federal government, it is subject to variation in levels of benefits.

Medicare and Medicaid: Evaluation

Medicare and Medicaid were not designed to change the structure of health care in the United States. These programs did not place physicians under the supervision of the federal government nor attempt to control the distribution or quality of medical practice. Instead they were based on preexisting patterns of insurance coverage, involving the participation of private health insurance companies, and they allowed physicians to continue to set their own fees and conduct business as usual.

In fact, Medicare and Medicaid turned out to be a financial boon to organized medicine and to hospitals as they channeled billions of dollars into health care. It can also be argued that Medicare and Medicaid contributed to rising prices in health care as they provided the opportunity to pass excessive demands for payment on to insurance companies instead of to the patients themselves. Of course, the general public does not really escape from paying higher prices, as the costs of the insurance companies have to be met. And to make matters worse, the Health Insurance Association of America estimated that $60 billion was lost to private and government insurers in 1989 through problems of fraud, abuse, and scandal. The U.S. Department of Health and Human Services found that for 1987 some $300 million was overpaid nationally on Medicare claims because of errors in paperwork by hospitals.

However, as Stevens (1971) notes, if the only problems in American health services were poor management and high incomes for physicians, there would not be the sense of massive urgency that has pervaded the U.S. health care situation in recent years. The problems in fact go to the very core of medical practice—its purpose to provide quality medical care for the entire population. What Medicare and Medicaid have accomplished on a national scale is basically two highly important measures. First, these programs may have been expensive and may not have met all the needs of the aged and the poor for which they were intended, but they have provided needed health services for the old and poverty stricken where these services were not previously available.

Second, Medicare and Medicaid established the precedent of the federal government's involvement in the administration of health care, and this involvement is the key to future health care planning and reorganization. And, according to Stevens, the time has long passed in the United States when the question of whether the federal government should intervene in health care delivery is debated. Federal government involvement in health care is now an important and substantial reality, and whatever happens in the future organization and scope of health care services in the United States is now dependent on federal government decisions.

One far-reaching measure is the 1983 federal legislation to curb Medicare spending by setting fixed amounts to be paid for services (DRGs) provided under its coverage. The new Medicare payment system was passed by Congress with relatively little debate as part of a plan to guarantee the financial status of the social security program. Hospitals make money if they keep costs below what Medicare pays and they can lose money if their costs exceed the rate. Under the law, hospitals cannot collect additional money from Medicare patients if they find federal money does not pay the entire bill. This situation requires hospitals to be both cost conscious and more efficient when it comes to treating patients covered by Medicare.

HEALTH REFORM

In the 1990s, the United States found itself the only First World country without national health insurance. The election of Bill Clinton to the United States presidency in 1992 marked the beginning of efforts to change this situation. All the problems of rising costs and increasing numbers of uninsured had pushed public demand for universal coverage to one of the top positions on the nation's political agenda. Previous presidential efforts had failed. Harry Truman had proposed a national health insurance program for all Americans in 1945 when health care costs consumed only 4 percent of GNP. But Truman's plan died in Congress after strong opposition from the AMA and concerns that such a program was a form of socialism. In 1974 Richard Nixon began pushing for a national health insurance scheme that was closely tied to the concept of HMOs, only to become politically crippled by the Watergate scandal that ultimately forced him to resign. Jimmy Carter suggested a plan during his first term in office but lost reelection in 1980.

Only Lyndon Johnson had success with his limited reforms that established Medicare and Medicaid in 1965.

However, in the late 1980s and early 1990s, several new developments took place. First, large corporations like Chrysler, appalled by the rising costs of health care in conducting business, openly called for a national health insurance program. Second, Congress showed a willingness to expand Medicare benefits for the elderly and extend Medicaid benefits to children and pregnant women living below the poverty line, while considering legislation that would require small businesses to furnish health insurance to their employees. And third, several states took the lead in developing their own health insurance programs.

Massachusetts, in a major innovation, enacted legislation in 1988 to provide a system of comprehensive health insurance for its citizens. The Massachusetts plan, which awaits full implementation in 1995 because of the state's fiscal problems, will provide health insurance to all residents who are unable to pay for private insurance and cannot qualify for Medicaid. Hawaii had been the first state to enact a health insurance program for its residents and back it up with money. Hawaii passed a health reform plan in 1974 that required all employers to contribute to health insurance for their workers and provided financial assistance to small businesses in meeting costs. The state plan, along with Medicare, Medicaid, and private insurance, eventually resulted in 98 percent of the population in Hawaii—the highest in the nation—having health insurance coverage. Programs to provide universal health insurance coverage to cover low-wage workers and the uninsured have been enacted in Oregon, Minnesota, Vermont, Florida, Washington, and Maryland. The Oregon plan guarantees health care to all its citizens but—in a controversial move—eliminates certain minor (superficial wounds) or untreatable (terminal AIDS infection) conditions from coverage to reduce costs. Elsewhere, Virginia, Illinois, Kansas, Kentucky, Missouri, and Rhode Island developed plans providing relatively inexpensive coverage to small businesses that cannot afford expensive benefits. A political initiative was begun in California in 1994 to try to establish a state-run, tax-payer financed health insurance system covering every resident.

These measures were all evidence of growing support for a national health insurance program and dissatisfaction with the fee-for-service system of financing health care. A 1990 Harris poll showed that 89 percent of Americans believed the nation's health care system needed a fundamental change; only 10 percent said the health system functioned well. This was a higher level of dissatisfaction with the health care delivery system than found in Italy and significantly higher than found in Great Britain, Germany, and Canada. A 1993 *New York Times*/CBS News poll found that 74 percent of those polled were satisfied with the quality of their care, but 72 percent wanted the government to intervene to control costs. Public attitudes supporting change may have reached their highest point ever. According to Allen Imershein and his colleagues (Imershein, Rond, and Mathis 1992), traditional health provider elites—physicians and hospitals—have come under attack from within and without the health care arena because of economic changes. Imershein and his colleagues predict that these elites will increasingly be displaced from their positions of dominance.

The Clinton Plan

President Clinton announced his plan for national health insurance in 1993.[4] At the time, this plan or a modified version of it, seemed likely to become reality. However, the proposal failed to clear Congress in 1994 and its future is uncertain as this book was being completed. Despite congressional inaction, national health insurance remains an important public issue and some type of reform seems likely in the near future as costs continue to rise and millions of Americans remain without health insurance. Since the Clinton plan is likely to be the starting point for the next round of national debate on health reform, the initial proposals are shown below.

Universal Coverage.   Every legal resident of the United States would have a standard level of health insurance benefits. The proposed benefit package covers the services of doctors and other health professionals, hospitals, emergency care, home health care, ambulances, outpatient laboratory tests, outpatient rehabilitation services such as physical therapy and speech pathology, durable medical equipment like prosthetic devices, and prescription drugs. Preventive care, including periodic medical checkups, screening, immunizations, prenatal care, and well-baby care would also be covered. Eyeglasses and dental care would be limited to children under eighteen years old. In the year 2000, preventive dental care for adults and expanded coverage for mental health and substance abuse treatment would be added. The standard benefit plan for mental health currently includes coverage for thirty outpatient visits and sixty hospital days per year. As for the elderly they would remain covered by Medicare but would receive a new benefit which would pay most of the cost of prescription drugs.

Organization.   The proposed new system of health care delivery would have three major components: health alliances, health care networks, and a National Health Board. Americans would be enrolled in regional *health alliances* run by the states. Health alliances would negotiate prices with health care networks and other providers, offer a range of programs to members, and collect premiums from employers and individuals. Companies with more than 5,000 employees would have the option of forming their own alliance and contracting directly with providers. Persons on Medicaid would join the regional alliances, thereby effectively ending the program. Medicare recipients would continue in that program or be integrated into the regional alliances.

The health alliances would offer three programs: an HMO plan, a fee-for-service plan, and a combination of the two. The HMO plan would be the least expensive with subscribers signing up with a health maintenance organization and consulting only doctors affiliated with that HMO. The fee-for-service plan would be the most expensive option and provide the widest choice of doctors. Patients could see any doctor they chose but would pay deductibles and 20 percent of costs for office visits and hospitalizations, up to a limit of $1,500 for an individual or $3,000 for a family each year. The combination plan would involve subscribers' joining an

---

[4]For details of the Clinton proposals, see Paul Starr, *The Logic of Health Care Reform*, rev. and enl. ed. (New York: Penguin Books, 1994); and White House Domestic Policy Council, *Health Security: The Official Text* (New York: Touchstone, 1993).

HMO to obtain most of their care but reserving the right to consult outside doctors by paying 20 percent of the fees for those visits. All physicians could charge fees only on the basis of a fee schedule approved by the region's health alliance.

Subscribers could not be turned away, regardless of their previous medical history, unless a plan were oversubscribed. The alliances would also publish information to help consumers compare the services and medical performance of the various plans and ensure that premiums would not increase faster than federally set limits.

The various *health care networks* would be organized by insurance companies who would create large conglomerates of doctors, hospitals, clinics, nursing homes, hospices, home health agencies, retail pharmacies, and medical equipment suppliers. Health insurers would become health care providers in that they would be responsible for managing the services provided. Presumably, the majority of these health networks would evolve into super HMOs in which physicians would be employees or be under some contractual obligation to the network. All would be required to offer the same basic benefits but could compete for subscribers by offering lower prices and high quality. This approach is known as managed competition—a method that combines free market forces with government regulation.

A *National Health Board*, consisting of seven members appointed by the president, would be created to monitor the entire system. The board would ensure compliance by the health alliances, adjust the standard benefits package as necessary, and set regional ceilings on spending. It would publish reports on the quality of care given by providers on a nationwide basis. The board would also monitor drug prices and require pharmaceutical companies to justify charges for drugs that seem unreasonably expensive.

Financing. The proposed average premium for the standard benefit package would be $1,932 for individuals and $4,360 for families a year. Employers would bear most of the costs for their employees by paying 80 percent of the health insurance premiums. Employers would have the option of paying more than 80 percent. Individuals and families would pay the difference between what their employer paid and the full cost of the plan they selected. Those enrolled in cheaper plans would pay less and in more expensive plans would pay more than average. The self-employed and unemployed would be responsible for the entire amount of the premium, but federal subsidies would be available for small businesses, low-wage workers, and the unemployed to obtain coverage. A cap on out-of-pocket personal expenses for health care, as previously noted, would be set at $1,500 for each individual or $3,000 per family per year. All Americans would be issued a national health identification card that would guarantee them access to needed services.

The financing of national health care would come not only from employers and employees but also from new taxes on items like cigarettes, savings from Medicaid, and spending limits on Medicare. Furthermore, in a major cost-reduction measure, there would be a standard medical claim form that would replace the hundreds of forms used by insurance companies today. This would greatly lessen administrative expenses, which can be as high as 25 percent of the cost of hospital care alone (Woolhandler, Himmelstein, and Lewontin 1993).

Major Changes

The effect of the Clinton administration proposals on the American health care delivery system would be profound. These changes would involve the general population, federal and state governments, physicians, hospitals, and health insurance companies. First, all Americans and legal residents of the United States would have guaranteed access to health care for the first time in history. Thus, the United States would join all other modern nations in providing universal or near universal health care coverage. Second, the federal government would become responsible for health care delivery for the nation as a whole. This would represent a major change in the function of the federal government and mean that access to health care had become a legal right for qualified persons. State governments, in turn, would be required to manage the regional health alliances within their jurisdiction.

Third, physicians would find that they would have even less autonomy than they have today. To be a full-fledged participant in the medical market, doctors would have to join a health care network run by insurance companies and most likely be part of an HMO. Those who refused to join could find it increasingly difficult to attract patients. Even when they treated patients who were not members of their network, their fees would be regulated. In addition, residency training programs for primary care physicians—family practitioners, internists, and pediatricians—would be expanded and programs for specialists reduced. Moreover, primary care physicians would act as gatekeepers to specialists; that is, patients could not go to specialists directly without the approval of their primary care doctor. Primary care doctors would be the big winners in this arrangement and their numbers would likely increase, as specialists would find fewer patients for their services or would be eliminated from treating patients belonging to other health care networks.

Fourth, hospitals would be affected because, when drawn into managed care networks, they would be under pressure to cut costs and some might not be able to survive. And fifth, health insurance companies would undergo significant change since they would have to organize, manage, and provide health care in accordance with government regulations and supervision. Many insurance companies might be unable to compete in this manner and be driven out of the market.

The Clinton plan was not passed by Congress when initially considered and there is no certainty that the plan will be adopted. A major criticism is the powerful role accorded to large health insurance companies in establishing health care networks and managing the delivery of care to patients. A serious question remains whether such companies—profit-making organizations—can provide quality care at affordable prices. Advertising, marketing of services, and the administrative costs of several different insurance companies would generate expenditures that health care delivery systems in Canada and Europe do not have. Basically, the country would have a corporate medical system run by insurance giants that would control hospitals, clinics, and laboratories and employ most physicians (Brown 1993; Woolhandler and Himmelstein 1993).

Other criticisms include the lack of choice regarding doctors and hospitals that some people might have if required by their health network to use only certain providers, the financial burden small and marginally profitable businesses might have in paying for health insurance premiums, and the extension of health care networks into small towns and rural areas where the population is too small to support managed competition. A town's only doctor or hospital cannot compete with itself.

When the plan was delivered to Congress in October, 1993, numerous interest groups lobbied legislators to adopt provisions favorable to them or to oppose it altogether. The issues and their solutions were complex and delays in bringing the health reform bill forward through various congressional committees gave vested interests more time to mobilize. The small business lobby strongly opposed measures requiring businesses with few employees to pay so much (80%) of the costs of health insurance for their workers. The American Medical Association opposed government control over health care delivery and losses in income for doctors. Not only physicians, but hospitals, drug companies, and insurance companies were opposed to price controls or global caps on health spending; labor unions and the elderly were against losses or caps on health benefits they now have; and consumer groups were dissatisfied with the powerful position of insurance companies, co-payments, deductibles, and the lack of immediate coverage for the uninsured. Lobbying efforts, lack of consensus between the Democrats and Republicans in Congress charged with drafting the legislation, and growing public uncertainty resulted in congressional inaction. In September 1994, the White House conceded there was no chance of passing national health insurance that year, but vowed to make it a priority again in 1995.

The Clinton plan marks the most ambitious effort ever to bring national health insurance to the United States. Whether the plan will eventually be successful is unknown as this book is being published. However, some type of national health reform eventually seems likely. The reason is that the problems which brought on the struggle for national health insurance remain unresolved to date. As large numbers of people continue to go without health insurance coverage and those with insurance have benefits cut by employers and health insurance companies because of cost-saving measures, pressures to act are likely to resurface.

HEALTH CARE: A RIGHT OR A PRIVILEGE?

According to Bryan Turner (1988), one way to understand politics in modern democracies is to view issues from the standpoint of conflict theory. Conflict theory takes the position that social inequality leads to conflict which leads to change. The conflict approach in sociology has its origins in the work of Karl Marx and Max Weber, but its focus is not just on class conflict but also on differences between interest groups as they maneuver for advantages in democratic political systems. Turner suggests that modern societies are characterized by conflict between democratic principles (which emphasize equality and universal rights) and the organization of economic services involving the production, exchange, and consumption of goods and services (which feature inequality). In other words, the ideology of advanced democracies promotes equality, but the reality of the capitalist economic system produces considerable inequality. Conflict, or tension, arises, states Turner, as democracies try to resolve this contradiction and bring equality to an economic system that is inherently unequal. It is therefore possible, concludes Turner (1988:52), "to conceptualize modern politics in terms of struggles by interest blocs and communities for political recognition of their needs and interests."

And this is exactly what is happening with respect to current measures at health reform. Several social scientists working in the tradition of conflict theory have argued that Americans would best be served by adopting a national health insurance system similar to those found in Europe (Ehrenreich 1978; Illich 1976; Navarro 1976, 1986, 1989; Waitzkin 1983, 1991). This argument is based on the traditional role of medical care as a commodity in the United States; that is, as a service to be bought and sold. Efforts to control costs are met with strong opposition because, as Paul Starr (1994) explains, the best organized interests in health benefit from the present system because the costs of health care equal incomes from health care. As Starr puts it:

> Rising costs have meant rising incomes; controlling costs means controlling incomes. The health care industry now represents a seventh of the U.S. economy, and the stakeholders in that industry—not just physicians, but hospitals, makers of medical equipment and pharmaceuticals, venture capitalists, and insurance companies—are not about to sit out a political battle that could so greatly affect their interests, in some cases their survival.[5]

In the final analysis, what health reform is really about is the issue of whether medical care is a *right* of all Americans or whether it is a *privilege*. As a commodity, medical care is a privilege. One argument is that such care is indeed a privilege, not a right, and if people want medical treatment they should pay for it. The difficulty of the training and the high value of the skills required to become a physician, as well as the time and effort put into providing care, should entitle doctors to receive high incomes. Others in the health field should be appropriately reimbursed for their services, too. This argument should not necessarily be construed to mean that the poor are unworthy of receiving medical care. Behind this argument is a generalized opposition to the welfare state; it is felt that the best way to help the poor is to provide them with jobs so that they can *buy* medical care like everybody else. To give the poor the highest quality of medical care available without improving the conditions of poverty within which they live is thought to be an exercise in futility.

However, a more socially responsible argument is that medical care does represent a special case. More in the nature of an opportunity rather than a commodity, quality health care should be available as a right of all Americans, regardless of living conditions or financial status.

---

[5]Paul Starr, *The Logic of Health Care Reform*, rev. and enl. ed. (New York: Penguin Books, 1994), pp. xxxvi–xxxvii.

The President's Commission for the Study of Ethical Problems in Medicine and Biomedical and Behavioral Research (1983) under the Reagan administration came to a similar conclusion several years ago. This commission examined the extent to which American society was obligated to provide for the health of the individual. It concluded that the trend in recent decades in the United States had been toward increasing the health care benefits of individuals and found a growing recognition that society has a moral obligation to ensure these benefits are distributed equally. But it was recognized by the commission that, while people have the ability through their choice of lifestyles and preventive measures to influence their health status, many health problems are beyond their control. For example, a person's health can be adversely affected by genetics, the environment, or even chance. While it seems reasonable for individuals to bear the responsibility for health outcomes based upon their informed and voluntary choice, people are not always fully informed about the consequences of their behavior and some health problems arise that individuals are unable to contain on their own.

Furthermore, the commission observed that a society's commitment to health care reflects some of its most basic attitudes about what it is to be a member of the human community. Therefore, when it comes to health care, individuals should not be entirely on their own. The commission concluded, accordingly, that society has an ethical obligation to ensure equitable access to health care for all. This obligation rests on the special importance of health care in relieving suffering, preventing premature death, restoring the ability to function, increasing opportunity, providing information about an individual's physical condition, and providing evidence of empathy and compassion. Individuals, in the commission's view, should still pay their fair share of the cost of their own health care, but the origins of health needs are too complex and their manifestations can be too severe to permit care to be regularly denied on the grounds that individuals are solely responsible for their own health.

It therefore appears that individuals should have a right to health care and society has an ethical obligation to provide it when it is justified on the basis of need and equity. But society's responsibility is balanced by the individual's responsibility. Individuals have the responsibility to maintain their own health; society has the responsibility to provide access to health care when needed.

Movement toward conceptualizing and establishing health care as a right in the capitalist economy of the United States is consistent with other measures associated with being a welfare state. The advent of the welfare state in Western society, as T. H. Marshall (1964) explained, is a culmination of processes that began in the eighteenth century. Marshall pointed out that the establishment of the welfare state is the latest phase in the evolution of citizens' rights in the West. To *civil* rights (gained in the eighteenth century), like freedom of speech and equality before the law, and *political* rights (acquired in the late eighteenth and nineteenth centuries), such as the right to vote and participate in the exercise of government, were added *social* rights (achieved in the late nineteenth and twentieth centuries) of protection from economic insecurity and the provision of at least a marginal level of economic welfare.

The emergence of these various rights of citizenship, all promoting equality, states Marshall, is a paradox, because they came during the same historical period as the rise of capitalism, which essentially is a system of inequality. Inequality in the capitalist system stems from the fact that it is based on private ownership of property and the gearing of economic activity to profit in the marketplace. Individuals are not equal in the amount of property they own or acquire, their position in relation to the production of goods and services in the marketplace, and the amount of profits (or losses) they derive from their work. As John Myles (1984:30) comments, "This marriage between a protective state and a capitalist economy was a union of opposites, for it required an accommodation between two opposing logics of distribution—one that attached rights to the possession of *property* and another that attached rights to *persons* in their capacity as citizens."

Essentially, what had taken place, in Marshall's (1964) view, was conflict between the rights of citizenship considered inherent in a democratic society by the general populace and the capitalist social class system. In the modern welfare state, individual rights of citizenship, not ownership and control of property, emerged as the basis for political representation and entitlement to public programs. Current efforts at health reform are an extension of the rights of citizenship to health care to United States. Canada and the nations of Western Europe had previously made health care a social right.

SUMMARY AND CONCLUSION

This chapter has examined the significant social debate regarding the rising cost of health care, problems in equity, and the unequal distribution of health services in the United States. These issues have been a focal point of concern in the interaction between medicine and society. Although organized medicine has consistently opposed social legislation that might affect the fee-for-service system of medical practice and the entrepreneurial role of the physician, the passage of Medicare and Medicaid signified the emergence of public awareness that the medical profession's interests were not always those of the general public. Current efforts at health reform proposed by the Clinton administration represent the beginning of a potentially profound change in the system of health care delivery in the United States—one that would guarantee access to health care for Americans and establish health as a social right.

Health Care in First World and Formerly Socialist Countries

15

To varying degrees, all nations of the world are faced with increased pressure of demands for quality health care and faced with rising costs of providing that care. This pressure has led to a renewed search for alternatives, among both developed and developing countries, with the result that interest and scholarship in the field of cross-national studies of health systems have significantly increased in recent years (Elling 1980; Field 1989; Gallagher 1989; Siegrist 1987a; World Bank 1993; World Health Organization 1981).

In this chapter, the focus is on health care in First World countries other than the United States and on former communist nations in Europe. Socialized forms of medicine common to Canada, Great Britain, Sweden, and Italy, will be discussed initially, followed by an examination of decentralized national health programs in Japan, Germany, France, and the Netherlands. The chapter will conclude by discussing changes in socialist medicine since the collapse of communist regimes in the former Soviet Union and Eastern Europe, as seen in Russia, Poland, and Hungary.

The value of studying the health care delivery systems of different countries is the insight provided into the norms values, culture, and national outlook of those societies. As Donald Light (1986) points out, medical care and health services are acts of political philosophy; therefore, social and political values underlie the choices made, the institutions formed, and the levels of funding provided.

Consequently, a nation's approach to health care is based upon its historical experience, culture, economy, political ideology, social organization, level of education and standard of living, and attitudes toward welfare and the role of the state.

In Western Europe the provision of health services became an important component of government policy in the last half of the nineteenth century. Behind this development was the desire of various European governments for a healthy population whose productivity could be translated into economic and military power. In some countries, providing national health insurance was also a means to reduce political discontent and the threat of revolution from the working class. Compulsory health was usually part of a larger program of social insurance intended to protect the income of workers when sick, disabled, unemployed, or elderly. Initially, protection was provided only to wage earners below a certain income level, but gradually benefits were extended to all or most of the population. Germany established the first system for national health insurance in 1883, followed by Austria in 1888, Switzerland and Great Britain in 1911, Russia in 1912, and the Netherlands in 1913.

Entitlements based on citizenship are aimed at providing people with welfare and health benefits, regardless of their position in society. The social welfare systems of Western Europe are more advanced in this direction than in the United States. Many Western Europeans receive comprehensive health insurance; protection of lost income due to illness, injury, or unemployment; and allowances to supplement family expenses for the maintenance of children, such as clothing, school lunches, and the like. These benefits are provided to all citizens, the affluent and the nonaffluent alike.

It was not until 1965 and the passage of Medicare and Medicaid that the United States provided health care benefits for some Americans—the aged and the poor. When European governments were introducing social insurance programs around the turn of the century, the U.S. government was not deeply involved in regulating either the economy or health services, nor was there a significant threat of social revolution from discontented workers. Moreover, Americans have traditionally been less committed to government welfare programs and more in favor of private enterprise in dealing with economic and social problems. Except for the elderly, participation in the welfare system is not considered normative in the United States and those Americans who do receive welfare tend to be stigmatized and socially devalued (Mead 1985). But in Western Europe, providing welfare and social security for the general population, not just the poor and elderly, is a normal feature of the state's role. This situation implies a fundamental difference in the social values of Americans and Western Europeans, with Americans stressing individualism and Western Europeans viewing government in a more paternalistic fashion.

In a study by Bernice Pescosolido, Carol Boyer, and Wai Ying Tsui (1985) on public evaluations of medical care in seven Western European nations (Austria, Finland, Great Britain, Italy, the Netherlands, Switzerland, and West Germany) and the United States, it was found that the poor in each country tended to give relatively positive evaluations. The more affluent, who had the greatest tax burden, tended to be more negative. However, those countries that had the most positive evaluations overall were those whose system of health benefits was considered by the population as the most innovative in guaranteeing health care. The lowest performance ratings were given to Italy and the United States. The highest ratings were awarded to Great Britain and the Netherlands, followed by Germany and Austria.

While there is much to be admired about American medicine, especially its level of technological advancement and general quality, other countries have been more effective in extending health services throughout its population. As Leonard Sagan explains:

> . . . many people believe that American medical care is largely responsible for the spectacular increase in life expectancy that has been achieved in the United States in the past century. They also believe that U.S. life expectancy exceeds that of most other postmodern countries. Both of these assumptions are simply wrong. During the recent period of rapidly rising consumption of medical services, the United States ranked eighteenth in the world in life expectancy from birth; although the life span continues to rise, the United States has nevertheless fallen behind such countries as Greece, Spain, and Italy, countries whose per-capita health expenditures are a fraction of ours.[1]

Sagan is correct on both counts. The United States does spend more on health care than any other country and does not rank in the first tier of nations in life expectancy. Table 15-1 shows the total health expenditures as a percentage of gross domestic product for selected countries for 1960–1991. In 1960, the United States was second only to Canada in health spending but forged into first place in 1970 and has held this position ever since—except for 1980 when Sweden spent a higher percentage of its GDP. Table 15-1 shows that for 1991, the United States spent 13.2 percent of its GDP on health, with Canada second at 10.0 percent; next is France at 9.1 percent, followed by Finland at 8.9 percent. The country with the lowest percentage of health expenditures among the countries shown in Table 15-1 is Greece (5.2 percent), followed by Denmark (6.5 percent) and Great Britain and Japan (6.6 percent). According to one observer: "Virtually no one in Canada or in western Europe—not even the fiercest critic—would want to import or even emulate the American system of financing and organizing health care" (Rodwin 1989:266).

The American system of health care delivery is clearly the most expensive in the world. Yet on the two most common measures of a country's overall level of health—infant mortality and life expectancy—the United States does not rank especially high. As shown in Table 15-2, Japan has the lowest infant mortality rate in the world at 4.6 per 1,000 live births in 1989. Sweden was second with a rate of 5.8 infant deaths per 1,000 live births. The United States is ranked twenty-fourth with an infant mortality rate in 1989 of 9.8 per 1,000 live births, which ranks just behind Italy and Greece, and just ahead of Israel.

---

[1]Leonard A. Sagan, *The Health of Nations* (New York: Basic Books, 1987), p. 195.

TABLE 15-1   Total Health Expenditures as a Percentage of Gross Domestic
Product: Selected Countries, Selected Years, 1960–1991

Country	1960	1965	1970	1975	1980	1985	1990	1991
Australia	4.6	4.9	5.0	5.7	6.5	7.0	8.2	8.6
Austria	4.6	5.0	5.4	7.3	7.9	8.1	8.3	8.4
Belgium	3.4	3.9	4.0	5.8	6.6	7.2	7.6	7.9
Canada	5.5	6.1	7.2	7.3	7.4	8.4	9.5	10.0
Denmark	3.6	4.8	6.1	6.5	6.8	6.2	6.3	6.5
Finland	3.9	4.9	5.7	6.3	6.5	7.2	7.8	8.9
France	4.2	5.2	5.8	6.8	7.6	8.6	8.8	9.1
Germany	4.7	5.1	5.5	7.8	7.9	8.2	8.3	8.5
Greece	3.2	3.6	4.0	4.1	4.3	4.9	5.4	5.2
Iceland	1.2	2.8	4.3	5.9	6.4	7.3	8.3	8.4
Ireland	4.0	4.4	5.6	7.7	8.5	8.0	7.0	7.3
Italy	3.3	4.0	4.8	5.8	6.8	6.7	8.1	8.3
Japan	2.9	4.3	4.4	5.5	6.4	6.6	6.5	6.6
Netherlands	3.9	4.4	6.0	7.7	8.2	8.3	7.2	7.2
New Zealand	4.4	4.5	5.1	6.4	7.2	6.6	7.3	7.6
Norway	3.3	3.9	5.0	6.7	6.6	6.4	7.4	7.6
Portugal	—	—	—	6.4	5.9	7.0	6.7	6.8
Spain	2.3	2.7	4.1	5.1	5.9	6.0	6.6	6.7
Sweden	4.7	5.6	7.2	8.0	9.5	9.4	8.6	8.6
Switzerland	3.3	3.8	5.2	7.0	7.3	7.7	7.8	7.9
United Kingdom	3.9	4.1	4.5	5.5	5.8	6.0	6.2	6.6
United States	5.2	6.0	7.4	8.4	9.2	10.6	12.2	13.2

Source: National Center for Health Statistics, *Health, United States, 1992* (Washington, D.C.:
U.S. Government Printing Office, 1993).

As for life expectancy, perhaps the best overall single measure of a nation's health, Table 15-3 shows that Japan has the highest life expectancy for
males at 76.2 years in 1989. Next comes Hong Kong, Greece, and Sweden. The
United States ranks twenty-first in life expectancy for males at 71.8 years. Table
15-3 indicates that males in Kuwait, Costa Rica, and Cuba lived longer on the
average than Americans. For females, Table 15-3 shows Japan with the highest
life expectancy at 82.5 years for 1989. France is next at 81.5 years, followed by
Switzerland and the Netherlands. The United States is shown in Table 15-3 to
have a life expectancy of 78.6 years for females, which is the sixteenth highest
position.

SOCIALIZED MEDICINE: CANADA, GREAT BRITAIN, SWEDEN, AND ITALY

Socialized medicine refers to a system of health care delivery in which health care
is provided in the form of a state-supported consumer service. That is, health care
is purchased but the buyer is the government, which makes the services available
at little or no additional cost to the consumer. There are several different forms of

TABLE 15-2 Infant Mortality Rates: Selected Countries, 1982 and 1989

Country	*INFANT MORTALITY RATE*	
	1982	1989
	Infant deaths per 1,000 live births	
Japan	6.6	4.6
Sweden	6.9	5.8
Finland	6.8	6.0
Singapore	10.7	6.6
Netherlands	8.3	6.8
Northern Ireland	13.7	6.9
Canada	9.1	7.1
Switzerland	7.7	7.3
Hong Kong	9.9	7.4
Germany (West)	10.9	7.4
France	9.5	7.5
Ireland	10.5	7.5
Germany (East)	11.4	7.6
Norway	8.1	7.7
Denmark	8.2	7.9
Australia	10.3	8.0
Spain	11.3	8.1
Austria	12.8	8.3
England and Wales	10.8	8.4
Belgium	11.1	8.6
Scotland	11.4	8.7
Italy	13.1	8.8
Greece	15.1	9.8
United States	11.5	9.8
Israel	13.9	9.9
New Zealand	12.0	10.2
Cuba	17.3	11.1
Czechoslovakia	16.2	11.3
Portugal	19.8	12.2
Costa Rica	19.4	13.9
Puerto Rico	17.1	14.3
Bulgaria	18.2	14.4
Hungary	20.0	15.7
Poland	20.2	16.0
Chile	23.6	17.1
Kuwait	22.8	17.3
Soviet Union (Former)	25.1	23.0
Romania	28.0	26.9

Source: U.S. National Center for Health Statistics, *Health, United States, 1990, 1992* (Washington, D.C.: U.S. Government Printing Office, 1991, 1993).

socialized medicine and the types that exist in Canada, Great Britain, Sweden, Italy, and Spain will be discussed in this section. Despite some differences between countries, what is common to all systems of socialized medicine is that the

TABLE 15-3   Life Expectancy at Birth, According to Sex: Selected Countries, 1989

MALE		FEMALE	
Country	Life Expectancy in Years	Country	Life Expectancy in Years
Japan	76.2	Japan	82.5
Hong Kong	74.3	France	81.5
Greece	74.3	Switzerland	81.3
Sweden	74.2	Netherlands	81.1
Switzerland	74.1	Canada	80.6
Israel	73.9	Spain	80.3
Netherlands	73.7	Sweden	80.1
Canada	73.7	Hong Kong	80.1
Spain	73.6	Norway	80.0
Italy	73.3	Italy	79.9
Norway	73.3	Australia	79.6
Australia	73.3	Greece	79.4
France	73.1	Germany (West)	79.2
England and Wales	72.9	Finland	79.0
Germany (West)	72.6	Austria	78.9
Kuwait	72.5	United States	78.6
Denmark	72.2	England and Wales	78.4
Cuba	72.2	Portugal	78.2
Austria	72.1	Belgium	78.2
Costa Rica	72.1	Denmark	77.9
United States	71.8	Israel	77.6
Ireland	71.7	New Zealand	77.3
Northern Ireland	71.4	Northern Ireland	77.3
New Zealand	71.4	Ireland	77.2
Singapore	71.4	Puerto Rico	77.2
Belgium	71.4	Costa Rica	76.9
Portugal	71.1	Singapore	76.7
Finland	70.9	Germany (East)	76.4
Scotland	70.6	Scotland	76.2
Germany (East)	70.1	Kuwait	75.8
Chile	70.0	Chile	75.7
Puerto Rico	69.1	Poland	75.5
Bulgaria	68.3	Cuba	75.3
Poland	66.7	Bulgaria	74.8
Romania	66.4	Soviet Union (Former)	73.9
Hungary	65.5	Hungary	73.9
Soviet Union (Former)	64.2	Romania	72.3

Source: U.S. National Center for Health Statistics, *Health, United States, 1992* (Washington, D.C.: U.S. Government Printing Office, 1993).

government (1) directly controls the financing and organization of health service in a capitalist economy, (2) directly pays providers, (3) owns most of the facilities (Canada is an exception), (4) guarantees equal access to the general population, and (5) allows some private care for patients willing to be responsible for their own expenses.

A summary of the key features of fee-for-service, socialized medicine, decentralized national health programs, and socialist medicine health care systems is shown in Table 15-4 (see also Field 1989). Fee-for-service and socialist systems are undergoing massive changes in the United States and in Russia and other ex-communist nations in Eastern Europe. At present, the United States is moving toward the decentralized national health model, while the former communist states appear headed more toward the socialized medicine approach. We will now examine socialized medicine, beginning with Canada.

Canada

The Canadian system of health care delivery is of particular interest to Americans because it is the system most often discussed as a future model for the United States (Bennett and Adams 1993; Evans 1984; 1986; Fuchs and Hahn 1990; Graig 1993; Iglehart 1986; Rodwin 1989; Vayda and Deber 1984). Like the United States, physicians in Canada are generally private, self-employed, fee-for-service practitioners. However, unlike in the United States, doctors' fees are paid by government-sponsored national health insurance according to a fee schedule negotiated with the provincial government. Most hospitals also operate on a budget negotiated with government officials at the provincial level. Thus, Canada essentially has a private system of health care delivery paid for almost entirely by public money. Private health insurance is generally prohibited except for covering only some supplemental benefits such as semiprivate room accommodations.

The publicly financed health care system is supported by taxes and premiums collected by the federal and provincial governments. Responsibility for providing health care rests with each province or territory, with the federal government supplementary funds. Virtually every Canadian has comprehensive insurance coverage for hospital and doctor expenses. Dental care, prescription drugs for persons under age sixty-five, ambulance service, private hospital rooms, and eye glasses are not covered.

TABLE 15-4   Types of Health Care Delivery Systems

	TYPES OF SYSTEMS			
Role of Government	**Fee-for-Service**	**Socialized Medicine**	**Decentralized National Health**	**Socialist Medicine**
Regulation	limited	direct	indirect	direct
Payments to providers	limited	direct	indirect	direct
Ownership of facilities	private and public	private and public	private and public	public
Public access	not guaranteed	guaranteed	guaranteed	guaranteed
Private care	dominant	limited	limited	abolished

Canada was late in adopting its version of socialized medicine. Universal hospital insurance was not provided until 1961 and coverage for physician fees was not passed until 1971 over the opposition of doctors. Prior to this period, Canadians paid their medical and hospital bills in a variety of ways—direct payments by patients, private health insurance, and municipal government payments. The health profile of Canadians with respect to infant mortality and life expectancy is somewhat better than for Americans. Table 15-2 shows that Canadians in 1989 had a lower rate of infant mortality than Americans (7.1 as compared to 9.8 deaths per 1,000 live births). Table 15-3 shows that Canadian males had a life expectancy of 73.7 years in 1989 compared to 71.8 years for American males; Canadian females had a life expectancy of 80.6 years compared to 78.6 years for American females.

The major problem facing Canada with respect to health care delivery is, as in most other major countries, one of rising costs. During the 1970s Canada's expenditures for health remained constant at about 7 percent of GDP and rose to over 8 percent in the early 1980s. The federal government realized it had no control over spending and enacted Bill C-37 in 1977 that limited federal contributions to national health insurance and made them independent of provincial health spending. Federal income and corporate taxes were also reduced, thereby giving the provinces room to increase their taxes in order to balance spending without increasing the overall tax rate. So while federal taxes went down, provincial taxes went up and taxation in general stayed at about the same level. Currently, the federal government pays about 30 percent of health care costs and the provinces the remaining 70 percent.

In 1984, the Canada Health Act was passed which reaffirmed the principle of universal access to health care and imposed penalties on provinces that allowed physicians to charge patients fees above government limits. By 1987, all provinces had banned extra billing by doctors. However, as Laurence Graig (1993:52) points out: "Although Canadian health care is essentially free at the point of service (patients never see a bill), it is by no means *free* to the individual." Canadians pay 15 to 20 percent more in income taxes than Americans, which means some of the affluent pay over half of their income in taxes.

Surveys consistently report that Canadians prefer their health care system—especially in contrast to the American model (Graig 1993; Rodwin 1989; Vayda and Deber 1984). Major reasons for the greater satisfaction of Canadians with their health care delivery system are its quality and lower cost. Canadian patients virtually pay nothing directly to doctors and hospitals. Rather, the government is the nation's purchaser of health services, paying a set fee to doctors for patient care and providing a set budget for operating costs to hospitals. For example, Canadian hospitals, unlike American hospitals, cannot make more money by providing more services. The essential difference between the United States and Canada in health spending, as Robert Evans (1986) explains, is that the Canadian system combines universal comprehensive coverage for the population combined with cost controls. "Universal coverage," as Evans (1986:597) points out, "is a necessary condition for government to engage in bilateral negotiations to exercise the leverage whereby cost escalation can be controlled." Since the government buys essentially all the care provided, it has the leverage to control the costs of that care. The biggest drawback to the Canadian system is longer waits for some medical procedures, like certain types of surgery and some diagnostic tests.

The American system of health care delivery, as Evans (1986) observes, combines the highest costs for health in the world with the highest proportion of expenditures by patients made directly to doctors and hospitals out of their own pockets. This system is something that Canadians do not want.

However, in the early 1990s, Canada experienced a crisis in health care as spending outstripped the government's ability to pay. Rising costs drove spending on health to 10 percent of the GDP in 1991. As shown in Table 15-1, this is the second highest percentage in the world after the United States, which spent 13.2 percent of its GDP on health that year. Aggravating the situation were an economic recession and lower tax revenues which reduced federal government contributions and caused the provinces to run up deficits to finance health care. About 30 percent of the total budgets of the ten provinces and two territories is spent on health. Some provinces have instituted cost-saving measures such as limiting hospital budgets and doctors' fees and significantly reducing amounts paid for Canadians' obtaining health care abroad, such as in the United States. Despite these problems, Canadians remain generally satisfied with their system of health care delivery and committed to keeping it (Bennett and Adams 1993; Graig 1993; Rodwin 1989).

Great Britain

The British National Health Service (NHS) was formed in 1948 after it was recognized that attempts spanning over thirty years had failed to finance health care by means of a national health insurance program that had limited benefits and covered only manual workers. A national health service is created by a government's nationalizing or taking over the responsibility for a nation's health care. Thus, the government becomes the employer for health workers, maintains facilities, and purchases supplies and new equipment through the use of funds collected largely by taxation. Little or no money is exchanged between the patient and the provider of services. Except for paying taxes, health services are essentially free to those who use them.

Although Germany was the first country to enact national health insurance, Britain established the first health care system in any Western society to offer free medical care to the entire population (Klein 1989). Prior to 1948, the quality of care one received in Britain clearly depended on one's financial resources; the poor suffered from a decidedly adverse situation. Thus, the Labor Party, which was in power after World War II, undertook to ensure that everyone would be able to receive medical treatment free of charge. To accomplish this the government had to take over privately owned hospitals. The National Health Service Act of 1948 reorganized British health care into three branches: (1) the Executive Councils, which are responsible for administering the system; (2) the Local Health Authority Services Branch, which is responsible for public health, outpatient care, home nursing, community care for the mentally ill, and homes for the aged; and (3) the Hospital and Specialist Services Branch, which is responsible for the management of all hospitals (except for a few private speciality hospitals) and physician specialists, who constitute the medical staff in British hospitals.

The first line of medical care in Great Britain remained the general practitioner who worked out of an office or clinic as part of either a solo or group practice. General practitioners are paid an annual capitation fee for each patient on their patient list as part of a contractual arrangement with the National Health Service. The general practitioner may have up to 3,500 patients on his or her list if a solo practitioner or up to 4,500 if the doctor is a member of a partnership and the average for the partnership does not exceed 3,500. The general practitioner is required to provide medical services free of charge. The patient (if over the age of sixteen) has the right to select his or her doctor and the doctor is free to accept or reject anyone as a full-time patient. But if a potential patient is rejected from joining a doctor's list, the doctor must still provide treatment if the person is not on any other physician's list or if the person's physician is absent. A higher capitation fee is paid for patients who are sixty-five years of age or older, and additional sums are paid by the government to meet certain basic office expenses, to join a group practice, for additional training, seniority, and for practicing medicine in areas that are underserved by physicians.

Except for emergencies, if treatment by a specialist (called "consultant" in the British system) or hospitalization is warranted, the general practitioner must refer the patient to a specialist. Generally, specialists are the only physicians who treat patients in hospitals. Specialists are paid a salary by the government. About 11 percent of the funds to support the National Health Service are derived from payroll deductions and employer's contributions; most of the revenue comes from general taxation. The average worker pays about 9 percent of his or her earnings for national health insurance, which is matched by employers.

Because of strong opposition from physicians when the National Health Service was first organized, physicians are also allowed to treat private patients and a certain number of hospital beds ("pay" beds) are reserved for this type of patient. Private patients are responsible for paying their own bills and most of them have health insurance from private insurance companies. The advantage of being a private patient is prestige, less time spent in waiting rooms and obtaining appointments, and, of course, privacy.

In addition to the medical care provided by the National Health Service, the British have a sickness benefit fund to supplement income while a person is sick or injured, death benefits paid to survivors, and maternity benefits.

The British Medical Association (BMA) had initially opposed both the enactment of national health insurance between 1911 and 1913 and the formation of the National Health Service after World War II, but each became law as the government was determined to institute the programs and enough inducements were offered to physicians to reduce the strength of their opposition (Jones 1981). In the face of strong government determination and skillful politics by the prime ministers at the time (Lloyd George in 1912 and Aneurin Bevan in 1946), the BMA was rendered ineffective. Both prime ministers managed to divide the loyalties of the BMA. Bevan, for example, refused to be drawn into lengthy negotiations with the BMA but provided concessions to teaching hospitals and consultants (specialists) and permitted the treatment of private patients in state hospitals to gain the support of many in the medical establishment. It also became increasingly clear to the medical profession that the government was going to turn the measure into law either with or without the support of the BMA.

In the end, the BMA became a partner with the government in instituting changes. Sentiment for cooperation with the government on the part of British physicians was established in the nineteenth century when the greatest threat to the BMA came from private organizations. These organizations were the medical aid institutions (commercial businesses) and the so-called friendly societies (insurance companies) that hired doctors as employees to provide less expensive medical services to their clients. In an effort to eliminate these external medical organizations, the BMA willingly worked with government agencies to control standards of medical practice. Consequently, it was through the involvement of the government in the medical market that the BMA became the most powerful and influential medical organization in Great Britain.

Initially, the National Health Service (NHS) was marked by controversy and subject to considerable criticism. The mode of capitation payments to general practitioners meant that the more patients seen by a physician, the more money the physician was able to make. Hence, there was a serious concern and some evidence that medical care was being provided in quantity rather than quality. A measure was introduced to pay physicians less for treating more patients, but as the population has increased the doctors have found it difficult to reduce their patient load. Also, the government and physicians have disputed the amount paid for capitation fees, with the physicians arguing that it is not enough. Disputes have taken place between general practitioners and specialists as well. Specialists have higher prestige and draw higher incomes—the average annual income of a specialist is approximately $100,000 compared to $60,000 for general practitioners. General practitioners have claimed that the NHS favors specialists not only in regard to income but also to fringe benefits (vacations, retirement, and so on) and have demanded that politicians and government administrators be more sensitive to their needs.

Consequently, conflict and problems concerning health care delivery in Britain are largely between health care providers and the government; there is little direct involvement by the general public (Gill 1994; Klein 1992; Ham 1992; Williams et al. 1993). As Derek Gill (1994) explains, it is the state's role to act as the protector of patients' rights and interests, but the structure of the NHS provides few channels for the public to voice its concerns directly.

The central problem faced by the British NHS is its lack of financial resources. Great Britain is not affluent and therefore is unable to spend as much money on welfare and medical services as some other countries. Moreover, the NHS has worked hard to hold down medical costs and only about 6.6 percent of Britain's GDP was spent on health care in 1991. This is well below the level of expenditures in the United States and Canada and less than that of most European countries. Though relatively successful in combating rising expenses, this policy has had its drawbacks. British doctors and nurses are paid considerably less, on the average, than their American counterparts. British physicians average about 60 percent less in pay than American doctors. Occasionally British doctors, nurses, or other health workers will go out on strike in order to increase their salaries. Many doctors, especially consultants, do a considerable amount of private work in order to increase their income.

British patients, on the other hand, have become increasingly dissatisfied with waiting for long periods of time in doctors' offices and for appointments to see them, as well as for long delays in obtaining elective surgery and what they perceive are low staffing levels in hospitals. In 1983, public confidence in the NHS was high, but by 1987 national surveys showed growing discontent. In 1983, some 55 percent of the population indicated satisfaction with the National Health Service, 20 percent were neither satisfied or dissatisfied, and 25 percent were dissatisfied; by 1987, only 41 percent were satisfied, 20 percent were still neither satisfied or dissatisfied, but the proportion dissatisfied had risen to 39 percent (Bosanquet 1988).

In order to improve the situation, the National Health Service received the largest increases in its budget in the early 1990s; furthermore, hospitals providing services to private patients were allowed to make a profit from those services instead of providing them at cost. Hospitals were also allowed to market their services to make them more attractive to private patients, and NHS patients could be admitted by their doctors to the best hospitals available—not just those in their district. These measures were intended by the government to improve efficiency, reduce delays in receiving treatment, and assist doctors and hospitals to increase their incomes by attracting more patients. Although these new measures signified the application of free-market methods to a state-financed system, public opinion polls show that support for the principle of state health care and greater government expenditures for health has risen since the early 1980s (Bosanquet 1988; Graig 1993).

In the meantime, the NHS has continued to introduce reforms (see Day and Klein 1991; Enthoven 1991; Gill 1994; Graig 1993; Klein 1992; Williams et al. 1993). Recent changes include making the NHS more responsive to the needs of patients by delegating as much power and responsibility as possible down to local health districts and hospitals. Hospitals can now be self-governing as NHS Hospital Trusts and can finance themselves by selling their services directly to district health authorities. Additionally, a contract with general practitioners allows large group practices with 11,000 or more patients to apply for their own budgets. General practitioners will be given higher incomes from capitation fees and encouraged to compete for patients. Patients, in turn, will be allowed to choose and change general practitioners more readily. And finally, the work of specialists will be audited and reviewed regularly to determine satisfactory performance.

Although reforms have been found necessary, the NHS has accomplished what it set out to do: provide free comprehensive medical care to the residents of Great Britain. It has shown significant results: The general health profile of Britain is among the highest in the world. Tables 15-2 and 15-3 show, for example, that the infant mortality rates for England and Wales are lower than in the United States, while life expectancy for males is higher and for females is slightly lower. On balance, health care in Britain is of a high quality despite problems (Klein 1989; Payer 1988; Sidel and Sidel 1982a; Stacey 1988). While significant inequalities in health remain between social classes (Armstrong 1989; Fitzpatrick and Scambler 1984; Macintyre 1986; Townsend, Davidson, and Whitehead 1990), these differences are relatively small when contrasted to the dramatic inequalities in health in Third World countries (Morgan, Calnan, and Manning 1985). Poor health among the lower classes in Britain is primarily due to the unhealthy lifestyles and living environment associated with poverty, rather than a lack of access to quality health care (Hart 1986, 1991; Reid 1989).

Sweden

Sweden, along with Great Britain, has demonstrated that a socialized system of health care delivery can be effective in a capitalist country through the formation of a national health service. The Swedish National Health Service is financed through taxation. Taxes in Sweden have been the highest in the world. However, tax reform in 1991 reduced the highest income tax rate from 72 to 51 percent. Sweden remains one of the world's most egalitarian countries when it comes to the provision of welfare benefits to the general population and inequities in living conditions have been reduced to a level that is more equal than in most other countries. Universal health insurance, old-age pensions, unemployment insurance, and job retraining programs protect employed Swedes and their families from concern about being pushed into poverty by poor health, old age, and unemployment. There are social class differences in health in Sweden with the lower class showing a less positive health profile than more affluent Swedes, but the difference is less pronounced than in most other countries (Diderichsen 1990; Lundberg 1986, 1992).

On practically every measure, the Swedes must be considered one of the world's healthiest populations overall. As shown in Table 15-2, Sweden has the second lowest infant mortality rate in the world (5.8 deaths per 1,000 live births). Table 15-3 shows that Sweden has the fourth highest life expectancy for males (74.2 years) and seventh highest for females (80.1 percent).

The Swedish National Health Service is the responsibility of the Ministry of Health and Social Affairs, which was established in its present form in 1964. Only particularly important health issues are decided by the Ministry. Most decisions pertaining to health policy are made by the National Board of Health and Welfare, which was established in 1968. This board plans, supervises, and regulates the delivery of health services at the county level. Physicians are employed by county councils and are paid according to the number of hours worked rather than the number of patients treated. Physicians are obligated to work a fixed number of hours per week, usually about forty to forty-two. It is generally left up to the doctor to decide what percentage of his or her time is to be spent on treating patients, doing research, or teaching. Physicians' salaries are standardized by specialty, place and region of work, and seniority.

A major characteristic of the national health service in Sweden is that general hospitals are owned by county and municipal governments. These local governments are responsible for maintaining and providing services. The state pays the general hospitals a relatively small amount of money from a health insurance fund, leaving the balance to be paid from local tax revenues. Enrollment in the government-sponsored health insurance program is mandatory for the entire population. Most of the money to support the insurance program comes from the contributions of employers and payroll deductions of employees. This insurance, a form of national health insurance, is used primarily to pay the salaries of physicians and other health workers. There are also some general practitioners in private practice whose fees are paid by the insurance fund and token payments from patients. Fees for all physicians, however, are set by the government and paid according to their schedule.

The Swedish health care system has some additional benefits other than generally free medical treatment. Excessive travel expenses to visit physicians and hospitals are paid by the government, and there is a cash sickness fund designed to protect a person's standard of living against losses of income due to illness or injury. Under this program people may receive up to 80 percent of the income they would be earning if they were able to work at their job. Drugs are either free or inexpensive, and financial supplements are paid to each woman giving birth to a child and to families with children under the age of sixteen regardless of income.

It would be somewhat misleading to consider the funding of Sweden's health care delivery system as an example of national health insurance since most of the revenues come from county councils. The total health bill in Sweden is met by contributions of approximately 70 percent from county taxes, 15 percent from the national government, and the remainder from miscellaneous sources.

While there is much to be admired about Sweden's system of welfare in general and health care in particular, the Swedes are heavily taxed to pay for it. And, as in most other countries, the cost of health care is rising. In 1991, health costs were 8.6 percent of the GDP, down from a high of 9.6 in 1980. However, pressure on government budgets intensified during the early 1990s because of a slowdown in the economy, rising unemployment, and tax reform.

Sweden nevertheless remains committed to universal and equal access to health services paid by public funding. County councils have been directed by the national legislature to remain responsible for health care delivery but pass the responsibility for nursing homes to municipalities and transfer part of their budgets to local health districts. This measure will allow the districts to purchase services from different primary care centers and hospitals, a development intended to promote competition between providers and greater freedom of choice for patients. These changes in Sweden's health services are not extreme; rather, they are intended to improve a highly successful system by introducing limited aspects of a free market.

Italy

Italy, like Great Britain and Sweden, has a national health service, the *Servizio Sanitario Nazionale* (SSN), which was established in 1979. The SSN provides free health care to Italy's fifty-eight million inhabitants. All citizens and legal residents are entitled by law to comprehensive care, including dental services. Small copayments are required for prescription drugs, eye glasses, and hospital care, but otherwise there are few personal expenses for health care. Workers also receive sickness benefits of 50 percent of their wages for the first twenty-one days of an illness and 67 percent thereafter for a total of six months' coverage.

The Ministry of Health in Rome is responsible for policy and budgeting, while regional offices supervise local health authorities, known as the *Unità Sanitaria Locale* (USL). Currently, there are about 650 USLs whose principal function is to administer benefits.

The system is organized so that general practitioners provide primary care and refer patients when necessary to specialists who work in hospitals. GPs are paid on a per capita basis, while specialists are salaried employees of USLs. Specialists in private practice who have a contract with a USL are paid by fee for service. Priority for hospitalization is determined by the seriousness of the patient's ailment. For people who can afford it, private hospitals are available. Patients pay all costs of private hospital care unless the hospital has an agreement with a USL, in which case part of the charges will be covered by national health insurance.

The *Servizio Sanitario Nazionale* is partially financed by contributions from workers and their employers. Workers have 1.3 percent of their salary deducted from their pay checks for health care and employers contribute another 9.65 percent—making the overall contribution 10.95 percent for each worker. The self-employed, farmers, elderly, and retired persons pay a health tax. These contributions cover about 41 percent of health care costs for the nation, with an additional 26 percent acquired from regional, provincial, and district taxes and 33 percent from patient copayments and private health insurance. Most private health insurance is intended to fill gaps in care not covered by the SSN, such as private hospital rooms and additional coverage for loss of income due to illness while sick, dentures, and other expenses. Most private health insurance plans are group policies provided to workers through employers or are purchased by the affluent. About 15.5 percent of the population has some type of private health insurance to supplement public care. When all health care costs are considered, Italians spend less than Americans. Table 15-1 shows that Italy spent 8.3 percent of its GDP in 1991 compared to 13.2 percent for the United States.

On the negative side, the SSN has major funding problems, long waits in doctors' offices and for some hospital services, and has been criticized for too much bureaucracy, waste, and inefficiency. Italians show relatively high levels of dissatisfaction with it (Hofmann 1990; Pescosolido et al. 1985). People in the lower class also have worse health, on the average, than those in the upper and middle classes—despite equal access to health care. The lower class has the most unhealthy living conditions and tends to use health services less efficiently and effectively than people in the classes above them (Piperno and Di Orio 1990). Besides important differences in health between socioeconomic groups, a regional difference exists with Italians in the less developed south showing poorer health than those in the industrialized north. Socioeconomic disparities are a major cause of regional differences in health because of the higher concentration of poor people in the south (Piperno and Di Orio 1990).

However, despite regional and class differences, the overall level of health in Italy is relatively high. Table 15-2 shows that Italy has a slightly lower infant mortality rate (8.8 deaths per 1,000 live births) than the United States, while Table 15-3 shows that Italian men (73.3 years) and women (79.9 years) have a higher life expectancy than their American counterparts. In fact, Italy has the tenth highest life expectancy in the world for both men and women. Like other industrialized societies, Italy continues to experience an improvement in its state of health.

DECENTRALIZED NATIONAL HEALTH PROGRAMS: JAPAN, GERMANY, THE NETHERLANDS, AND FRANCE

Decentralized national health programs differ from systems of socialized medicine in that government control and management of health care delivery is more indirect. The government acts primarily to regulate the system, not operate it. Often the government functions in the role of a third party mediating and coordinating health care delivery between providers and the organizations involved in the financing of services. In decentralized national health programs, the government (1) indirectly controls the financing and organization of health services in a capitalist economy, (2) regulates payments to providers, (3) owns some of the facilities, (4) guarantees equal access to the general population, and (5) allows some private care for patients willing to be responsible for their own expenses. In this section, the decentralized national health care systems in Japan, Germany, the Netherlands, and France will be discussed.

Japan

Japan spent 6.6 percent of its GDP on health care in 1991 (half of that of the United States), but the Japanese have achieved striking results over the last thirty years. For example, in 1955 the average life expectancy of a Japanese was more than four years less than that of an American. By 1967, Japan's life expectancy had passed that of the United States and currently, as shown in Table 15-3, is the highest in the world for both males (76.2 years) and females (82.5 years). Japanese rates for infant mortality, listed in Table 15-2, are also lower than any other country (4.6 per 1,000 live births in 1989).

Japan has a national health insurance plan, introduced in 1961, but its benefits are relatively low by Western standards. Japanese patients pay 30 percent of the cost of health services, with the national plan paying the remainder. However, patients are reimbursed by the plan for expenses over 60,000 yen ($580) for medical care during any given month; low-income patients are reimbursed for amounts spent over 33,600 yen ($325) monthly. People over seventy years of age have all of their costs covered. Patients are allowed to choose their own doctors and encouraged to visit them regularly, which more than likely promotes the longevity of the Japanese since health problems can be diagnosed during early stages. About one-third of Japanese doctors are in private practice and paid on a fee-for-service basis and the rest are full-time, salaried employees of hospitals. Physicians not on a hospital staff cannot treat their patients once they are hospitalized.

Physician fees for office visits and examinations are quite low because the government sets fees. Regardless of seniority or geographical area, all Japanese doctors in private practice are paid the same amount for the same procedures according the government's uniform fee schedule. Fee revisions are negotiated by the Central Social Medical Care Council in the Ministry of Health and Welfare comprised of eight providers (doctors, dentists, and a pharmacist), eight payers (four insurers, two from the government, and two from management and labor), and four who represent public interests (three economists and a lawyer); however, any changes in fees are ultimately decided by the Ministry of Finance because government subsidies must be kept within general budgetary limits (Ikegami 1991, 1992). In effect, the government virtually determines fees for doctors and hospitals. Hospitals costs tend to be low because the government refuses to pay high costs in that area as well.

The government fee schedule is the primary mechanism for cost containment. Providers are prohibited by law for charging more than the schedule allows. Japanese doctors do receive a substantial supplementary income from the drugs they prescribe (25 or more percent of the price of the drug) and the Japanese use more prescription drugs than patients anywhere (Graig 1993; Powell and Anesaki 1990; Wolferen 1989). Private practitioners in Japan earn significantly more (about four times as much) than hospital-based doctors (Ikegami 1991).

The Japanese national health insurance plan does not cover all Japanese. Instead, the government encouraged private organizations to keep government involvement at a minimum by setting up their own welfare programs. Part of the normative structure of the Japanese business world is that companies are responsible for taking care of their own employees. In Japan this responsibility includes providing retirement plans, helping retired employees find post-retirement work, arranging vacations, offering low-cost loans for housing, and providing medical care. Consequently, there are separate programs of health services for employees of large companies, small and medium-sized companies, and public and quasi-public institutions. Some large companies even employ doctors and own hospitals. There is also a program for citizens who are not covered under other plans. Consequently, the entire Japanese population is covered by some type of health insurance plan and the average Japanese has a much greater measure of security concerning health care than the average American (Graig 1993; Ikegami 1991, 1992; Powell and Anesaki 1990; Sonoda 1988; Steslicke 1989; Yamamoto 1983).

The concept of having a decentralized system of health care based largely on occupation is supported by Japanese businessmen, who generally provide more benefits than they are required by law. Business leaders oppose a heavy welfare burden for government; they want to pay less in taxes and avoid the governmental administrative overhead required for a large public welfare system (Vogel 1979). The tax burdens in welfare states like Sweden and Great Britain are undesirable, as is the type of welfare system in the United States. Also important is the desire of Japanese businesses to provide security to their employees in exchange for employee loyalty and productivity. This policy gives large Japanese corporations an advantage in attracting workers because of the greater benefit packages they can offer. This, of course, means that some Japanese have better health care benefits than others, although the overall provision of health benefits in Japan is highly equitable.

Nakoki Ikegami (1992) notes that it can be argued that the excellent health of the Japanese population and relatively low medical costs are more a reflection of lifestyles and economic conditions than the health care delivery system. Ikegami says that this argument may well be accurate, but he calls attention to the fact that universal coverage without rationing care is a major achievement. While no health system can be perfect because demands can easily exceed resources, the Japanese have established the most efficient system in the world: It is relatively low cost, effective, and equitable.

However, there are problems. Some 80 percent of all Japanese hospitals are privately owned by physicians, but many facilities are old and lack space. Because the Japanese government limits how much they can charge, Japanese hospitals are often required to admit more and more patients in order to meet their expenses. Overcrowding has therefore become common in most hospitals. The average length of hospitalization in Japan is also longer than in the West. Hospital administrators complain that it is difficult to finance updated facilities or hire additional personnel without increases in the amounts charged to patients.

There are typically long waits at doctors' offices and clinics as well because Japanese physicians do not use an appointment system. Basically, it is a case of first come, first served and some patients begin lining up outside the doctor's office before it opens. Furthermore, relationships between doctors and patients in Japan tend to be more impersonal than in the United States. Patients are told little about their diagnoses, the treatment prescribed, or types of drugs being administered. "Doctors," state Margaret Powell and Masahira Anesaki (1990:174), "tend to explain away the problem in soothing terms without necessarily providing precise information about what exactly the problem is." The doctor–patient relationship is based on trust and the traditional Japanese cultural value of deference to authority. A patient requesting information directly would be seen as questioning the physician's authority, judgment, and knowledge. Therefore, patients are to rely on what doctors tell (or usually do not) tell them.

According to Hiroyuki Hattori and his colleagues (1991), doctors will disclose the fact that a patient has terminal cancer to the patient's family (as a form of substitute consent) but not to the patient. As few as 5 percent of all patients dying of cancer may be aware they have the disease (Powell and Anesaki 1990). This situation may be changing somewhat because of court decisions verifying patient rights, the possibility of malpractice suits, and growing public concern about full disclosure of information (Hattori et al. 1991; Powell and Anesaki 1990). There is also growing dissatisfaction among some patients about how they are personally treated by doctors and many prefer self-care, if possible, over consulting with a doctor (Haug et al. 1991). In the meantime, the Japanese medical profession remains highly self-regulated and adverse to public scrutiny (Powell and Anesaki 1990).

Other problems are due to changes in the health of the Japanese. Kyoichi Sonoda (1988) notes that larger percentages of Japanese reported they were sick over the previous year. About one in seven Japanese reports having felt ill. Disease patterns are also changing. As seen in Table 15-5, heart disease is on the rise and is now the second leading cause of death after cancer. Historically, Japan has had low mortality rates from heart disease in comparison to Western societies. This trend undoubtedly influences higher levels of life expectancy among the Japanese, especially among males. The traditional low-fat, low-protein and high carbohydrate Japanese diet of fish, rice, and green vegetables is a major factor in this situation (Powell and Anesaki 1990). Also the stress-reducing aspects of Japanese culture, such as strong group solidarity and cooperation in dealing with problems and after-work socializing by males on a regular basis with close friends in bars or noodle shops, may be important (Matsumoto 1971). These drinking places are often designed to encourage relaxation and allow a temporary escape from the tensions of modern living. After-work socializing with co-workers seems to have become a routine activity in the lifestyles of many men in industrial Japan.

However, Table 15-5 depicts a significant rise in heart disease since 1950. Presumably, a more Westernized lifestyle and increase in the consumption of animal fats and proteins—associated with Western diets—have promoted more heart disease, along with the stresses of living in a dynamic, hard-working, and densely populated society (Cohen et al. 1979; Powell and Anesaki 1990). According to Table 15-5, heart disease was responsible for only 5.9 percent of all

TABLE 15-5   Percentage of Deaths by Major Causes, Japan, 1950–1990

Cause of Death	1950	1960	1970	1980	1985	1990
Tuberculosis	13.5	4.5	2.2	0.9	0.6	0.4
Cancer	7.1	13.3	16.8	22.4	25.0	26.5
Heart Disease	5.9	9.7	12.5	17.1	18.8	20.2
Stroke	11.7	21.2	25.4	22.5	17.9	14.9
Diabetes/Hypertension	1.3	2.6	3.6	3.4	2.9	2.3
Pneumonia/Bronchitis	8.6	6.5	4.9	5.4	6.8	9.1
Accidents/Harmful Actions	3.6	5.5	6.1	4.0	3.9	3.9
Other	48.3	36.7	28.5	24.3	24.1	22.7
Totals	100.0	100.0	100.0	100.0	100.0	100.0

Source: Ministry of Health and Welfare, Japan, 1992.

deaths in Japan in 1950 but rose to cause 20.2 percent of all deaths in 1990. Table 15-5 also shows a consistent rise in the percentage of deaths from cancer from 7.1 percent of all deaths in 1950 to 26.5 percent in 1990. The shift toward higher fat in Japanese diets has contributed to a rise in colon and pancreatic cancers and heavy smoking among Japanese males has led to an acceleration in mortality rates from lung cancer (Wynder et al. 1991). The Japanese also have the highest rates of stomach cancer in the world. Increases in death rates from cancer and heart disease, as well as the highest mortality rates from stroke of any advanced country, suggest that increases in life expectancy for the Japanese may be slowing down and perhaps reaching a limit.

These changes, combined with the rapid growth of Japan's elderly population, are likely to place tremendous pressure on Japan's health care delivery system in the future. The proportion of people living to old age is increasing in Japanese society faster than in any other country in the world and this situation is going to require a significant response from Japan's system of health care delivery (Cockerham 1991).

Germany

The structure of health care delivery in the Federal Republic of Germany has not changed significantly since 1883 and the reforms instituted by Bismarck's administration in imperial Germany. The program established at that time was based on three principal components: (1) compulsory insurance, (2) free health services, and (3) sick benefits. Employees, self-employed, unemployed, old-age pensioners, and certain categories of domestic workers providing infant and child care, home help, and the like are all required to be insured by one of Germany's public health insurance organizations. There are 1,169 public health insurance groups and membership in a particular health plan is usually determined by such factors as occupation or place of employment. For example, there are plans for miners, craftsmen, seamen, and farmers, and some large business corporations sponsor their own program for the people they employ. Germany's largest public health insurance organization, consisting of several local sickness funds, is the *Allgemeine Ortskrankenkassen* (AOK). The AOK, which insured about half the population of western Germany, is now expanding into eastern Germany, along with other health insurance organizations, with the unification of the two German states in 1990. The AOK originally insured only blue-collar workers but broadened its membership base to include the general population.

As John Myles (1984) pointed out, Bismarck's welfare measures in the late nineteenth century were both a response to democratization and an attempt to suppress it. That is, Bismarck wanted to defuse the demands for political rights from an increasingly well-organized and leftist-oriented working class by providing them with social rights that linked workers to the state rather than to labor unions or socialist political parties. Included in Bismarck's plan was the first national health insurance program ever. David Childs and Jeffrey Johnson (1981:99) summarize the outcome: "Whatever view we might now take of Bismarck's motives in introducing these schemes, there can be no doubt that they were excellent for their time and they became a model for both subsequent German governments and for foreign governments."

Following Germany's defeat in World War II and the incorporation of its eastern lands into a separate communist state, West Germany became a multiparty republic in 1949. The Federal Republic's constitution, the Basic Law, guarantees the social welfare of its citizens, continues the comprehensive social welfare system developed by Bismarck, and now includes the East Germans. The program that currently exists includes health insurance, old-age pensions, sickness benefits for income lost to illness or injury, unemployment insurance, and family assistance in the form of allowances for children, rent (especially for the elderly), and public funds for the construction of low-income housing.

Approximately 90 percent of all Germans participate, involuntarily or voluntarily, in the nation's public health insurance program. The remainder consist generally of civil servants, the self-employed, and white-collar workers with yearly incomes above the government ceiling ($36,000 in the west and about $29,000 in the east), but they can take out private insurance. In the state plan, health care is free to the individual and covers medical and dental treatment, drugs and medicines, and hospital care as needed. In the event of illness, the employer must continue to pay the employee's full wages for six weeks, and then the health insurance fund provides the individual with his or her approximate take-home pay for up to seventy-eight weeks. If the illness is more protracted, benefits are continued under a welfare plan unless the person is permanently incapacitated and is entitled to a disability pension. About 12.9 percent of a worker's monthly gross earnings goes to pay for health insurance, with half the contribution made by the employee and half by the employer.

According to Erwin Scheuch (1987), the current welfare system in Germany makes it possible for its citizens to demand the most in all welfare programs. Thus, Germans, on the average, appear to have a different mentality about the welfare state than Americans. All Germans can use its services whenever and as long as it is necessary; therefore, they can approach the social welfare system for health care, pensions, and other benefits with an exceptionally strong sense of personal entitlement. A distinctive psychological orientation on the part of Germans, in comparison to Americans, helps us to understand the different approaches to welfare. The German word *anspruchsdenken* cannot be translated literally into English, but essentially means a "mentality of entitlement." It signifies a readiness on the part of the individual to claim and use the welfare benefits to which he or she is entitled by law. The fact that *anspruchsdenken* has no equivalent in English underscores the lack of a corresponding mentality in American society (Cockerham, Kunz, and Lueschen 1988a).

Public health insurance plans are coordinated by the National Federation of Health Insurance. The insurance plan will issue a medical certificate to members and their dependents periodically. This certificate is presented to a physician when services are rendered. The physician then submits the certificate to his or her association of registered doctors, which all physicians are required to join. Payment is made to the physician through the doctors' association according to a fee schedule agreed upon by the association and the public health insurance plans. Hospital fees and payments are handled in the same manner (Glaser 1987; Iglehart 1991; Kirkman-Liff 1991; Knox 1993; Wysong and Abel 1991).

As the preceding discussion indicates, the German government does not play a major role in the financing of health services. The government's primary function is one of administration. The Federal Ministry of Labor and Social Affairs exercises general supervision of the health care delivery system through state ministries and local health boards. According to Donald Light (1986; Light and Schuller 1986), this form of health service organization is one of corporatism and represents a unique contribution by Germany to the provision of health care. Corporatism in the German context consists of (1) compulsory membership on the part of the population in a national health plan and (2) a set of institutions situated between the government and its citizens with the authority to manage health care under government auspices.

Approximately 50 percent of Germany's physicians are general practitioners, which is a relatively high percentage compared to the United States. Most German doctors practice medicine in private offices or clinics on a solo basis. Few work in a group practice. German physicians are well paid, earning somewhat more, on average, than American doctors. Health care costs rose significantly during the 1970s and the government put pressure on physicians and hospitals to keep down costs. Table 15-1 shows that between 1985 and 1991, health costs increased only slightly, from 8.2 to 8.5 percent of the GDP. The Health Care Reform Act of 1989 helped limit costs by increasing the amounts paid by persons insured voluntarily in the public health plan, adding a small copayment for prescription drugs, establishing price ceilings for most drugs, and other measures. More recently, the Health Structure Act of 1993 mandated price cuts for drugs; lower incomes for doctors and dentists, along with compulsory retirement at age sixty-eight; increased copayments for patients; and limits on hospital budgets. Beginning in 1997, Germans are free to choose the public health insurance fund to which they wish to belong.

Table 15-2 shows that Germany (West and East) had lower infant mortality rates than the United States in 1989. The U.S. infant mortality rate was 9.8 per 1,000 compared to 7.4 for West Germany and 7.6 for East Germany. Table 15-3 indicates that both West German men and women had a slightly higher life expectancy. For men, the West Germans showed a life expectancy of 72.6 years in 1989 and American men were listed at 71.8 years; for women, the West German figures were 79.2 years versus 78.6 years for Americans. East German men lived an average of 70.1 years and women 76.4 years, which will pull the all-German average down in future rankings. Almost half of all deaths are due to diseases of the heart and circulatory system (Huppmann and Wilker 1988; Siegrist 1987a, 1988).

Generally, the overall level of health of the German people and the quality of care available to them is very similar to the United States. Germans in the western portion of the country participate in health lifestyles to about the same extent as Americans (Abel 1991; Cockerham, Kunz, and Lueschen 1988a); for example, trends in smoking reduction took place somewhat later than in the United States but followed the same pattern (Scheuch 1989; Wetterer and Troschke 1986).

West Germans and Americans also show similar overall levels of psychological distress (Cockerham, Kunz, and Lueschen 1988b). And, as in the United States and elsewhere, the lower class in Germany has the poorest overall health and lowest utilization of preventive care (Kirchgëssler 1990; Siegrist 1989). As German medical sociologist Johannes Siegrist (1989:359) explains: ". . . we can summarize that the main burden of social inequality in [health care] is no longer underutilization of health services in situations of acute help-seeking, but a lack of awareness of long-term concern about health."

When it comes to health, the most striking difference between Germans and Americans, especially as the Germans reduce the differences between the western and eastern parts of their country, is not the general level of health but rather the manner in which health services are organized and funded.

The Netherlands

Health care delivery in the Netherlands is based on the German system which was imposed on the Dutch when their country was occupied by German forces during World War II. After the war, the Dutch kept the health care system with a few modifications. About 66 percent of the Dutch population receives health care through public health insurance funds similar to those in Germany. The funds are organized on a regional basis, membership is compulsory for individuals and families below a certain income (about $30,000), and the insured is not entitled to choose among the various funds. The insurance funds receive revenue from a single national fund, which is supported by state subsidies and contributions of 2.85 percent from employees and 4.95 percent from employers—an amount equal to 8 percent of an employee's wages. Sickness benefits for payment of wages when ill for a period of six weeks are provided, after which 70 percent of wages are paid up to twelve months. Dental care, eye glass lenses, drugs, and hospital care are provided.

The remaining 34 percent of the Dutch population has private health insurance. As in Germany, these are civil servants, the self-employed, and people with the highest incomes. Employees who purchase private insurance receive a contribution from their employers equal to what would be paid for public insurance. There are several different private health insurance companies, both profit and nonprofit, and various types of health plans. Physicians are divided into general practitioners (GPs) and specialists, with GPs providing a "gatekeeper" role since all referrals to specialists and hospitals come through them (Kirkman-Liff 1991). Patients have limited choice of a GP, since they usually register with one in their area. GPs have an average of 2,350 registered patients; they are paid on a fee-for-service basis for patients with private insurance and on a per capita basis for patients with public insurance. Specialists are paid on a fee-for-service basis from both private and public insurers. Hospitals are all nonprofit and receive an operating budget annually from both private and public health insurance funds.

The population of the Netherlands is relatively small (some 14.9 million people), but the country is one of the most densely populated in the world (about

438 persons per kilometer). The Dutch have distinct social classes, but differences are not extreme. In fact, the Netherlands has one of the lowest levels of poverty in Europe (Davis 1992). By taxing wealth heavily and providing generous welfare benefits to the less affluent, there has been a redistribution of income to reduce class distinctions. The lowest income tax rate is 38.4 percent and the highest 60 percent; there is also a net wealth tax of 0.8 percent for persons earning large amounts. According to Flora Lewis (1987:256), egalitarianism is expressed not only in material goods, but in welfare benefits. People living on welfare or unemployment insurance receive 80 percent of their previous salary for six months, then 75 percent for up to two years and an extra month's allowance for holidays. "Dutch officials," states Lewis, "explained that everybody had a right to an annual vacation and it would be unjust to exclude the poor."

Consequently, the Netherlands has achieved a degree of socioeconomic equity beyond that of most nations. Yet the Dutch upper and middle classes still have lower mortality rates, higher life expectancy, and better health than the lower class (Kunst, Looman, and Mackenbach 1990; Spruit 1990). They are also more likely to live a healthy lifestyle (Stevens et al. 1994). Positive changes in the health of the Dutch begin first in the upper classes, such as smoking cessation and favorable changes in diet; as a result, lung cancer and heart disease are less prevalent at the top of society and more prevalent at the bottom (Kunst, Looman and Mackenbach 1990). Still, on every measure, the Netherlands has one of the healthiest populations in the world. Table 15-2 shows infant mortality to be fifth lowest in the world at 6.9 infant deaths per 1,000 live births, while Table 15-3 shows life expectancy to be seventh highest for men at 73.7 years and fourth highest for women at 81.1 years.

France

Unlike Germany, which began its social welfare system in the 1880s, France did not have similar developments until 1930. A law passed in 1901 did authorize numerous private organizations to offer health plans on a nonprofit basis to specific occupational groups, but the 1930 legislation laid the legal foundation for a national welfare system by subsidizing health care, housing, and old-age benefits for low-income families. The entire system, known as the *Sécurité Sociale*, was reorganized in 1945 after World War II and expanded to include practically the entire population.

However, there is no single organization providing health insurance on a nationwide basis. Rather, the French insurance system is divided between occupational groups. Professionals, businessmen, craftsmen, civil servants, farmers, and other occupations have their own organizations. For family and old-age benefits, a similar system exists. Unlike Germany, where the several public health insurance plans are regulated by a single administrative system, France has several channels of regulation and administration for the financing and provision of welfare services, including health care. Consequently, there is a minimum level of centralization in France's social welfare system. All of the various insurance organizations are nonprofit, supervised by a particular government agency (one among many) and responsible just to their members. As Isidor Wallimann points out:

> Germany, Switzerland, the U.S.A. (and as a rule all or most modern welfare states) tend towards having one insurance system covering all citizens irrespective of their occupational or class location. This is also true for health insurance where states—such as Sweden, Great Britain, Germany, however not the U.S.A. or Switzerland—intend to provide coverage against illness for the entire population. It must be concluded, therefore, that the French welfare state is very unique in that it covers the entire population against such things as old age and illness by means of an insurance system which is not only more decentralized but also organized around the occupational or class location of individuals.[2]

How can uniformity and equality in covering the entire population be achieved with so many different insurance organizations? The answer is that the French welfare system is neither uniform nor equal (Guillemard 1986; Rodwin and Saudier 1993; Wallimann 1986)—but everyone does receive a level of health benefits adequate to meet hospital and most physician costs. The French health insurance system provides universal coverage, freedom of choice in doctors and hospitals, and diversity with respect to financing (Fielding and Lancry 1993; Rodwin and Sandier 1993).

The major differences are in pension plans. Everyone is required to belong to a national insurance plan and all such plans are supervised by various government agencies. The Department of Agriculture, for example, manages the health insurance organization for farmers and agricultural workers, and the Department of Social Affairs and National Security controls the salary and wage earner's health plan. These agencies all follow national policy, which provides some uniformity and coordination; otherwise, there are many differences and inequalities. Different organizations have different rates of contributions and levels of benefits. Persons in well-paid occupations pay more in contributions and receive more in benefits, particularly in old-age pensions. Consequently, France's social welfare system is divided along socioeconomic lines and subject to greater class conflict than found in most other Western states.

Some 70 percent of all French hospitals are in the public sector, and hospital bills for serious illnesses in both public and private hospitals are completely covered by the patient's national health insurance plan and most of the bill for less serious problems are also met. Patients pay doctors directly for their services and are then reimbursed for 75 percent of their costs by their insurance. Physician and hospital fees are negotiated with the government and paid according to a fixed schedule. The organization of France's hospital system tends to be extremely complicated and poorly planned; the Ministry of Health makes hospital policy, national insurance plans finance its operation, and there is no effective means of

---

[2]Isidor Wallimann, "Social Insurance and the Delivery of Social Services in France." *Social Science and Medicine*, 23 (1986), 1307.

controlling costs (Pouvouville and Renaud 1985). Nevertheless, the portion of France's GDP spent on health was 9.1 percent in 1991, which is well below that of the United States but higher than that of any other West European country.

France differs from other Western states in its method of financing social insurance, including health benefits. The French depend less on taxes on personal income to meet their social needs than any other Western country (Wallimann 1986). About 42 percent of the funds come from contributions made by employers and employees, 39 percent from property tax, and 19 percent from income tax. Employees contribute about 6 percent of their wages and salaries, while employers pay 12.6 percent of their payrolls for health benefits. Thus, "France is unique in that employers pay an unusually high share of all contributions into the social insurance system" (Wallimann 1986:1310). Other countries, like the United States, Canada, Great Britain, and Germany, have equal percentages of contributions from employers and employees. But in France, employers are required to contribute heavily to social welfare because of the political success of socialists and labor unions in attempting to reduce or eliminate altogether the contributions of workers.

While the French lack a centralized system of health care financing and organization and some occupational groups have better insurance benefits than others, can it be claimed that the quality of care is poor? Generally, it appears that French medical care is quite good (Ardagh 1987; Payer 1988; Pouvourville and Renaud 1985). Tables 15-2 and 15-3 show that infant mortality is lower in France than in the United States (7.5 deaths per 1,000 live births) in 1989, while life expectancy for French men is higher (73.1 years). Life expectancy for French women, however, is the second highest in the world (81.5 years).

In the 1980s, the French government placed a strong emphasis upon health education and the promotion of healthy lifestyles (Letourmy 1986). Such programs are in line with the fact that a significant gap in health and mortality continues to persist between the social classes in France (Fox 1989). Per capita spending on health care has risen, however, and French hospitals are, on the average, more modern than those in Britain (Ardagh 1987). The French also spend more on medication than other Europeans, with the government reimbursing 70 percent of their costs, and efforts are under way to change this measure in order to reduce government health expenditures.

SOCIALIST MEDICINE: ALTERATIONS IN RUSSIA, POLAND, AND HUNGARY

Socialist medicine is a system in which health care is a state-provided public service (Field 1989). The state controls, organizes, finances, and allocates health care directly to all citizens free of charge. Typically, there are no third-party organizations or insurance companies interposed between health care providers and patients. The state owns all facilities and pays a salary to all health care workers. There is no private health insurance and no private practitioners. Socialist medical systems (1) directly control the financing and organization of health services in a socialist (communal) economy, (2) pays providers directly, (3) owns all facilities, (4) guarantees equal access, and (5) bans private care.

However, the socialist model of health care delivery was severely altered when communism collapsed in Eastern Europe and the former Soviet Union during 1989 to 1991. Centralized planning, rigid control of the economy, unrealistic quotas for the production of goods, and shoddy products, along with a lack of incentives for workers and a relatively low standard of living, marked the economic failure of communism (Dahrendorf 1990). When the Soviet Union's last president, Mikhail Gorbachev, opened the door to reform, the communist system in Europe simply fell apart—changing much of socialist medicine in the process. In this section we will review the situation in Russia, Poland, and Hungary.

Russia

Currently the old Soviet system of health care delivery remains largely in place in Russia—although reforms are expected.[3] Comprehensive health care remains free to the general population. However, people who can afford it pay for health care out of their own pocket and use the best doctors and hospitals; they also receive faster and higher quality services. There is no health insurance system, public or private. So Russians have two choices: use the existing public system in which care is free or pay the same health care providers to give them better service.

The central government continues to finance health services out of its general revenues. In 1989, 3.4 percent of the GDP was spent on health care in the former Soviet Union as a whole (Rowland and Telyukov 1991) and most likely reflects expenditures in the Russian Republic. This is a lower percentage in comparison to other industrialized countries and less than one would expect, given the magnitude of health problems in the country. According to Elena Mezentseva and Natalia Rimachevskaya (1992), health care costs have typically been "financed on the basis of the so-called *residual principle,* that is from funds left over after providing for the needs of the sectors of the economy which were given investment priority: defence, heavy industry, and agriculture."

The ownership and operation of all health facilities are the responsibility of the Ministry of Health, which is also charged with the training of health workers. Management duties are delegated from the Ministry of Health to subordinate agencies in the Russian Republic's provinces and regions down to local neighborhoods and rural areas. Most of the population receives health care at polyclinics located in cities or in rural health centers. A particular health practitioner will be responsible for a designated number of people. A physician who gives primary care, for example, will be assigned about 2,000 people on the basis of what district they live in. Patients are free to select their own doctor if they are willing to pay them; otherwise, they utilize the physician to whom they are assigned.

[3]For discussions of health care delivery in the former Soviet Union, see Albrecht and Salmon 1987; C. Davis 1989; Field 1967, 1985; Knaus 1981; Mezentseva and Rimachevskaya 1990, 1992; Rowland and Telyukov 1991; Sidel and Sidel 1982a.

Russia has about 4.6 doctors for every 1,000 persons which is about double the ratio in the United States. The majority (66 percent) are women, a trend that holds true for other health workers as well (Mezentseva and Rimachevskaya 1990). However, men hold 85 percent of the academic positions in medicine (Knaus 1981). Men also hold the majority of medical posts in the Ministry of Health. Thus, Russian women are more likely to be medical practitioners than medical professors, administrators, and policy makers. According to William Knaus (1981), the former Soviet government diverted large numbers of women into medicine during the early 1930s because of a critical need for doctors and a shortage of manpower. Medicine was one area where it was felt that women could adequately replace men. Many working-class women who had been nurses and even hospital orderlies suddenly found themselves promoted to doctor and were sent to medical schools for training. Knaus explains that:

> Many had no ambitions beyond a weekly paycheck. The Soviet government responded in kind with a low wage scale and a social status for medicine that treated the new physician with no more respect given a factory worker. Professionalism was not rewarded nor even encouraged. Medicine became a job and women were the ones chosen to do it.[4]

Consequently, Soviet medicine came to consist of significantly larger numbers of women. Men came to consider professions like engineering more attractive than female-dominated medicine. Russian doctors do enjoy some status and prestige, yet the highest prestige in Russian society goes to such occupations as airline pilots. Russian doctors are all paid salaries by the state that differ according to training, skill, seniority, and level of responsibility. Salaries are in the same range as those paid to high school teachers and skilled manual workers; physicians are not among the best-paid professionals in Russia. They are paid about 70 percent of the average salary of an industrial worker (Mezentseva and Rimachevskaya 1992; Rowland and Telyukov 1991). Physicians are supported in their work by large numbers of nurses and *feldshers*, who are similar in training and duties to physician assistants and nurse practitioners in the United States.

Through the early 1990s, Russia's economy continued to falter and the overall standard of living declined. Especially shocking was the decline in life expectancy that accompanied a society in crisis. Table 15-6 shows that in 1960, life expectancy for males in the former Soviet Union was 65.3 years but declined to 65.1 by 1987 and 64.2 in 1989. Preliminary figures for 1993 released by the Russia State Committee on Statistics showed life expectancy in Russia for males stood at 60 years. For females, life expectancy rose between 1960 and 1989 to 73.9 years but fell in Russia to 72 years in 1993. Never before in the period since World War II has such a dramatic drop in life expectancy taken place. Increased mortality from heart disease, accidents, alcoholism, and violence, among males thirty to sixty

---

[4]William A. Knaus, *Inside Russian Medicine* (Boston: Beacon Press, 1981), p. 83.

TABLE 15-6 Life Expectancy at Birth in the Former Soviet Union and Russian Republic, Selected Years, 1960–1993

Year	Male	Female
Soviet Union		
1960	65.3	72.7
1987	65.1	73.9
1989	64.2	73.9
Russia		
1993*	60.0	72.0

*Preliminary figures.
Sources: *Population of the USSR*, 1962; U.S. National Center for Health Statistics, 1991, 1993; and Russia State Committee on Statistics, 1994.

years of age, is responsible for this decline (Knaus 1981; Mezentseva and Rimachevskaya 1992).

There has also been a fluctuation in infant mortality for reasons that are unexplained. In 1971, infant mortality in the old Soviet Union was 22.9 deaths per 1,000 live births; Table 15-2 shows that in 1982 infant mortality had risen to 25.1 deaths per 1,000 births but dropped to 23 per 1,000 by 1989. More recent figures for Russia indicate that infant mortality was 17.8 deaths per 1,000 births in 1992 and rose to 19.3 per 1,000 in 1993. Changes may be related to the use of cigarettes and alcohol during pregnancy, as well as a diet low in animal protein but high in grains, potatoes, and fat causing low birth weights; also the long Russian winters may reduce the availability of fresh vegetables and other sources of vitamins for the diets of pregnant women. The relationship of low birth weight to high infant mortality is important because undernourished babies are particularly at high risk for pneumonia, which accounted for about half of all infant deaths in the former Soviet Union.

Other health-related developments in Russia are the rising death rate and falling birth rate. As depicted in Figure 15-1, Russia's birth rate dropped from 17 births per 1,000 people in 1984 to a provisional rate in 1993 of 9.2 per 1,000. During the same period, Russia's death rate rose from 11 to 14.6 deaths for every 1,000 persons. Declining birth rates are not unusual in today's world; increasing death rates, however, are highly unusual for a major country. Russian society clearly has serious problems as it struggles with forging a democratic political system and strong free market economy. Without an economic recovery, health reforms will be difficult. Plans include a major restructuring of the health care delivery system to allow competition among providers, private ownership of facilities, and the establishment of health insurance financed by contributions from workers, employers, and government subsidies.

FIGURE 15-1   Birth and Death Rates in the Former Soviet Union
                  and Russian Republic, 1984–1993 (per 1,000 people).

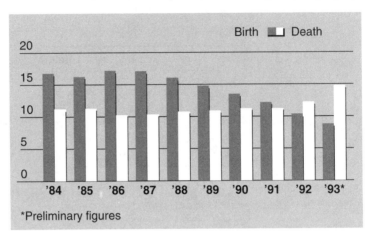

Source: Russia State Committee on Statistics, 1994.

In the meantime, the Russian people have access to a basic no-frills approach to medical care. To obtain better, more personalized care, patients give doctors, nurses, and ward attendants money or gifts for extra consideration (Davis 1989). Otherwise, the average citizen has little ability to influence the course of his or her treatment.

Poland

Poland is another formerly socialist country which has a deteriorating state of health. Life expectancy is declining and morbidity rates for heart disease and cancer are rising. Rates for tuberculosis are twice the average for Europe. There have also been significant increases in the incidence of influenza and hepatitis. Table 15-3 shows that life expectancy in Poland in 1989 for men was 66.7 years and for women 75.5 years. Polish government figures for 1991 indicate that life expectancy had dropped to 66.1 years for men and 75.3 years for women. The decrease in life expectancy for men in 1991 was largely due to premature deaths of men age forty-five to sixty-four. Infant mortality, however, is improving. Table 15-2 shows that Poland had an infant mortality rate of 20.2 deaths per 1,000 births in 1982 and 16.0 in 1989. For 1991, the rate is 14.2 deaths per 1,000 births.

      In spite of recent democratic changes, reform of the health care delivery system in Poland is hampered by an economic recession which has lowered the efficiency of the system and the standard of living of the majority in the population (Wnuk-Lipinski 1990). As in more affluent societies, health inequities are greatest in the lower class and have worsened in recent years. In spite of a Soviet-style health system which provided free health care before 1989, social inequalities in health remain (Wnuk-Lipinski 1990). Currently, most health care in Poland is provided by personnel and facilities organized and supported by the state. Health care is financed by the central budget, while income earned is paid back into the budget. Cooperative and private clinics supplement the government system. Cooperative clinics are established and run by industrial and farm worker groups to provide outpatient care; physicians are paid by the state but are allowed to have some private patients. Unlike state-run clinics, patients have the liberty to choose their physician in cooperative clinics. Private practices, clinics, and hospitals have also been allowed since 1988. Poland intends to have multiple forms of medical practice in the future, to include state, cooperative, private, religious, and investor-owned facilities.

Hungary

Health conditions in the former socialist state of Hungary are also in need of improvement. Table 15-2 shows that infant mortality declined from 20 deaths per 1,000 live births in 1982 to 15.7 per 1,000 in 1989. However, Table 15-3 shows that life expectancy for men in 1989 stood at 65.5 years which exceeds only the former Soviet Union for that year. In 1987, Hungary had a slightly higher level of life expectancy for males with an average of 65.7 years. Life expectancy for women was 73.9 years which equaled the Soviet Union and exceeded only Romania. Female life expectancy in Hungary in 1989 was the same as in 1987. By European standards, life expectancy in Hungary is low.

Between 1948 and 1989, Hungary operated a Soviet-style health care delivery system characterized by central planning and control, subsidized by the state, and providing free health care to the general population under the Uniform State Health Service Act of 1950. This act officially eliminated health insurance and made free health care a right of all citizens. Private practice was not forbidden but in reality existed only in dentistry. The health system was financed by the government's central budget.

With the fall of communism, Hungary has revamped its health care delivery system. Most people are enrolled in a compulsory national health insurance plan which is supported by contributions from workers, employers, and government funds. Only those individuals and families with substantial incomes can remain outside the national health plan. Patients are allowed free choice of health care providers. General practitioners are paid by the insurance fund on a per capita basis; specialists are paid on a fee-for-service basis. Hospitals are paid on a service rendered basis according to a fee schedule of Diagnostic Related Groups (DRGs)—similar to the DRG system used for Medicare in the United States. Private health insurance is available for the affluent and private medical care has been legalized. Hungary is still undergoing the transformation of its health services and its short-term goal is to increase efficiency while the country moves more fully into a capitalist economic system.

CONCLUSION

This review of the organization and social policy of health care in First World and formerly socialist countries suggests that no nation has an ideal system of dealing with health problems. All nations are faced with rising demands for quality health care in the face of limited resources, and in most countries the high cost of care has presented special problems in achieving a desired outcome. Exact comparisons between nations in terms of the effectiveness of their respective health care delivery systems are difficult because of varying political structures, diet, climate, degree of technological advancement, social commitment to national health care, and cultures, which have an impact on the overall health profile of a particular country. Sweden, for example, appears to have a much more effective approach to the provision of medical care than the United States as measured in terms of infant mortality and life expectancy. Yet Sweden has a much smaller and more homogeneous population than the United States and fewer social class differences. It is much easier for the Swedes to focus on health care and mobilize their financial resources to cope with it. Nevertheless, it can be said that the United States has an overall level of health that places it among the world's healthiest nations but not at the top.

Japan has been particularly successful in its approach to health; health care is both low cost and readily accessible to the general public. The Japanese have the lowest infant mortality and highest life expectancy for both men and women in the world. Economic conditions in Japan and Japanese lifestyles may be the primary factors in this development, but the health care delivery has undoubtedly made a major contribution. Yet the Japanese situation is one that other capitalist countries may not necessarily want since business corporations have the expense of providing their own health benefits, people in the national plan are responsible for up to 30 percent of the cost of their care monthly, and the use of prescription drugs is the highest in the world.

Europe has special problems in regard to health. As Denny Vågerö and Raymond Illsley (1992) explain, the period after World War II produced a general improvement in health in most European countries. Although inequities between social classes were recreated in each new generation, this trend occurred at successively higher levels so that all socioeconomic groups benefited. However, Vågerö and Illsey point out that from the mid-1960s on, health care delivery on the basis of welfare capitalism in Western Europe and socialism in Eastern Europe came to increasingly differ. As discussed in this chapter, the formerly socialist countries Russia, Poland, and Hungary experienced a period of decreasing life expectancy and increasing mortality—especially for men. The emergence of this East-West health division leaves Europe with a difficult public health challenge for the 1990s.

Obvious worldwide trends are appearing and are likely to have an effect on health care policy in the future. These trends are: (1) Considerable attention is being paid to the cost of health care and controls over such costs are an important aspect of health policy; (2) preventive medical services are receiving increasing emphasis in developed societies as more attempts are being made to keep well people healthy; (3) efforts are being made to design a more effective administration of large health care systems, and (4) there is more demand and increased responsiveness on the parts of governments and policy makers to provide a health care system that meets national needs. While different countries are taking different approaches to solve health problems, all countries appear to be moving toward a system that will eliminate inequities.

Health Care in Other Countries

16

T his chapter focuses on health care delivery in countries that are not First World or formerly socialist nations. All countries of the world face the problem of meeting the almost unlimited demand for health care with limited resources. To have a more complete appreciation of the various approaches to health care, it is necessary to look beyond North American, European, and Japanese delivery systems. In this chapter we will review how fee-for-service (South Africa), socialized (Saudi Arabia and Kenya), decentralized national (Mexico), and socialist (China) health care systems cope with the challenge of providing health resources to their populations.

FEE-FOR-SERVICE: SOUTH AFRICA

The Republic of South Africa has been experiencing massive social change in recent years, with the end of white rule coming in 1994. According to South African medical sociologist H.C.J. van Rensburg (1991; Rensburg, Fourie, and Pretorius 1992), the major features of South African health care up to the present result from a lengthy molding process of more than three centuries. While various native tribes in the region had their own system of traditional healers, the first Western medical care arrived shortly after 1652 when the Dutch East India Company established a refueling station at what later became Capetown. In 1795 the British occupied the Cape area and the descendants of the early Dutch—the Boers who later became known as Afrikaners—moved into the hinterlands. Eventually, the British obtained control over the region after defeating the Zulus in the late nineteenth century and the Boers in the early twentieth century. The new country that was set up in 1910—the Union of South Africa—sealed cooperation between whites. Other racial and ethnic groups were not consulted.

The health care system that had developed in the meantime was unplanned, uncoordinated and fragmented along racial lines. As Rensburg explains, political unification had little meaning in terms of a unified health care system. The structure of health care delivery was divided in several ways. First, there was a dominant Western and scientific component which existed largely in urban areas and traditional healing which mostly took place in rural regions. The former served whites and some urban blacks, while the latter was used exclusively by blacks. Even today, there is a dual system of health care and many South African blacks use traditional healing or a combination of traditional and Western medicine (Pretorius, de Klerk, and Rensburg 1993). Second, a racially differentiated Western system arose which divided health care providers and hospitals. Whites were given health care by whites, blacks by blacks, Asians by Asians, and so forth. Each racial group had its own practitioners, but whites controlled the official health care system for the nation as a whole. Third, a mixed funding system came into being which featured a private fee-for-service system, similar to that of the United States, and a public system financed by the government which served the poor and elderly. Again, the former approach was principally for whites and those who could afford private care at the hands of physicians of their own race, and the latter was largely for blacks and other racial minorities.

Efforts to establish a nonracial, national health service failed in the 1940s, and, in 1948, a nationwide policy of apartheid, or separation of the races, officially divided the entire society—including health care. Whites maintained power through an all-white government that controlled the police and armed forces and imposed a strict system of racial segregation in jobs, schools, townships, and health care delivery. People were registered with the government according to race and classified as either white, Asian, coloured (mixed race), or black. Ten separate departments of health for the nation were initially established, but reforms in 1983 reduced the number to three (Andersson and Marks 1988; de Beer 1986; Rensburg and Benatar 1993).

Considerable inequality in levels of health care exists among the races in South Africa. The highest quality care is in the fee-for-service private sector and used principally by whites (Rensburg and Fourie 1988). Inequality in health care is matched with inequality in employment, education, housing, and overall quality of life. It is therefore not surprising that racial differences in health persist (Rensburg 1991; Rensburg and Benatar 1993). As Rensburg and Benatar explain:

> . . . the tendency to separate people of different race or colour has for decades and even centuries dominated the scene in the organisation, provision, and distribution of health care, engraving undeniably race-differ-

TABLE 16-1   Life Expectancy by Race and Gender in South Africa,
1980–1985 and 1990–1995 (estimated)

	MALES		*FEMALES*	
	1980–1985	**1990–1995***	**1980–1985**	**1990–1995***
Whites	66.8	67.2	74.3	74.9
Asians	63.1	63.7	69.8	70.7
Coloureds	55.4	56.9	63.5	64.8
Blacks	55.1	56.9	62.5	64.0

*Based on South African Government estimates.

Source: Adapted from H.C.J. van Rensburg, A. Fourie, and E. Pretorius, *Health Care in South Africa* (Pretoria: Academica, 1992).

entiated imprints on the health care system. Consequently grave race-related disparities, inequalities, fragmentation and discrimination in health care and health-determining spheres of life, with divergent outcomes, are reflected in the health indices and health statuses of the different "colour" groups in south Africa.[1]

For example, Table 16-1 shows the life expectancy for the four major racial groups in South Africa by gender for the years 1980 to 1985 and estimates for 1990 to 1995. For both time periods, Table 16-1 shows that white males and females had higher life expectancy than (in order) Asians, coloureds, and blacks. Whites also have the lowest infant mortality rates at 13 deaths per 1,000 live births in 1980 to 1985, compared to 18.9 for Asians, 56 for coloureds and 82 for blacks. Heart disease is the leading cause of death for adult whites, Asians, and coloureds, but ranks third for blacks. The leading cause of death for adult blacks—which is indicative of the quality of life available to them—is accidents, poisonings, and violence. Accidents, poisonings, and violence are the fourth leading cause of death for whites behind cancer and respiratory disease but rank second for Asians and coloureds.

Disparities in levels of health care are likewise reflected in inequities in resources. Whites, with 13.5 percent of the total population, had 74.8 percent of the physicians in 1988. Nonwhites, comprising 86.5 percent of the population, had 25.2 percent of the doctors. Recent breakdowns by specific races in percent of doctors were not available, but 1980 figures show that 1.3 percent of all physicians were black. The percentage of medical students in 1988 was white (75.2), black (11.1), Asian (10.9), and coloured (2.8). Whites make up 45.6 percent of the nurses, while some 43.1 percent of nurses are black, 8.9 percent coloured, and 2.3 percent Asian. About 25 percent of all hospitals are for whites and 75 percent are nonwhite.

[1]H.C.J. van Rensburg and S.R. Benatar, "The Legacy of Apartheid in Health and Health Care," *South African Journal of Sociology* 24 (1993), 99.

All of this is likely to change, however, as South Africa moves toward racial equality following the all-races election in 1994 that voted blacks into positions of national leadership for the first time in history. Earlier, in 1990, the structure of health care delivery had been changed when public hospitals were opened to all races, hospital apartheid was ended, and the three racially separate departments of health were directed to be phased out. Other changes are not known at present, but it is highly likely that all vestiges of racial discrimination in health care delivery will be ended and some type of national health insurance program will be instituted to provide equal access to health.

SOCIALIZED MEDICINE: SAUDI ARABIA AND KENYA

Socialized medicine is practiced in different environments. This section discusses socialized health care in a wealthy country (Saudi Arabia) and a relatively poor nation (Kenya).

Saudi Arabia

Saudi Arabia is a desert kingdom whose native population, as Eugene Gallagher and Maureen Searle (1984) and others (Mackey 1987) explain, is Arab and Islamic to a degree extreme even for the Middle East. Ruled by a king who is an absolute monarch, Saudi Arabian society is characterized by the traditional segregation of women from public life and strong extended family relationships. Saudi Arabia is included in this chapter as an example of a form of socialized medicine provided by one of the most affluent nations of the world. As late as 1945, Saudi Arabia was a poor country largely inhabited by nomadic Bedouin tribes. Sandra Mackey (1987) points out that most Saudis lived in tents or small, poorly ventilated houses made of straw and mud. There was no electricity, education, or medical care. But in the 1950s, money from oil revenues began pouring into the country and during the 1970s Saudi Arabia became a world power because of its wealth and reserves of oil. Between 1970 and 1979, revenues increased from $1.2 billion to $65 billion annually and reached $125 billion in the early 1980s before oil prices declined. Currently, oil brings about $45 billion in revenues. With so much money coming into the country in such a relatively short period of time, Saudi Arabia experienced an unprecedented spurt of economic growth and modernization.

The oil revenues are paid to the king who distributes funds to manage the nation. Although the exact population of Saudi Arabia is not known, it probably numbers around 11 million people (7 million Saudis and 4 million foreign nations). Saudis pay no income tax and are assured an adequate standard of living by their government. Any higher living standard is to be earned by the individual, with the government ready to guarantee grants and loans for housing and business ventures. Mackey describes the situation as follows:

The oil boom made the Saudis rich. They were not only statistically rich, as reckoned by dividing oil revenues by the number of people, but also in the sense that the Saudis commanded high disposable incomes and lived in one of the world's most benevolent welfare states. Huge oil revenues coupled with Saudi Arabia's small population enabled the House of Saudi to give every Saudi citizen a share of prosperity on a scale few rulers have ever matched. Through careful management, there would have been enough money to make every citizen a ward of the state. King Faisal early rejected this idea, choosing instead to press Saudis into the work force while cushioning them against serious need with grants, loans, subsidies, and government services. By 1980 this combination was providing a per capita income from employment of almost $2500 a month, supplemented by a pantheon of government programs that added another 29 percent to personal income.[2]

Massive amounts of money were channeled into housing, education, and medical care. Where in 1970 there had been 47 hospitals, 7,165 hospital beds, and 789 physicians, in 1990 there were 87 modern hospitals, nearly 20,000 beds, and more than 7,500 physicians. The King Faisal Medical City in the capital of Riyadh, opened in 1975, was intended to be the best equipped medical center in the world. In addition, there were four medical schools, five nursing schools, and other institutions for training dentists, pharmacists, and medical technicians. Health care in government hospitals is free and if it is necessary for a Saudi citizen to go abroad for specialized medical treatment, the expenses for that person and at least one other family member will be paid by the government.

Saudi Arabia, however, has both a public and private system of health care delivery. Yet as Gallagher and Searle (1985) observe, Saudi affluence provides two important contrasts with most other developing nations. First, the resources of government medicine are of a high quality and are well distributed throughout the urban and vast desert areas of the kingdom. Second, with the spread of wealth in the population, more families are able to become medical consumers in the private sector, thereby reducing the number of people dependent upon public health care. While private and public medicine may not provide the same standard of care, the gap between "first-class" private care and "second-class" government medicine, in Gallagher and Searle's view, is substantially narrower than that found in other developing nations. Providing high quality medical care to those in need is one way in which the government, with its wealth, can benefit the public in a manner consistent with Saudi political culture and the teachings of Islam. Gallagher and Searle state:

> Citizens are entitled to receive modern health services within the public sector without such services becoming the object of political contention, such as occurs increasingly in Western nations. Public provision for

[2]Sandra Mackey, *The Saudis: Inside the Desert Kingdom* (Boston: Houghton Mifflin, 1987), pp. 217–218.

health care has strong popular appeal. Anyone can become ill, need health care, and benefit from its application. When, as in Saudi Arabia, it is provided in a monarchic system of government, health care can be endowed with a sense of patrimonial solitude for the ill and ailing. This imagery has strong meaning within the symbolic context of extended-family concern for kinsmen, which is very powerful in Saudi Arabia.[3]

Consequently, unlike other aspects of modernization involving Western culture such as bureaucracy, structure, and the Protestant work ethic, the provision of Western-style health care to Saudi Arabia's population has not produced severe strains in Saudi society. But the transition to a modern medical system has not been without challenges, despite ample funding. Two problems in particular are not typical of Western societies. One is the lack of trained Saudi medical professionals and the other is health care for women. While there are over 7,500 physicians in Saudi Arabia, about 85 percent of them are foreigners. There are also equally high percentages of foreigners working as nurses. It will be several years before enough Saudi physicians and other health personnel are able to provide Saudi Arabia with "medical self-sufficiency" (Gallagher and Searle 1984).

The position of females in Saudi society presents some special considerations for health care providers. Women are segregated from men in educational institutions and hospitals; women are also not allowed to drive automobiles nor can they travel abroad without the permission of the senior male member of their family. While separate hospital facilities and clinics can be established for women or different hours arranged for medical consultations if separate facilities are not available, female patients may have to be treated by foreign male physicians because of the shortage of Saudi doctors. To meet the health needs of women and avoid dependence on male physicians, about 50 percent of all Saudi medical students are female. Thus, medicine is one of the few professions open to women in Saudi Arabia. As Gallagher and Searle (1985) note, females are segregated in varying degrees throughout the Middle East for pre-Islamic reasons of male honor and female virtue, but this practice is more strictly observed in Saudi Arabia than in most other societies in the region. As a result, Saudi medicine is confronted with the requirement to comply with the culture's division of the sexes wherever possible. This is seen in Saudi medical education where medical schools have both a male and female campus; even though English is the language of instruction, Western textbooks are used, and many of the faculty are neither Saudi nor Muslim—Saudi and Islamic values prevail. As Gallagher (1988b) observed, all students dress conservatively, participate in daily prayers, and shun the consumption of pork and alcohol. The students are rigidly segregated by sex in the same school. Gallagher provides an example:

> Several male students asked that the main (male) library curtain off the windows facing the central campus courtyard so that they would not be able to view female students crossing the yard en route to lab sessions.

[3]Eugene B. Gallagher and C. Maureen Searle, "Health Services and the Political Culture of Saudi Arabia," *Social Science and Medicine*, 21 (1985), 259.

Although the females always wore the full black cloaks (*abbayas*) that were required when they moved off the female campus, the complainants said that the female students were too much of a distraction from their studies. The library installed curtains in response. The curtains were moveable, however, so that students could open or close them according to the sensibilities of whoever was in the library.[4]

Gallagher provides other examples, such as students complaining the non-Muslim faculty did not understand Islam, demanding the library cancel subscriptions to magazines like *Scientific American* and *Psychology Today* because they contained liquor ads and articles about sex, and refusing to perform clinical clerkships outside of Saudi Arabia in other Arab states they felt were too permissive.

Infant mortality rates in Saudi Arabia are still somewhat high with 1991 rates of 32 infant deaths per 1,000 live births. In comparison to other countries in the region, Saudi Arabia shows lower infant mortality rates than countries like Yemen, where 1991 rates were 109 per 1,000. But, as far back as 1986, rates were 26 in the United Arab Emirates, 26 in Bahrain, and 19 in Kuwait. Therefore, Saudi Arabia still has some distance to cover before becoming one of the world's healthiest nations. Nevertheless, progress in health is being made. In 1976, the average life expectancy of a Saudi was 45 years; by 1981 life expectancy had risen to 54 years and in 1991 life expectancy reached 69 years.

Kenya

Kenya is located in East Africa and covers an area approximately the size of France. As a result of one of the highest birth rates in the world (45 births per 1,000 persons in 1991) and declining mortality, the population of Kenya increased from 5.4 million in 1948 to 24 million in 1990. With a rapidly rising population and a depressed agricultural economy, based largely on the production of coffee and tea, Kenya has serious economic and social problems—although the economy is somewhat better than other nations in the region. Kenya is included in this chapter as an example of the type of socialized health care delivery system developed by a relatively poor Third World country.

Kenya has a national health service that employs physicians and other health personnel and owns hospitals, but private practitioners, mission clinics run by church organizations, and traditional native folk healers are also available. The Kenyan national health care system was established in the early 1950s under a colonial administration and includes regional and district hospitals and a network of rural health clinics. Modern, Western-style health care in Kenya, as elsewhere in Africa, is primarily provided by the state, concentrated almost exclusively in major urban centers, and inherited largely without modification from former colonial powers, which, in Kenya's case, was Great Britain. This is the situation not only in Kenya, but also in Nigeria (Ityavyar 1988), Ghana (Fosu 1989),

[4]Eugene B. Gallagher, "Convergence or Divergence in Third World Medical Education? An Arab Study," *Journal of Health and Social Behavior*, 29 (1988), 391–392.

and throughout Africa south of the Sahara (Alubo 1990; Ungar 1989), including South Africa (Rensburg et al. 1992).

Despite good intentions, Kenyan health policy is typical of other African states in that most of the national health budget is spent in the capital of Nairobi. S. Ogoh Alubo (1990) notes, for example, a period when Kenya spent 40 percent of its entire health budget on Nairobi's National Kenyatta Hospital and only 2 percent went to rural health clinics. On the average, urban health institutions in Kenya receive 80 to 85 percent annually of the total national health budget. Almost every hospital is located in an urban center. The best educated and most wealthy members of Kenyan society also live in urban areas, especially in Nairobi and Mombassa, and they demand and receive the highest quality public health services in the country (Mwabu 1984).

Consequently, there is a considerable disparity between urban–rural health care. Some 85 percent of Kenya's population lives in rural areas where dispensaries and clinics are poorly equipped and understaffed by trained personnel. Kenya has some 10,000 physicians, which is approximately 50 doctors for every 100,000 persons, but less than 10 percent of Kenya's physicians are located in rural settings. This means that about 5 medical doctors are available for every 100,000 rural residents; however, some estimates are that the ratio is closer to 3 doctors per 100,000 rural dwellers (Mwabu 1984). Another major problem that rural residents face is that they must often travel great distances to reach a health clinic; even though care is free—as it is for all Kenyans who use public facilities— travel expenses, a lack of transportation and roads in rural areas, and the time involved are major considerations in making the decision to seek medical care. In some areas, professional health care is simply not available.

Cheryl Bentsen (1991) studied the Maasai tribe in Kenya and found they rarely get sick. When they do, they treat themselves with home remedies, cauterize wounds with hot ash, drink medicinal soups made from roots and bark, or, if these measures fail, visit a herbalist or traditional healer. Physicians are visited only for emergencies unless a clinic is nearby. She reports on the case of one Maasai warrior who did visit a medical doctor. The man had been severely gored by a water buffalo but had managed to make his way to a remote clinic. The doctor, a novice, feeling that the man would not survive the long drive over back roads to Nairobi, where modern medical care was available, performed surgery. He lacked experience, anesthesia, and blood for transfusion. The only painkiller was aspirin, and the doctor propped a textbook in front of him so he could refer to it during the operation. The next morning, when the doctor went to check on his patient, he was gone. But months later, the man returned in good health with the gift of a goat. Despite a lack of experience and equipment, the surgery was successful.

Many people turn to traditional folk healers, even in large cities, not only for treatment, but also to find out why they contract certain illnesses and who is responsible (Fosu 1989). Traditional healers are widely available to the African public, although their popularity varies, and they remain the most common source of health care in rural Africa (Good 1987). Traditional healers are inexpensive, effective in reducing anxiety and stress, and embedded in the culture of the groups they serve; consequently, they are likely to persist as health providers in a developing country like Kenya where there is an acute shortage of trained health professionals (Good 1987; Fosu 1989).

Although the Kenyan health care system is financed by revenues from the country's general budget and public services are provided at no cost, there are sometimes small fees for physician consultations and charges for drugs. Private care is also available to those persons who want it and can afford it. Kenya has a medical school and nursing schools for the training of their own health professionals, and health care delivery remains an important government priority in the nation's development. Infant mortality has risen in Kenya from 64 deaths per 1,000 births in 1978 to 67 per 1,000 in 1991 which is still significantly lower than in neighboring countries. In 1991, for example, the infant mortality rate in Ethiopia was 130 per 1,000, while the rate in Rwanda was 111, Tanzania 115, and Uganda 188. Life expectancy in Kenya in 1991 was 59 years which compares to 48 years in Ethiopia and 51 in Tanzania. Health conditions may be far from Western standards in Kenya, but they are better than elsewhere in East Africa. As Kenya moves through the 1990s, it confronts increasingly serious problems in public health other than funding. Many people, perhaps a majority in rural areas, are infected with malaria. But the most life-threatening epidemic at present is AIDS, which, while not as prevalent in Kenya as in nearby Zaire, Rwanda, and Uganda, is nevertheless extensive and spreading throughout the population. About 100,000 people were believed to be HIV-infected in Kenya in 1993 and about 2 million are expected to be so by the year 2000.

DECENTRALIZED NATIONAL HEALTH: MEXICO

Mexico has a decentralized national health system covering most of the general population through a variety of programs that fall into one of three broad categories. First, there are the public social security organizations that provide both health insurance and old-age benefits for specific groups of private and government employees. Second is the health care provided through the government's Ministry (Secretariat) of Health and Welfare or SSA (*Secretaria de Salubridad y Asistencia*), which is the primary source of care for the majority of persons not covered by a social security organization—especially the urban poor. And third is the private health care system, which consists of various private practitioners, hospitals and clinics, and charitable organizations.

The largest health plan in Mexico covers workers in the private sector and is administered by the Mexican Social Insurance Institute or IMSS (*Instituto Mexicano de Segura Social*). The IMSS was established in 1943 as a compulsory government-sponsored social security program for salaried workers in Mexico City and surrounding areas and is financed by contributions from workers, employers, and the state. The program was extended to other metropolitan areas during 1943–1945 and salaried agricultural workers were added in 1954; and, in 1973, legislation was enacted that provided for the extension of IMSS social insurance to everyone with jobs in the private sector, including those who could not afford to contribute financially. Known as the IMSS Social Solidarity Program, health services are provided free of charge to low-income workers and their families in return for approximately ten days of work in public projects. The level of benefits available for low-income members, however, is not comprehensive and is limited to general medical and maternity care. Furthermore, despite efforts to expand the IMSS program to rural areas, more than 90 percent of the IMSS membership is urban.

Another health plan, which provides the most extensive and generous benefits of any social security program, was established in 1960 for government workers and is administered by the Social Insurance Institute of State Employees (ISSSTE or *Instituto de Seguridad y Servicios Sociales Para los Trabajadores del Estado*). The IMSS and ISSSTE programs are by far the largest health insurance plans in Mexico. Other social security programs with health insurance are available to members of the armed forces (ISSSFAM) and the state-run oil industry (PEMEX). Approximately 45 percent of Mexico's population is covered by these various social security plans.

The Ministry or Secretariat of Health and Welfare (SSA), created in 1943, is responsible for Mexico's overall health policy and provides health care directly to the urban poor through its own hospitals and clinics. Nearly 20 percent of the population is dependent on the SSA to meet their health needs. Another 15 percent of the population utilizes the private sector. According to Peter Ward (1985), private medicine is not just for the wealthy. "The poor make extensive use of the private sector," states Ward (1985:111), "for 'lightweight' consultations, and they may also receive private treatment paid by their employer—a feature of patronage that remains widespread throughout Mexico."

In theory, Mexico has a national health system; yet in reality, not everyone has access to it (Ward 1985; Warner 1991). Exact figures are not known, but some 15 to 20 percent of the population lacks ready access to modern health care. Most of these persons live in rural areas, including highly isolated sections of the country. Many of them have no health insurance, or if they do have some type of coverage, physicians and clinics are not available locally. Consequently, they turn to a variety of sources, either public health care, private doctors and hospitals, nuns, folk healers, or rely on self-treatment. James Young's (1981) study of medical choice in a small Mexican village illustrates the manner in which some rural Mexicans obtain health care. Young found that the villagers:

> . . . do not utilize modern medical treatment more frequently because such services are inaccessible. When a trip to a doctor might cost at least a week's income, and the ill person must be transported on a slow, uncomfortable, and often overcrowded bus for an hour or more, it is not surprising that less expensive and more convenient alternatives are often chosen. Since many households have quite limited resources that must be allocated among a number of essential needs, it seems justifiable, though perhaps regrettable, that illnesses not considered life threatening are found to not warrant the sacrifice of household resources that a physician's treatment would entail.[5]

---

[5]James Clay Young, *Medical Choice in a Mexican Village* (New Brunswick, N.J.: Rutgers University Press, 1981), p. 173.

The villagers in Young's study clearly recognized that physicians were able to provide cures better than any other form of healing—but distance, inconvenience, travel expenses, and low-cost physician fees were important barriers. Doctors were usually consulted in only relatively serious circumstances. The most frequent response to illness was self-care, utilizing a variety of traditional herbal or commercially purchased remedies. Other sources of care in the village included folk healers (*curanderos*), a small dispensary operated by local Catholic nuns, and a medical station staffed by a solitary practical nurse with a ninth-grade education.

Despite its nationwide program of social insurance, Mexico has a serious problem of maldistribution of services. More than 35 percent of all doctors are located in the Mexico City area, which has only 20 percent of the population; consequently, Mexico City has a surplus of physicians, while other parts of the country have a shortage. Even though health clinics are established throughout the country, rural areas are likely to be served by a nurse (Warner 1991). For the country as a whole, there are approximately eighty physicians per 100,000 people and about 75 percent of all doctors are employed in some type of government-sponsored health program—although some have both a public and private practice. The remaining 25 percent are private, fee-for-service practitioners. In border areas near the United States, affluent Mexicans and others covered by some type of U.S. health insurance visit American doctors; some Americans, in turn, especially the poor and near poor without Medicaid, seek the services of less expensive Mexican physicians and buy drugs at cheaper prices in Mexican pharmacies. Many drugs in the United States requiring prescriptions, including some antibiotics and pain killers, are sold over the counter in Mexico. Crossing the U.S.-Mexico border, from one side or the other, to obtain health services is a fact of life for some people (Warner 1991).

The overall health of the Mexican population is improving. Life expectancy in 1991 was 70 years compared with 63 years in 1972; infant mortality was 36 deaths per 1,000 births in 1991 as contrasted with 80 per 1,000 in 1965. Approximately 6 percent of Mexico's GDP was spent on health care in the late 1980s. Health care delivery in major urban centers in Mexico is often of high quality, especially in the national medical institutes in Mexico City; in rural areas, however, access to modern medicine is limited and difficult to obtain. Overall, Mexico has established a generally effective national system of health care delivery, despite being a developing nation and having an often troubled economy that has affected public spending on health care.

But significant problems remain. As is the case in Africa (Fosu 1989), Mexican health care is oriented toward curative rather than preventive medicine; hence, there has not been a large scale effort to prevent illness through public health programs intended to improve nutrition, water, sewage systems, and training in hygiene (Ward 1985). In addition, the various social health insurance plans differ in the levels of benefits provided and the decentralized system of health care delivery promotes a lack of coordination, planning, and fiscal control in a country that lacks great national wealth. And, most importantly, a significant segment of the population in rural areas lacks access to modern health services.

However, as Ward (1985:110) explains, "at least, [health care] coverage has . . . been extended to the not so powerful, and specifically to wider section of the working population that includes both blue- and white-collar workers." Mexico's health policy emphasizes continued improvement in the health of the general population, with a particular focus on meeting the basic health needs of the underprivileged. Health care for the urban poor seems to be Mexico' s highest priority at this point in the development of its health care delivery system.

SOCIALIST MEDICINE: CHINA

The People's Republic of China is one of the few countries practicing socialist medicine. Prior to the 1949 revolution, there were few Western-trained physicians in China and these doctors generally lived in major cities where they commanded high fees for their work. Except for a few missionary doctors in the countryside, the bulk of the Chinese population received medical care from folk practitioners and shamans. There was a heavy death toll from disease, poor sanitation, and widespread ignorance about health matters. In 1949, the average life expectancy of a Chinese was only thirty-two years.

Improvement in health became one of the major goals of the Red Chinese government after it came to power following the civil war with Nationalist forces. One of the first public health measures was the "Patriotic Health Movement," in which millions of Chinese killed flies, removed trash, and worked to improve sanitation. Two other measures were also important. First, traditional Chinese medicine was revived, featuring the use of herbal medicines and techniques like acupuncture, in which pain is controlled by the insertion of needles into certain designated points in the body. Even though its therapeutic value is not fully understood, traditional Chinese medicine is still used today throughout China with considerable effectiveness for many health problems. Often traditional medicine is used in conjunction with Western medicine, and while Chinese physicians are trained largely in either the traditional or the Western approach, all receive some training in both disciplines. China is the only country that consistently treats traditional and scientific medicine equally, making both of them legally available and encouraging Western-style physicians to learn traditional methods (Jingfeng 1988).

Second, the so-called barefoot doctors movement was begun, in which 1.8 million paramedical personnel were eventually trained in rudimentary medicine and sent to rural areas to provide basic medical treatment and assist in efforts at preventive medicine and public health (Rosenthal 1987; Sidel and Sidel 1982a, 1982b). Through this movement, the majority of the population was able to have at least some routine access to medical care.

China's attempts at improving its health care system suffered a serious setback during the Cultural Revolution of 1966 to 1977. The Cultural Revolution was intended by China's leaders to be a mass movement of the people that would expose corruption and rid the government of unnecessary bureaucracy. Many influential people were subjected to severe public criticism and even persecuted by revolutionary groups such as the Red Guards, whose membership included thousands of young students. Schools and universities were closed as young people abandoned their studies to participate in revolutionary activities. Factions developed within the movement itself, and this period of Chinese history is marked with chaos as power struggles were waged within the hierarchy of the government and the Communist party. There was a widespread disruption of work and education, and many people lost their lives in the street fighting, torture, and pressure to commit suicide that followed. For nearly four years, there was virtually no medical research or training of medical students. Thousands of doctors were forced to leave their positions and were sent into the countryside to work with peasants in agricultural communes. When medical education was resumed in 1970, the time for training was cut from eight years after high school to three years, with emphasis on practical and applied medicine. Almost anyone could gain admission to medical school and few or no examinations were given during training. The quality of Chinese doctors declined accordingly and the old system has now returned, but many valuable years were lost in regard to both medical education and research.

Today an extensive network of health care facilities exists in China. Clinics providing preventive medicine, birth control measures, and first aid are readily available in both rural areas and urban neighborhoods. People with serious illnesses or injuries are referred to district and regional hospitals. Many communes and factories have their own clinics or hospitals. Medical care for workers is paid for by welfare funds that the communes and factories set up with money obtained by the sale of goods and crops. Funds to support public employees and others are derived largely from income at the national level generated by economic production as in the former Soviet system. For the individual, medical care has been essentially free, except for small charges when hospitalized or for some drugs that are generally inexpensive and easily obtained. China is completely self-sufficient in the manufacture of drugs and costs have gone down considerably since 1950. Rising costs and the growth in demand from an increasingly large elderly population have led China to consider reforms intended to reduce state expenditures for health care. Current measures include increasing the portion paid by individuals and state-run enterprises for health services. One approach being tested is to have individuals pay 10 to 20 percent of charges for outpatient care and 5 percent for hospitalization.

In 1991, the average life expectancy in China was 69 years. Precise figures concerning infant mortality are difficult to obtain, but in 1949 it is estimated that about 120 infant deaths per 1,000 births occurred in China's cities and the rate in the countryside was 200 deaths per 1,000 births; the rate estimated for China overall in 1991 was 38 deaths per 1,000 births. In 1984, Chinese government figures show that China had one million doctors of traditional Chinese and Western medicine, which is one doctor per every 1,000 persons. Acute infectious diseases have been brought under control or eliminated and effective treatment of parasitic diseases has greatly improved the overall health of the Chinese people, with cardiovascular diseases most prevalent among lower socioeconomic groups (Siegrist, Bernhardt, Feng, and Schettler 1990). Heart disease and cancer are now the major health problems in most parts of the country. By modern standards, medical science in China is still not highly developed and much of its medical technology is outdated. Improvement in health care delivery, however, remains a major goal of the society.

CONCLUSION

Countries throughout the world are confronted with major challenges in providing health care, as is indicated by this discussion of selected countries that are not First World or formerly socialist nations. Rising costs and demand in excess of resources are common almost everywhere. Countries like Saudi Arabia, which have wealth, are obviously in a better position than less affluent nations in meeting the health needs of citizens. Developing countries which lack resources, which is the case for the great majority, find it especially hard to meet needs as seen in the case of Kenya. However, the health situation in Kenya is better than in most other African countries south of the Sahara—which speaks to the fact that health services for most Africans are inadequate or nonexistent.

In many developing countries, modern health care is concentrated in urban areas and rural residents are often left to cope with illness on their own or seek out traditional healers. Modern medical care may be an unaffordable luxury. In such countries, health policy is usually oriented toward meeting basic health needs (curing), rather than prevention or the expansion of specialized services (Fosu 1989). Whereas levels of health are much worse in some countries than in others, the World Bank (1993) reports that life expectancy in developing nations rose from 46 years in 1960 to 63 years in 1990. Widespread use of immunizations and the effective treatment of diarrhea with oral fluids were cited by the World Bank for saving about three million lives a year. Successes, however, can be diminished by the rise of new and deadly problems, such as AIDS, drug-resistant forms of malaria and tuberculosis, and the growing consumption of tobacco in Third World countries. Waste, inefficiency, and theft hamper the delivery of health services in some countries as well. Consequently, the world has considerable distance to travel before health for all can be a global certainty.

The search for an optimal form of health care delivery goes on. The fee-for-service approach, like that of the United States and South Africa, has a tradition of discrimination and inequality. Fee-for-service also tends to inflate costs and create incentives for excessive and unnecessary care. Since the collapse of Marxist and socialist-style health systems in Europe and their failure to promote high levels of health, the influence of these models in the world has been significantly reduced. Only China and Cuba still operate a purely socialist system and China shows some signs of change by increasing payments from patients. Cuba is sliding into poverty because of a failing economy and has a severe shortage of drugs, equipment, and high-quality facilities. Thus, most of the countries of the world appear to be moving toward some type of socialized or decentralized national health system—incorporating various forms of universal coverage and limited or managed competition.

References

ABEL, THOMAS. 1991 "Measuring health lifestyles in a comparative analysis: Theoretical issues and empirical findings." *Social Science and Medicine*, 32:899–908.

ABEL, THOMAS, and WILLIAM C. COCKERHAM. 1993 "Lifestyle or lebensführung? Critical remarks on the mistranslation of Weber's 'class, status, party.' " *Sociological Quarterly*, 34:551–556.

ABEL, THOMAS, WILLIAM C. COCKERHAM, GUENTHER LÜESCHEN, and GERHARD KUNZ. 1989 "Health lifestyles and self-direction in employment among American men: A test of the spillover effect." *Social Science and Medicine*, 28:1269–1274.

ABERCROMBIE, NICHOLAS, ALAN WARDE, KEITH SOOTHILL, JOHN URRY, and SYVLIA WALBAY. 1988 *Contemporary British society*. Oxford, U.K.: Polity Press.

ADAY, LUANN, and RONALD ANDERSEN. 1975 *Development of indices of access to medical care*. Ann Arbor: Health Administration Press.

ADAY, LUANN, RONALD ANDERSEN, and GRETCHEN V. FLEMING. 1980 *Health Care in the U.S.: Equitable for whom?* Beverly Hills, Calif.: Sage.

ADLER, ISRAEL, AND JUDITH T. SHUVAL. 1978 "Cross pressures during socialization for medicine." *American Sociological Review*, 43:693–704.

AGBONIFO, P. O. 1983 "The state of health as a reflection of the level of development of a nation." *Social Science and Medicine*, 17:2003–2006.

ALBRECHT, GARY L., 1984 "Large urban public hospitals: An analysis of competing explanatory paradigms," pp. 221–256 in *Research in the sociology of health care*, Vol. 3, J. Roth (ed.). Greenwich, Conn.: JAI.

ALBRECHT, GARY L., and JUDITH A. LEVY. 1982 "The professionalization of osteopathy: Adaptation in the medical marketplace," pp. 161–206 in *Research in the sociology of health care*, Vol. 2, J. Roth (ed.). Greenwich, Conn.: JAI.

———. 1984 "A sociological perspective of physical disability," pp. 45–106 in *Advances in medical social science*, Vol. 2, J. Ruffini (ed.). New York: Gordon & Breach.

ALBRECHT, GARY L., and J. WARREN SALMON. 1987 "Anomalies in Soviet health care." *Journal of Medical Practice Management*, 2:288–296.

ALEXANDER, JEFFREY A., and MARY L. FENNELL. 1986 "Patterns of decision making in multi-hospital systems." *Journal of Health and Social Behavior*, 27:14–27.

ALEXANDER, JEFFREY A., MICHAEL A. MORRISEY, and STEPHEN M. SHORTELL. 1986 "Effects of competition, regulation, and corporatization on hospital-physician relationships." *Journal of Health and Social Behavior*, 27:220–235.

ALFORD, ROBERT R. 1975 *Health care politics*. Chicago: University of Chicago Press.

ALLEN, GILLIAN, and ROY WALLIS. 1976 "Pentecostalists as a medical minority," pp. 110–137 in *Marginal medicine*, R. Wallis and P. Morley (eds.). New York: The Free Press.

ALLMAN, RICHARD M., WILLIAM C. YOELS, and JEFFREY MICHAEL CLAIR. 1993 "Reconciling the agendas of physicians and patients," pp. 29–48 in *Sociomedical Perspectives on Patient Care*, J. Clair and R. Allman (eds.). Lexington, KY: University of Kentucky Press.

ALUBO, S. OGOH. 1990 "Debt crisis, health and health services in Africa." *Social Science and Medicine*, 31:639–648.

AMERICAN MEDICAL ASSOCIATION. 1991 "Hispanic Health in the United States." *Journal of the American Medical Association*, 265:248–252.

ANDERSEN, RONALD, and LUANN ADAY. 1978 "Access to medical care in the U.S.: Realized and potential." *Medical Care*, 16:533–546.

ANDERSEN, RONALD, and ODIN W. ANDERSON. 1979 "Trends in the use of health services," pp. 371–391 in *Handbook of medical sociology*, 3rd ed., H. Freeman, S. Levine, and L. Reeder (eds.). Englewood Cliffs, N.J.: Prentice Hall.

ANDERSEN, RONALD, JOANNA KRAVITS, and ODIN W. ANDERSON (eds.). 1975 *Equity in health services: Empirical analyses in social policy*. Cambridge, Mass.: Ballinger.

ANDERSEN, RONALD, SANDRA ZELMAN LEWIS, AIDA L. GIACHELLO, LUANN ADAY, and GRACE CHIU. 1981 "Access to medical care among the Hispanic population of the southwestern United States." *Journal of Health and Social Behavior*, 22:78–79.

ANDERSSON, NEIL, and SHULA MARKS. 1988 "Apartheid and health in the 1980s." *Social Science and Medicine*, 27:667–681.

ANNANDALE, ELLEN C. 1989 "The malpractice crisis and the doctor–patient relationship." *Sociology of Health and Illness*, 11:1–23.

ANSPACH, RENEE R. 1988 "Notes on the sociology of medical discourse: The language of case presentation." *Journal of Health and Social Behavior*, 29:357–374.

ANTONOVSKY, AARON. 1972 "Social class, life expectancy and overall mortality," pp. 5–30 in *Patients, physicians and illness*, 2nd ed., E. Gartly Jaco (ed.). New York: The Free Press.

———. 1979 *Health, stress, and coping*. San Francisco: Jossey-Bass.

APPLE, DORRIAN. 1960 "How laymen define illness." *Journal of Health and Social Behavior*, 1:219–225.

ARBER, SARA. 1989 "Gender and class inequalities in health: Understanding the differentials," pp. 250–279 in *Health inequalities in European countries*, J. Fox (ed.). Aldershot, U.K.: Gower.

———. 1993 "Chronic illness over the life course: Class inequalities among men and women in Britain," pp. 39–64 in *Medical Sociology: Research on chronic illness*, T. Abel, S. Geyer, U. Gerhardt, J. Siegrist, and W. van den Heuvel (eds.). Bonn: Informationszentrum Sozialwissenschaften.

ARDAGH, JOHN. 1987 *France today*. London: Penguin.

ARLUKE, ARNOLD, LOUANNE KENNEDY, and RONALD C. KESSLER. 1979 "Reexamining the sick-role concept: An empirical assessment." *Journal of Health and Social Behavior*, 20:30–36.

ARLUKE, ARNOLD, and JACK LEVIN. 1982 "Second childhood." *Public Communication Review*, 1:21–25.

ARMSTRONG, DAVID. 1989 *An outline of sociology as applied to medicine*, 3rd Ed. London: Wright.

ASELTINE, ROBERT H., JR., and RONALD C. KESSLER. 1993 "Marital disruption and depression in a community sample." *Journal of Health and Social Behavior*, 34:237–251.

ASKENASY, ALEXANDER R., BRUCE P. DOHRENWEND, and BARBARA S. DOHRENWEND. 1977 "Some effects of social class and ethnic group membership on judgments of the magnitude of stressful life events: A research note." *Journal of Health and Social Behavior*, 18:432–439.

ATKINSON, THOMAS, RAMSAY LIEM, and JOAN H. LIEM. 1986 "The social costs of unemployment: Implications for social support." *Journal of Health and Social Behavior*, 27:317–331.

AVERY, CHARLENE. 1991 "Native American medicine: Traditional healing." *Journal of the American Medical Association*, 265:2271, 2273.

AVISON, WILLIAM R., and R. JAY TURNER. 1988 "Stressful life events and depressive symptoms: Disaggregating the effects of acute stressors and chronic strains." *Journal of Health and Social Behavior*, 29:253–264.

BARNARTT, SHARON N. 1990 "A review of medical sociology textbooks." *Teaching Sociology*, 18:372–376.

BARNETT, TONY, and PIERS BLAIKE. 1992 *AIDS in Africa*. New York: Guilford.

BAUMANN, BARBARA. 1961 "Diversities in conceptions of health and physical fitness." *Journal of Health and Social Behavior*, 2:39–46.

BAUWENS, ELEANOR. 1977 "Medical beliefs and practices among lower-income Anglos," pp. 241–270 in *Ethnic medicine in the Southwest*, E. Spicer (ed.). Tucson: University of Arizona Press.

BAYER, RONALD. 1986 "AIDS, power, and reason." *Milbank Quarterly*, 64:168–182.

BECKER, HOWARD S. 1973 *Outsiders: Studies in the sociology of deviance*. 2nd ed. New York: The Free Press.

BECKER, HOWARD S., and BLANCHE GREER. 1958 "The fate of idealism in medical school." *American Sociological Review*, 23:50–56.

BECKER, HOWARD S., BLANCHE GREER, EVERETT C. HUGHES, and ANSELM STRAUSS. 1961 *Boys in white: Student culture in medical school*. Chicago: University of Chicago Press.

BECKER, LANCE B., BEN H. HAN, PETER M. MEYER, FRED A. WRIGHT, KARIN V. RHODES, DAVID W. SMITH, JOHN BARRETT, and the CPR Chicago Project. 1993 "Racial differences in the incidence of cardiac arrest and subsequent survival." *New England Journal of Medicine*, 329:600–606.

BECKER, MARSHALL H. 1979 "Psychosocial aspects of health-related behaviors," pp. 253–274 in *Handbook of medical sociology*, H. Freeman, S. Levine, and L. Reeder (eds.). Englewood Cliffs, N.J.: Prentice Hall.

BECKER, MARSHALL H. (ed.). 1974 *The health belief model and personal health behavior*. San Francisco: Society for Public Health Education, Inc.

BECKER, MARSHALL H., and LOIS A. MAIMAN. 1975 "Sociobehavioral determinants of compliance with health and medical care recommendations." *Medical Care*, 13:10–24.

BECKER, MARSHALL H., LOIS A. MAIMAN, JOHN P. KIRSCHT, DON P. HAEFNER, and ROBERT H. DRACHMAN. 1977 "The health belief model and prediction of dietary compliance: A field experiment." *Journal of Health and Social Behavior*, 18:348–366.

BECKER, MARSHALL H., and IRWIN M. ROSENSTOCK. 1989 "Health promotion, disease prevention, and program retention," pp. 284–305 in *Handbook of medical sociology*, 4th ed., H. Freeman S. Levine (eds.). Englewood Cliffs, N.J.: Prentice Hall.

BELLIN, SEYMOUR S., and H. JACK GEIGER. 1972 "The impact of a neighborhood health center on a patient's behavior and attitudes relating to health care: A study of low income housing." *Medical Care*, 10:224–239.

BENDIX, REINHARD. 1960 *Max Weber: An intellectual portrait*. New York: Doubleday.

BENHAM, LEE, and ALEXANDRA BENHAM. 1975 "Utilization of physician services across income groups, 1963–1970," pp. 97–103 in *Equity in health services: Empirical analyses in social policy*, R. Andersen, J. Kravits, and O. Anderson (eds.). Cambridge, Mass.: Ballinger.

BENNETT, ARNOLD, and ORVILL ADAMS (eds.). 1993 *Looking North for Health: What we can learn from Canada's health care system*. San Francisco: Jossey-Bass.

BENNETT, F. J. 1987 "AIDS as a social phenomenon." *Social Science and Medicine*, 25:529–539.

BENOIT, CECILIA. 1989 "The professional socialisation of midwives: Balancing art and science." *Sociology of Health & Illness*, 11:160–180.

BENOLIEL, JEANNE Q. 1975 "The realities of work: Commentary on Howard Leventhal's information-processing model," pp. 175–188 in *Humanizing health care*, J. Howard and A. Strauss (eds.). New York: Wiley-Interscience.

BENTSEN, CHERYL. 1991 *Maasai Days*. New York: Anchor.

BEN-SIRA, ZEEV. 1976 "The function of the professional's affective behavior in client satisfaction: A revised approach to social interaction theory." *Journal of Health and Social Behavior*, 17:3–11.

———. 1980 "Affective and instrumental components in the physician-patient relationship: An additional dimension of interaction theory." *Journal of Health and Social Behavior*, 21:170–180.

BERGER, PETER L., and THOMAS LUCKMANN. 1967 *The social construction of reality*. New York: Anchor.

BERKANOVIC, EMIL. 1972 "Lay conceptions of the sick role." *Social Forces*, 51:53–63.

BERKANOVIC, EMIL, and LEO G. REEDER. 1973 "Ethnic, economic, and social psychological factors in the source of medical care." *Social Problems*, 21:246–259.

———. 1974 "Can money buy the appropriate use of services? Some notes on the meaning of utilization data." *Journal of Health and Social Behavior*, 15:93–99.

BERKANOVIC, EMIL, CAROL TELESKY, and SHARON REEDER. 1981 "Structural and social psychological factors in the decision to seek medical care for symptoms." *Medical Care*, 19:693–709.

BERKMAN, LISA F. and LESTER BRESLOW. 1983 *Health and ways of living: The Alameda County study*. Fairlawn, N.J.: Oxford University Press.

BICE, T. W., R. L. EICHHORN, and P. D. FOX. 1972 "Socioeconomic status and use of physician services: A reconsideration." *Medical Care*, 10:261–271.

BIRD, CHOLE E., and ALLEN M. FREMONT. 1991 "Gender, time use, and health." *Journal of Health and Social Behavior*, 32:114–129.

BLACKBURN, CLARE. 1991 *Poverty and Health*. Milton Keynes, U.K.: Open University Press.

BLACK REPORT. 1980 *Inequalities in health: Report on a research working group*. London: Department of Health and Social Services.

BLACKWELL, ELIZABETH. 1902 *Essays in medical sociology*. London: Bell.

BLAIR, STEVEN N., HAROLD W. KOHL III, RALPH S. PAFFENBARGER, DEBRA G. CLARK, KENNETH H. COOPER, and LARRY W. GIBBONS. 1989 "Physical fitness and all-cause mortality." *Journal of the American Medical Association*, 262:2395–2401.

BLAXTER, MILDRED. 1983 "Health services as a defence against the consequences of poverty in industrialised societies." *Social Science and Medicine*, 17:1139–1148.

———. 1990 *Health and lifestyles*. London: Tavistock.

BLAXTER, MILDRED, and RICHARD CYSTER. 1984 "Compliance and risk-taking: The case of alcohol liver disease." *Sociology of Health and Illness*, 6:290–310.

BLOOM, SAMUEL W. 1963 *The doctor and his patient*. New York: The Free Press.

———. 1973 *Power and dissent in the medical school*. New York: The Free Press.

———. 1986 "Institutional trends in medical sociology." *Journal of Health and Social Behavior*, 27:265–277.

———. 1988 "Structure and ideology in medical education: An analysis of resistance to change." *Journal of Health and Social Behavior*, 29:294–306.

———. 1990 "Episodes in the institutionalization of medical sociology: A personal view." *Journal of Health and Social Behavior*, 31:1–10.

BOOTH, ALAN, and PAUL AMATO. 1991 "Divorce and psychological stress." *Journal of Health and Social Behavior*, 32:396–407.

BOSANQUET, NICK. 1988 "An ailing state of national health," pp. 93–108 in *British social attitudes, the 5th report*, R. Jowell, S. Witherspoon, and L. Brook (eds.). Aldershot, U.K.: Gower.

BOSK, CHARLES L. 1979 *Forgive and remember: Managing medical failure*. Chicago: University of Chicago Press.

BOSK, CHARLES L., and JOEL E. FRADER. 1990 "AIDS and its impact on medical work: The culture and politics of the shop floor." *Milbank Quarterly*, 68, 1:257–279.

BOULTON, MARY, DAVID TUCKETT, CORAL OLSON, and ANTHONY WILLIAMS. 1986 "Social class and the general practice consultation." *Sociology of Health and Illness*, 8:325–350.

BOURNE, PETER. 1970 *Men, stress, and Vietnam*. Boston: Little, Brown.

BOWLING, ANNE. 1981 Delegation in general practice: A study of doctors and nurses. London: Tavistock.

BRAITHWAITE, RONALD L., and SANDRA E. TAYLOR (eds.). 1992 *Health issues in the black community*. San Francisco: Jossey-Bass.

BRENNER, M. HARVEY. 1973 *Mental illness and the economy*. Cambridge, Mass.: Harvard University Press.

———. 1987a "Economic change, alcohol consumption and disease mortality in nine industrialized countries." *Social Science and Medicine*, 25:119–132.

———. 1987b "Relation of economic change to Swedish health and social well-being, 1950–1980." *Social Science and Medicine*, 25:183–196.

BRENNER, M. HARVEY, and ANNE MOONEY. 1983 "Unemployment and health in the context of economic change." *Social Science and Medicine*, 17:1125–1138.

BROADHEAD, ROBERT S. 1983 *The private lives and professional identity of medical students*. New Brunswick, N.J.: Transaction.

BROOKS, CHARLES H. 1980 "Social, economic, and biologic correlates of infant mortality in city neighborhoods." *Journal of Health and Social Behavior*, 21:2–11.

BROOKS-GUNN, JEANNE, and FRANK F. FURSTENBERG. 1990 "Coming of age in the era of AIDS: Puberty, sexuality and contraception." *Milbank Quarterly*, 68, no. 1:59–84.

BROWN, E. RICHARD. 1979 *Rockefeller medicine men: Medicine and capitalism in America*. Berkeley: University of California Press.

BROWN, GEORGE W., and TIRRIL HARRIS. 1978 *Social origins of depression: A study of psychiatric disorder in women*, New York: The Free Press.

BROWN, JULIA S., and MAY E. RAWLINSON. 1977 "Sex differences in sick role rejection and in work performance following cardiac surgery." *Journal of Health and Social Behavior* 18:276–292.

BROWN, LAWRENCE D. 1986 "Introduction to a decade of transition." *Journal of Health Politics, Policy and Law*, 11:569–584.

BROWN, PHIL. 1993 "Health policy notes." *Medical Sociology Newsletter*, Fall:4–8.

BURDYS, GRACE. 1987 *Planning for the nation's health: A study of twentieth-century developments in the United States*. Westport, Conn.: Greenwood Press.

BURY, MICHAEL. 1991 "The sociology of chronic illness: A review of research and prospects." *Sociology of Health and Illness*, 13:451–468.

CALNAN, MICHAEL. 1987 *Health & illness: The lay perspective.* London: Tavistock.

———. 1989 "Control over health and patterns of health-related behaviour." *Social Science and Medicine*, 29:131–136.

CAMPBELL, JOHN D. 1978 "The child in the sick role: Contributions of age, sex, parental status, and parental values." *Journal of Health and Social Behavior*, 19:35–51.

CANNON, WALTER B. 1932 *The wisdom of the body.* New York: W. W. Norton & Co., Inc.

CARPENTER, MICK. 1993 "The subordination of nurses in health care: Towards a social divisions approach," pp. 95–130 in *Gender, work and medicine*, E. Riska and K. Wegar (eds.). London: Sage.

CARTWRIGHT, ANN. 1964 *Human relations and hospital care.* London: Routledge & Kegan Paul.

CASSELL, ERIC J. 1985 *Talking with patients, Vol. 2.* Cambridge, Mass.: MIT Press.

———. 1986 "The changing concept of the ideal physician." *Daedalus*, 115:185–208.

CATALANO, RALPH, and C. DAVID DOOLEY. 1977 "Economic predictors of depressed mood and stressful life events in a metropolitan community." *Journal of Health and Social Behavior*, 18:292–307.

CAWLEY, JAMES F. 1985 "The physician assistant profession: Current status and future trends." *Journal of Public Health Policy*, 6:78–99.

CENTERS FOR DISEASE CONTROL AND PREVENTION. 1987 "Protective effect of physical activity on coronary heart disease." *Morbidity and Mortality Weekly Report*, 36 (July 10): 426–430.

CHALFANT, H. PAUL, and RICHARD KURTZ. 1971 "Alcoholics and the sick role: Assessments by social workers." *Journal of Health and Social Behavior*, 12:66–72.

CHARMAZ, KATHY. 1983 "Loss of self: A fundamental form of suffering in the chronically ill." *Sociology of Health and Illness*, 5:168–195.

———. 1991 *Good days, bad days: The self in chronic illness and time.* New Brunswick, N.J.: Rutgers University Press.

CHILDS, DAVID, and JEFFREY JOHNSON. 1981 *West Germany: Politics and society.* London: Croom Helm.

CLAIR, JEFFREY MICHAEL. 1993 "The application of social science to medical practice," pp. 12–28 in *Sociomedical Perspectives on Patient Care*, J. Clair and R. Allman, (eds.). Lexington, KY: University of Kentucky Press.

CLARK, MARGARET. 1959 *Health in the Mexican-American culture.* Berkeley: University of California Press.

CLAUS, LISABETH M. 1983 "The development of medical sociology in Europe." *Social Science and Medicine*, 17:1591–1597.

CLEARY, PAUL D., and DAVID MECHANIC. 1983 "Sex differences in psychological distress among married people." *Journal of Health and Social Behavior*, 24:111–121.

CLEARY, PAUL D., DAVID MECHANIC, and JAMES R. GREENLEY. 1982 "Sex differences in medical care utilization: An empirical investigation." *Journal of Health and Social Behavior*, 23:106–119.

COCKERHAM, WILLIAM C. 1983 "The state of medical sociology in the United States, Great Britain, West Germany, and Austria." *Social Science and Medicine*, 17:1513–1527.

———. 1988 "Medical sociology," pp. 575–599 in *Handbook of Sociology*, N. Smelser (ed.). Newbury Park, Calif.: Sage.

———. 1990 "A Test of the relationship between race, socioeconomic status, and psychological distress." *Social Science and Medicine*, 31:1321–1326.

———. 1991 *This aging society.* Englewood Cliffs, N.J.: Prentice Hall.

———. 1992 *Sociology of mental disorder*, 3rd Ed. Englewood Cliffs, N.J.: Prentice Hall.

COCKERHAM, WILLIAM C., THOMAS ABEL, and GUNTHER LÜESCHEN. 1993 "Max Weber, formal rationality, and health lifestyles." *Sociological Quarterly*, 34:413–425.

COCKERHAM, WILLIAM C., MORTON C. CREDITOR, UNA K. CREDITOR, and PETER B. IMREY. 1980 "Minor ailments and illness behavior among physicians." *Medical Care*, 18:164–173.

COCKERHAM, WILLIAM C., GERHARD KUNZ, and GUENTHER LUESCHEN. 1988a "Social stratification and health lifestyles in two systems of health care delivery: A comparison of America and West Germany." *Journal of Health and Social Behavior*, 29:113–126.

———. 1988b "Psychological distress, perceived health status, and physician utilization in America and West Germany." *Social Science and Medicine*, 26:829–838.

COCKERHAM, WILLIAM C., GUENTHER LUESCHEN, GERHARD KUNZ, and JOE L. SPAETH. 1986a "Social stratification and self-management of health." *Journal of Health and Social Behavior*, 27:1–14.

———. 1986b "Symptoms, social stratification, and self-responsibility for health in the United States and West Germany." *Social Science and Medicine*, 22:1263–1271.

COCKERHAM, WILLIAM C., KIMBERLY SHARP, and JULIE WILCOX. 1983 "Aging and perceived health status." *Journal of Gerontology*, 38:349–355.

COE, RODNEY M. 1978 *Sociology of medicine*, 2nd ed. New York: McGraw-Hill.

COHEN, J. B., S. L. SYME, C. D. JENKINS, A. KAGAN, and S. J. ZYZANSKI. 1979 "Cultural context of type A behavior and risk for CHD: A study of Japanese American males." *Journal of Behavioral Medicine*, 2:375–384.

COLE, STEPHEN. 1986 "Sex discrimination and admission to medical school, 1929–1984." *American Journal of Sociology*, 92:529–567.

COLE, STEPHEN, and ROBERT LEJEUNE. 1972 "Illness and the legitimation of failure." *American Sociological Review*, 37:347–356.

COLUMBOTOS, JOHN. 1969 "Social origins and ideology of physicians: A study of the effects of early socialization." *Journal of Health and Social Behavior*, 10:16–29.

CONGER, RAND D., FREDERICK O. LORENZ, GLEN H. ELDER, JR., RONALD L. SIMONS, and XIAOJIA GE. 1993 "Husband and wife differences in response to undesirable life events." *Journal of Health and Social Behavior*, 34:71–88.

CONRAD, PETER. 1975 "The discovery of hyperkinesis: Note on the medicalization of deviant behavior." *Social Problems*, 23:12–21.

———. 1986a "The social meaning of AIDS." *Social Policy*, 21:51–56.

———. 1986b "The myth of cut-throats among premedical students: On the role of stereotypes in justifying failure and success." *Journal of Health and Social Behavior*, 27:150–160.

———. 1988a "Health and fitness at work: A participant's perspective." *Social Science and Medicine*, 26:545–550.

———. 1988b "Learning to doctor: Reflections on recent accounts of the medical school years." *Journal of Health and Social Behavior*, 29:323–332.

CONRAD, PETER, and JOSEPH W. SCHNEIDER. 1980 *Deviance and medicalization: From badness to sickness*. St. Louis: Mosby.

COOLEY, CHARLES H. 1962 *Social organization*. New York: Schocken.

———. 1964 *Human nature and the social order*. New York: Schocken.

COOMBS, ROBERT H. 1978 *Mastering medicine: Professional socialization in medical school*. New York: The Free Press.

COSER, ROSE L. 1956 "A home away from home." *Social Problems*, 4:3–17.

COULTON, CLAUDA, and ABBIE K. FROST. 1982 "Use of social and health services by the elderly." *Journal of Health and Social Behavior*, 23:330–339.

CRANDALL, LEE A., and R. PAUL DUNCAN. 1981 "Attitudinal and situational factors in the use of physician services by low-income persons." *Journal of Health and Social Behavior*, 22:64–77.

CRAWFORD, ROBERT. 1984 "A cultural account of health: Control, release, and the social body," pp. 60–103 in *Issues in the political economy of health care*, J. McKinley (ed.). New York: Tavistock.

CROOG, SYDNEY H., and DONNA F. VER STEEG. 1972. "The hospital as a social system," pp. 274–314 in *Handbook of medical sociology*, 2nd ed., H. Feeman, S. Levine, and L. Reeder (eds.). Englewood Cliffs, N.J.: Prentice Hall.

CRUMP, JEREMY. 1989 "Athletics," pp. 44–77 in *Sport in Britain: A social history*. Cambridge, U.K.: Cambridge University Press.

CUMPER, G. E. 1983 "Jamaica: A case study in health development." *Social Science and Medicine*, 17:1983–93.

DAHRENDORF, RALF. 1979 *Life chances*. Chicago: University of Chicago Press.

———. 1990 *Reflections on the Revolution in Europe*. New York: Random House.

DAVIDSON, LAURIE, and LAURA KRAMER GORDON. 1979 *The sociology of gender*. Chicago: Rand McNally.

DAVIS, CHRISTOPHER M. 1989 "The Soviet health system: A national health service in a socialist society," pp. 233–262 in *Success and crisis in national health systems*, M. Field (ed.). London: Routledge.

DAVIS, FRED. 1966 "Problems and issues in collegiate nursing education," pp. 138–175 in *The nursing profession*, F. Davis (ed.). New York: John Wiley.

———. 1972 *Illness, interaction, and the self*. Belmont, Calif.: Wadsworth.

DAVIS, FRED, and VIRGINIA OLESEN. 1963 "Initiation into a women's profession: Identity problems in the status transition of coed to student nurse," *Sociometry*, 26:89–101.

DAVIS, HOWARD H. 1992 "Social stratification in Europe," pp. 17–35 in *Social Europe*, J. Bailey (ed.). London: Longman.

DAVIS, MARADEE A. 1981 "Sex differences in reporting osteoarthritic symptoms: A sociomedical approach." *Journal of Health and Social Behavior*, 22:298–310.

DAWBER, THOMAS R., WILLIAM B. KANNEL, and LORNA P. LYELL. 1963 "An approach to longitudinal studies in the community: The Framingham study." *Annals of the New York Academy of Sciences*, 107:539–566.

DAY, PATRICIA, and RUDOLF KLEIN. 1991 "Britain's health care experiment." *Health Affairs*, Fall:39–59.

DEAN, ALFRED, BOHDAN KOLODY, and PATRICIA WOOD. 1990 "Effects of social support from various sources on depression in elderly persons." *Journal of Health and Social Behavior*, 31:148–161.

DEAN, KATHRYN. 1989 "Self-care components of lifestyles: The importance of gender, attitudes and the social situation." *Social Science and Medicine*, 29:137–152.

DE BEER, CEDRIC. 1986 *The South African disease: Apartheid health and health services*. Trenton, N.J.: African World Press.

DEFRIESE, GORDON H., and JO ANNE EARP. 1989 "Care and treatment of acute illness," pp. 205–235 in *Handbook of Medical Sociology*, 4th ed., H. Freeman and S. Levine (eds.). Englewood Cliffs, N.J.: Prentice Hall.

DENTON, JOHN A. 1978 *Medical sociology*. Boston: Houghton Mifflin.

DEVRIES, RAYMOND G. 1993 "A cross-national view of the status of midwives," pp. 131–146 in *Gender, work and medicine*, E. Riska and K. Wegar (eds.). London: Sage.

DEWOLFF, P., and J. MEERDINK. 1954 "Mortality rates in Amsterdam according to profession," pp. 53–55 in *Proceedings of the world population conference*, Vol. 1. New York: United Nations.

D'HOUTAUD, A., and MARK G. FIELD. 1984 "The image of health: Variations in perception by social class in a French population." *Sociology of Health and Illness*, 6:30–59.

————. 1986 "New research on the image of health," pp. 233–258 in *Concepts of health, illness and disease*, C. Currer and M. Stacey (eds.). Leamington Spa, U.K.: Berg.

DIDERICHSEN, FINN. 1990 "Health and social inequities in Sweden." *Social Science and Medicine*, 31:359–367.

DOHRENWEND, BARBARA S. 1973 "Life events as stressors: A methodological inquiry." *Journal of Health and Social Behavior*, 14:167–175.

DOHRENWEND, BARBARA S., LARRY KRASNOFF, ALEXANDER R. ASKENSASY, and BRUCE P. DOHRENWEND. 1978 "Exemplification of a method for scaling life events: The PERI life events scale." *Journal of Health and Social Behavior*, 19:205–229.

DOHRENWEND, BRUCE P. 1975 "Sociocultural and social-psychological factors in the genesis of mental disorders." *Journal of Health and Social Behavior*, 16:365–392.

DOHRENWEND, BRUCE P. and BARBARA SNELL DOHRENWEND. 1981 "Life stress and illness: Formulation of the issues," pp. 1–27 in *Stressful life events and their contexts*, B. Dohrenwend and B. Dohrenwend (eds.). New York: Prodist.

DOOLEY, DAVID, and RALPH CATALANO. 1984 "Why the economy predicts help-seeking: A test of competing explanations." *Journal of Health and Social Behavior*, 25:160–176.

DREWS, FREDERICK A. 1986 *A healthy life: Exercise, behavior, nutrition.* Benchmark Press.

DUBOS, RENÉ. 1959 *Mirage of health.* New York: Harper & Row.

————. 1969 *Man, medicine, and environment.* New York: Mentor.

————. 1981 "Health and creative adaptation," pp. 6–13 in *The nation's health*, P. Lee, N. Brown, and I. Red (eds.). San Francisco: Boyd & Fraser.

DUFF, RAYMOND S., and AUGUST B. HOLLINGSHEAD. 1968 *Sickness and society*, New York: Harper & Row.

DURBIN, RICHARD L., and W. HERBERT SPRINGALL. 1974 *Organization and administration of health care.* St. Louis, Mo.: C. V. Mosby.

DURKHEIM, EMILE. 1950 *The rules of sociological method.* New York: The Free Press.

————. 1951 *Suicide.* New York: The Free Press.

————. 1956 *The division of labor in society.* New York: The Free Press.

————. 1961 *The elementary forms of religious life.* New York: Collier.

DUTTON, DIANA B. 1978 "Explaining the low use of health services by the poor: Costs, attitudes, or delivery systems? *American Sociological Review*, 43:348–368.

————. 1979 "Patterns of ambulatory health care in five different delivery systems." *Medical Care*, 17:221–241.

————. 1986 "Social class, health, and illness," pp. 31–62 in *Applications of social science to clinical medicine and health policy*, L. Aiken and D. Mechanic (eds.). New Brunswick, N.J.: Rutgers University Press.

DWYER, JEFFREY W., LESLIE L. CLARKE, and MICHAEL K. MILLER. 1990 "The effect of religious concentration and affiliation on country mortality rates," *Journal of Health and Social Behavior*, 31:185–202.

EARICKSON, ROBERT J. 1990 "International behavioral responses to a health hazard: AIDS." *Social Science and Medicine*, 31:951–962.

ECKBERG, DOUGLAS LEE. 1987 "The dilemma of osteopathic physicians and the rationalization of medical practice." *Social Science and Medicine*, 25:1111–1120.

EHRENREICH, BARBARA, and DIERDRE ENGLISH. 1979 "The 'sick' women of the upper classes," pp. 123–143 in *The cultural crisis of modern medicine*, J. Ehrenreich (ed.). New York: Monthly Review Press.

EHRENREICH, JOHN. 1978 "Introduction: The cultural crisis of modern medicine," pp. 1–35 in *The cultural crisis of modern medicine*, J. Ehrenreich (ed.). New York: Monthly Review Press.

EITINGER, L. 1964 *Concentration camp survivors in Norway and Israel.* London: Allen & Unwin.

————. 1973 "A followup of the Norwegian concentration camp survivors." *Israel Annals of Psychiatry and Related Disciplines,* 11:199–209.

ELDER, R. G. 1963 "What is the patient saying?" *Nursing Forum,* 2:25–37.

ELINSON, JACK. 1985 "The end of medicine and the end of medical sociology." *Journal of Health and Social Behavior,* 26:268–275.

ELLING, RAY H. 1980 *Cross-national study of health systems.* New Brunswick, N.J.: Transaction.

ELLISON, CHRISTOPHER G. 1991 "Religious involvement and subjective well-being." *Journal of Health and Social Behavior,* 32:80–99.

ELSTON, MARY ANN. 1993 "Women doctors in a changing profession: The case of Britain," pp. 27–61 in *Gender, work and medicine,* E. Riska and K. Wegar (eds.). London: Sage.

ENGLE, GEORGE L. 1971 "Sudden and rapid death during psychological stress: folklore or folkwisdom?" *Annals of Internal Medicine,* 74:771–782.

————. 1977 "The need for a new medical model: A challenge for biomedicine." *Science,* 196:129–135.

ENSEL, WALTER M., and NAN LIN. 1991 "The life stress paradigm and psychological distress." *Journal of Health and Social Behavior,* 32:321–341.

ENTHOVEN, ALAIN C. 1991 "Internal market reform of the British health service." *Health Affairs,* Fall:60–70.

EVANS, ROBERT G. 1984 *Strained mercy: The economics of Canadian health care.* Toronto: Butterworth.

————. 1986 "Finding the levers, finding the courage: Lessons from cost containment in North America." *Journal of Health Politics, Policy and Law,* 11:585–616.

EVANS, ROBERT G., and GREGORY L. STODDART. 1990 "Producing health, consuming health care." *Social Science and Medicine,* 31:1347–1364.

FAIRBANKS, DIANNE TIMBERS, and RICHARD L. HOUGH. 1981 "Cross-cultural differences in perceptions of life events," pp. 63–84 in *Stressful life events and their contexts,* B. Dohrenwend and B. Dohrenwend (eds.). New York: Prodist.

FARIS, ROBERT E. and H. WARREN DUNHAM. 1939 *Mental disorders in urban areas.* Chicago: University of Chicago Press.

FEATHERSTONE, MIKE. 1987 "Lifestyle and consumer culture." *Theory, Culture and Society,* 4:5–70.

FENWICK, RUDY, and CHARLES M. BARRESI. 1981 "Health consequences of marital-status change among the elderly: A comparison of cross-sectional and longitudinal analyses." *Journal of Health and Social Behavior,* 22:106–116.

FERRARO, KENNETH F. 1980 "Self-ratings of health among the old and old-old." *Journal of Health and Social Behavior,* 21:377–383.

————. 1993 "Are black older adults health-pessimistic?" *Journal of Health and Social Behavior,* 34:201–214.

FERRARO, KENNETH F., and TAMMY SOUTHERLAND. 1989 "Domains of medical practice: Physicians' assessment of the role of physician extenders." *Journal of Health and Social Behavior,* 30:192–205.

FIELD, MARK G. 1967 *Soviet socialized medicine: An introduction.* New York: The Free Press.

————. 1985 "Soviet life, 1985: In sickness and health." *Wilson Quarterly,* Autumn:1–14.

————. (ed.). 1989 *Success and crisis in national health systems.* London: Routledge.

FIELDING, JONATHAN E., and PIERRE-JEAN LANCRY. 1993 "Lessons from France—'Vive la différence.' " *Journal of the American Medical Association,* 270:748–756.

FILLENBAUM, GERDA G. 1979 "Social context and self-assessment of health among the elderly." *Journal of Health and Social Behavior*, 20:45–51.

FIORENTINE, ROBERT. 1987 "Men, women, and the premed persistence: A normative alternatives approach." *American Journal of Sociology*, 92:1118–1139.

FISHER, SUE. 1984 "Doctor-patient communication: A social and micro-political performance." *Sociology of Health and Illness*, 6:1–27.

FISHER, SUE, and ALEXANDRA DUNDAS TODD. 1990 *The social organization of doctor-patient communication*, 2nd Ed. Norwood, N.J.: Ablex.

FITTON, FREDA, and H. W. K. ACHESON. 1979 *The doctor/patient relationship: A study in general practice*. London: Department of Health and Social Security.

FITZPATRICK, RAY, and GRAHAM SCAMBLER. 1984 "Social class, ethnicity, and illness," pp. 54–86 in *The experience of illness*, R. Fitzpatrick, J. Hinton, S. Newman, G. Scrambler, and J. Thompson (eds.). London: Tavistock.

FLAHERTY, JOSEPH, and JUDITH RICHMAN. 1989 "Gender differences in the perception and utilization of social support: Theoretical perspectives and an empirical test." *Social Science and Medicine*, 28:1221–1228.

FLOGE, LILIANE, and DEBORAH M. MERRILL. 1986 "Tokenism reconsidered: Male nurses and female physicians in a hospital setting." *Social Forces*, 64:925–947.

FLOOD, ANN BARRY, and W. RICHARD SCOTT. 1978 "Professional power and professional effectiveness: The power of the surgical staff and the quality of surgical care in hospitals." *Journal of Health and Social Behavior*, 19:240–254.

FOSU, GABRIEL B. 1989 "Access to health care in urban areas of developing societies." *Journal of Health and Social Behavior*, 30:398–411.

FOUCAULT, MICHEL. 1973 *The birth of the clinic*. London: Tavistock.

FOX, A.J. (ed.). 1989 *Health inequalities in European countries*. Aldershot, U.K.: Gower.

FOX, JOHN W. 1980 "Gore's specific sex-role theory of mental illness: A research note." *Journal of Health and Social Behavior*, 21:260–267.

FOX, RENÉE. 1957 "Training for uncertainty," pp. 207–241 in *The student-physician*, R. K. Merton, G. Reader, and P. L. Kendall (eds.). Cambridge, Mass.: Harvard University Press.

———. 1985 "Reflections and opportunities in the sociology of medicine." *Journal of Health and Social Behavior*, 26:6–14.

FOX, RENÉE C., LINDA H. AIKEN, and CARLA MESSIKOMER. 1990 "The culture of caring: AIDS and the nursing profession." *Milbank Quarterly*, 67:226–258.

FREEBORN, DONALD K., and BENJAMIN J. DARSKY. 1974 "A study of the power structure of the medical community," *Medical Care*, 12:1–12.

FREEMAN, HOWARD E., and SOL LEVINE. 1989 "The present status of medical sociology," pp. 1–13 in *Handbook of medical sociology*, 4th ed., H. Freeman and S. Levine (eds.). Englewood Cliffs, N.J.: Prentice Hall.

FREEMAN, HOWARD E., SOL LEVINE, and LEO G. REEDER. 1972 "Present status of medical sociology," pp. 501–522 in *Handbook of medical sociology*, 2nd ed., H. Freeman, S. Levine, and L. Reeder (eds.). Englewood Cliffs, N.J.: Prentice Hall.

FREIDSON, ELIOT. 1960 "Client control and medical practice." *American Journal of Sociology*, 65:374–382.

———. 1970a *Profession of medicine*. New York: Dodd, Mead.

———. 1970b *Professional dominance*. Chicago: Aldine.

———. 1975 *Doctoring together*. New York: Elsevier North-Holland.

———. 1989 *Medical work in America: essays on health care*. New Haven, Conn.: Yale University Press.

FREUND, PETER E. S., and MEREDITH B. MCGUIRE. 1991 *Health, illness, and the social body.* Englewood Cliffs, N.J.: Prentice Hall.

FRIEDMAN, MEYER, and RAY H. ROSENMAN. 1974 *Type A behavior and your heart.* New York: Fawcett.

FRIES, JAMES F. 1980 "Aging, natural death, and the compression of morbidity." *New England Journal of Medicine*, 303:130–135.

FUCHS, VICTOR R. 1974 *Who shall live?* New York: Basic Books.

———. 1986 *The health economy.* Cambridge, Mass.: Harvard University Press.

FUCHS, VICTOR R., and JAMES S. HAHN. 1990 "How does Canada do it? A comparison of expenditures for physicians' services in the United States and Canada." *New England Journal of Medicine*, 323:884–890.

FULLER, THEODORE D., JOHN N. EDWARDS, SANTHAT SERMSRI, and SAIRUDEE VORAKITPHOKATORN. 1993 "Gender and health: Some Asian evidence." *Journal of Health and Social Behavior*, 34:252–271.

FUNCH, DONNA P., and JAMES R. MARSHALL. 1984 "Measuring life stress: Factors affecting fall-off in the reporting of life events." *Journal of Health and Social Behavior*, 25:453–464.

GALLAGHER, EUGENE B. 1976 "Lines of reconstruction and extension in the Parsonian sociology of illness." *Social Science and Medicine*, 10:207–218.

———. 1988a "Modernization and medical care." *Sociological Perspectives*, 31:59–87.

———. 1988b "Convergence or divergence in third world medical education? An Arab study." *Journal of Health and Social Behavior*, 29:385–400.

———. 1989 "Sociological studies of third world health and health care: An introduction." *Journal of Health and Social Behavior*, 30:345–352.

GALLAGHER, EUGENE B., and C. MAUREEN SEARLE. 1984 "Cultural forces in the formation of the Saudi medical role." *Medical Anthropology*, 8:210–221.

———. 1985 "Health services and the political culture of Saudi Arabia." *Social Science and Medicine*, 21:251–262.

———. 1989 "Content and context in health professional education," pp. 437–454 in *Handbook of medical sociology*, 4th ed., H. Freeman and S. Levine (eds.). Englewood Cliffs, N.J.: Prentice Hall.

GALVIN, MICHAEL L., and MARGARET FAN. 1975 "The utilization of physicians' services in Los Angeles County, 1973." *Journal of Health and Social Behavior*, 16:75–94.

GATCHEL, ROBERT J., ANDREW BAUM, and DAVID S. KRANTZ. 1989 *An introduction to health psychology.* New York: Random House.

GAY, E. GREER, JENNIE J. KRONENFELD, SAMUEL L. BAKER, and ROGER L. AMIDON. 1989 "An appraisal of organizational response to fiscally constraining regulation: The case of hospitals and DRGs." *Journal of Health and Social Behavior*, 30:41–55.

GEERTSEN, REED, MELVILLE R. KLAUBER, MARK RINDFLESH, ROBERT L. KANE, and ROBERT GRAY. 1975 "A re-examination of Suchman's views on social factors in health care utilization." *Journal of Health and Social Behavior*, 16:226–237.

GEIGER, H. JACK. 1975 "The causes of dehumanization in health care and prospects for humanization," pp. 11–36 in *Humanizing health care*, J. Howard and A. Strauss (eds.). New York: Wiley-Interscience.

GEORGOPOULOS, BASIL F., and FLOYD C. MANN. 1972 "The hospital as an organization," pp. 304–311 in *Patients, physicians and illness*, 2nd ed., E. Jaco (ed.). New York: Macmillan.

GERHARDT, UTA. 1989a *Ideas about illness: An intellectual and political history of medical sociology.* London: Macmillan.

———. 1989b "The sociological image of medicine and the patient." *Social Science and Medicine*, 29:721–728.

———. 1989c "Sociology on medicine: Understanding medical sociology's critical stand-point," pp. 31–48 in *Health and illness in America and Germany*, G. Lüschen, W. Cockerham, and G. Kunz (eds.). Munich: Oldenbourg.

GERTH, H. H., and C. WRIGHT MILLS (eds.). 1946 *From Max Weber: Essays in sociology*. New York: Oxford University Press.

GIBBS, JACK. 1971 "A critique of the labeling perspective," pp. 193–205 in *The study of social problems*, Earl Rubington and Martin S. Weinberg (eds.). New York: Oxford University Press.

GILL, DEREK. 1994 "A national health service: Principles and practice," pp. 480–494 in *The sociology of health and illness: Critical perspectives*, 4th Ed., P. Conrad and R. Kern (eds.). New York: St. Martin's Press.

GILLICK, MURIEL R. 1984 "Health promotion, jogging, and the pursuit of the moral life." *Journal of Health Politics, Policy and Law*, 9:369–387.

GINZBERG, ELI. 1991 "Access to health care for Hispanics." *Journal of the American Medical Association*, 265:238–241.

GLASER, BARNEY G., and ANSELM M. STRAUSS. 1965 *Awareness of dying*. Chicago: Aldine.

GLASER, WILLIAM A. 1987 *Paying the hospital*. San Francisco: Jossey-Bass.

GLASSNER, BARRY. 1988 *Bodies*. New York: G. P. Putnam.

———. 1989 "Fitness and the postmodern self." *Journal of Health and Social Behavior*, 30:180–191.

GLIK, DEBORAH C. 1990 "The redefinition of the situation: The social construction of spiritu-al healing experiences." *Sociology of Health and Illness*, 12:151–168.

GLIK, DEBORAH C., WILLIAM B.WARD, ANDREW GORDON, and FASSU HABA. 1989 "Malaria treatment practices among mothers in Guinea." *Journal of Health and Social Behavior*, 30:421–435.

GOCHMAN, D. S. 1971 "Some correlates of children's health care beliefs and potential behav-ior." *Journal of Health and Social Behavior*, 12:148–154.

GOFFMAN, ERVING. 1959 *The presentation of self in everyday life*. New York: Anchor.

———. 1961 *Asylums*. New York: Anchor.

GOLD, MARSHA R. 1991 "HMOs and managed care." *Health Affairs*, 10:189–206.

GOLDBERG, KENNETH C., ARTHUR J. HARTZ, STEVEN J. JACOBSEN, HENRY KRAKAUER, and ALFRED A. RIMM. 1992 "Racial and community factors influencing coronary artery bypass graft surgery rates for all 1986 Medicare patients." *Journal of the American Medical Association*, 267:1473–1477.

GOLDSTEIN, MICHAEL S. 1992 *The health movement: Promoting fitness in America*. New York: Twayne.

GOOD, CHARLES M. 1987 *Ethnomedical systems in Africa*. New York: Guilford.

GOODE, WILLIAM J. 1957 "Community within a community." *American Sociological Review*, 22:194–200.

———. 1960 "Encroachment, charlatanism, and the emerging profession: Psychology, soci-ology, and medicine," *American Sociological Review*, 25:902–914.

GORDON, GERALD. 1966 *Role theory and illness*. New Haven, Conn.: College and University Press.

GORE, SUSAN. 1978 "The effect of social support in moderating the health consequences of unemployment." *Journal of Health and Social Behavior*, 19:157–165.

———. 1981 "Stress-buffering functions of social supports: An appraisal and clarification of research models," pp. 202–222 in *Stressful life events and their contexts*, B. Dohrenwend and B. Dohrenwend (eds.). New York: Prodist.

———. 1989 "Social networks and social supports in health care," pp. 306–331 in *Handbook of medical sociology*, 4th ed., H. Freeman and S. Levine (eds.). Englewood Cliffs, N.J.: Prentice Hall.

GORE, SUSAN, ROBERT H. ASELTINE, JR., and MARY ELLEN COLTON. 1992 "Social structure, life stress, and depressive symptoms in a high school-aged population." *Journal of Health and Social Behavior*, 33:97–113.

GORE, SUSAN, and THOMAS W. MANGIONE. 1983 "Social roles, sex roles, and psychological distress: Additive and interactive models of sex differences." *Journal of Health and Social Behavior*, 24:300–312.

GORTMAKER, STEVEN L. 1979 "Poverty and infant mortality in the United States." *American Sociological Review*, 44:280–297.

GORTMAKER, STEVEN L., JOHN ECKENRODE, and SUSAN GORE. 1982 "Stress and the utilization of health services: A time series and cross-sectional analysis." *Journal of Health and Social Behavior*, 23:25–38.

GOSS, MARY E. 1963 "Patterns of bureaucracy among hospital staff physicians," pp. 170–194 in *The hospital in modern society*, E. Freidson (ed.). New York: The Free Press.

GOULDNER, ALVIN. 1970 *The coming crisis of western sociology*. New York: Basic Books.

GOVE, WALTER R., and MICHAEL HUGHES. 1979 "Possible causes of the apparent sex differences in physical health: An empirical investigation." *American Sociological Review*, 44:126–146.

GOVE, WALTER R., MICHAEL HUGHES, and CAROLYN BRIGGS STYLE. 1983 "Does marriage have positive effects on the psychological well-being of the individual?" *Journal of Health and Social Behavior*, 24:122–131.

GOVE, WALTER R., and JEANNETTE F. TUDOR. 1973 "Adult sex roles and mental illness." *American Journal of Sociology*, 78:812–835.

GRAHAM, SAXON. 1972 "Cancer, culture, and social structure," pp. 31–39 in *Patients, physicians and illness*, 2nd ed., E. Jaco (ed.). New York: The Free Press.

GRAHAM, SAXON, and LEO G. REEDER. 1972 "Social factors in chronic illness," pp. 63–107 in *Handbook of medical sociology*, 2nd ed., H. Freeman, S. Levine, and L. Reeder (eds.). Englewood Cliffs, N.J.: Prentice Hall.

GRAIG, LAURENCE A. 1993 *Health of nations*, 2nd ed. Washington, D.C.: Congressional Quarterly, Inc.

GREEN, HARVEY. 1986. Fit for America: Health, fitness, sport, and American society. New York: Pantheon.

GREENLEY, JAMES R., and RICHARD A. SCHOENHERR. 1981 "Organization effects on client satisfaction with humaneness of service." *Journal of Health and Social Behavior*, 22:2–18.

GREY, BRADFORD H. 1991 *The profit motive and patient care: The changing accountability of doctors and hospitals*. Cambridge, Mass.: Harvard University Press.

GUILLEMARD, ANNE-MARIE. 1986 "State, society and old-age policy in France: From 1945 to the current crisis." *Social Science and Medicine*, 23:1319–1326.

HAAS, JACK, and WILLIAM SHAFFIR. 1977 "The professionalization of medical students: Developing competence and a cloak of competence." *Symbolic Interaction*, 1:71–88.

———. 1982 "Taking on the role of doctor: A dramaturgical analysis of professionalization." *Symbolic Interaction*, 5:205–222.

HAFFERTY, FREDERIC W. 1986 "Physician oversupply as a socially constructed reality." *Journal of Health and Social Behavior*, 27:358–369.

HAINES, VALERIE A., and JEANNE S. HURLBERT. 1992 "Network range and health." *Journal of Health and Social Behavior*, 33:254–266.

HALL, OSWALD. 1946 "The informal organization of the medical profession." *Canadian Journal of Economics and Political Science*, 12:30–44.

———. 1948 "The stages of a medical career." *American Journal of Sociology*, 53:327–336.

HAM, CHRISTOPHER. 1992 *Health policy in Britain*, 3rd ed. London: Macmillan.

HAMILTON, V. LEE, CLIFFORD L. BROMAN, WILLIAM S. HOFFMAN, and DEBORAH S. RENNER. 1990 "Hard times and vulnerable people: Initial effects of plant closing on autoworkers' mental health." *Journal of Health and Social Behavior*, 31:123–140.

HAMMOND, JUDITH. 1980 "Biography building to insure the future: Women's negotiation of gender relevancy in medical school." *Symbolic Interaction*, 3:35–49.

HARE, A. PAUL. 1976 *Handbook of small group research*, 2nd ed. New York: The Free Press.

HARRIS, DANIEL M., and SHARON GUTEN. 1979 "Health-protective behavior: An exploratory study." *Journal of Health and Social Behavior*, 20:17–29.

HART, NICKY. 1986 "Inequalities in health: The individual versus the environment." *Journal of Royal Statistics Society*, 149:228–246.

———. 1989 "Sex, gender, and survival: Inequalities of life chances between European men and women," pp. 109–141 in *Health inequalities in European countries*, J. Fox (ed.). Aldershot, U.K.: Gower.

———. 1991 "The social and economic environment and human health," pp. 151–180 in *Oxford textbook of Public Health*, Vol. 1, W. Holland, R. Detels, and G. Knox (eds.). Oxford, U.K.: Oxford University Press.

HATTORI, HIROYUKI, STEPHEN M. SALZBERG, WINSTON P. KIANG, TATSUYA FUJIMIYA, YUTAKA TEJIMA, and JUNJI FURUNO. 1991 "The patient's right to information in Japan—Legal rules and doctor's opinions." *Social Science and Medicine*, 32:1007–1016.

HAUG, MARIE, HIROKO AKIYAMA, GEORGEANN TRYBAN, KYOICHI SONODA, and MAY WYKLE. 1989 *Social Science and Medicine*, 33:1011–1022.

HAUG, MARIE, and BEBE LAVIN. 1981 "Practitioner or patient—Who's in charge?" *Journal of Health and Social Behavior*, 22:212–229.

———. 1983 *Consumerism in medicine*. Beverly Hills, Calif.: Sage Publications, Inc.

HAYES, DIANE, and CATHERINE E. ROSS. 1987 "Concern with appearance, health beliefs, and eating habits." *Journal of Health and Social Behavior*, 20:17–29.

HAYES-BAUTISTA, DAVID E. 1976a "Modifying the treatment: Patient compliance, patient control, and medical care." *Social Science and Medicine*, 10:233–238.

———. 1976b "Termination of the patient-practitioner relationship: Divorce, patient style." *Journal of Health and Social Behavior*, 17:12–21.

HEINZELMANN, F. 1962 "Determinants of prophylaxis behavior with respect to rheumatic fever." *Journal of Health and Social Behavior*, 3:73–81.

HELZER, JOHN E. 1981 "Methodological issues in the interpretations of the consequences of extreme situations," pp. 108–129 in *Stressful life events and their contexts*, B. Dohrenwend and B. Dohrenwend (eds.). New York: Prodist.

HENDERSON, LAWRENCE J. 1935 "Physician and patient as a social system." *New England Journal of Medicine*, 212:819–823.

HERZLICH, CLAUDINE. 1973 *Health and illness*. London: Academic Press.

HERZLICH, CLAUDINE, and JANINE PIERRET. 1986 "Illness: Causes to meaning," pp. 71–96 in *Concepts of health, illness and disease*, C. Currer and M. Stacey (eds.). Leamington Spa, U.K.: Berg.

———. 1987 *Illness and self in society*, E. Forster (trans.). Baltimore, Md.: Johns Hopkins University Press.

HEYDEBRAND, WOLF V. 1973 *Hospital bureaucracy*. New York: Dunellen.

HILDRETH, CAROLYN J., and ELIJAH SAUNDERS. 1992 "Heart disease, stroke, and hypertension in blacks," pp. 90–105 in *Health issues in the black community*, R. Braithwaite and S. Taylor (eds.). San Francisco: Jossey-Bass.

HILLIER, SHEILA. 1987 "Rationalism, bureaucracy, and the organization of the health services: Max Weber's contribution to understanding modern health care systems," pp. 194–220 in *Sociological theory and medical sociology*, G. Scambler (ed.). London: Tavistock.

HINES, RALPH. 1972 "The health status of black Americans: Changing perspectives," pp. 40–50 in *Patients, physicians and illness*, 2nd ed., E. Jaco (ed.). New York: The Free Press.

HJERMANN, I., K. VELVE BYRE, I. HOLME, and P. LEREN. 1981 "Effect of diet and smoking intervention on the incidence of coronary heart disease." *Lancet*, 8259:1303–1310.

HOCHSCHILD, ARLIE RUSSELL. 1973 "A review of sex role research." *American Journal of Sociology*, 78:1011–1029.

HOFMANN, PAUL. 1990 *That fine Italian hand.* New York: Henry Holt.

HOLLINGSHEAD, AUGUST B. 1973 "Medical sociology: A brief review." *Milbank Memorial Fund Quarterly*, 51:531–542.

HOLLINGSHEAD, AUGUST B., and FREDERICK C. REDLICH. 1958 *Social class and mental illness: A community study.* New York: John Wiley.

HOLLINGSWORTH, J. ROGERS. 1981 "Inequality in levels of health in England and Wales, 1891–1971." *Journal of Health and Social Behavior*, 22:268–283.

HOLLMANN, W., H. LIESEN, R. ROST, H. HECK, and J. SATOMI. 1985 Präventive Kardiologie: Bewegungsmangel und körperliches Training aus epidemiologischer und experimenteller Sicht." *Zeitschrift für Kardiologie*, 74:46–54.

HOLLOWAY, JOSEPH E. (ed.). 1990 *Africanisms in American culture.* Bloomington: Indiana University Press.

HOLLOWAY, ROBERT G., JAY W. ARTIS, and WALTER E. FREEMAN. 1972 "The participation pattern of 'economic influentials' and their control of a hospital board of trustees," pp. 312–324 in *Patients, physicians, and illness*, 2nd ed., E. Jaco (ed.). New York: Macmillan.

HOLMES, T. H., and M. MASUDA. 1974 "Life change and illness susceptibility," pp. 45–72 in *Stressful life events: Their nature and effects*, B. S. Dohrenwend and B. P. Dohrenwend (eds.). New York: John Wiley.

HOLMES, T. H., and R. H. RAHE. 1967 "The social readjustment rating scale," *Journal of Psychosomatic Research*, 11:213–225.

HOLOHAN, ANN. 1977 "Diagnosis: The end of transition," pp. 87–97 in *Medical encounters: The experience of illness and treatment*, A. Davis and G. Horobin (eds.). New York: St. Martin's Press.

HOOKER, RODERICK S. 1991 "The military physician assistant." *Military Medicine*, 156:657–660.

HOUGH, RICHARD L., DIANNE TIMBERS FAIRBANKS, and ALMA M. GARCIA. 1976 "Problems in the ratio measurement of life stress." *Journal of Health and Social Behavior*, 17:70–82.

HOUSE, JAMES S. 1974 "Occupational stress and coronary heart disease." *Journal of Health and Social Behavior*, 15:12–27.

HOUSE, JAMES S., ANTHONY J. MCMICHAEL, JAMES A. WELLS, BERTON H. KAPLAN, and LAWRENCE R. LANDERMAN. 1979 "Occupational stress and health among factory workers." *Journal of Health and Social Behavior*, 27:139–160.

HOUSE, JAMES S., VICTOR STRECHER, HELEN L. METZNER, and CYNTHIA A. ROBBINS. 1986 "Occupational stress and health among men and women in the Tecumseh Community Health Study." *Journal of Health and Social Behavior*, 27:62–77.

HOWARD, JAN, and BARBARA L. HOLMAN. 1970 "The effects of race and occupation on hypertension mortality." *Milbank Memorial Fund Quarterly*, 48:263–296.

HOWARD, JAN, and ANSELM STRAUSS (eds.). 1975 *Humanizing health care.* New York: Wiley-Interscience.

HOWELL, MARY C. 1979 "Pediatricians and mothers," pp. 201–211 in *The cultural crisis of modern medicine*, J. Ehrenreich (ed.). New York: Monthly Review Press.

HUGHES, EVERETT C., HELEN MACGILL, and IRWIN DEUTSCHER. 1958 *Twenty thousand nurses tell their story.* Philadelphia: Lippincott.

HUMMER, ROBERT A. 1993 "Racial differences in infant mortality in the U.S.: An examination of social and health determinants." *Social Forces*, 72:529–554.

HUNT, CHARLES W. 1989 "Migrant labor and sexually transmitted disease: AIDS in Africa." *Journal of Health and Social Behavior*, 30:353–373.

HUPPMANN, GERNOT, and FRIEDRICH-WILHELM WILKER. 1988 *Medizinische psychologie medizinische soziologie.* Munich: Urban & Schwarzenberg.

HURLEY, ROGER. 1971 "The health crisis of the poor," pp. 83–112 in *The social organization of health*, P. Dreitzel (ed.). New York: Macmillan.

HYDE, DAVID R., and PAYSON WOLFF. 1954 "The American Medical Association: Power, purpose and politics in organized medicine." *Yale Law Journal*, 63:938–1022.

IDLER, ELLEN L. 1987 "Religious involvement and the health of the elderly: Some hypotheses and an initial test." *Social Forces*, 66:226–238.

IDLER, ELLEN L., and STANISLAV V. KASL. 1992 "Religion, disability, depression, and the timing of death." *American Journal of Sociology*, 97:1052–1079.

IGLEHART, JOHN K. 1986 "Canada's health care system." *New England Journal of Medicine*, 315:202–208.

———. 1991 "Health policy report: Germany's health care system." *New England Journal of Medicine*, 324:503–508, 1750–1756.

IKEGAMI, NAOKI. 1991 "Japanese health care: Low cost through regulated fees." *Health Affairs*, Fall: 87–109.

———. 1992 "The economics of health care in Japan." *Science*, 258:614–618.

ILLICH, IVAN. 1976 *Medical nemesis: The expropriation of health.* New York: Pantheon.

ILLSLEY, R., and P. G. SVENSSON (eds.). 1986 *The health burden of social inequities.* Copenhagen: World Health Organization Regional Office for Europe.

IMERSHEIN, ALLEN W., PHILIP C. ROND III, and MARY P. MATHIS. 1992 "Restructuring patterns of elite dominance and the formation of state policy in health care." *American Journal of Sociology*, 97:970–993.

ITYAVYAR, DENNIS A. 1988 "Health services inequalities in Nigeria." *Social Science and Medicine*, 27: 1223–1235.

JACOBSON, DAVID E. 1986 "Types and timing of social support." *Journal of Health and Social Behavior*, 27:250–264.

JANZ, NANCY K., and MARSHALL H. BECKER. 1984 "The health belief model: A decade later." *Health Education Quarterly*, 11:1–47.

JARVIS, GEORGE K., and HERBERT C. NORTHCOTT. 1987 "Religion and differences in morbidity and mortality." *Social Science and Medicine*, 25:813–814.

JASPERS, KARL. 1988 *On Max Weber*, J. Dreijmans (ed.). New York: Paragon House.

JENKINS, C. DAVID. 1971 "Psychologic and social precursors of coronary disease." *New England Journal of Medicine*, 284:244–255, 307–317.

———. 1983 "Social environment and cancer mortality in men." *New England Journal of Medicine*, 308:395–398.

JINGFENG, CAI. 1988 "Integration of traditional Chinese medicine with western medicine—Right or wrong?" *Social Science and Medicine*, 27:521–529.

JOHNSON, MALCOLM. 1975 "Medical sociology and sociological theory." *Social Science and Medicine*, 9:227–232.

JONES, PHILIP R. 1981 *Doctors and the BMA.* Westmead U.K.: Gower.

JONES, RUSSELL A., H. JEAN WIESE, ROBERT W. MOORE, and JOHN V. HALEY. 1981 "On the perceived meaning of symptoms." *Medical Care*, 19:710–717.

JOOSTEN, J. 1989 "The structure of the concept of 'health' in the Dutch population." *Colloque INSERM*, 178:71–84.

KANNEL, W. B. 1982 "Meaning of the downward trend in cardiovascular mortality." *Journal of the American Medical Association*, 247:877–880.

KAPLAN, GIORA, VITA BARELL, and AYALA LUSKY. 1988 "Subjective state of health and survival in elderly adults." *Journal of Gerontology*, 43:S114–S120.

KAPLAN, HOWARD B. 1989 "Health, disease, and the social structure," pp. 46–68 in *Handbook of medical sociology*, 4th ed., H. Freeman and S. Levine (eds.). Englewood Cliffs, N.J.: Prentice Hall.

KAPLAN, HOWARD B., ROBERT J. JOHNSON, CAROL A. BAILEY, and WILLIAM SIMON. 1987 "The sociological study of AIDS: A critical review of the literature and suggested research agenda." *Journal of Health and Social Behavior*, 28:140–157.

KASER, MICHAEL. 1976 *Health care in the Soviet Union and Eastern Europe*. Boulder, Colo: Westview Press.

KASL, S., and S. COBB. 1966 "Health behavior, illness behavior, and sick role behavior." *Archives of Environmental Health*, 12:246–266.

KASS, LEON R. 1976 "Medical care and the pursuit of health," pp. 1–22 in *New directions in public health care: An evaluation of proposals for national health insurance*. San Francisco: Institute for Contemporary Studies.

KASSEBAUM, G., and B. BAUMANN. 1965 "Dimensions of the sick role in chronic illness." *Journal of Health and Social Behavior*, 6:16–27.

KASTELER, JOSEPHINE, ROBERT L. KANE, DONNA M. OLSEN, and CONSTANCE THETFORD. 1976 "Issues underlying prevalence of 'doctor-shopping' behavior." *Journal of Health and Social Behavior*, 17:328–339.

KAWAHITO, HIROSHI. 1990 "Karoshi and its background," pp. 4–13 in *Karoshi*, National Defense Council for Victims of Karoshi (eds.). Tokyo: Mado-Sha.

KEGELES, S. S. 1963 "Why people seek dental care: A test of a conceptual formulation." *Journal of Health and Social Behavior*, 4:166–173.

KELLETT, ANTHONY. 1982 *Combat motivation*. Boston: Kluwer.

KENDALL, PATRICIA, and GEORGE G. READER. 1988 "Innovations in medical education of the 1950s contrasted with those of the 1970s and 1980s." *Journal of Health and Social Behavior*, 29:279–293.

KENDALL, PATRICIA L., and HANAN C. SELVIN. 1957 "Tendencies toward specialization in medical training." pp. 153–174 in *The student-physician*, R. Merton, G. Reader, and P. Kendall (eds.). Cambridge, Mass.: Harvard University Press.

KESSLER, RONALD C. 1979 "Stress, social status, and psychological distress." *Journal of Health and Social Behavior*, 20:259–272.

KESSLER, RONALD C., and PAUL D. CLEARY. 1980 "Social class and psychological distress." *American Sociological Review*, 45:463–478.

KESSLER, RONALD C., JAMES S. HOUSE, and J. BLAKE TURNER. 1987 "Unemployment and health in a community sample." *Journal of Health and Social Behavior*, 18:51–59.

KESSLER, RONALD C., KATHERINE A. MCGONAGLE, SHANYANG ZHAO, CHRISTOPHER B. NELSON, MICHAEL HUGHES, SUZANN ESHLEMAN, HANS-ULRICH WITTCHEN, and KENNETH S. KENDLER. 1994 "Lifetime and 12-month prevalence of DSM-III-R psychiatric disorders in the United States." *Archives of General Psychiatry*, 51:8–19.

KESSLER, RONALD C., and JANE D. MCLEOD. 1984 "Sex differences in vulnerability to undesirable life events." *American Sociological Review*, 49:620–631.

KESSLER, RONALD C., and JAMES A. MCCRAE. 1981 "Trends in the relationship between sex and psychological distress: 1957–1976." *American Sociological Review*, 46:443–452.

———. 1982 "The effect of wives' employment on the mental health of married men and women." *American Sociological Review*, 47:217–227.

KESSLER, RONALD C., and HAROLD W. NEIGHBORS. 1986 "A new perspective on the relationships among race, social class, and psychological distress." *Journal of Health and Social Behavior*, 27:107–115.

KESSLER, RONALD C., J. BLAKE TURNER, and JAMES S. HOUSE. 1989 "Unemployment, reemployment, and emotional functioning in a community sample." *American Sociological Review*, 54:648–657.

KICKBUSCH, ILONA. 1989 "Self-care in health promotions." *Social Science and Medicine*, 29:125–130.

KIEV, ARI. 1968 *Curanderismo: Mexican-American folk psychiatry*. New York: The Free Press.

KIMMERLE, RONALD. 1987 "Jogging—zur Entstehung und Entwicklung einer kollektiven Bewegüng im Sport." *Sportwissenschaft*, 17:121–150.

KIRCHGÄSSLER, K.-U. 1990 "Health and social inequities in the Federal Republic of Germany." *Social Science and Medicine*, 31:249–256.

KIRKMAN-LIFF, BRADFORD L. 1991 "Health insurance values and implementation in the Netherlands and the Federal Republic of Germany." *Journal of the American Medical Association*, 265:2496–2502.

KIRSCHT, JOHN P. 1974 "The health belief model and illness behavior," pp. 387–408 in *The health belief model and personal health*, M. H. Becker (ed.). San Francisco: Society for Public Health Education, Inc.

KLEIN, RUDOLF. 1989 *The politics of the NHS*, 2nd ed. London: Longman.

———. 1992 "In search of the perfect health care system: Britain's pursuit of the global mirage." *International Journal of Health Services*, 3:187–194.

KNAUS, WILLIAM A. 1981 *Inside Russian Medicine*. Boston: Beacon Press.

KNIGHT, ROSEMARY A., and DAVID A. HAY. 1989 "The relevance of the health belief model to Australian smokers." *Social Science and Medicine*, 28:1311–1314.

KNOWLES, JOHN H. (ed.). 1963 *Hospitals, doctors, and the public interest*. Cambridge, Mass.: Harvard University Press.

———. 1973 "The hospital," pp. 91–102 in *Life and death and medicine*, San Francisco: W. H. Freeman & Company Publishers.

KNOX, RICHARD. 1993 *Germany's health system*. New York: Faulkner & Gray.

KOBASA, SUZANNE C., SALVATORE R. MADDI, and SHEILA COURINGTON. 1981 "Personality and constitution as mediators in the stress-illness relationship." *Journal of Health and Social Behavior*, 22:368–378.

KOOS, EARL. 1954 *The health of Regionville*. New York: Columbia University Press.

KOSA J., and L. S. ROBERTSON. 1969 "The social aspects of health and illness," pp. 35–68 in *Poverty and health*, John Kosa, Aaron Antonovsky, and K. Zola (eds.). Cambridge, Mass.: Harvard University Press.

KOSA, JOHN, AARON ANTONOVSKY, and IRVING K. ZOLA (eds.). 1969 *Poverty and health*. Cambridge, Mass.: Harvard University Press.

KOTARBA, JOSEPH A., and PAMELA BENTLEY. 1988 "Workplace wellness participation and the becoming of self." *Social Science and Medicine*, 26:551–558.

KRAUSE, ELLIOTT A. 1971 *The sociology of occupations*. Boston: Little, Brown.

———. 1977 *Power & illness*. New York: Elsevier North-Holland.

KRAUSE, NEAL M. 1987 "Stress in racial differences in self-reported health among the elderly." *Gerontologist*, 27:72–76.

KRAVITS, JONNA, and JOHN SCHNEIDER. 1975 "Health care need and actual use by age, race and income," pp. 169–187 in *Equity in health services: Empirical analyses in social policy*, R. Andersen, J. Kravits, and O. Anderson (eds.). Cambridge, Mass.: Ballinger.

KRONENFELD, JENNIE J. 1978 "Provider variables and the utilization of ambulatory care services." *Journal of Health and Social Behavior*, 19:68–76.

KRONENFELD, JENNIE J., KIRBY L. JACKSON, KEITH E. DAVIS, and STEVEN N. BLAIR. 1988 "Changing health practices: The experience from a worksite health promotion project." *Social Science and Medicine* 26:515–524.

KUNST, A. E., C. W. N. LOOMAN, and J. P. MACKENBACH. 1990 "Socio-economic mortality differences in the Netherlands in 1950–1984: A regional study of cause-specific mortality." *Social Science and Medicine* 31:141–152.

KUO, WEN H., and YUNG-MEI TSAI. 1986 "Social networks, hardiness and immigrant's mental health." *Journal of Health and Social Behavior*, 27:133–149.

KURTZ, RICHARD A., and H. PAUL CHALFANT. 1984 *The sociology of medicine and illness.* Boston: Allyn & Bacon.

LAGASSE, RAPHAEL, PERRINE C. HUMBLET, ANN LENAERTS, ISABELLE GODIN, and GUIDO F. G. MOEN. 1990 "Health and social inequities in Belgium." *Social Science and Medicine,* 31:237–248.

LAGUERRE, MICHAEL. 1987 *Afro-Caribbean folk medicine.* South Hadley, Mass.: Bergin & Garvey.

LAHELMA, EERO, and TAPANI VALKONEN. 1990 "Health and social inequities in Finland and elsewhere." *Social Science and Medicine,* 31:257–266.

LAROCCO, JAMES M., JAMES S. HOUSE, and JOHN R. P. FRENCH, JR. 1980 "Social support, occupational stress, and health." *Journal of Health and Social Behavior,* 21:202–218.

LAU, RICHARD R., MARILYN JACOBS QUADREL, and KAREN A. HARTMAN. 1990 "Development and change of young adults' preventive health beliefs and behavior: Influence from parents and peers." *Journal of Health and Social Behavior,* 31:240–259.

LAUER, ROBERT. 1974 "Rate of change and stress." *Social Forces,* 52:510–516.

LAUFER, ROBERT S., M. S. GALLOPS, and ELLEN FREY-WOUTERS. 1984 "War stress and trauma: The Vietnam veteran experience." *Journal of Health and Social Behavior,* 25:65–85.

LAVIN, BEBE, MARIE HAUG, LINDA LISKA BELGRAVE, and NAOMI BRESLAU. 1987 "Change in student physicians' views on authority relationships with patients." *Journal of Health and Social Behavior,* 28:258–272.

LEBLANC, ALLEN J. 1993 "Examining HIV-related knowledge among adults in the U.S." *Journal of Health and Social Behavior,* 34:23–36.

LECLERC, ANNETTE. 1989 "Differential mortality by cause of death: Comparison between selected European countries," pp. 92–108 in *Health inequalities in European countries,* J. Fox (ed.). Aldershot, U.K.: Gower.

LEE, RANCE P. L. 1983 "Problems of primary health care in a newly developed society: Reflections on the Hong Kong experience." *Social Science and Medicine,* 17:1433–1439.

LEFTON, MARK. 1984 "Chronic disease and applied sociology: An essay in personalized sociology." *Sociological Inquiry,* 54:466–476.

LENNON, MARY CLARE. 1987 "The psychological consequence of menopause: The importance of timing of a life stage event." *Journal of Health and Social Behavior,* 23:353–366.

LENNON, MARY CLARE, and SARAH ROSENFIELD. 1992 "Women and mental health: The interaction of job and family conditions." *Journal of Health and Social Behavior,* 33:316–327.

LETOURMY, ALAIN. 1986 "Qui veut, en France, d'un mode de vie plus sain?" *Social Science and Medicine,* 22:125–133.

LEVENTHAL, HOWARD. 1975 "The consequences of personalization during illness and treatment: An information-processing model," pp. 119–162 in *Humanizing health care,* J. Howard and A. Strauss (eds.). New York: Wiley-Interscience.

LEVENTHAL, H., G. HOCHMAN, and I. ROSENSTOCK. 1960 "Epidemic impact on the general population in two cities," pp. 14–23 in *The impact of Asian influenza on community life.* Washington, D.C.: U.S. Department of Health, Education and Welfare.

LEVINE, CAROL. 1990 "AIDS and changing concepts of family." *Milbank Quarterly,* 68:33–58.

LEVINE, SOL. 1987 "The changing terrains in medical sociology: Emergent concerns with quality of life." *Journal of Health and Social Behavior,* 28:1–6.

LEVINE, SOL, JACOB J. FELDMAN, and JACK ELINSON. 1983 "Does medical care do any good?" pp. 394–401 in *Handbook of health, health care, and the health professions,* D. Mechanic (ed.). New York: The Free Press.

Levinson, Richard M., and M. Zan York. 1974 "The attribution of 'dangerousness' in mental health evaluations." *Journal of Health and Social Behavior*, 15:328–335.

Levy, Jerrold E. 1983 "Traditional Navajo health beliefs and practices," pp. 118–178 in *Disease change and the role of medicine: The Navajo experience*, J. Kunitz (ed.). Berkeley: University of California Press.

Lewis, Flora. 1987 *Europe*. New York: Simon and Schuster.

Liem, Ramsay, and Joan Liem. 1978 "Social class and mental illness reconsidered: The role of economic stress and social support." *Journal of Health and Social Behavior*, 19:139–156.

Light, Donald, Jr. 1979 "Uncertainty and control in professional training," *Journal of Health and Social Behavior*, 20:310–322.

———. 1983 "Medical and nursing education: Surface behavior and deep structure," pp. 455–478 in *Handbook of health, health care, and the health professions*, D. Mechanic (ed.). New York: Free Press.

———. 1986 "Comparing health care systems: Lessons from East and West Germany," pp. 429–443 in *The sociology of health and illness*, 2nd ed., P. Conrad and R. Kern (eds.). New York: St. Martins.

———. 1988 "Toward a new sociology of medical education." *Journal of Health and Social Behavior*, 29:307–322.

———. 1989 "Social control and the American health care system," pp. 456–474 in *Handbook of medical sociology*, 4th ed., H. Freeman and S. Levine (eds.). Englewood Cliffs, N.J.: Prentice Hall.

Light, Donald W., and Alexander Schuller (eds.). 1986 Political values and health care: The German experience. Cambridge, Mass.: MIT Press.

Lin, Nan, and Walter M. Ensel. 1989 "Life stress and health: Stressors and resources." *American Sociological Review*, 54:382–399.

Lin, N. R., R. S. Simeone, W. M. Ensel, and W. Kuo. 1979 "Social support, stressful life events, and illness: A model and an empirical test." *Journal of Health and Social Behavior*, 20:108–119.

Lin, Nan, Mary W. Woelfel, and Stephen C. Light. 1985 "The buffering effect of social support subsequent to an important life event." *Journal of Health and Social Behavior*, 26:247–263.

Link, Bruce. 1983 "Reward system of psychotherapy: Implications for inequities in service delivery." *Journal of Health and Social Behavior*, 24:61–69.

Link, Bruce G., Bruce P. Dohrenwend, and Andrew E. Skodol. 1986 "Socio-economic status and schizophrenia: Noisome occupational characteristics as a risk factor." *American Sociological Review*, 51:242–258.

Linn, Bernard S., and Margaret W. Linn. 1980 "Objective and self-assessed health in the old and very old." *Social Science and Medicine*, 14:311–315.

Lipowski, Z. J. 1970 "Physical illness, the individual and the coping process." *Psychiatry in Medicine*, 1:91–101.

Lorber, Judith. 1975 "Good patients and problem patients: Conformity and deviance in a general hospital." *Journal of Health and Social Behavior*, 16:213–225.

———. 1984 *Women physicians: Careers, status, and power*. New York: Tavistock.

———. 1993 "Why women physicians will never be true equals in the American medical profession," pp. 62–76 in *Gender, work, and medicine*, E. Riska and K. Wegar (eds.). London: Sage.

Loscocco, Karyn A., and Glenna Spitze. 1990 "Working conditions, social support, and the well-being of female and male factory workers." *Journal of Health and Social Behavior*, 31:313–327.

Lubkin, Ilene Morof. 1986 *Chronic illness: Impact and interventions*. Boston: Jones and Bartlett.

Ludmerer, Kenneth. 1985 *Learning to heal*. New York: Basic Books.

LUNDBERG, OLLE. 1986 "Class and health: Comparing Britain and Sweden." *Social Science and Medicine*, 23:511–517.

———. 1992 "Health inequalities in Sweden: Levels and trends." *International Journal of Health Services*, 3:167–174.

LÜSCHEN, GÜNTHER, WILLIAM C. COCKERHAM, and GERHARD KUNZ. 1987 "Deutsche und amerikansiche Gesundheitskultur—oder what they say when you sneeze." *Mensch Medizin Gesellschaft*, 12:59–69.

McFARLANE, ALLAN H., GEOFFREY R. NORMAN, DAVID L. STREINER, and RANJAN G. ROY. 1983 "The process of social stress: Stable, reciprocal, and mediating relationships." *Journal of Health and Social Behavior*, 24:160–173.

McINTIRE, CHARLES. 1984 "The importance of the study of medical sociology." *Bulletin of the American Academy of Medicine*, 1:425–434.

McINTOSH, JIM. 1974 "Processes of communication, information seeking and control associated with cancer: A selective review of the literature." *Social Science and Medicine*, 8:167–187.

McKEOWN, THOMAS 1979 *The role of medicine*. Oxford, U.K.: Blackwell.

McKINLAY, JOHN B. 1972 "Some approaches and problems in the study of the use of services—An overview." *Journal of Health and Social Behavior*, 13:115–152.

———. 1973 "Social networks, lay consultation and help-seeking behavior." *Social Forces*, 51:275–291.

McKINLAY, JOHN B., and SONJA M. McKINLAY. 1981 "Medical measures and the decline of mortality," pp. 12–30 in *The sociology of health and illness*, P. Conrad and R. Kern (eds.). New York: St. Martin's Press.

McKINLAY, JOHN B., SONJA M. McKINLAY, and ROBERT BEAGLEHOLE. 1989 "Trends in death and disease and the contribution of medical measures," pp. 14–45 in *Handbook of medical sociology*, 4th ed., H. Freeman and S. Levine (eds.). Englewood Cliffs, N.J.: Prentice Hall.

McLANAHAN, SARA, and JENNIFER L. GLASS. 1985 "A note on the trend in sex differences in psychological distress." *Journal of Health and Social Behavior*, 26:328–336.

McLEOD, JANE D., and RONALD C. KESSLER. 1990 "Socioeconomic status differences in vulnerability to undesirable life events." *Journal of Health and Social Behavior*, 31:162–172.

MacGRAW, RICHARD M. 1975 "Medical specialization and medical coordination," pp. 588–606 in *Medical behavioral science*, T. Millon (ed.). Philadelphia: Saunders.

MacINTYRE, SALLY. 1986 "The patterning of health by social position in contemporary Britain: Directions for sociological research." *Social Science and Medicine*, 23:393–415.

———. 1989 "The role of health services in relation to inequalities in health in Europe," pp. 317–332 in *Health inequalities in European countries*, J. Fox (ed.). Aldershot, U.K.: Gower.

MACKEY, SANDRA. 1987 *The Saudis: Inside the desert kingdom*. Boston: Houghton Mifflin.

MADDOX, GEORGE L., and THOMAS A. GLASS. 1989 "Health care of the chronically ill," pp. 236–261 in *Handbook of medical sociology*, 4th ed., H. Freeman and S. Levine (eds.). Englewood Cliffs, N.J.: Prentice-Hall.

MADSEN, WILLIAM. 1973 *The Mexican-Americans of south Texas*, 2nd ed. New York: Holt, Rinehart, & Winston.

MAKOFSKY, DAVID. 1977 "Malpractice and medicine." *Society*, 14:25–29.

MANNING, PHILIP. 1992 *Erving Goffman and Modern Sociology*. Stanford, Calif.: Stanford University Press.

MARCUS, ALFRED C., and TERESA E. SEEMAN. 1981 "Sex differences in reports of illness and disability: A preliminary test of the 'fixed-role obligations' hypothesis." *Journal of Health and Social Behavior*, 22:174–182.

MARCUS, ALFRED C., and JUDITH M. SIEGEL. 1982 "Sex differences in the use of physician services: A preliminary test of the fixed role hypothesis." *Journal of Health and Social Behavior*, 23:186–197.

MARMOR, THEODORE R. 1973 *The politics of Medicare*. Chicago: Aldine.

MARMOT, M. G., M. J. SHIPLEY, and GEOFFREY ROSE. 1984 "Inequalities in death—Specific explanations of a general pattern." *Lancet*, 83:1003–1006.

MARSHALL, JAMES R., DAVID I. GREGORIO, and DEBRA WALSH. 1982 "Sex differences in illness behavior: Care seeking among cancer patients." *Journal of Health and Social Behavior*, 23:197–204.

MARSHALL, ROBERT J., JR., JOHN P. FULTON, and ALBERT F. WESSEN. 1978 "Physician career outcomes and the process of medical education." *Journal of Health and Social Behavior*, 19:124–138.

MARSHALL, T. H. 1964 *Class, citizenship, and social development*. Chicago: University of Chicago Press.

MARTIN, CLAUDIA J., and DAVID V. MCQUEEN (eds.). 1989 *Readings for a new public health*. Edinburgh, U.K.: Edinburgh University Press.

MARTIN, LINDA G. 1988 "The aging of Asia." *Journal of Gerontology* , 43:S99–S113.

MARTIN, STEVEN C., ROBERT M. ARNOLD, and RUTH M. PARKER . 1988 "Gender and medical socialization." *Journal of Health and Social Behavior* , 29:333–343.

MASON, TONY (ed.). 1989 *Sport in Britain: A social history*. Cambridge: Cambridge University Press.

MATSUMOTO, Y. SCOTT. 1971 "Social stress and coronary heart disease in Japan," pp. 123–149 in *The social organization of health* , H. Dreitzel (ed.). New York: Macmillan.

MATT, GEORG E., and ALFRED DEAN. 1993 "Social support from friends and psychological distress among elderly persons: Moderator effects of age." *Journal of Health and Social Behavior*, 34:187–200.

MAUKSCH, HANS. 1972 "Nursing: Churning for a change?" pp. 206–230 in *Handbook of medical sociology*, 2nd ed., H. E. Freeman, S. Levine, and L. G. Reeder (eds). Englewood Cliffs, N.J.: Prentice-Hall.

MEAD, GEORGE HERBERT. 1934 *Mind, self, and society*. Chicago: University of Chicago Press.

MEAD, LAWRENCE M. 1985 *The social obligations of citizenship*. New York: Free Press.

MECHANIC, DAVID. 1962a "The concept of illness behavior." *Journal of Chronic Diseases*, 15:189–194.

———. 1962b *Students under stress: A study of the social psychology of adaptation*. New York: The Free Press.

———. 1964 "The influence of mothers on their children's health attitudes and behavior." *Pediatrics*, 33:444–453.

———. 1972 *Public expectations and health care*. New York: Wiley-Interscience.

———. 1978 *Medical sociology*, 2nd ed. New York: The Free Press.

———. 1979 "Correlates of physician utilization: Why do major multivariate studies of physician utilization find trivial psychosocial and organizational effects?" *Journal of Health and Social Behavior*, 20:387–396.

MECHANIC, DAVID, and RONALD J. ANGEL. 1987 "Some factors associated with the report and evaluation of back pain." *Journal of Health and Social Behavior*, 28:131–139.

MECHANIC, DAVID, and EDMUND H. VOLKART. 1961 "Stress, illness behavior, and the sick role." *American Sociological Review*, 25:51–58.

MERENSTEIN, JOEL H., HARVEY WOLFE, and KATHLEEN M. BARKER. 1974 "The use of nurse practitioners in a general practice." *Medical Care*, 12:437–444.

MERTON, ROBERT. 1938 "Social structure and anomie." *American Sociological Review*, 3:672–682.

MERTON, ROBERT K., GEORGE G. READER, and PATRICIA KENDALL. 1957 *The student-physician*. Cambridge, Mass.: Harvard University Press.

MEITLIN, CURT, and JOSEPH WOELFEL. 1974 "Interpersonal influence and symptoms of stress." *Journal of Health and Social Behavior*, 15:311–319.

MEZENTSEVA, ELENA, and NATALIA RIMACHEVSKAYA. 1990 "The Soviet country profile: Health of the U.S.S.R. population in the 70s and 80s—An approach to a comprehensive analysis." *Social Science and Medicine*, 31:867–877.

———. 1992 "The health profile of the population in the republics of the former Soviet Union: An analysis of the situation in the 70s and 80s." *International Journal of Health Sciences*, 3:127–142.

MILLER, MICHAEL H. 1973 "Who receives optimal medical care?" *Journal of Health and Social Behavior*, 14:176–182.

———. 1974 "Work roles for the associate degree graduate." *American Journal of Nursing*, 74:468–470.

MILLER, STEPHEN J. 1970 *Prescription for leadership: Training for the medical elite*. Chicago: Aldine.

MILLMAN, MARCIA. 1977a "Masking doctors' errors." *Human Behavior*, 6:16–23.

———. 1977b *The unkindest cut*. New York: Morrow.

MIROWSKY, JOHN. 1985 "Depression and marital power: An equity model." *American Journal of Sociology*, 91:557–592.

MIROWSKY, JOHN, and CATHERINE E. ROSS. 1983 "Paranoia and the structure of powerlessness." *American Sociological Review*, 48:228–239.

———. 1989 *Social causes of psychological distress*. New York: Aldine de Gruyter.

MISHLER, ELLIOT G. 1984 *The discourse of medicine: Dialectics of medical interviews*. Norwood, N.J.: Ablex.

MIZRAHI, TERRY. 1986 *Getting rid of patients: Contradictions in the socialization of physicians*. New Brunswick, N.J.: Rutgers University Press.

MONTEIRO, LOIS. 1973 "Expense is no object . . .: Income and the physician visits reconsidered." *Journal of Health and Social Behavior*, 14:99–115.

MORA, GEORGE. 1985 "Historical and theoretical trends in psychiatry," pp. 1–75 in *Comprehensive textbook of psychiatry*, Vol. 1, 4th ed., A. Freedman, H. Kaplan, and B. Sadock (eds.). Baltimore: Williams & Wilkins.

MORGAN, MYFANWY, MICHAEL CALNAN, and NICK MANNING. 1985 *Sociological approaches to health and medicine*. London: Croom Helm.

MORSE, EDWARD V., GERALD GORDON, and MICHAEL MOCH. 1974 "Hospital costs and quality of care: An organizational perspective." *Milbank Memorial Fund Quarterly*, 52:315–346.

MORSE, JANICE M., DAVID E. YOUNG, and LISE SWARTZ. 1991 "Cree Indian healing practices and Western health care: A comparative analysis." *Social Science and Medicine*, 32:1361–1366.

MOSKOS, CHARLES C., JR. 1970 *The American enlisted man*. New York: Russell Sage.

MOSS, GORDON E. 1973 *Illness, immunity, and social interaction*. New York: John Wiley.

MOSSEY, JANA M., and EVELYN SHAPIRO. 1982 "Self-rated health: A predictor of mortality among the elderly." *American Journal of Public Health*, 8:800–808.

MULLEN, PATRICIA D., JAMES C. HERSEY, and DONALD C. IVERSON. 1987 "Health behavior models compared." *Social Science and Medicine*, 24:973–981.

MUNAKATA, TSUNETSUGU. 1992 "Effective health policy for AIDS prevention in Japan: Suggestions from an international KABP comparison," pp. 223–228 in *Behavioral medicine: An integrated approach to health and illness*, S. Araki (ed.). New York: Elsevier.

———. 1994 *AIDS in Japan*. Tokyo: Akashi Shoten.

MUTCHLER, JAN E., and JEFFREY A. BURR. 1991 "Racial differences in health and health care service utilization in later life: The effect of socioeconomic status." *Journal of Health and Social Behavior*, 32:342–356.

MWABU, GERMANO MWIGA. 1984 "A model of household choice among medical treatment alternatives in rural Kenya." Unpublished Ph.D. Dissertation, Boston University.

MYLES, JOHN F. 1978 "Institutionalization and sick role identification among the elderly." *American Sociological Review*, 43:508–521.

————. 1984 *Old age in the welfare state.* Boston: Little, Brown.

NATHANSON, CONSTANCE A. 1975 "Illness and the feminine role: A theoretical review." *Social Science and Medicine*, 9:57–62.

————. 1977a "Sex, illness, and medical care: A review of data, theory, and method." *Social Science and Medicine*, 11:13–25.

————. 1977b "Sex roles as variables in preventive health behavior." *Journal of Community Health*, 3:142–155.

————. 1980 "Social roles and health status among women: The significance of employment." *Social Science and Medicine*, 14A:463–471.

NATIONAL CENTER FOR HEALTH STATISTICS. 1983 *Health, United States, 1983.* Washington, D.C.: U.S. Government Printing Office.

————. 1984 *Health Indicators for Hispanic, black, and white Americans.* Series 10. No. 148. U.S. Department of Health and Human Services.

————. 1985 *Health, United States, 1985.* Washington, D.C.: U.S. Government Printing Office.

————. 1987a "Prevalence of known diabetes among black Americans." *Advance data from vital and health statistics.* No. 130. Hyattsville, Md.: U.S. Department of Health and Human Services.

————. 1987b *Health care coverage by age, sex, race, and family income: United States, 1986. Advance data from vital and health statistics.* No. 139. Hyattsville, Md.: U.S. Department of Health and Human Services.

————. 1988 *Health, United States, 1987.* Washington, D.C.: U.S. Government Printing Office.

————. 1989 "Characteristics of persons dying of diseases of heart." *Advance Data for Vital and Health Statistics.* No. 172. Hyattsville, Md.: U.S. Department of Health and Human Services.

————. 1990 *Health, United States, 1989.* Washington, D.C.: U.S. Government Printing Office.

————. 1991 *Health, United States, 1990.* Washington, D.C.: U.S. Government Printing Office.

————. 1993 *Health, United States, 1992.* Washington, D.C.: U.S. Government Printing Office.

NAVARRO, VICENTE. 1976 *Medicine under capitalism.* New York: Prodist.

————. 1986 *Crisis, health, and medicine: A social critique.* New York: Tavistock.

————. 1989 "Why some countries have national health insurance, others have national health services, and the U.S. has neither." *Social Science and Medicine*, 28:887–898.

NELKIN, DOROTHY, DAVID P. WILLIS, and SCOTT V. PARRIS. 1990 "Introduction." *Milbank Quarterly*, 68, no. 1:1–9.

NEW, PETER KONG-MING. 1958 "The osteopathic students: A study in dilemma," pp. 413–421 in *Patients, physicians, and illness*, E. Jaco (ed.). Glenco, Ill.: The Free Press.

NEWACHECK, PAUL W., and LEWIS H. BUTLER. 1983 "Patterns of physician use among low-income, chronically ill persons." *Medical Care*, 21:981–988.

NEWMAN, JOY P. 1986 "Gender, life strains, and depression." *Journal of Health and Social Behavior*, 27:161–178.

NISBET, L.A., and D. V. McQUEEN. 1993 "Anti-permissive attitudes to lifestyles associated with AIDS." *Social Science and Medicine*, 36:949–955.

NOELLE-NEWMAN, ELISABETH. 1983 *Eine demoskopische Deutschstunde.* Zurich: Interform.

NOLEN, WILLIAM A. 1970 *The making of a surgeon.* New York: Random House.

NORRIS, FRAN H., and STANLEY A. MURRELL. 1984 "Protective function of resources related to life events, global stress, and depression in older adults. *Journal of Health and Social Behavior*, 25:424–437.

NORTHCOTT, HERBERT C. 1980 "Women, work, and health." *Pacific Sociological Review*, 23:393–404.

OBBO, CHRISTINE. 1993 "HIV transmission through social and geographical networks in Uganda." *Social Science and Medicine*, 36:949–955.

OLESEN, VIRGINIA L. 1989 "Caregiving, ethical and informal: Emerging challenges in the sociology of health and illness." *Journal of Health and Social Behavior*, 30:1–10.

OLESEN, VIRGINIA L., and ELVI W. WHITTAKER. 1968 *The silent dialogue*. San Francisco: Jossey-Bass.

OLMSTED, DONALD W., and KATHERINE DURHAM. 1976 "Stability of mental health attitudes: A semantic differential study." *Journal of Health and Social Behavior*, 17:35–44.

OTTEN, MAC W., STEVEN M. TEUTSCH, DAVID F. WILLIAMSON, and JAMES S. MARKS. 1990 "The effect of known risk factors on the excess mortality of black adults in the United States." *Journal of the American Medical Association*, 268:845–850.

PAFFENBARGER, RALPH S., JR., ROBERT T. HYDE, ALVIN L. WING, and CHUNG-CHENG HSIEH. 1986 "Physical activity, all-cause mortality, and longevity of college alumni." *New England Journal of Medicine*, 314:605–613.

PAFFENBARGER, RALPH S., JR., ROBERT T. HYDE, ALVIN WING, I-MIN LEE, DEXTER L. JUNG, and JAMES KAMPERT. 1993 "The association of changes in physicial-activity level and other lifestyle characteristics with mortality among men." *New England Journal of Medicine*, 32:538–545.

PARRY, GLENYS. 1986 "Paid employment, life events, social support, and mental health in working-class mothers." *Journal of Health and Social Behavior*, 27:193–208.

PARSONS, TALCOTT. 1951 *The social system*. Glencoe, Ill.: The Free Press.

———. 1975 "The sick role and role of the physician reconsidered." *Milbank Memorial Fund Quarterly*, 53:257–278.

———. 1979 "Definitions of health and illness in light of American values and social structure," pp. 120–144 in *Patients, physicians, and illness*, 3rd ed., E. Jaco (ed.). New York: The Free Press.

PARSONS, TALCOTT, and RENÉE FOX. 1952. "Illness, therapy and the modern urban American family." *Journal of Social Issues*, 8:31–44.

PAUL, JOHN R. 1966 *Clinical epidemiology*. Chicago: University of Chicago Press.

PAVALKO, ELIZA K., GLEN H. ELDER, JR., and ELIZABETH C. CLIPP. 1993 "Worklives and longevity: Insights from a life course perspective." *Journal of Health and Social Behavior*, 34:363–380.

PAYER, LYNN. 1988 *Medicine and culture*. London: Penguin Books.

PEARLIN, LEONARD I. 1989 "The sociological study of stress." *Journal of Health and Social Behavior*, 30:241–256.

PEARLIN, LEONARD I., MORTON A. LIEBERMAN, ELIZABETH G. MENAGHAN, and JOSEPH T. MULLAN. 1981 "The stress process." *Journal of Health and Social Behavior*, 22:337–356.

PEARLIN, LEONARD I., and SCHOOLER, CARMIN. 1978 "The Structure of Coping." *Journal Health and Social Behavior*, 23:2–17.

PERROW, CHARLES. 1963 "Goals and power structures: A historical case study," pp. 112–146 in *The hospital in modern society*, E. Friedson (ed.). New York: The Free Press.

PESCOSOLIDO, BERNICE A. 1992 "Beyond rational choice: The social dynamics of how people seek help." *American Journal of Sociology*, 97:1096–1138.

PESCOSOLIDO, BERNICE A., CAROL A. BOYER, and WAI YING TSUI. 1985 "Medical care in the welfare state: A cross-national study of public evaluation." *Journal of Health and Social Behavior*, 26:276–296.

PETO, RICHARD, ALAN D. LOPEZ, JILLIAN BOREHAM, MICHAEL THUN, and CLARK HEATH, JR. 1992 "Mortality from tobbaco in developed countries: Indirect estimation from national vital statistics." *Lancet*, 339:1268–1278.

PFLANZ, MANFRED, and JOHANN J. ROHDE. 1970 "Illness: Deviant behavior or conformity." *Social Science and Medicine*, 4:645–653.

PHIFER, JAMES F., KRZYSZTOF Z. KANIASTY, and FRAN H. NORRIS. 1988 "The impact of natural disaster on the health of older adults: A multiwave prospective study." *Journal of Health and Social Behavior*, 29:65–78.

PIPERNO, ALDO, and FERDINANDO DI ORIO. 1990 "Social differences in health and utilization of health services in Italy." *Social Science and Medicine*, 31:305–312.

POLEDNAK, ANTHONY P. 1989 *Racial & ethnic differences in disease*. New York: Oxford University Press.

POLLNER, MELVIN. 1989 "Divine relations, social relations, and well-being," *Journal of Health and Social Behavior*, 30:92–104.

PORTER, SAM. 1992 "Women in a women's job: The gendered experience of nurses." *Sociology of Health & Illness*, 14:510–527.

POUVOURVILLE, GERARD DE, and MARC RENAUD. 1985 "Hospital system management in France and Canada: National pluralism and provincial centralism." *Social Science and Medicine*, 20:153–166.

POWELL, KENNETH E., PAUL D. THOMPSON, CARL J. CASPERSEN, and JULIETTE S. KENDRICK. 1987 "Physical activity and the incidence of coronary heart disease." *Annual Review of Public Health*, 8:253–287.

POWELL, MARGARET, and MASAHIRA ANESAKI. 1990 *Health care in Japan*. London: Routledge.

PRESCOTT, PATRICIA A., and SALLY A. BOWEN. 1985 "Physician–nurse relationships." *Annals of Internal Medicine*, 103:127–133.

PRESIDENT'S COMMISSION FOR THE STUDY OF ETHICAL PROBLEMS IN MEDICINE AND BIOMEDICAL AND BEHAVIORAL RESEARCH. 1983 *Securing access to health care, Vol. 1*. Washington, D.C.: U.S. Government Printing Office.

PRESTHUS, ROBERT. 1978 *The organizational society*. Rev. ed. New York: St. Martin's Press.

PRETORIUS, ENGELA, G.W. DE KLERK, and H.C.J. VAN RENSBURG. 1993 *The traditional healer in South African health care*. Pretoria: Human Sciences Research Council.

PROHASKA, THOMAS R., GARY ALBRECHT, JUDITH A. LEVY, NOREEN SUGRUE, and JONG-HWA KIM. 1990 "Determinants of self-perceived risk for AIDS." *Journal of Health and Social Behavior*, 31:384–394

PSATHAS, GEORGE. 1968 "The fate of idealism in nursing school." *Journal of Health and Social Behavior*, 9:52–64.

QUAH, STELLA R. 1989 "The social position and internal organization of the medical profession in the third world: The case of Singapore." *Journal of Health and Social Behavior*, 30:450–466.

RADELET, MICHAEL L. 1981 "Health beliefs, social networks, and tranquilizer use." *Journal of Health and Social Behavior*, 22:165–173.

RADLEY, ALAN. 1989 "Style, discourse and constrain in adjustment to chronic illness." *Sociology of Health & Illness* 11:230–252.

RADO, S. 1949 "Pathodynamics and treatment of traumatic war neurosis (traumatophobia)." *Psychosomatic Medicine*, 43:363–398.

RAGLAND, DAVID R., and RICHARD J. BRAND. 1988 "Type A and mortality from coronary heart disease." *New England Journal of Medicine*, 318:65–69.

RANK, STEVEN G., and CARDELL K. JACOBSON. 1977 "Hospital nurses' compliance with medication overdose orders: A failure to replicate." *Journal of Health and Social Behavior*, 18:188–193.

RANSFORD, H. EDWARD. 1986 "Race, heart disease worry, and health protective behavior." *Social Science and Medicine*, 12:1355–1362.

RASMUSSEN, HOWARD. 1975 "Medical education—Revolution or reaction." *Pharos*, 38:53–59.

REEDER, LEO G. 1972 "The patient-client as a consumer: Some observations on the changing professional-client relationship." *Journal of Health and Social Behavior*, 13:406–412.

REEDER, LEO G., and EMIL BERKANOVIC. 1973 "Sociological concomitants of health orientations: A partial replication of Suchman." *Journal of Health and Social Behavior*, 14:134–143.

REID, IVAN. 1989 *Social class differences in Britain*, 3rd ed. Glasgow, U.K.: Fontana Press.

RENSBURG, H.C.J. VAN. 1991 "South African health care in change." *South African Journal of Sociology*, 22:1–10.

RENSBURG, H.C.J. VAN, and S.R. BENATAR. 1993 "The legacy of apartheid in health and health care." *South African Journal of Sociology*, 24:99–111.

RENSBURG, H.C.J. VAN, and A. FOURIE. 1988 "Privatisation of South African health care: In whose interest?" *Curationis*, 11:1–6

RENSBURG, H.C.J. VAN, A. FOURIE, and E. PRETORIUS. 1992 *Health Care in South Africa: Structure and dynamics*. Pretoria: Academia.

RISKA, ELIANNE, and KATARINA WEGAR. 1993 "Women physicians: A new force in medicine?" pp. 77–93 in *Gender, work and medicine*, E. Riska and K. Wegar (eds.). London: Sage.

RITCHEY, FERRIS J. 1981 "Medical rationalization, cultural lag, and the malpractice crisis." *Human Organization*, 40:97–112.

RITCHEY, FERRIS J., MARK LA GORY, and JEFFREY MULLIS. 1991 "Gender differences in health risks and physical symptoms among the homeless." *Journal of Health and Social Behavior*, 32:33–48.

RITZER, GEORGE, and DAVID WALCZAK. 1988 "Rationalization and the deprofessionalization of physicians." *Social Forces*, 67:1–22.

ROBERTS, ROBERT E., and EUN SUL LEE. 1980 "Medical care use by Mexican-Americans: Evidence from the human population laboratory studies." *Medical Care*, 43:266–281.

ROBERTS, ROBERT E., and STEPHEN J. O'KEEFE. 1981 "Sex differences in depression reexamined." *Journal of Health and Social Behavior*, 22:394–400.

ROBINSON, BEVERLY J. 1990 "Africanisms and the study of folklore," pp. 211–224 in *Africanisms in American culture*, J. Holloway (ed.). Bloomington: Indiana University Press.

RODENSTEIN, MARIANNE. 1987 "Wandlüngen des gesundheitsverstandnisses in der moderne." *Mensch Medizin Gesellschaft*, 12:292–298.

RODRÍGUEZ, JOSEP A., and LOUIS LEMKOW. 1990 "Health and social inequities in Spain." *Social Science and Medicine*, 31:351–358.

RODWIN, VICTOR G. 1989 "New ideas for health policy in France, Canada, and Britain," pp. 265–285 in *Success and crisis in national health systems*, M. Field (ed.). London: Routledge.

RODWIN, VICTOR G., and SIMONE SANDIER. 1993 "Health care under French national health insurance." *Health Affairs*, Fall:111–131.

ROEBUCK, JULIAN, and ROBERT QUAN. 1976 "Health-care practices in the American Deep South," pp. 141–161 in *Marginal medicine*, R. Wallis and P. Morely (eds.). New York: The Free Press.

ROGLER, LLOYD H., and AUGUST B. HOLLINGSHEAD. 1965 *Trapped: Families and schizophrenia*. New York: Wiley.

ROGOFF, NATALIE. 1975 "The decision to study medicine," pp. 109–129 in *The student-physician*, R. K. Merton, G. Reader, and P. L. Kendall (eds.). Cambridge, Mass.: Harvard University Press.

ROOS, NORALOU P., JOHN R. SCHERMERHORN, and LESLIE L. ROSS, JR. 1974 "Hospital performance: Analyzing power and goals." *Journal of Health and Social Behavior*, 15:78–92.

ROSEN, GEORGE. 1979 "The evolution of social medicine," pp. 23–50 in *Handbook of medical sociology*, 2nd ed., H. Freeman, S. Levine, and L. Reeder (eds.). Englewood Cliffs, N.J.: Prentice-Hall.

ROSENBERG, CHARLES E. 1987 *The care of strangers: The rise of America's hospital system*. New York: Basic Books.

ROSENBERG, EMILY J., and BARBARA S. DOHRENWEND. 1975 "Effects of experience and ethnicity on ratings of life events as stressors." *Journal of Health and Social Behavior*, 16:127–129.

ROSENFIELD, SARAH. 1980 "Sex differences in depression: Do women always have higher rates?" *Journal of Health and Social Behavior*, 21:33–42.

———. 1989 "The effects of women's employment: Personal control and sex differences in mental health." *Journal of Health and Social Behavior*, 30:77–91.

———. 1992 "The costs of sharing: Wives' employment and husbands' mental health." *Journal of Health and Social Behavior*, 33:213–225.

ROSENSTOCK, IRWIN. 1966 "Why people use health services." *Milbank Memorial Fund Quarterly*, 44:94-127.

ROSENTHAL, MARILYNN M. 1987 *Health care in the People's Republic of China*. Boulder, Colo.: Westview Press.

ROSS, CATHERINE E., and RAYMOND S. DUFF. 1982 "Returning to the doctor: The effect of client characteristics, type of practice, and experiences with care." *Journal of Health and Social Behavior*, 23:119–131.

ROSS, CATHERINE E., and JOAN HUBER. 1985 "Hardship and depression." 26:312–327. *Journal of Health and Social Behavior*.

ROSS, CATHERINE E., and JOHN MIROWSKY. 1979 "A comparison of life-event-weighting schemes: Change, undesirability and effect-proportional indices." *Journal of Health and Social Behavior*, 20:166–177.

ROSS, CATHERINE E., JOHN MIROWSKY, and JOAN HUBER. 1983 "Dividing work, sharing work, and in-between: Marriage patterns and depression." *American Sociological Review*, 48:809–823.

ROSS, CATHERINE E., JOHN MIROWSKY, and PATRICIA ULBRICH. 1983 "Distress and the traditional female role: A comparison of Mexicans and Anglos." *American Journal of Sociology*, 89:560–682.

ROTH, JULIUS, and PETER CONRAD (eds.). 1987 *The experience and management of chronic illness*. Newbury Park, Calif.: Sage.

ROUECHÉ, BERTON. 1967 *Annals of epidemiology*. Boston: Little, Brown.

———. 1978 "Annals of medicine." *The New Yorker* (August 21):63–70.

ROWLAND, DIANE, and ALEXANDRE V. TELYUKOV. 1991 "Soviet health care from two perspectives." *Health Affairs*, Fall:71–86.

RUCH, LIBBY O. 1977 "Multidimensional analysis of the concept of life change." *Journal of Health and Social Behavior*, 18:71–83.

RUCH, LIBBY O., and SUSAN MEYERS CHANDLER. 1983 "Sexual assault trauma during the acute phase: An exploratory model and multivariate analysis." *Journal of Health and Social Behavior*, 24:174–185.

RUCH, LIBBY O., SUSAN MEYERS CHANDLER, and RICHARD A. HARTER. 1980 "Life change and rape impact." *Journal of Health and Social Behavior*, 21:248–260.

RUDERMAN, FLORENCE. 1981 "What is medical sociology?" *Journal of the American Medical Association*, 245:927–929.

RUESCHMEYER, DIETRICH. 1972 "Doctors and lawyers: A comment on the theory of professions," pp. 5–19 in *Medical men and their work*, E. Freidson and J. Lorber (eds.). Chicago: Aldine.

RUGGIE, MARY. 1992 "The paradox of liberal intervention: Health policy and the American welfare state." *American Journal of Sociology*, 97:919–944.

RUNDALL, THOMAS G. 1978 "Life change and recovery from surgery." *Journal of Health and Social Behavior*, 20:418–427.

RUNDALL, THOMAS G., and JOHN R. C. WHEELER. 1979 "The effect of income on use of preventive care: An evaluation of alternative explanations." *Journal of Health and Social Behavior*, 20:397–406.

RUSHING, WILLIAM A. 1984 "Social factors in the rise of hospital costs," pp. 27–114 in *Research in the sociology of health care, Vol. 3*, J. Roth (ed.). Greenwich, Conn.: JAI.

———. 1985 "The supply of physicians and expenditures for health services with implications for coming physician surplus." *Journal of Health and Social Behavior*, 26:297–311.

RUTSTEIN, DAVID. 1967 *The coming revolution in medicine.* Cambridge, Mass.: MIT Press.

SAGAN, LEONARD A. 1987 *The health of nations.* New York: Basic Books.

SAKANO, JUNKO, and YOSHIHIKO YAMAZAKI. 1990 *Survey of the role of white-collar workers as family members in the Tokyo area.* University of Tokyo: Department of Health Sociology.

SALLOWAY, JEFFREY C. 1973 "Medical utilization among urban gypsies." *Urban Anthropology*, 2:113–126.

SAWARD, ERNEST W. 1973 "The organization of medical care," pp. 129–135 in *Life, death, and medicine.* San Francisco: W. H. Freeman.

SAWYER, DARWIN O. 1980 "Normative conflict and physician use: A latent structure approach." *Journal of Health and Social Behavior*, 21:156–169.

SCAMBLER, GRAHAM, and ANTHONY HOPKINS. 1986 "Being epileptic: Coming to terms with stigma." *Sociology of Health and Illness*, 8:26–43.

SCHEFF, THOMAS J. 1966 *Being mentally ill.* Chicago: Aldine.

SCHEFFLER, RICHARD M., and OLIVIA D. STINSON. 1974 "Characteristics of physician's assistants: A focus on speciality." *Medical Care*, 12:1019–1030.

SCHEUCH, ERWIN K. 1987 "Entwicklung der Bevölkerungsstruktur and unser Gesundheitswesen." *Mensch Medizin Gesellschaft*, 12:135–143.

———. 1989. "Recent social changes and their consequences for the health care system in the Federal Republic of Germany," pp. 147–166 in *Health and illness in America and Germany*, G. Lüschen, W. Cockerham, and G. Kunz (eds.). Munich: Oldenbourg.

SCHIFF, ROBERT L., DAVID A. ANSELL, JAMES E. SCHLOSSER, AHAMED H. IDRIS, ANN MORRISON, and STEVEN WHITMAN. 1986 "Transfers to a public hospital." *New England Journal of Medicine*, 314:552–557.

SCHOENDORF, KENNETH C., CAROL J. R. HOGUE, JOEL C. KLEINMAN, and DIANE ROWLEY. 1992 "Mortality among infants of black as compared to white college-educated parents." *New England Journal of Medicine*, 326:1522–1526.

SCHULMAN, SAM. 1972 "Mother surrogate—After a decade," pp. 233–239 in *Patients, physicians and illness*, E. Jaco (ed.). New York: The Free Press.

SCHWARTZ, MIRIAM A. 1984 "A sociological interpretation of the controversy over 'unnecessary surgery,' " pp. 159–200 in *Research in the sociology of health care, Vol. 3*, J. Roth (ed.). Greenwich, Conn.: JAI.

SCOTT, RICHARD W. 1982 "Managing professional work: Three models of control for health organizations." *Health Services Research*, 17:213–230.

SCULLY, DIANA, and PAULINE BART. 1979 "A funny thing happened on the way to the orifice: Women in gynecology textbooks," pp. 212–226 in *The cultural crisis of modern medicine*, J. Ehrenreich (ed.). New York: Monthly Review Press.

SECCOMBE, KAREN. 1989 "Ethnicity or socioeconomic status? Health differences between elder Alaska natives and whites." *Gerontologist*, 29:551–556.

SEEMAN, M., and J. W. EVANS. 1962 "Alienation and social learning in a reformatory." *American Journal of Sociology*, 69:270–284.

SEEMAN, MELVIN, and TERESA E. SEEMAN. 1983 "Health behavior and personal autonomy: A longitudinal study of the sense of control in illness." *Journal of Health and Social Behavior*, 24:144–160.

SEGALL, ALEXANDER. 1976 "The sick role concept: Understanding illness behavior." *Journal of Health and Social Behavior*, 17:162–168.

SEGALL, ALEXANDER, and JAY GOLDSTEIN. 1989 "Exploring the correlates of self-provided health care behaviour." *Social Science and Medicine*, 29:153–161.

SELYE, HANS. 1956 *The stress of life.* New York: McGraw-Hill.

SHAPIRO, MARTIN. 1978 *Getting doctored.* Kitchener, Ontario, Canada: Between the Lines.

SHARP, KIMBERLY, CATHERINE E. ROSS, and WILLIAM C. COCKERHAM. 1983 "Symptoms, beliefs, and use of physician services among the disadvantaged." *Journal of Health and Social Behavior*, 24:255–263.

SHEHAN, CONSTANCE L., MARY ANN BURG, and CYNTHIA A. REXROAT. 1986 "Depression and the social dimensions of the full-time housewife role." *Sociological Quarterly*, 27:403–422.

SHORTELL, STEPHEN M. 1973 "Patterns of referral among internists in private practice." *Journal of Health and Social Behavior*, 14:335–348.

SHORTER, EDWARD. 1991 *Doctors and their patients.* New Brunswick, N.J.: Transaction.

SHUVAL, JUDITH T. 1990 "Health in Israel: Patterns of equality and inequality." *Social Science and Medicine*, 31:291–304.

SIDEL, VICTOR W., and RUTH SIDEL. 1982a *A health state: An international perspective on the crisis in United States medical care.* Rev. ed. New York: Pantheon.

———. 1982b *The Health of China.* Boston: Beacon Press.

SIEGEL, KAROLYN, and BEATRICE J. KRAUSS. 1991 "Living with HIV infection: Adaptive tasks of seropositive gay men." *Journal of Health and Social Behavior*, 32:17–32.

SIEGRIST, JOHANNES. 1984 "Threat to social stress and cardiovascular risk." *Psychotherapy and Psychosomatics*, 42:90–96.

———. 1987a *Social inequities in health: Evaluating the European region.* Copenhagen: World Health Organization Regional Office for Europe.

———. 1987b "Impaired quality of life as a risk factor in cardiovascular disease." *Journal of Chronic Diseases*, 40:571–578.

———. 1988 *Medizinische soziologie.* Munich: Urban & Schwarzenberg.

———. 1989 "Steps toward explaining social differentials in morbidity: The case of West Germany," pp. 353–371 in *Health inequalities in European countries*, J. Fox (ed.). Aldershot, U.K.:Gower.

SIEGRIST, JOHANNES, RALPH BERNHARDT, ZONGCHEN FENG, and GOTTHARD SCHETTLER. 1990 "Socioeconomic differences in cardiovascular risk factors in China." *International Journal of Epidemiology*, 19:905–910.

SIEGRIST, JOHANNES, KLAUS DITTMAN, KARIN RITTNER, and INGBERT WEBER. 1982 "The social context of active distress in patients with early myocardial infarction." *Social Science and Medicine*, 16:443–453.

SIEGRIST, JOHANNES, RICHARD PETER, ASTRID JUNGE, PETER CREMER, and DIETER SEIDEL. 1990 "Low status control, high effort at work and ischemic heart disease: Prospective evidence from blue-collar men." *Social Science and Medicine*, 31:1127–1134.

SIEGRIST, JOHANNES, KARIN SIEGRIST, and INGBERT WEBER. 1986 "Sociological concepts in the etiology of chronic disease: The case of ischemic heart disease." *Social Science and Medicine*, 22:247–253.

SIGERIST, HENRY E. 1960 "The special position of the sick," pp. 10–11 in *Henry E. Sigerist on the sociology of medicine*, M. Roemer (ed.). New York: MD Publications.

SIMMONS, L., and H. WOLFF. 1954 *Social science in medicine.* New York: Russell Sage.

SIMON, ROBIN W. 1992 "Parental role strains, salience of parental identity and gender differences in psychological distress." *Journal of Health and Social Behavior*, 33:25–35.

SMITH, ALLEN C., and SHERRYL KLEINMAN. 1989 "Managing emotions in medical school: Students' contacts with the living and the dead." *Social Psychology Quarterly*, 52:56–69.

SMITH, H. L. 1955 "Two lines of authority: The hospital's dilemma." *Modern Hospital*, 84:59–64.

SMITH, RICHARD. 1987 *Unemployment and health*. Oxford, U.K.: Oxford University Press.

SNOW, LOUDELL F. 1977 "Popular medicine in a black neighborhood," pp. 19–25 in *Ethnic medicine in the Southwest*, E. Spicer (ed.). Tucson: University of Arizona Press.

———. 1978 "Sorcerers, saints and charlatans: Black folk healers in urban America." *Culture, Medicine, and Psychiatry*, 2:69–106.

SONODA, KYOICHI. 1988 *Health and illness in changing Japanese society*. Tokyo: University of Tokyo Press.

SONTAG, SUSAN. 1978 *Illness as metaphor*. New York: Farrar, Straus, and Giroux.

SORENSEN, GLORIAN, PHYLLIS PIRIE, AARON FOLSOM, RUSSELL LUEPKER, DAVID JACOBS, and RICHARD GILLUM. 1985 "Sex differences in the relationship between work and health: The Minnesota Heart Survey." *Journal of Health and Social Behavior*, 26:379–394.

SORENSEN, JAMES R. 1974 "Biomedical innovation, uncertainty, and doctor-patient interaction." *Journal of Health and Social Behavior*, 15:366–374.

SPARER, GERALD, and LOUISE M. OKADA. 1974 "Chronic conditions and physician use patterns in ten urban poverty areas." *Medical Care*, 12:549–560.

SPRUIT, INGEBORG P. 1990 "Health and social inequities in the Netherlands." *Social Science and Medicine*, 31:319–329.

SROLE, LEO, T. S. LANGNER, S. T. MICHAEL, M. K. OPLER, and T. A. C. RENNIE. 1962 *Mental health in the metropolis: The midtown Manhattan study*, Vol. 1. New York: McGraw-Hill.

STACEY, MARGARET. 1988 *The sociology of health and healing*. London: Unwin Hyman.

STAHL, S. M., and G. GARDNER. 1976 "A contradiction in the health care delivery system: Problems of access." *Sociological Quarterly*, 17:121–129.

STARR, PAUL. 1982 *The social transformation of American medicine*. New York: Basic Books.

———. 1994 *The logic of health care reform*, Rev. and enl. ed. New York: Penguin.

STEIN, LEONARD I. 1967 "The doctor-nurse game." *Archives of General Psychiatry*, 16:699–703.

STEIN, LEONARD I., DAVID T. WATTS, and TIMOTHY HOWELL. 1990 "The doctor-nurse game revisited." *New England Journal of Medicine*, 322:546–549.

STERN, BERNARD F. 1927 *Social factors in medical progress*. New York: Columbia University Press.

STESLICKE, WILLIAM E. 1989 "Health care and the Japanese state," pp. 101–127 in *Success and crisis in national health systems*, M. Field (ed.). London: Routledge.

STEVENS, FRED, JOS DIEDERIKS, JOUKE VAN DER ZEE, and GÜNTHER LÜSCHEN. 1994 "Health lifestyles, health concerns, and social position in the Netherlands and Germany." *European Journal of Public Health* (forthcoming).

STEVENS, ROSEMARY. 1971 *American medicine and the public interest*. New Haven, Conn.: Yale University Press.

———. 1989 *In sickness and in wealth: American hospitals in the twentieth century*. New York: Basic Books.

STEWART, MIRIAM J. 1989 "Social support: Diverse theoretical perspectives." *Social Science and Medicine*, 28:1275–1282.

STEWART, WALTER F., RICHARD B. LIPTON, DAVID D. CELENTANO, and MICHAEL L. REED. 1992 "Prevalence of migraine headaches in the United States." *Journal of the American Medical Association*, 267:64–69.

STOLLER, ELEANOR PALO. 1984 "Self-assessments of health by the elderly: The impact of informal assistance." *Journal of Health and Social Behavior*, 25:260–270.

STRAUS, ROBERT. 1957 "The nature and status of medical sociology." *American Sociological Review*, 22:200–204.

STRAUSS, ANSELM. 1966 "Structure and ideology of the nursing profession," pp. 60–104 in *The nursing profession*, F. Davis (ed.). New York: John Wiley.

———. 1970 "Medical ghettos," pp. 9–26 in *Where medicine fails*, A. Strauss (ed.). Chicago: Aldine.

———. 1975 *Chronic illness and the quality of life*. St. Louis, Mo.: C. V. Mosby.

STRAUSS, ANSELM and JULIET M. CORBIN. 1988 *Shaping a new health care system*. San Francisco: Jossey-Bass.

STRAUSS, ANSELM, LEONARD SCHATZMAN, DANUTA EHRLICH, RUE BUCHER, and MELVIN SABSHIN. 1963 "The hospital and its negotiated order," pp. 147– 169 in *The hospital in modern society*, E. Freidson (ed.). New York: The Free Press.

SUCHMAN, EDWARD A. 1963 *Sociology and the field of public health*. New York: Russell Sage.

———. 1965a "Social patterns of illness and medical care." *Journal of Health and Social Behavior*, 6:2–16.

———. 1965b "Stages of illness and medical care." *Journal of Health and Social Behavior*, 6:114–128.

SUDMAN, SEYMOUR, and HOWARD E. FREEMAN. 1989 "Access to health care services in the U.S.A.: Results and methods," pp. 177–196 in *Health and illness in America and Germany*, G. Lüschen, W. Cockerham, and G. Kunz (eds.). Munich: Oldenbourg.

SUSSER, MERVYN, KIM HOPPER, and JUDITH RICHMAN. 1983 "Society, culture, and health," pp. 23–49 in *Handbook of health, health care, and the health professions*, D. Mechanic (ed.). New York: The Free Press.

SUSSER, M. W., and W. WATSON. 1971 *Sociology in medicine*, 2nd ed. New York: Oxford University Press.

SVARSTAD, BONNIE L. 1986 "Patient-practitioner relationships and compliance with prescribed medical regimens," pp. 438–459 in *Applications of social science to clinical medicine and health policy*, L. Aiken and D. Mechanic (eds.). New Brunswick: N.J.: Rutgers University Press.

SYME, LEONARD. 1975 "Social and psychological risk factors in coronary heart disease." *Modern Concepts of Cardiovascular Disease*, 44:17–21.

SYTKOWSKI, PAMELA A., WILLIAM B. KANNEL, and RALPH B. D'AGOSTINO. 1990 "Changes in risk factors and the decline in mortality from cardiovascular disease." *New England Journal of Medicine*, 322:1635–1641.

SZASZ, THOMAS S. 1974 *The myth of mental illness*, rev. ed. New York: Harper & Row.

SZASZ, THOMAS, and MARC HOLLENDER. 1956 "A contribution to the philosophy of medicine: The basic models of the doctor-patient relationship." *Journal of the American Medical Association*, 97:585–588.

TALLER, STEPHEN L., and ROBERT FELDMAN. 1974 "The training and utilization of nurse practitioners in adult health appraisal." *Medical Care*, 12:40–48.

TANNER, JAMES L., WILLIAM C. COCKERHAM, and JOEL L. SPAETH. 1983 "Predicting physician utilization." *Medical Care*, 21:360–369.

TAYLOR, SANDRA E. 1992 "The mental health status of black Americans: An overview," pp. 20–34 in *Health Issues in the Black Community*, R. Braithwaite and S. Taylor (eds.). San Francisco: Jossey-Bass.

TESSLER, RICHARD, DAVID MECHANIC, and MARGARET DIMOND. 1976 "The effect of psychological distress on physician utilization: A prospective study." *Journal of Health and Social Behavior*, 17:353–364.

THOITS, PEGGY A. 1987 "Gender and marital status differences in control and distress: Common stress versus unique stress explanations." *Journal of Health and Social Behavior*, 28:7–22.

THOMPSON, JAMES. 1984 "Compliance," pp. 109–131 in *The experience of illness*, R. Fitzpatrick, S. Newman, G. Scambler, and J. Thompson (eds.). London: Tavistock.

TIERNEY, KATHLEEN J., and BARBARA BAISDEN. 1979 *Crisis intervention programs for disaster victims: A source book and manual for smaller communities*. Rockville, Md.: National Institute of Mental Health.

TOTMAN, RICHARD. 1979 *Social causes of illness*. New York: Pantheon.

TOWNSEND, J. MARSHALL. 1976 "Self-concept and the institutionalization of mental patients: An overview and critique." *Journal of Health and Social Behavior*, 17:263–271.

TOWNSEND, PETER, and NICK DAVIDSON (eds.) and MARGARET WHITEHEAD. 1990 *Inequalities in health*. London: Penguin Books.

TREVIÑO, FERNANDO M., M. EUGENE MOYER, R. BURCIAGA VALDEZ, and CHRISTINE A. STROUP-BENHAM. 1991 "Health insurance coverage and utilization of health services by Mexican Americans, mainland Puerto Ricans, and Cuban Americans." *Journal of the American Medical Association* 265:233–237.

TUCHMAN, BARBARA W. 1978 *A distant mirror: The calamitous 14th century*. New York: Random House.

TURNER, BRYAN S. 1984 *The body and society*. Oxford: Blackwell.

———. 1987 *Medical power and social knowledge*. London: Sage.

———. 1988 *Status*. Milton Keynes, U.K.: Open University Press.

———. 1992 *Regulating bodies: Essays in medical sociology*. London: Routledge.

TURNER, HEATHER, ROBERT B. HAYS, and THOMAS J. COATES. 1993 "Determinants of social support among gay men: The context of AIDS." *Journal of Health and Social Behavior*, 34:37–53.

TURNER, R. JAY. 1981 "Social support as a contingency in psychological well-being." *Journal of Health and Social Behavior*, 22:357–367.

TURNER, R. JAY, and WILLIAM R. AVISON. 1992 "Innovations in the measurement of life stress: Crisis theory and the significance of event resolution." *Journal of Health and Social Behavior*, 33:35–50.

TURNER, R. JAY, and SAMUEL NOH. 1983 "Class and psychological vulnerability among women: The significance of social support and personal control." *Journal of Health and Social Behavior*, 24:2–15.

TUXWORTH, W., A. M. NEVILL, C. WHITE, and C. JENKINS. 1986 "Health, fitness, physical activity, and morbidity of middle aged male factory workers." *British Journal of Industrial Medicine*, 43:733–753.

TWADDLE, ANDREW. 1969 "Health decisions and sick role variations: An exploration." *Journal of Health and Social Behavior*, 10:105–114.

———. 1973 "Illness and Deviance." *Social Science and Medicine*, 7:751–762.

UEHATA, TETSUNOJYO. 1991 "Karoshi due to occupational, stress-related cardiovascular injuries among middle-aged workers in Japan." *Journal of Science of Labor*, 67:20–28.

ULBRICH, PATRICIA M., GEORGE J. WARHEIT, and RICK S. ZIMMERMAN. 1989 "Race, socioeconomic status, and psychological distress: An examination of differential vulnerability." *Journal of Health and Social Behavior*, 30:131–146.

UMBERSON, DEBRA, CAMILLE B. WORTMAN, and RONALD C. KESSLER. 1992 "Widowhood and depression: Explaining long-term gender differences in vulnerability." *Journal of Health and Social Behavior*, 33:10–24.

UNGAR, SANFORD J. 1989 *Africa: The people and politics of an emerging continent*. New York: Simon & Schuster.

U.S. DEPARTMENT OF HEALTH AND HUMAN SERVICES. 1985 *Black & Minority Health*. Washington, D.C.: U.S. Government Printing Office.

VÅGERÖ, DENNY, and RAYMOND ILLSLEY. 1992 "Inequality, health and policy in east and west Europe." *International Journal of Health Sciences*, 3:225–239.

VALKONEN, TAPANI. 1987 "Social inequality in the face of death." Unpublished manuscript. Helsinki: Department of Sociology, University of Helsinki.

―――. 1989 "Adult mortality and level of education: A comparison of six countries," pp. 142–162 in *Health inequalities in European countries*, J. Fox (ed.). Aldershot, U.K.: Gower.

VANFOSSEN, BETH E. 1981 "Sex differences in mental health effects of spouse support and equity." *Journal of Health and Social Behavior*, 22:130–143.

VAYDA, EUGENE, and RAISA B. DEBER. 1984 "The Canadian health care system: An overview." *Social Science and Medicine*, 18:191–197.

VELIMIROVIC, B. 1987 "AIDS as a social phenomenon." *Social Science and Medicine*, 25:541–552.

VERBRUGGE, LOIS M. 1976 "Females and illness: Recent trends in sex differences in the United States." *Journal of Health and Social Behavior*, 17:387–403.

―――. 1983 "Multiple roles and physical health of women and men." *Journal of Health and Social Behavior*, 24:16–30.

―――. 1985 "Gender and health: An update on hypotheses and evidence." *Journal of Health and Social Behavior*, 26:156–182.

―――. 1986 "From sneezes to adieux: Stages of health for American men and women." *Social Science and Medicine*, 22:1195–1212.

―――. 1989 "The Twain meet: Empirical explanations of sex differences in health and mortality." *Journal of Health and Social Behavior*, 30:282–304.

VLADECK, BRUCE C. 1983 "Equality, access, and the costs of health services," pp. 1–18 in *Securing access to health care*, Vol. 3, President's Commission for the Study of Ethical Problems in Medicine and Biomedical and Behavioral Research. Washington, D.C.: U.S. Government Printing Office.

VOGEL, EZRA F. 1979 *Japan as number one*. Cambridge, Mass.: Harvard University Press.

VOLKART, E. H. (ed.). 1951 *Social behavior and personality*. New York: Social Science Research Council.

WAITZKIN, HOWARD. 1983 *The second sickness: Contradictions of capitalist health care*. New York: The Free Press.

―――. 1985 "Information giving in medical care." *Journal of Health and Social Behavior*, 26:81–101.

―――. 1989 "A critical theory of medical discourse: Ideology, social control, and the processing of social context in medical encounters." *Journal of Health and Social Behavior*, 30:220–239.

―――. 1991 *The politics of medical encounters*. New Haven, Conn.: Yale University Press.

WALDRON, INGRID. 1981 "Why do women live longer than men?" pp. 45–66 in *The sociology of health and illness*, P. Conrad and R. Kern (eds.). New York: St. Martin's Press.

―――. 1983 "Sex differences in illness incidence, prognosis and mortality: Issues and evidence." *Social Science and Medicine*, 17:1107–1123.

WALLE, ETIENNE VAN DE. 1990 "The social impact of AIDS in Sub-Saharan Africa." *Milbank Quarterly*, 68:110–132.

WALLIMANN, ISIDOR. 1986 "Social insurance and the delivery of social services in France." *Social Science and Medicine*, 23:1305–1317.

WALLIS, ROY, and PETER MORLEY. 1976 "Introduction," pp. 9–19 in *Marginal medicine*, R. Wallis and P. Morley (eds.). New York: The Free Press.

WAN, THOMAS T. II. 1982 "Use of health service by the elderly in low income communities." *Milbank Memorial Fund Quarterly*, 60:82–107.

WAN, THOMAS T. H., and SCOTT J. SOIFER. 1974 "Determinants of physician utilization: A causal analysis." *Journal of Health and Social Behavior*, 15:100–108.

WARBASSE, JAMES. 1909 *Medical sociology*. New York: Appleton.

WARD, PETER. 1985 *Welfare politics in Mexico*. London: Allen & Unwin.

WARDWELL, WALTER I. 1979 "Limited and marginal practitioners," pp. 230–250 in *Handbook of medical sociology*, 3rd ed., H. Freeman, S. Levine, and L. Reeder (eds.). Englewood Cliffs, N.J.: Prentice-Hall.

———. 1980 "The present and future role of the chiropractor," pp. 25–41 in *Modern developments in the principles and practice of chiropractic*, S. Haldeman (ed.). New York: Appleton-Century-Crofts.

———. 1982 "The state of medical sociology—A review essay," *Sociological Quarterly*, 23:563–571.

WARHEIT, GEORGE J., CHARLES E. HOLZER III, and SANDRA A. AREY. 1975 "Race and mental illness: An epidemiologic update." *Journal of Health and Social Behavior*, 16:243–256.

WARHEIT, GEORGE J., CHARLES E. HOLZER III, and JOHN J. SCHWAB. 1973 "An analysis of social class and racial differences in depressive symptomatology." *Journal of Health and Social Behavior*, 14:291–298.

WARNECKE, RICHARD B. 1973 "Non-intellectual factors related to attrition from a collegiate nursing program." *Journal of Health and Social Behavior*, 14:153–167.

WARNER, DAVID C. 1991 "Health issues in the U.S.-Mexican border." *JAMA*, 265:242–247.

WEBER, MAX. 1958 *The Protestant ethic and the spirit of capitalism*. New York: Scribner.

———. 1978 *Economy and society*, 2 vols, G. Roth and C. Wittich (eds.). Berkeley: University of California Press.

WEINER, HERBERT. 1985 "Schizophrenia: Etiology," pp. 650–651 in *Comprehensive textbook of psychiatry*, Vol. 1, 4th ed., H. Kaplan and B. Sadock (eds.). Baltimore: William & Wilkins.

WEISS, GREGORY L., and LYNNE E. LONNQUIST. 1994 *Sociology of health, healing, and illness*. Englewood Cliffs, N.J.: Prentice Hall.

WEITZ, ROSE. 1989 "Uncertainty and the lives of persons with AIDS." *Journal of Health and Social Behavior*, 30:270–281.

WEITZ, ROSE, and DEBORAH SULLIVAN. 1986 "The politics of childbirth: The re-emergence of midwifery in Arizona." *Social Problems*, 33:163–175.

WELCH, SUSAN, JOHN COMER, and MICHAEL STEINMAN. 1973 "Some social and attitudinal correlates of health care among Mexican-Americans." *Journal of Health and Social Behavior*, 14:205–213.

WENGER, NANETTE K. 1982 "Coronary heart disease in women: Myth and fact." *Hospital Practice*, 17:114A-X.

WESSEN, ALBERT F. 1972 "Hospital ideology and communication between ward personnel," pp. 325–342 in *Patients, physicians and illness*, 2nd ed., E. Jaco (ed.). New York: Macmillan.

WEST, CANDACE. 1984 "When the doctor is a 'lady': Power, status and gender in physician-patient encounters." *Symbolic Interaction*, 7:87–106.

WETHINGTON, ELAINE, and RONALD C. KESSLER. 1986 "Perceived support, received support, and adjustment to stressful life events." *Journal of Health and Social Behavior*, 27:78–89.

WETTERER, ANGELIKA, and JURGEN VON TROSCHKE. 1986 *Smoker motivation*. Berlin: Springer.

WHEATON, BLAIR. 1980 "The sociogenesis of psychological disorder: An attributional theory." *Journal of Health and Social Behavior*, 21:100–124.

WHITE HOUSE DOMESTIC POLICY COUNCIL. 1993 *Health security: The official text*. New York: Touchstone.

WHITEHEAD, MARGARET. 1990 "The health divide," pp. 222–356 in *Inequalities in health*, P. Townsend and N. Davidson (eds.) and M. Whitehead. London: Penguin Books.

WILDMAN, RICHARD C., and DAVID RICHARD JOHNSON. 1977 "Life change and Langner's 22-item mental health index: A study and partial replication." *Journal of Health and Social Behavior*, 18:179–188.

WILKINSON, RICHARD G. 1986 *Class and health.* London: Tavistock.

WILLIAMS, DAVID R. 1990 "Socioeconomic differentials in health: A review and redirection." *Social Psychology Quarterly*, 53:81–99.

WILLIAMS, DAVID R., DAVID T. TAKEUCHI, and RUSSELL K. ADAIR. 1992 "Socioeconomic status and psychiatric disorder among blacks and whites." *Social Forces*, 71:179–194.

WILLIAMS, RORY. 1983 "Concepts of health: An analysis of lay logic." *Sociology*, 17:187–205.

WILLIAMS, SIMON J., MICHAEL CALNAN, SARAH L. CANT, and JOANNE COYLE. 1993 "All change in the NHS? Implications of the NHS reforms for primary care prevention." *Sociology of Health & Illness*, 15:19–43.

WILSON, ROBERT N. 1963 "The social structure of a general hospital." *Annals of the American Academy of Political Science*, 346:67–76.

———. 1970 *The sociology of health.* New York: Random House.

WINKLEBY, MARILYN A., DARIUS E. JATULIS, ERICA FRANK, and STEPHEN P. FORTMANN. 1992 "Socioeconomic status and health: How education, income, and occupation contribute to risk factors for cardiovascular disease." *American Journal of Public Health*, 82:816–820.

WNUK-LIPINSKI, EDMUND. 1990 "The Polish country profile: Economic crisis and inequalities in health." *Social Science and Medicine*, 31:859–866.

WOLFEREN, KAREL VAN. 1989 *The Enigma of Japanese power.* New York: Knopf.

WOLINSKY, FREDERIC D. 1988 *The sociology of health: Principles, professions, and issues*, 2nd ed. Belmont, Calif.: Wadsworth.

WOLINSKY, FREDERIC D., RODNEY M. COE, DOUGLASS K. MILLER, JOHN M. PRENDERGAST, MYRA J. CREEL, and M. NOEL CHAVEZ. 1983 "Health services utilization among the noninsitutionalized elderly." *Journal of Health and Social Behavior*, 34:325–336.

WOLINSKY, FREDERIC D., RAY R. MOSELY III, and RODNEY M. COE. 1986 "A cohort analysis of the use of health services by elderly Americans." *Journal of Health and Social Behavior*, 27:209–219.

WOLINSKY, FREDERIC D., and SALLY R. WOLINSKY. 1981 "Expecting sick-role legitimation and getting it." *Journal of Health and Social Behavior*, 27:229–242.

WOOLHANDLER, STEFFIE, and DAVID U. HIMMELSTEIN. 1993 *The national health program book.* Monroe, Maine: Common Courage Press.

WOOLHANDLER, STEFFIE, DAVID U. HIMMELSTEIN, and JAMES P. LEWONTIN. 1993 "Administrative costs in U.S. hospitals." *New England Journal of Medicine*, 329:400–403.

WORLD BANK. 1993 *World development report: Investing in health.* New York: Oxford University Press.

WORLD HEALTH ORGANIZATION. 1981 *Health services in Europe*, 3rd ed., Vol. 1. Copenhagen: World Health Organization.

———. 1986 "Life-styles and health." *Social Science and Medicine*, 22:117–124.

WYNDER, ERNST, L., YASUYUKI FUJITA, RANDALL E. HARRIS, TAKESHI HIRAYAMA, and TOMOHIKO HIYAMA. 1991 "Comparative epidemiology of cancer between the United States and Japan." *Cancer*, 67:746–763.

WYSONG, JERE A., and THOMAS ABEL. 1991 "Universal health insurance and high-risk groups in West Germany: Implications for U.S. health policy." *Milbank Quarterly*, 68:527–560.

YAMAMOTO, MIKIO. 1983 "Primary health care and health education in Japan." *Social Science and Medicine*, 17:1419–1431.

YAMAZAKI, YOSHIHIKO, and JUNKO SAKANO. 1991 "Lifestyle and stress of Japanese workers." Paper presented to the International Conference on Return to Work, Production, and Administration to Capitalism, Chemitz, Germany (October).

YOSHIDA, KAREN K. 1993 "Reshaping of self: A pendular reconstruction of self and identity among adults with traumatic spinal cord injury." *Sociology of Health & Illness,* 15:217–245.

YOUNG, JAMES CLAY. 1981 *Medical choice in a Mexican village.* New Brunswick, N.J.: Rutgers University Press.

ZBOROWSKI, MARK. 1952 "Cultural components in responses to pain." *Journal of Social Issues,* 8:16–30.

ZOLA, IRVING K. 1966 "Culture and symptoms—An analysis of patients' presenting complaints." *American Sociological Review,* 31:615–630.

———. 1972 "Medicine as an institution of social control." *Sociological Review,* 20:487–504.

———. 1982 *Missing pieces: A chronicle of living with a disability.* Philadelphia: Temple University Press.

———. 1989 "Toward the necessary universalizing of a disability policy," *Milbank Quarterly,* 67, Supp. 2:401–428.

———. 1991 "Bringing our bodies and ourselves back in: Reflections on a past, present, and future 'medical sociology.' " *Journal of Health and Social Behavior,* 32:1–16.

Name Index

Abel, T., 90, 92, 97, 306
Abercrombie, N., 60
Acheson, H., 178
Adair, R., 55
Adams, O., 291, 293
Aday, L., 118, 120, 122, 126
Adler, I., 197
Agbonifo, P., 25
Aiken, L., 26, 31–32
Albrecht, G., 133–134, 231, 311
Alexander, F., 154
Alexander, J., 234, 239
Allen, G., 136–137
Allman, R., 176
Alubo, S., 326
Amato, P., 67, 76
Andersen, R., 41, 109, 117–118, 120, 122, 126–127, 182
Anderson, O., 41, 109, 120, 126
Andersson, N., 320
Annandale, E., 252
Anesaki, M., 62, 301–303
Angel, R., 37–38
Anspach, R., 199
Antonovsky, A., 57, 81, 162
Apple, D., 127
Arber, S., 57–58, 60
Ardagh, J., 99, 310

Arey, S., 55
Arluke, A., 124, 158, 164
Armstrong, D., 297
Arnold, R., 181
Aseltine, R., 67, 76, 87
Atkinson, T., 73, 78
Avery, C., 147
Avison, W., 86

Bailey, C., 31
Baisden, B., 80
Barell, V., 37
Barker, K., 220
Barnett, T., 29
Bart, P., 180
Baum, A., 62
Baumann, B., 127, 162
Bauwens, E., 135, 140
Bayer, R., 32
Beaglehole, R., 5
Becker, H., 10, 165, 167, 195–196, 198, 214
Becker, M., 93, 103, 105–106, 128
Bellin, S., 120
Benatar, S., 320–321
Bendix, R., 92
Benham, A., 120

371

Subject Index

SUMMARY A contemporary account of medical sociology, grounded in current research and sociological theory. This edition includes new chapters on health care in Third World Countries, the First World and formerly Socialist countries, and discusses health reform in the US and Clinton's proposals.